B & I
11/5/84
34.95

√

Principles of
Water Resources Planning

ALVIN S. GOODMAN
Polytechnic Institute of New York

with the assistance of

David C. Major
Clark University

David H. Marks
Massachusetts Institute of Technology

Jerome Delli Priscoli
Institute for Water Resources,
U.S. Army Corps of Engineers

Elizabeth E. Salmon
Dane County, Wisconsin, Board of Supervisors
Dane County Regional Planning Commission
Madison, Wisconsin, Metropolitan Sewerage District

William R. Walker
Virginia Polytechnic Institute
and State University

PRENTICE-HALL, INC., ENGLEWOOD CLIFFS, NEW JERSEY 07632

Library of Congress Cataloging in Publication Data

Goodman, Alvin S.
  Principles of water resources planning.

  Includes bibliographical references and index.
  1. Water resource development.   I. Major, David C.
II. Title.
TC405.G633 1984   333.91′15   83-4575
ISBN   0-13-710616-5

Printed in the United States of America

10 9 8 7 6 5 4 3 2 1

Editorial-production supervision and interior design: Paul Spencer
Cover design: 20/20 Services, Inc.
Manufacturing buyer: Anthony Caruso

ISBN   0-13-710616-5

Prentice-Hall International, Inc., *London*
Prentice-Hall of Australia Pty. Limited, *Sydney*
Editora Prentice-Hall do Brasil, Ltda., *Rio de Janeiro*
Prentice-Hall Canada Inc., *Toronto*
Prentice-Hall of India Private Limited, *New Delhi*
Prentice-Hall of Japan, Inc., *Tokyo*
Prentice-Hall of Southeast Asia Pte. Ltd., *Singapore*
Whitehall Books Limited, *Wellington, New Zealand*

Contents

Three

ELEMENTS OF PROJECT FORMULATION AND APPRAISAL **54**

Four

ESTIMATES OF POPULATION AND WATER NEEDS **72**

Five

IDENTIFICATION AND PRELIMINARY EVALUATION OF PROJECTS

105

Six

COMPREHENSIVE REGIONAL PLANNING

158

Seven

PUBLIC INVOLVEMENT IN WATER RESOURCES PLANNING

181

Contents

Eight

ECONOMIC ANALYSES 197

Nine

FINANCIAL ANALYSES 243

Contents

Sixteen

SOCIAL IMPACT ASSESSMENT

488

Seventeen

LEGAL AND INSTITUTIONAL ASPECTS

505

Eighteen

ADMINISTRATION OF PLANNING PROGRAMS

522

Contents

Contents

Preface

This book has been designed for use as an undergraduate or graduate text, and as a guide for practitioners in the field of water resources planning and management. It should be useful to engineers, economists, planners, legal and management specialists, and environmental, social, and political scientists.

The subject of water resources planning is too broad and has too many methodological options to be covered completely in a single volume. The objective of this book has, therefore, been more limited—to present the principles of water resources planning and to provide a reasonable selection of additional descriptive and analytical material. All references used for this book are listed at the ends of the chapters; these references are a rich source of information for further study.

The first half of the book stresses the engineering and economic planning aspects of water resources studies that should be understood by all students and practitioners in water resources planning, whatever their basic academic disciplines. The second half provides additional material on specialized methods used in water resources planning and on other subjects needed to round out the field. Those who employ these specialized methods should have advanced training and experience in their respective professional disciplines in order to perform at an effective and reliable level. A knowledge of advanced mathematics is needed for only a few sections; in these areas a perspective may be gained from the connecting discussions.

The scope of this book was influenced by experience gained in teaching a graduate course in water resources planning for some twenty years at Northeastern University, New York University, and the Polytechnic Institute of New York. The initial version of this book was prepared using government agency publications and consulting engineering practice as the principal sources of information and illustrations. The chapters were then supplemented with selected materials from the very extensive body of literature and research reports in the field of water resources planning. Thus, this book emphasizes both the principles and the actual practice of water resources planning. The reader will find that some of the methods employed in practice are not fully and rigorously in agreement with the principles of planning.

I tested this version of the book in a graduate course in water resources planning; in 28 contact hours we covered the first nine chapters and selected material in the remaining chapters. Following this effort, I was fortunate in securing the assistance of five colleagues who teach and practice in the water resources planning field and who are eminent in specific professional disciplines. These individuals, with their chapter involvement, are: David C. Major, Clark University, economics and multiobjective planning, Chapters 1–10; David H. Marks, Massachusetts Institute of Technology, systems analysis, including mathematical optimization, Chapters 11–13; Jerome Delli Priscoli, Institute for Water Resources of the U.S. Army Corps of Engineers, socioeconomic and environmental assessments, Chapters 14–16; Elizabeth E. Salmon, Dane County Board of Supervisors and Regional Planning Commission, and Metropolitan Sewerage District, Madison, Wisconsin, public involvement process, Chapter 7; and William R. Walker, Virginia Polytechnic Institute and State University, legal and institutional aspects, Chapters 5 and 17. Revisions that were made to produce this version of the book included selective excisions and reworking to reduce the text to manageable length, extensive revisions of some material (in particular for Chapters 7, 16, and 17), and other editorial changes to improve definitions or clarify discussions.

I believe our joint effort resulted in a much improved version of the book, which, considering the interdisciplinary nature of the water resources planning field, could not have been done as effectively by any single individual. Nevertheless, as author and final arbiter, I gladly accept responsibility for all material, including changes to material presented by my assistants.

I also wish to acknowledge the encouragement and help received from a number of other individuals. In particular, thanks are due to Eugene O'Brien, Partner, and Andrzej Jezierski, former Head of Water Resources Division, Tippetts-Abbett-McCarthy-Stratton, Engineers, Architects and Planners, New York. The writer has been associated with TAMS since 1951, and many of the case studies discussed in the book are based on the firm's projects. Others who reviewed material in the first version of the text include Thomas Fitzgerald and Scott Emery, TAMS; Verne H. Scott, University of California, Davis; Edith Brown Weiss, Georgetown University Law Center; and Li Ti Xian, Tianjin University, China.

In the preparation of the manuscript, assistance was received from a number of highly capable individuals, including Carolyn G. Magliolo, Marie Rothenberg, Carolyn Coleman, and Dianna Rullan of TAMS; and Elaine Cummings, Kay Kamara, Pam McCarthy, Pat James, and Carol Devlin of the Polytechnic Institute of New York.

Finally, I wish to express my heartfelt appreciation to my wife, Nettie, who has always encouraged my professional efforts and was a particularly patient partner through the long hours needed to write this book.

Alvin S. Goodman

ONE

Introduction

1.1 CONCEPTUAL FRAMEWORK AND SCOPE

This book describes the general process of and detailed methodologies employed in planning projects involving water and related land resources. A *project* consists of constructed facilities and other measures that control, utilize, or limit the use of water. *Planning* activities include the identification, formulation, and analysis of projects. Planning activities are also included in subsequent phases of project implementation, including design, construction, and operation. Engineers, but not all other professionals in the water resources field, distinguish between planning and *design*, applying the latter term to the preparation of detailed engineering studies, drawings, and specifications for structures, equipment, and other components of a project. Water resources planning methods are based on *scientific, legal, ethical, judgmental*, and other concepts.

Although water resources projects have been constructed for thousands of years, modern water resources planning has evolved over only about 50 years. In the United States, it extends from the enactment of the Flood Control Act of 1936, which initiated the requirement for benefit-cost analysis. Until recently, water resources planning in the United States was carried out almost entirely by engineers. Economists and natural resource planners have been represented extensively in the literature for many years, but have had influential roles in professional practice and in the promulgation of policies and rules of government agencies only since about 1950. Ecologists, sociologists, and other environmental and social scientists have also participated in important water resource planning, particularly since the passage of the National Environmental Policy Act in 1969, which requires the preparation of an environmental impact statement for every significant federal action.

1

The sponsor of a water resources project may be a federal, state, or local government agency, an investor-owned or municipal public utility, an industrial firm, or a private entrepreneur. A planner may be on the staff of one of these organizations, from a governmental regulating agency, or in a firm of consulting engineers or planners, or may work as an individual or as a member of a public interest group. Planners receive academic training in disciplines such as engineering, architecture, city and regional planning, economics, sociology, political science, law, and the biological sciences. Effective water resources planning often requires a synthesis of methodologies based on several or all of these disciplines.

A government sponsor determines the attractiveness of a project after consideration of a number of factors, including engineering feasibility, economic and financial viability, environmental and socioeconomic impacts, legal and institutional constraints, and political acceptability. A private venturer, whose principal aim is a profitable project, must also make a multifaceted analysis, since such a sponsor must ration the available water, land, capital, personnel, and other resources; must adhere to various governmental regulations; and needs to consider public opinion and political acceptability.

Projects vary in the types of water needs they meet or the water-related problems they solve. The physical, environmental, and social setting in which planning takes place also differs from one location to another. Thus, the planner, in adopting a general approach and detailed methodologies, should recognize that a diversity of issues and constraints exist for different projects. This book describes a number of techniques that have been previously employed on projects of various types, and the experiences of these projects can serve to guide the planning of projects in the future. For most projects it is likely that the good planner will want to make appropriate modifications to suit the new set of conditions under which his or her responsibilities must be carried out.

The emphasis in this book is on practical state-of-the-art methods that are suitable in the professional practice of water resources planning. Historical and theoretical details are included only to the extent needed as a foundation for such methods. The book includes many examples taken from actual project reports. Most of these reports are of recent origin. Others are used because the technology they present is still valid and pedagogically useful. The book also describes methodologies developed during planning research or in governmental regulatory activities. Some of these techniques have not been fully tested, but are judged by the author and his associates to warrant serious consideration for their implementation.

Sections in this and other chapters will show that many U.S. governmental agencies at the federal, state, and local levels are involved in the planning of water resources projects. Although it has always been recognized that different federal agencies have different legal mandates and public constituencies, various approaches have been attempted to impose uniform procedures of project formulation and analysis, to eliminate perceived incorrect and inconsistent analyses, and to permit projects proposed by different agencies to be compared. An executive agency, the U.S. Water Resources Council (WRC), was established in 1965 and, in 1973, issued a set of "Principles and Standards for Planning Water and Related Land Resources" that applied to all federal planning activities that were not of a regulatory nature. The "Principles and Standards" were revised in 1979 and 1980 and "Procedures" for detailed evaluation were published by the WRC in 1979 and 1980. The "Principles, Standards, and Procedures" were replaced in 1983 by "Economic and Environmental Principles and Guidelines for Water and Related Land Resources Implementation Studies," which were only applicable to the water resources project plans of the Corps of Engineers, Bureau of Reclamation, Tennessee Valley Authority, and Soil Conservation Service.* Debate continues on the federal guidelines and on the location and functions of a coordinating agency. This is a good illustration both of the development of criteria and the transitory nature of government institutions. As might be expected, these documents are not fully satisfactory or unanimously accepted, but they are a praiseworthy attempt to provide detailed, explicit guidance on investment criteria for water projects. The reader, thus cautioned, should consider these documents, together with the other concepts and techniques that are presented in this book, in determining a course of action.

Chapters 1 and 2 present definitions of terms used in water resources planning, the historical and professional setting in which planning takes place, the nature of water as a resource, and the fundamental engineering and economic concepts that should guide water resources planning. Chapters 3 to 6 describe the application of these principles in the estimation of population and water needs, and in the identification, formulation, and preliminary analysis of projects. Such projects may range from a single project meeting a single-purpose need to a regional system in a multiunit, multipurpose, and multiobjective framework. In these chapters, the emphasis is on engineering and planning approaches, but with additional analysis of the economic and environmental consequences of projects and other factors that should be considered in these studies. Chapter 7 deals with the problems and techniques of public involvement in the planning process.

Chapters 1 to 7 provide the general basis of water resources planning, including additional important considerations and practical examples. Chapters 8 to 17 provide further elaboration of the techniques of analysis using the specialized methods of various professional disciplines. Chapters 8 to 10 cover many details of economic and financial analyses for a variety of different types of water resources projects. Chapters 11 to 13 describe mathematical modeling and other approaches for handling problems of risk and uncertainty and for formulating projects that are optimal, primarily but not exclusively according to economic criteria. Chapters 14 to 16 present methodologies for evaluating the environmental and socioeconomic impacts of projects. Chapter 17 reviews important legal and institutional aspects. Finally, Chapter 18 suggests approaches for scheduling the monetary and personnel resources to carry out water resources planning.

*Documents issued from 1973 to 1980 will usually be referred to in this book as the Water Resources Council "Principles and Standards" and "Procedures." Page references will be to the Federal Register (see the list of References at the end of this chapter for volumes in the Register). The 1983 document will be referred to as "Principles and Guidelines" and page references will be to a separate publication available from the U.S. Government Printing Office.

1.2 PURPOSES OF WATER RESOURCES DEVELOPMENT AND MANAGEMENT

Water resources planning techniques are used to determine what measures should be employed to meet water needs, take advantage of opportunities for water resources development, and preserve and enhance natural water resources and related land resources.

Water resources are developed or managed for the following *purposes* and functions:

- Water supply for municipal and industrial uses
- Water supply for rural uses
- Water supply for thermal-electric power plant cooling
- Irrigation, including water supply
- Flood control and damage prevention
- Hydroelectric power
- Navigation
- Water quality management, including wastewater treatment and disposal and flow augmentation
- Recreation
- Commercial fishing and trapping
- Drainage, sedimentation control, land stabilization, erosion control, and other measures for management of urban and rural lands and watersheds

In addition to the foregoing purposes and functions, for which economic benefits can usually be estimated, the growing "environmental movement" has encouraged policies to plan and manage water resources for the preservation and enhancement of:

- Natural water and related land areas, including aesthetic values
- Archeological, historical, biological, and geological resources
- Ecological systems
- Water, land, and air quality

Planning, development, and management of water resources may also be used to further the general welfare, including:

- Regional economic development
- Income distribution
- Health and safety
- Educational and cultural opportunities
- Emergency preparedness
- Other measures to improve the "quality of life"

1.3 GENERAL DEFINITIONS IN WATER RESOURCES PLANNING

The *goals* of water resources planning may be advanced by the use of constructed facilities, or *structural* measures, or by management and legal techniques that do not require constructed facilities. The latter are *nonstructural* measures and may include rules to limit or control water and land use (e.g., flood warning systems, restrictive zoning on floodplains) which complement or substitute for constructed facilities. A *project* may consist of one or more structural or nonstructural measures. The implementability of a structural or nonstructural measure, or a *system* of measures, depends not only on technical effectiveness but also on acceptability from other standpoints, such as economic, financial, environmental, social, legal, and institutional *impacts*.

Whereas the terms *purpose, goal,* and *objective* have similar meanings in ordinary usage, they are different in water resources planning. Traditionally, a *purpose* has referred to a category of water needs and problems (e.g., municipal and industrial water supply, flood control), while a *goal* or objective implies a broader value. Except when one or the other term is preferred in a particular discipline, this book will not distinguish between *goals* and *objectives*. Some water resource planners believe it is useful to consider a goal as a general societal aim such as the "improvement of the quality of life" and to express an objective in more specific (monetary or other) terms such as "maximization of net benefits." *Policies* are related to the goals and objectives and to the various *constraints* which restrict development and management within specified bounds.

When various projects are elements of a regional plan (or even when a single project emphasizes different types of values), multiple purposes and objectives may be considered. Water resources planning objectives have changed in the United States in response to changing national values and the political process. Under the Water Resources Council "Principles and Guidelines" of 1983, the single objective considered by federal agencies is "national economic development." *Beneficial* and *adverse* effects are evaluated for this objective and also for "environmental quality," "regional economic development," and "other social effects." A plan that is optimal for the national economic development objective produces maximum *net* economic *benefits* (benefits minus costs). Other plans may emphasize environmental quality, nonstructural measures, or other approaches. Since these plans would not generally be the same, *trade-offs* that increase some values at the expense of others would have to be considered in order to obtain a recommended plan.

The methodologies of water resources planning may be categorized as *principles, standards*, and *procedures*. As defined by the Water Resources Council (1973, p. 24780), *principles* provide the broad policy framework for planning activities and include the conceptual basis for planning. *Standards* provide for uniformity and consistency in comparing, measuring, and judging beneficial and adverse effects of alternative plans. *Procedures* provide more detailed methods for carrying out the various levels of planning activities, including the measurement of beneficial and adverse effects, and the comparison of alternative plans for action. Principles, standards, and procedures are all subject to change over time. The principles, being most fundamental, are expected to evolve relatively slowly, while the standards and procedures are expected to change more readily with the development of data and techniques. The term *guidelines* may be applied when the standards and procedures are not fully binding on the planner.

Rouse and Ince (1957) have made a study of the history of hydraulics and Biswas (1970) has written a history of hydrology. These are major specialty areas of water resources planning and engineering. According to Biswas, there is recorded evidence of water resources works extending to 3200 BC. Rouse and Ince suggest that the first leader in hydraulics was probably Archimedes (287–212 BC), who established the elementary principles of buoyancy and flotation. Modern hydraulics has its origins in the early nineteenth century when, for example, Manning (1816–1897) proposed several formulas for open-channel flow resistance.

Thirteen outstanding papers were presented on "Water Resources Planning in America: 1776–1976" on the occasion of an observance of the bicentennial in 1976 by the American Society of Civil Engineers (*Proceedings of Water Resources Planning and Management Division*, March 1979 and March 1980). The interested reader will find papers on the historical development of water resources planning (Weber, Schad, Schwarz, and Linsley), western water planning (Keith et al.), and on the historical perspective of modern topics of concern, including economic analysis (James and Rogers), environment (Ortolano), social aspects (Willeke), system planning (Burges), hydrology (Linsley), water quality (Hey and Waggy), public health (Dworsky and Berger), and food and agricultural policies (Heady). Goodman (1976) has reported on the status of education and training in water resources planning.

Over the past 50 years, water resources planning has evolved from a relatively straightforward methodology to a complex procedure. This is illustrated by the planning of a community water supply. Traditionally, the first step was to project the needs of the population and industry for water, usually by extrapolating historical trends. The next step was to determine the yield and quality of various surface water and groundwater sources, and to make preliminary layouts and cost estimates of the facilities needed to withdraw water from each source, treat the water, and convey it to the community. This process involved not only the application of formulas but also much engineering judgment and experience. Each of the better solutions was analyzed to determine its structural and hydraulic integrity and its effectiveness in providing the water needed. The least-cost solution was usually adopted, and final planning consisted of preparing the designs and arranging for the necessary lands, water rights, and rights-of-way, so that the project could be constructed.

Planning is now more broadly based. Instead of emphasizing a single project to meet a specific defined requirement, all needs and opportunities for water resource development are considered in a region such as a river basin. Many projects are planned for more than one purpose and more than one objective, and include both structural and nonstructural measures.

From engineering and economic standpoints, the planning of water resource projects in a multiunit, multipurpose, multiobjective regional context is a logical evolution from the old methods, consistent with the development of modern techniques such as systems analysis, operations research, and computer programming. The major changes, in addition to these technological developments, have resulted from the inclusion of additional areas of consideration that are not quantifiable in the traditional sense (as are hydrologic, hydraulic, structural, cost, service, and other engineering factors). These nontraditional areas cover such topics as fish and wildlife; water-based recreation; aesthetics; wild and scenic rivers; preservation of ecological values; historic, social, and cultural values; and the restoration or enhancement of the quality of water bodies and associated land resources.

1.5 GENERALIZED PROCESS OF WATER RESOURCES PLANNING AND MANAGEMENT

The following phases are usually involved in the planning and management of a major water resources project (adapted from American Society of Civil Engineers, 1974).

- *Establishment of goals and objectives*—broad policies; legal and other constraints
- *Problem identification and analysis*—collection of data; projection of demand/supply relationships; uses of water and land; opportunities for development and management
- *Solution identification and impact assessment*—structural solutions; non-structural (management) solutions; preliminary assessment of impacts
- *Formulation of alternatives and analysis*—criteria and procedures for comparison of alternatives; formulation of alternative systems of structural and nonstructural measures; detailed assessment of impacts
- *Recommendations, including priorities and schedules for implementation*
- *Decisions*
- *Implementation*—organizations for action, if required
- *Operation and management*

The modern water resources planning organization should carry out its work with the participation of those who would be directly affected by the organization's projects (beneficially or adversely), all government agencies having jurisdiction, public interest groups, and other interested organizations and individuals. Such participation should be both formal (e.g., hearings, interagency committees, license and permit applications), and informal (e.g., brochures, response to inquiries). Information from these entities and their reactions to proposals will often sharpen the goals and objectives, assist in identifying and analyzing problems and solutions, provide guidance in the formulation and analysis of alternatives, and indicate the acceptability and preference for possible recommendations.

In proceeding from the initial to the final phases of the planning and management process, the work in one phase can suggest changes in one or more of the other phases. This effect can be referred to as *feedback*, and the linkages may be in both forward and backward directions. Even when the water resource system plan is implemented, it should be updated from time to time during the operation and management phase.

The methods of water resources planning range from fairly simple techniques employing substantial professional judgment to sophisticated mathematical optimization approaches. The selection of methods for a planning effort depends on the type of project; the formal requirements of the planning organization; the available personnel, money, and equipment for investigations; and the capabilities and preferences of the planning staff.

1.6 TASKS FOR WATER RESOURCES PLANNING PROJECT

An outline of tasks for planning an urban flood control project will provide a perspective of the complexity of a typical water resource project and an indication of the different professional specialties involved. Some of the activities in the following list overlap (e.g., environmental studies will begin before the structures are finally selected).

- Management and coordination
- Analysis of basic data—maps, aerial photos, stream flow, etc.
- Determination of needs for flood control
  - —delineation of area affected by floods
  - —determination of floodplain characteristics
  - —forecast of future activities in affected area
  - —estimates of existing and future flood damages
- Consideration of alternative ways of meeting needs
  - —upstream reservoir
  - —local protective works for urban area
  - —nonstructural measures
- Studies for reservoir
  - —selection of site
  - —selection of capacity
  - —selection of type of dam and spillway
  - —layout of structures
  - —analysis of foundations of structures
  - —development of construction plan
  - —cost estimates of structures
  - —layout and cost estimates of access roads, bridges, communication facilities, construction camp, etc.
  - —identification and estimates of requirements for lands, relocations, easements, etc.
  - —consideration of reservoir for multipurpose use with pertinent analyses of layouts, capacities, costs, etc.
- Studies for local protective works—levees, walls, river shaping and paving, interior pumping stations
- Studies of nonstructural measures—land use controls, flood warning systems, flood proofing, etc.
- Formulation of optimal combination of structural and nonstructural components for flood control project

- Economic analyses
- Financial analyses
- Assessments of environmental impacts—ecological, archeological, historical, geological, air and water quality, land sedimentation and erosion, etc.
- Sociological impact assessment
- Public information and participation programs
- Report preparation

The planning activities shown by the list above constitute the work needed to prepare a *feasibility* report. The level of engineering detail for such a report is higher than for a *preliminary* report, but lower than for the design of a project.

1.7 PROFESSIONAL SPECIALISTS IN WATER RESOURCES PLANNING

The list of tasks for the flood control planning project indicates that at least the following skills would have to be represented:

- Engineers—civil, structural, hydraulic, hydrologic, geotechnical, construction, cost estimating, mechanical, electrical, surveying and mapping, drafting
- Urban/regional land planning specialists
- Architects
- Economic and financial specialists
- Environmental specialists—biological sciences of various types, forestry, archeological, historical, geological, water and air quality, soils
- Sociologists
- Real estate and relocation specialists
- Public information specialists
- Report production specialists

If the project has multipurpose development opportunities, additional specialists may be needed to study them. Irrigation planning, for example, would involve soil and crop agronomists and other farm specialists, agricultural economists, and irrigation engineers. If sophisticated systems analyses are employed, computer specialists would be needed.

1.8 AVAILABILITY OF WATER

On a global basis, at any given moment, the distribution of water over the earth is shown by the percentages in Figure 1.1. The percentages of groundwater and surface water do not indicate their overall availabilities. Much of the groundwater is located far from points of need, or at depths and in aquifer materials that make retrieval impossible or uneconomic. Much surface water is flowing water that replenishes the volume of a stream typically on the average of 30 times per year.

Although there is enough water worldwide for everyone, its distribution is quite

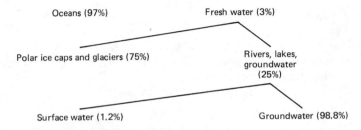

Oceans (97%) Fresh water (3%)

Polar ice caps and glaciers (75%) Rivers, lakes,
groundwater
(25%)

Surface water (1.2%) Groundwater (98.8%)

Figure 1.1 Distribution of water on earth. (From Wolman, 1962.)

variable. Population intensities and water availabilities often are not compatible. People live in water-deficient areas (e.g., the southwestern United States) because of attractive climatic or cultural reasons, or because relocation is impractical due to political, societal, or economic constraints. Areas that are deficient in precipitation for agriculture often have excellent soils and are thus good candidates for irrigation. Some of the best economic developments lie in the floodplains of streams, but they must be protected to survive and grow. The water resource planner is thus challenged to overcome the problems of too little or too much water, to develop the best logistics and facilities to meet water needs, and to take advantage of other opportunities for development, preservation, and enhancement.

Table 1.1 shows estimates for the average annual water balances of the world. A major uncertainty in such estimates comes from the difficulty of estimating precipitation on and evaporation from the oceans due to lack of observed data. Also, as discussed by Biswas (1979), such a global picture does not give a correct impression of the tremendous variability of water with regard to both space and time.

In the case of rural and urban water supply, the World Health Organization (1976) carried out a survey on the extent of water supply and sewerage at the end of 1975, to which 67 developing countries responded. In urban communities, some 130

TABLE 1.1 AVERAGE ANNUAL WATER BALANCE OF WORLD

	Volume (thousands of cubic kilometers)		
Regions	*Precipitation*	*Evaporation*	*Runoff*
Africa	20.7	17.3	3.4
Asia	30.7	18.5	12.2
Australia	7.1	4.7	2.4
Europe	6.6	3.8	2.8
North America	15.6	9.7	5.9
Latin America	28.0	16.9	11.1
Antarctica	2.4	0.4	2.0
Total, land areas	111.0	71.0	40.0
Oceans	385.0	425.0	−40.0
Total, world	496.0	496.0	0.0

Source: Baumgartner and Reichel (1975).

million people (25%) had no access to potable water by house connections or standpipes. In rural areas, almost 1000 million people (80%) did not have reasonable access to safe water. Considering both rural and urban populations together, only 35% (638,000,000) were adequately served. These are averages. There are several countries where 91 to 100% of the urban population was served while in other countries less than 5% of the rural population was served. Biswas (1979) found large variations and enormous insufficiencies of water for other major sectoral uses: agriculture, industry, and hydroelectric. Biswas also identified a number of places where there have been severe social and environmental impacts of water development, where conflicts have occurred between federal and local jurisdictions, and between neighboring states, and where problems have involved international waters. He concluded that the problem of water availability in the future is basically that of rational management.

1.9 USE OF WATER IN THE UNITED STATES

The U.S. Geological Survey has published reports containing estimates of water withdrawals in the United States for every fifth year since 1950. Nonwithdrawal or on-site uses for navigation, recreation, and water quality management are not included. The Geological Survey categories of withdrawals are public supply (for domestic, commercial, and industrial uses); rural (domestic and livestock); irrigation; self-supplied industrial (including thermoelectric power generation); and hydroelectric power. The changes in water withdrawals during the period 1950–1975 are shown in Figure 1.2.

The physical limit of water supply in the United States is the annual runoff of 1200 billion gallons per day. The Geological Survey estimates that the maximum economically dependable supply based on extensive measures to reduce evaporation and increase recharge is about 500 billion gallons per day. Neither the limit of runoff nor the dependable supply can be compared directly with total use since the latter may represent multiple uses of the same water. It is significant, however, that the total consumption in 1975 of 95 billion gallons per day was less than 20% of the estimated 500 billion gallons of economically dependable supply.

The foregoing figures indicate that the nation as a whole has adequate water supplies. The problems that exist are due to the variability of climate, landforms, and geology, and the distribution of population and industry whose requirements do not match water availabilities. The greatest shortages of water occur in the southwestern United States, but problems of logistics and expense of developing sources and conveyance facilities may exist anywhere in the nation. The uneven distribution of surface flows throughout the year result in floods, droughts, and problems of inadequate supply. Groundwaters fluctuate less than surface flows, but are subject to overpumping. Other problems result from the degradation of water quality by natural causes and human activities. Application of good water resources planning techniques is needed not only to solve the problems of meeting needs, but also to take advantage of the opportunities that exist for improved conservation and enjoyment of water and related land resources.

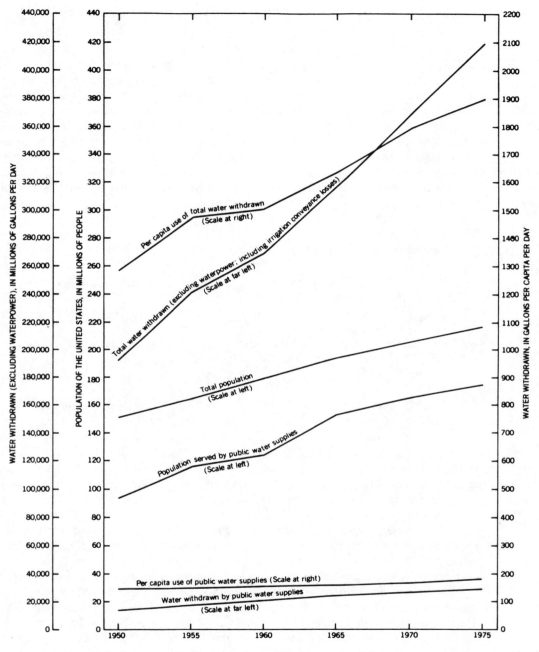

Figure 1.2 Trends of population and withdrawals of water in the United States. (From Murray and Reeves, 1977.)

TABLE 1.2 USE OF EXISTING RESERVOIR STORAGE IN THE UNITED STATES

Primary Purpose	Number of Dams	Total Maximum Storage (millions of acre-feet)
Irrigation	6,329	150.083
Hydroelectric	1,372	167.768
Flood control	7,776	300.678
Navigation	187	125.355
Water supply	7,279	267.187
Recreation	16,639	263.986
Debris control	344	190.907
Farm ponds	4,546	197.796
Other	4,779	111.456
	49,249	1,875.216

Source: McDonald (1977).

1.10 MAGNITUDE OF THE WATER RESOURCES FIELD IN THE UNITED STATES

Many water resources developments involve the construction of dams. In 1977, there were about 50,000 dams in the United States with a total of about 1900 million acre-feet of storage. Table 1.2 shows the primary uses of this storage. It does not distinguish between single-purpose and multiple-purpose projects and does not reflect the large variation of reservoir use among regions. Of these dams, 5500, including most of the largest, are owned and operated by the federal government. The remainder are owned by state and local governments, by public and private utilities, by industries and private corporations, and by individuals (McDonald 1977). In 1976, there were approximately 1400 conventional hydroelectric plants in the United States. They had a total capacity of 65 million kilowatts and an average annual energy production of 287.8 billion kilowatt-hours; this output was about 15% of the total electric energy production in 1976 (U.S. Federal Power Commission, 1976).

The Consulting Panel on Water Resource Planning to the United States National Water Commission (U.S. National Water Commission, 1972) estimated in 1972 that a total cumulative expenditure of $302.6 billion in 1971 dollars had been made for water resources development in the United States, distributed by sources of funds and purpose in Table 1.3. The table shows clearly that the federal government, state and other local government agencies, and private entities all have important roles in the water resources field in the United States. Lovell et al. (1968) estimated the 1975 annual level of expenditures for construction of water-oriented facilities at $12 billion in 1967 dollars.

The average annual investment in water resources in the United States involves 600,000 persons in direct construction, based on an approximate analysis by Lovell et al. (1968) of the labor component. They also estimated that over 50,000 engineers and other professionals are involved in planning, design, construction, education, and research; in the regulatory agency activities; and in the maintenance and operation of facilities for the control and utilization of water.

TABLE 1.3 TOTAL ESTIMATED CAPITAL EXPENDITURES IN THE UNITED STATES TO 1972 (Millions of 1971 Dollars)

	Federally Financed	State and Locally Financed	Privately Financed	Total
Hydropower	9,100	3,100	6,100	18,300
Flood control	24,700	1,900	1,400	27,900
Navigation	16,400	1,600	—	18,000
Wastewater disposal	8,900[a]	56,200	4,500	69,500
Storm sewers	—	30,300	3,100	33,400
Municipal water	6,500[a]	67,000	9,100	82,600
Industrial water	6,500[a]	4,700	14,300	25,500
Irrigation	10,400	3,400	13,600	27,400
Total	82,500	168,100	52,000	302,600

[a]Includes facilities at federally owned establishments.
Source: U.S. National Water Commission (1972).

1.11 WATER RESOURCES INSTITUTIONS

The Consulting Panel on Water Resources Planning of the United States National Water Commission (U.S. National Water Commission, 1972) listed the many institutions in the United States having an interest in water. The complex of jurisdictions in the United States was also shown by the U.S. Water Resources Council "Coordination Directory" (1979). In addition to over 30 federal agencies, many other governmental units are found at interstate regional, state, intrastate regional, and local levels. These institutions have many functions ranging from planning, design, and construction to licensing, monitoring, and research. Over the years, many attempts have been made through informal interagency organizations, reorganizations, and formal agencies (e.g., Water Resources Council) to establish uniform standards for planning, to reduce overlapping activities, and to improve planning efficiency. These attempts have met with varying degrees of success.

Water resources planners, in the United States and elsewhere, often perform studies in foreign countries and for international study and financing institutions. The latter include the Agency for International Development (AID) of the U.S. Department of State; the International Bank for Reconstruction and Development (World Bank); the United Nations (UN Development Programme, Food and Agriculture Organization, World Health Organization, UNESCO, etc.); Organization of American States; Inter-American, Asian and African Development Banks; and various regional organizations and affiliates of the major global institutions.

REFERENCES

AMERICAN SOCIETY OF CIVIL ENGINEERS, "Organization of TCWRPM to Meet Environmental, Economic, Social, Political Considerations in Water Resources Planning and Management," Task Committee for Program Development on Environmental Evaluation and Other Interrelated Aspects, Francis W. Montanari et al., January 1974 (unpublished).

AMERICAN SOCIETY OF CIVIL ENGINEERS, "Water Resources Planning in America: 1776–1976," papers in *Proc. Am. Soc. Civil Eng.*, vol. 105, no. WR1, March 1979; and vol. 106, no. WR1, March 1980.

BAUMGARTNER, A., and E. REICHEL, *The World Water Balance*, R. Oldenbourg, Munich, 1975.

BISWAS, ASIT K., *History of Hydrology*, North-Holland, Amsterdam, 1970.

BISWAS, ASIT K., "Water: A Perspective on Global Issues and Politics," *Proc. Am. Soc. Civil Eng.*, vol. 105, no. WR2, September 1979.

BURGES, STEPHEN J., "Water Resource Systems Planning in U.S.A.: 1776–1976," *Proc. Am. Soc. Civil Eng.*, vol. 105, no. WR1, March 1979 (discussed by Harry Wiersema, vol. 106, no. WR1, March 1980).

DWORSKY, LEONARD B., and BERNARD B. BERGER, "Water Resources Planning and Public Health: 1776–1976," *Proc. Am. Soc. Civil Eng.*, vol. 105, no. WR1, March 1979.

GOODMAN, ALVIN S., "Education and Training in Water Resources Planning," *Proc. Am. Soc. Civil Eng.*, vol. 102, no. WR2, November 1976.

HEADY, EARL O., "Food and Agricultural Policies," *Proc. Am. Soc. Civil Eng.*, vol. 104, no. WR1, March 1979.

HEY, DONALD L., and W. HENRY WAGGY, "Planning for Water Quality: 1776–1976," *Proc. Am. Soc. Civil Eng.*, vol. 105, no. WR1, March 1979.

JAMES, L. DOUGLAS, and JERRY R. ROGERS, "Economics and Water Resources Planning in America," *Proc. Am. Soc. Civil Eng.*, vol. 105, no. WR1, March 1979 (discussed by David A. Bella, vol. 106, no. WR1, March 1980).

KEITH, JOHN E., KEITH WILDE, JAY C. ANDERSEN, and ALLEN LE BARON, "Western Economic Development and Water Planning: Bureau of Reclamation," *Proc. Am. Soc. Civil Eng.*, vol. 105, no. WR1, March 1979.

LINSLEY, RAY K., "Hydrology and Water Resources Planning: 1776–1976," *Proc. Am. Soc. Civil Eng.*, vol. 105, no. WR1, March 1979a.

LINSLEY, RAY K., "Two Centuries of Water Planning Methodology," *Proc. Am. Soc. Civil Eng.*, vol. 105, no. WR1, March 1979b.

LOVELL, LEONARD A., CLARENCE L. FREEMAN, and ALVIN S. GOODMAN, "Riven Basin Planning for Private Development," *Proc. Am. Soc. Civil Eng.*, paper 5946, no. PO1, May 1968.

McDONALD, RICHARD J., "Estimates of National Hydroelectric Power Potential at Existing Dams," U.S. Army Corps of Engineers, Institute for Water Resources, July 20, 1977.

MURRAY, C. RICHARD, and E. BODETTE REEVES, "Estimated Use of Water in the United States in 1975," *U.S. Geol. Surv. Circ. 765*, 1977.

ORTOLANO, LEONARD, "Water Planning and the Environment: 1776–1976," *Proc. Am. Soc. Civil Eng.*, vol. 105, no. WR1, March 1979.

ROUSE, HUNTER, and SIMON INCE, "History of Hydraulics," Iowa Institute of Hydraulic Research, State University of Iowa, 1957.

SCHAD, THEODORE M., "Water Resources Planning—Historical Development," *Proc. Am. Soc. Civil Eng.*, vol. 105, no. WR1, March 1979 (discussed by Ellis L. Armstrong and by A. C. Chaturvedi, vol. 106, no. WR1, March 1980).

SCHWARZ, HARRY E., "Water Resources Planning—Its Recent Evolution," *Proc. Am. Soc. Civil Eng.*, vol. 105, no. WR1, March 1979.

U.S. FEDERAL POWER COMMISSION (now Federal Energy Regulatory Commission), "Hydroelectric Power Resources of the United States, January 1, 1976."

U.S. NATIONAL ENVIRONMENTAL POLICY ACT, 1969.

U.S. NATIONAL WATER COMMISSION, "Water Resources Planning," Consulting Panel on Water Resource Planning, May 1972.

U.S. WATER RESOURCES COUNCIL, "Principles and Standards for Planning Water and Related Land Resources," Federal Register (vol. 38, no. 174, pp. 24778-24869), September 10, 1973; (vol. 44, no. 242, pp. 72978-72990), December 14, 1979; (vol. 45, no. 190, pp. 64366-64400), September 29, 1980.

U.S. WATER RESOURCES COUNCIL, "Procedures for Evaluation of National Economic Development (NED) Benefits and Costs in Water Resources Planning (Level C)," (Federal Register, vol. 44, no. 242, pp. 72892-72976), December 14, 1979; "Procedures for Evaluation of National Economic Development (NED) Benefits and Costs and Other Social Effects (OSE) in Water Resources Planning (Level C), Final Rule" (Federal Register, vol. 45, no. 190, pp. 64448-64466), September 29, 1980; "Environmental Quality Evaluation Procedures for Level C Water Resources Planning, Final Rule" (vol. 45, no. 190, pp. 64402-64446), September 29, 1980.

U.S. WATER RESOURCES COUNCIL, "Water Resources Coordination Directory," November 1979.

U.S. WATER RESOURCES COUNCIL, "Economic and Environmental Principles and Guidelines for Water and Related Land Resources Implementation Studies," March 10, 1983.

WEBER, EUGENE W., "Water Planning—Overview," *Proc. Am. Soc. Civil Eng.*, vol. 105, no. WR1, March 1979.

WILLEKE, GENE E., "Social Aspects of Water Resources Planning," *Proc. Am. Soc. Civil Eng.*, vol. 105, no. WR1, March 1979.

WOLMAN, ABEL, "Water Resources," National Academy of Sciences—National Research Council, Washington, D.C., Publication 1000-B, 1962.

WORLD HEALTH ORGANIZATION, "Community Water Supply and Wastewater Disposal," Doc. A29/12/Rev. 1, Geneva, 1976.

TWO

Some Basic Engineering and Economic Planning Concepts

2.1 SCOPE

This chapter continues the definition of important terms used in water resources planning which was begun in Chapter 1, and introduces many of the engineering and economic concepts that are a basis for the detailed planning methodologies discussed in the chapters to follow. The factors that determine the geographic area within which projects are located or provide services are described, and the needs, problems, and other issues that should be addressed for various project purposes are listed. Methods are outlined for comparing projects and for determining whether a project is economically justified. The differences between economic and financial analyses are identified, and specifics are discussed such as the estimate of capital investment and annual costs, the selection of an interest rate for discounting, the equivalency calculations that utilize the interest rate, and the variation of demand for products and services with price. Chapter 1 indicated the difference between planning according to purpose and planning according to objective. This chapter considers systems of objectives which have been used in economically advanced countries such as the United States and in developing countries. This chapter also discusses some of the differences in public and private approaches to the planning of projects, including economic and financial analyses.

2.2 PLANNING AREA

The Consulting Panel on Water Resources Planning in a report to the U.S. National Water Commission (1972) recommended establishing the geographic area of interest for planning so that a minimum of external effects need to be taken into account and that subareas are "united by economic interests, political interests, physical characteristics, or common areawide development problems." The *river basin* often meets these criteria. As noted in U.S. Senate Document 97 (U.S. President's Water Resources Council, 1962, p. 3):

> River basins are usually the most appropriate geographical units for planning the use and development of water and related land resources in a way that will realize fully the advantage of multiple use, reconcile competitive uses through choice of the best combination of uses, coordinate mutual responsibilities of different agencies and levels of government and other interests concerned with resource use.

A river basin encompasses the *drainage area* extending upstream from the mouth of the main stream of the area, and is defined by outlining the drainage divide between this and adjacent basins on a topographic map (see Figure 2.1). The geologic structure sometimes indicates an underground water system with somewhat different boundaries than shown on the surface. Water balance estimates and other hydrologic studies involve subbasins as well as the river basin as a whole.

Because of legislative or political factors, or because data are organized by such divisions, the study area may be selected to have governmental boundaries (e.g., state, county). Eligibility requirements for specific government programs (e.g., for sewerage, water supply, and wastewater treatment) may require consistency with specific area-wide plans. The projects in a river basin may also have *service areas* that extend beyond the boundaries of the drainage area. The output of a hydroelectric project may be fed into a power utility's regional transmission and distribution system whose boundaries are determined by the franchises awarded by a state regulatory authority. The water supply for a large city may be conveyed in a long pipeline extending from a water body to a location many miles away (e.g., New York City obtains one-third of its supply from the Delaware River Basin).

2.3 NEEDS AND OPPORTUNITIES OF WATER RESOURCES FACILITIES AND PROGRAMS

The following outline is an introductory checklist covering important issues, primarily of an engineering nature, that should be treated in planning studies for various types of water resource development and management programs. In addition, there are environmental, political, economic, financial, social, legal, institutional, and other issues that determine whether it is practical to implement a project. These are discussed from a variety of perspectives in other chapters.

Water Supply for Municipal and Industrial Uses and for Thermal-Electric Power Plant Cooling. Present and future demands for municipal and industrial water.

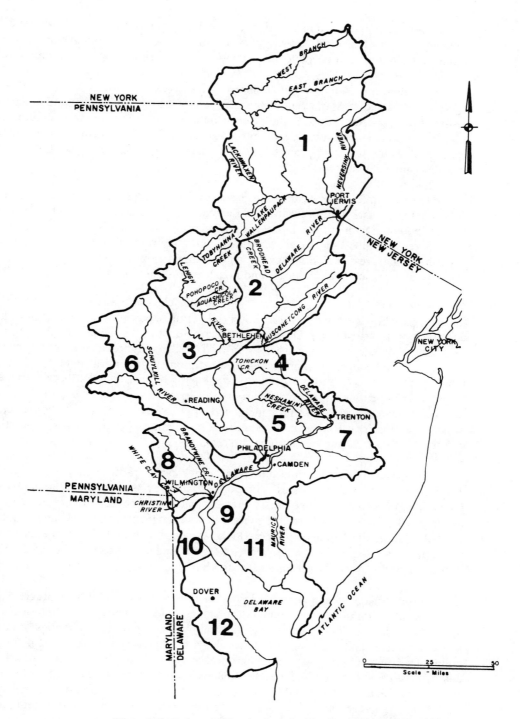

Figure 2.1 Delaware River basin and subbasins. (From TAMS, 1972.)

Total requirements and consumptive uses for thermal-power plants. Alternative sources of supply: location, arrangement of works, quantity and quality of available water, cost. Associated needs for transmission and distribution of water supplies.

Irrigation and Agricultural Drainage. Land classifications in terms of irrigability. Present extent of irrigation and dry farming. Market potential and projected demands for various crops. Suitable crop patterns and their water requirements, allowing for consumed water, precipitation, and irrigation practices. Alternative sources of water supply. Arrangement and cost of required water supplies and of irrigation and drainage works.

Flood Control. Areas that are prone to floods, extent of past flooding, and flood damages sustained. Present flood damage potential. Future increases in flood damage potential with growth of population and economic activity. Present and future alternatives for flood damage reduction, including reservoir construction; local structural measures, including levees and stream improvements to increase flow capacity and reduce bank damage; and nonstructural measures.

Hydroelectric Power. Present and future electric system load variations (annual, monthly, weekly, daily, and hourly) in terms of power or capacity (kilowatts) and energy (kilowatt-hours). Other system characteristics that determine the types of generating, transmission, and distribution facilities. For hydroelectric developments serving isolated industrial plants, mining operations, agricultural developments or municipalities, the variations in capacity and energy requirements of these activities. Location, physical arrangements, appropriate capacity, and cost of potential hydroelectric developments. Appropriateness and opportunity for isolated hydroelectric projects serving industrial plant or other needs. Relation of pumping and generating cycles in the case of pumped storage projects.

Navigation. Present and potential waterborne traffic volumes. Effect of alternative transportation modes (competitive highway, rail, and air facilities) on projections of water traffic volumes. Present and potential recreational navigation. Minimum depths for navigation. Minimum flows to maintain depths. Water supplies needed to maintain depths or to serve locks. Arrangement and cost of measures for maintaining and enhancing water transportation, including constructing reservoirs, deepening and widening river channels, and building locks and canals.

Water Quality Management. Location, quantity, and pollution characteristics of wastewater discharges from population centers and industries. Characteristics of non–point-source pollution due to agricultural fertilizers, forestry activities, mining, and other urban and rural uncontrolled runoff. Evaluation of present and potential pollution. Effects of pollution on appearance, and chemical, physical, and biological characteristics of water body. Effects of unsatisfactory water quality on uses of water, health, and fish and wildlife and other ecological systems. Minimum flows for fish and wildlife maintenance, aesthetics, and other requirements. Problems of sedimentation. Alternative measures to improve water quality, including improved urban and rural drainage, wastewater treatment, diversion of pollution discharges, and low-flow augmentation by reservoirs.

Water-Based Recreation. Present and potential demands for recreation, such as for swimming, boating, fishing, hunting, picnicking, hiking, scenic enjoyment, and observation of wildlife. Present and potential locations and characteristics of recreational areas (area, depth, shoreline length, quality of water and land). Existing and potential capacities for recreation users, facilities, and costs to make recreation areas accessible and enjoyable.

Fish and Wildlife. Inventory of important forms of fish and wildlife and supporting vegetation and marine life. Identification of endangered species. Past and potential ecological changes due to natural changes and human activities. Structural and nonstructural measures to preserve and enhance fish, wildlife, and other ecological forms.

Watershed Management. Identification and evaluation of measures for land stabilization, erosion control, and sediment management; for enhancement of water, land, and air quality; and for improvement of recreation and other water-based activities and uses. Preservation of outstanding archeological, historical, cultural, and aesthetic features.

2.4 GENERAL PRINCIPLES OF PROJECT ANALYSIS

Introduction. The most important problems are to choose among alternative projects and to determine the optimum scale (size) of a project. Other problems include allocation of costs among the several functions of a multiple-purpose project, and the allocation of costs to those who benefit from the project. Analytic aids may also be used to plan a budget; for example, one may analyze the benefits and costs for each item in a budget or one may determine how much benefit would be lost if a budget item is deleted or reduced in amount.

The concepts used in project planning studies may be quite different from those used by accountants. The planner or economist is interested in estimating future effects in terms of physical quantities, benefits, and costs; the values of the benefits and costs may be different from the monetary revenues and expenditures. The accountant is usually interested in keeping track of past costs. The information developed by accountants, however, may be very useful in making estimates of project costs. Higher authority may have to approve the analyst's assumptions for period of analysis, interest rate, method of depreciation, accounting for positive and negative impacts on various objectives, and so on.

There is undoubtedly much room for expansion of the use of analytic aids in analyzing public works. However, there are many engineering projects (e.g., for water supply to meet municipal and industrial needs) for which the solutions are obvious and for which detailed studies of alternatives are not undertaken. Such projects to meet clearly defined needs or to meet legal requirements do not, therefore, require a sophisticated economic or financial study.

The following paragraphs describe some of the approaches used in typical project analyses.

Analysis of Alternatives.   Most analyses require the comparison of alternatives. Such analyses may include: (1) comparison of two or more projects; (2) comparison of various scales (size of project or size of an element of a project); and (3) comparison of a project with no project at all (this is the problem of project justification).

Tangible Values.   In a business setting, a choice among alternatives is determined primarily by analysis of financial costs, revenues, and other sources of income. For public works, both financial and economic analyses are needed, and the former require the estimates to be made in monetary terms. For economic analysis, beneficial and adverse impacts are in terms of real income productivity; they are not necessarily reflected in revenues and outlays.

Comparison When Costs Are Specified.   When two or more alternatives have essentially equivalent costs, the problem is to compare the benefits or services. This situation often occurs when a public agency authorizes a specific budget for a general area of public services, and wishes to receive maximum output for each dollar expended.

Comparison When Benefits Are Specified.   When two or more alternatives provide essentially equivalent benefits, or provide essentially the same services, the problem is to compare the costs. An example is when the quality of effluent is specified for a wastewater treatment plant which receives influent of known quantity and quality. The costs may be in terms of the investment required or, more preferably, on a *life-cycle* basis (equivalent annual or present-worth values). For some alternatives, the costs may be directly related to quantities of material or work (e.g., dams constructed of similar materials); for this case, the comparison may be in terms of the quantities rather than the dollar costs.

Comparison when Alternatives Have Varying Benefits and Costs.   When two or more alternatives differ in both benefits and costs, they can be compared by one or more of the following measures:

1. Present worth, with stipulated interest rate used; $PW(B - C)$
2. Equivalent uniform annual cash flow with a stipulated interest rate used for computations; average annual $(B - C)$
3. Prospective rate of return (calculated rate on the investment); (net operating revenue)/(depreciated investment) or comparable public works calculation
4. Benefit-cost ratio
5. Internal rate of return, which is the rate that equates present worths of benefits and costs

Comparisons on Present Worth or Annual Basis. Benefits and costs are computed in terms of present worth or annual amounts. If the benefits and costs vary from year to year over the period of analysis, the procedure is:

1. Convert all of these "time streams" of benefits and costs into present worth quantities; or
2. Convert the present-worth quantities of benefits and costs into equivalent uniform annual amounts of benefits and costs over the period of analysis.

The present-worth method is the conceptually correct method of comparing benefits and costs over time, and discounted $B - C$ is the preferred quantity to compare in project design (see Bierman and Smidt, 1966, and Eckstein, 1961). Other methods are variants of this (annual equivalents), give correct results in restricted circumstances (internal rate of return), or are theoretically incorrect although perhaps of some practical use (e.g., payout period). In water resources planning, if other methods are used but there is any question as to recommendations, calculations should be redone using the present-worth method.

Interest Rate. The comparisons of alternatives usually involve mathematical operations with formulas containing an interest rate. This rate is usually expressed on an annual basis. It may be referred to as a "discount rate"; it is used not only in present-worth calculations, but also in determinations of future worth or equivalent annual amounts.

Period of Analysis. The period of analysis should be at least as long as the payout period for funds borrowed to build the project, and should not exceed the "economic life" of the project. The average economic life of many structures and machines may be obtained from schedules of the U.S. Internal Revenue Service. If the period of analysis is 100 years (say for a dam project) and a piece of equipment lasts 20 years (say a motor), the piece of equipment is assumed to be replaced four times during the 100 years. (One way to do this is to depreciate the piece of equipment five times using a "sinking fund" each time; salvage value at the end is taken into account if the piece of equipment is assumed to last, for example, 22 years.)

With and Without Analysis. The effects of a project are the differences *with* and *without* the project, which is not the same as "before" and "after." If the latter principle is adhered to, the project may be incorrectly credited with developments unrelated to the project itself. Substantial changes may be expected in the regional economy, for example, whether the project is constructed or not.

Values Based on Prices. Market prices are relevant to financial and economic analyses in different ways. In financial analyses, prices represent financial flows that may or may not have to be adjusted for taxes, subsidies, or other financial considerations. For economic analyses, market prices may represent a good estimate of true economic value, or alternatively they may have to be adjusted for differences between market price and true economic value by the use of "simulated" values (called "shadow" or "economic accounting" prices).

Physical Comparability. In addition to economic and financial analyses, the planner must take account of other effects that often cannot be estimated satisfactorily in economic or financial terms. These include differences in *uncertainties* of construction and operation. With respect to uncertainties, the term *risk* is preferred when the probability can be estimated for the events (e.g., floods and droughts) that produce uncertainty. The following are some uncertainties of an engineering nature.

- Alternative solutions that are apparently equivalent do not, in fact, produce the same results. One project may be inherently better from an engineering point of view, it may have a longer life, or the benefits it achieves may be more certain.
- Some solutions may offer greater flexibility than others from the point of view of potential future modifications of the project purposes to suit possible future needs. For example, a flood control reservoir project may offer greater feasibility for possible future "multiple-purpose" use than an alternative local protection project (involving levees, floodwalls, and channel modifications).
- Some solutions include components that are more or less susceptible to unforeseen problems and consequent increases in costs. For example, dam sites in an area may have serious foundation problems which are not susceptible to advance evaluation based on limited explorations.

Multiunit, Multipurpose, Multiobjective Considerations. Regional (e.g., basin) studies may involve multiunits with various development stages, multipurpose facilities, and multiobjective considerations. The latter may include economic, environmental, or other objectives. When projects involve multiple purposes, there will be special problems in deciding how costs and benefits are to be analyzed for each of the purposes. One important issue is assigning costs of a dam and reservoir to various projects or purposes benefiting from water storage; the *separable cost-remaining benefits* method and other techniques are discussed in Chapter 8.

Sensitivity and Risk Analyses. Financial (or economic) analyses require forecasts of expenditures (or economic costs) and revenues (or benefits). Conclusions may differ depending on such forecasts. Modern techniques include "sensitivity" and "risk" analyses. In sensitivity analysis, one or more elements are varied over a range of possible values and a range of results is determined. In probability or *risk* analysis, input, output, or both are derived using statistical probability concepts (e.g., probability equals 60% that $B/C \geq 1.5$, probability equals 80% that $B/C \geq 1.2$, etc.).

Financial analyses are needed for both public and private projects. They include the preparation of the following types of documents:

- Estimates of the investment cost and annual cost of the project, in terms of monetary requirements
- Schedule showing the breakdown of the investment cost by years, with separate accounts of expenditures for construction and for the other categories of costs needed to bring the project into operation
- Estimates of portions of investment cost in domestic and foreign funds, especially in the case of developing countries whose foreign currencies are in short supply
- Plan for financing the costs of the project investment, including the sources of funds and the terms for repayment of each category of borrowings
- Estimates of costs; revenues from the sale of water and other services; and required subsidies on a year-by-year basis extending from the completion of construction to the date when the repayment of all borrowings is completed and beyond if appropriate
- Plan for the required annual subsidies, if any, working funds to enable operation to commence, and for financing to meet temporary cash flow requirements
- Additional statements of a financial nature depending on the regulatory and financial institutions involved in the project

Economic analyses are needed, in addition to financial analyses, for most public projects, especially when water resources projects are analyzed at a national level. Some of the elements of the description that follows may be considered by private enterprises, but it is rare that they will be treated as formally.

Economic analyses treat all economic costs and benefits. Economic effects of public works may involve beneficial or adverse effects in addition to construction and operating costs and user benefits. Economic feasibility implies that the discounted benefits of constructing and operating the project will exceed the discounted costs over its useful life. Indicators such as the benefit-cost ratio, net benefits, and internal rate of return are used to demonstrate economic feasibility. All costs and benefits that can be accounted for as being attributable to the project should be included in the analyses.

A variety of methods exist for determining benefits of a project. A benefit is not the same as revenue, since the actual or perceived beneficial effects of a project may be greater or less than the revenue to recover project costs. Unlike the services of a private business, many public services are offered without expectation of full or even partial reimbursement of costs. On the other hand, there are many times when prices charged for public services are set equal to costs, but when the benefits in terms of consumer satisfactions are actually greater than revenues. The "Principles and Guidelines" of the U.S. Water Resources Council (1983, p. 9) include the following measurement standard for goods and services valued for the National Economic Development account:

The general measurement standard of the value of goods and services is defined as the willingness of users to pay for each increment of output from a plan. Such a value would be obtained if the "seller" of the output were able to apply a variable unit price and charge each user an individual price to capture the full value of the output to the user. Since it is not possible in most instances for the planner to measure the actual demand situation, four alternative techniques can be used to obtain an estimate of the total value of the output of the plan: willingness to pay based on actual or simulated market price; change in net income; cost of the most likely alternative; and administratively established values.

For a water supply serving municipal, industrial, or thermal power needs, a minimum measure of benefits may be the cost of an alternative that would provide comparable service in terms of quantity and quality of water that would in fact be utilized in the absence of the water supply project under consideration. For a hydroelectric power project, the benefits may be equivalent to the cost of an alternative power project (usually thermal-electric) providing equivalent power and energy. For an irrigation project, the benefits may be evaluated in terms of increased agricultural income attributable to the water supply. For flood control, the benefits may be determined as the damages prevented by the project. For navigation, the benefits may be the cost savings of waterborne commerce in comparison with alternative modes of transportation. Recreational benefits may be in terms of perceived values based on the type of recreational activity and the money people are willing to spend while reaching and engaging in the activity.

The examples of benefits outlined above are in terms of *direct user benefits*. The *direct costs* are usually related to the investment and annual costs of the financial analyses. In addition, both benefits and costs may be increased for *externalities* due to other effects on the economy that may be caused by the project. External economies include such effects as a reduction in downstream water treatment costs that is external to a plan for flood control and hydropower purposes. A plan may also cause external diseconomies, as when a reservoir stores low flows and reduces the flows downstream that are available to dilute wastewater discharges, thereby increasing the cost of treatment. Externalities are not usually evaluated in a financial analysis but should be included in an economic analysis.

As noted earlier, economic analyses may be based on benefits and costs that are adjusted by *shadow pricing*. Shadow prices, particularly in developing countries, are used when market prices do not indicate the true costs to the national economy. Additional adjustments called *weights* are also used in some countries to express government policy to favor or discourage use of specific resources.

If a project is determined to be economic on the basis of a benefit-cost analysis, it is justified from a public standpoint provided that, when budget constraints exist, the services of such a project are considered of high enough priority for implementation as compared with the use of valuable resources (capital, skilled labor, etc.) for other purposes.

In engineering economy studies involving business decisions, the terms *financial* and *economic* are often used interchangeably. In some fields of public works also, no distinction is made between the two terms. However, whether or not the terms are used interchangeably, the analyst should always make clear which objective is being studied—the financial or the national income (economic) objective.

Sunk Costs. It is a general rule of economic analysis that costs already committed and for which the sponsor is liable do not enter into a comparison of alternatives or a decision as to whether or not to proceed with a project. This is consistent with the fact that such "sunk costs" would apply to both the "with" and "without" conditions and therefore cancel out in decision-making considerations. In financial analyses, however, all cash flows, including carryover obligations, may have to be considered. For such analyses, the analyst may include sunk costs with an appropriate footnote to the calculations, or may make two sets of calculations, with and without the sunk costs.

Transfer Payments. These are payments such as taxes and subsidies. These are not properly included in national income (economic) analyses, since the national income objective is concerned with real income and productivity effects. However, they are properly taken into account in financial analyses and in studies of impacts on regional and group income accounts (Marglin 1967; Major 1977).

Inflation. In economic analyses, calculations are made in terms of constant dollars. In practice, the analysis is usually made in terms of prices in effect during the planning phase. This assumes that general inflation rates would have an equal effect on future benefits and costs which, after conversion to constant dollar values, could be discounted at a specified interest rate. This approach should be modified if different components of the benefits and costs are affected differently by inflation. In financial analyses, an analysis on a year-by-year basis makes it possible to take account of assumed inflation rates for any component of costs, revenues, and subsidies.

2.6 INVESTMENT COST

Financial analyses of water resources projects that involve constructed facilities start with estimates of investment cost and annual cost. Table 2.1 shows a recommended form of summary investment cost estimate for a hydroelectric project.

Most water resource projects in the United States are executed through purchase contracts for major equipment and for construction. The costs for such contracts depend on estimates of labor, materials, equipment, business overhead, financing charges, and profit. Contracts are awarded by the sponsor, or "owner" (private or public), after proposals (tenders, bids) are received from contractors and evaluated for cost and other considerations. The proposals are based on plans and specifications provided by the owner of the project. In some cases, the owner acts as his own contractor to carry out all or a portion of the construction ("force account" method).

The costs of the contract awards, together with the costs of lands, land rights, and possibly separate water rights, constitute the total direct construction costs, not

TABLE 2.1 BRIDGE CANYON PROJECT: SUMMARY OF TOTAL PROJECT
INVESTMENT (DOLLARS)

Description	Amount
Production Plant	
Land and land rights	200,000
Structures and improvements	7,801,000
Reservoirs, dams, and waterways	47,758,000
Turbines and generators	27,840,000
Accessory electrical equipment	1,528,000
Miscellaneous power plant equipment	2,184,000
Roads	10,303,000
Subtotal	97,614,000
Transmission Plant	
Land and land rights	1,272,000
Clearing land	42,000
Switching station, Bridge Canyon	7,916,000
Switching station requirements beyond Bridge Canyon	19,833,000
Towers and footings	11,019,000
Overhead conductors and devices	14,908,000
Roads and trails	554,000
Subtotal	55,544,000
General Plant	
General plant	75,000
Subtotal	75,000
Total Direct Construction Costs, Not Including Contingencies	153,233,000
Contingencies	15,704,000
Total Direct Construction Costs, Including Contingencies	168,937,000
Engineering, supervision of construction, and Department	
of Water and Power overhead	14,680,000
Subtotal	183,617,000
Net interest during construction, at 3½% annually	9,898,000
Total Project Investment	193,515,000

Source: TAMS (1960).

including contingencies. Contingencies are usually applied as percentages of direct construction cost components and cover extra costs that are paid to contractors during construction due to differences between estimated quantities of construction and the quantities actually realized at the project site, omissions of incidental items of work, unforeseen difficulties at the site, changes in plans, and other uncertainties not definable when the contracts are awarded.

Engineering supervision of construction (by engineer and/or owner, not by the contractor) and owner's overhead assignable to the project are applied as percentages of the subtotal of direct costs, including contingencies. The resulting subtotal represents the total costs, not including interest during construction.

If investment costs are estimated as of the date when construction is completed and operation starts, it is necessary to add interest during construction for borrowed funds or for equivalent expected returns on equity funds used for the construction. These financing costs may be based on a detailed schedule showing when various payments to contractors and for other costs are required. An approximate estimate may be based upon applying the full annual interest rate for one-half of the construction period.

For the example shown in Table 2.1, the ratio of investment cost to direct field cost without contingencies for estimates made in 1960 was 1.27. For more typical projects with several years of construction at recent (1983) financing costs, such a ratio would be 1.6 or greater.

2.7 ANNUAL COST

Table 2.2 shows a summary annual cost estimate for the same project. The operation and maintenance item applies to labor, supplies, and replacement of short-lived equipment and materials. General administrative expenses are for a portion of the overhead of the central offices of the owner. Renewals and replacements apply only to major structural or machine elements and are estimated as an annual amount to preserve the equity of the investment and keep the project in operative order. Debt service covers interest and amortization based upon repaying the investment cost of the project within the useful life of the project; in this example, the amount shown was estimated by applying a "capital recovery factor" based on 45 years and 3½% interest to the investment cost of $193,515,000. Finally, license fees are included for payments to the Federal Power Commission (now the Federal Energy Regulatory Commission).

For purposes of a financial analysis, the components of the annual cost estimate may be quite different depending on the method used for assigning general administration expenses, providing for renewals and replacements ("sinking fund," straight-line method, or other accounting method), and financing. With respect to the latter term, the capital recovery factor provides an estimate of equal annual payments over the project period to pay back the funds borrowed to cover the investment cost. This is equivalent to paying an amount for interest each year, while accumulating

TABLE 2.2 BRIDGE CANYON PROJECT: SUMMARY OF ANNUAL CHARGES (DOLLARS)

Description	Amount
Operation and maintenance	
Generation	348,300
Transformation	124,300
Transmission line	212,700
General administrative expenses	185,000
Renewals and replacements	1,007,300
Debt service on investment	8,602,400
FPC license fees	101,600
Total Annual Charges	10,581,600

Source: TAMS (1960).

the investment amount by means of a sinking fund and repaying it in a lump sum at the end of the project period. When the owner uses equity funds for construction, the "debt service" term does not apply and provision must be made instead for a return on equity each year and for depreciation of the investment over the project period (or a shorter period using accounting rules permitted by regulatory authorities and the income tax rules).

If the owner is not a public entity, the investment cost and particularly the annual cost estimates would include allowances for taxes. Insurance costs may be shown as a separate item if they are not included in owner's overhead. If the project is constructed in a developing country, the estimates of investment and annual costs should be shown by separate components for foreign ("hard") currency and local ("soft") currencies since they may be subject to different financing terms. (An example of this is given in Chapter 9.) When estimates are made for a central government project, the period for capital recovery and applicable interest rate may be established by government rule for the purposes of the estimates, since money is not generally borrowed for each project separately. Special studies are needed when the project is constructed in stages to meet a growing demand or in accordance with the availability of funds. Also, a project may be financed by bonds whose terms are fixed by law, or where the repayment schedule is arranged to provide for annual amounts that vary from year to year to meet a progressive growth in revenues.

The estimates shown in Tables 2.1 and 2.2 are in terms of *financial costs*. They may have to be adjusted to estimate *economic* costs.

2.8 RELATIONSHIPS BETWEEN PRICE AND DEMAND AND MEASURES OF MONETARY VALUE

Section 2.5 indicated that the economic value of a product or service from a water resource project is correctly estimated as the amount users are willing to pay for the product or service. The variation of this value can be shown conceptually by a curve of price per unit versus units of demand; this is the line AC on Figure 2.2. The demand curve is constructed in principle on the assumption of constant prices for other goods, constant incomes, and constant preferences. When any of these change, the demand for system outputs may shift. (A good basic reference on the demand curve is Dorfman, 1978.)

The price *elasticity* of demand is defined as $(dQ/Q)/(dP/P)$. If, for example, the price is increased by 100% and this results in a 20% decrease in demand, the elasticity is 0.2. The elasticity is less for necessities than for "luxuries." In water resource terms, domestic water supply is generally underpriced with respect to its real value and demand for this product is relatively inelastic within typical ranges of price. However, the demand for certain large industrial water consumers can become elastic when prices, while still modest for domestic water supply, are increased to the point where conservation measures and alternatives (e.g., air cooling) become economic.

Economic profitability as reflected in the demand curve may not be a reasonable criterion by which to assess public projects. There may be other objectives, or the underlying income distribution that gives rise to the demands in question might

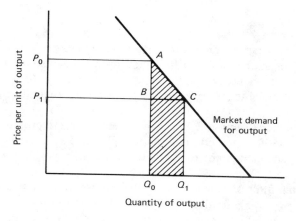

Figure 2.2 Total value or willingness to pay for increased output.

not be acceptable. Nonetheless, analysts will usually wish to consider economic profitability as one dimension of project evaluation. In considering this dimension, care must be taken in using actual market prices as a reflection of willingness to pay, as these may include large distortions from monopolistic practices or government policies. If the market value is used to estimate benefits, it will also understate expected satisfaction where the increment to supply is sufficient to affect price. An examination of the total satisfaction from a project would have to consider the excess of what consumers are willing to pay for its products over what they actually pay. The difference is called *consumers' surplus*. In Figure 2.2, P_0 represents the amount that consumers are willing to pay for the last unit purchased when Q_0 units are available; this is the market clearing price for that quantity. If market price is reduced to P_1, they will buy Q_1 units. Assume that a project increases output by $Q_1 - Q_0$. The total expenditure they will make will be represented by the shaded rectangle CBQ_0Q_1, but the value of their satisfaction is $CABQ_0Q_1$. The difference, or the shaded triangle CAB, represents the consumers' surplus.

The change in the price caused by the increased production of a project may be negligible if the product or service is nationally or internationally traded or the increase is proportionally small. However, if the increased amount of product or service substantially reduces local prices, the value per unit would go down and the economy of existing projects may also be affected.

The goods and services that enter into the construction and operation of a water resources project are generally traded, although often in a distorted market. Therefore, the market prices, modified for distortions and adjusted by shadow pricing if appropriate, may be used on the cost side of the benefit-cost analysis. Where the project inputs are substantial relative to the market for these inputs, an examination of the demand curve for inputs may be necessary (Dasgupta et al. 1972).

It is often not practical, however, to use the market approach for the evaluation of benefits. This is because a market may not exist for a product or service or it may not be possible to interpret the demand curve because of inadequate data. Thus, other methods are utilized in practice. Some of these were mentioned in Section 2.5.

2.9 DISCOUNT (INTEREST) RATE

As mentioned in Section 2.4, when the analyses of water resources projects involve the comparison of alternatives in economic (or financial) terms, they usually require the use of formulas involving an *interest* rate, especially when the lives of the alternatives, or the timing of benefits (or revenues) and costs (or expenditures), are different.

At the end of this chapter (Section 2.15), a number of simple problems are solved using the formulas. Other methods of comparing projects or elements of projects (suboptimization) in economic and financial terms are discussed in Chapters 8, 9, and 10.

In financial accounting, *interest* is money paid for the use of borrowed funds. *Profit* is paid for the use of ownership funds (equity funds). The term *rate of return* is also used; this may refer to the interest rate which the lender receives, or the profit rate which the owner receives; it may also refer to the overall rate that a government agency earns on a capital investment or which a business earns on its employment of both lenders' and owners' funds. For the economic objective, it refers to the real national income return on the investments whether or not there is a financial return.

The interest rate is almost always expressed as an annual rate. The "financial" rate may be thought of as being made up of percentages for: (1) risk of loss; (2) administrative expenses in handling securities; and (3) pure gain or interest, that which compensates the lender for forgoing the use of his or her money during the time the borrower has it and which creates incentive for the accumulation of capital.

In economy calculations for public works, the analyst should usually assume that interest applies whether all the money comes from borrowed funds or all or part of the money comes directly from tax income or other revenues; this will take account of the fact that tax income and other revenues may be used to reduce a public debt or may have other alternative uses. The interest (or *discount*) rate used in public works studies may be different from the *financial* rate a government pays for borrowed money; for example, it may be a *social* or *opportunity cost* rate. In practice, the appropriate interest rate for financial or economic analyses may be:

1. Cost of borrowing set by supply and demand for money in the open market.
2. Cost of borrowing set by law or formal agreement.
3. Minimum attractive rate when business uses available funds.
4. Opportunity cost when government uses tax income and borrowings, which implies an equivalent rate of return in alternative uses (approximated by some economists as average rate of return in private sector).
5. Social rate set by a government agency, which may encourage or discourage projects—a lower rate may be more appropriate for public projects than would be reflected in the market behavior of individuals having a shorter life or taking a different view of the risks of investing money. Such a rate is appropriately used with a shadow price on capital (Marglin 1967; Major 1977).

6. U.S. federal government projects—weighted average yield on outstanding long-term borrowings; this is determined for each fiscal year and is not allowed to change by more than ¼ of 1% in any year.

2.10 MULTIOBJECTIVE PLANNING IN THE UNITED STATES

2.10.1 Historical Development of National Objectives

The U.S. Inter-Agency Committee on Water Resources in its "Proposed Practices for for Economic Analysis of River Basin Projects" ("Green Book," issued May 1950 and revised May 1958) recognized (p. 5) that "the ultimate aim of river basin projects and programs, in common with all other productive activity, is to satisfy human needs and desires." Although it "recognized that public policy may be influenced by other than economic considerations," the report restricted itself to the economics of project development and justification in terms of benefits and costs from the standpoint of aggregate consumption principles as applied to the unadjusted market place. Presumably, any broader considerations related to the public welfare were taken into account in the practices of the individual agencies. In fact, since the adoption of the Green Book principles was not mandatory, emphases on different objectives could be continued if they were implicit in the legal and institutional framework under which the agency (e.g., Bureau of Reclamation) operated. Since agencies had specialized missions and political constituencies, concern with noneconomic objectives was not uncommon.

U.S. Senate Document 97 (U.S. President's Water Resources Council, 1962) took a broader view of planning policies that were desirable from a national viewpoint, and specified policies that were supposed to be applied uniformly by the agencies except when prevented by law (the President's Water Resources Council consisted of the secretaries of the principal federal agencies dealing with water resources). The basic objective in the formulation of plans was stated (p. 1) "to provide the best use, or combination of uses, of water and related land resources to meet all foreseeable short and long-term needs." In "pursuit of this basic conservation objective," planning would fully consider the following objectives and make "reasoned choices" between them when they conflict:

1. Development
2. Preservation
3. Well-being of people

Development included both national development and regional development, and applied to the various purposes of water and related land resources development and management (water supply, navigation, outdoor recreation when provided or enhanced by development works, etc.). Preservation was defined (p. 2) as "proper stewardship in the long-term interest of the Nation's national bounty" and referred to such aspects as protection and rehabilitation of resources; maintenance and use for recreational purposes of natural water and land areas; and preservation and management of areas of natural beauty, historical, and scientific interest. It stated that the

> Well-being of all the people shall be the overriding determinant in considering the best use of water and related land resources. Hardship and basic needs of particular groups within the general public shall be of concern, but care shall be taken to avoid resource use and development for the benefit of a few or the disadvantage of many. In particular, policy requirements and guides established by the Congress and aimed at assuring that the use of natural resources, including water resources, safeguard the interests of all of our people shall be observed.

Following the establishment of a Water Resources Council (WRC) in 1965 replacing the President's Water Resources Council, the WRC in 1967 appointed a Special Task Force to review and revise the then current evaluation practices (according to Senate Document 97). Following a preliminary report in June 1969, the Task Force presented recommended principles and standards for planning in July 1970. The set of objectives recommended in the 1970 report were: (1) national economic development; (2) environmental quality; (3) social well-being; and (4) regional development. This document recommended the use of four accounts (tables) that displayed the beneficial and adverse effects toward each objective. After further study, review, field testing, and public hearings, the Council published its "Proposed Principles and Standards" on December 21, 1971, which retained as objectives national economic development, quality of the environment, and regional development. Although the system of accounts was to include "social factors," these were not given equal status as a major national planning objective. Finally, after further comments were received and various governmental agencies were consulted, the Water Resources Council on September 10, 1973, established its "Principles and Standards for Planning Water and Related Land Resources" in which a complete display or accounting would be made on only two objectives: National Economic Development and Environmental Quality. For each alternative plan, the beneficial and adverse effects on regional development and social well-being were, however, to be displayed (p. 24782) "where appropriate."

The "Principles and Standards" were revised in 1979 and 1980 and "Procedures" for detailed evaluation were developed and published by the Water Resources Council for the National Economic Development objective in 1979 and 1980 and for the Environmental Quality objective in 1980. The categories for presentation were revised somewhat and renamed National Economic Development (NED), Environmental Quality (EQ), Regional Economic Development (RED), and Other Social Effects (OSE).

In 1983, in order "to reduce the burden on agencies in complying with detailed and legally binding technical rules" (Federal Register, vol. 48, no. 48, March 10, 1983), the "Principles and Standards" and "Procedures" were replaced by "Principles and Guidelines" based on the single NED objective (p. iv). The NED account would be required, while other information would be included in the EQ, RED, and OSE accounts, or "in some other appropriate format" (p. v).

2.10.2 Water Resources Council System of Accounts

A system of accounts was specified by the WRC in 1973 and illustrated by tables for a hypothetical project. Table 2.3 displays the effects on the National Economic Development (NED) objective. Chapter 10 discusses NED evaluation procedures. Chapter 15 provides information on the Environmental Quality (EQ) procedures. Chapters 14 and 16 discuss methods for studying Regional Economic Development (RED) effects and Other Social Effects (OSE).

The WRC published extensive guidelines for the NED and EQ accounts in 1983 in its "Principles and Guidelines." This document provided much less information for the RED and OSE accounts. Other material is available in the WRC 1973 document for the Regional Development (RD) and Social Well-Being (SWB) accounts and in the publications of other federal agencies.

TABLE 2.3 BENEFICIAL AND ADVERSE EFFECTS FOR A PLAN—NATIONAL ECONOMIC DEVELOPMENT (ADDITIONAL TABLES FOR EACH ALTERNATIVE PLAN)

Components	Measures of Effects
I. Beneficial effects	
A. Value of increased outputs of goods and service.	
Examples include:	
1. Flood control	$1,000,000
2. Power	1,000,000
3. Water supply	1,000,000
4. Irrigation	1,000,000
5. Recreation	1,000,000
6. Use of labor resources otherwise unemployed or underemployed in construction or installation of the plan	1,000,000
B. Value of output resulting from external economics.	
Examples include:	
1. Economics of scale in subsequent processing	1,000,000
2. Reduced transportation costs as result of road relocation	1,000,000
Total beneficial effects	8,000,000
II. Adverse effects	
A. Value of resources required for a plan. Examples include:	
1. Project construction and OMR	3,000,000
2. Project pumping power	1,000,000
3. Labor resources displaced and subsequently unemployed	500,000
B. Losses in output resulting from external diseconomics.	
Examples include:	
1. Diseconomics of scale in subsequent processing for displaced activities	500,000
2. Increased transportation costs as result of road relocation	1,000,000
Total adverse effects	6,000,000
Net beneficial effects	2,000,000

Source: U.S. Water Resources Council (1973, pp. 24834-5).

2.10.3 Noneconomic Objectives

Section 1.11 indicated that many institutions in the United States at federal, state, and local levels are involved in the planning of water resources projects. Section 2.10.1 has discussed the evolution of the objectives of federal agencies in the planning of these projects. It is expected that the composition and roles of agencies will continue to change in the future in accordance with the changes in legislative, executive, and legal directives that reflect new leadership and societal values. Despite changes in agency structure and rules (some of them substantial), however, it is likely that water resources planning agencies in the United States, and for that matter, in other countries with advanced economies, will continue to be guided by considerations that extend beyond the purely economic.

Engelbert (1968) states that social noneconomic considerations have always permeated water policy decision-making processes. He lists these considerations under four broad headings. *Ethical* considerations include the sustenance and protection of human life and the conservation of resources for future generations. *Social policy* considerations facilitate regional and national growth, influence the spatial distribution of population, and promote the public's general welfare. Standards of *due process* are procedures whereby individual rights are secured and maintained. They consciously establish water institutions and procedures that will minimize social conflict. *Aesthetic* factors are society's interest in using and conserving water resources to protect the beauty, quality, and reliability of the natural environment.

In considering the public objectives in managing the water resources of the Colorado Basin, a report of the National Academy of Sciences (1968) also recognized the need to *satisfy political obligations* together with other economic and noneconomic goals.

2.10.4 Mix of Economic and Noneconomic Objectives

Most planning for water resource projects in the public sector (and even in the private sector, although perhaps not as explicitly) involves the need to consider both economic and noneconomic objectives. The emphasis may be on the economic objectives with the noneconomic objectives considered as constraints or taken into account less explicitly (i.e., by judgment of the planners), the two types of objectives may be considered on a par with each other, or other approaches may be used in planning. One of the difficulties is to establish the relative importance of the objectives and their components, and measures of the degree of accomplishment. In this connection, James and Lee (1971) have raised a number of questions for a diversified set of six economic and noneconomic objectives.

A comprehensive water resources study by the U.S. North Atlantic Regional Water Resources Study Coordinating Committee (1972) considered the three objectives of national efficiency, regional development, and environmental quality. This study has been discussed by Major (1977) and by Wollman (1976).

Plans were formulated emphasizing each of the three objectives and a recommended mixed objective program was also developed. The first costs for these programs differed substantially; in 1970 prices, they were as follows:

	Billions of dollars
National efficiency	28.2
Regional development	37.6
Environmental quality	44.6
Recommended mixed objectives	
Water management	21.8
Land management	2.9
Environmental management	12.5
Total	37.2

2.11 OBJECTIVES OF DEVELOPING COUNTRIES

The United Nations Industrial Development Organization (in its "Guidelines for Project Evaluation," prepared by Dasgupta, Sen, and Marglin, 1972) recommended that project analysis consider the following objectives for *developing countries* (pp. 29–33):

1. Aggregate consumption
2. Income redistribution
3. Growth rates of national income
4. Employment level
5. Self-reliance
6. Merit wants

Aggregate consumption is the basic economic or national income (National Economic Development) objective; it is measured by the willingness to pay for system inputs and outputs. It may be necessary to adjust these prices for the imperfections of the market (e.g., by shadow pricing). Another issue relates to aggregating consumption over time; this requires an appropriate social rate of discount, which can vary from year to year. If society considers that the consumption of poor persons should be given greater weight than that of rich persons, this is taken into account by the separate income redistribution objective (see World Bank publications, e.g., Squire and van der Tak, 1975). One approach to the income redistribution objective is to measure this benefit by the amount of consumption accruing to the poorest group or poorest region, and weighing this amount in order to consider it with the aggregate consumption objective.

Expansion of employment, or a reduction in unemployment, if it is considered to be important primarily for its impact on aggregate consumption or on income distribution, is largely taken into account by these measures. It may, however, be taken as a separate objective if "unemployment may be thought to be a denial of human dignity, and its reduction may be preferred irrespective of considerations of total consumption and its distribution. Then the size of unemployment may be a measure of costs, i.e., of negative benefits" (Dasgupta et al. 1972, p. 32).

Self-reliance may be a goal when it is desired to reduce dependence on richer countries because of chronic shortages of savings or of foreign exchange. Such dependence may be estimated in terms of the trade deficit (gap between imports and exports) or by the deficit in the overall balance of payments.

Merit wants are objectives whose national importance is not determined by individuals in their capacity as consumers. Employment and self-reliance are considered to be examples of merit wants. A particularly good example of merit wants is education.

The UN publication treats the problems of evaluating the extent to which projects advance each of the objectives and discusses their combination into measures of "aggregate national economic profitability." In this treatment consumption is used as the basic unit of account. This requires that other types of benefits must be weighed to consider them in terms of equivalent units. This, in turn, involves establishing equivalencies between different types of benefits. The approach outlined in the UN publication (Dasgupta et al. 1972, p. 34) is to obtain a weighted sum of benefits. Thus, if the planner considers that, at the margin, a_1 units of B_1 *are equivalent to* a_2 units of B_2 and to a_3 units of B_3, the aggregate measure of benefits is

$$B = a_1 B_1 + a_2 B_2 + a_3 B_3$$

In order to express total benefits in terms of B_1 the coefficients are divided by a_1,

$$B = B_1 + \frac{a_2}{a_1} B_2 + \frac{a_3}{a_1} B_3$$

or

$$B = B_1 + C_2 B_2 + C_3 B_3$$

where C_2 and C_3 express the equivalencies between amounts of B_1 and B_2 and between B_1 and B_3, respectively. These weights (C_2 and C_3) thus represent the rates at which the planner is ready to substitute one kind of benefit for another.

Objectives such as those outlined above, based on UN guidelines, may often be expressed in other ways. For example, in Chapter 6, the master plan for the Vardar/Axios River Basin in Yugoslavia and Greece (TAMS, 1978) will be discussed, where the following planning categories were important in formulating alternative plans:

- Economic sector development (agricultural, industrial, electric power)
- Balanced regional development
- Engineering and economic feasibility
- Financial viability

No attempt was made to obtain a single measure encompassing the various planning categories with this system of objectives. It is clear, however, that new projects, if they pass appropriate economic feasibility tests, generally also result in increased employment and self-reliance. Balanced regional development relates to income redistribution among regions as well as groups. Since both economic and financial analyses considered foreign exchange, the concept of self-reliance was again involved.

The approach to project formulation did not consider trade-offs through an analytical procedure involving equivalence of units of alternative objectives. Weightings were, however, considered implicitly through extensive consultations and reliance on the judgments of personnel of the United Nations and representatives of the two countries who could interpret the economic, institutional, and political consequences of alternative plans. Another example of this by Major and Lenton (1979) is discussed in Chapter 13.

In discussing the objectives of developing countries, Wiener (1972, p. 84) recognizes their need to achieve short-term and medium-term economic targets before it is meaningful to introduce long-term goals. Thus, "achievement of reasonable nutritional, educational, housing, clothing and leisure levels must precede attempts to set comprehensive and more sophisticated aims." He points out, however, that while expanding the "classical" means of production (land, water, capital, and labor), a developing country should also consider diverting substantial resources to improving the "politico-administrative" dimension with the object of improving *growth capacity* and, ultimately, of *priming a process of cumulative growth.*

Wiener (p. 148) divides objectives into "direct or final objectives" concerned with production of commodities and services and "indirect" or "instrumental objectives," which are the means and tools that have to be created and employed to reach a direct objective. His recommended direct objectives are similar to those outlined earlier: increasing aggregate sectorial production, improving the balance of payments, reducing unemployment, improving the distribution of added production between regions or between producer groups within the sector, and increasing the propensity to save. Instrumental objectives comprehend the expansion and improvement of planning capacity, volume of transformation inputs (human resources trained and motivated to transform responses of the basic producer and his institutions), and institutional space at all levels.

The UNIDO guidelines, in developing a system of objectives for industrial development, do not lay any stress on the quality of the environment or other intangible descriptors applying to the quality of human life. Although these aspects are not ignored in developing countries, they are not considered as explicitly as in the more economically advanced countries (in particular, the United States). Subsequent chapters, in discussing planning approaches and actual planning cases, will describe the important role of noneconomic objectives. It will be emphasized that noneconomic factors can, in fact, be on a par with or even more important than economic performance in formulating a project and achieving its implementation.

2.12 APPROACHES TO PROJECT FORMULATION, ANALYSIS, AND RANKING WITH MULTIOBJECTIVES

There are a number of different approaches used in multiobjective planning. These methods include:

- Maximization of one objective, with constraints (specified values or limits) on the other objectives
- Formulation of alternative plans, each emphasizing a different objective, and from this developing a mixed objective plan through a consensus or bargaining process among the participants in the planning process and the decision makers
- Use of an explicit system of weights to make the several objectives commensurable, thus permitting the maximization of a "utility" or "welfare" function, or the use of trade-off relationships that allow the increase (or decrease) in the value of one objective at the expense (or gain) of another until the marginal rates of change of all objectives are equal
- Use of target values of components of all objectives, with functions to express penalties for failures to meet these targets

In subsequent chapters, these methods will often be employed; however, they may not be identified with a recognized formal method of multiobjective optimization. In many cases the treatment of objectives is limited to their implicit consideration in the rationale or value judgments of the planners who develop a particular procedure for project formulation or analysis.

Later chapters consider methods for obtaining optimal plans, including mathematical optimization techniques. The following section on social welfare provides an introduction to theoretical concepts underlying these methods.

2.13 SOCIAL WELFARE FUNCTION, INDIFFERENCE CURVES, AND TRADE-OFFS

Welfare economics aims to establish rules whereby resources (land, water, capital, labor, etc.) are allocated in order to maximize net social (i.e. economic) benefits. In classical theory, the welfare functions that are maximized refer to individuals or families and their aggregated benefits. For a detailed exposition of the theoretical basis of welfare or, more generally, "utility" functions, the reader is referred to the works of Samuelson (1948) and Graaf (1963), which expand the work by classical economists (e.g., Marshall and Pigou) in the field of welfare economics. In multiobjective analysis, the concept may be extended to consider various objectives and the levels of attainment of these objectives. The general expression for a welfare function would be

$$W = f(A, B, C, \ldots)$$

In this equation, A, B, C, ... stand for the objectives. If social welfare increases linearly with increases in the quantity of attainment of the various objectives, the following form of the welfare function may be written:

$$W = a_1 A + a_2 B + a_3 C + \ldots$$

This equation is similar to that suggested by Dasgupta et al. (1972) in the UN guidelines. When W is a scalar quantity, the a values are in appropriate units to permit the conversion of objectives (each of which may be in different units) into a measure of welfare. If each of the objectives is in the same units, the a values could be weights that consider the relative importance of each of the objectives, and thus sum up to 1.0. The values of W and each of the objectives need not be in terms of monetary units; and scalar quantities that describe the "utility" or relative utility of plans could be used for comparing one alternative plan with another. This approach is further discussed using the mathematical principles of "multiattribute utility theory" in Chapter 13.

As conceived for water resource project analysis, the methods of measurement of utility are established by a government agency or by an individual planner to express societal preferences. These preferences represent ethical judgments for society that may not necessarily be the same as the measures of well-being of individuals (or families) as perceived in classical welfare economics. James and Lee (1971) have discussed the role of welfare economics in planning.

Indifference curves are a means of visualizing the relative preferences that individuals or society holds with respect to various objectives. Figure 2.3 shows various curves plotted on a chart of net discounted income benefits toward national and regional objectives. The curves, W_1, W_2, . . . may be referred to as indifference curves or, in this case, as social preference curves. Each point on the W_1 curve shows a mix of contributions to the national and regional objectives which is considered by society to be equivalent to the mix at any other point on the same curve. The points on the W_2 curve show the equivalent of contributions perceived with respect to the two objectives for another (generally higher) level of combined income benefits.

In Figure 2.3 is shown another curve BC, which represents the boundary of the "feasible set" of water resource development and management alternatives that are considered within limits that are set by physical, budgetary, and other constraints. This curve is known as the net benefit *transformation curve* since it indicates how net benefits toward one objective may be transformed or traded for net benefits toward the other objective. In this case, point A represents the socially optimal combination of net benefits toward the two objectives since it achieves a balance between the contributions toward the two objectives while providing for the maximum feasible welfare. This point is located at the intersection of the transformation curve with the tangent indifference curve. The negative of the slope of the tangent line at this point shows the relative weights given to national and regional income, or for the substitution of one for the other.

The example of Figure 2.3 is intended to be conceptual. The indifference curves W_1, W_2, and W_3 are not necessarily parallel to each other, and many different shapes of transformation curves are also possible. Furthermore, if more objectives were considered, the W and T relationships would be mapped as surfaces (or higher forms) and it would be impossible, except in relatively simple cases, to demonstrate the optimization graphically.

If the various objectives are expressed in monetary terms, or in other numerical units, it may be possible to perform the optimization using mathematical techniques. Such techniques are discussed in Chapter 13. In some cases, trade-offs are made in the objectives, or components of the objectives, in the iterative processes of planning

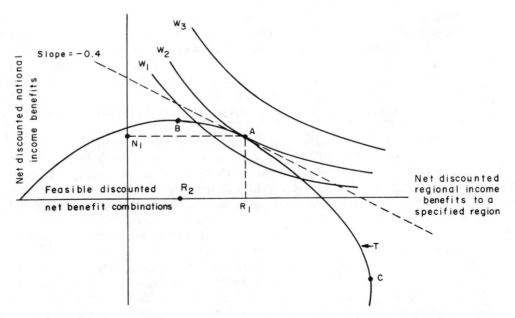

Figure 2.3 Multiobjective theory. T is the net benefit transformation curve; W_1, $W_2, \ldots$ are the social preference curves. (From Major, 1977. Copyrighted by the American Geophysical Union.)

such as those discussed in Chapter 6. This involves substantial judgment and experience on the part of the planners as well as suboptimization procedures such as comparative estimates of cost or benefit-cost ratio, scoring systems for comparing alternatives, and displays such as those of the U.S. Water Resources Council in its system of accounts.

2.14 DIFFERENCES BETWEEN PRIVATE BUSINESS ECONOMICS AND PUBLIC WATER RESOURCES PROJECT POLICIES

This section presents some general observations on the behavior of managers of private business and government decision makers involved in water resources project formulation, authorization, implementation, and operation. Some of these concepts have been previously discussed by Grant and Ireson (1960, p. 436-8).

Success in private business is generally measured by the profits that are earned and returned to the owners of the business. There is no such general standard of success to measure the performance of decision makers (agency officials) for public water resources projects (although there are cases where revenues must equal or exceed financial costs and this may be analogous to the concept of "profit"). Analyses of public water resources projects compare economic benefits and costs and the net benefits may also have some similarities to "profit." The types, amounts, and impacts of project products and services, however, must also be acceptable in a governmental and public sense. A project must be justified "on balance" considering not only the financial and economic effects but also the set of environmental, social, institutional, political, and other impacts. The techniques for analyzing the effects of water resources projects may be complex, may require application by an inter-disciplinary team, and may not be well understood by nonspecialists. This has often led to distrust of the results of water resources analysis by elected officials and the public.

The management of a private business is generally unified in attempting to improve operating efficiencies and secure profits. The general body of "owners" of the business do not participate actively in the planning and decision making of the business. Although the business, especially if it is large or of the public utility type, often engages in activities of a public service nature, these activities may be motivated by a desire to improve its "image" and gain support for its business policies, be required as a condition of permits or licenses, or be undertaken to take advantage of favorable tax treatment. This unified owner interest and focus on policies related to its basic business purpose does not apply to public water resources projects. When water resources projects are considered, there are many "owners" or interests that are often in conflict with each other and that may participate in the planning process from the early stages to project implementation and later. These may include government agencies, politicians, business enterprises, trade associations and unions, public interest groups, and individuals. These parties may act for reasons ranging from purely altruistic motives to entirely self-serving.

A private business sells goods and services in the marketplace at prices that are generally equal to or less than the value that customers place on these outputs (this statement may require qualification in the case of customers served by public utilities dealing in essential commodities or services). Users of water resources project outputs, on the other hand, may benefit at little or no cost to themselves. In the United States, this is the case for most of the benefits provided by federally sponsored reservoir projects for navigation, flood control, water quality management, and recreation. Many other types of water resources projects are heavily subsidized by the federal government or by a combination of federal and local government agencies. The costs for such activities are ultimately borne by the taxpayers, but the taxes paid by any single organization or individual may have no relationship to the benefits received by that entity. Even if beneficiaries of water resources projects pay for project services, prices are often set near or below costs, and may be substantially less than the real values of the services. If this is done, it should be done for clearly stated reasons relating to legitimate and agreed-upon national objectives, such as regional or group income objectives; it should not be the result of actions by well-organized and powerful beneficiaries acting outside the legitimate political process.

In the United States and other countries, capital, labor, and other basic resources are never enough to proceed with all projects. Rationing, through the process of project authorization and financing, is carried out with a large amount of political input. As pointed out by Grant and Ireson (1960): "Politics is always a factor in public business, and even in cases where political favoritism of the 'pork barrel legislation' type does not enter into the picture, this political control is operative." In addition to the question of whether an expenditure for a public works project is really desirable in a community sense for a nation, region, or locality, the question always arises whether it will appear justifiable to public officials, legislators, and interest groups and individuals who "may not have the technical background or openness of mind for proper appreciation of all of the factors in the case. . . . Particularly does it create difficulties in the way of getting a planned coordinated development for the future, as contrasted with piecemeal construction where each decision is made only to meet a present emergency. . . . The short and uncertain tenure of office of many public officials is an obstacle to a carrying out of a consistent policy that is not so likely to exist in private business." This last problem is not restricted to public projects; short-term considerations of the managers of a private business often differ from those for overall profit maximization.

The legal requirements pertaining to public water resources projects are usually greater in number and more complex than those pertaining to most business decisions. In addition to the legal guidelines on project formulation, analysis, and reporting, there are important problems of water and related land rights; participation in the process for government authorization and approval of construction funds; civil service requirements for personnel and other legal requirements concerning purchases, construction, and operating requirements of regulatory agencies and other government authorities who issue licenses and permits and monitor operations; government legislation and agency regulations outlawing or limiting certain types of construction or areas in which they can be built; requirements for environmental impact statements and other assessments; and other constraints not generally applicable to private businesses.

The criteria for financial and economic analyses are often quite different for government and private projects. An analysis for a public project usually takes a longer view than a business that adopts a shorter period of analysis, for reasons of risk considerations and to take advantage of income tax laws. The public works project also takes a longer view in the selection of an interest rate; in the United States, federal agencies use an interest rate based on long-term obligations, while private business uses the interest rate for current borrowings. The public works project does not not have to pay most taxes, whereas the private business needs to consider this in its annual costs (in comparing public and private projects, many analysts prefer to include taxes forgone in the costs of government projects reasoning that these amounts must be paid indirectly by the taxpayer). The longer period of analysis, the lower interest rate for discounting, and the omission of taxes when taken together often produce numerically better economic results for a public project than for a privately sponsored competitive project.

2.15 CALCULATIONS INVOLVING DISCOUNT RATE

The following symbols are commonly used for interest formulas:

i = interest rate per interest period
n = number of interest periods

P = present sum of money

F = future sum of money at the end of n periods (i.e., equivalent to P with interest i)

A = amount of each end-of-period payment or receipt in a uniform series of n periods, the entire series equivalent to P or F, with interest i

Calculations are made using conversion factors. The numerical values of these conversion factors are obtained from tables or computed individually from the formulas. The Appendix contains tables for the conversion factors needed for most calculations taken from a World Bank publication (Gittinger 1973).

Some simple problems are given in the following to illustrate the uses of the conversion formulas. For additional problems more oriented to water resources analyses, the reader is referred to Kuiper (1965, 1971), James and Lee (1971), Linsley and Franzini (1979), and Gittinger (1972). There are also many references in engineering economics texts (e.g., Degarmo and Canada 1973; Grant et al. 1976; Institution of Civil Engineers, 1969).

Given P, to find F

$$F = P(1 + i)^n$$

where the conversion factor may be represented by (F/P, i, n) and is the "single-payment compound factor" or "compounding factor for 1."

Example 2.1:

$1.0 million is borrowed for 25 years at 7% interest. What amount must be repaid in a lump sum at the end of the twenty-fifth year?

$$F = P(F/P, 0.07, 25) = 1,000,000 \times 5.4274 = \$5,430,000$$

Example 2.2:

What is the equivalent future worth at the end of 10 years at 10% interest of three $100,000 investments, one made now, one at the beginning of the third year, and one at the beginning of the fifth year?

$$F_1 = P_1(F/P, 0.10, 10) = 100,000 \times 2.5937 = 259,400$$
$$F_2 = P_2(F/P, 0.10, \ 8) = 100,000 \times 2.1436 = 214,400$$
$$F_3 = P_3(F/P, 0.10, \ 6) = 100,000 \times 1.7716 = \underline{177,200}$$
$$\$651,000$$

Given F, to find P

$$P = F\left[\frac{1}{(1 + i)^n}\right]$$

where the conversion factor may be represented by (P/F, i, n) and is the "single-payment present worth factor" or "discount factor for 1."

Example 2.3:

$1.0 million is estimated to be needed 25 years from now. What amount should be invested at 7% interest to provide for this?

$$P = F(P/F, 0.07, 25) = 1,000,000 \times 0.1842 = \$184,200$$

Example 2.4:

What is the equivalent present worth at 10% interest of three $100,000 investments, one made now, one at the end of the third year, and one at the end of the tenth year from now?

$$
\begin{aligned}
P_1 &= F_1(P/F, 0.10, \ \ 0) = 100,000 \times 1.0 \quad \ \ = \quad 100,000 \\
P_2 &= F_2(P/F, 0.10, \ \ 3) = 100,000 \times 0.7513 = \quad \ \ 75,100 \\
P_3 &= F_3(P/F, 0.10, 10) = 100,000 \times 0.3855 = \quad \ \ 38,600 \\
&\hspace{7cm} \overline{\quad \$213,700}
\end{aligned}
$$

Given F, to find A

$$A = F\left[\frac{i}{(1 + i)^n - 1}\right]$$

where the conversion factor may be represented by $(A/F, i, n)$ and is the "uniform series sinking fund factor."

Example 2.5:

$1.0 million is estimated to be needed 25 years from now. What uniform end-of-year amount should be placed in a sinking fund at 10% interest to provide this amount?

$$A = F(A/F, 0.10, 25) = 1,000,000 \times 0.0102 = \$10,200$$

Example 2.6:

What uniform amount at the end of each of 10 years at 7% interest is equivalent to $1.0 million 10 years from now?

$$A = F(A/F, 0.07, 10) = 1,000,000 \times 0.0724 = \$72,400$$

Given P, to find A

$$A = P\left[\frac{i(1 + i)^n}{(1 + i)^n - 1}\right]$$

where the conversion factor may be represented by $(A/P, i, n)$ and is the "uniform series capital recovery factor."

Example 2.7:

The capital investment in a project is $10 million. What annual year-end payments are needed at 7% interest to amortize the investment in 20 years?

$$A = P(A/P, 0.07, 20) = 10,000,000 \times 0.0944 = \$944,000$$

Example 2.8:

What uniform amount at the end of each of 10 years at 10% interest is equivalent to a payment made now of $1 million?

$$A = P(A/P, 0.10, 10) = 1,000,000 \times 0.1627 = \$162,700$$

Given A, to find F

$$F = A \left[\frac{(1 + i)^n - 1}{i} \right]$$

where the conversion factor may be represented by $(F/A, i, n)$ and is the "uniform series compound amount factor" or "compounding factor for 1 per annum."

Example 2.9:

If $1000 is set aside at 7% interest at the end of each year, what is the future value of deposits made for 15 years?

$$F = A(F/A, 0.07, 15) = 1,000 \times 25.1290 = \$25,129$$

Example 2.10:

What is the equivalent future worth of 10 end-of-year payments of $10,000 each at 10% interest?

$$F = A(F/A, 0.10, 10) = 10,000 \times 15.937 = \$159,400$$

Given A, to find P

$$P = A \left[\frac{(1 + i)^n - 1}{i(1 + i)^n} \right]$$

where the conversion factor may be represented by $(P/A, i, n)$ and is the "uniform series present worth factor" or "present worth of an annuity factor."

Example 2.11:

How much should be deposited now in a fund at 7% interest to provide for 20 year-end payments of $1000?

$$P = A(P/A, 0.07, 20) = 1,000 \times 10.5940 = \$10,594$$

Example 2.12:

What is the equivalent present worth at 10% interest of a series of 20 year-end amounts of $1000 each?

$$P = A(P/A, 0.10, 20) - \$1,000 \times 8.5136 = \$8,513$$

A Few More Examples

Example 2.13:

A present investment of $100,000 is expected to yield a return of $10,500 a year for 15 years. What is the approximate rate of return?

This calculation requires a trial-and-error approach as follows:

Try $i = 0.07$; $A = 100,000 (A/P, 0.07, 15) = 100,000 \times 0.1098$
    $= \$10,980$ NG
Try $i = 0.06$; $A = 100,000 (A/P, 0.06, 15) = 100,000 \times 0.1030$
    $= \$10,300$ NG

The correct value for i is between 7 and 6%; and may be estimated by interpolation.

Example 2.14:

A present investment of $100,000 will not be made unless it can be recovered at 10% interest. If the return is $15,000 per year, how many years of operation must be guaranteed at this level?

This calculation requires a trial-and-error approach as follows:

Try $n = 11$; $P = A(P/A, 0.10, 11) = 15,000 \times 6.4951 = \$97,427$ NG
Try $n = 12$; $P = A(P/A, 0.10, 12) = 15,000 \times 6.8137 = \$102,205$ NG

The correct value for n is between 11 and 12 years and may be estimated by interpolation.

Example 2.15:

A new pipeline is to be installed. The investments and costs for pumping are as follows:

Diameter of Pipe (in.)	Investment in Pipeline	Cost per Hour for Operation and Maintenance, Including Pumping
8	$20,000	$2.50
12	25,000	0.40
16	40,000	0.10

The pipe is used for pumping for 2000 hours per year. What is the most economic size of pipeline if it is needed for 10 years and there is no salvage value at the end of that time? The applicable discount rate is 10%.

Solution in terms of annual cost:

Capital Recovery	=	$A = P(A/P, i, n)$
8-in. line		$A = 20,000(A/P, 0.10, 10)$
		$= 20,000 \times 0.1627 = \$3254$
12-in. line		$A = 25,000 \times 0.1627 = \$4067$
16-in. line		$A = 40,000 \times 0.1627 = \$6508$
Annual Pumping Cost		
8-in. line		$2.5 \times 2000 = \$5000$
12-in. line		$0.4 \times 2000 = \$800$
16-in. line		$0.1 \times 2000 = \$200$
Total Annual Cost		
8-in. line		$8254
12-in. line		$4867 (most economic)
16-in. line		$6708

Alternate solution in terms of present worth:

Present Worth	=	$P = A(P/A, i,n)$
8-in. line		$P = 5000(P/A, 0.10, 10)$
		$= 5000 \times 6.1446 = \$30,723$
12-in. line		$P = 800 \times 6.1446 = \$4916$
16-in. line		$P = 200 \times 6.1446 = \$1229$
Total Present Worth		
8-in. line		$50,723
12-in. line		$29,916 (most economic)
16-in. line		$41,229

If a more precise solution were required, the total annual costs for 8-, 10-, 12-, 14-, and 16-in. pipe could be determined; a graph of diameter versus total annual cost plotted; and the diameter selected corresponding to the lowest annual cost.

Example 2.16:

Projects A and B are to be compared in terms of their benefit-cost ratios and net benefits (benefits minus costs) on a present worth basis and on an annual basis over a 12-year period of analysis. The applicable discount rate is 10%. Project A requires 1 year for construction and provides 5 years of benefits after construction. Project B requires 2 years for construction and provides 10 years of benefits after construction. The following table shows the benefits and costs for projects A and B in thousands of dollars. Each amount is an end-of-year value. Which is the more economic project?

Year	Project A			Project B		
	Construction Cost	Operation Costs	Benefits	Construction Cost	Operation Costs	Benefits
1	100			100		
2		10	20	100		
3		10	40		20	40
4		10	60		20	60
5		10	80		20	80
6		10	100		20	100
7					20	120
8					20	140
9					20	160
10					20	180
11					20	200
12					20	200

SOLUTION: PRESENT-WORTH BASIS AT 10% INTEREST RATE

Year	C	B	$B-C$	Factor	Present Worth		
					C	B	$B-C$
Project A							
1	100	0	-100	0.909	90.90	0	-90.90
2	10	20	10	0.826	8.26	16.52	8.26
3	10	40	30	0.751	7.51	30.04	22.53
4	10	60	50	0.683	6.83	40.98	34.15
5	10	80	70	0.621	6.21	49.68	43.47
6	10	100	90	0.565	5.65	56.50	50.85
					125.36	193.72	68.36

$$B/C \text{ ratio} = \frac{193.72}{125.36} = 1.55; \quad \text{net benefits} = 193.72 - 125.36 = \$68.36 \text{ thousand}$$

Year	C	B	B − C	Factor	Present Worth C	Present Worth B	Present Worth B − C
Project B							
1	100	0	−100	0.909	90.90	0	−90.90
2	100	0	−100	0.826	82.60	0	−82.60
3	20	40	20	0.751	15.02	30.04	15.02
4	20	60	40	0.683	13.66	40.98	27.32
5	20	80	60	0.621	12.42	49.68	37.26
6	20	100	80	0.565	11.30	56.50	45.20
7	20	120	100	0.513	10.26	61.56	51.30
8	20	140	120	0.466	9.32	65.24	55.92
9	20	160	140	0.424	8.48	67.84	59.36
10	20	180	160	0.386	7.72	69.48	61.76
11	20	200	180	0.351	7.02	70.20	63.18
12	20	200	180	0.319	6.38	63.80	57.42
					275.08	575.32	300.24

$$B/C \text{ ratio} = \frac{575.32}{275.08} = 2.09; \quad \text{net benefits} = 575.32 - 275.08 = \$300.24 \text{ thousand}$$

Project B is more economic than Project A.

ALTERNATE SOLUTION: ANNUAL BASIS AT 10% INTEREST RATE FOR 12 YEARS

Capital recovery factor = 0.1467

Project A
Annual benefits = 193.72 × 0.1467 = 28.42
Annual costs = 125.36 × 0.1467 = 18.39
B/C ratio = 1.55
Net benefits = $10.03 thousand

Project B
Annual benefits = 575.32 × 0.1467 = 84.40
Annual costs = 275.08 × 0.1467 = 40.35
B/C ratio = 2.09
Net benefits = $44.05 thousand (more economic)

Note that B/C ratios are the same on a present-worth and an annual basis.

A Few More Remarks. The single-payment present-worth factor is the reciprocal of the single-payment compound amount factor, indicating the relationship of P and F via a single factor. A similar remark may be made for F and A, since the uniform series compound amount factor is the reciprocal of the sinking fund factor. Finally, P and A are similarly related since the uniform series present-worth factor is the reciprocal of the capital recovery factor.

The capital recovery factor is equal to the interest rate plus the sinking fund factor. Thus, if the capital investment is managed by means of loans, the investors may be repaid in a series of uniform annual payments (apply capital recovery factor to principal) or the investors may receive only interest each year on the principal and the full principal in a lump sum at the end of the loan period; this lump sum is available when annual payments are made into a sinking fund and accumulated at compound interest.

Repayment of the investment cost by *amortization* using a sinking fund is equivalent to "writing off" the investment by *depreciation* using a sinking fund. The latter concept may also be used to estimate the remaining value of an investment after a specified number of years (equal to original value minus depreciation by means of a sinking fund). The existing value of an investment may need to be estimated for purposes of setting an allowable revenue that provides for a lawful rate of return on investment, as is often the case with public utilities. There are also other methods used for depreciation; these include the straight-line method and other procedures used in accounting practice. These are often advantageous when taking advantage of the income tax laws. Such considerations are beyond the scope of this book but are discussed in any current text on engineering economics.

REFERENCES

BIERMAN, HAROLD, JR., and SEYMOUR SMIDT, *The Capital Budgeting Decision*, 2nd ed., Macmillan, New York, 1966.

DASGUPTA P., A. SEN, and S. MARGLIN, "Guidelines for Project Evaluation," United Nations Industrial Development Organization, Vienna, 1972.

DEGARMO, E. P., and J. K. CANADA, *Engineering Economy*, 5th ed. Macmillan, New York, 1973.

DORFMAN, ROBERT, *Prices and Markets*, 3rd ed. Prentice-Hall, Englewood Cliffs, N.J., 1978.

ECKSTEIN, OTTO, *Water Resource Development*, Harvard University Press, Cambridge, Mass., 1961.

ENGELBERT, ERNEST A., "Water Pricing: A Social Decision-Making Process," *Proc. Water Pricing Policy Conf.*, Rep. 13, University of California Water Resources Center, March 1968.

GITTINGER, J. PRICE, *Economic Analysis of Agricultural Projects*, International Bank for Reconstruction and Development, Johns Hopkins University Press, Baltimore, Md., 1972.

GITTINGER, J. PRICE, ed. *Compounding and Discounting Tables for Project Evaluation*, International Bank for Reconstruction and Development, Johns Hopkins University Press, Baltimore, Md., 1973.

GRAAF, J. DE V., *Theoretical Welfare Economics*, Cambridge University Press, New York, 1963.

GRANT, EUGENE L., and W. GRANT IRESON, *Principles of Engineering Economy*, 4th ed., Ronald Press, New York, 1960.

GRANT, EUGENE L., W. GRANT IRESON, and RICHARD S. LEAVENWORTH, *Principles of Engineering Economy*, 6th ed., J Wiley, New York, 1976.

INSTITUTION OF CIVIL ENGINEERS (U.K.). *An Introduction to Engineering Economics*, 1969.

James, L. Douglas, and Robert E. Lee, *Economics of Water Resources Planning*, McGraw-Hill, New York, 1971.

Kuiper, Edward, *Water Resources Project Economics*, Butterworth, Kent, England, 1971.

Kuiper, Edward, *Water Resources Development*, Butterworth, Kent, England, 1965.

Linsley, Ray K., and Joseph B. Franzini, *Water Resources Engineering*, 3rd ed., McGraw-Hill, New York, 1979.

Major, David C., "Multiobjective Water Resource Planning," *Am. Geophys. Union Water Resources Monogr. 4*, 1977.

Major, David C., and Roberto L. Lenton, *Applied Water Resource Systems Planning*, Prentice-Hall, Englewood Cliffs, N.J., 1979.

Marglin, S. A., *Public Investment Criteria*, MIT Press, Cambridge, Mass., 1967.

National Academy of Sciences, "The Range of Objectives in Planning for the Use of Colorado Water," in *Water and Choice in the Colorado Basin: An Example of Alternatives in Water Management*, Publ. 1689, Washington, D.C., 1968.

Samuelson, Paul A., *Foundations of Economic Analysis*, Harvard University Press, Cambridge, Mass., 1948.

Squire, Lyn, and Herman G. van der Tak, *Economic Analysis of Projects*, Johns Hopkins University Press, Baltimore, Md., 1975.

TAMS (Tippetts-Abbett-McCarthy-Stratton, New York), "Bridge Canyon Development—Amendment to Application for License before the Federal Power Commission," Dept. of Water and Power of the City of Los Angeles, September 1960.

TAMS (Tippetts-Abbett-McCarthy-Stratton, New York), "Water Resources Study for Power Systems, Delaware River Basin," March 1972.

TAMS (Tippetts-Abbett-McCarthy-Stratton, New York), and Massachusetts Institute of Technology, Cambridge, "Integrated Development of the Vardar/Axios River Basin—Yugoslavia—Greece," December 1978.

U.S. Inter-Agency Committee on Water Resources, "Proposed Practices for Economic Analysis of River Basin Projects," May 1950; rev. May 1958.

U.S. National Water Commission, "Water Resources Planning," Consulting Panel on Water Resources Planning, May 1972.

U.S. North Atlantic Regional Water Resources Study Coordinating Committee, "North Atlantic Regional Water Resources Study," North Atlantic Division, U.S. Army Corps of Engineers, New York, 1972.

U.S. President's Water Resources Council, "Policies, Standards, and Procedures in the Formulation, Evaluation, and Review of Plans for Use and Development of Water and Related Land Resources," 87th Cong., 2nd sess., Senate Doc. 97, 1962.

U.S. Water Resources Council, "Procedures for Evaluation of Water and Related Land Resource Projects," Report by the Special Task Force, June 1969.

U.S. Water Resources Council, "Findings and Recommendations," "Principles for Planning Water and Land Resources," "Standards for Planning Water and Land Resources," Report by the Special Task Force, July 1970.

U.S. Water Resources Council, "Proposed Principles and Standards for Planning Water and Related Land Resources," December 21, 1971.

U.S. Water Resources Council, "Principles and Standards for Planning Water and Related Land Resources," September 10, 1973; rev. December 14, 1979; rev. September 29, 1980.

U.S. WATER RESOURCES COUNCIL, "Procedures for Evaluation of National Economic Development (NED) Benefits and Costs in Water Resources Planning (Level C)," December 14, 1979; rev. September 29, 1980.

U.S. WATER RESOURCES COUNCIL, "Environmental Quality Evaluation Procedures for Level C Water Resources Planning," September 29, 1980.

U.S. WATER RESOURCES COUNCIL, "Economic and Environmental Principles and Guidelines for Water and Related Land Resources Implementation Studies," March 10, 1983.

WIENER, AARON, *The Role of Water in Development*, McGraw-Hill, New York, 1972.

WOLLMAN, NATHANIEL, "Water Resources Models: A Historical Summary," in *Economic Modeling for Water Policy Evaluation*, R. M. Thrall et al., eds., North-Holland/American Elsevier, 1976.

THREE

Elements of Project Formulation and Appraisal

3.1 SCOPE

This chapter and the next three discuss the process whereby projects are identified, formulated, appraised, and implemented. The focus of these chapters is on the engineering and planning aspects of the process; there is also discussion of the additional aspects of project assessment (such as economic, environmental, and institutional) that are elaborated on in subsequent chapters.

This chapter begins by outlining a typical sequence of studies for an engineering project, proceeding from preliminary studies to project construction and operation. Regional studies and studies to meet specific investigative or legal requirements are then discussed. Studies by engineers and other specialists lead to recommendations for project implementation (or not). These recommendations are usually reviewed before approval by decision makers in a government agency, private business, or banking institution. Various guidelines are presented for these appraisals; the criteria for appraisal may differ for an economically developed country such as the United States and for a developing country, where the review may be undertaken by an international funding agency. This chapter concludes with a review of some recent trends in project evaluation.

3.2 SEQUENCE OF STUDIES
FOR A SINGLE ENGINEERING PROJECT

This section assumes that the general location and purpose of the prospective project have already been determined by an earlier screening process or other means of designation. The following describes a typical five-stage sequence of reports, documents, and actions for the project, including the preliminary (or reconnaissance) report, the feasibility report, the contract documents, and activities during construction and operation.

3.2.1 First Stage: Preliminary (or Reconnaissance) Report

This consists of office studies, field studies, and the preparation of a report. The report prepared as a result of these studies should answer the following questions:

- Is a feasible project likely?
- What are approximate estimates of capacity and cost?
- What additional studies are needed to confirm feasibility?

The investigation begins with *office studies*, using available information contained in previous reports, maps, and data. Much of this is available from federal, state, and local governmental agencies. Utilities, private firms, newspapers, libraries, and other sources should also be contacted. Basic materials include maps and photographs (topographic maps, land surveys, county and city tax maps, transportation maps, aerial photographs); geologic and soil surveys and data; climatological data; stream flow and ground water records; water quality and sediment measurements; information on ecological and environmental conditions; and data and forecasts pertinent to the specific purpose of the project (e.g., projection of water supply requirements, or electric power demands; characteristics of existing water supply, or electric generation and transmission systems; etc.).

Office studies may be adequate to make initial determinations of the general arrangement of the project components, the capacity of the project or the services it can provide, and its cost. Better estimates can be made by supplementing office studies by *field reconnaissance and surveys*. This work is needed to confirm the estimates made in office studies, to suggest changes in them, and to obtain detailed information concerning such matters as needed relocations in cases where the available maps are not recent. Topographic surveys, stream measurements, and geological and soils investigations may be needed, but these should be kept to a minimum, consistent with the nature of the preliminary report. The personnel involved in this work are normally engineers and geologists, but they may also include environmentalists and other specialists.

3.2.2 Second Stage: Feasibility Report

If the project sponsor determines that additional studies are warranted based on the preliminary report and other considerations, a feasibility report will be prepared. This report should contain enough information to permit a decision on whether or not to implement the project. This implies technical studies more detailed than those required for the preliminary report, financial and economic analyses, and a plan for project implementation. The feasibility report should include the following:

- Descriptions and analyses of the data
- Confirmation of construction feasibility based on additional field and laboratory investigations, studies of project arrangements and individual project features, and analysis of construction methods (sources of construction materials, access to the project site, diversion of water during construction, etc.)
- Final recommendations for arrangement of project works, preliminary plans and other analyses to determine the principal quantities of construction, a reliable cost estimate, and discussions of the design criteria
- Construction schedule showing the timing and costs of project features
- Economic analyses of the project
- Financial analyses projecting the year-by-year costs, revenues, and subsidies for the project
- Plans for financing construction, and for managing the construction and operation of the project
- Institutional and legal requirements
- Assessments of the environmental and social impacts of construction and operation, and other impact studies if required

Depending on the extent of detailed drawings and of analyses needed to confirm construction feasibility and make reliable estimates of project cost, the work in this phase consists of designs in addition to planning studies. Many references (e.g., the publication on the design of small dams by the U.S. Department of the Interior, Bureau of Reclamation, 1973) are available for guidance.

3.2.3 Third Stage: Final Design and Preparation of Contract Documents

Contract documents include plans and specifications which are sufficiently detailed to obtain tenders (bids) from qualified construction and equipment contractors. The plans (drawings) and specifications are based on additional studies of the details of project works, the logistics of construction, other aspects related to temporary and permanent facilities, and the performance of contractors. The contract documents also contain additional information on the responsibilities of the project sponsor and the contractor. Various forms to be completed by the contractor provide information on the contractor's legal status and financial capabilities, set forth the quantities and prices for construction and for equipment, and elaborate on the construction methods proposed by the contractor.

The sponsor and engineers review the tenders made by contractors. A major factor is the prices offered by a contractor, but other factors considered may include the reputation and previous experience of the contractor, the specific working methods proposed to carry out the construction or manufacture of equipment, and in the case of the latter, the operating efficiency of the equipment to be provided.

Contractors' tenders are usually ranked after weighting the factors, in order to determine which tenders are in the sponsor's best interest, and awards are made accordingly.

3.2.4 Fourth Stage: Construction

Additional detailed drawings needed during construction are prepared by the sponsor's engineers and by the contractors subject to the sponsor's approval. Payments to the contractors are usually made based on measurements of work in progress or completed, in accordance with the terms of the contract documents. Usually, a percentage of each payment is withheld by the sponsor and released only when the work is entirely completed and accepted. Supervision of construction by the sponsor's engineers often includes field layout of major works, approval of contractors' choices of working procedures and materials, interpretation of the plans and specifications, approval of the contractors' drawings needed to supplement the engineers' drawings, inspection of construction activities and of finished work to ensure conformance with plans and specifications, measurement of quantities of construction, and certifications required as a basis for payments to the contractors.

3.2.5 Fifth Stage: Operation

The sponsor may employ outside engineers and other consultants to assist in operation for a limited period, train operators, prepare manuals for operation and maintenance, and monitor the performance of the various features (structural, hydrologic, hydraulic, etc.). Studies of operating rules may continue as experience develops.

3.3 FORMULATION OF A SINGLE ENGINEERING PROJECT

The engineers (or the interdisciplinary team of specialists) that formulate a water resources project define the arrangement of project components, and sufficient details concerning their sizes and functions so that realistic cost estimates can be prepared. Project formulation relates to stages 1 to 3, above; it begins in a rudimentary way in the reconnaissance level work required for the preliminary report, is refined and elaborated in the feasibility report stage, and undergoes additional changes and detailed definition in the preparation of the plans and specifications for the contract documents.

During project formulation, the planner evaluates the available data and conceives a plan to utilize water and related land resources to meet project needs. This work draws on scientific training, experience with other projects of similar type or with similar components, and imagination and judgment to lay out a project that fits the available topographic, geologic, and soils conditions. Account is also taken of information on water volumes and flow rates, nature and magnitude of project products and services that are desired, and existing or potential constraints. Constraints may include legal limitations on water or land involving quantities or uses; practical limitations on relocations, land purchase, and easements permitted for buildings, roads, railroads, utilities and other human-made features; or obvious unsuitability of a site for certain types of developments (e.g., a type of dam may be unsuitable for certain topographic configurations, geology, or construction material availabilities). In most cases more than one layout is possible. A good planner will eliminate the most unsuitable alternatives while assessing the remaining alternatives fairly and comprehensively. With some sites and service requirements, the planner may be able to proceed directly to the optimal solution. In the more usual case, alternative layouts will need to be prepared and examined for cost, function, construction suitability, and other factors.

The planner may approach a solution for a site starting with the perspective of a water need of a particular type and magnitude (e.g., municipal and industrial water supply) and then consider the possibilities for modifying the project to make it suitable for multipurpose operations (e.g., recreation, hydroelectric power). Or, the planner may from the beginning examine a variety of plans that exploit the site for all the opportunities for multipurpose development.

The formulation of a project as discussed above emphasizes structural details, costs, project services, reliability, safety, and other engineering matters. It is necessary, however, to consider the impacts of a project that are not primarily of an engineering or cost nature. If the formulation team is dominated by engineers, it will be necessary to consult with or have formal assessments by other specialists at various stages to ensure that environmental, sociological, institutional, and other factors are adequately taken into account. Otherwise, projects may be proposed that cannot be implemented. At the early stages of planning, impact analysis can be limited to identifying the most obvious problems, but studies at later stages need to be more comprehensive.

As the work of formulation proceeds, the planner gains an improved under-standing of site conditions, advantages and disadvantages of alternative project arrangements, and possible opportunities for using the site to produce more or different project services. The planner is, therefore, better able to communicate with the sponsor of the project, and reconsideration of project objectives and purposes, scale, or other aspects may result from such communication.

As an example of the formulation process, the process of considering and assessing alternatives for protecting an urban riverside community against flood damage will be discussed here. Alternative projects are to be evaluated utilizing possible methods of reducing flood damages to existing buildings and other facilities and reducing flood risk to permit additional urban growth. As outlined in Section 1.6, three principal approaches to reducing flood damage may be considered: (1) management measures; (2) local protection facilities; and (3) upstream flood control reservoirs.

The first approach is primarily a nonstructural solution. It includes some or all of the following components: (a) zoning, to limit the types of land uses permitted to those which may not be severely damaged by floods (e.g., agriculture, recreation, wild areas), and to specify the types of construction if facilities are permitted; (b) protection of individual properties, by waterproofing the lower floors of existing buildings; (c) flood warning system, to evacuate residents and to move valuables; and

(d) flood insurance, to recognize the risks of floods and to provide compensation when damages are not avoidable at acceptable cost.

The second approach emphasizes the construction of levees or walls to prevent inundation from floods below some specified design flood flow (often the highest flood of record). Additional works may include drainage and pumping facilities for areas that are sealed off from precipitation runoff to the river by the levees; and modifications to increase the hydraulic capacity or stability of the river, such as changes in profile or direction, channelization, and paving.

The third approach is based on the construction of one or more reservoirs upstream from the community. This implies the availability of site(s) that are suitable for a dam, spillway, and outlet works, and a large enough reservoir to capture the volume of a design flood and release it at nondamaging rates. Alternative sites as well as alternative layouts of works enter into this analysis. This approach to flood control lends itself to consideration of multipurpose reservoir uses; these may typically be recreation, hydroelectric energy generation, and water supply.

Depending on the risk that floods will occur which are larger than the design flood for local protection works, or the design floods for upstream reservoirs, these second and third approaches should also include management (nonstructural) elements such as those in the first approach.

Some of the structural alternatives for a flood control project are shown in Figures 3.1 to 3.5 from the pioneering studies of flood control in the Miami Conservancy District (Woodward 1920). Details of the nonstructural and structural components of projects appear in Linsley and Franzini (1979), Davis and Sorenson (1969), Kuiper (1965), planning and design manuals and other publications of federal agencies with important design and construction functions in the water resources field (U.S. Bureau of Reclamation, Corps of Engineers, Soil Conservation Service, and Tennessee Valley Authority), and reference books in specialty fields such as irrigation engineering, hydroelectric engineering, municipal and industrial water supply, and wastewater treatment and disposal.

3.4 REGIONAL STUDIES

Regional studies differ greatly from single-project studies, and among themselves, in their level of detail and focus on specific projects. The U.S. Water Resources Council (1973, p. 24825) classified planning studies into three categories, depending on relative emphasis on regional needs and problems and on individual projects, and the period of time within which these needs would be met or problems solved.

Framework studies and assessments (Level A) are the most general since they determine the extent of water and land problems and needs for a large geographic area over the long term. They set forth the general approaches for the solution of problems, and they can also recommend specific plans and programs that do not require further study. They also describe the additional planning studies that are needed.

Regional or river basin plans (Level B) are reconnaissance-level evaluations of water and land resources for a selected area, with a focus on middle-term (15 to 25

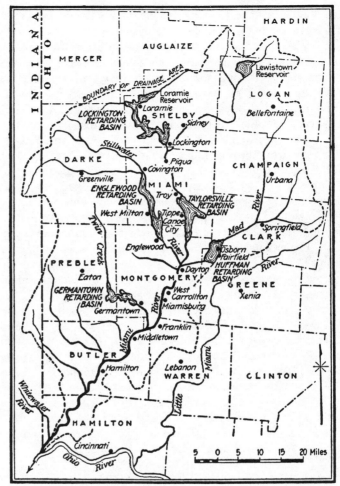

Figure 3.1 Location of retarding basins in Miami Valley. (From Woodward, 1920.)

years) needs and desires. Planning studies consider the effects of alternative projects in a multipurpose, multiobjective setting, and possible trade-offs.

Implementation studies (Level C) are programs or project feasibility studies that focus on action plans to follow in the near term and midterm (next 10 to 15 years). These studies often result from the findings of the framework studies and assessments and the regional or river basin studies.

Under this classification, the structural and nonstructural components of an individual project would not necessarily be identified until the Level B regional or river basin plans. A reconnaissance-level or somewhat more detailed study would be carried out in the Level B work to ensure that the structural and nonstructural

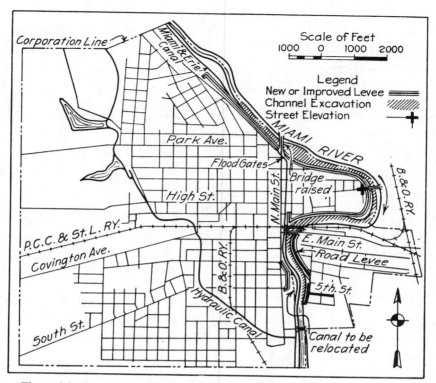

Figure 3.2 Map of Piqua, Ohio, showing local flood protection works. (From Woodward, 1920.)

measures included in a regional or river basin system are realistic. A feasibility study to provide a basis for project authorization would be completed under the Level C designation, specifically related to the regional system of projects and their interrelationships. The Water Resources Council "Principles and Guidelines" (1983) present methods for implementation studies.

3.5 OTHER TYPES OF STUDIES

Engineers and other planning specialists may be engaged in studies with a somewhat different focus or level of specificity than indicated by the categories described earlier for single projects and regional plans. Some of these are as follows:

- Single-purpose studies on a national level (e.g., for water supply, hydroelectric power, navigation).
- Single-purpose studies on a regional level (e.g., river basin, service area).
- Studies meeting the needs of a specific sponsor (e.g., hydroelectric power and water supply for thermal power plants for an electrical power utility; water supply for a municipal utility or industry).

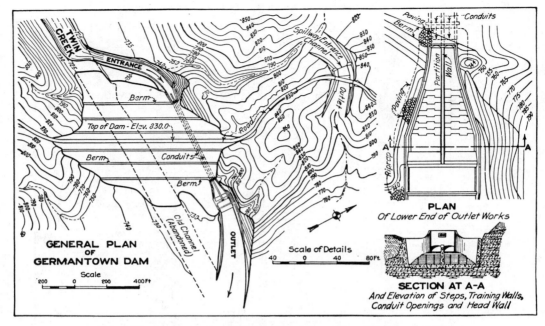

Figure 3.3 General layout of Germantown Dam. (From Woodward, 1920.)

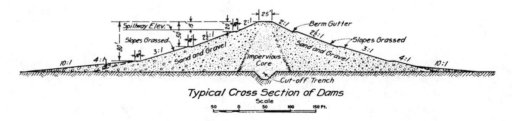

Figure 3.4 Cross section through earth dam. (From Woodward, 1920.)

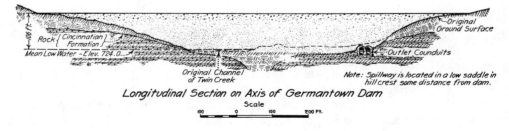

Figure 3.5 Longitudinal section of dam. (From Woodward, 1920.)

- Preparation of an application to a regulatory agency for a license or permit for a project (e.g., U.S. Federal Energy Regulatory Commission), or to a funding agency or institution (e.g., World Bank).
- Investigation of an existing facility for safety or adequacy (for stability, adequacy of foundations, spillway capacity and its adequacy, etc.).
- Investigation of the failure of a structure (to determine reasons for failure that has already occurred; hydraulic profile and damages that may result from a dam break, etc.).
- Special assessments of a water resource project in terms of its impact on the air, water, and land environments; on economic systems; or its socioeconomic effects.
- Preparation of an environmental impact statement, as required for every significant federal government action under the National Environmental Policy Act (1969).
- Review of study, report, or proposal by another agency or engineer. This may involve problems of professional ethics that need to be resolved according to local laws or customs.

3.6 PROJECT APPRAISAL

Project appraisal is the process by which a reviewing authority determines whether a water resources project meets appropriate criteria for authorization and/or funding, or whether a regional plan meets appropriate standards for proceeding with implementation studies of one or more component projects. The following sections deal primarily with government-sponsored projects but, for completeness, considerations applying specifically to a private business are also discussed. The analyses for the United States and other economically advanced countries may differ from appraisals of projects in developing countries that are subject to international lending agencies review.

The following sections emphasize the *results* of planning rather than the *process* of planning, but of course the latter must be carefully considered when appraising recommended plans and confirming the validity of the rejection of alternatives. Planners in national, regional, and local organizations, not specifically governed by the appraisal guidelines in this chapter, will be able to use them to formulate their own appraisal procedures while conforming to their institutional missions and incorporating specific considerations that apply to the conditions in their project and service areas.

3.7 U.S. GOVERNMENT AGENCY APPRAISAL GUIDELINES

3.7.1 National Water Commission Guidelines

The Consulting Panel on Water Resource Planning to the U.S. National Water Commission (1972) suggested that eight criteria should apply to a "good" plan. The following is a list of these criteria, with some explanation of terms.

1. *Be a document that is, indeed, a plan*, including display of alternative courses of action and recommendations on the desired course of action in terms of explicit structural or nonstructural measures.
2. *Meet stated goals.*
3. *Cover a rational planning area.*
4. *Have adequate detail to fit the type of action proposed*, depending on whether it is a policy, framework, appraisal, or implementation plan and whether it is functional, sectoral, or multisectoral (land use, water resources, energy supply, etc.) in scope.
5. *Fit into a multisectoral plan*, or anticipate the components of such a plan.
6. *Illuminate the alternatives that were considered*, including the advantages and disadvantages of each.
7. *Equitably allocate the resources*, based on reliable information on direct and indirect costs, economic benefits, and intangible consequences.
8. *Have proper balance to meet uncertainties*, by devising plans that maintain flexibility, so that adjustments to future conditions can be made readily and avoiding irrevocable allocations of water resources if feasible.

As discussed in Section 2.10, each federal agency in the United States followed its own guidelines until about 1950. Subsequently, rules that would apply to most agencies evolved and have continued to undergo revisions. The following outlines the Water Resource Council guidelines in effect in 1981. These guidelines have not applied to the Environmental Protection Agency, Federal Energy Regulatory Agency, and others with special regulatory authority.

3.7.2 Water Resources Council Guidelines

Criteria that influenced the U.S. federal water agencies, in addition to their own agency guidelines, might be said to date from at least 1950, as discussed in Section 2.10 (see Major, 1977, for a more extensive review of these criteria). The most ambitious attempts at agency-wide criteria have been those of the Water Resources Council, dating from its establishment in 1965.

The WRC "Principles and Standards" (1973, 1979, 1980) and "Principles and Guidelines" (1983) have provided guidelines for formulating alternative plans. Under the "Principles and Standards" at least three plans are prepared as a basis for formulating a recommended plan. These include plans focusing on two objectives—National Economic Development and Environmental Quality—and a primarily nonstructural plan (WRC, 1980, p. 64393).

The "Principles and Guidelines" focus on a plan that "reasonably maximizes" a single NED objective, with other plans formulated to "reduce net NED benefits in order to further address other federal, state, local, and international concerns. . . . " The results of project formulation and analysis are displayed in a series of tables. Alternative plans, including the NED plan, are formulated in consideration of four tests (WRC, 1983, p. 7):

Completeness is the extent to which a given alternative plan provides and accounts for all necessary investments or other actions to ensure the realization of the planned effects. This may require relating the plan to other types of public or private plans if the other plans are crucial to realization of the contributions to the objectives.

Effectiveness is the extent to which an alternative plan alleviates the specified problems and achieves the specified opportunities.

Efficiency is the extent to which an alternative plan is the most cost-effective means of alleviating the specified problems and realizing the specified opportunities, consistent with protecting the nation's environment.

Acceptability is the workability and viability of the alternative plan with respect to acceptance by state and local entities and the public and compatibility with existing laws, regulations, and public policies.

3.8 CONSIDERATIONS APPLYING TO APPRAISALS BY PRIVATE BUSINESS

It is necessary to distinguish between the characteristics of a public utility in the water resources field and a private enterprise governed by the more general rules applying in the marketplace. (DeGarmo and Canada, 1973, and Grant et al., 1976, are useful for further elaboration of the material in this section.)

The private enterprise that is not a public utility is discussed first. In many cases, the needs of a business enterprise may be very specific and the best plan may be expressible in rather direct terms. If an industry requires water for processing, it can consider purchasing water from a municipal or other public utility or providing the water itself. In this case it must consider the amounts of water needed now and in the future, the costs and flexibility of providing the water by alternative means, and perhaps some other practical factors, such as the difficulties of securing necessary permits, and tax aspects of purchasing rather than self-development.

If a private firm considers a water resources project, not as a necessary adjunct to a manufacturing process, but as an inherently commercial project, the firm will be interested primarily in the financial efficiency of the project, that is, the annual rate of return on the project investment or other financial criterion, and how it compares with the expected results of alternative financial investments. If the firm can develop a financial package involving others, the return on the smaller invested capital may be increased.

The discussion above should not imply that least cost of alternatives or financial return on investment are the only factors influencing an investment decision in private business. As outlined by DeGarmo and Canada (1973), nonmonetary values of importance may include economic laws, general business conditions, social and human values, personal or corporate objectives, consumer likes and dislikes, and government regulations. In this connection, the discussion in Section 2.14 is also pertinent.

Public utilities are investor owned or are owned by governmental bodies. The latter are municipalities or regional agencies which operate within a small area or, in the case of federal government operations, may extend over a large area (e.g., Tennessee Valley Authority). These enterprises are distinguished by their right of eminent domain to acquire property rights (land, water, real estate) and their exclusive franchise for service in a specified geographic area. Such utilities are usually regulated by federal and state bodies in the United States, which set rates for selling products and services, establish and monitor standards of service, and prescribe accounting procedures. Rates and allowable earnings are usually established to secure a fair return, after taxes, on the value of the utility's property. Because of the stability and long-range nature of its services, high capital intensity of its investments, and lower functional depreciation, utilities in the water resources field (water supply, power, irrigation) can generally amortize their investments over a longer period than can other private business enterprises. Since the needs for projects are defined by the growth of demand, the public utility cannot avoid an investment merely because a greater return could be earned in a non-water resource activity, as can other private enterprises. However, it will lay stress on how to provide products and services in the most efficient manner. In this connection, the aspects of rate setting and income tax liabilities will be very important.

3.9 APPRAISALS OF PROJECTS IN DEVELOPING COUNTRIES

3.9.1 Appraisals by the World Bank

This discussion is based largely on the appraisal guidelines of the World Bank in reviewing an application for a loan by a governmental or quasi-governmental organization in a developing country. Until recently, these guidelines, with their nearly exclusive emphasis on the national income objective, were not fully appropriate for project reviews for countries that may also place stress on other objectives (such as environmental quality in the United States). Now, however, the World Bank has developed criteria to implement its concern with other impacts, such as the effects of projects on lower-income groups. This multiobjective broadening of the World Bank's criteria makes its procedures more generally applicable than previously. An agency in a developing country submits a loan application in order to fulfill its responsibility to provide water supply, electricity, or other services to a particular area. At the same time, the World Bank is interested in determining whether the project is important to the regional or national economy and to the improvement of the general welfare and standard of living.

The following outlines concerns of importance to the World Bank. (For details on World Bank procedures, see King, 1967, Krombach, 1970, and Baum, 1970).

Creditworthiness. Before any project presented to the World Bank for financing undergoes appraisal, the Bank assesses whether the terms and amounts of the loan (or credit) being applied for are within the limits which the country can reasonably be expected to service, taking into account all existing and future foreign debts. The Bank judges this based on its previous activities within the country and its contacts with the prospective borrower.

Scope of Appraisal. The appraisal of the project itself usually involves a number of different aspects, including economic, technical, commercial, financial, institutional, organizational, and managerial aspects.

Economic Aspects. This appraisal determines whether: (1) the sector involved (e.g., agricultural, power, etc.) is a priority for the economic development of the country concerned; and (2) whether the project is of sufficiently high priority in this sector to justify investment in it. The first question should preferably be answered by reference to a study of the entire economy which has produced an overall economic development program, including the identification of priority sectors and the requirements that are projected for goods and services in each sector. Often, however, such comprehensive plans either do not exist or are not reliable. Many projects are thus selected not with reference to an overall plan but rather to meet specific identified needs (e.g., to overcome a shortage of electric power), or to take advantage of identified special opportunities (e.g., to produce agricultural crops that have a ready market).

The second question should preferably be answered by reference to a more detailed plan for the specific sector in which the water resource project is placed (e.g., power sector, including thermal and hydroelectric alternatives) in which the projects have been compared in comprehensive economic terms. This implies the evaluation of benefits and costs, adjusted for accounting (shadow) prices if appropriate, the determination of indicators of merit such as the internal rates of return, and the comparison of these indicators with those for other investments in the country having comparable risks. Other economic aspects should also be considered when establishing an order of priority for the various projects. For example, a basic investment in a project with lower economic returns (or possibly no revenues) may set the stage for the development of projects with much more attractive returns. Other factors affecting priorities may include foreign exchange requirements and earnings of the project, and effects of the project in reducing unemployment or in improving health and distribution of income. The analysis also needs to take account of infrastructure costs that are not included as part of the project cost estimates, and also opportunities created by the project for related enterprises.

Technical Aspects. This appraisal involves a review of the detailed engineering plan for construction and operation of the project. In this connection, the World Bank not only carries out its own appraisal, but requires assurance that a qualified engineering staff has prepared the plan. The scale of the project should be suitable considering the possibilities for physical exploitation of the available site, the time expected for the demands for project services to increase to the project capacity, and the needs to conserve scarce capital. The location and layout of project features are reviewed for adequacy and appropriateness. The design criteria employed for preliminary plans and expected for subsequent detailed designs if the project is approved are also reviewed. The appraisal considers whether the proposed plan is the least cost or otherwise best solution among the alternatives. The construction schedule is analyzed for potential causes of delay. The underlying assumptions for the cost estimates are considered, and the estimates are reviewed to determine that they are complete and that they contain adequate contingencies (for omissions, physical contingencies, and price increases), allowance for interest during construction, and provisions for working capital. The projections of cost during operation of the project should be prepared for various levels of project usage.

Commercial Aspects. This appraisal includes a review of the arrangements for buying materials and services needed to construct the project. In this respect, the World Bank insists on procedures to obtain best value for money expended, which normally involves competitive bidding, internationally if practicable. Consulting engineers can often be usefully employed to evaluate bids to take account not only of price but also quality, experience and reliability of the supplier, efficiency of the project, terms of delivery and payment, and other factors. The Bank's appraisal extends to the arrangements for obtaining the materials, power, and labor to maintain and operate the project, and the procedures for marketing the goods and services provided by the project.

Financial Aspects. This appraisal determines the soundness of the financial plans for both construction and operation phases of the project. The financing plan for construction must cover all the monies involved, the sources from which they will be obtained, and the amounts and terms for repayment of each loan. In addition to loans from an international agency such as World Bank, monies may be obtained from banks within the country, from surplus funds made available from existing operations, and from governmental appropriations. A financial analysis must also be made of financial liquidity, projecting costs expected during the operation phase, and the revenues and other funds to pay such costs and to repay both foreign exchange and domestic loans. The financial return on the investment is also estimated if the project is revenue earning. If the loan application is submitted by an ongoing enterprise, various financial statements will be reviewed, including those projected for the future in which the new project is integrated with other operations.

Institutional, Organizational, and Managerial Aspects. The World Bank reviews the organizational arrangements for construction and for operation. It wants to be assured that the organization functions in a businesslike manner and, in some projects, it has conditioned its assistance on the creation of an autonomous operating authority insulated from political pressures and rigidities of governmental administrative procedures.

The Bank places particular stress on adequate management skills. If such skills are not fully available locally among engineers, accountants, lawyers, and other trained individuals, outside organizations or individuals may be needed, at least during the initial stages of operation and to provide management training to local personnel. Management tasks include the development and administration of rate policies, monitoring financial performance, and setting technical standards for operation. Training programs need to extend to both office and field operations.

Project Completion Report. The World Bank, in addition to the appraisals prior to approving a loan, discussed above, also prepares a Project Completion

Report after the completion of of an individual project (World Bank, 1976), which is designed to evaluate the success of the implementation and to analyze the deficiencies that were revealed.

3.9.2 Appraisals by the U.S. Agency for International Development

The Agency for International Development (AID) procedures manual for feasibility analysis of water and land use projects (1976) relates to such projects as technical assistance, training, or research; commodity support, development bank, and sector programs; and construction and resource development. Projects considered may or may not be revenue producing. The manual is based on four general feasibility criteria for development assistance:

1. The economic and technical soundness of the activity to be financed
2. The relationship of the activity to other development activities being undertaken or planned and its likely contribution to realizable long-range objectives
3. The likelihood of the activity contributing to the achievement of self-sustaining growth
4. The likelihood of the activity contributing to the development of either or both of the following:
   a. Educational or other institutions and programs directed toward social progress
   b. Economic resources or the increase of productive capacities in furtherance of development assistance

The following checklist for preliminary project appraisal prepared for AID (1971) exhibits many similarities to the factors considered important by the World Bank.

- Sources and types of information in the country and from secondary sources such as World Bank and AID.
- Examination of previous projects of a similar nature so that steps are planned to avoid or minimize difficulties already experienced in such projects.
- Engineering and data requirements needed to ascertain that it is physically possible to implement a proposed project and to establish its physical characteristics in sufficient detail to allow estimates of construction and operating costs.
- Alternative projects adequately considered, and proposed project formulated to cope with uncertainties.
- Costs adequately estimated; indigenous materials used instead of imported materials when possible; standards for construction; costs including investments for adequate roads, utilities, and other infrastructure to service the project to accommodate expansion of public institutions serving to regulate the project, and to relocate persons displaced by the project.

- Estimates of demand and valuations of output, including consideration of market demands caused by economic, demographic, and institutional factors; nonmarket services provided through infrastructure projects such as education and public health facilities. Probabilities of projected needs or demands being realized. Valuation of projected output at market prices and accounting (shadow) prices. Valuation for projects having outputs not sold for a price; indirect benefits and indivisible benefits (e.g., improved public health and environment). Selection of least-cost alternatives where quantification and/or monetary valuation of output is not feasible.

- Organization and management aspects, including identification of project sponsorship (policymakers, sponsoring entities); organizational structure or form; legal arrangements; management authority and autonomy; availability and arrangements for training required managerial and technical personnel and skilled labor and meeting unskilled labor requirements; organizational headquarters physical facilities; and extent to which organization and management would be affected by administration of the "project's environment," existing and pending legislation and government regulations, and social and environmental impacts of project.

3.10 RECENT TRENDS IN PROJECT EVALUATION

The Water Resources Council "Principles and Standards" (1973, 1979, 1980) adopted environmental quality as a coequal objective with national economic development, and also considered regional economic development and other social effects. Such an approach indicates that in an advanced economy such as the United States, society as a whole is willing to accept a smaller rate of economic growth in order to accommodate environmental and other social concerns.

Revisions of the "Principles and Standards" (1979 and 1980) included enhanced consideration of water conservation and nonstructural alternatives as desirable aspects of planning to be emphasized. Water conservation consists of actions that will: (1) reduce the demand for water; (2) improve efficiency in use and reduce losses and waste; (3) improve land management practices to conserve water. In addition, a primarily non-structural plan was to be prepared and included as a candidate plan whenever structural project or program alternatives are considered. This involves a combination of nonstructural or demand-reducing measures, including modifications in public policy, management practice, regulatory policy, and pricing policy.

The WRC "Principles and Standards" of 1983 replaced the "Principles and Standards" and focus on the single national economic development objective, but environmental, conservation, and nonstructural measures are mentioned prominently in considering alternative plans (pp. 6–7).

The World Bank and agencies in the United States (e.g., U.S. Army Corps of Engineers, Institute of Water Resources) have developed in recent years improved methods to determine the social impacts of projects. The World Bank and other international financial agencies, and national and local government agencies in both economically advanced and developing countries, have developed an increased awareness of the environmental impacts of projects and of the need to prepare environmental assessments so that enlightened decisions can be made when projects are rejected or authorized. Although the level of commitment to noneconomic impacts is understandably less in the poorer countries for whom water resource development is needed for survival and attainment of an acceptable standard of living, it is clear that societies are aiming toward balanced development considering "quality of life" as well as "quantity." In this context, quality of life comprehends not only the human environment and the ecological values relating to other forms of life, but also such aspects as aesthetics, cultural, anthropological, and historical values, and the restoration of waters and related land damaged by human activities.

REFERENCES

BAUM, WARREN C., "The Project Cycle," *Finance and Development*, June 1970.

DAVIS, C. V., and K. E. SORENSON, eds., *Handbook of Applied Hydraulics*, 3rd ed., McGraw-Hill, New York, 1969.

DE GARMO, E. P., and J. K. CANADA, *Engineering Economy*, 5th ed., Macmillan, New York, 1973.

GRANT, EUGENE L., W. GRANT IRESON, and RICHARD S. LEAVENWORTH, *Principles of Engineering Economy*, 6th ed., Wiley, New York, 1976.

KING, JOHN A., JR., *Economic Development Projects and Their Appraisal*, World Bank book published by Johns Hopkins University Press, Baltimore, Md., 1967.

KROMBACH, JURGEN, "Financing of Water Supply and Sewerage Projects in Developing Countries," *Proc. Columbia Univ. Semin. Pollut. Water Resources*, September 1970.

KUIPER, EDWARD, *Water Resources Development*, Butterworth, Kent, England, 1965.

LINSLEY, RAY K., and JOSEPH B FRANZINI, *Water Resources Engineering*, 3rd ed., McGraw-Hill, New York, 1979.

MAJOR, DAVID C., "Multiobjective Water Resource Planning," *Am. Geophys. Union Water Resources Monogr. 4*, 1977.

U.S. AGENCY FOR INTERNATIONAL DEVELOPMENT, "Appraisal Guidelines for Development," Draft, September 1971.

U.S. AGENCY FOR INTERNATIONAL DEVELOPMENT, "Feasibility and Analysis Procedures Manual, Benefit-Cost Evaluations—Water and Land Use Projects," January 1976.

U.S. DEPARTMENT OF THE INTERIOR, BUREAU OF RECLAMATION, *Design of Small Dams*, 2nd ed., U.S. Government Printing Office, Washington, D.C., 1973.

U.S. NATIONAL WATER COMMISSION, "Water Resources Planning," Consulting Panel on Water Resources Planning, May 1972.

U.S. WATER RESOURCES COUNCIL, "Principles and Standards for Planning Water and Related Land Resources," September 10, 1973; rev. December 14, 1979; rev. September 29, 1980.

U.S. WATER RESOURCES COUNCIL, "Economic and Environmental Principles and Guidelines for Water and Related Land Resources Implementation Studies," March 10, 1983.

WOODWARD, SHERMAN M., "Hydraulics of the Miami Flood Control Project," State of Ohio Miami Conservancy District, 1920.

WORLD BANK, "Operations Evaluation—World Bank Standards and Procedures," June 1976.

FOUR

Estimates of Population and Water Needs

4.1 SCOPE

Forecasts of population and water needs are necessary ingredients of local and regional planning. They are important for determining the location and types of projects that are required, for establishing the functional characteristics and scale of project components and estimating their cost, and for projecting the benefits expected after the projects are placed in operation. Estimates of population and water needs can be based on an interpretation of data on historical trends. If such data are unavailable or inadequate, water requirements must be estimated by other approaches, such as adapting typical unit demands that have been compiled by various authorities.

In addition to the problems of estimating population and water needs, this chapter treats other factors that have become important in modern planning, primarily for water supply but also for other project purposes; these include the effects of price on demand, water conservation and other nonstructural approaches, and inter-relationships of water and energy. This chapter shows how mathematical models are used to forecast population and water needs; these models often consider related economic activities. More sophisticated mathematical models that focus on the interrelationships of water resources project construction and regional economic growth are described in Chapter 14.

4.2 DATA FOR DEMOGRAPHIC STUDIES

Demography is the science of population. It refers to the number of persons and their arrangement in space; structure (e.g., sex and age groupings); the growth or decline of population (total or one of its units); components of change in terms of births, deaths, and migrations; and economic characteristics such as economic activity, employment status, occupation, industry, and income (Shryock et al. 1976).

There are large variations of population density in the United States and throughout the world. The following factors affect population distribution (United Nations, 1973):

- Climate (temperature, precipitation)
- Landforms (topography, including altitude and slope, swamps, marshes, and deserts)
- Soils
- Energy resources and mineral raw materials
- Space relationships (accessibility as affected by distance from seacoast, natural harbors, navigable rivers and fall lines, the heads of river navigation)
- Cultural factors
  —historical (recency of discovery and settlement)
  —political (boundaries, including buffer zones and controls and migration and trade; government policies)
  —types of economic activities
  —technology (state of the arts; type of farming; highway, rail, water, and air transportation facilities)
  —social organization
- Demographic factors (variations in natural increase; variations in net migration)
- Economic characteristics (employed and unemployed economically active population; homemakers, students, income recipients, and other noneconomically active population; income)

The most comprehensive source of demographic information in the United States is the Bureau of the Census. Its "Environmental/Socioeconomic Data Sources" (1976) and "Profile of Census Programs" (1978) are excellent guides to the data it collects. In the latter document, which was prepared for water planners, the Bureau states that its principal functions include:

- Decennial censuses of population and housing (after 1986, also a mid-decade census of population)
- Quinquennial census of agriculture, state and local governments, manufacturers, mineral industries, commercial fisheries, business, construction industries, and transportation
- Current surveys which provide information on many of the subjects covered in the censuses at weekly, monthly, quarterly, annual, or other intervals
- Compilation of current statistics on U.S. foreign trade, including data on imports, exports, and shipping
- Special censuses at the request and expense of state and local government units

Each Bureau report includes discussions of terminology, population surveyed or enumerated, reliability of estimates, sources of error, and any allocations or comparability with reports or data. Data are processed for a number of different geographic levels. The most common are:

- Standard Metropolitan Statistical Area and Component Areas (SMSAs; central city of over 50,000 population and the surrounding metropolitan county or counties)
- Census Tract (small, homogeneous, relatively permanent area; average 4000 population; all SMSAs are entirely tracted)
- Block Group or Enumeration District (subdivisions of census tracts, places, and minor civil divisions; average 1000 population)
- Block (identified in all urbanized areas and other selected areas; average 100 population)

Most population projections are based on a time-series analysis of current and past demographic data, or cohort-survival techniques. Other types of economic growth studies also require demographic data. For example, the "Bureau of Reclamation Economic Assessment Model (BREAM)" prepared by Mountain West Research, Inc. (1978) is organized around five component submodels:

- Demographic
- Construction worker
- Economic
- Labor market
- Community allocation

The demographic data for BREAM are obtained from the Census Bureau and from other federal, state, and local governmental agencies and private entities (e.g., project employment from construction contractors, and nonresident college population from local institutions).

Where census data are unavailable or inadequate, other sources that may be used (Shryock et al. 1976) include tax office records, city directories, church membership records, postal delivery stops, permits for new residential construction and for demolition, telephone subscribers, and water, electric, and gas meters. Registration systems may also be useful, such as those that include vital events (e.g., births and deaths), arrivals and departures at international boundaries, workers in jobs covered by social insurance plans, and voters. United Nations publications provide data on international movements. A comprehensive guide to data sources, other than the census materials, in the categories of demography, public services, social well-being, economy, social structure, and community response, was prepared for the Corps of Engineers by Flynn and Schmidt (1977).

4.3 POPULATION PROJECTIONS

For almost every water resource project, population projections (total and areal distribution) are needed to accomplish one or more of the following:

- Estimate demands for specific outputs of the water resource project (municipal water supply, power, recreation, etc.).

- Assess the likelihood that a project built to exploit a water resource will find an adequate market.
- Schedule the implementation, including stage development, of water resource projects.
- Provide the population component in a regional economic model. Such a model predicts one or more of the following: the need for various types of project outputs, the economic impacts attributable to the water resources development, and the community facilities that are needed to serve the construction and permanent project populations.

Population projections should be made for near-, mid-, and long-term needs (25 years or more in the future). In many cases, an inaccurate forecast would merely mean that the schedule for implementation of a group of phased projects must be sped up or slowed down. In other cases, serious problems may arise. For example, a project may be a financial (or economic) failure if inadequate revenues (or benefits) are realized due to overoptimistic projections. The record of long-range projections is not good. Low estimates made in the economic depression of the 1930s in the United States did not compare favorably with post–World War II values due to birthrate increases and the acceleration of migration to urban areas. Also, extrapolations based on post–World War II growth appear too high for the 1980s, due to a leveling off and reduction of the birthrate.

The basic equation of balance in population studies is

$$P_t = P_0 + B - D + I - O$$

where

P_t = population at end of period
P_0 = population at beginning of period
B = births
D = deaths
I = inmigration
O = outmigration

Population projections may be based on a time-series analysis of data for P as a whole or for each of the components of the equation. Further disaggregations may be in terms of any common property, or "cohort" (e.g., all people born in a given year). Another general approach is to establish relationships to historical trends and projections for the nation as a whole or for SMSAs or other defined region for which reliable projections are already available from governmental agencies.

Some general estimating principles have been suggested by Shryock et al. (1976):

- More accurate estimates can generally be made for an entire country than for the geographic subdivisions of the country.
- More accurate estimates can generally be made for the total population of an area than for the demographic characteristics of the population of the area.

TABLE 4.1 ERRORS IN POPULATION FORECASTS

	Average Error (%)	
Forecasting Method	*10-Year Forecast*	*20-Year Forecast*
Graphical extrapolation of past population growth	34.9	61.8
Projections based on exponential growth pattern	33.0	61.0
Projections based on linear growth pattern	14.2	18.8
Projections based on ratio of area to projected population of region	9.3	15.6
Projections based on S-shaped growth pattern	8.8	10.6

Source: McJunkin (1964).

- In general, assuming that the available data are of good quality, direct data are to be preferred to indirect data from the standpoint of the accuracy of the resulting estimates, either in preparing separate estimates or in elaborating a single estimate.
- An estimate may be checked by comparing it with another estimate derived by an equally accurate or more accurate method using different data and assumptions.
- Interpolation is more reliable than extrapolation.
- The quality of the base data, the quality of data used to allow for change since the base data, and the period of time that has elapsed since the base data all have a major effect in the accuracy of the final estimate.

4.3.1 Extension of Historical Data

Schmitt and Crosetti (1953) prepared projections for 1940 and 1950, based on census data for 1890–1930 for the five largest cities in each of four census regions. Average errors for five different methods are shown in Table 4.1. McJunkin also analyzed the forecast accuracies of methods used by other investigators (Schmitt and Crosetti 1953; Siegel et al. 1954).

4.3.2 Historical and Goal-Oriented Projections

Both population and economic projections were made for the Appalachian Water Resources Survey (AWRS) by the Corps of Engineers, Office of Appalachian Studies (OAS) (U.S. Department of the Army, 1969), in connection with comprehensive development studies focused on water resource projects. Separate projections were made for population, employment by industry group, per capita income, and gross output per employee. Data and projections were grouped by 27 economic subregions, 28 water areas, and 59 state planning subregions. Historically, there was a downward trend in the Appalachian region for population, employment, and income as compared with values for the United States as a whole. The goal of the

TABLE 4.2 APPALACHIA POPULATION PROJECTIONS FOR TWO SCENARIOS (Water Area B-1) (Thousands)

Year	Historical and Projected		Development Benchmarks	
	Employment	*Population*	*Employment*	*Population*
1960	324	878	324	878
1980	409	1122	418	1272
2000	533	1445	717	1867
2020	667	1772	1100	2878

Source: U.S. Department of the Army, Corps of Engineers (1969).

Appalachian Regional Development Act of 1965 and its extensions was to provide economic stimuli to reverse the downward trend.

Two sets of projections were prepared, based on two different "scenarios." One, by the U.S. Department of Commerce, Office of Business Economics (OBE), was called the "Historical and Projected" projection since it was based on an extension of historical trends. The other, by the OAS, was called the "Development Benchmarks" population and was based on changing the historical trends.

For the "Historical and Projected" projections, a group of assumptions was used to develop national totals and then these were disaggregated (from nation to major regions to states). For the "Development Benchmarks," assumptions were based on a quantification of goal-oriented statements in the Appalachian Regional Development Act:

- After 1980, population will be a constant percent of U.S. population.
- Labor force participation will increase to the projected national rate, and the population per worker will decline from 2.7 in 1960 to 2.58 by 2020.
- Per capita income will increase to at least 95% of national average by 2020.

The first two assumptions affected the population projections and the third was added for the income projections. The OBE and OAS projections for 1980 were about the same, but there were large differences for subsequent years. For example, Table 4.2 shows the population values for one of the "water areas."

4.3.3 Cohort Projections

Population projections were made for Kingston, Jamaica, and surrounding area in connection with a comparative study of water supply projects by Tippetts-Abbett-McCarthy-Stratton and Mattis, Demain, Beckford and Associates (TAMS, 1977). The approach in this study was to review and compare existing projections and to develop a range of growth possibilities. The best documented projections had been made by Roberts (1976) of the Census Research Programme of the University of West Indies and by the Town Planning Department (Jamaica, 1973). Other

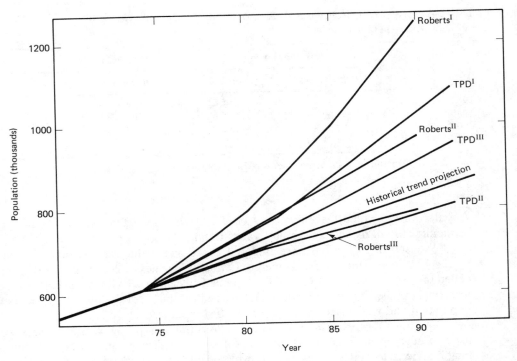

Figure 4.1 Population projections for Kingston and St. Andrew, Jamaica. (From TAMS, 1977.)

projections had been made by the Ministry of Mining and Natural Resources and United Nations agencies (Archer 1975; Jamaica, 1972; United Nations, 1975).

Roberts made projections of population components (cohorts) for the country as a whole in conjunction with internal migrations among the 14 parishes of Jamaica. He placed particular emphasis on movements to the parish in which Kingston is located because he found that the capital city "exerts such a strong attractive force on all other parish populations." Roberts assumed three scenarios. Projection I illustrated the results of completely uncontrolled growth by assuming no reduction in fertility from the high levels observed in 1970, constant mortality, and no external migration. Projection II introduced a growth constraint in the form of declining fertility levels by assuming that fertility would fall to replacement level by 1985 and thereafter remain constant. Projection III added a second constraint on growth in the form of external migration corresponding to the fairly high levels of the 1960s. The Town Planning Department also made three projections. Projection I, the highest by the agency, was based on a constant growth rate and stable fertility rates. Projection II was the lowest and took account of declining fertility. Projection III was a midrange estimate. The various projections by Roberts and TPD were adjusted so that they all extended from the base population census figure determined by surveys in 1974, as shown on Figure 4.1. This figure also shows a "historical trend" projection obtained by graphical extension of the historical growth trend experienced in the period 1960–1974.

Estimates of Population and Water Needs   Chap. 4

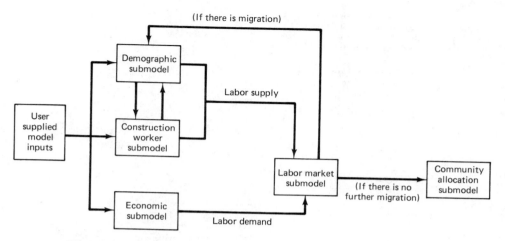

(If there is migration)

Demographic submodel

Labor supply

User supplied model inputs

Construction worker submodel

Labor market submodel

(If there is no further migration)

Community allocation submodel

Economic submodel

Labor demand

Figure 4.2 Bureau of Reclamation economic assessment model, BREAM. (From Mountain West Research, Inc., 1978.)

An analysis was made to determine whether the densities of population implied by the projections were reasonable. The high rate of growth implied by the Roberts I projection (a doubling of population in 16 years) did not appear possible due to a lack of available open land space, except land reserved for official buildings and public amenities. If Kingston were to reach the densities envisaged in the Roberts I and TPD I projections, there would have to be radical and immediate changes in building patterns as well as significant investments in public high-density housing. The assumptions in the Roberts I and TPD I projections of constant fertility rate and no external migration were also judged to be unrealistic. For these reasons, these projections were not considered to be within the range of feasible growth patterns.

For the purpose of studying various water supply options, it was decided to adopt the Roberts II projection as the "high" projection and the TPD II as the "low." The extension of the historical trend lay between these limiting projections and was named the "most likely" projection. It was judged that any growth over and above the historical growth trend would take the form of "spillover" into suburban areas surrounding Kingston.

4.3.4 Projections Taking Account of Project Impact

The Bureau of Reclamation Economic Assessment Model (BREAM) is described in a report by Mountain West Research, Inc. (1978). The data requirements for this model were described in Section 4.2. This model is based on relatively straightforward cause-and-effect relationships. (More complex models for population and economic projections related to project impact are described in Chapter 14.)

Interrelationships among the major components of BREAM are represented schematically in Figure 4.2. The model evaluates the consistency of the labor supply projections obtained from analysis of the area's population with the labor demand

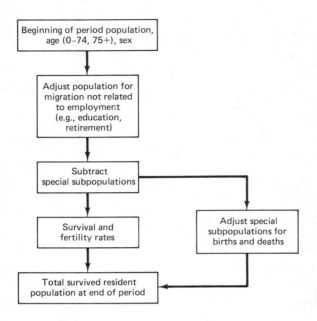

```
┌─────────────────────────┐
│ Beginning of period population, │
│   age (0-74, 75+), sex   │
└─────────────────────────┘
            │
            ▼
┌─────────────────────────┐
│  Adjust population for   │
│   migration not related  │
│      to employment       │
│     (e.g., education,    │
│       retirement)        │
└─────────────────────────┘
            │
            ▼
┌─────────────────────────┐
│        Subtract          │────────┐
│  special subpopulations  │        │
└─────────────────────────┘        ▼
            │          ┌──────────────────────┐
            ▼          │   Adjust special      │
┌─────────────────────────┐ subpopulations for │
│    Survival and          │   births and deaths│
│   fertility rates        │ └──────────────────┘
└─────────────────────────┘        │
            │                      │
            ▼                      │
┌─────────────────────────┐        │
│  Total survived resident │◄──────┘
│ population at end of period│
└─────────────────────────┘
```

Figure 4.3 Demographic submodel for BREAM. (From Mountain West Research, Inc., 1978.)

implied by analysis of the area's economy. In the event that the supply and demand for labor are not in balance, adjustments are assumed to occur principally by migration, although some change in the number of unemployed can also be expected. Once equilibrium is achieved in the labor market, no further migration occurs and levels of population, employment, and income are established for each county in the local impact area. The model then disaggregates the county population projections and allocates them to the communities within each county. The following summary of the five analytic components of the BREAM model is based on the report.

Demographic Submodel.   The principal input into the demographic submodel is county population, disaggregated by age and sex. Age and sex specific survival rates are applied to each cohort (i.e., each age/sex specific group) to compute the effect of deaths on the county population. Age-specific fertility rates are then applied to the females in each age group to estimate the number of births. This procedure yields an estimate of the "survived" population of the county. Further adjustments are made in the demographic submodel for special subpopulations such as those that are independent of local labor market conditions (e.g., retirement migration), for large college populations, or for a large military installation. Figure 4.3 summarizes the cohort-survival process.

Construction Worker Submodel.   The construction worker submodel is used whenever a project is under consideration for which some part of the construction labor force may have to immigrate to the study area because the project's labor demands exceed the supply available in the local labor market. Once the project labor requirements have been specified, the submodel begins by determining the composition of the construction force between local and nonlocal workers. After the number of nonlocal workers is determined (i.e., the number of immigrating workers), the construction worker submodel estimates the demographic characteristics of the workers that will be accompanied by their families and it makes an estimate of the community allocation of the immigrating workers.

Economic Submodel. The economic submodel is an "export-base" model which determines both income and employment. The export-base model for a community focuses on the growth of economic activities having outputs that are exported from the community, and the increases of employees and personal income related to such growth. Export-base and other types of models of economic growth are discussed in Chapter 14.

Labor Market Submodel. The population calculated in the demographic submodel and the total employment estimate calculated in the economic submodel are the principal inputs into the labor force and migration process. The locally available supply of labor is calculated by applying age/sex specific labor force participation rates to the population. Labor demand is estimated by multiplying the total employment figure from the economic submodel by an implied multiple-job holding and commutation rate, and this results in what is called adjusted employment. If the supply of labor is in balance with demand for labor, no further adjustments are made to population, employment, or income projections at the county level and the model goes on to the community allocation process. If, however, there is an imbalance in the supply and demand for labor, in- or outmigration is assumed to occur until the imbalance is eliminated. Whenever migration occurs, it is necessary to iterate through the demographic submodel so that the county population can be appropriately adjusted. The basic relationships of the labor market submodel are diagrammed in Figure 4.4.

Community Allocation Submodel. Once equilibrium has been established in the local labor market, county totals for population, employment, and income are fixed and it only remains to allocate the population to communities within each county. School age population for each community is also allocated and the estimated number of households is determined. The population is allocated by component of population change, which allows different allocation schemes to be used for natural increase (births minus deaths), retirement migration, employment-related migration, and migration of nonlocal construction workers.

The community allocation submodel comes into play at the end of each projection period after the population for each county in the local impact area has been determined. The allocation procedure addresses each of the principal components of population change individually. Population change from the previous year is equal to the natural increase (births minus deaths) plus retirement migration plus employment-related migration. Employment migration can be further subdivided into nonlocal construction workers and all other employment migration components. Each component is allocated according to one of four community distributions generated by the model. Three of the options are based on the community's share of the county's

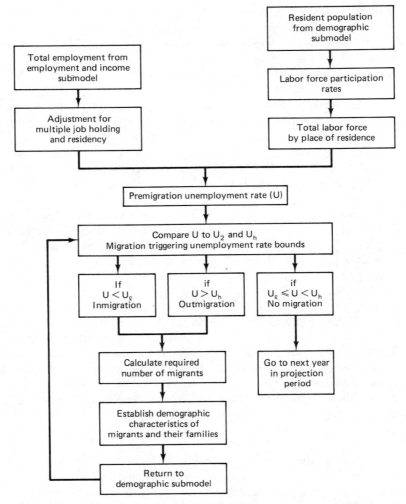

Figure 4.4 Labor market submodel for BREAM. (From Mountain West Research, Inc., 1978.)

population for previous years. The fourth option is used if there are nonlocal construction workers; they and their families are then allocated on a project-by-project basis according to the allocation coefficients calculated in the construction worker submodel.

4.4 ECONOMIC/DEMOGRAPHIC PROJECTIONS

The U.S. Water Resources Council "Principles and Guidelines" (1983, pp. 4–5) state that:

The forecasts of with-and-without-plan conditions . . . should be based on . . . national/ regional projections of income, employment, output, and population. . . . Appropriate national and regional projections should be used as an underlying forecasting framework. . . . National projections used in planning are to be based on a full employment economy. . . . Forecasts should be made for selected years over the period of analysis to indicate how changes in economic and other conditions are likely to have an impact on problems and opportunities.

Economic/demographic projections are needed for estimates in the various "accounts" prepared by federal agencies for alternative projects. For the National Economic Development account, projections are needed not only to provide a basis for user demands and their reflection in water user benefits, but also for other types of economic evaluations for a project. In addition to being important in National Economic Development account preparation, projections are essential for evaluating the effects included in the Regional Economic Development and Other Social Effects accounts. Indirectly, population, industry, and other elements of economic/demographic characteristics of a region also affect changes in the Environmental Quality account.

Economic/demographic projections are also needed for the preparation of an environmental impact statement (EIS), which is required for any U.S. federal agency action that significantly affects the quality of the human environment, in accordance with the National Environmental Policy Act of 1969. The Council on Environmental Quality guidelines for the EIS (1973) emphasize the importance of both direct and indirect consequences of policies or actions.

In the regional development program for Appalachia, increased rates of population and economic growth were, *in themselves*, considered to be important goals of development. This is discussed in Chapter 14. Such regional goals are important (and perhaps most important in developing countries) for some areas. Economic/demographic projections are needed in estimating real resource flows and transfers in regional income accounting procedures.

Figure 4.5 shows a sequence of seven steps in the economic/demographic assessment process, as presented by Chalmers and Anderson (1977) of Mountain West Research, Inc. for the U.S. Bureau of Reclamation. The first four steps correspond to an assessment of the population, employment, and income impacts of a proposed action. The last three steps carry the impact analysis down to the community facilities and the fiscal implications of the proposed action. The BREAM mathematical model was formulated to implement this approach. An outline of this model and the components relating principally to population were given in Section 4.3.4 and the economic submodel will be discussed further in Chapter 14. The BREAM formulation focuses on the community effects of a proposed action and does not emphasize the broader economic impacts that could result.

A representative economic base study was prepared by the National Planning Association (1967) for the Chesapeake Basin, in connection with studies by federal agencies of water quality in the Chesapeake Bay Drainage Basin, including the Susquehanna River, and the formulation of a comprehensive plan for the development of the water and related land resources of the Susquehanna River Basin. The

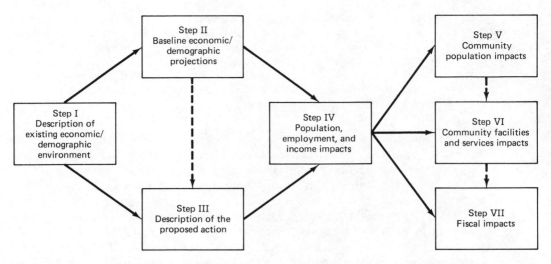

Figure 4.5 Steps in economic/demographic assessment process. (From Chalmers and Anderson, 1977.)

economic base study was a prerequisite to the preparation of water quality control and water resource development programs and had three principal components: an analysis of economic structure, the identification and analysis of growth forces, and projections of economic growth.

The first component included a detailed analysis of the past and present economic structure of the basins and its relation to the national economy. This considered the population; labor force and employment; personal income; and status and trends in the principal economic activities, including agriculture; mining, forestry, and commercial fisheries; manufacturing; transportation and utilities; recreation and tourism; and service, trade, and construction activities. The analysis was developed on a subregion and county basis. The analyses covered the characteristics of the area's resources and their past and present use in conjunction with associated industries.

The structure of the basin's economy was examined to identify and analyze those growth forces that could reasonably be expected to operate effectively in the future in fostering and sustaining economic growth. Special attention was directed to those industries of the basins that rely heavily upon the availability of water of sufficient quantity and of suitable quality.

Projections of economic growth started with an analysis of the future pattern of national economic growth for the purpose of relating the region to the national economy. The economic growth was measured in terms of population, employment, gross national product, and total and per capita income. Projections were made for the basin and subregions in terms that would facilitate their translation into water requirement and quality estimates. The measures of economic development in the projections are shown in Table 4.3. The relationship of water resource development to economic growth was investigated to estimate to what extent an accelerated rate of development would alter the basin's projected rate of overall economic growth.

TABLE 4.3 MEASURES OF ECONOMIC DEVELOPMENT IN ECONOMIC BASE STUDY

1. Population of the area
   a. Urban and rural
   b. Labor force
   c. Households
2. Industrial development
   a. Employment by industrial categories (for major water-using industries, employment given by a three- or four-digit industrial classification; other industrial categories may be grouped together)
   b. Product output for major water-using industries where possible
3. Agriculture
   a. Farm population
   b. Livestock number
   c. Acres irrigated by crop categories
   d. Production for different types of food processing
   e. Water quantities needed
4. Recreation
   a. Types of water use
   b. Some measure of amount of use by types
5. Projection dates
   1960—base year for all projections; 1970—short-term projection; 1985—first long-term projections; 2020—final long-term projection

Source: National Planning Association (1967).

Chapter 14 discusses other techniques that may be used to evaluate the economic impacts of investments in water resource developments. Some of these approaches recognize that public investments not only have an effect on the existing economic structure but may also create the economic and physical conditions that induce additional economic growth.

4.5 WATER RESOURCE NEEDS FOR WATER SUPPLY

4.5.1 Definitions

Water demand is discussed in Section 2.8 (the effect of price on the change of demand) and in Section 4.7 (data on this relationship). Categories of water demand include public water uses (domestic, commercial, industrial, and public), rural (domestic, livestock), irrigation, and self-supplied industrial (cooling and processing, thermoelectric and hydroelectric power). Water demands vary continuously and are expressed for annual, monthly, daily, hourly, or other time periods.

Withdrawal uses are from diversion of water from groundwater or surface water sources. *Nonwithdrawal uses* are on-site uses such as navigation, water-based recreation, and wastewater disposal by dilution. Water is also needed for natural vegetation and wildlife.

Consumptive use is the portion of the water withdrawn that is no longer available for further use because of evaporation, transpiration, incorporation into manufactured products and crops, or use by human beings and livestock. The terms "consumption" and "demand" are often used interchangeably in public water supply technology; since little of the water withdrawn for this purpose is consumed, this usage is not recommended.

4.5.2 Trends in Withdrawals

Trends in population, water withdrawals, and water consumed in the United States during the period 1950–1975 are shown in Figure 1.2 and Table 4.4. The average daily per capita total water withdrawn was over 1900 gallons in 1975 compared with

TABLE 4.4 CHANGES IN WATER WITHDRAWALS AND WATER CONSUMED IN THE UNITED STATES, 1950–1975 (Billion Gallons per Day) (Partial figures may not add to total because of independent rounding)

	1950	1955	1960	1965	1970	1975	Percent Increase or Decrease 1970–1975[a]
Total population (millions)	150.7	164	179.3	193.8	205.9[b]	217.5[c]	5.6
Total withdrawals	200	240	270	310	370	420	11.7
Public supplies	14	17	21	24	27	29	7.9
Rural domestic and livestock	3.6	3.6	3.6	4.0	4.5	4.9	10.3
Irrigation	110[d]	110	110	120	130	140	10.9
Self-supplied thermoelectric power use	40[e]	72	100	130	170	190	18.0
Other self-supplied industrial use	37[e]	39	38	46	47	44	−5.6
Sources from which water was withdrawn							
Fresh groundwater	34	47	50	60	68	82	21.7
Saline groundwater	f	0.65	0.38	0.47	1.0	1.0	−6.0
Fresh surface water	160[g]	180	190	210	250	260	5.1
Saline surface water	10[g]	18	31	43	53	66	30.9
Reclaimed sewage	f	.2	0.1	0.7	0.5	0.5	2.2
Water consumed by off-channel uses	d	f	61	77	87[h]	95[h]	9.9
Water used for hydroelectric power	1100	1500	2000	2300	2800	3300	20.7

[a]Calculated from original unrounded computer printout figures for the two years.
[b]Including Puerto Rico.
[c]Including Puerto Rico and Virgin Islands.
[d]Including an estimated 30 bgd in irrigation conveyance losses.
[e]Estimated distribution of 77 bgd reported by MacKichan (1951).
[f]Data not available.
[g]Distribution of 170 bgd of fresh water and saline water reported by MacKichan (1951).
[h]Fresh water only.
Source: Murray and Reeves (1977).

about 1300 gallons in 1950. The per capita daily withdrawals for public water supplies increased to 133 gallons in 1975 from 70 gallons in 1950. When only the 175 million persons served by public supplies are considered, the value for 1975 was 168 gallons per capita per day.

There is a generally increasing demand for water throughout the world. In many developing regions, much of the demand is unsatisfied because of inadequate water supplies. Per capita uses in the United States vary markedly from one region to another and differ from those in other countries. Technological developments may affect both water demand and water supply in the future, as shown in Table 4.5.

TABLE 4.5 TECHNOLOGICAL ADVANCES THAT WILL AFFECT FUTURE WATER DEMAND

To Increase Future Demand for Water

Gas production from coal
Electric power generation by conventional nuclear reactors
Surface transportation using electric power
Transport of solids by water slurry pipeline
Fire hazard area irrigation
Forest and rangeland irrigation
Solution mining

To Decrease Future Demand for Water

Electric power generation by gas-cooled nuclear reactors
Electric power generation by nuclear fusion
Electric power generation by fuel cells
Electric power generation by magnetohydrodynamics
Electric power generation in open-cycle engines
Electric power generation by use of wind and water power
Recirculation cooling pond development
Cooling tower design and utilization in industry
Industrial cooling systems using air
Water as dilutent for wastes
No-rinse washing/laundry technology
Bioprocessing to provide food
Artificial antitranspirants
Genetic development of plants to withstand drought and salinity
Subirrigation and unsaturated leaching strategy
Landscaping with artificial materials

To Increase and/or Decrease Future Demand for Water,
Direction Uncertain or Different Directions in Different Regions

Conversion of solar energy to heat and power
Power generating units for meeting peak demands
Electric power transmission over long distances
Oil shale conversion to liquid fuels
Advanced communications systems
Central electric versus on-site total energy systems
Geothermal energy
Regional environmental management of bays and estuaries
Vegetation management

Source: National Academy of Sciences (1971).

4.5.3 Public Water Supplies

Differences in demand for water are attributed to both natural and economic factors. More water is used in warm, drier regions than in humid areas due to more lawn watering, bathing, and air conditioning. Water may be run continuously to prevent freezing of pipes in extremely cold weather. Of various climatic influences, precipitation appears to have the greatest effect on per capita residential demand primarily since it affects the lawn watering required. The living standards of the population also affect the demand, which is greater for higher-income residential districts. Good predictive models for municipal use have been developed based on three variables: population, average annual per capita income, and annual rainfall (Lauria and Chiang 1975).

When conservation measures are implemented during water shortages, water demand may not fully recover when ample supplies again become available. Rates of water use increase with water pressures in the distribution system. Public needs for fighting fires may be small on an annual basis, but the high demand for short periods may control the design of the distribution system.

Table 4.6 shows the components of water demand (domestic, commercial, industrial, and public), for a representative public water supply in the United States of 150 gallons per capita per day (gpcd). The ratio of maximum to average daily demand may range from 1.5 to 3.5, with an average of 2.0, while the ratio of maximum to average hourly demand may range from 2.0 to 7.0, with an average of 4.5.

4.5.4 Commercial Water Demand

As shown in Table 4.6, a representative value of commercial water use is 20 gallons per capita per day, with a range of 10 to 130 gallons. Table 4.7 shows typical average water requirements for apartments, motels, hotels, office buildings, shopping centers, and miscellaneous commercial activities. Other estimates for commercial uses are shown in Table 4.8.

TABLE 4.6   TYPICAL WATER DEMAND IN THE UNITED STATES

	Quantity (gpcd)	
Class	*Normal Range*	*Average*
Domestic or residential	20–90	55
Commercial	10–130	20
Industrial	20–80	50
Public, and unaccounted for	10–50	25
Total	60–250	150

Source: Fair, Geyer, and Okun (1971).

Estimates of Population and Water Needs   Chap. 4

TABLE 4.7 COMMERCIAL WATER DEMAND IN THE UNITED STATES

Class	Demand per Unit
Apartment buildings	156 gpd/unit
Motels	69 gpd/unit
Hotels	307–407 gpd/room
Office buildings	0.070–0.084 gpd/ft^2
Shopping centers	0.015–0.18 gpd/ft^2
Laundromats	184 gpd/washer
Commercial laundries	251 gpd/washer
Washmobile	330 gpd/car/hour
Service station	472 gpd/lift

Source: Residential Water Use Research Project of the Johns Hopkins University and the Office of Technical Studies of the Architectural Standards Division of the Federal Housing Administration, cited in Clark, Viessman, and Hammer (1977).

TABLE 4.8 COMMERCIAL WATER DEMAND IN THE UNITED STATES

Types of Establishments	gpd
Airports (per passenger)	3–5
Apartments, multiple family (per resident)	60
Bath houses (per bather)	10
Camps	
Construction, semipermanent (per worker)	50
Day with no meals served (per camper)	15
Luxury (per camper)	100–150
Resorts, day and night, with limited plumbing (per camper)	50
Tourist with central bath and toilet facilities (per person)	35
Cottages with seasonal occupancy (per resident)	50
Courts, tourist, with individual bath units (per person)	50
Clubs	
Country (per resident member)	100
Country (per nonresident member present)	25
Dwellings	
Boarding houses (per boarder)	50
Additional kitchen requirements for nonresident boarders	10
Luxury (per person)	100–150
Multiple family apartments (per resident)	40
Rooming houses (per resident)	60
Single family (per resident)	50–75
Estates (per resident)	100–150
Factories (gal per person per shift)	15–35
Hotels with private baths (two persons per room)	60
Hotels without private baths (per person)	50
Institutions other than hospitals (per person)	75–125
Hospitals (per bed)	250–400

(Continued)

TABLE 4.8 *(continued)*

Types of Establishments	*gpd*
Laundries, self-serviced (gal per washing, i.e., per customer)	50
Motels with bath, toilet, and kitchen facilities (per bed space)	50
With bed and toilet (per bed space)	40
Parks	
Overnight with flush toilets (per camper)	25
Trailers with individual bath units (per camper)	50
Picnic areas	
With bath houses, showers, and flush toilets (per picnicker)	20
With toilet facilities only (gal per picnicker)	10
Restaurants with toilet facilities (per patron)	7–10
Without toilet facilities (per patron)	2½–3
With bars and cocktail lounge (additional quantity per patron)	2
Schools	
Boarding (per pupil)	75–100
Day with cafeteria, gymnasiums, and showers (per pupil)	25
Day with cafeteria, but no gymnasiums or showers (per pupil)	20
Day without cafeteria, gymnasiums, or showers (per pupil)	15
Service stations (per vehicle)	10
Stores (per toilet room)	400
Swimming pools (per swimmer)	10
Theaters	
Drive-in (per car space)	5
Movie (per auditorium seat)	5
Workers	
Construction (per person per shift)	50
Day (school or offices per person per shift)	15

Source: U.S. Public Health Service (1962).

4.5.5 Industrial Water Demand

As shown in Table 4.6, a water use of 50 gallons per capita per day is typical for the industrial water component of a public water supply system. This estimate, however, is not appropriate for communities with large water-using industries or with industries

TABLE 4.9 INDUSTRIAL WATER DEMAND IN THE UNITED STATES

Beer	470 gal/barrel
Canned apricots	80 gal/No. 2 case
Canned lima beans	250 gal/No. 2 case
Coke	3,600 gal/ton
Leather (tanned)	16,000 gal/ton
Paper	39,000 gal/ton
Steel	35,000 gal/ton
Woolens	140,000 gal/ton

Source: From *Water-Resources Engineering*, Third Edition, by Ray K. Linsley and Joseph B. Franzini. Copyright 1979, 1972, 1964 by McGraw-Hill, Inc. Used with the permission of McGraw-Hill Book Company.

providing their own supply. Table 4.9 shows some water requirements of selected industries. Most of the water used by industry is for cooling and the amount used can be reduced with extensive recirculation. Table 4.10 gives estimates of maximum, average, and minimum uses for various industries.

4.5.6 Water Demand for Energy

As shown in Table 4.4, hydroelectric power plants are by far the largest users of water in the United States. This is essentially a nonconsumptive use and the water is generally available after power production for other uses.

TABLE 4.10 WITHDRAWAL FOR INDUSTRIAL USES (Gallons per Unit)

Product or User	Maximum	Average	Minimum	Conservation Technique
Steam power generation (kWh)	170	80	0.45 (cooling)	Recycling of cooling water through natural draft cooling towers
			1.20 (theoretical)	Recycling through cooling towers
			1.32 (actual)	Recycling through cooling towers
Petroleum refining (gal crude oil)	44.5	18.3	0.8 (actual)	Information insufficient
			1.0 (actual)	Information insufficient
			1.73 (actual)	Complete recirculation through both cooling towers and cooling ponds
Finished steel (tons)	65,000	40,000	1,400	Complete recycling through cooling towers, reuse of all flows
			4,000	Recycling through cooling ponds
Soaps, edible oils (lb)	7.5		1.57	Recycling through cooling towers and colloidal separation
Carbon black (lb)	14	4	0.25	Maximum use of air cooling devices
Natural rubber (processing) (lb)	6		2.54	Information insufficient
Butadiene (lb)	305	160	13	Theoretical estimate based on complete recycling through cooling towers
Glass containers (tons)	667		118	Cooling water recirculated
	507		192	Cooling water recirculated
Automobiles (passenger) (units)	16,000		12,000	Sprays substituted for immersion rinses
Trucks, buses (units)	20,000		15,000	Sprays substituted for immersion rinses

Source: Hudson and Abu-Lughod (1956).

TABLE 4.11 WATER REQUIREMENTS FOR PRODUCING ENERGY IN THE UNITED STATES

Source	Consumption	Water (gal/million Btu)
Western coal mining	6–14.7 gal/ton	0.24–0.61
Eastern coal mining	15.8–18.0 gal/ton	0.66–0.75
Oil shale	145.4 gal/bbl	30.1
Coal gasification	72–158 gal/mscf	72–158
Nuclear power plants	0.8 gal/kWh	234.5
Oil and gas production	17.3 gal/bbl	3.05
Refineries	43 gal/bbl	7.58
Fossil-fuel power plants	0.41 gal/kWh	120.2
Gas processing plants	169 gal/mscf	1.67

Source: U.S. Water Resources Council (1974).

As shown in Table 4.11, the average consumptive use of cooling water for a fossil-fuel power generating plant is 0.41 gallons per kilowatt-hour. The actual water intake is much greater. Table 4.12 shows water withdrawals and consumptions for various cooling techniques. Unit water requirements for energy-related activities are also shown in Tables 4.10 and 4.13. Water requirements for synthetic fuel production have been analyzed by Probstein and Gold (1978).

4.5.7 Irrigation and Rural Water Demands

Table 4.14 shows the water supplied by federal irrigation projects to farms having different crop patterns, growing seasons, and precipitation. Water supplied by an irrgation project must be greater than the consumptive use less effective precipitation. The consumptive uses for various crops and native plants in the United States are shown in Table 4.15. Other information for estimating consumptive water use and water supply requirements for various crops are available from many sources (e.g., Kaser 1969; American Society of Civil Engineers, 1974; U.S. Department of Agriculture, 1976). Rural requirements other than for irrigation are shown in Tables 4.16 and 4.17.

TABLE 4.12 COMPARISON OF FOUR COOLING TECHNOLOGIES

	Once-through	Cooling Pond	Wet Tower	Dry Tower
Water withdrawal (acre-feet/yr)	537,500	11,425	11,100	0
Water consumption (acre-feet/yr)	6,950	10,375	11,100	0
Electricity generated (kWh/yr)	8.15×10^9	8.15×10^9	8.10×10^9	7.58×10^9
Electricity generated (once-through = 100)	100	100	99	93

Source: Hirsch, et al. (1977).

Estimates of Population and Water Needs Chap. 4

TABLE 4.13 WATER USES IN ENERGY-RELATED ACTIVITIES
(acre-feet per quadrillion Btu of product)

Activity	Process Water	Evaporation	Waste Water	Total	Sources
Nuclear power stations (LWR)	—	537,200	55,600	592,800[a]	Davis and Wood (1974)
Fossil-fueled power stations	—	358,100	37,100	395,200[b]	Gold et al. (1977)
Coal gasification, high-Btu gas	32,500	68,100	2,800	103,400	Gold et al. (1977)
Oil shale conversion	21,700	32,000	8,000	61,700	Dickinson et al. (1976) Gold et al. (1977)
Coal gasification, low-Btu gas	1,000	56,000	700	57,700	Chandra et al. (1978) Kimmel et al. (1976)
Coal liquefaction	2,800	36,700	17,500	57,000	McNamee et al. (1976)
Nuclear fuel processing	—	37,400	3,900	41,300	Davis and Wood (1974)
Coal slurry pipeline	—	—	—	34,000	Gold et al. (1977) Palmer et al. (1977)
Oil refining	—	16,000	6,200	22,200	Davis and Wood (1974)
Underground coal mining	—	7,700	—	7,700	James et al. (1977) Nehring et al. (1976)
Strip coal mining, revegetation	—	3,400	—	3,400	Gold et al. (1977)
Strip coal mining, no revegetation	—	1,800	—	1,800	Gold et al. (1977)

[a]Equivalent to 0.66 gallon/kWh.
[b]Equivalent to 0.44 gallon/kWh.
Source: Buras (1979).

The total water requirement for irrigation consists of the water needed by the crops plus the losses in delivery and application of the water; the latter may typically range from 25% for a canal system to nothing for spray irrigation. Soil, climate, and other physical factors affect the total water requirement.

4.5.8 Water Demand Projections

Values of water demand such as those given in the foregoing paragraphs and tables should be used only when historical data on water use in the project area or comparable locations are not available. When information on historical demand is available it should be taken into account as discussed below for studies of the water supply needs of Kingston, Jamaica, by TAMS (1977). In these studies it was found convenient to calculate per capita water demand, or consumption, as the total production divided by total population. Such a value differs from those based on water sales or on utility customers.

TABLE 4.14 AVERAGE USE OF WATER ON FEDERAL IRRIGATION PROJECTS

State	Project	Average Elevation	Years Considered	Area Irrigated (acres)	Predominating Character of soils
Ariz.–Calif.	Yuma	120	1917–1926	51,950	Medium
California	Orland	250	1917–1926[a]	14,554	Light
Colorado	Grand Valley	4,700	1916–1925	10,139	Heavy
	Uncompahgre	5,500	1917–1926	61,178	Medium
Idaho	Boise	2,500	1917–1925[b]	145,616	Light
	King Hill	2,750	1921–1927	6,460	Very light
	Minidoka, S. Side Pumping	4,200	1917–1926	44,945	Medium
Montana	Huntley	3,000	1917–1926	19,406	Heavy
	Lower Yellowstone	1,900	1917–1926	17,540	Heavy
	Milk River	2,200	1917–1926	16,793	Heavy
	Sun River, Fort Shaw	3,700	1917–1926	7,650	Heavy
	Sun River, Greenfields	3,700	1919–1926	9,867	Medium
Nevada	Newlands	4,000	1917–1926	38,808	Medium
New Mexico	Carlsbad	3,100	1917–1926	22,535	Medium
N.M.–Texas	Rio Grande	3,700	1919–1926	96,847	Medium
Oregon	Klamath	4,100	1917–1926	43,325	Medium
	Umatilla	470	1916–1925	10,970	Light
South Dakota	Belle Fourche	2,800	1917–1926	45,164	Heavy
Washington	Okanogan	1,000	1921, 1923 1925	5,260	Light
	Yakima, Sunnyside	800	1917–1926	91,726	Medium
	Yakima, Tieton	1,500	1917–1926	27,607	Light
Wyoming	Shoshone, Frannie	4,150	1922–1926	7,963	Heavy
	Shoshone, Garland	4,400	1917–1926	32,380	Medium
Wyo.–Neb.	North Platte	4,100	1919–1926	107,694	Medium

[a]1918, 1920, and 1924 omitted because of heavy water shortage.
[b]1924 omitted because of water shortage.
Source: From "Irrigation," by Rolland F. Kaser, Sec. 33 in *Handbook of Applied Hydraulics*, edited by C. V. Davis and K. E. Sorensen. Copyright 1969 by McGraw-Hill Book Company. Used with the permission of McGraw-Hill Book Company.

Figure 4.6 shows the trends of water production, population, and per capita demand in the Water Commission service area between 1960 and 1976. The figure shows that per capita consumption did not rise in the later years. This was largely due to the unavailability of water rather than to static demand. Summer water restrictions were in existence since 1968. In 1975, there were restrictions during 194 days of the year. It was thus reasonable to assume that potential demand was significantly higher than actual demand.

Two projections of per capita demand were made. The first, which gave a potential per capita demand of 100 imperial gallons per day by year 2000, was based

Crops Grown (% of Total Area)					Precipitation (ft)		Water Delivered to Farms (acre-ft/ acre)	Water Delivered Plus Growing Season Prec. (ft)
Alfalfa, Hay, and Pasture	Small Grain	Furrow Crops	Trees	Irrigation Season	Before Growing Season	During Growing Season		
39	3	58	—	Jan.–Dec.	0.33	0.33	3.01	3.34
53	5	19	23	Jan.–Nov.	1.02	0.37	3.17	3.55
36	24	33	7	Apr.–Nov.	0.27	0.48	3.61	4.09
47	25	25	3	Apr.–Oct.	0.26	0.55	5.76	6.31
53	31	13	3	Apr.–Oct.	0.43	0.38	3.60	3.98
75	7	11	6	Apr.–Nov.	0.41	0.35	7.01	7.36
50	28	22	—	Apr.–Oct.	0.32	0.53	2.54	3.07
42	34	24	—	May–Sept.	0.37	0.63	1.39	2.02
45	33	22	—	May–Sept.	0.33	0.71	1.34	2.05
73	22	5	—	Apr.–Oct.	0.18	0.91	0.65	1.56
75	20	5	—	May–Oct.	0.23	0.60	1.54	2.14
23	75	2	—	May–Oct.	0.28	0.65	1.28	1.93
85	11	4	—	Mar.–Nov.	0.15	0.25	2.88	3.13
33	4	63	—	Jan.–Nov.	0.06	0.86	2.36	3.22
37	8	53	2	Feb.–Dec.	0.06	0.60	2.89	3.49
77	21	2	—	Apr.–Sept.	0.68	0.18	1.43	1.61
85	1	6	8	Mar.–Nov.	0.40	0.35	5.02	5.37
62	22	16	—	May–Sept.	0.48	0.86	1.22	2.08
9	—	3	88	May–Sept.	0.51	0.42	2.60	3.02
57	7	21	15	Mar.–Oct.	0.27	0.21	3.29	3.50
44	12	11	33	Apr.–Sept.	0.44	0.16	2.51	2.67
72	17	11	—	Apr.–Oct.	0.11	0.39	2.19	2.58
59	28	13	—	Apr.–Nov.	0.09	0.33	2.38	2.71
36	26	38	—	May–Sept.	0.47	0.81	2.23	3.04

on extending the historical trend prior to the imposition of restrictions. It was believed more reasonable to adopt another estimate which implicitly accounts for such factors as changing demand patterns already brought about by continued summer restrictions which resulted in the adoption of measures to conserve water, and some degree of price sensitivity. This gave an estimate of per capita demand of 90 imperial gallons by year 2000, which was applied equally to all consumers in the region. These per capita demands include industrial requirements but not irrigation demand. It was assumed that existing irrigation projects would continue to be served by their sources of supply or by compensation arrangements for some of the projects considered, and that new projects would be served by other local supplies.

TABLE 4.15 CONSUMPTIVE USE BY VARIOUS CROPS AND NATIVE PLANTS IN THE WESTERN UNITED STATES

Crop	Quantity (ft/yr)
Alfalfa	2.8–3.1
Beets	2.0
Citrus	1.9
Cotton	2.4–2.5
Peaches	2.5
Wheat	1.2–1.5
Wild hay	2.6

Source: From *Water-Resources Engineering*, Third Edition, by Ray K. Linsley and Joseph B. Franzini. Copyright 1979, 1972, 1964 by McGraw-Hill, Inc. Used with the permission of Mc-Graw Hill Book Company.

TABLE 4.16 RURAL WATER DEMAND IN THE UNITED STATES

Class	Quantity (gpcd)
Rural dwellings	50
Rural schools, overnight camps, and factories (not including manufacturing uses)	25
Wayside resturants	10
Work and construction camps	45
Resort hotels	100
Rural hospitals	200
Farm animals	2–20

Source: Fair, Geyer, and Okun (1971).

TABLE 4.17 WATER FOR LIVESTOCK

	gpd/Animal
Beef cattle and steers	12
Dairy cows	
Ordinary dairy herds (dry and producing cows)	15
High-producing cows (12 gal of milk or more per day)	35
Goats	2
Hogs	4
Horses and mules	12
Sheep	2
Chickens	0.05–0.10
Ducks	0.06–0.18
Turkeys	0.10–0.18

Source: U.S. Public Health Service (1962).

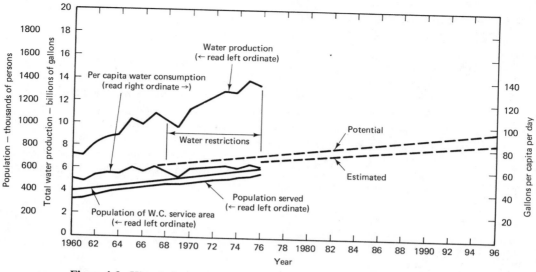

Figure 4.6 Historical and projected water consumption for Water Commission service area, Jamaica. (From TAMS, 1977.)

The projected water demand by 2000 for the total region, assuming "most likely" population growth (see Section 4.3.3), would be 115.8 million imperial gallons per day. For purposes of sensitivity analyses, demand projections for the entire region were made for "high" and "low" populations as well as for the "most likely" population. The implications of these different possibilities lie in the timing of any future water supply scheme, in the incremental capacity needed by year 2000, and in the financial returns of the project.

The forecasts discussed above are based on single projections of overall per capita demand. This approach is reasonable when industrial and irrigation requirements are not important components of the total demand. When these are important components, it is advisable to formulate a predictive model incorporating projections for the separate components of demand, using sample data for selected activities and estimates of typical requirements such as those given in preceding sections. Lauria and Chiang (1975) describe a model for predicting water requirements for North Carolina based on a previously developed input–output model for 58 industrial sectors in four regions (three regions within the state plus the "rest of the world") and a set of industrial water usage coefficients developed from published sources of data. Forecasts for the major regions were disaggregated to county levels based on employment. Economic growth models, including input-output models, are discussed in Chapter 14.

4.5.9 Water Resource Needs for Other Purposes

These needs cannot be expressed as easily using generalized estimates such as those given above for water demands. A brief review of the principal considerations affecting needs for water supplies and for other purposes is given in Section 2.3.

4.6 WATER CONSERVATION AND OTHER NONSTRUCTURAL ALTERNATIVES

Adverse impacts of water resource development (e.g., environmental, social, legal) can often be prevented or mitigated by reducing the scale of the project to fit smaller needs or by substituting management techniques and other nonstructural alternatives. Project cost will generally also be reduced by this approach.

The Water Resources Council "Principles and Standards" (1979 revisions, pp. 72989-90) and "Principles and Guidelines" (1983, pp. 6–7) emphasize these alternatives to the traditional structural measures in addressing water resources problems and needs. The following are various methods that can be used for different types of water resource purposes:

Municipal and Industrial Water Supply. Reduce the level and/or alter the pattern of demand by metering, leak detection, and changes in repair rate structures, regulations on use such as plumbing codes, education programs, and drought contingency planning. Modify the management of existing water development and supplies by recycling, reuse, and pressure reduction. Increase upstream watershed management and the conjunctive use of ground and surface waters.

Irrigation Water Supply. Reduce the level and/or alter the time pattern of use through irrigation scheduling, modified water rate structures, leak detection and repair, recycling, and reuse. Modify the management of existing water development and supplies by tailway recovery and phreatophyte controls.

Recreation and Fish and Wildlife. Enhance the management of existing sites and manage capacity by distributing the users of existing sites.

Hydroelectric Power. Reduce the level and/or time pattern of demand by time of day pricing, utility loans for insulation, appliance efficiency standards, educational programs, interregional power transfers, and increased transmission efficiency.

Navigation. Make lockage changes to reduce congestion, improve the scheduling of lock arrivals, and use switch boats for locking through tows.

Flood Hazard Reduction. Reduce the susceptibility to flood damage by land use regulations, redevelopment and relocation policies, disaster preparedness, flood proofing, flood forecasting and warning systems, floodplain information, floodplain acquisition, and floodplain easements. Reduce the adverse burden of flooding by flood insurance and flood emergency relief programs. Protect natural storage areas such as wetlands for site detention of floodwaters and use human-made areas such as building roofs and parking lots.

4.6.1 Conservation of Public Water Supplies

Additional information on the conservation of water supplies is provided in this subsection and the next two sections.

In addition to conserving water, a reduced municipal water demand reduces the cost of water supply works, water treatment and distribution, and wastewater collection, treatment, and disposal. It also reduces the energy required to operate these facilities and the energy required for hot water heating. The costs for implementing conservation measures can be less than the costs of new supplies in a growing economy (Maddaus and Feuerstein 1979).

Howe and Linaweaver (1967) studied 10 metered and 8 nonmetered cities in the western United States and found an average daily demand of 458 gallons per dwelling unit for the metered cities and 692 for the unmetered cities. According to Hanke (1970), the installation of universal metering in Boulder, Colorado, reduced the average daily demand from 212 gallons per capita to 168 gallons. Both studies indicated an even greater proportional drop in peak demands.

The use of water-saving devices in water closets, shower heads, and faucets can reduce daily per capita household demand by 14 to 16.6 gallons (Flack 1980; Maddaus and Feuerstein 1979). Clouser and Miller (1980) have estimated the savings for a community equipped with such devices at 20% of total demand. Flack (1980) states that reducing system pressures, controlling losses in distribution mains to 10 to 15% of total delivery, using household pressure reducers, and fixing plumbing leaks can all be effective conservation measures.

Very substantial reductions in demand have been made during droughts. Clouser and Miller (1980) reported that when water conservation measures were adopted in Marin County, California, including bans on car washing, installation of water-saving devices, and water consumption quotas, water use was reduced by 65%. Even when the drought ended and control measures were removed or relaxed, the residential demand remained 45% below pre-drought levels.

4.7 PRICE ELASTICITIES OF WATER DEMAND

The effect of price changes on water demand was described in Section 2.8. A number of studies have been made of the price elasticity of domestic water in the United States. Howe and Linaweaver (1967) found an average annual weighted price elasticity of −0.40 for 21 metered areas; this means that an increase in price of 100% would cause a 40% drop in demand. A review by Cassuto and Ryan (1979) of 13 other published studies showed a range of price elasticities of −0.02 to −0.75 with a median of about −0.5. Elasticities are often low in the United States at least partly because of the low prices generally charged for water.

Sonnen and Evenson (1979) state that, based on a model developed for the Corps of Engineers, choosing a numerical conservation target to be achieved is more meaningful than manipulations of price. This model was for urban demands and did not evaluate elasticities for self-supplied commercial, industrial, or agricultural uses.

Very few studies have been carried out to show the price elasticities of commercial and industrial water. Lynne et al. (1978) estimated the following price elasticities for various commercial establishments in the Miami, Florida, area: department stores, −1.07; grocery stores and supermarkets, −0.72; motels and hotels, −0.11 to −0.24; eating and drinking establishments, −0.17; and other commercial businesses, −0.48. Bower (1966) has noted that water is simply one input to a production process and that where the supply is not limited, it is analyzed in economic terms by an industry in the same manner as other factor inputs. Factors affecting the use of industrial water utilization include the technology of the production process, the quality requirements of the final product, the quality of the raw inputs, effluent controls, and water cost. The most common response to increases in water costs is to increase the extent of recirculation. That substantial variations in water requirements of commercial and manufacturing enterprises are possible is clear from the data given in Sections 4.5.4 to 4.5.6. The same conclusion applies to agricultural demand, as shown in Section 4.5.7 and discussed further in the following section.

4.8 WATER/ENERGY RELATIONSHIPS

The increased costs of energy from fossil fuels in the United States in the 1970s and increased costs and shortages in many other countries have led to an emphasis on both domestic production of energy and conservation of energy. Energy is needed to construct and operate water facilities. Water is needed to process fuels and produce energy. Thus, project assessment will tend increasingly to include the evaluation of energy impacts. The estimates of water requirements for producing energy (Section 4.5.6) and the energy savings that accompany water conservation efforts (Section 4.6) are two types of information for energy impact assessment.

Hampton and Ryan (1980) have reported on a comprehensive nationwide reconnaissance-level assessment of water needs for energy development for 1985–2000. This study considered the increased needs of traditional producers as well as the development needs of previously unexploited energy resources such as oil, shale, and synthetic fuels, which are highly intensive water users. They found that water for energy demands will not be adequately satisfied by year 2000 unless proper planning measures are instituted. They also found that offstream and instream water requirements for other purposes (which are often protected by institutional and legal rights) may constrain energy development in areas with known fossil-fuel supplies. In many areas in the western United States, the increase of fossil-fuel production would be at the loss of presently irrigated land, since the use of water for production of grass, hay, and pasture in such areas cannot compete economically with energy-related industry (Hansen 1976).

Plotkin et al. (1979) indicate there are substantial opportunities for conservation in both energy and agricultural development in the western states. A Soil Conservation Service study (U.S. Department of Agriculture, 1976) also showed the potential for water savings through crop selecton.

Growers in California used several energy and water strategies in response to drought conditions in 1976–1977. Water used for irrigation was reduced by the installation of sprinkler and drip systems and by more careful attention to times of application. Scarce water supplies were maintained and augmented by phreatophyte control, lining of ditches, and use of reclaimed water. Energy consumption was reduced by the need to pump less water due to the conservation measures noted above and by improvement in the maintenance and efficiencies of wells, pumps, and motors (Ritschard and Tsao 1980). Some of these strategies involved adverse effects (excessive groundwater drawdowns, ground subsidence, salt imbalances). It has been reported (U.S. Energy Research and Development Administration, 1976) that energy savings associated with water utilization in agriculture can be as high as 25% in a normal year. A collection of articles on energy and water use forecasting is available through the American Water Works Association (1980).

4.8.1 Water Energy Models

Buras (1979) found that existing energy-economy models do not explicitly take account of the availability of water resources for energy-related activities. His research was aimed at demonstrating the feasibility of integrating water resources availabilities and water consumption data into energy-economy models.

Hagan and Roberts (1980) have made energy-balance calculations for several different types of water resources projects. For a reservoir project to supply irrigation water they considered the energy used to construct and maintain the facilities and to deliver the stored water to service areas, energy consumed by people traveling for recreation and fishing, and the reduction of power due to release of water from the reservoir for fish and wildlife preservation.

Brill et al. (1977) studied the coal reserves in the Ohio River Basin by: (1) developing a mathematical model of a regional water resources system and the interlocking energy production system; (2) developing an optimization procedure for use in planning a regional allocation pattern for supplying water to major energy facilities as well as for other water needs; and (3) demonstrating the impact that the development of a large energy industry could have on the allocation of water resources in this large basin.

Energy can also be modeled in the context of a complete ecological system. This is discussed in Chapter 15 for Environmental Assessments.

REFERENCES

AMERICAN SOCIETY OF CIVIL ENGINEERS, Irrigation and Drainage Division Committee on Irrigation Water Requirements, "Consumptive Use of Water and Irrigation Water Requirements," 1974.

AMERICAN WATER WORKS ASSOCIATION, "Energy and Water Use Forecasting," Denver, Colo., 1980.

ARCHER, H. V., "Projection for the Water Commission Service Area," Ministry of Mining and Natural Resources, Jamaica, 1975.

BOWER, BLAIR T., "The Economics of Industrial Water Utilization," in Water Research, Allen V. Kneese and Stephen C. Smith, eds., Johns Hopkins University Press, Baltimore, Md., 1966.

BRILL, E. DOWNEY, JR., S. GIRAY VELIOGLO, and ROBERT W. FUESSLE, "Water and Energy Systems: A Planning Model," J. Water Resources Plann. Manage. Div., Proc. Am. Soc. Civil Eng., vol. 103, no. WR1 May 1977.

BURAS, NATHAN, "Determining the Feasibility of Incorporating Water Resource Constraints in Energy Models," Electric Power Research Institute, Palo Alto, Calif., Report EA. 1147, August 1979.

CASSUTO, ALEXANDER E., and STUART RYAN, "Effect of Price on the Residential Demand for Water within an Agency," *Water Resources Bull.*, vol. 15, no. 2, April 1979.

CHALMERS, J. A., and E. J. ANDERSON, "Economic/Demographic Assessment Manual," Mountain West Research, Inc., November 1977.

CHANDRA, K., et al., 1978, "Economic Studies of Coal Gasification Combined Cycle Systems for Electric Power Generation," Electric Power Research Institute, Palo Alto, Calif., Rep. AF-642, Project 239, 1978.

CLARK, J. W., W. VIESSMAN, and M.J. HAMMER, *Water Supply and Pollution Control*, 3rd ed., IEP–Dun-Donnelley, New York, 1977.

CLOUSER, RODNEY L., and WILLIAM L. MILLER, "Household Water Use: Technology Shifts and Conservation Implications," *Water Resources Bull.*, vol. 16, no. 3, June 1980.

DAVIS, G. H., and L. A. WOOD, "Water Demands for Expanding Energy Development," *U.S. Geol. Surv. Circ. 703*, Reston, Va., 1974.

DEBLER, E. B., "Use of Water on Federal Irrigation Projects", *Trans. Am. Soc. Civil Eng.*, vol. 94, 1930.

DICKINSON, E. M., et al., "Synthetic Liquid Fuels Development: Assessment of Critical Factors," vol. II, Energy Research and Development Administration, Rep. ERDA 76-129/2, Washington, D.C., 1976.

FAIR, G. M., J. C. GEYER, and D. A. OKUN, *Elements of Water Supply and Wastewater Disposal*, 2nd ed., Wiley, New York, 1971.

FLACK, J. ERNEST, "Achieving Urban Water Conservation," *Water Resources Bull.*, vol. 16, no. 1, February 1980.

FLYNN, CYNTHIA B., and ROSEMARY T. SCHMIDT, "Sources of Information for Social Profiling," Department of Sociology, University of Kansas, December 1977.

GOLD, H., et al., "Water Requirements for Steam-Electric Power Generation and Synthetic Fuel Plants in the Western United States," EPA Rep. 600/7-77-037, U.S. Environmental Protection Agency, Washington, D.C., 1977.

HAGAN, ROBERT M., and EDWIN B. ROBERTS, "Energy Impact Analysis in Water Project Planning," *J. Water Resources Plann. Manage. Div., Proc. Am. Soc. Civil Eng.*, vol. 106, no. WR1, March 1980.

HAMPTON, NORMAN F., and BENNETT Y. RYAN, JR., "Water Constraints in Emerging Energy Production," *Water Resources Bull.*, vol. 16, no. 3, June 1980.

HANKE, S. H., "Demand for Water under Dynamic Conditions," *Water Resources Res.*, vol. 6, no. 5, October 1970.

HANSEN, DEE C., "Water Available for Energy—Upper Colorado River Basin," *J. Water Resources Plann. Manage. Div., Proc. Am. Soc. Civil Eng.*, vol. 102, no. WR2, November 1976.

HIRSCH, R. M., J. C. JAMES II, and J. E. SCHEFTER, "Residuals Management," *Proc. Symp. River Qual. Assess.*, Am. Water Resources Assoc. Annu. Meet., Tucson, Ariz., 1977.

HOWE, CHARLES H., and F. P. LINAWEAVER, JR., "The Impact of Price on Residual Water Demand and Its Relation to System Design and Price Structure," *Water Resources Res.*, vol. 3, no. 1, February 1967.

HUDSON, H. E., JR., and J. ABU-LUGHOD, "Water Requirements," in *Water for Industry*, American Association for the Advancement of Science, Washington, D.C., 1956. Copyright 1956 by the American Association for the Advancement of Science.

JAMAICA TOWN PLANNING DEPARTMENT and UNITED NATIONS SPECIAL FUND PROJECT, "The Kingston Regional Plan," 1972.

JAMAICA TOWN PLANNING DEPARTMENT, "Kingston Metropolitan Area Land Use Study," 1973.

JAMES, I. C., II, and T. D. STEELE, "Application of Residuals Management for Assessing the Impacts of Alternative Coal-Development Plans on Regional Water Resources," *3rd Int. Symp. Hydrol.*, Colorado State University, Fort Collins, Colo., 1977.

KASER, ROLLAND F., "Irrigation," Sect. 33 in *Handbook of Applied Hydraulics*," C. V. Davis and K. E. Sorensen, ed., McGraw-Hill, New York 1969.

KIMMEL, S., et al., "Economics of Current and Advanced Gasification Processes for Fuel Gas Production," EPRI Rep. AF-244, Project 239, 1976.

LAURIA, DONALD T., and CHENG H. CHIANG, "Models for Municipal and Industrial Water Demand Forecasting in North Carolina," Water Resources Research Institute of the University of North Carolina, North Carolina State University, Raleigh, November 1975.

LINSLEY, RAY K., and JOSEPH B. FRANZINI, *Water Resources Engineering*, 3rd ed., McGraw-Hill, New York, 1979.

LYNNE, GARY D., WILLIAM G. LUPPOLD, and CLYDE KIKER, "Water Price Responsiveness of Commercial Establishments," *Water Resource Bull.*, vol. 14, no. 3, June 1978.

MACKICHAN, K. A., "Estimated Use of Water in the United States, U.S. Geol. Survey Circ. 115, 1950.

McJUNKIN, FREDERICK E., "Population Forecasting by Sanitary Engineers," *J. Sanit. Eng. Div.*, *Proc. Am. Soc. Civil Eng.*, vol. 90, no. SA4, August 1964.

McNAMEE, G. P., et al., "Economics of Current and Advanced Gasification Processes for Fuel Gas Production," EPRI Rep. AF-244, Project 239, 1976.

MADDAUS, WILLIAM O., and DONALD L. FEUERSTEIN, "Effect of Water Conservation on Water Demands," *J. Water Resources Plann. Manage. Div.*, *Proc. Am. Soc. Civil Eng.*, vol. 105, no. WR2, September 1979.

MOUNTAIN WEST RESEARCH, INC., "Bureau of Reclamation Economic Assessment Model (BREAM) Technical Description," January 1978.

MURRAY, C. RICHARD, and E. BODETTE REEVES, "Estimated Use of Water in the United States in 1975," *U.S. Geol. Surv. Circ. 765*, 1977.

NATIONAL ACADEMY OF SCIENCES, "Potential Technological Advances and Their Impact on Anticipated Water Requirements," 1971.

NATIONAL PLANNING ASSOCIATION, "Economic Base Study for Chesapeake Basin," February 1967.

NEHRING, R., et al., "Coal Development and Government Regulation in the Northern Great Plains," RAND Rep. R-1981-NSF/RC, Rand Corporation, Santa Monica, Calif., 1976.

PALMER, R. N., et al., "Comparative Assessment of Water Use and Environmental Implications of Coal Slurry Pipelines," *U.S. Geol. Surv. Open File Rep. 77-698*, 1977.

PLOTKIN, STEPHEN E., HARRIS GOLD, and IRVIN L. WHITE, "Water and Energy in the Western Coal Lands," *Water Resources Bull.*, vol. 15, no. 1, February 1979.

PROBSTEIN, RONALD F., and HARRIS GOLD, "*Water in Synthetic Fuel Production*," MIT Press, Cambridge, Mass., 1978.

RITSCHARD, RONALD L., and KAREN TSAO, "Energy and Water Consumption Strategies in Irrigated Agriculture," *Water Resources Bull.*, vol. 16, no. 2, April 1980.

ROBERTS, G. W., "Assessing Internal Migration in a Small Country Illustrated from the Position of Jamaica," *Symp. Popul.*, Minsk, USSR, 1976.

SCHMITT, R. C., and A. H. CROSETTI, "Short-Cut Methods of Forecasting City Population," *J. Mark.*, vol. 17, 1953.

SHRYOCK, H. S., J. S. SIEGEL, and Associates: *The Methods and Materials of Demography*, condensed edition by E. G. Stockwell, Academic Press, New York, 1976.

SIEGEL, J. S., H. S. SHRYOCK, and B. GREENBERG, "Accuracy of Postcensal Estimates of Population for States and Cities," *Am. Sociol. Rev.*, vol. 19, 1954.

SONNEN, MICHAEL B., and DONALD E. EVENSON, "Demand Projections Considering Conservation," *Water Resources Bull.*, vol. 15, no. 2, April 1979.

TAMS (Tippetts-Abbett-McCarthy-Stratton, New York, and Mattis Demain Beckford & Associates Ltd., Kingston), "Comparative Study of Water Supply Projects for Kingston and Surrounding Area," July 1977.

UNITED NATIONS, "The Determinants and Consequences of Population Trends," vol. I, Series A, *Popul. Stud. 50*, 1973.

UNITED NATIONS SECRETARIAT, Department of Economic and Social Affairs, Population Division, "Population of Kingston and St. Andrew," 1975.

U.S. BUREAU OF THE CENSUS, "Environmental/Socioeconomic Data Sources," 1976.

U.S. BUREAU OF THE CENSUS, Center for Census Use Studies, "Profile of Census Programs," January 1978.

U.S. COUNCIL ON ENVIRONMENTAL QUALITY, "Preparation of Environmental Impact Statements: Guidelines," Federal Register, vol. 38, pp. 20550-62, August 1, 1973.

U.S. DEPARTMENT OF AGRICULTURE, SOIL CONSERVATION SERVICE, "Crop Consumptive Irrigation Requirements and Irrigation Efficiency Requirements for the United States," 1976.

U.S. DEPARTMENT OF THE ARMY, Corps of Engineers, Office of Appalachian Studies, "Development of Water Resources in Appalachia," Main Report, Part IV, Planning Concepts and Methods, September 1969.

U.S. ENERGY RESEARCH and DEVELOPMENT ADMINISTRATION, "Report of Proceedings of ERDA Workshop on Energy Conservation in Agricultural Production," 1976.

U.S. PUBLIC HEALTH SERVICE, "Manual of Individual Water Supply Systems," Publ. 24 (rev.), 1962.

U.S. WATER RESOURCES COUNCIL, "Principles and Standards for Planning Water and Related Land Resources," September 10, 1973; rev. December 14, 1979; rev. September 29, 1980.

U.S. WATER RESOURCES COUNCIL, "Project Independence," 1974.

U.S. WATER RESOURCES COUNCIL, "Economic and Environmental Principles and Guidelines for Water and Related Land Resources Implementation Studies," March 10, 1983.

FIVE

Identification and Preliminary Evaluation of Projects

5.1 SCOPE

Methodologies are needed for identifying and performing preliminary analyses of potential projects in a region, to determine which of the projects should be studied in more detail. These *screening* methodologies range from simple procedures that are appropriate for primarily engineering considerations and single-purpose projects to complex procedures that are applied in multipurpose and multiobjective planning. This chapter focuses on procedures leading to the selection of one or a few projects, while Chapter 6 deals with the approach for a regional system of interrelated projects. Screening methodologies may incorporate constraint mapping and various planning aids such as basic data inventories, remote sensing, generalized estimates, overlays, and computerized approaches. Chapters 1 and 3 have indicated the importance of environmental considerations in modern planning of water and related land resources. This chapter discusses this subject further from three standpoints: environmental and social impacts, prevention or mitigation of adverse environmental impacts, and comparison of environmental impacts together with economic, engineering, and other factors in the screening process. Other aspects of environmental and socioeconomic planning are discussed in Chapters 14 to 16.

5.2 SCREENING

The screening techniques that are appropriate depend on the specific goals of studies, the amount and completeness of information that is already available, and the time and resources that can be expended. In any method, the investigator attempts to ensure that all meritorious projects receive adequate consideration.

The process of screening involves evaluation of all existing and potential projects in a river basin or other defined geographic area for one or more purposes and objectives of water resources development. It may lead to the selection of outstanding projects on which to focus further investigations directed to early construction or to a ranking of all potential projects that appear attractive for a long-term program of development. The studies may also assess the adequacy of the available information for existing and potential projects as a basis for more comprehensive planning.

Screening presupposes that a reasonable amount of information has already been collected on the topography, geology, and hydrology of the study area. If this is not the case, as in many economically underdeveloped regions in the world, time must be allowed for programs to collect such data, by aerial or ground surveys, geological investigations, and stream gagings. The minimum time for this work may be two to five years, depending on the variability of stream flow and other aspects.

When studies are made with emphasis on single-purpose development, the screening techniques adopted should accomplish one or more of the following:

1. Identify the set of projects within a defined geographic area that satisfy specified minimum criteria.
2. Determine which of the idenified projects are sufficiently attractive to be retained for more detailed studies and which should be "screened out." This process may involve one or several stages of assessment and elimination of projects.
3. Assess the data for each retained project, for completeness and adequacy, for further evaluations as in items 4 and 5 below.
4. Determine an order of merit of the retained projects, when each project is considered for single-purpose independent operation.
5. Formulate a schematic plan of existing and potential projects (location, interconnection with the river system and with other projects, hydrologic interrelationships, etc.) for systems studies. The systems studies could include mathematical optimization studies for single or multiple purposes, sometimes specifically referred to as "screening models," or could include other studies of integrated operation leading to a regional or "master" plan.

The following sections will describe methods appropriate for categories 1 through 4. The methods of category 5 are covered in Chapters 6, 12, and 13.

5.3 CONSTRAINT MAPPING

Early in the screening process, the planner should identify those areas where constraints would prevent the siting of a water resources project. In any region, federal and state legislation protects specific environmental and cultural resources from development. These include national wilderness areas, registered historical sites, and known habitats of endangered species. In addition, certain natural, social, and other characteristics may cause areas to be unsuitable for further consideration. Exclusions depend on the type of project and will vary among the different regions of the country. Map overlay methods to show restricted areas and for other project suitability analyses are described in Section 5.13.5.

5.4 SCREENING BASED LARGELY ON ENGINEERING CONSIDERATIONS

This section is based on the work of Tippetts-Abbett-McCarthy-Stratton (TAMS) in screening seven river basins in the northeastern United States with a total area of over 85,000 square miles (Freeman and Dixon 1976). Types of projects studied by screening methods, each with its own set of site selection criteria, included:

- Natural runoff catchment storage reservoirs, on-stream
- Seasonal pumped-storage reservoirs, off-stream
- Pumped-storage hydroelectric plants
- Circulating water consumptive use reservoirs for thermal electric generating plants, both fossil- and nuclear-fueled
- Conventional hydroelectric developments, including combination with pumped-storage features, flood control, irrigation, municipal water, recreation, etc.
- Reservoirs for low-flow augmentation in connection with pollution abatement
- Potential lake developments having physical features attractive to area development, including industrial, residential, and recreational possibilities (i.e., "new town" development)
- Energy parks, including, at one general location, interacting sites for thermal power plants with cooling water supplies, conventional hydroelectric plants, pumped-storage hydroelectric plants, and water supplies for other needs of the complex

Order of Studies.   When nonengineering considerations are not important for a particular project purpose being investigated or when such considerations can be taken into account after the engineering studies are largely completed, the screening can proceed as follows:

1. Establish site selection criteria.
2. Perform in-office studies to identify all sites that appear to satisfy the criteria, prepare preliminary cost estimates, and establish a preliminary ranking of sites. This step completes the "preliminary" screening.
3. Perform field reconnaissance of sites meeting site selection criteria, and having a cost below a specified cut-off level.
4. Adjust cost estimates and other analyses as a result of field reconnaissance.
5. Update the ranking of sites, based essentially on cost. This step completes the "secondary" screening.

At this point, adjustments can be made to the ranking to take account of uncertainties of an engineering nature such as problems of structural stability, adequacy of foundations, sources and amounts of construction materials, and variability of water. Other adjustments can also be made for nonengineering considerations, if problems have been identified by the office and field studies; these could include adverse environmental impacts; physical and social disruptions from relocations of population, structures, railroads, roads, and utilities; and other legal, institutional, political, and social issues that would affect the practicality of implementing a project. The following details of the screening procedure were developed for the investigation of reservoir sites.

Site Selection Criteria. The planner considers the functional requirements of projects and draws on past experience to establish the site selection criteria. In this phase, the planner should review information on existing projects of the type to be inventoried, paying special attention to the characteristics of economical operating projects. The requirements for identifying a reservoir storage site may include a minimum drainage area to ensure adequate inflows of water, a location for dam and reservoir of minimum volume to provide adequate storage and regulation of seasonal inflows, and a location for a spillway of adequate capacity to pass specified flood flows. Criteria can be used to limit the amount of work in a screening investigation. For instance, if all potential sites having at least 50 square miles of drainage area are to be identified, changing the criterion to 25 square miles will increase the number of sites included by a factor of about 3.

The following is a set of appropriate criteria for natural runoff on-stream catchment reservoirs in the northeastern United States:

1. The damsite shall have a drainage area of at least 50 square miles.
2. The reservoir shall have a live storage adequate to regulate the flows in a 5-year drought cycle.
3. The reservoir shall have additional storage to allow for evaporation, seepage, and dead storage (below outlet level).
4. The spillway site shall provide for a capacity to pass a peak outflow in cubic feet per second of $10,000A^{0.5}$, where A is the drainage area in square miles. This is very conservative and some leeway may be allowed in this requirement.
5. The reservoir shall not be located in areas requiring extensive relocations or where such construction is known to be illegal.

In-Office Studies. The office studies evaluate all previous studies of specific sites, and identify additional sites by careful perusal of maps and aerial photographs, following the streams on these maps to discover topographic features that permit dam, reservoir, and spillway construction. Transparent overlays and tables are useful for showing the location and principal features of potential developments and providing space for additional comments based on these and other studies. Because of the large areas to be covered and many sites to be studied, all computation procedures and estimates should be standardized. Maps, photos, and other basic data should be filed for ready reference since time spent searching for such information is wasteful.

The inventory studies are carried out initially using only readily available topographic, geologic, and hydrologic information. In the United States, "quadrangle" maps published by the U.S. Geological Survey (USGS) are available at scales of 1:62,500 and 1:24,000, aerial photographs at 1:20,000 scale are available from various governmental sources, and extensive stream flow data are also published by the USGS. This allows basic information to be assembled at minimum engineering cost, and inventory studies can be accomplished in a relatively short period of time. The aerial photographs should be the most recent since available quadrangle maps may not have been updated to show industrial and residential construction and transportation routes which would interfere with development.

Previous studies are especially important when water resource investigations are to be conducted within the continental United States or other economically advanced countries. Few new dam sites or reservoir sites will be identified except where new technology has made construction feasible. For instance, the development of large pumps and/or reversible pump-turbines may make a reservoir, previously limited in size by a deficient drainage area, economically feasible. Thus, the deficient flow from a small drainage area on a tributary stream can be augmented by seasonal pump-in from the main stream, with or without generation of seasonal electric energy through discharge back to the main stream. Also, new methods of cutoff construction such as chemical grouting, slurry trench, or drilled concrete caisson piles may now make a dam with a permeable-foundation feasible, where 25 to 50 years ago costs of construction would have been prohibitive. The planner must be aware that other changes occur with time. Where previously, costs of relocating a railroad may have been prohibitive, many railroads in the northeastern United States still appearing on maps have been taken out of service since the end of World War II.

A thorough investigation should include both existing reservoirs (for possible redevelopment to larger size) and all sites previously studied by other agencies. A list of reservoirs studied in the past for any purpose should be prepared as a prerequisite to a proper preliminary screening for a basin study.

Generalized hydrologic relationships based on regional studies should be prepared to determine whether individual sites meet the criteria. Using data for the existing gaging stations, a map may be prepared with lines of average runoff per square mile. Regulation studies may also be made using these data and results plotted as a dimensionless ratio of regulated flow to average flow versus dimensionless ratio of required live storage to average annual runoff volume. For example, for the Susquehanna Basin, analyses of the most severe historical drought for 1-, 2-, and 3-year periods of operation gave the following values:

Period (years)	Regulated Flow as Percent of Average Flow	Required Storage as Percent of Average Annual Runoff
1	25	12
2	40	26
3	52	51

Generalized cost relationships in the form of graphs and nomographs should be prepared if they are not already available. Such relationships can cover structure, fill, excavation, lands and relocations, and other features.

After identifying the sites meeting the criteria for drainage area and having valley topography suitable for a dam and spillway, a rough calculation can be made based on map data of storage versus reservoir elevation, and the dam and spillway arrangement can be tentatively selected. Hydrologic relationships can be used to determine the scale of the project and an abbreviated cost estimate can be made using the cost relationships. This process should permit an approximate ranking of sites using a simple cost parameter. For a reservoir, this parameter may be in terms of dollars per acre-foot of storage or dollars per cubic foot per second of water supplied. The parameter can be used to establish cutoff points at which to eliminate poor sites in this early phase of screening. It will generally be found that the unit costs of a reservoir project will be lowest when the site is developed to its maximum hydrologic capacity, as limited by the topography of the site or the level at which excessive relocations are required; this is because the reservoir surface, and hence the rate of addition of volume, increases as the dam height increases.

The first screening may result in a large number of identified sites meeting the criteria and having unit costs below cutoff levels. To make the number of sites retained more manageable, more detailed abbreviated cost estimates may be applied to the better sites taking account, in the case of the reservoirs, of costs of water conveyance systems, pumping costs, and other ancillary facilities, and reexamining aerial photographs and other sources of information for relocations and other problems that would increase construction costs. If the reservoir is to be used for hydroelectric power, the costs of the power installation can be included, and the cost parameter can be dollars per installed kilowatt of capacity or cents per kilowatt-hour of energy. From the list of sites that have been reranked in order of unit cost, the best, perhaps 50% or less, will then be subjected to more intensive study.

Field Reconnaissance, Adjustment of Cost Estimates, and Reranking of Sites. The field reconnaissance should be made by specialists experienced in project layout and cost estimating, geology, and soils. They can check whether the general layout prepared in the office is reasonable or whether changes are indicated, make a preliminary assessment of the adequacy of foundations for structures, locate materials in the area that are needed for construction, and identify any obvious problems of design and construction. They can determine if there are any serious problems of access and relocation that may not have been evident from maps and other office references. Social and environmental evaluations may be limited due to personnel and time limitations, but problems such as severe social dislocations or obvious environmental impacts should be considered.

The value of field reconnaissance in the basin study cannot be overemphasized. It is through field observations that the investigator gains an understanding of the project sites and the entire basin terrain. Rapidly changing conditions accompanying new highway construction and urbanization of formerly rural areas will affect the choice of one site over another. In some cases, a single sign of real estate developers entering an area may preclude building major reservoirs for water storage.

If conditions allow, the field reconnaissance should be made without publicity in order to discourage real estate speculation or overreaction by individuals and public interest groups that may follow the dissemination of information that a site is being considered for reservoir development. No commitment should be stated or implied concerning any site because such commitments are not justified at this level of investigation.

As the result of the field reconnaissance work, the cost estimates may be revised, new cost parameters calculated in terms of unit of service or product, and a reordering of projects made.

Investigating Team. The team performing the screening described above should consist of a hydrologist, a hydraulic engineer, a civil-layout engineer who is also experienced in cost estimating, a photogrammetrist and aerial photograph interpreter, and a geologist. Depending on the purpose of the projects, additional specialists are needed, such as a hydroelectric engineer, environmental engineer, or recreation planning specialist.

Order of Work. The sequence indicated can be followed when the time period of the study and the seasons of the year permit the studies to be conducted in proper order. Where this is not the case, various phases of the work will have to be conducted concurrently. Field reconnaissance may be started immediately after a rough preliminary screening and, while preliminary and secondary screenings are carried out, adjustments between the different divisions of work may be made continually. Field reconnaissance trips may be made up to the time of completion of the studies and preparation of a consistent set of preliminary and secondary screening documents. When the phases of work overlap, some reduction in efficiency can be expected.

5.5 SCREENING THAT INCLUDES CONSIDERATION OF MULTIPLE PURPOSES AND OBJECTIVES

If multiple purposes of development are considered, the outline and explanation presented above is too simple. Identification and assessment of the various purposes and possible trade-offs may take place at various points in the study. If environmental and social considerations are important (especially when multiobjective planning is specified), these aspects cannot be ignored even at the earliest stage of the study and should be evaluated formally when establishing the final ranking of projects. For this work, matrices or tables are often used to show the interactions between development actions and their socioeconomic and environmental impacts, with numerical values applied to indicate the importance of these impacts. Weighting procedures permit estimation of the relative contributions of the projects to the designated purposes and objectives, and to other factors influencing site selection. Such methods are discussed in detail in Chapters 13, 15, and 16. An example will suffice to demonstrate the technique here.

The Florida Power and Light Company (Jopling 1974) has developed a method to evaluate and compare many potential thermal power plant sites using a matrix system that utilizes a number of weighting factors the company considers important in the selection of such sites. The system, which is illustrated by Tables 5.1 and 5.2, gives a heavy weight to:

1. Water supply and cooling systems development
2. Land availability
3. Compatibility of land use
4. Environmental impact

TABLE 5.1   EVALUATION SYSTEM FOR HYPOTHETICAL POWER PLANT SITE

	Weighting Factor (WF)	Rating (R)	Evaluation Points (WF × R)
1. Capability of cooling system development	3	5	15
2. Proximity to load center	1	3	3
3. Land availability	3	5	15
4. Compatibility of land use	3	5	15
5. Resource consumption			
a. Water consumption	3	3	9
b. Land utilization, amount	1	1	1
c. Land utilization, critical environmental importance	2	5	10
6. Accessibility			
a. To rail transportation	1	5	5
b. To highway transportation	1	5	5
c. To water transportation	1	5	5
d. To a port	1	3	3
7. Suitable soil foundation conditions	1	3	3
8. Cost of transmission connections	1	5	5
9. Environmental impact			
a. Water quality impact	3	5	15
b. Terrestrial biological impact	3	3	9
c. Aquatic biological impact	3	2	6
d. Construction effects	1	5	5
e. Aesthetics	1	3	3
f. Air quality impact	2	5	10
g. Noise impact	1	5	5
h. Transmission system routing	1	5	5
i. Impact on fuel delivery corridors	2	3	6
10. Process water supply	1	5	5
11. Population density	2	5	10
12. Socioeconomic impact			
a. Community services	1	5	5
b. Area economy	1	3	3
13. System compatibility	3	1	3
Site evaluation quality (total)			184

Source: Jopling (1974).

TABLE 5.2 COMPARISON OF POWER PLANT SITES USING EVALUATION SYSTEM

Site	Site Evaluation Quality	Ranking	Ranking
1	79	8	
2	92	5	
3	80	7	
4	140	2	2
5	102	4	4
6	60	9	
7	115	3	3
8	175	1	1
9	88	6	

Key 1 PPSEI Weighting Factors		Key 2 PPSEI Rating Scale	
Weight	Criteria	Rating	Criteria
1	Least important	1	Very poor site
2	Moderately important	2	Poor site
3	Highly important	3	Fair site
		4	Good site
		5	Very good site

Source: Jopling (1974).

Up until the passage of the National Environmental Policy Act of 1969, factors 1, 2, and 3 were considered most important. It is the addition of the last factor, environmental impact, that has complicated the site screening process and increased the cost of engineering and other professional services connected with site selection. Many studies involving a large number of sites use matrix systems like that of the Florida Power Company.

Some systems are computerized and print out, graphically, possible locations on maps. Some matrix evaluation methods are based on map and computer studies. The validity of such methods is no better than the field reconnaissance and detailed field investigations used to develop input to the studies. First "broad brush" eliminations of obviously unsatisfactory areas can sometimes be accomplished solely by map studies. However, real knowledge of a service area and suitability of sites can be obtained only by field examinations and engineering analyses based on adequate geotechnical, topographic, and environmental data.

The work activity chart shown in Figure 5.1 illustrates the total effort needed to select a site considering the technical and environmental characteristics of a large number of potential sites. A screening process such as that outlined in the figure is a practical requirement in a country such as the United States which has advanced economic development, strong environmental movement, access of the general public to the decision-making process, and layers of authorities who must approve a project before it can be implemented. The figure shows various phases leading successively to smaller lists of "priority," "potential," and "preferred" (recommended) sites.

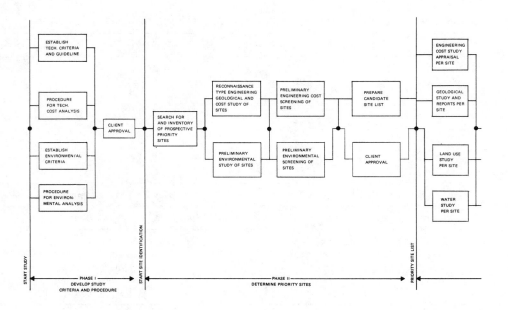

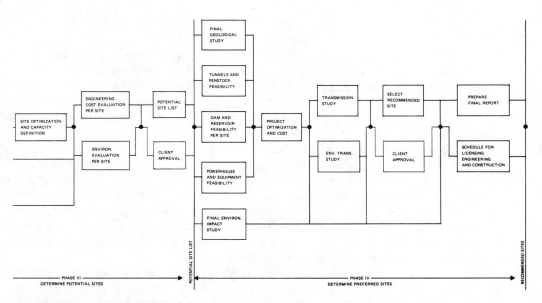

Figure 5.1 Work activity chart for screening hydroelectric project sites. (From Freeman and Dixon, 1976.)

5.6 REVIEW AND ADJUSTMENT OF PROJECT DATA BASE FOR PRELIMINARY COMPARISONS OF ALTERNATIVES

The problem discussed in this section is how to compare a number of alternative projects with different outputs and other characteristics. Any methodology for this problem should be based on reevaluating key physical relationships, updating costs, and performing other adjustments to permit comparison of the projects in terms suitable for a single-purpose project (e.g., cost per unit of output for water supply) or terms suitable for a multipurpose project (e.g., net benefits or benefit-cost ratio). An example of this approach is the screening study made in 1977 by TAMS in connection with additional water supplies for Kingston, Jamaica (Goodman and Jezierski 1979). The study involved the review of six major surface water supply schemes previously proposed and three groundwater sources.

The study included review and evaluation of existing reports, development of new data, and field work. Emphasis was placed on checking or establishing fundamental data on population and water demands, hydrology, geology, and hydrogeology. The alternative layouts followed closely the alignments and other engineering features as indicated in the available reports, since the scope of work did not include redesign or new designs for any of the structures. In order to provide a realistic and relatively uniform basis for comparisons of the projects, however, the office and field studies were designed to the greatest practical extent to bring the various schemes into a similar focus from a number of important standpoints. These included reliability of construction and operation of facilities, integration with other existing and future projects in the water supply and distribution system, compatibility in the context of a master plan, and safe yield.

The recommended master plan was based on the development of surface water supply sources. The Blue Mountain range, the source of most of the surface water supplies reviewed, extends along an east-west axis and divides the island of Jamaica into two approximately equal halves. The drainage areas of rivers flowing north and south from the ridge area are limited. This, and the variability of runoff, are the main contributors to the problems of water resource development in the area. Continuous records of the river flows available for the study, with one notable exception, were remarkably sparse and this necessitated correlations in order to develop synthesized records. The analyses emphasized the low flows that occurred during the periods represented by these records and the regulation of flows that was possible by operation of impounding reservoirs. The criteria adopted in the estimation of safe yields of surface supplies were equivalent to a return period of 1 in 25 years (estimated safe yield not attained every 25 years on the average) and were considered adequate for the planning of this water supply system.

Studies determined that groundwater supplies would not offer a long-term solution to the problem of water supply in the Kingston area because of inadequate yields and problems such as saline intrusion that would become worse with additional pumping. It was recommended that available groundwater supplies should either be developed to satisfy interim water supply requirements or reserved for future use. Groundwater development was also considered for compensating irrigators whose surface water supplies would be diverted to Kingston for municipal use. Estimates of yields of groundwater supplies were based on field observations, analysis of well logs, and review of the literature, including previous electrical analog modeling.

The potential of reused wastewater was also examined. Proper reuse of existing and future sewage flows would have a beneficial effect on the availability of water. Treated sewage effluents could be used to recharge the freshwater aquifers and create a barrier against saltwater intrusion. Treated sewage effluents could also be used for crop cultivation, which would free groundwater supplies now being used for irrigation. These groundwater supplies could then be diverted for domestic use. It was determined, however, that reuse of wastewater would not be feasible for either the present or the near future. Such water resources management techniques imply energy-intensive systems and high initial capital investments. In addition, long-term studies of the environmental impact of each alternative system must be conducted. The pressure injection of sewage effluents into deep wells to form a saltwater barrier must be based on pilot programs to determine if full-scale operations will be effective.

In developing comparative cost estimates, all information and basic physical data on sites and structures were obtained from published reports and pertinent backup information. Project components or structures were not redesigned. In order to produce a fair representation of project costs on a consistent level, however, structural dimensions were changed to reflect proper construction procedures. For example, provisions were made for overbreak in tunnels and a flat excavated invert to allow construction. Also, available geological information was utilized to establish firm rock lines and excavation limits. The tunnel section that had been proposed for two of the routes was considered to be inadequate to allow safe and efficient construction for the long lengths between portals, and was increased in diameter. When more adequate preliminary detail was available in a study of one project, it was applied to another project to better represent quantities of excavation, concrete and reinforcement. Unit prices were increased to reflect inflation since the dates of the original estimates; U.S. Bureau of Reclamation and *Engineering News-Record* indexes were used for this purpose. Costs of mechanical equipment were estimated with the aid of manufacturers' quotations.

As a result of this effort, each scheme was represented for purposes of comparative analysis by an alignment; principal dimensions of diversion structures, tunnels, pipelines, compensation wells, treatment facilities, and other project features; and estimates of construction quantities and total cost and unit cost of water. Contingencies of 15 to 25% were applied to the construction cost, depending on the information available on a given project and the level to which it was studied in the past. Estimates of investment cost also included engineering, supervision and administration costs, and interest during construction. Annual costs included amortization of debt and operation, maintenance, and replacement costs.

Comparative estimates for the six alternative water supply schemes and for a first priority scheme proposed are shown in Table 5.3 in terms of investment costs, annual costs, and cost per million imperial gallons per day (migd) if full output is assumed to be accepted into the water system with the completion of each phase of construction. This table compares the adjusted values with those from previous studies.

Scheme	This Study				Date	Previous Studies			
	Yield (migd)	Investment Cost ($1000 U.S.)	Annual Cost ($1000 U.S.)	Cost/migd per Year ($1000 U.S.)		Yield (migd)	Investment Cost ($1000 U.S.)	Annual Cost ($1000 U.S.)	Cost/migd per Year ($1000 U.S.)
Blue Mountain— Southern Route					June 1972				
Phase I	16.4	66,787	8,640	527		13.5	36,985	4,834	358
Phase II	15.4	94,086	12,484	811		20.0	40,008	5,987	299
Phase III	14.2	55,584	7,722	544		21.0	29,749	4,557	217
Phase IV	33.1	53,991	7,934	240		38.0	61,864	9,706	255
	79.1	270,448	36,780	465		92.5	168,606	25,084	271
Blue Mountain— Northern Route					June 1968				
Phase I	12.0	51,445	6,572	548		23.0	34,200	4,462	194
Phase II	8.2	32,415	4,206	513		22.0	10,000	1,317	60
Phase III	10.0	23,042	2,945	295		26.0	14,000	1,862	72
Rosemount Dam scheme	30.2	106,902	13,723	454	Oct. 1976	71.0	58,300	7,605	107
Konigsberg Dam scheme	27.7	111,515	14,493	523	June 1975	50.0	25,600	3,338	67
Mahogany Vale scheme (without hydropower)	72.1	169,108	23,118	321	Sept. 1967	100.0	89,100	11,619	116
	27.2	129,078	17,596	647		30.0	112,395	14,758	492
Mahogany Vale scheme (with hydropower)	94.8	396,452	50,078	528[a]	Oct. 1976	94.8	177,300	23,120	244
TAMS—first priority scheme	16.4	49,502	6,853	418					

[a] Maximum cost, before allocation of costs to hydropower and water supply.
Source: TAMS (1977).

Requirements for the master plan included the provision of adequate water supplies to satisfy the anticipated growth of water demand in Kingston and surrounding area between approximately 1982 and 2000. It was also desirable that the first phase of the master plan be adequate for 7 years (1982–1989) of demand growth. Figure 5.2 shows the estimates of water demand of the total region to be served. These estimates were based on predictions of population and unit demands which are discussed in Chapter 4. Table 5.4 shows comparative estimates for several master plans, including one based on the recommended first priority scheme. These were selected for further engineering, economic, and financial analysis.

The most practical and economic plan for three-phased development is indicated by the selection of projects shown on Figure 5.2 in relation to water demand growth, and on Figure 5.3 in terms of regional layout. Detailed schedules of construction cost estimates in local and foreign currencies and economic and financial analyses of the project are discussed in Chapters 8 and 9.

Figures 5.4 and 5.5 show (at reduced scale) a suggested presentation requiring two 11- by 17-inch sheets, for one alternative at the preliminary planning level. One sheet provides the essential informaton on physical characteristics and the other sheet covers costs and construction schedule.

The summary tables and figures (Tables 5.3 and 5.4, Figures 5.2 and 5.3) are the basis for the final selection of a plan. Additional tabular information and drawings

TABLE 5.4 COMPARATIVE ESTIMATES FOR ALTERNATIVE MASTER PLANS

Scheme	Yield (migd)	Investment Cost ($1000 U.S.)	Annual Cost ($1000 U.S.)	Cost/imgd per Year ($1000 U.S.)
Blue Mountain—Southern Route				
Phase I	16.4	66,787	8,640	527
Phase II	15.4	94,086	12,484	811
Phase III	14.2	55,584	7,722	544
Phase IV	33.1	53,991	7,934	240
	79.1	270,488	36,780	465
Blue-Mountain—combined Northern Route and Yallahs River Diversion				
Phase I	16.4	49,502	6,853	418
Phase II	16.1	97,348	12,864	799
Phase III	30.2	101,735	13,173	436
	62.7	248,585	32,890	525
Recommended master plan				
Phase I (first priority)	16.4	49,502	6,853	418
Phase II	16.1	97,348	12,864	799
Phase III	30.0	68,694	9,113	304
	62.5	215,454	28,830	461

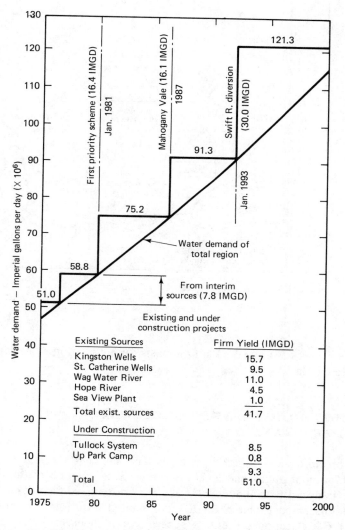

Figure 5.2 Kingston water supply: installation schedules for master plan. (From TAMS, 1977.)

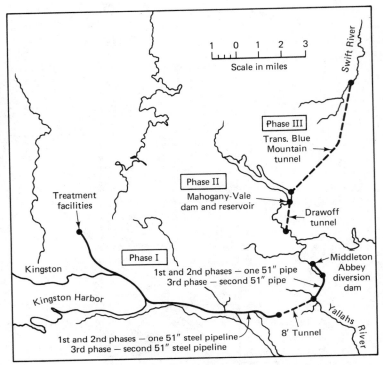

Figure 5.3 Kingston water supply: recommended master plan. (From TAMS, 1977.)

(such as Figures 5.4 and 5.5) are the basis for authorizing more detailed designs for the selected plan.

5.7 REVIEW AND ADJUSTMENT OF PROJECT DATA FOR MASTER PLANNING

The problem discussed here is to adjust and augment a data base so that equitable consideration of single- and multipurpose projects can proceed, in which each project can be analyzed both individually and in a systems context. The preceding section treated this same problem for a more limited case (single-purpose public water supply). This section presents a general comprehensive methodology. It is based partly on studies that led to a recommended master plan for integrated development of the Vardar/Axios Basin in Yugoslavia and Greece (TAMS, 1978). In work prior to these studies, various governmental agencies and consulting firms had prepared reports on individual projects, at different times and with different levels of detail. Not all of the elements discussed below were applied to the Vardar/Axios studies.

In the course of investigations of this type, a schematic diagram should be prepared indicating existing and potential projects, the sources of their water supplies, and their interconnections with the river system and other projects. An inventory and examination should be made of the numerous reports and other information documents. Preliminary evaluations should be made of principal project features such as layout and sizes of principal project components, operational characteristics such as spillway design floods and mean water yields, adequacy of foundations, estimates of construction costs, and unusual or special construction problems or relocations. The projects studied in a large river basin may vary from a small direct pumping scheme covering a few hundred acres of irrigated land to large multipurpose projects involving reservoir storage for irrigation, hydropower, municipal and industrial, thermal power plant cooling, and recreation uses. This information, together with additional data processing, defines the basic system of projects and the physical and economic data needed for comprehensive systems analysis.

The procedure assumes that all projects with significant potential value (in the basin and outside the basin, but serving its population) have already been identified. It also assumes that at least preliminary studies have already been carried out for each project.

For purposes of alternative system studies, information should preferably be available concerning each project at more than one level of development. Feasibility of stage development should also be investigated. Three levels of development are usually adequate to define trends of cost and benefits. Information for fewer levels of development may be considered due to restrictive topography and geology, hydrologic limitations, unacceptable flooding of large communities, or other reasons.

The information described above should be put into tables and perhaps other types of exhibits. Fairly large exhibits are needed to show all the information. Since projects are to be compared, the exhibits should be arranged to show both the information that is available and the information that is lacking, and deficiencies to be overcome if possible. To the extent practicable, the information should be shown in quantitative terms. Where quantitative expressions are not available, descriptive material can be put into tables. Dates for information should be indicated to show where updating of costs will probably be necessary and possibly for other reasons (e.g., environmental and socioeconomic studies have been carried out only in recent years). The tables should be organized so that, for several levels of development of a project, it is clear which items are the same and which are different.

The tables should then be examined to determine what adjustments are needed. All cost estimates should be adjusted to a common basis with suitable indexes such as the *Engineering News-Record* construction indexes that are used in the United States. If there are large differences in percentage allowances for construction contingencies, engineering, and interest during construction, they should be adjusted, unless there are obvious differences in risks or other reasons. In the case of major physical features such as spillways, diversion schemes, and waterways that have a hydrologic and hydraulic basis, criteria should be established for recurrence interval for the hydrologic events, limiting velocities, and so on, and adjustments made to the

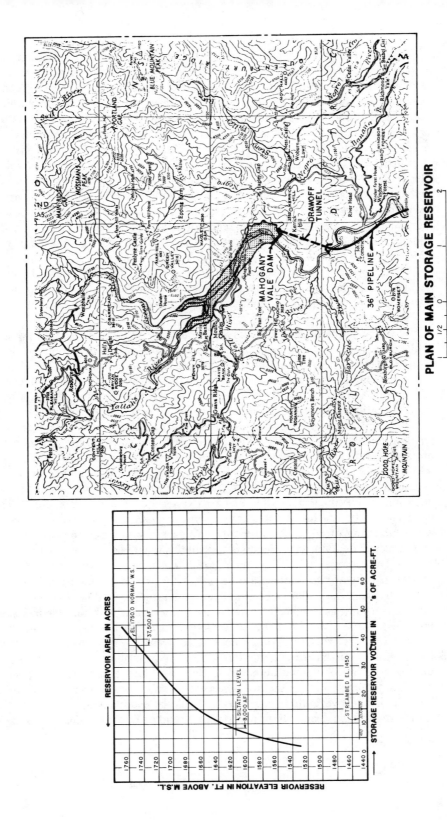

Figure 5.4 Kingston water supply: Mahogany Vale alternative, physical characteristics. (From TAMS, 1977.)

PROJECT PERTINENT DATA

DESCRIPTION	UNIT OR DATUM	VALUE
DAM AND RESERVOIR (MAHOGANY VALE DAM)		
Height of Dam	Ft	320
Type of Dam		Embankment Dam
Streambed Elevation	Ft M S L	1450
Top of Dam Elevation	"	1770
Full Reservoir Elevation	"	1750
Max Reservoir Elevation	"	1765
Dead Storage Elevation	Ft	1618
Dead Storage Volume	Ac-Ft	8000
Live or Usable Storage Volume	"	29500
Total Storage Volume	"	37500
Estimated Average Safe Yield	MGD	27.0
Estimated Life of Reservoir	Years	50
Area submerged by Max W.S. of Reservoir	Acres	1000
Spillway Design Capacity	CFS	150000
Outlet Works Capacity	CFS	100
WATER CONVEYANCES		
Tunnels		
Drawoff 6'-0"ø Tunnel Length	Ft	5000
Conveyance Capacity	imgd	
Pipelines Total length	Ft	115585
Pipeline 30"ø from Negro River Intake, Length	Ft	5835
Pipeline 36"ø from Yallahs Drawoff Tunnel to Cambridge Hill Tank, Length	Ft	32050
Pipeline 42"ø From Cambridge Hill Tank to Mona Reservoir, Length	Ft	77700
Conveyance Capacity	imgd	50
TERMINAL FACILITIES		
Installed Capacity	imgd	50

MAIN STORAGE DAM-PLANS AND SECTIONS

Figure 5.4 (continued)

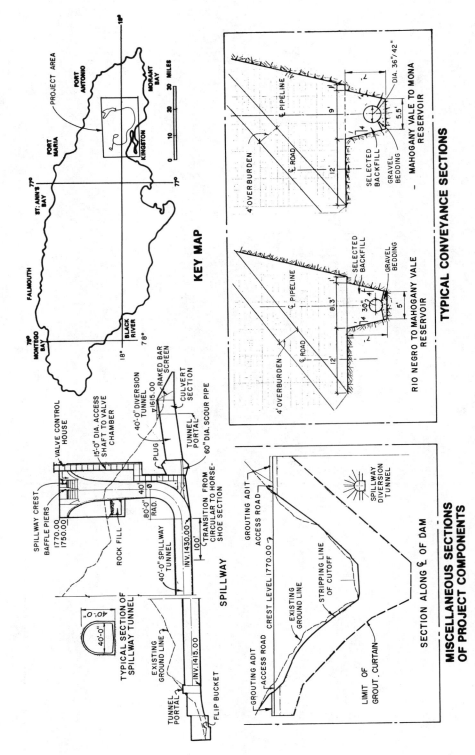

KEY MAP

TYPICAL SECTION OF SPILLWAY TUNNEL

SPILLWAY

TYPICAL CONVEYANCE SECTIONS

MAHOGANY VALE TO MONA RESERVOIR

RIO NEGRO TO MAHOGANY VALE RESERVOIR

SECTION ALONG ₵ OF DAM

MISCELLANEOUS SECTIONS OF PROJECT COMPONENTS

Figure 5.4 *(continued)*

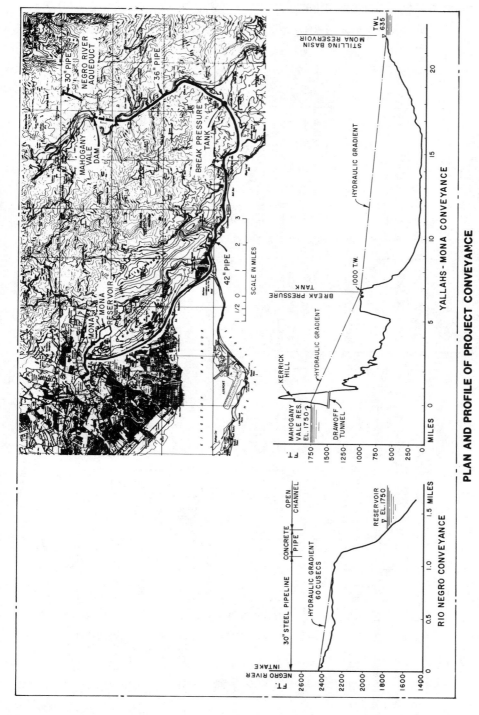

PLAN AND PROFILE OF PROJECT CONVEYAMCE

NOTES AND SPECIAL COMMENTS
1). Considerable damage to concrete may be expected due to high velocity of flow and cavitation at the elbow of Glory Hole Spillway.
2). A concrete arch gravity dam with overflow spillway is the most likely choice for this narrow site with steep abutments. The overflow spillway would provide adequate spilling capacity avoiding the extensive excavation of the steep abutments required by other spillway.

Figure 5.4 (continued)

125

DAM, RESERVOIR AND SPILLWAY

ITEM	UNIT	UNIT PRICE	INDEX	ADJ. UNIT PRICE	QUANTITY	AMOUNT	TOTAL COSTS
Land & Land Rights	Acres			500	1000	500,000	
Relocations	L.S.					2,000,000	
Reservoir Clearing	Acres			500	500	250,000	
Excavation Dam	C.Y.			4.00	150,000	600,000	
Foundation Treatment	Job					1,000,000	
Embankment Impervious	C.Y.			6.00	760,000	4,560,000	
Embankment Transition Material	C.Y.			4.00	694,000	2,776,000	
Embankment Filter Material	C.Y.			12	138,000	1,656,000	
Rip-Rap	C.Y.			15	54,000	810,000	
Embankment Pervious Shell	C.Y.			4	1,380,000	5,520,000	
Clearing & Grubbing	Acres			1000	100	100,000	19,772,000
Spillway Excavation Open Cut	C.Y.			3.00	115,600	346,800	
Spillway & Diversion Tunnel Excavation	C.Y.			35	248,100	8,683,500	
Concrete-Spillway (Incl. Tunnel Lining)	C.Y.			105	95,700	10,048,500	
Steel Supports	lbs.			0.50	4,762,000	2,381,000	
Reinf. Steel	lbs.			0.40	5,226,200	2,090,480	
Conc. in Tunnel Plug	C.Y.			90	1870	168,300	
Conc. In Spillway Outlet	C.Y.			100	15,000	1,500,000	
Mech. Equipment	L.S.					300,000	
Misc.	L.S.				1,000,000	1,000,000	26,518,580
							46,290,580

NEGRO RIVER DIVERSION DAM

ITEM	UNIT	UNIT PRICE	INDEX	ADJ. UNIT PRICE	QUANTITY	AMOUNT	TOTAL COSTS
Rock Excavation	C.Y.			6	200	1,200	
Concrete in Weir	C.Y.			80	100	8,000	
Concrete in Intake	C.Y.			115	200	23,000	
Reinforcement	lbs.			0.40	20,000	8,000	
Land & Land Rights	Acres			2,000	2	4,000	
Clearing & Grubbing	Acres			1000	5	5000	49,200
Pipe Bridge	L.S.			25000	1	25,000	
30" Pipe	lbs.			0.60	632,000	379,275	
Pipeline Overburden Excavation	C.Y.			0.4	33,280	13,320	
Pipeline Rock Bench Excavation	C.Y.			5	46,040	230,200	
Pipeline Rock Trench Excavation	C.Y.			8	10,075	80,600	
Pipe Bedding	C.Y.			12	1,090	13,080	
Selected Backfill	C.Y.			2	7,930	15,860	
Concrete Anchor Etc.	C.Y.			80	100	8,000	
Road Surfacing	C.Y.			12	1,300	15,600	
Seeding & Topsoil	S.Y.			1.75	6,030	10,560	
Drainage Ditches	L.S.					14,000	805,495
Open Channel Excav.	C.Y.			4	3,060	12,240	
Open Channel Conc.	C.Y.			150	816	122,400	
Reinforcement	lbs.			0.4	24,400	9,760	144,400
							999,095

Figure 5.5 Kingston water supply: Mahogany Vale alternative, cost estimates. (From TAMS, 1977.)

DERIVATION OF CAPITAL EXPENDITURES AND ANNUAL COSTS (IN 1000'S U.S. $)

DESCRIPTION	COST OF CONST.	CONTINGENCIES, ENG. & ADMIN, INTEREST *	TOTAL INVESTMENT COSTS	ESTIMATED SERVICE LIFE IN YEARS	12% CAPITAL RECOVERY FACTOR	ANNUAL CAPITAL RECOVERY	ANNUAL PUMPING POWER				OTHER OPERATION, MAINT. & REPLACEMENT		OTHER ANNUAL COSTS		TOTAL ANNUAL COSTS	REMARKS
							PUMPING HEAD	ASSUMED OPERATING HOURS/YEAR	PUMPING POWER PER YEAR	ANNUAL POWER COSTS	% ASSUMED	COSTS	A	B		
STORAGE DAM AND RESERVOIR	46,290.6	1.62	74,990.8	50	0.1204	9,029.0					1	750.0			9,779.0	
NEGRO RIVER DIVERSION DAM AND PIPELINE	999.0	1.62	1,618.4	40	0.1213	194.5					1	16.0			210.5	
INTAKE	1,904.0	1.62	3,084.5	40	0.1213	374.2					1	30.9			405.1	
PIPELINES	20,607.2	1.62	33,383.7	35	0.1223	4,082.8					2	667.7			4,750.5	
MONA RESERVOIR	237	1.62	383.9	50	0.1204	46.2					1	38.4			84.6	
TREATMENT WORKS	8400	1.62	13,608.0	30	0.1241	1,688.8					3	408.2			2,097.0	
IRRIGATION WATER WELLS	1,240	1.62	2,008.8	20	0.1339	269.0									269.0	WC not responsible for operation of wells
OTHER COMPONENTS A																
OTHER COMPONENTS B																
TOTALS	79,677.8		129,078.1			15,684.5						1,911.2			17,595.7	

* THIS MULTIPLIER IS MADE UP OF THE
FOLLOWING COMPONENT OF COST :

COST LEVEL	DESCRIPTION	%
(A)	CONSTRUCTION COSTS	100
(B)	CONTINGENCIES	15
	APPLIED TO (A)	
(C)	ENGINEERING AND ADMINISTRATION	12
	APPLIED TO ((A)+(B))	
(D)	INTEREST DURING CONSTRUCTION	12 / ANNUM
	APPLIED TO 1/2 ((A)+(B)+(C))	
	FOR PERIOD OF CONSTRUCTION	
	1.15 x 1.12 x 1.26 = 1.62	

Figure 5.5 (continued)

INTAKE, YALLAH/KINGSTON PIPELINE

ITEM	UNIT	UNIT PRICE	INDEX	ADJ. UNIT PRICE	QUANTITY	AMOUNT	TOTAL COSTS
Drawoff Tunnel Excavation	C.Y.	35			14,200	497,000	
Tunnel Concrete	C.Y.	105			7,850	824,250	
Steel Supports	lbs.	0.50			175,000	87,500	
Reinf.	lbs.	0.40			450,750	180,300	
Misc., inc. Mech. Equipm't	L.S.					315,000	1,904,050
PIPELINES							
Yallah/Kingston Pipeline Excav. Overburden	C.Y.	0.40			689,660	275,870	
Pipeline Excavation Rock Bench	C.Y.	5.0			1,106,780	5,533,900	
Pipeline Excavation Rock Trench	C.Y.	8.0			216,805	1,734,440	
Land & Land Rights	Acres	2,000			50	100,000	
Clearing & Grubbing	Acres	1,000			245	245,000	
Pipe Bedding	C.Y.	12			24,390	292,680	
36" φ Pipe	lbs.	0.6			4,327,000	2,596,050	
42" φ Pipe	lbs.	0.6			13,856,500	8,313,900	
Pipeline Conc. Bridges	L.S.	Average 25,000			21	525,000	
Pipeline Backfill	C.Y.	2.0			156,480	312,960	
Road Surfacing	C.Y.	12			24,390	292,680	
Seeding & Topsoil	S.Y.	1.75			134,140	234,750	
Break Pressure Tank	L.S					50,000	
Misc.	L.S.					100,000	20,607,230
							22,511,280

MONA RESERVOIR, MONA TREATMENT WORKS, COMPENSATION WATER WELLS

ITEM	UNIT	UNIT PRICE	INDEX	ADJ. UNIT PRICE	QUANTITY	AMOUNT	TOTAL COSTS
MONA RESERVOIR							
Spillway Basin & Mains		Taken from Humphreys & Sons Report V.I, P.39. According to 1977 (x 2.15)				34,400	
Inlet & Outlet Works		Same				202,100	236,500
TREATMENT WORKS **							8,400,000
Compensation Water Wells		Same					1,240,300
							9,876,500

** Estimated

Figure 5.5 (continued)

CONSTRUCTION SCHEDULE

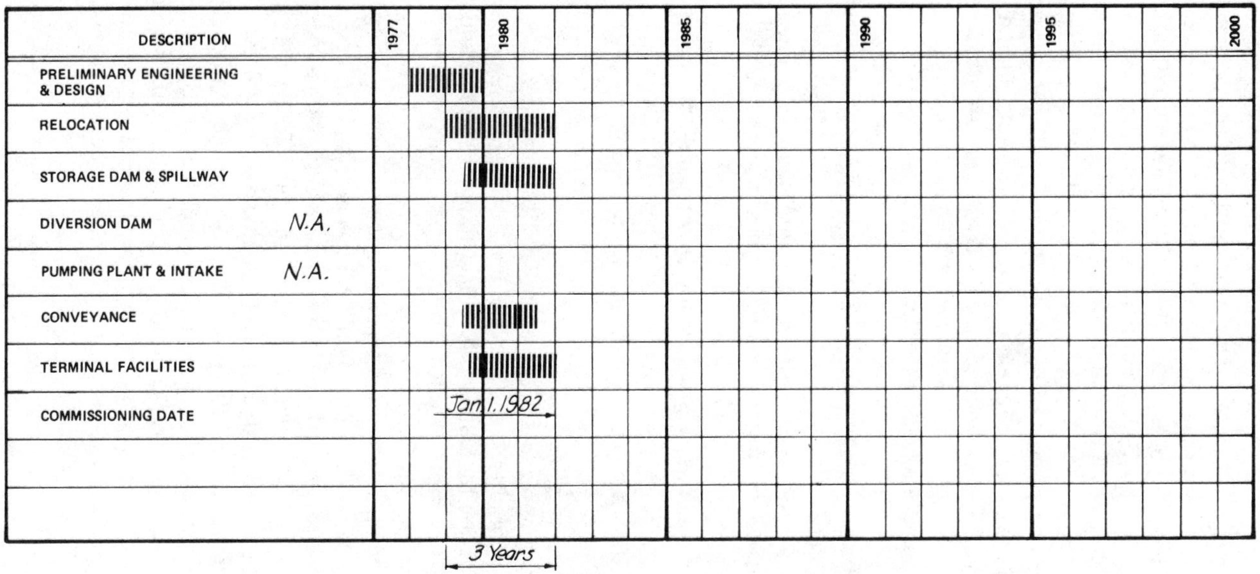

DESCRIPTION	1977	1980	1985	1990	1995	2000
PRELIMINARY ENGINEERING & DESIGN	▓					
RELOCATION	▓▓▓					
STORAGE DAM & SPILLWAY	▓▓▓					
DIVERSION DAM	N.A.					
PUMPING PLANT & INTAKE	N.A.					
CONVEYANCE	▓▓					
TERMINAL FACILITIES	▓▓					
COMMISSIONING DATE	Jan 1, 1982					

├─ 3 Years ─┤

SUMMARY			REMARKS
SAFE YIELD	MIGD	27.2	(9928.0x10^6 igals/yr)
COMPARATIVE INVESTMENT COST	$U.S.	129,078.1	1000's
COMPARATIVE ANNUAL COST	$U.S.	17,595.7	1000's
COMPARATIVE UNIT COSTS INVESTMENT PER MIGD	$U.S.	4,745	1000's
COST PER THOUSAND IGALLONS	$U.S.	1.77	

NOTE: THESE RESULTS ARE FOR COMPARISON OF SCHEMES, AND WOULD REQUIRE ADJUSTMENTS TO REFLECT FINAL CRITERIA FOR ECONOMIC AND FINANCIAL ANALYSES. UNIT COSTS SHOWN CORRESPOND TO FULL PRODUCTION AND ARE NOT IDENTICAL WITH AVERAGE UNIT COSTS OVER THE PROJECTS USEFUL LIFE WHEN SATISFYING ACTUAL INCREMENTAL DEMANDS.

Figure 5.5 (continued)

project features and cost estimates if they are substantially out of line. If hydropower projects have different capacity factors (ratio of average to maximum power) but will be expected to operate in a similar manner, the factors should be adjusted. If there are some obviously poor layouts of project features, their revision should be considered. These measures should not take an inordinate amount of time at this stage of the work; the emphasis should be on adjusting estimates for comparative purposes.

Rough comparisons should then be made among the projects, to eliminate those that obviously should not be considered further. This should be done on the basis of cost per unit reservoir volume or per cfs of yield in the case of a flow regulation project, or some other measures of unit cost of output (construction cost or present worth value) or economic indicator (e.g., benefit-cost ratio). Projects should be eliminated at this stage very cautiously, eliminating only those that are obviously inferior; concurrence or, at least, advice of the sponsor's staff should be sought.

Several types of studies should now be undertaken to:

1. Adjust projects in accordance with known opportunities for resources development and known user demands.
2. Adjust layouts and cost estimates in accordance with information obtained by field examinations; these consider construction conditions, access, relocations, etc.
3. Estimate principal features such as reservoir volumes for additional levels of development.
4. In general, to fill in the missing pieces of data in the inventory tables to the extent feasible.

It is important in comparing and ranking projects that all be compared on an equitable basis. However, this is not always easily done. For instance, some projects may have had more field examination than others, such as drilling or better mapping. Others may have been subjected to a more detailed level of design. Factors should be applied to account for these different levels of study between projects. Usually, the geologic evaluation of a site is the most important consideration or variable affecting project construction costs. All sites considered should be given a uniform geologic evaluation by a geologist knowledgeable of the geology of the region, with a view to reflecting this evaluation in project costs. Much of this work depends on the field examinations, but office map studies and other analyses should also be utilized.

The projects should then be reexamined to rank projects, considering benefits, cost, importance in meeting broad national objectives, and other factors. Systems of projects, including alternative operating rules, can then be formulated using various levels of the better projects, as indicated by this ranking. No standard procedure for such formulation of systems is suitable for all problems. The concurrence or advice of the sponsor's staff should again be sought.

To review, the screening process in preparation for master or comprehensive planning (discussed in Chapter 6) should consist of the following steps:

1. Inventory of project information

2. First adjustment of project features and costs, to meet minimum planning criteria
3. Elimination of obviously unsuitable projects
4. Field examinations and additional office studies, second adjustment of project features and costs, estimates of features and costs for additional levels of development
5. Ranking of projects
6. Formulation of alternative systems of projects

Modifications of these procedures may be indicated by experience in examining the projects. Also, certain complications (such as alternative projects overlapping in a river reach or using the same water) may have to be resolved in special ways. Time and personnel available for the studies is also an important consideration. Overlapping of the steps and shortcutting of some of the procedures may be necessary.

5.8 ROLE OF ENVIRONMENTAL CONSIDERATIONS IN WATER RESOURCES AND RELATED LAND PLANNING

The U.S. National Water Commission (1973) has placed the following perspective on the importance of considering environmental effects in the planning of water resources developments:

To speak of the environmental effects of man's development activities is to speak of a variety of consequences, some good and some bad. The construction of a dam and reservoir may be used to illustrate the point. The development could affect:

1. The biology of the natural environment—some ecosystems could be damaged and others benefited.
2. The recreational potential of the area—white water canoeing might be eliminated while water skiing is made possible.
3. The esthetic values of the area—a canyon beautiful to some for its colorful formations could be inundated to form a tranquil lake, equally beautiful to others.
4. The spiritual feelings some people hold for the area—some might experience a sense of esthetic loss if a dam obliterated a unique geographical or historical place of interest while others might feel a sense of pride or accomplishment in the building of a structure, the taming of nature, the creation of employment, and the provision of additional useable supplies of water and energy.

As diverse as the environmental consequences of development may be, ranging from ecological effects to attitudinal responses based on philosophical concepts of value, they reflect a shared national concern for the effects of environmental change on people—on their life support systems, their standard of living, their recreational opportunities, and their spiritual well-being. It is often a matter of people's preferences for one set of values over another. But it may also be a matter of man's ability to keep the planet Earth in a healthful and agreeable condition in which he and his descendents can live and prosper.

Chapters 1 to 3 have indicated the importance of environmental considerations and other nonengineering/economic aspects in site selection, project formulation, and evaluation. Inadequate consideration of these aspects may also result in difficulties of project implementation, such as those related to public acceptance, government regulatory agency approvals, and legal and institutional conflicts. Thus, in every stage of project planning, including the identification and preliminary evaluation stage, it is important to consider these aspects. The following three sections provide reviews of environmental impacts, public health and other biological aspects of water resources planning, and of methods of preventing or mitigating adverse environmental impacts. Some social impacts of projects are also included. These sections are followed by a brief discussion of environmental impacts that were considered in a comparative analysis of alternative sites for reservoir construction. More formal and detailed analyses of projects in terms of their environmental and social impacts are described in Chapters 15 and 16, respectively.

5.9 TYPES OF ENVIRONMENTAL IMPACTS AND INTERRELATIONSHIPS OF LAND AND WATER

5.9.1 Reservoir Development

A reservoir project is the basis for a discussion of the ways in which the construction, operation, and management of a water resources project impact on the various components of environmental quality. Ortolano (1973) has classified water resources development activities potentially influencing the environment, building on studies by Aggerholm (1972), Arthur D. Little (1971), and the U.S. Army Corps of Engineers. The six categories are: (1) preconstruction activities; (2) construction activities; (3) project structures and facilities; (4) operation and maintenance activities; (5) project outputs and their associated "induced" effects; and (6) nonstructural activities.

Before the main construction activities for a reservoir commence, it is usual to begin the purchase and destruction or relocation of highways and buildings and to construct access roads. Such activities may have environmental impacts, in addition to causing dislocations and inconvenience of travel for the residents and businesses in the project area. Land speculation and changes in land utilization may result in anticipation of the project (particularly if changes in water configurations, recreation opportunities, and floodplain protection are included). Construction activities that have environmental impacts include those related to the housing and services for construction workers, the operation of construction equipment (air pollution, noise, delays), excavation and earth-moving operations (spoil disposal, river turbidity), and care of water during construction (diversions and other changes in flow). In addition to the user benefits of reservoir construction, the project outputs may induce other recreational land development and industrial plants, and other economic growth may occur as the indirect result of the reservoir. Finally, nonstructural measures such as floodplain zoning or land purchase may change the patterns of land development and rates of economic growth.

Hagan and Roberts (1972) have identified many environmental impacts of water storage and diversion projects and have classified them according to their location in areas of impoundment, areas downstream from the impoundment or diversion or both, along the conveyance route, and in the areas of project water use. Table 5.5 is a summary based on their studies of the major environmental impacts identified in these four locations; the table also includes socioeconomic effects. Table 5.6 lists environmental and socioeconomic factors of concern to persons affected by these projects.

5.9.2 Other Interrelationships of Land and Water

Human development and the associated use of land affects water in ways other than reservoir development. These actions may affect project planning, impede or prevent project approval, or result in legal adversary proceedings (see Chapter 17 for a detailed discussion of water law in the United States). The impacts result from physical alterations to the land itself, from release to the hydrologic cycle of various substances associated with particular land use activities, and from the withdrawal of water.

TABLE 5.5   ENVIRONMENTAL IMPACTS FOR WATER AND DIVERSION PROJECTS

1. Disturbs Natural State of Area—Changes land areas to water areas; changes wild rivers to controlled rivers; changes landforms, vegetation, fish, wildlife, and other biota; affects microclimate
2. Modifies Stream Flows Downstream of Reservoir—Reduces flood peaks; reduces or raises minimum flows; may introduce abnormal and variable flows; affects scouring and sedimentation
3. Affects Groundwater Levels, Seepage, Waterlogging
4. Modifies Evaporation and Transpiration
5. Affects Water Temperature, Stratification, and Salinity
6. Changes Physical, Chemical, and Bacteriological Water Quality Characteristics
7. Alters Erosion, Sediment Production, and Transport—Erodes banks; causes landslides; deposits sediment in reservoir and stream
8. Submerges Land Areas—Exposes banks during drawdown, causes loss of archaeological and historic sites, displaces people and business; causes loss of farmland; alters aquatic and riparian habitat for plants, insects, fish, wildlife
9. Modifies Types and Quantities of Fish and Wildlife Production, Including Anadromous Fish
10. Modifies Recreational Potential of Water and Land Areas—Increases people pressures on natural areas and introduces infrastructure problems
11. Increases Opportunities for Development of Surrounding Lands for Urban and Vacation Housing, and for Increased Urban, Commercial, and Industrial Growth—With potential for air, noise, land, and water pollution and increased infrastructure requirements
12. Interferes with Land Access and May Introduce Plant, Insect, and Animal Pests
13. Alters Population and Economic, Social, and Political Life of Area with Associated Environmental and Socioeconomic Impacts

Source: Based on Hagan and Roberts (1972).

TABLE 5.6 SOME FACTORS AFFECTING INDIVIDUAL RECOGNITION AND DEGREE OF CONCERN OVER ENVIRONMENTAL IMPACT OF WATER PROJECTS

Persons Living in Area of Water Impoundment or Diversion, or Both

1. Landowners Affected Directly by Project—Concern depends on whether land area is submerged, provided with new vista or shoreline frontage, subjected to increased seepage or higher water table, and receives better flood protection.

2. Area Residents Concerned About:
    a. Effects on general economy of area from loss in agricultural production from submerged area, payroll arising from project construction and operation, development of adjacent areas for housing and industry, and altered recreational opportunities and travel;
    b. Effects on tax base;
    c. Effects on local government costs for public services—police, fire, roads, schools, social programs;
    d. Anticipated effects on future development and economy of area.

3. Sensitivities to Ecological Issues—These sensitivities may be secondary to above considerations with many individuals.

Persons Living in Area Served by Water Project

1. Farmers, Landowners, and Residents of Rural Areas—In districts receiving augmented or new water supplies: increased land values and crop income, improved economic conditions for rural communities, higher tax base for local governments.

2. Urban Areas—Augmented water supply may eliminate or lessen periodic water shortages for present populations; improve water quality; allow increased land development, new industry, increased construction, and higher population, with economic benefits to some residents; permit expansions of industry and population unwanted by some residents.

3. Undeveloped Areas—New water supply permits settlement and urbanization of previously unoccupied or sparsely settled districts.

4. Sensitivities to Ecological Issues—With many individuals, these sensitivities are secondary to the previous considerations.

Persons Living Outside Areas of Origin or Service

1. Farmers and Rural Communities Already Adequately Supplied with Water—May suffer economically from produce of new irrigated areas.

2. Rural and Urban Dwellers:
    a. May be concerned about possible future costs to them for water projects (through taxation);
    b. May deplore disturbance of natural conditions of wild rivers;
    c. May be concerned about maintenance of beaches along seacoast;
    d. May desire to boat, fish, and hunt in undisturbed areas;
    e. May be concerned about effects of project on commercial fishing and continued availability of seafood;
    f. May welcome new opportunities for fishing and water-based recreation on newly created lakes;
    g. May be concerned about continued opportunities for dilution and transport of wastes from their communities.

3. Sensitivities to Ecological Issues—Many individuals consider these issues of compelling importance.

Source: Hagan and Roberts (1972).

The clearing of vegetation is usually one of the steps in land development for urban or commercial uses and, to a certain extent, for agricultural uses. This can have three major environmental impacts: (1) the rate and quantity of runoff increases, while infiltration decreases because the soil loses its capacity to absorb water; (2) erosion of the bare soil increases, producing sediment which becomes a burden in waterways and may diminish water quality, or which becomes trapped in reservoirs and reduces their storage capacity (erosion not only strips away topsoil, but also deteriorates the beds and banks of watercourses); and (3) any function performed by the vegetation of filtering pollutants from runoff is lost.

The replacement of vegetative cover with impervious roofs and paved areas will reduce erosion but will tend to accentuate other problems associated with increased runoff and reduced infiltration. When impervious surfaces collect precipitation and rapidly direct it into watercourses, groundwater recharge is blocked, streams experience rapid fluctuations, flood peaks are increased, and low flows of dry periods are diminished. In addition, pollutants that have been deposited on the land surface are leached from the ground and may be washed downstream.

Filling and draining wetlands may result in particularly severe impacts. Lying at the interface between uplands and aquatic systems, wetlands are the location of intensive biological activity whose destruction causes harmful effects on both terrestrial and aquatic systems. Wetlands also have very important roles in the hydrologic cycle. A number of examples of hydrologic function and related water quality effects have been shown (U.S. Senate Committee on Public Works, 1976). Wetlands act as a buffer against rapid hydrologic fluctuations. The natural storage of floodwaters reduces flood peaks and the severity and duration of droughts by causing excess waters to be gradually absorbed or released. The U.S. Army Corps of Engineers estimated that a 40% reduction in wetlands along the Charles River in Massachusetts would elevate flood stages 2 to 4 feet. By slowing the velocity of floodwaters, wetlands reduce damages when flooding does occur. Bridges below a Pennsylvania wetland that had been preserved were unharmed after widespread flooding, whereas similar bridges elsewhere were destroyed. Wetlands purify the water that flows through them and thus mitigate the effects on the aquatic system caused by land development. A study of Lake Minnetonka in Minnesota for the period from June 1969 to May 1970 showed that although 77,000 pounds of phosphorus was released into the watershed, only 50,300 pounds reached the lake. Wetlands help to prevent siltation of downstream areas by slowing the flow of water, thus decreasing the erosion of stream banks and settling out a portion of the sediment load. Finally, wetlands are important sites of groundwater recharge in some areas.

Another impact of land use on water arises from pollutants. The runoff from a construction site, for example, may carry 40,000 times as much sediment as the runoff from unaltered watersheds (Wildrick et al. 1976). Other substances, such as agricultural chemicals, are deposited on land and subsequently carried by runoff into water bodies. Leachates from landfills for the disposal of wastes may have a severe impact on the quality of surface waters and groundwaters. The waste generated by a land use activity may be deliberately discharged into adjacent waters. The type of land use directly affects the type and quantity of pollutants that enter receiving waters.

The amount of water withdrawn for land uses is directly related to the character of the land use, its intensity, and the techniques used in the consumption of water (U.S. National Water Commission, 1973). For example, if a section of land is used for a thermal-electric power generating plant, much more water will be needed than if it is used as a nonimproved pasture needing no other water than rainfall.

Not only do land uses have an impact on water, but conversely, the quality, quantity, and location of water have a substantial impact on land uses. The availability of sufficient quantities of clean water determines whether lands can be used for many purposes. Industry, agriculture, and residential development cannot occur without adequate supplies of water. The critical importance of water quantity and quality is also reflected in the market values of land associated with available water.

Because land and water are so closely related as physical systems, programs for the development or management of these resources also tend to be functionally related. For example, a decision that is made in a land use management program will affect whether the goals of a water quality improvement program are met. Similarly, the construction of a project for water quality improvement or the control of floods is likely to affect the success of land use planning. There are many examples of these types of interrelationships and, unfortunately, they often arise as unintended secondary effects rather than as well-conceived interactions. Better integration of land and water management can help to harmonize conflicting programs or to use programs in mutually reinforcing ways.

Many governmental programs designed for the protection and improvement of water quality provide excellent examples of how land and water management programs need to be better integrated. One of the most notorious has been the effect of sewage treatment construction on land use patterns. Such facilities are typically designed with excess capacity in order to avoid problems of early obsolescence. The availability of sewers, however, often stimulates growth in areas that are unsuitable or unprepared to accommodate it. Runoff and other nonpoint sources of pollution can then cause water quality degradation as severe as that which the facilities were intended to correct. Also, because of the need to increase tax revenues to finance the local share of the cost of building and operating these facilities, local governmental officials may be reluctant to implement measures to control growth.

On the other hand, the failure to build new water pollution control facilities can have equally severe impacts on land use patterns and the growth management plans of local governmental officials. (Williams 1978). When connections from new buildings threaten to exceed a treatment plant's capacity, a moratorium may be required on new hookups. Unless alternative treatment systems are available, this action translates into a moratorium on new construction. Similar restrictions on industrial usage of land may result from the enforcement of effluent limitations in areas with badly degraded water quality.

The linkage between land and water management has become most evident in the control of nonpoint sources of water pollution. The traditional emphasis of water pollution control programs has been on regulating the discharge of wastes from point sources such as sewage treatment plants and industrial facilities. Water quality goals, however, cannot be achieved with such a limited approach because much of the pollutant load comes from nonpoint sources such as runoff from construction sites, agricultural operations, and urban streets. Land use control is necessary if the nonpoint sources are going to be controlled (U.S. Environmental Protection Agency, 1975).

Floodplain management is another need that requires an integrated land and water management approach. Flooding is a natural and necessary hydrologic phenomenon. Problems occur because structures are built that are susceptible to damage within the floodplain. Often, the least costly and least environmentally damaging method of preventing flood damage is to restrict land use within the floodplain. In many cases structural improvements have been made to the flood channel at great cost, permitting additional encroachment on the floodplain and negating any reduction in flood damage potential.

Wetlands protection is another need of environmental management which cannot be solved by traditional autonomous water management or land use controls. The hydrologic benefits of wetlands have been described above. Wetlands also provide excellent wildlife habitat, timber, open space, and recreational areas. The degradation of wetlands and the loss of their water control functions generally come from changing land use patterns, such as conversion to agricultural use or housing development. Although wetlands may be threatened by certain water management actions, such as lowering water levels in a river to provide water supply or channelizing streams to reduce flooding, these actions are generally taken to accommodate land use changes.

Although a close physical relationship exists between land and water resources, and their management programs should be at least functionally related, as discussed above, this has not been adequately reflected in the multitude of decisions, laws, and institutions that affect natural resources. Land and water have frequently been used and abused, studied and regulated, spoken of and acted upon as though they were entirely separate systems. Even people who understand that there is a relationship between what is done on the land and what happens to nearby water, and vice versa, frequently exhibit a lack of concern for the impact of their own actions on the environment. When they cause environmental damages, they may even gain substantial economic benefit by ignoring the effects.

Because neither ethics nor economics have effectively restrained environmental degradation, government has had to intervene. However, governmental regulations and the actions of government agencies have often failed to integrate land and water management adequately. One reason is that the people who staff government agencies may lack sufficient information on environmental problems or may not be sufficiently concerned. They may also be subject to political pressure from interests that may sustain economic costs from effective environmental regulations. Other reasons suggested by commentators implicate institutional factors. Government has historically attacked problems in a piecemeal rather than a comprehensive manner. Numerous single-purpose agencies have been created to deal with such specific problems as a need for roads, flood protection, or irrigation water. The emphasis of these agencies has been on achieving narrow goals while other factors have been deemed less important. This approach has compounded other problems, even as it has helped resolve the one for which it was designed. Thus, problem solvers have often failed to recognize the synergism involved and to consider secondary impacts, such as stimulus to growth and development. Even federal agencies have been slow to perceive, and often unable to correct, undesirable secondary effects because correction would require departure from the single-purpose missions typically thrust on these agencies by legislation. When adherence to this assigned role has been the standard by which the Congress and client groups have measured their effectiveness, more efficient and cost-effective methods outside the scope of traditional activity may be ignored by such an agency. For example, an agency that was created, staffed, and funded to build dams would tend to promote the construction of dams to control floods and not adequately consider less expensive alternatives of floodplain management if the latter solution would not be implemented by that agency (U.S. National Water Commission, 1973).

Numerous undesirable consequences have flowed from the failure to integrate and coordinate land and water management effectively. Despite considerable progress, the environment still is not generally managed as an integrative, holistic, natural system. Numerous decisions regarding development or regulatory activities are being made each day without adequate consideration of their effect on the resources as a whole or on other governmental programs. The quality of the environment, therefore, continues to be degraded.

The problems caused by lack of integration are most acute when programs are conflicting and inconsistent. For example, one arm of government may authorize the destruction of wetlands, while another seeks to protect them. Although conflict is necessary and beneficial as long as there are different points of view, in many cases too much effort is spent on such interagency struggles. Such counterproductive action not only wastes energy, but the potential benefits of having programs reinforce one another may also be lost.

5.10 PUBLIC HEALTH AND RELATED ASPECTS OF WATER RESOURCES PLANNING

There are many direct and indirect public health benefits that result from water resources development. More varied and increased agricultural yields assist in improving nutrition. Better water supplies and wastewater treatment reduce the incidence of waterborne diseases. Recreation opportunities and environmental quality enhancement raise the spirit and morale. Economic benefits of water resources development increase income, which improves the standard of living and associated health care.

Along with these benefits, however, adverse effects to the public health may also occur. According to a United Nations report (Lagler 1969), deforestation in the USSR led to an increase in tick-borne encephalitis, increased rice growing in Asia brought epidemics of mosquito-borne encephalitis, and urbanization without adequate drainage is still contributing to the spread of filariasis. The same report recommends that advisors on public health biology and sanitation be associated at an early stage for each new reservoir project in a developing country to provide guidance on the studies and to anticipate infections that might break out. Water resources projects can pose threats to health through the inadvertent improvement of the habitat for certain disease vectors. Not only are water bodies themselves involved, but changes to the countryside during project construction can radically alter the insect and snail populations which act as carriers of many infections. Problems can also arise from resettlement of populations, either to make way for a project or to provide the labor needed for construction and operation (e.g., irrigation projects), since parasites travel with the people.

Domestic water supplies are essential to human survival but can carry disease when inadequately treated or improperly conveyed from the source. Rural water supplies from lakes may be foci of schistosomiasis (bilharziasis). Quiet water in beds of aquatic weeds makes an ideal habitat. Irrigation projects in the tropics and subtropics are other places where this snail-borne infection may occur.

Anthropod-borne infections include malaria, onchocerciasis, trypanosomiasis, filiariasis, and virus infections. Many species of mosquito which may be found in quiet water with vegetation act as malaria vectors. In addition to their importance as a disease vector, mosquitos can cause serious nuisance problems. According to Hayes (1976), mosquitos are the principal vector associated with water resources projects in the United States. Onchocerciasis (river blindness) is associated with flowing waters of streams in which the small blackfly vector spends its preadult life. Spillways from dams also provide breeding sites. The tsetse fly is a vector associated with lakeside and riverside which carries trypanosomiasis (sleeping sickness). Virus infections,

TABLE 5.7 CHARACTERISTICS OF WATER-RELATED DISEASES

Parasites	Diseases Transmitted	Intermediate Host	Infection Route
Nematoda:			
Onchocerca volvulus	River blindness (onchocerciasis)	Black fly (*Simulium*)	Bite
Wuchereira bancrofti	Elephantiasis (filariasis)	Several mosquitoes	Bite
Protozoa:			
Plasmodium spp.	Malaria	Anopheles mosquito	Bite
Trypanosoma gambiense	African sleeping sickness	Tsetse fly (*Glossina* p.)	Bite
Trematoda:			
Schistosoma haematobium	Urinary schistosomiasis	Aquatic snail (*Bulinus*)	Percutaneous
Schistosoma mansoni	Intestinal schistosomiasis	Aquatic snails (*Biompholaria; Australorbis*)	Percutaneous
Schistosoma japonicum	Visceral schistosomiasis	Amphibious snail (*Oncomelania*)	Percutaneous
Viruses:			
Over 30 mosquito-borne viruses are associated with human infections	Encephalitis; dengue	Several mosquitoes	Bite

Source: Biswas (1980).

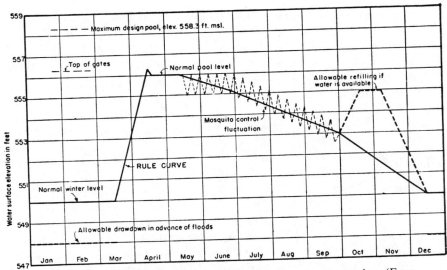

Figure 5.6 Rule curve for reservoir to control mosquito propagation. (From Bowden, 1941.)

particularly yellow fever, are spread by mosquitos and may be found in open water and in jars used to store water.

Table 5.7 summarizes the characteristics of the more important water-related diseases. Biswas has discussed the enormous social costs of water resource developments in spreading disease in the developing countries. He has also discussed the problems of aquatic weeds, which are a great nuisance in blocking water passages, increasing evaporation, and improving the habitat for disease vectors.

In addition to the effects of the vectors themselves, the use of pesticides, herbicides, and other poisons in connection with agriculture (and fishing in some places) and for control of diseases may themselves also cause problems when they are washed into public water supplies.

Hayes (1976) and Biswas (1980) suggest measures that may be taken in design, maintenance, and operation to prevent or reduce problems. Bowden (1941) has described a rule curve for reservoir operation to reduce mosquito problems; this is illustrated on Figure 5.6.

5.11 METHODS OF PREVENTING OR MITIGATING ADVERSE ENVIRONMENTAL IMPACTS OF RESERVOIR DEVELOPMENT

The methods of the U.S. Bureau of Reclamation (Keating 1973; Stamm 1973; Fairchild 1973) are representative of methods for preventing or mitigating environmental impacts. The following is based largely on their practices for reservoirs, but many methods are also applicable to other water resources facilities.

Preconstruction and Construction Activities. Perform construction by methods that will prevent the entrance or accidental discharge of pollutants into surface or underground water sources. Use barriers, settling ponds, or other means to prevent excessively turbid water from entering watercourses. Operate equipment or vehicles that do not emit excessive exhaust gases or produce excessive noise. Keep dusts produced during manufacture, handling, and storage of cements and other materials from entering the atmosphere. Keep dust from other activities to acceptable levels. Do not disrupt the natural landscape any more than is absolutely necessary (some areas may be specifically designated for protection from damage). Clearing of vegetation from reservoir areas, structure sites, transmission line rights-of-way, and other locations should be controlled so that no trees are cut outside designated areas. Cut trees and brush should be disposed of properly. Erosion and unvegetated slopes of cuts and fills on access and construction roads should be minimized by controlling their routing, holding them to minimum length, and siting them for later permanent use. Where roads and other areas are not permanent, prepare and seed as soon as possible after construction is completed.

Project Structures and Facilities. Alignment of transmission lines along principal highways should be avoided where possible. Towers and conductors should be placed where shielded by natural topography whenever possible, and should avoid areas of high amenity value such as historic sites and recreation areas. Route roads to blend with the natural topography rather than by the shortest route. Protect channel banks downstream from a dam with embankments and armor rock. Design structures to fit them into the natural scenery of the area where they are built, and maintain a low-profile appearance if possible. Provide multilevel intakes to make downstream water of suitable quality with respect to temperature, oxygen, turbidity, nutrients, dissolved minerals, and other components. Include fish ladders or other facilities for migratory or anadromous fish, and enhance fishing by attraction techniques and stocking. Replace areas taken for project facilities with equivalent areas for fish, wildlife, and flora.

Operation and Maintenance Activities. Operate reservoir to reduce drawdowns that may affect recreation or other purposes. Operate reservoir to reduce mosquito propagation for disease control. Release water of suitable quality by selection of intake level, and reduce variability of discharges that cause environmental problems downstream. Manage reservoirs to provide high biological productivity of desirable species. By zoning or easements, acquire facilities to preserve important historical, cultural, or natural aspects. Properly locate and operate a visitor's center and other tourist facilities. Acquire and maintain downstream floodplain areas for recreation development or protection for other reasons.

5.12 ENVIRONMENTAL SCREENING FOR RESERVOIR PROJECT

The environmental screening of a water resources project should identify potential problems related to environmental impacts and should determine their importance. A report on the Pond Hill Reservoir in Pennsylvania, which was prepared for the Pennsylvania Power and Light Company by the firm of Tippetts-Abbett-McCarthy-Stratton (TAMS, 1979), is a representative example of such screening. To operate the Susquehanna Steam Electric Station (SES), water will be withdrawn from the Susquehanna River. While some of this water will be returned to the river, approximately two-thirds will evaporate during the cooling process for the power plant. The anticipated average rate of loss is 50 cubic feet per second.

The environmental studies (TAMS, 1979) considered the options for low-flow augmentation and the environmental consequences of constructing a reservoir to supplement Susquehanna River flow when necessary. It was determined that the construction of a new reservoir with the capacity to replace water that is withdrawn for the operation of the SES was the most economically desirable and reliable means of meeting low-flow-augmentation requirements. The following is a summary analysis of the environmental impacts of constructing such a reservoir at the Pond Hill site.

The potentially adverse impacts on the environment and community include the following:

- Pond Hill Creek will be permanently altered—about 1.4 miles of it from free flowing to reservoir status, the remaining 0.8 mile to a partially regulated stream with minimum flows maintained.
- About 260 acres of land will be inundated or covered by the embankment. Vegetation in this area will be lost together with some wildlife and other stream bank communities.
- The borrow area within the site boundary will be disturbed and reclaimed, temporarily resulting in an increase in noise and dust.
- Fluctuating water levels, to the extent that the project is used for low-flow augmentation, will result in exposed areas and alter aquatic habitat for the period of drawdown.
- There will be an increase in traffic as workers commute to and from the area during construction.

The potentially beneficial impacts on the environmental and the community include the following:

- The reservoir will provide a makeup water supply to the Susquehanna River during low-flow conditions.
- In the reservoir area there will be an increase in waterfowl, and aquatic and lakeshore wildlife.
- Recreational uses compatible with the reservoir operation and requirements of the habitat will be possible.

In earlier studies, TAMS investigated 13 potential reservoir sites capable of meeting augmentation water supply storage requirements for consumptive water use at the SES. An environmental evaluation of the 13 sites defined the constraints of each with respect to both ecology and the human environment. A technical evaluation identified whether a reservoir could be constructed at each site and determined the approximate cost of construction. The environmental and technical elements were used in combination to determine that Pond Hill was the optimal reservoir site. The environmental assessment was limited to environmental concerns associated with reservoir development which were of particular importance or of potentially significant impact. Each site was analyzed according to 11 factors. The reservoir environmental evaluation matrix for Pond Hill and two alternative sites is shown on Figure 5.7.

5.13 PLANNING AIDS

5.13.1 Types of Planning Aids

Many types of planning aids can be used to facilitate the screening investigations and other studies discussed in this chapter. Some of these aids are required routinely. Other aids permit a more comprehensive and interdisciplinary examination of a study area or allow a perspective that may otherwise not be evident. Finally, some of the techniques can assist the planning process by reducing the amount of technical effort required, particularly when repetitive tasks are needed or where the planning process requires a number of iterations. The planning aids are grouped into the following categories:

- Basic data
- Aerial photos, satellites, and remote sensing
- Generalized estimates
- Overlays and other techniques for suitability mapping
- Computerized data banks and displays

Other planning techniques, which serve both in sophisticated (e.g., mathematical) analysis of alternative plans and as aids to more direct (e.g., judgmental) approaches, are discussed in Chapters 6 and 11 to 16.

5.13.2 Basic Data

Useful information for water resources studies is available from government agencies and nongovernmental entities. Many types of data appear in publications issued on a regular basis. Other data are in agency files, and are made available when requested. The U.S. Bureau of Reclamation manual on *Design of Small Dams* (1973) lists many types of materials together with their sources in the United States. Chapter 4 discussed demographic and economic data and estimates of water demands.

The National Water Data Exchange (NAWDEX) is an interagency computerized program managed and coordinated by the U.S. Geological Survey. A "Master Water Data Index" contains information for over 189,000 surface water sites and over 116,000 groundwater sites at which data are, or have been, collected by almost 400 organizations. The data base may be queried by geographic location, type of data (stream flow, water quality, etc.), specific types of data (biological, chemical, sediment, etc.), and many other criteria. Such data are provided in

Key: Rating as a potential reservoir relative to other sites studied	Sites		
	Pond Hill	Graves Pond Creek	Little Meshoppen Creek
● Good reservoir site ◐ Fair reservoir site ○ Poor reservoir site			
Residential activity 0–2 residences — good 3–6 residences — fair > 6 residences — poor	●	◐	◐
Development below dam 0–5 residences — good 6–15 residences — fair > 15 residences — poor	●	◐	○
Active agricultural land affected 0–25 acres — good 26–75 acres — fair > 75 acres — poor	●	○	●
Agricultural capability of soils within site Predominantly Class IV–VIII — good Significant amount of Class III — fair Significant amount of Class I and II — poor	●	◐	●
Length of stream inundated ≤ 1.5 miles — good 1.6–2.9 miles — fair ≥ 3.0 miles — poor	●	●	○
Stream fishery quality Small (intermittent flow) unstocked — good Other unstocked streams — fair Stocked streams — poor	●	●	◐
Quality of reservoir water source Good to excellent quality — good Fair to good quality — fair Poor to fair quality — poor	○	◐	●
Potential impact on water source Never withdraw more than 10% of flow — good Normally, flows not reduced below long-term median — fair Flows sometimes reduced to conservation flow — poor	●	●	●
Wildlife habitat Worse than average (for sites studied) — good Average quality (for sites studied) — fair Better than average (for sites studied) — poor	○	◐	○
Character/length of water conduit route Tunnel, or pipeline less than 1.0 mile long — good Pipeline 1.0–3.0 miles long — fair Pipeline more than 3.0 miles long or pipeline of any length which traverses sensitive area — poor	◐	●	◐
Area exposed by drawdown < 150 acres — good 150–200 acres — fair > 200 acres — poor	●	◐	○

Figure 5.7 Reservoir environmental evaluation matrix. (From TAMS, 1979.)

statistical summaries or by site location map-plot overlays (Edwards 1980). Uniform procedures have been published by an interagency committee of the U.S. federal government to guide water data collection (U.S. Department of the Interior, Geological Survey, 1977).

5.13.3 Aerial Photos, Satellites, and Remote Sensing

Aerial photos are the basis for most topographic maps used for water resources planning. Ground surveys provide control for the aerial work and are needed for small contour interval mapping for detailed plans. Aerial maps are used for many other purposes, such as agricultural soil classifications and geological interpretations. They can also be used to check details on maps when topography and extent of development are in doubt. Except where dense forest cover obscures large areas from view, airphotos reveal every natural and human-made detail on the ground (U.S. Department of the Interior, Bureau of Reclamation, 1973). Identification of features is facilitated by stereoscopic examination. Virtually the entire area of the United States is covered by aerial photography, most often at a scale of 1:20,000. This scale has been found satisfactory for engineering and geologic interpretation of surface materials. Large-scale photos may be needed for more detailed work, such as for reservoir clearing estimates and geologic reconnaissance mapping of dam sites.

Low-altitude flights to reconnoiter potential project sites are often undertaken, particularly when available maps are deficient, to gain a perspective of potential projects and to assist in the establishment of data collection programs. Such flights can also include photography to document conditions such as human-made developments and water quality problems of interest to water resources planners. The California State Water Resources Control Board's (1978) low-altitude aerial surveillance program has been used to detect point-source pollution discharges and nonpoint sources of water quality problems (erosion and agricultural wastes). Photography is by hand-held, single-lens-reflex, 35-mm cameras using both true- and false-color (infrared) films and occasionally black-and-white films.

High-altitude conventional photography and remote sensing procedures based on aircraft and satellites have found increasing use in recent years. Remote sensing involves the gathering of technical information at spectral or electromagnetic ranges that are beyond the human senses; such imagery requires translation and interpretation into forms that are useful for water resources planning. Some applications have been the following:

- Panchromatic black-and-white, color, and color infrared photographs and thermal infrared imagery for delineating flood boundaries in the southeastern United States (Moore and North 1974)
- Satellite imagery to determine extent of flooding in Louisiana, merging flood maps with computerized land use maps (Schwertz et al. 1976).
- Review of remote sensing techniques for river basin studies, including distribution and seasonal changes, of hydrologic characteristics, land use, population and industry, soils, geology, and stream characteristics; identification of critical areas and integration with mathematical planning models (Link and Shindala 1973)

- Remote sensing via satellite to define input parameters in terms of land cover for urban hydrologic planning models in Virginia (Jackson et al. 1977)
- Satellite image-processing techniques to produce cropland and crop-type statistics for input into agricultural water demand prediction procedures in California (Estes et al. 1978)
- Use of earth-orbiting satellites as a means of collecting hydrologic data from widely dispersed, often remote sites using small transmitters in Canada (Halliday 1979)
- Inventory of inland lakes and human-made impoundments in India by means of satellite data (Thiruvengadachari et al. 1980)
- Prediction of temperatures in discharge plume of thermal power plant, based on surface temperatures obtained by means of infrared imagery, in New York (Cataldo et al. 1978)
- Use of satellite systems in the United States to derive aerial snow cover maps for selected river basins, monitoring river ice breakup, identifying water areas in floods, and making rainfall estimates (McGinnis et al. 1980)

5.13.4 Generalized Estimates

Estimates of materials for construction can be based on plotted curves, nomographs, equations, or other relationships (e.g., for embankment dams as function of height and length; spillways as function of length and capacity; conduits as function of length, diameter, and head; and powerhouse as function of head and capacity). Hydrologic relationships can be generalized for a specific region (e.g., for mean flow as a function of area, variations of flow as a function of mean flow, and reservoir storage as a function of mean flow and maximum time between fillings). Finally, cost relationships are often available (e.g., for treatment plants as a function of capacity and organic removal percentage, hydroelectric power and pumping plants as a function of capacity and head, dams as function of height and type, and wells as a function of capacity and head).

Generalized relationships are available in the literature, or are derived by the water resource planner based on studies of one or more representative sites in the region of study. Once available, they can be used to reduce study effort when many repetitive calculations are needed. Figure 5.8 provides estimates of installed capacity and energy cost for small hydroelectric power stations based on drainage area and head.

Generalized estimates can be computerized and coordinated with water and land data to assist in the screening of project alternatives. The U.S. Army Corps of Engineers has developed an extensive computer-based methodology for area-wide planning studies (MAPS), to assist planners in producing a comprehensive array of alternatives for regional water supply (Walski 1980). The program consists of various modules, including the following:

- Water balance—Given hydrologic and water use data, identifies water source problems, selects capacities of treatment and transmission facilities, and assesses adequacy of existing and proposed reservoirs.

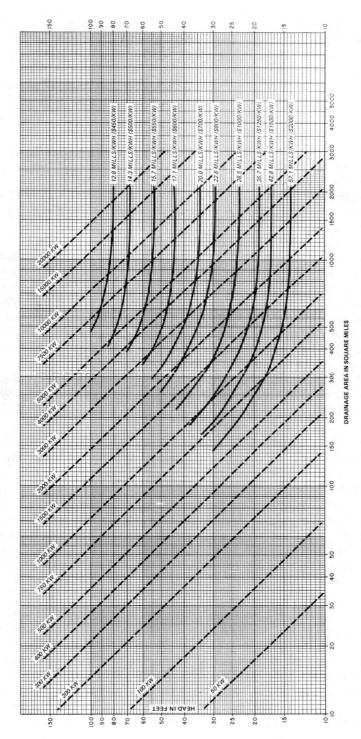

Figure 5.8 Typical maximum installed capacity and minimum energy cost for small hydropower plants at existing dams in the northeastern United States. (From O'Brien et al., 1979.)

- Design modules—Given controlling physical dimensions and flows, carries out engineering calculations to determine economic scale and estimates costs of force mains, gravity mains, open channels, pipelines, pump stations, reservoirs, storage tanks, tunnels, water treatment plants, and well field.
- Hardy-Cross network analysis—Determines heads at nodes and flows in pipes for a looped or tree-structured pipe system.
- Amortization—Computes present worth and annual costs of projects.

5.13.5 Overlays and Other Techniques for Suitability Mapping

McHarg (1968, 1969) is probably the most significant contributor to the development of this approach, which is applicable principally to the land planning aspects of water resources projects.

Transparencies of environmental characteristics are overlaid on a regional base map. Various colors, or various shades of one color, are used to indicate the areal extent and value of each variable (e.g., features of historic value, habitats, geologic features, scarce ecological associations) with respect to its capability or suitability for a specified land use (e.g., conservation, passive recreation, active recreation, residential development, commercial–industrial development, highway routing). These suitability maps for individual land uses can be combined into composite land use maps (e.g., residential and commercial–industrial development, passive and active recreation).

Maps for individual land uses or composite land use can be further combined by superpositioning. Areas of compatibility and conflict can be shown by using various colors and shades of colors to indicate the intensity of compatibility or conflict. Partitioned areas can be rated for their suitability for various purposes using schemes involving numerical scores or combinations of letters and numbers.

The Canadian Department of Regional Economic Expansion (n.d.) has been developing a land inventory covering about 1 million square miles which provides land capability for agriculture, forestry, recreation, and wildlife. Maps at a scale of 1:50,000 and a central computerized data bank are features of this system. The sector maps are based on soil surveys, interpretation of air photos, and field surveys of forest and wildlife resources. Land use planning maps have also been prepared from an analysis of individual sector compatibility maps, supplemented by information on present land use and socioeconomic conditions.

The U.S. Environmental Protection Agency, Region 1 (1978), has suggested that a number of features be evaluated by overlays while preparing environmental assessments for wastewater facility plans in the New England states. These features are shown on Table 5.8. A typical overlay system incorporates five exhibits. The base map shows the planning area boundary with major roads and railroads, and rivers and lakes. Overlays on the base map show the existing and proposed wastewater treatment works, areas not subject to further development, areas whose characteristics inhibit development, and areas with legal or institutional protection.

Map overlays were used for analyzing and aggregating economic and social environmental data in a planning model developed by the Battelle–Columbus

TABLE 5.8 SUGGESTED FEATURES TO BE EVALUATED BY OVERLAY SYSTEMS
(Wastewater facility plans in New England states)

Areas Unlikely to Experience Future Development

1. Fully developed areas
2. Privately owned forests
3. Publicly owned lands

Features That Inhibit Development

1. Slopes unsuitable for development
2. Soil conditions unsuitable for construction
3. Land adjoining certain sites—airports, industrial areas, disposal sites, mines, quarries
4. Hazardous areas

Areas to Be Protected or Enhanced by Legal or Institutional Protection

1. Sole source aquifers
2. Areas of particular scenic value
3. Prime and unique agricultural land
4. Wetlands
5. Endangered species and other significant wildlife habitats
6. Recreation sites
7. Cultural resources
8. Coastal zones
9. Floodplains
10. Wild and Scenic Rivers

Source: U.S. Environmental Protection Agency (1978).

Laboratories for use in the South Carolina coastal zone (Nehman et al. 1975). A Land Use Trade-Off Model (LUTOM) defines locations within a region which are "best" suited for each size and type of desired land use. The methodology aggregates the values from overlays applied to partitioned resource units. Policies defined to constrain development (such as restrictions on use, desirable types and rates of economic growth, and water quality standards) result in no-development ratings or exclusion of some land uses. Economic, environmental, and social suitability of land for various uses is expressed by a numerical score. Finally, compatibility between adjacent land units is analyzed on a scale of 5 to 1 for low to high compatibility. Thus, an industrial, high-pollutant area would having a rating of 5 when considered against a residential area having fewer than three dwelling units per acre. The compatibility indexes are based on considering nine factors grouped in three areas for pollution potential, ecology, and aesthetics.

Map-overlay methods were used in Texas as a planning aid to select a water conveyance canal minimizing environmental impact (Wells et al. 1975). Ten overlay maps were used to show the distribution of the following features throughout the study area: soils, water, vegetation, geology, topography, land use, transportation, cultural and historic areas, human-made structures, and natural resource features. Various shadings corresponding to value ratings were applied to the maps for soils, water, and vegetation. The darkest shadings indicated the highest values that would be affected under the conditions of change induced by construction of the canal. The maps for soils, water, and vegetation were superimposed and the other maps were then laid down in any order. The naked eye, aided by a light-intensity scanner, identified the areas with the darkest spots. Initial "macro-corridors" for the canal were obtained by connecting points having the lowest value points, independent of engineering and operational considerations. A field check was made by means of a low-level flight. This was followed by more detailed analyses to select a final route taking account of engineering and environmental design considerations, including surface and sub-surface drainage, need for stream crossings by the canal, local human and wildlife circulation patterns in areas ajacent to the canal, agricultural systems, environmental aesthetics, and recreation potentials.

Krauskopf and Bunde (1972) extended the concepts of overlays to a computerized method for screening alternative project sites or routes. Under this procedure, a set of factors (determinants) are selected that should influence the location of the facility under consideration; these determinants concern engineering cost and environmental and social impacts. Each determinant is, in turn, described by a model that is a linear function of a number of data variables which should influence it; the variables are grouped into components with the influence of each variable reflected by a weight within the component. The data variables are "objective" data, which are determined on a cellular basis for the entire area under consideration and are kept in computer storage. The data are retrieved to determine the value of each determinant for each cell. This leads to a "determinant surface" in the form of a symbolic map with the highest-value cells, represented by the most dense point character, indicating areas most restrictive to the location of the facility under consideration. "Alternative representation surfaces" may be obtained by combining determinants; this process requires a weighting of the determinants to reflect their relative importance. The method can be used to suggest the most attractive sites or routes. Another approach is to place any facility or route on any alternative or determinant surface and calculate its impact on resources (e.g., acres of land) and its "effective cost" in terms of the values of determinants and combinations of determinants.

A comparative evaluation of methods for producing land suitability maps has been made by Hopkins (1977). He indicates that any method requires: (1) a procedure for identifying parcels of land that are homogeneous; and (2) a procedure for rating these parcels with respect to suitability for each land use. With a *gestalt* method, homogeneous regions are determined through direct field examination or maps without consideration of individual factors such as slopes, soils, vegetation, and so on. *Mathematical combinations* include various methods by which superimposed overlay values are considered, including ordinal methods and linear or nonlinear combinations based on weighting values of the factors. *Factor combination* is based on obtaining a composite map of regions that are homogeneous with respect to all factors and establishing a suitability rating for each of these. *Cluster* analysis is similar except that homogeneous regions are identified by a scheme that involves successive pairing of the most similar sites or groups of sites based on an index of similarity. Other logical combinations are based on *rules of combination* or *hierarchical methods*.

5.13.6 Computerized Data Banks and Displays

Much of the progress in these activities has profited from the research and development work carried on at the Harvard Laboratory for Computer Graphics and Spatial Analysis (1971) and applied in resources planning studies (e.g., U.S. Department of the Army, Corps of Engineers, 1971).

One of the more versatile data management systems is the HEC-SAM system assembled at the Hydrologic Engineering Center of the U.S. Army Corps of Engineers (Davis 1978) for application to comprehensive floodplain studies. This system and others that are discussed in this section consider existing and projected land uses as an important factor in the evaluations that are made; in this respect, they are similar to the overlay techniques described in the preceding section.

As shown by the outline on Figure 5.9, the HEC-SAM system is designed to evaluate present and alternative future basinwide development patterns in terms of flood hazards, economic damage potential, and environmental consequences. Displays are generated in grid or polygon format. The computer programs for detailed planning are standard Corps of Engineers tools that have been in use for a number of years. The system output includes: (1) grid map graphic displays of the data variables, attractiveness, and impact analysis results; and (2) detailed numeric printout of runoff hydrographs, flow exceedence frequency relationships, expected annual damages, storm pollutographs and time traces of erosion, and a range of water quality parameters for the existing and the selected future development patterns. The output corresponds to the complete range of technical output of comprehensive floodplain assessments.

The Louisiana Environmental Management System (LEMS) serves as a central data collection and retrieval system for various state agencies for environmental reviews and other water resource planning activities (Whitehurst et al. 1975). Data from federal and state agency sources are stored and retrieved in relation to the state plane coordinate system. The output may be in the form of tabulations and statistical analyses (from line printers), graphs and maps (from incremental plotters), cathode ray tube images, and automatic three-dimensional drawings. Topographic, hydrologic, and other data from separate sources can be automatically combined and plotted at the same scale into a combined overlay. Available scales are 1:633,600 (1 inch = 10 miles) for statewide distributions, 1:200,000 (1 inch = 3.16 miles) for regional problems, and 1:1,200 (1 inch = 100 feet) for local studies and engineering maps. The system also includes a group of techniques that provide a generalized environmental assessment; for a particular geographic site, the system describes: (1) the current condition; (2) the future condition if the present growth rates and changes remain in effect; and (3) the future condition resulting from selected superimposed processes that interrupt or modify normal national change or cultural growth.

The LEMS system has been used for water quality management planning and for multiple-purpose river basin planning. For studies of the Tensas River Basin, the system provided varying amounts of information (i.e., different amounts of field work and normal operations were required) on the following aspects:

- Historical and archaeological inventories

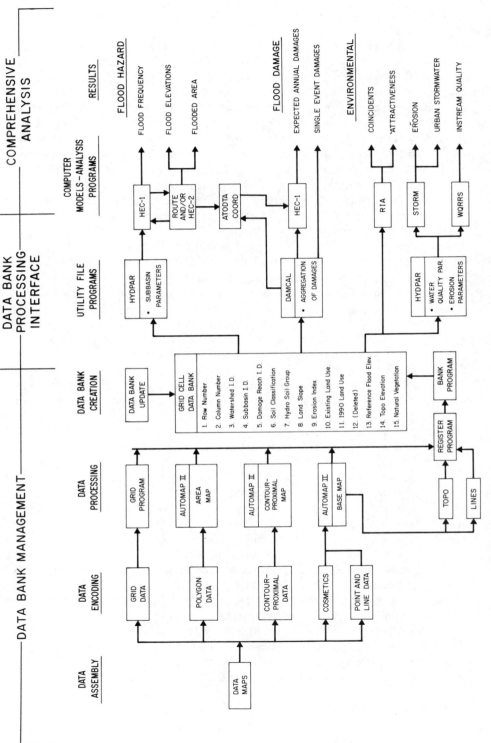

Figure 5.9 Spatial data management and comprehensive analysis system (HEC-SAM). (From Davis, 1978.)

- Demographic and economic statistics
- Land use and land ownership maps
- Transportation, hydrology, and geology
- Ecologically oriented uses
- Recreational uses and aesthetics
- Biological elements (aquatic, terrestrial, and vegetational)
- Impact assessment for proposed action

A land Data Management System (Land DMS) was designed to produce tables and maps for metropolitan land and water resources planning by the Southeastern Wisconsin Regional Planning Commission (SEWRPC). The basic areal unit is a cell having a nominal area of 2.5 acres, whose coordinates are tied to the state plane coordinates. The system has assisted in the planning of "environmental corridors," in the study of diffuse source pollution abatement alternatives, and in the preparation of input data for hydrologic–hydraulic simulation models (Walesh et al. 1977).

In the Menomonee River watershed, the SEWRPC wished to delineate environmental corridors and to devise various means whereby the majority of the area in the corridors could be reserved in an open and essentially natural state. Such corridors have at least three of the following elements: floodlands; soils that are limited for urban development; and wetlands, woodlands, wildlife habit, areas of rugged terrain and large relief, and significant geological formations and physiographic features. Maps needed for this study were produced partly by computer and partly manually. Using a system of value ratings for selected land types, the land DMS was programmed to determine the sum of the assigned numerical values for each cell in the watershed and to produce a map on which the point total was shown for each cell having one or more corridor elements. This map was supplemented manually with information relative to rugged terrain and high-relief topography, significant geological formations and physiographic features, potential outdoor recreation and related open-space sites, historic sites and structures, and scenic areas and vistas.

The ADAPT (Areal Design and Planning Tool) system was developed and applied to water quality management studies of the lower James River in Virginia (Grayman et al. 1975). The system consists of a computer file system, a series of mathematical submodels, and a set of display routines for producing computer-generated maps. These maps are based on information stored in the data file or determined by the various submodels. Information is stored for each Unit Planning Area (UPA) in a triangulated representation obtained by "digitizing" the topography (Figure 5.10).

Each triangle is referenced individually and as part of a subarea such as a drainage basin or political jurisdiction. For purposes of land-based designs, information stored for each triangle included depth to bedrock, depth to water table, existing sewers, type and intensity of present land use, and as projected at 10-year intervals. Three-dimensional maps were computer generated for topography and land values. The model was used for the planning of sewers and treatment facilities and to determine the effect of waste discharges on the water quality of the stream.

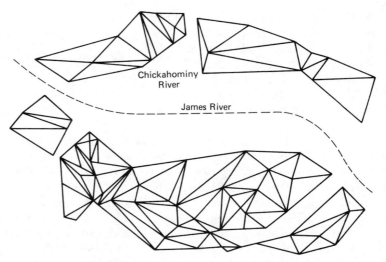

Chickahominy
River

James River

Figure 5.10 Triangulated representation of topographical map. (From Grayman et al., 1975.)

REFERENCES

AGGERHOLM, D., "Environmental Impact Statements—The Policy Practice Gap," U.S. Army, Corps of Engineers, Institute for Water Resources, 1972.

BISWAS, ASIT K., "Environment and Water Development in Third World," *J. Water Resources Plann. Manage. Div., Proc. Am. Soc. Civil Eng.*, vol. 106, no. WR1, March 1980.

BOWDEN, N.W., "Multiple Purpose Reservoir Operation," *Civil Eng.*, November 1941.

CALIFORNIA STATE WATER RESOURCES CONTROL BOARD, "Manual of Practice—Low Altitude Aerial Surveillance for Water Resources Control," July 1978.

CANADIAN DEPARTMENT OF REGIONAL ECONOMIC EXPANSION, "A Guide for Resource Planning, the Canada Land Survey," n.d.

CATALDO, JOSEPH C., RICHARD R. ZAVESKY, and ALVIN S. GOODMAN, "Prediction of Temperatures Due to Heated Discharges," *J. Power Div., Proc. Am. Soc. Civil Eng.*, vol. 104, no. PO2, April 1978.

DAVIS, DARRYL W., "Comprehensive Flood Plain Studies Using Spatial Data Management Techniques," *Water Resources Bull.*, vol. 14, no. 3, June 1978.

EDWARDS, MELVIN D., "Water Data and Services Available from Participants in the National Water Data Exchange," *Water Resources Bull.*, vol. 16, no. 1, February 1980.

ESTES, JOHN E., JOHN R. JENSEN, and LARRY R. TINNEY, "Remote Sensing of Agricultural Water Demand Information: A California Study," *Water Resources Res.*, vol. 14, no. 2, April 1978.

FAIRCHILD, WARREN D., "Planning Water Resource Projects to Maximize Environmental Benefits," *Am. Soc. Civil Eng., Nat. Meet. Water Resources Eng.* , 1973.

FREEMAN, C. N., and J. H. DIXON, "Inland Site Location in the Northeast with Emphasis on Water Supply Needs," in *Civil and Environmental Aspects of Energy Complexes*, A. S. Goodman, ed., American Society of Civil Engineers, New York, 1976.

GOODMAN, ALVIN, S., and ANDRZEJ JEZIERSKI, "Master Plan for Water Supply, Kingston, Jamaica," *Water Resources Plann. Manage. Div. Am. Soc. Civil Eng., Spec. Conf. Water Syst.*, Houston, 1979.

GRAYMAN, WALTER M., R. M. MALES, W. E. GATES, and A. W. HADDER, "Land Based Modeling System for Water Quality Management Studies," *J. Hydraul. Div., Proc. Am. Soc. Civil Eng.*, vol. 101, no. HY5, May 1975.

HAGAN, ROBERT M., and EDWIN B. ROBERTS, "Ecological Impacts of Water Projects in California," *J. Irrig. Drain. Div., Proc. Am. Soc. Civil Eng.*, paper 8780, no. IR1, March 1972.

HALLIDAY, ROBERT A., "Satellite Data Collection in Canada," *Am. Soc. Civil Eng. Conv.*, Boston, April 1979.

HARVARD UNIVERSITY LABORATORY FOR COMPUTER GRAPHICS AND SPATIAL ANALYSIS, SYMVU Manual," Cambridge, Mass., 1971.

HAYES, RICHARD O., "Impact of Water Resources on Vector-Borne Disease," *J. Water Resources Plann. Manage. Div., Proc. Am. Soc. Civil Eng.*, vol. 102, no. WR2, November 1976.

HOPKINS, LEWIS D., "Methods for Generating Land Suitability Maps: A Comparative Evaluation," *Am. Inst. Plann. J.*, October 1977.

JACKSON, THOMAS J., ROBERT M. RAGAN, and WILLIAM N. FITCH, "Test of Landsat Based Urban Hydrologic Modeling," *J. Water Resources Plann. Manage. Div.*, Proc. Am. Soc. Civil Eng., vol. 103, no. WR1, May 1977.

JOPLING, David C., "Plant Site Evaluation Using Numerical Ratings," *Power Eng.*, March 1974.

KEATING, WILLIAM H., "Construction of Reclamation Projects to Enhance Environment," *Am. Soc. Civil Eng., Nat. Meet. Water Resources Eng.*, 1973.

KRAUSKOPF, THOMAS M., and DENNIS C. BUNDE, "Evaluation of Environment Impact through a Computer Modelling Process," in *Environmental Impact Analysis: Philosophy and Methods*, Robert Ditton and Thomas Goodale, eds., University of Wisconsin Sea Grant Program, 1972.

LAGLER, KARL F., ed., "Man-Made Lakes—Planning and Development," U.N. Development Programme, FAO, Rome, 1969.

LINK, L. E., and ADNAN SHINDALA, "Utilization of Remote Sensing in River Basin Studies," *Water Resources Bull.*, vol. 9, no. 5, October 1973.

ARTHUR D. LITTLE, INC., "Transportation and Environment, Synthesis for Action—Impact of National Environmental Policy Act of 1969 on the Department of Transportation," vol. I, Washington, D.C., 1971.

MCGINNIS, DAVID F., JR., R. A. SCOFIELD, S. R. SCHNEIDER, and C. P. BERG, "Satellites as Aid to Water Resource Managers," *J. Water Resources Plann. Manage. Div. Proc. Am. Soc. Civil Eng.*, vol. 106, no. WR1, March 1980.

MCHARG, IAN, "A Comprehensive Highway Route—Selection," *Highway Res. Rec. 246*, 1968.

MCHARG, IAN, *Design with Nature*, Natural History Press, New York, 1969.

MOORE, GERALD K., and GARY W. NORTH, "Flood Inundation in the Southeastern United States from Aircraft and Satellite Imagery," *Water Resources Bull.*, vol. 10, no. 5, October 1974.

NEHMAN, GERALD, G. BOLES, N. DEE, and J. GRIFFIN, "Land Use and Environmental Planning:

An application in the South Carolina Coastal Zone," *Water Resources Bull.*, vol. 11, no. 4, August 1975.

O'BRIEN, EUGENE, ALEXANDER C. GEORGE, and CLAYTON C. PURDY, "Evaluation of Small Hydroelectric Potential," Tippetts-Abbett-McCarthy-Stratton, New York, April 1979.

ORTOLANO, LEONARD, ed., "Analyzing the Environmental Impacts of Water Projects," Stanford University, Dept. of Civil Engineering, March 1973.

SCHWERTZ, EDDIE, L., JR., BRADLEY E. SPICER, and HENRY T. SVEHLAK, "Near Real-Time Mapping of the 1975 Mississippi River Flood in Louisiana Using Landsat Imagery," *Water Resources Bull.*, vol. 12, no. 6, December 1976.

STAMM, GILBERT G., "Managing Water Resources Projects to Maintain Environmental Benefits," *Am. Soc. Civil Eng., Nat. Meet. Water Resources Eng.*, 1973.

TAMS (Tippetts-Abbett-McCarthy-Stratton, New York, and Mattis Demain Beckford & Associates Ltd., Kingston), "Comparative Study of Water Supply Projects for Kingston and Surrounding Area," July 1977.

TAMS (Tippetts-Abbett-McCarthy-Stratton, New York, and Massachusetts Institute of Technology, Cambridge), "Integrated Development of the Vardar/Axios River Basin—Yugoslavia–Greece," December 1978.

TAMS (Tippetts-Abbett-McCarthy-Stratton, New York), "Environmental Report, Pond Hill Reservoir," February 1979.

THIRUVENGADACHARI, S., P. S. RAO, and K. R. RAO, "Surface Water Inventory through Satellite Sensing," *J. Water Resources Plann. Manage. Div., Proc. Am. Soc. Civil Eng.*, vol. 106, no. WR2, July 1980.

U.S. DEPARTMENT OF THE ARMY, Corps of Engineers, Institute for Water Resources, "Honey Hill, a Systems Analysis for Planning the Multiple Use of Controlled Water Areas," IWR Rep. 71–9, 1971.

U.S. DEPARTMENT OF THE INTERIOR, Bureau of Reclamation, *Design of Small Dams*, 2nd ed., U.S. Government Printing Office, Washington, D.C., 1973.

U.S. DEPARTMENT OF THE INTERIOR, Geological Survey, "National Handbook of Recommended Methods of Water-Data Acquisition," 1977.

U.S. ENVIRONMENTAL PROTECTION AGENCY, "Guidelines for Areawide Waste Treatment Management Planning," 1975.

U.S. ENVIRONMENTAL PROTECTION AGENCY, Region 1, "Environmental Assessment Manual," June 1978.

U.S. NATIONAL WATER COMMISSION, "New Directions in U.S. Water Policy," June 28, 1973a.

U.S. NATIONAL WATER COMMISSION, "Policies for the Future," 1973b.

U.S. SENATE COMMITTEE ON PUBLIC WORKS, 34th Cong., 2nd sess., Hearings on S. 2770, Sect. 404, Proposed Amendments to the Federal Water Pollution Control Act, 1976.

WALESH, STUART G., LOIS A. KAWATSKI, and PAUL J. CLAVETTE, "Land Data Management System for Resource Planning," *J. Water Resource Plann. Manage. Div., Proc. Am. Soc. Civil Eng.*, vol. 103, no. WR2, November 1977.

WALSKI, THOMAS M., "Maps—A Planning Tool for Corps of Engineers Regional Water Supply Studies," *Water Resources Bull.*, vol. 16, no. 2, April 1980.

WELLS, DAN W., et al., "Procedure for Selecting a Minimal Environmental Impact Routing for a Water Conveyance Canal," *Water Resources Bull.*, vol. 11, no. 4, August 1975.

WHITEHURST, CHARLES A., ELVIN J. DANTIN, and DONALD HARANG, "The Louisiana Environmental Management System and Its Utility in Water Resource Planning," *Water Resources Bull.*, vol. 11, no. 4, August 1975.

WILDRICK, J., et al., "Urban Water Runoff and Water Quality Control," Virginia Water Resources Research Center, 1976.

WILLIAMS, C., "The Influence of Environmental Law on Nebraska Land Use," *Nebr. Law Rev.*, no. 57, 1978.

SIX

Comprehensive Regional Planning

6.1 SCOPE

Chapter 5 described various methodologies for identifying and performing preliminary analyses of projects in a region. This chapter discusses the planning process
extending from these preliminary studies through the preparation of a plan for
developing and managing the water resources in a region. Such a plan can emphasize
either single-purpose or multipurpose development. The following are usually
established for each component unit of the plan: scale, principal operational
characteristics, relationship with other units when all are operated as a system, and
schedule for implementation. Single purpose regional plans are discussed for
municipal and industrial water supply and for water quality management. A
multipurpose regional plan is described which considers irrigation, power, municipal
and industrial water supply, water quality, and flood control. The chapter also
describes a framework analysis at a national level which includes a study of water
balances and the identification of critical water-related problems.

6.2 DEFINITIONS OF MASTER, COMPREHENSIVE, AND INTEGRATED PLANNING

In water resources planning, *master planning* is the formulation of a phased
development plan to: (1) meet the estimated requirements for a single water resource
purpose over a specified period of time; or (2) exploit the opportunities for single and

multipurpose water resource projects in a defined geographic area over a specific period of time or until all justified projects are completed. The plan can include a single project in various phases or a multiunit system of projects, and can encompass both structural and nonstructural elements. When the studies involve multiunit, multipurpose, and multiobjective planning, and consideration of both structural and nonstructural alternatives, the terms *comprehensive planning* or *integrated planning* are often applied.

Regional plans of this type often include a schedule showing the phased development of programs; sufficient information on the characteristics of each project to indicate clearly general physical arrangements, scale, controlling parameters (such as dam elevation, capacities, etc.); and a schedule of investment costs. They may also include concise statements or tables summarizing contributions to specified planning objectives and project impacts (economic, environmental, social, and others).

These plans are based on a review of previous reports on individual projects; on discussions with planners in governmental agencies and other organizations, and with private individuals; on the results of screening studies; and on topographic, geological, hydrologic, and other information. In many instances, previous studies must be reevaluated and new groupings, stagings, and modifications of physical features must be made to achieve the desired formulations.

Master (or comprehensive, or integrated) planning studies do not include detailed "feasibility" report studies of individual projects which are needed for final authorization and financing of projects. Such studies may already have been completed before or during the master plan studies because of earlier initiatives by various organizations. If so, they should be made consistent with the master plan.

6.3 OUTLINE OF A COMPREHENSIVE PLANNING REPORT FOR A RIVER BASIN

This section outlines a recommended composition of a report that is a synthesis of various comprehensive planning studies for river basins carried out in the United States (e.g., Allegheny River Basin, 1971) and other countries, both industrialized and developing. For a specific project, the outline should be modified to take account of local factors such as: (1) the organization sponsoring the studies and its planning objectives; (2) the planning criteria that may already by established by governmental (regional, national, international) authorities or special institutions (e.g., the World Bank); (3) the economic sectors (industrial, agriculture, etc.) in the region and their existing development; (4) types of needs and opportunities for water resources development; and (5) other factors (legal, economic, environmental, social, etc.) that are important to planning.

A summary section (often referred to as an *Executive Summary*) should be placed at the beginning of the report. This contains a brief description of the studies and presents the principal conclusions and recommendations. It provides an introduction to the remainder of the report by giving an overall perspective of the studies. Its importance is indicated by the fact that it may be the only planning document read by decision makers and policy reviewers who do not have the time or responsibility to examine the planning analyses supporting the recommendations. Information should include location, drainage area, and other principal physical features of the study area; water resources needs and opportunities for municipal and industrial water supply, water quality management, and other project purposes; compact descriptions and/or tables summarizing the single- and multipurpose projects with their structural and nonstructural elements constituting the proposed comprehensive plan; and recommendations for further studies if any. The report as a whole includes details on the above and the study methodologies.

Chapter I (*Introduction*) should discuss the study objectives; outline the scope of the studies and report; state the authorization for the work; make reference to the previous reports and studies bearing on the project; and include appropriate acknowledgments of cooperating organizations and individuals.

Chapter II (*Planning Principles*) should discuss the planning objectives (e.g., adequate water supply, economic development, increased employment opportunities, environmental protection and conservation); legal and other constraints relating to water and related land resources; and planning criteria (e.g., benefit-cost, interest rate, water quality standards). The general planning methodology should also be described. The detailed methodologies should be described by means of tables, graphics, other exhibits, and discussions in the chapters that follow.

Chapter III (*Study Area and Economic Profile*) should describe the study area (location, drainage area, political and geographic subdivisions, general topography and vegetation, pattern of streams and other water bodies, important urban centers, etc.). An economic profile should include data on existing conditions and projections for population and employment; manufacturing, commerce, recreation, and other activities with economic impact; and supporting infrastructure such as transportation routes, communications, and water and power distribution.

Chapter IV (*Water Resources Needs*) should analyze the current status and projected needs for project purposes (municipal and industrial water supply, water quality management, floodplain management, electric power, etc.). In this sense, the term "needs" comprehends both "basic needs" and reasonable "aspirations." This chapter presents information on existing problems (e.g., floods and droughts), and the new or more intensified problems expected in the future due to economic growth, degradation by wastes, increasing demand for services to meet expectations for a higher standard of living, and other important changes in the river basin.

Chapter V (*Water Resources Opportunities*) should assess the surface water resources (location, precipitation pattern, runoff pattern, floods, low flows, withdrawals, degree of existing flow regulation, opportunities for increased flow regulation); the groundwater resources (location, variations of groundwater surface, withdrawals, estimates of yield, extent of physical connection with surface waters and opportunities for conjunctive use); the existing and potential reservoir sites (location, area and capacity, effect on downstream flows, availability of sites for single and multipurpose development); and the opportunities for nonstructural management (floodplain zoning, water conservation, and other measures).

Chapter VI (*Plan Alternatives*) should present information on various plans for single- and multipurpose development, including structural and nonstructural measures that meet (partially or fully) the planning objectives, constraints, and criteria. At this level, the assessment is approximate but should reflect enough study work to enable preliminary comparisons (e.g., site location, range of scale and construction cost, and capacity to provide water, power, and other services so that the extent of meeting needs and rough unit costs can be judged). Plans should be eliminated that cannot be implemented because of gross defects such as excessive unit costs or conflict with extensive existing development. Reconnaissance-level environmental and social assessments may be appropriate for these studies to identify the possible impacts on nonengineering/economic objectives and thus to help indicate the range of choice in comprehensive planning. The involvement of various government agencies, private organizations, and the general public may be required or desirable for establishing and/or reviewing the formulations; for certain types of projects, the public involvement program may be defined by law.

Chapter VII (*Recommended Plans*) should describe the proposed plans and should provide information on the analyses leading to their selection. These include project layouts, cost estimates, economic (and perhaps financial) analyses, and environmental and social assessments at the level needed for these studies.

Chapter VIII (*Project Implementation*) should include a schedule for the implementation of the various projects staged to meet the needs, and the annual capital investments that must be provided. Recommendations should also be included on unresolved problems that should be studied; and on the feasibility reports, applications for licenses and permits, and other documents that will be required before final approval and implementation of the projects. Of particular importance is an analysis of the organization, professional personnel, and outside consultants needed to perform final planning, design, construction, and operation.

The next several sections describe master (or comprehensive, or integrated) planning studies that have actually been carried out, with various degrees of sophistication and adherence to the scope of the outline above.

6.4 MASTER PLAN OF SINGLE-PURPOSE PROJECTS TO MEET MUNICIPAL WATER SUPPLY NEEDS

Master plans may be formulated for a single purpose or for multiple purposes. As an example of a single-purpose master plan, Chapter 5 described the studies of water supplies to meet the needs of Kingston, the capital city of Jamaica (TAMS, 1977). As discussed in Chapter 5, screening studies considered six major surface water supply schemes and three groundwater sources. The resulting recommendations provided for a first-stage priority project and a phased master plan to beyond the year 2000. Tables in that chapter showed the estimated yields and costs for each of the surface water supply projects. Figures showed the presentation style for the layout, cost estimates, and schedule of projects.

6.5 INTEGRATED PLAN OF SINGLE- AND MULTIPURPOSE PROJECTS TO MEET VARIOUS NEEDS IN A SPECIFIED GEOGRAPHIC AREA

The following discussion draws on the Executive Summary volume of a report prepared for the United Nations on the integrated development of the 24,000-square kilometer Vardar/Axios River Basin in Yugoslavia and Greece (TAMS, 1978). The master plan formulation for the basin considered over 150 projects for municipal and industrial water supply, cooling water for thermal power plants, irrigation, hydro-power, maintenance of water quality, flood control, recreation, and navigation.

General Concepts of Integrated Development. The integrated development of the Vardar/Axios Basin includes a system of projects scheduled to meet the needs and aspirations of Yugoslavia [in particular, the Socialist Republic of Macedonia (SRM)] and Greece. It includes recommendations for cost-sharing arrangements (see Chapter 8 of this book for the methodology employed for such recommendations). Institutional, managerial, and financial arrangements were not part of the studies. Legal, social, and environmental impacts were not fully analyzed but were taken into account in some planning criteria.

The considerations that guided the detailed methodology for formulating the master plan included: economic sector development (principally agricultural, municipal and industrial, and electric power); balanced regional development; engineering and economic feasibility of facilities; and compatibility with existing power and hydraulic systems.

Each water resource development project differs from other projects in its regulation of flows, water supply withdrawals, and consumption of water. Its hydrologic reliability and economic performance depend on the flows available to it, which are often modified by projects upstream. The project, in turn, affects the operation of other projects which are downstream. In order to account properly for these interrelationships and to test plans for integrated development, systems analyses were made. After hydrologic and economic analyses were made for each project individually, systems analyses were used to study subbasins and the entire Vardar/Axios basin from these standpoints. Project configurations for 1985, 2000, and 2025 were considered appropriate for both short- and long-term assessments.

For the formulation of a basin plan and a schedule for implementing projects, the preferences expressed by a Coordinating Directorate composed of representatives of Yugoslavia and Greece (working through a UN Project Manager and two Co-Managers representing the individual governments) were followed as closely as practicable. In some cases, adjustments were made to improve reliability with the available water. Priorities of project purposes such as municipal and industrial water supplies, irrigation, and hydroelectric power were taken into account where water was limited and it was necessary to change the size or operation of some projects. In determining whether projects were satisfactory from a hydrologic standpoint, criteria were established in terms of the percentage of time that water requirement targets were met.

In general, the ultimate development of the projects was considered close to the maximum size proposed in the engineering reports made available for the master plan studies by the governments. It was concluded that with some exceptions, there was enough water in the basin to meet the contemplated goals for irrigation and other needs with integrated development.

Basin Planning Approach. An essential preliminary step in the planning of the development of the basin was an assessment of the water requirements throughout the basin in the years 1985, 2000, and 2025 as well as an assessment of water available in the basin and of potential hydraulic works.

The master plan was developed in a series of steps, generally proceeding from individual project examination, through subbasin studies, to complete basin simulations. Because of the very large number of projects to be considered and the complexity of their interactions, it was necessary to adopt computerized techniques of analysis.

Early in the study, a schematic diagram was prepared indicating existing and potential projects, the sources of their water supplies, and their interconnections with the river system and other projects. This diagram is too detailed for reproduction here, but Figure 6.1 shows the structure of such a diagram. This work was accomplished by the completion of an inventory, examination of reports and other information documents, and evaluation of principal project features.

The work described above, referred to as "preliminary screening," is discussed in Chapter 5 of this book. These techniques, together with additional data processing, defined the basic system of projects and the physical and economic data needed for comprehensive systems analysis. Economic and financial criteria applying to the systems analysis, and other planning considerations were taken into account in the course of formulating the master plan.

Computer Analyses. Prior to undertaking the simulation for the entire basin, water balance analyses were carried out for each project at a subbasin level. These subbasin analyses resulted in adjustments to the required capacities of reservoirs and the modification of irrigation projects to be compatible with available water supplies. These investigations were also useful in providing an initial evaluation of the project configurations and interrelationships comprehended by the schematic diagram mentioned above, and led to the evaluation of basin configurations by simulation models called MITTAMS and EXTG1. These models accommodated a large number of projects and an enormous quantity of data, and provided measures of performance in hydrologic and economic terms. They were also effective in accounting for the complementarity between projects and purposes (for example, water used in a reservoir for hydropower and for recreation can be released for use in other projects downstream).

The simulation models reproduced the interactions among the elements of the system and described the outcome of operating the system under a given set of inputs and operating assumptions. By successive and systematic runs of the models, the response to the variations in inputs or operating conditions or both were evaluated.

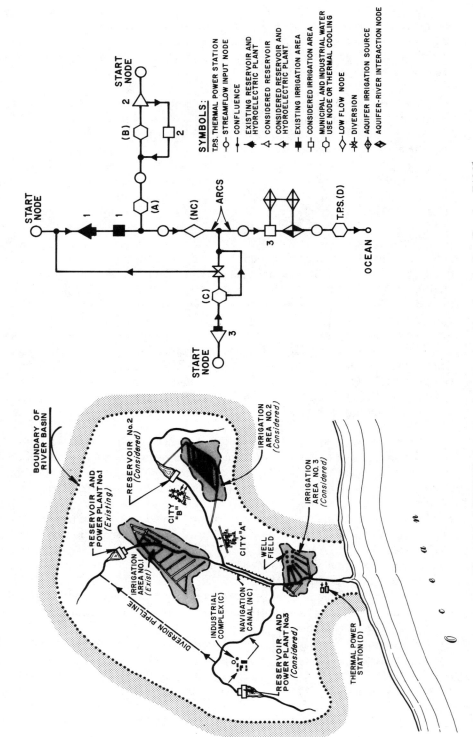

SYMBOLS:

T.P.S. THERMAL POWER STATION

—○— STREAMFLOW INPUT NODE

—●— CONFLUENCE

◄ EXISTING RESERVOIR AND HYDROELECTRIC PLANT

△ CONSIDERED RESERVOIR

◁ CONSIDERED RESERVOIR AND HYDROELECTRIC PLANT

■ EXISTING IRRIGATION AREA

▣ CONSIDERED IRRIGATION AREA

□ MUNICIPAL AND INDUSTRIAL WATER USE NODE OR THERMAL COOLING

◇ LOW FLOW NODE

◇ DIVERSION

◈ AQUIFER IRRIGATION SOURCE

◈ AQUIFER-RIVER INTERACTION NODE

Figure 6.1 MITTAMS. A water resource system and its schematization. (Based on TAMS, 1978.)

When used in conjunction with engineering and economic criteria, the results of these runs allowed: (1) the systematic comparison of alternative configurations of water resources projects in the basin; and (2) the evaluation of the effect of the upstream development on the flows at the border and the consequent downstream development.

Twelve models were used to prepare input data and to carry out the simulation studies. They are summarized in the following list.

Program Code	Purpose
MITTAMS	Large-time-increment (one month) simulation program for evaluating the hydrological and economic consequences of various plans in a multiunit, multipurpose basin project. A multiyear historic or synthetic hydrologic record was used for the Vardar portion of the basin.
EXTGW1	Extension of MITTAMS to consider conjunctive use of surface water and groundwater through a finite difference integration of the fundamental equations of groundwater flow. Used for the Axios portion of the basin, with border flows obtained from MITTAMS and with corresponding hydrologic record for the Axios portion of the basin.
AQUIFEM	Finite-element model of groundwater flow, for short-time-interval integration of the fundamental equations of groundwater flow. Used for the Axios portion of the aquifers for data assessment, reconciliation of data, simulation of past conditions, and forecast of the response of the aquifers to massive pumping. Results provided input data for EXTGW1.
ALUCEM	Agricultural Land Use Capability Estimation Model for processing and analyzing agricultural data for river basin and economic sector studies. Data banks were created to obtain crop and livestock budgets, budget summaries, and project summaries of costs and income. Water requirement estimates were made.
REAP	Cost analysis program for projects in the basin which determined investment and annual costs, in financial and economic terms, including adjustments for interest during construction and shadow pricing.
IPSUB	Subbasin hydrologic reliability program, used in screening studies, to obtain hydrologically reliable subsystems for inclusion in MITTAMS model.
EPA	Steady-state water quality simulation model, utilizing the Streeter–Phelps equations, for analysis of the biochemical oxygen demand and dissolved oxygen conditions in the main river and its tributaries.
PUDDLES	Runge–Kutta integration of the storage equation, for routing of floods in reservoirs.
MULTIPLE CORRELATION MODEL	Used to fill the gaps of some hydrologic records by correlation with simultaneous records at several other stations.
FLOW GENERATION MODEL	Model for generating simultaneous synthetic records at characteristic stations, through first-order Markov chain and cross-correlation techniques.
HIMP	Used to determine flows at start nodes for the MITTAMS and EXTGW1 models, through correlations with the records at characteristic stations and other stations used in the analysis.
BENNY	Used to determine the unit cost of services, for individual projects, using financial prices.

Planning Considerations. In developing the master plan for the Vardar/Axios River Basin, several considerations appeared appropriate for multiunit, multiobjective planning in the SRM and Greece. In the formulation of individual projects, and of a balanced system of projects within the context of an optimum basin plan, attention was given to the following broad planning categories.

1. *Economic Sector Development.* The planning emphasized the need to develop the basin *agricultural sector* to the maximum extent compatible with the availability of land and water. Areas that are suitable for irrigation were identified by SRM and Greek agricultural planning organizations, and cropping patterns were selected by the planners with the assistance of counterpart agricultural experts. The selections in many cases reflected not only efficiencies with respect to land capabilities and markets but, for certain crops such as rice, recognized other objectives—regional preferences and the desire to be independent of imports. This led to the projections of water requirements and financial and economic estimates. In subsequent subbasin and overall basin systems analyses, the irrigation projects were retained at full development scale, except when water shortages were severe enough to reduce hydrologic reliability and economic performance to unacceptable levels. Agricultural development should result in the improvement of the standard of living of the population of the region, both rural and urban; contribute to regional indepen-dence by reducing imports and increasing the potential for exports; and increase farm employment and related agro-processing opportunities, and thus enhance the stability of rural activities and discourage excessive migration to urban areas. Shadow pricing procedures (see Chapters 8 and 10) in the economic analyses of agricultural projects adjusted the values of unskilled labor, imported materials, and agricultural products that may be exported or substituted for imports.

Importance was also placed on growth in the *industrial sector* and related urban growth. These requirements, from a water resources standpoint, were expressed in terms of municipal and industrial water supplies, criteria for water quality manage-ment, and cooling water supplies for thermal power generation. In most parts of the basin, adequate water supplies can be obtained for these needs. Where conflicts might occur among various purposes, special efforts were made in the planning procedures to resolve them. For example, the study of alternative systems showed that the dependability of water for thermal power generation could be improved by relocating one or more proposed generating units. For the few places where serious deficiencies would remain with respect to municipal and industrial water supply or stream water quality, recommendations were made for additional groundwater exploration and for wastewater treatment. Some recommendations were also made to transfer certain industrial demands from water deficient to surplus areas.

It was recognized that the development of the *electric power sector* must proceed parallel with the growth of agriculture and industry. Since there is the option of thermal power, multipurpose reservoirs (except for one reservoir having an important flood control function) would be operated so that the production of hydroelectric power would generally be subordinate to the release of water supplies for irrigation and for municipal and industrial purposes. Within physical and hydrologic limitations, the reservoirs and hydroelectric power projects were planned for maximum development. Dependable (or firm) energy output in kilowatt-hours per month for each plant was determined by computer simulation analyses as a function of water available 95% of the time on a monthly basis. Dependable (or firm) capacity in megawatts was determined as a function of dependable energy and plant capacity factor appropriate for electric system service. The best installed capacity for each plant should be selected by the regional electric power enterprise based on these studies and electrical systems considerations. Using this approach, the major hydroelectric plants were justified at the maximum hydrologic levels as having benefit-cost ratios exceeding unity. In the economic analyses of hydroelectric projects, careful attention was given to shadow pricing of the hydroelectric works that require substantial foreign exchange and of the thermal alternatives used for benefit estimates that require imported fuel (see Chapters 8 and 10). For this purpose, existing lignite reserves were assumed to be adequate only for already projected thermal plants and not for substitutes for hydroelectric plants.

The benefit-cost ratios computed for the hydroelectric plants were minimum estimates since they account only partially for the values of such plants in power system operations to accommodate rapid and fluctuating changes in power demand or in enhancing the stability of the electric system. Thus, a benefit-cost ratio for a hydroelectric project close to unity did not necessarily indicate that a project just passed the test for economic feasibility. Minor hydroelectric projects at reservoirs constructed essentially for irrigation showed variable performance from hydrologic and economic standpoints.

Irrigation, municipal and industrial and cooling water supplies, and hydro-electric power facilities are the principal purposes of development. Flood control, recreation, and navigation were also included as purposes of development. Flood control and recreation would share reservoir costs and provide benefits but would not generally have a major effect on the selection and formulation of multipurpose projects. Inclusion of navigation would have a major effect only in the operation of one reservoir which would have to provide all its water supply to navigation rather than irrigation.

2. *Balanced Regional Development.* The river basin is naturally divided into independent regions of different sizes, separated by mountains and constituting entities with their own populations and resources. Although some regions are better endowed with water resources than others, it was considered that there was much merit, where possible, in distributing projects among the separate regions and implementing them according to a schedule that would not weigh heavily in favor of one region over another. The implementation of these projects by 1985, 2000, or 2025 was assumed for basin systems analyses largely in accordance with the preferences of the Coordinating Directorate. Also, any reductions of project size (particularly irrigation) that would improve benefit-cost ratio or increase reliability with respect to water availability were made very cautiously, recognizing that there might be conflicts with regional plans and aspirations.

An initial project schedule for construction was prepared on the basis of priority according to benefit-cost ratio. It was realized that such an approach alone would not adequately reflect social goals. Thus, this schedule was modified following receipt of the views of the Coordinating Directorate. The resulting schedule was part of the recommended master plan that was subjected to final economic and financial analysis.

3. *Engineering and Economic Feasibility.* Engineering and economic data

were presented in the report for evaluation of projects, individually and in terms of basin performance. Most of this information required processing to adjust data to make them suitable for systems analyses (see Section 5.7). Engineering reviews were used to recommend changes in physical project features and to indicate changes in cost estimates. Prior to the studies for this report, the projects had been studied by others within a limited framework for hydrologic and economic feasibility. The systems analyses, performed at subbasin and basin levels, provided additional results by which to judge hydrologic and economic feasibility.

Economic analyses were based on comparisons of benefits and costs that were adjusted by shadow pricing. Shadow prices reflect adjustments to financial values where market prices do not indicate the true costs to the national economy. (See Chapter 8 for further discussion of the economic analyses.) Indicators of economic viability that were considered included:

- Benefit-cost ratio
- Net benefits (benefits minus costs)
- Internal rate of return

4. *Financial Implications.* A project, if it has an economic benefit-cost ratio greater than 1, is justified from a national standpoint provided that the services of such a project are considered of high enough priority for implementation compared with the use of valuable resources for other purposes. However, the results of the benefit-cost analyses do not provide sufficient information on financial viability during the course of each project's actual construction and operation, as discussed below.

In the preparation of a schedule of overall expenditures it was assumed that the capital necessary for investment in the projects of the master plan would not be a constraint in selecting and scheduling projects. This assumption appeared reasonable, based on discussions with the UN Project Manager and the Co-Managers. Such an assumption, however, may require reconsideration in any negotiations between the countries and when each government considers projects for five-year plans and similar documents.

For each project in the master plan the average unit cost of services was estimated. In each case where a project was recommended for inclusion in the master plan, it was justified in terms of improved agricultural income for irrigation, or when compared with alternative methods of providing services for other types of projects. However, the cost of water or power may appear high when compared with existing projects, since new projects usually cost more than projects already paid for or fully subsidized or built when construction costs were much lower.

Financial analyses, on an annual basis, of all costs, revenues, and subsidies were not carried out but will be needed before a financial decision for implementation is made for each project.

In addition to the planning categories discussed above (economic sector development, balanced regional development, engineering and economic feasibility, and financial implications), the planners considered several other types of criteria for project evaluation, as discussed below.

Priorities and Reliability Criteria. *Priorities* were established for the several demands upon basin flows, following discussions with each of the Co-Managers. In order of priority, the major water demands for the SRM were as follows:

- Municipal and industrial
- Thermal cooling for power plants
- Irrigation
- Hydropower
- Maintenance of water quality

Some water will be supplied from Axios Basin sources for water supply of industries in the Axios Plain. There are no other major water requirements for municipal, industrial, or power needs in the Greek portion of the basin that must be supplied directly from basin flows. Accordingly, the corresponding order of priority for major water demands in Greece was reduced to:

- Irrigation
- Municipal and industrial
- Maintenance of water quality (for Axios River, in practice that recorded at the border)

In most of the systems analyses, navigation was not included. Separate systems analyses were made assuming high priority for navigation to determine impacts in the event that the Danube–Aegean Navigation Project is approved in the future.

Reliability criteria are a means of evaluating hydrologic performance of a given water resource development project. In this study reliability was defined as the percentage of time that specified water requirements are met. The reliability targets for each of the several flow demand elements were set as follows:

Demand Element	Reliability Target (%)
Municipal and industrial	95
Thermal cooling	95
Irrigation	80
Navigation	95

The reliability computations were all on a monthly time basis except for irrigation, which was calculated for annual time periods. The 80% irrigation target expresses the goal that in 2 years out of 10 during all the years of simulation an irrigation project could sustain a water shortage in one or more months of the irrigation season.

Requirements for hydropower generation were expressed in terms of dependable energy, defined as that energy which would be available 95% of the time, calculated on a monthly basis. The reliability target was then, by definition, 95%.

Requirements for water quality were expressed in terms of maximum milligram per liter concentrations of carbonaceous biochemical oxygen demand (BOD), and minimum milligram per liter concentrations of dissolved oxygen. The monthly reliability target for flows to satisfy water quality requirements was 99%. In those cases where flows were slightly below minimum standards, consideration was given to the recuperative ability of the waterway downstream from the pollution source to restore river flows in a relatively short distance to acceptable water quality levels; this consideration, however, did not arise at the border, where flows were well within established quality criteria.

No account is taken of the magnitude of the shortages in the definition of reliability presented above. The seriousness of a shortage was reflected in a penalty that reduces benefits, computed by means of a "loss function" defined for each type of water use. The percentage reliability was therefore recognized as only an index of performance; cases may arise when low reliability is associated with minor shortages and small shortfall losses, as defined by the respective loss function. Accordingly, both reliability and economic indicators were evaluated as measures of performance.

Border Flows (Yugoslav–Greek Agreement of 1970). In June 1970, an agreement was concluded between the government of the Socialist Federal Republic of Yugoslavia and the government of Greece to coordinate their efforts with the assistance of the United Nations in the preparation of an integrated development plan for the Vardar/Axios River Basin. A part of that agreement was concerned with the establishment of certain minimum flows at the international border between the two countries. The mean monthly flows for the period of May through September, incorporated in the 1970 agreement, were used as flow indicators under various conditions of basin development.

6.6 REGIONAL WATER QUALITY MANAGEMENT PLANS

In recent years, the largest expenditures in water resources planning and development in the United States have been for the formulation of regional waste management plans and the planning and construction of waste treatment and disposal facilities. The principal legal authorities for these programs are the Federal Water Pollution Control Act of 1972 (PL 92-500), the regulations of the federal Environmental Protection Agency, and the related water quality management acts and regulations of the individual states. Activities financially supported and regulated by the federal government are often referred to as "303," "208," or "201" programs, corresponding to three sections of PL 92-500.

Although the high cost of wastewater treatment is recognized in various congressional directives and also has an effect on how various types of pollutants are handled, analyses of benefits and costs in comparable economic terms are not generally made in 303, 208, and 201 studies. Overall, the regulations that apply to water quality management programs emphasize two types of requirements: (1) standards for minimum levels of wastewater treatment (effluent standards) for municipal and industrial wastes; and (2) standards for water quality of receiving waters, which may require higher wastewater treatment levels than in (1).

Planning on a regional basis considers water- and land-related resources and other factors bearing on quality management. The following is a summary of the relationships of the 303-208-201 planning process (Dobrowolski and Grillo 1977):

> Section 303 provides for the preparation of basin plans. The area studied in such a plan is the drainage basin of one or more navigable rivers. Effluent limitations, schedules for compliance, and total maximum daily loads for pollutants are established for discharges in the basin. Water quality standards are evaluated or revised, and schedules of compliance are implemented for the standards. The study must also provide for the disposition of all residual wastes from any waste treatment processes. Finally, an inventory and ranking, in order of priority, of needs for construction of waste treatment works to meet the goals set forth in other sections of the law are included in the basin plans.

> Section 208 provides for the preparation of areawide waste treatment management plans. The area involved can be within any jurisdiction, i.e., municipal, county, or the boundary of a planning agency. The plan identifies the facilities necessary to meet the municipal and industrial waste treatment needs of the area over a twenty-year period. Construction priorities, implementation schedules, and financial requirements for the initiation and completion of the treatment works are included. A regulatory program must be established to ensure timely completion of the projects, and agencies capable of carrying out the plan must be identified. Processes to control pollution from non-point, mine-related, and construction sources must be determined. The study must provide for the disposal of all residual wastes generated in the area.

> Section 201 provides grants for the planning and construction of specific treatment works. The area involved can be a municipality or within the boundaries of any intermunicipal or interstate agency (sewer authority). The grants are for waste treatment management plans which are consistent with the recommendations of the 303 and 208 plans, where these have been prepared.

Section 209 of the 1972 federal legislation provides for regional or river basin planning studies by river basin commissions and federal–state interagency efforts. In terms of the classification of regional studies in Section 3.4, these multipurpose, multiobjective studies are of the Level B type. Although not so designated, it appears that (as limited by the water quality management focus) the Section 303 and Section 208 studies are similar to Level B and the Section 201 studies are similar to the Level C (implementation) type.

The fact that there is no legal requirement for benefit-cost analyses does not mean that planners cannot strive for cost effectiveness. In the context of water quality planning the concept of cost effectiveness is interpreted broadly (Lienesch and Emison 1976):

> Cost effectiveness has generally been viewed as a project evaluation technique for choosing the monetary least-cost alternative from various treatment alternatives. It has consequently focused on the conventional approach of treatment as the major means for pollution abatement. Section 208 shifts the emphasis for cost effectiveness to a consideration of environmental, social, political, economic as well as monetary costs for all means of pollution abatement. As a result, cost effectiveness broadens its scope to include consideration of all means for reducing pollution and adds social, political,

environmental and economic costs as criteria for evaluation. This is a new thrust in alternative assessment for it has broader considerations for plan evaluation. This new direction has major importance since it clearly calls for noncapital intensive solutions to be considered on equal terms with construction efforts for pollution abatement. This recognizes that the entire system of pollution from generation, to transportation, to discharge must be reviewed if alternatives are to be truly cost effective in achieving their intended objectives.

Some of the problems that derive from land and water interrelationships are discussed in Section 5.9.2. There are a number of technical planning and design issues that must be considered in the development of a regional water quality management plan. Among these are:

- Effects of nonpoint sources of pollution (particularly agricultural and forestry)
- Effects of saltwater intrusion and other groundwater/surface water interface problems, when groundwater is overpumped or when disposal of treated wastes to surface waters replaces on-site disposal
- Alternatives of surface water, subsurface water, and land disposal schemes
- On-site disposal versus use of collection systems and centralized treatment and disposal plants
- Cost savings due to the economies of scale inherent in fewer wastewater treatment plants versus the added collection costs of extended intercepter sewers
- Optimal treatment level of each of the wastewater treatment plants whose location has been identified in order to meet water quality standards of receiving waters
- Long pipeline for offshore ocean discharge versus stream or near-shore discharge of wastewaters requiring higher treatment levels
- Processes for handling difficult-to-treat wastes, such as are discharged from certain industries and pharmaceutical and chemical plants, and the amount of pretreatment required for these wastes

Some of these technical problems are amenable to analyses by the methods of systems analysis and operations research. Chapter 12 discusses the use of programming and simulation techniques for such problems.

An important component of the planning process under the Federal Water Pollution Control Act and the guidelines of the Environmental Protection Agency is the involvement of all interested government and nongovernment agencies and the general public (see Chapter 7 for an extended discussion of public involvement procedures). The following reviews a case study that incorporates technical factors and citizen preferences. In this study "citizen" input implies input from representatives of government agencies and interested individuals from the general public.

6.7 MULTIOBJECTIVE METHODOLOGY FOR WATER QUALITY MANAGEMENT INCORPORATING CITIZEN PREFERENCES

Phillips (1978) evaluated alternatives in the Nassau County portion of the Nassau–Suffolk Areawide Wastewater Management Study ("208 Study"). Five objectives were considered: cost, environmental quality, reliability, implementability (as related to institutional and other factors), and energy utilization. The study was carried out in two phases. It was determined that the number of possible alternative diversion and treatment combinations was over 600,000. In Phase One, a mixed-integer programming screening model was used to reduce the large number of alternatives down to a manageable number based on cost; in this phase environmental quality constraints limited the number of alternatives considered. Phase Two utilized a three-step approach to evaluate further the screened alternatives. Step 1 used a questionnaire to estimate citizen preferences for the selected objectives. Step 2 performed a technical evaluation of each alternative based on how well it satisfied each objective. Step 3 combined the results of Steps 1 and 2 to generate a ranking of the final alternatives.

Following the formulation of a least-cost plan in Phase One corresponding to the mixed-integer programming solution, sensitivity analyses were carried out varying the degree of treatment, the replacement of equipment at old plants, and incorporating new areas into the management plan. As a result of these studies, additional plans were formulated and four alternatives were subsequently selected for evaluation in Phase Two. The following paragraphs provide additional information on Phase Two.

Step 1. Citizen Participation. Three citizen groups were selected whose interests span environmental planning to economic growth; these were the Marine Resources Council (MRC), the Technical Advisory Committee (TAC), and the Citizens Advisory Committee (CAC). A general discussion with each group included a visual presentation and a question-and-answer period. Following this two-way exchange of information, two questionnaires were administered to estimate the weight the citizens attached to each of the five objectives. Figure 6.2 shows the results of this procedure.

The first questionnaire was based on a pairwise ranking. Two objectives were paired, and each respondent was asked to indicate his or her preference of how much more important one objective is than another by means of a ratio. The order of the objectives was rearranged to ensure unbiased results. The second questionnaire was based on rankings. The respondent was asked to consider all five objectives, and to select a place on a scale of 1 to 10 where each objective ranked according to preference. The respondent was also asked to put an upper bound on the dollars he or she would be willing to pay for an excellent long-term solution to the environmental problems of the area; the purpose of this question was to develop an absolute dollar figure below which the relative weights generated are valid.

Step 2. Technical Evaluation. A technical evaluation was made to determine how each alternative compares with all other alternatives in fulfilling a specific

Objective	CAC	TAC	MRC	Overall adjusted weights
Cost	15	17	16	16
Environment	24	25	25	25
Reliability	22	21	21	21
Implementability	20	21	20	20
Energy	19	16	18	18

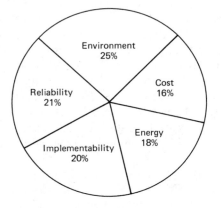

Figure 6.2 Comparison of final weights for objectives. (From Phillips, 1978.)

objective. The cost and environmental constraints have been mentioned previously. Reliability was determined in terms of the percentage of time an existing plant met its permit criteria for BOD removal. Implementability was determined as a score on a scale of 1 to 10 based on interviews with appropriate officials, who were asked to consider citizen acceptance, existence of a capable management agency, acceptance by existing institutions, regulatory agency acceptance, and adequate financial base. The energy objective was rated by evaluating the total annual energy budget for each alternative.

Step 3. Multiobjective Decision Matrix. This matrix combined technical evaluations and objective weights using the techniques of additive weighting, as shown in Figure 6.3, to obtain an overall evaluation index (I) for each alternative. Each objective weight is multiplied by an appropriate relative value for an alternative. The combinations are summed in the vertical direction giving the final score (index) for each alternative. The value of this index (I) for an alternative depends on the designated scale of values. The highest scores (indices) will determine the final alternatives. Stated mathematically, the objective function to be maximized is:

$$I = \sum_{i=1}^{n} W_i V_{ij}, \text{ where } j \text{ varies from 1 to } m$$

n = number of objectives (five in this case)
m = number of alternatives
W_i = weight of importance the citizen places on objective i (dimensionless)
V_{ij} = relative value of alternative j in fulfilling objective i

Other analyses of the final decision matrix included an error analysis of the

Alternatives

	1	2	3	$\cdots$	m
1	$(W_1)V_{11}$	$(W_1)V_{12}$	$(W_1)V_{13}$		$(W_1)V_{1m}$
2	$(W_2)V_{21}$	$\cdots$	$\cdots$		$\cdots$
3	$\cdots$	$\cdots$	$\cdots$		$\cdots$
4	$\cdots$	$\cdots$	$\cdots$		$\cdots$
5	$\cdots$	$\cdots$	$\cdots$		$(W_5)V_{5m}$

Objectives

Figure 6.3 Multiobjective decision matrix. (From Phillips, 1978.)

results and the calculation of a confidence interval and a midpoint for each alternative in terms of the multiobjective index. In this case, there was a fairly even distribution of results, indicating the relative equality of plans. This may have been because of the prior screening of Phase One. In the more typical situation, the results would be likely to yield a more distinct ranking of the plans.

6.8 PLAN FORMULATION PROCEDURE— WATER RESOURCES COUNCIL GUIDELINES

The Water Resources Council "Principles and Standards" of 1973, as amended in 1979, and 1980, describe a process of plan formulation, comparison, and selection. These rules were replaced by the "Principles and Guidelines" of 1983. Both the 1983 guidelines and the superseded rules are believed to be of much interest to water resources planners. They are similar in many respects to the other procedures discussed earlier in this book, although more formal and more detailed.

Planning Process. Under the "Principles and Standards," planning is carried out for two objectives: National Economic Development (NED) and Environmental Quality (EQ). The planning process consists of six major steps with additional iterations. All of the phases apply to Level B studies (regional and river basin studies) and Level C studies (implementation studies). Level A studies (framework studies and assessments such as the national assessment described in Section 6.9) are carried out by "any appropriate planning process" and may involve only the first two steps. The "Principles and Guidelines," applying only to implementation studies and focusing on a single objective (NED), list the six major steps (WRC, 1983, p. 2):

1. Specification of the water and related land resources problems and opportunities (relevant to the planning setting) associated with the federal objective and specific state and local concerns
2. Inventory, forecast, and analysis of water and related land resource conditions within the planning area relevant to the identified problems and opportunities
3. Formulation of alternative plans
4. Evaluation of the effects of the alternative plans
5. Comparison of alternative plans

6. Selection of a recommended plan based upon the comparison of alternative plans

   Iterations will frequently occur upon completion of the comparison of plans (Step 5), but may occur at any step. This process "may sharpen the planning focus or change its emphasis as new data are obtained or as the specification of problems or opportunities changes or becomes more clearly defined" (WRC, 1983, p. 2). Reasons for iteration given in an earlier document, when two objectives (NED and EQ) were considered, are the following (WRC, 1980, p. 64400):

- More detail is needed as basis for selecting a recommended plan.
- The consideration of alternative plans reveals significant shortfalls in alleviating the problems or realizing the opportunities of one or both of the objectives.
- Information on resource capability and alternative plans suggests that the initial specification of problems or opportunities was in error and requires modification.
- Public policy changes occurring during the planning study suggest the need for change in emphasis for the NED or EQ objectives.
- The consideration of alternative plans reveals significant adverse effects.

   "Scoping" and Inventory.   The first two major steps are completed by means of "scoping," and inventory and forecasting methods. Scoping is used to identify significant issues and their ranges. Scoping is emphasized near the beginning of the planning process and is continued throughout the project. This process includes affected federal, state, and local agencies and other interested groups and persons.
   Problems and opportunities are specified for current and future conditions, associated with the NED objective and state and local concerns. Such issues are defined so that "meaningful levels of achievement can be identified. This will facilitate the formulation of alternative plans in cases in which there may be financial, environmental, technical, legislative, or administrative constraints on the total alleviation of a problem or realization of an opportunity. . . . The potential for alleviating problems and realizing opportunities is determined during inventorying and forecasting" (WRC, 1983, p. 2). Alternative plans should be based on the most likely conditions in the future with and without the plan. Forecasts are made for selected years over the period of analysis to indicate how changes in economic and other conditions are likely to have an impact on problems and opportunities (WRC, 1983, pp. 5–6). The inventory determines the quantity and quality of water and related land resources, and identifies opportunities for protection and enhancement of those resources (WRC, 1983, p. 6).

   Formulation of Alternative Plans.   An alternative plan (Step 3) "consists of a system of structural and/or nonstructural measures, strategies, or programs formulated to alleviate specific problems or take advantage of specific opportunities associated with water and related land resources in the planning area" (WRC, 1983,

p. 6). The National Economic Development plan considers all beneficial and adverse effects that are attributable to the plan in economic terms, and "reasonably maximizes" contributions to NED. Other alternative plans are formulated "to address other federal, state, local, and international concerns not fully addressed by the NED plan." The number and variety of alternative plans is governed by: (1) the problems and opportunities associated with the water and related land resources in the study area; (2) the overall resource capabilities of the study area; (3) the available alternative measures; and (4) preferences of and conflicts among state and local entities and different segments of the public (WRC, 1983, pp. 7–8).

Alternative plans are formulated in consideration of four tests: completeness, effectiveness, efficiency, and acceptability. These tests are described in Section 3.7.2.

Detailed procedures for formulating plans based on two objectives were included in the 1979 version of the "Principles and Standards." This approach aimed at the satisfaction of the component needs of the objectives using combinations of plan elements. As a first approximation, the component needs that are complementary are arrayed—that is, the satisfaction of one component by a plan element does not preclude satisfaction of other components or add materially to the cost of satisfying other components. A given alternative plan is initially formulated as a set of component needs and plan elements that are essentially in harmony. This plan is then adjusted by identifying and analyzing relevant alternative means of meeting each of the component needs. This step considers the effectiveness of each alternative means of contributing to the satisfaction of a component need, and the extent of complementarity or conflict among component needs in relation to that means. In formulating a given alternative plan, initial consideration is limited to its orientation toward one of the objectives. Further additions are made for the component needs of another objective, provided that their inclusion does not significantly diminish the contributions of the overall plan to the objective toward which the plan is oriented (WRC, 1979, p. 72989).

Accounts.   The evaluation, comparison, and plan selection (Steps 4, 5, and 6) of the various alternative plans are facilitated by means of "accounts," which are displays in tabular form. Four accounts are used to organize the information on the effects of alternative plans. Effects of an alternative plan in each account are the differences between the projected conditions "with the plan" and projected conditions "without the plan." The National Economic Development (NED) account lists the beneficial and adverse effects of a plan on the national economy. The Environmental Quality (EQ) account shows effects expressed in appropriate quantitative units or qualitative terms. The Regional Economic Development (RED) account shows the regional incidence of NED effects, income transfers, and employment effects. The Other Social Effects (OSE) account shows urban and community impacts; effects on life, health, and safety; displacement of people, businesses, and farms; long-term effects on the productivity of resources, such as agricultural land; and energy requirements and energy conservation (WRC, 1983, pp. 12–13).

These four accounts encompass "all significant effects of a plan on the human environment" and "social well-being" effects as required by various laws (WRC, 1983, p. 8).

Plan Selection.   After consideration of the various alternative plans and their impacts, and after the appropriate iterations (WRC, 1983, pp. 14–15):

> The planning process leads to identification of alternative plans that could be recommended or selected. The culmination of the planning process is the selection of the recommended plan or the decision to take no action. The selection should be based on a comparison of the effects of alternative plans. . . . The alternative plan with the greatest net economic benefit consistent with protecting the Nation's environment (the NED plan) is to be selected unless . . . there is some overriding reason for selecting another plan, based upon other federal, state, local and international concerns.

Plans are not to be recommended for federal development if they would physically or economically preclude nonfederal plans that would likely be undertaken in the absence of the federal plan and that would more effectively contribute to the federal objective (NED) when comparably evaluated (WRC, 1983, p. 15).

Under the "Principles and Standards," a recommended plan (when considered on the basis of the with-plan versus without-plan comparison) was formulated to have combined beneficial NED and EQ effects that outweigh combined adverse NED and EQ effects. This allowed a plan lacking net NED benefits to be recommended if net EQ benefits were sufficiently large, even though EQ benefits were not stated in monetary terms (WRC, 1980, p. 64399).

6.9 FRAMEWORK STUDIES AND ASSESSMENTS

A classification of regional studies based on their level of detail and focus on specific types of projects was given in Section 3.4. The broadest studies were termed framework studies and assessments. The "Second National Water Assessment" by the U.S. Water Resources Council (1978) is an example of this type. It was based on analyses of data for the 1975 base year and projections for 1985 and 2000. The country was divided into 21 water resource regions and 106 subregions for the purpose of data collection and analysis, and to incorporate input from various federal, state, and regional sources. The assessment provided estimates of water balances based on appraisals of water supply and water use, and identified critical problems. Water supply and water use projections were projected from a socioeconomic baseline for 1975. Two futures were considered: the national future, representing the federal viewpoint, and the state–regional future, representing state and/or regional viewpoints. A regional report was prepared for each of the 21 water resource regions. Water uses analyzed included "offstream" (withdrawal) uses and "instream" uses such as fish and wildlife needs, hydroelectric generation, navigation, and recreational activities.

To assist in identifying the nation's critical water problems, a water supply adequacy analysis model was developed. It was based on the concept of a balance

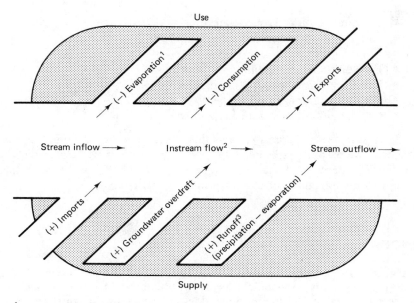

Use

(−) Evaporation[1] (−) Consumption (−) Exports

Stream inflow → Instream flow[2] → Stream outflow →

(+) Imports (+) Groundwater overdraft (+) Runoff[3] (precipitation − evaporation)

Supply

[1] Includes only evaporation from man-made reservoirs.
[2] Includes flow requirements for navigation, hydroelectric, conveyance to meet downstream treaty and compact commitments, fish and wildlife habitat maintenance, waste assimilation, recreation, sediment transport, and freshwater inflow to estuaries.
[3] Includes precipitation minus natural evaporation from the land surfaces and plant transpiration, and drainage to groundwater.

Figure 6.4 Water balance elements. (From U.S. Water Resources Council, Second National Water Assessment, 1978.)

between water use and water supply, and took into consideration both groundwater and fresh surface water. This model, which is shown schematically in Figure 6.4, was used to provide a subregional analysis for each of the water resources regions and subregions. Subregions have water inflow or supply from upstream subregions, interbasin imports, precipitation runoff, and groundwater. Requirements for water include interbasin exports, consumption, and evaporation, which are deducted from the potential supply. Goundwater recharge is accounted for in the model and is not considered a loss.

Comparison of water supply and water use data showed that the nation's water supplies generally are sufficient to meet water needs for all beneficial purposes. However, major water problems were identified in most of the 21 water resources regions, and local problems of varying intensity were found in nearly all of the 106 subregions. Maps were prepared that showed the locations of major problems.

The assessment reviewed the following critical problems:

- Inadequate surface water supply
- Overdraft of groundwater
- Pollution of surface water

- Contamination of groundwater
- Quality of drinking water
- Flooding
- Erosion and sedimentation
- Dredging and disposal of dredged material
- Wet-soils drainage and wetlands
- Degradation of bay, estuary, and coastal water

Assessment programs such as this, since they provide guidance for national or regional water policies, should be updated periodically. Water resource problem profile statements can be used to target programs for effective water management and to assess the adequacy of current programs and policies.

REFERENCES

ALLEGHENY RIVER BASIN REGIONAL WATER RESOURCES PLANNING BOARD, "Allegheny River Basin, New York, Alternatives for Water Resources Development and Management," report preparation by Tippetts-Abbett-McCarthy-Stratton, March 1971.

DOBROWOLSKI, FRANK, and LEONARD GRILLO, "Experience with the 303-208-201 Study Relationships," *Water Resources Bull.*, vol. 13, no. 3, June 1977.

LIENESCH, WILLIAM C., and GERALD A. EMISON, "Planning for Implementation under Section 208," *J. Water Resources Plann. Manage. Div., Proc. Am. Soc. Civil Eng.*, vol. 102, no. WR2, November 1976.

PHILLIPS, KEVIN J., "Multi-objective Analysis Applied to Areawide Wastewater Management," Ph.D. thesis, Polytechnic Institute of New York, June 1978.

TAMS (Tippetts-Abbett-McCarthy-Stratton, New York, and Mattis Demain Beckford & Associates Ltd., Kingston), "Comparative Study of Water Supply Projects for Kingston and Surrounding Area," July 1977.

TAMS (Tippetts-Abbett-McCarthy-Stratton, New York, and Massachusetts Institute of Technology, Cambridge), "Integrated Development of the Vardar/Axios River Basin—Yugoslavia–Greece," December 1978.

U.S. WATER RESOURCES COUNCIL, "Principles and Standards for Planning Water and Related Land Resources," September 10, 1973; rev. December 14, 1979; rev. September 29, 1980.

U.S. WATER RESOURCES COUNCIL, "Second National Water Assessment, the Nation's Water Resources 1975–2000," December 1978.

U.S. WATER RESOURCES COUNCIL, "Economic and Environmental Principles and Guidelines for Water and Related Land Resources Implementation Studies," March 10, 1983.

SEVEN

Public Involvement in Water Resources Planning

7.1 INTRODUCTION

The trend in planning is toward a more "open" process in which the organization sponsoring a plan or project and its staff seek an increasing level of interaction with all entities that have an actual or perceived interest in the plan or project. This trend is in accord with ethical behavior in democratic types of societies and has also emerged as a practical response to heightened environmental and social concerns. In the United States it has been formalized by federal mandates for public participation in natural resources planning.

The public participation process provides information to generate public interest and increase understanding of a plan or proposal. Interaction with the public elicits information and encourages a continuing dialogue. By these means, planners establish credibility for the plan or project and the agency or firm involved.

This chapter provides an overview of program requirements and suggestions for the design of an effective public participation component of the planning process.

7.2 PURPOSES AND BENEFITS OF PUBLIC PARTICIPATION

Increased public participation in water resources planning and decision making has arisen as a result of mounting public pressure on decision makers. Opposition to some proposals has resulted in long delays or abandonment of projects which have been perceived as unacceptable. Planners have recognized that big or complex projects need the support of many groups to be acceptable. Effective participation is the way to gain public acceptance of worthwhile projects or, alternatively, to recognize early which projects are not likely to be acceptable.

Public involvement in planning may be justified as good management practice since it often presents opportunities to:

- Identify legal requirements, funding limitations, or other constraints and ensure that the plan is compatible with them.
- Take advantage of technical expertise that may be available in the various publics involved.
- Identify and clarify positions of different groups and individuals affected by the plan.
- Identify sensitive issues and ways of preventing or reducing adverse impacts.
- Overcome conflicts and reach a consensus when there are different points of view with respect to plan components, particularly when multiple objectives are involved.
- Gain support for the project or project implementation.

7.3 REQUIREMENTS FOR PUBLIC PARTICIPATION

At all levels of government, planners and decision makers have long recognized the need for public participation. Requirements in federal programs have changed significantly in forms and focus in the last two decades in an attempt to balance the recognized need for public information and comment and the added time and money such requirements may entail.

The Federal Water Pollution Control Act Amendments of 1972 (PL 92-500) acknowledged the need for public participation in water quality management programs, by advising on priorities, contributing to regulations, and monitoring compliance. It also led to the establishment of explicit guidelines for providing information, accepting public comments, conducting public hearings and meetings, and ensuring a more balanced public input through specifying the makeup of advisory committees. "Probably no Federal law has been so explicit in specifying opportunities and requirements for citizen involvement [Conservation Foundation, 1976]."

Another recognition of the importance of public participation can be found in the U.S. Water Resources Council "Principles and Guidelines" for implementation studies, which state (WRC, 1983, p. 3):

Interested and affected agencies, groups and individuals should be provided opportunities to participate throughout the planning process. The responsible federal planning agency should contact and solicit participation of: other federal agencies; appropriate regional, state, and local agencies; national, regional and local groups; other appropriate groups such as affected Indian tribes; and individuals. A coordinated public participation program should be established with willing agencies and groups.

Efforts to secure public participation should be pursued through appropriate means such as public hearings, public meetings, workshops, information programs, and citizen committees.

The WRC guidelines (pp. 105–106) especially emphasize the interdisciplinary approach and extensive public involvement process required by the National Environmental Policy Act of 1969.

Earlier guidelines of the Water Resources Council also emphasized the importance of coordination and review in Level A (framework studies) and Level B (regional or river basin plans) (WRC, 1973, p. 24859).

7.4 FACTORS THAT CONTRIBUTE TO EFFECTIVE PUBLIC PARTICIPATION

Salmon (1979) has identified a number of factors that should be considered in designing an effective public participation program. These relate to the dissemination of information, interaction of the agency and the public, establishment of credibility, and conforming to laws and funding requirements. The eight factors considered most important are discussed below.

7.4.1 Preplanning

Natural resource use and allocation, and the formulation of the structural and nonstructural components of projects, are rarely single-issue items. The initial step in any planning process should be to define the scope of the program and the main issues that will be of concern to the public. This should include some basic research on the community that will be affected. The information needed will include such things as:

- The general characteristics of the community, including socioeconomic data
- Local values and concerns relevant to the project, including attitudes about the resource under consideration and the agency or firm doing the planning
- The history of similar projects, if any, including interest groups or individuals involved in these earlier projects or programs
- Community experience with citizen participation and community cohesiveness
- The political decision-making framework in the community
- Local groups or individuals who are interested in or affected by the proposal

This information can be gained from local newspapers and libraries and from conversations with local leaders.

Also important is detailed information on the plan or proposal under study. Some water resource projects may require many changes in values and/or life-styles and thus be relatively controversial, requiring an extensive effort to involve differing interests. Other projects may require public understanding of new or complex resource problems and solutions and may necessitate intensive educational efforts. The complexity, amount of data available, time available for information generation and dissemination, and the resources of those affected by the issue must be considered in designing a public participation program.

Using information about the community and the nature of the planning process or project, the planner can determine more effectively the scale of public involvement needed. Some problems will be too small or not affect community values enough to warrant extensive allocation of time and money. Others may involve strong values or major changes or be extremely complex and require maximum public discussion.

In designing opportunities for citizen participation, it is helpful to seek the advice of local leaders and elected officials in reviewing information, identifying interested groups or individuals, and deciding how to involve people. If the plan or project involves federal mandates for participation, attention also must be paid to conformance to these rules.

7.4.2 Agency/Firm Policy

Although technical phases of agency programs normally have well-defined require-ments and standards for information collection and evaluation, relatively few agencies have defined their expectations and procedures for public participation. Policies concerning when citizens will be involved, who will represent citizens, what channels of communication will be established, and what decision-making power citizens will be given should be addressed and formalized.

Public attitudes about a planning agency or firm are bound to influence acceptance of the planning process and plan. Thus, care should be take to provide measures to enhance public confidence. Stated goals on the involvement of citizens in a consistent, valid, and equitable manner and design of a clear decision-making process with timely citizen participation built into the total planning effort can be of substantial benefit in instilling public confidence.

7.4.3 Resources

Successful public participation programs cost time and money. Trained staff, money, and time must be available. Although many staff members may be involved with citizens, in general each study should be managed by only one person to ensure program responsibility and continuity.

Attributes in staff that contribute to the success of a public involvement program include: sensitivity, the willingness to listen, a positive attitude on the program and the public's role in decision making, the ability to organize information and groups, written and oral communication skills, and a flexible approach. Training in citizen participation skills is also important.

Knowledge of group dynamics is also helpful, and in the case of certain situations, essential. According to Spencer (1979), it is particularly difficult to deal with issues that involve:

- Multiple groups

- Controversy, disagreement, and lack of consensus with respect to values, as reflected in awareness of a problem, priority given to it, and the intensity of concern
- Technical difficulties, as reflected by the state of the art and its level of sophistication
- Time constraints
- Money constraints
- Significant changes in the organizational structure
- Significant changes in resource allocation pattern
- Low level of coalition development
- Lead organization that has little power, authority, or responsibility and a history of failures
- Small and unskilled planning staff
- Low technical quality of the proposal
- Turbulent environment

Because such issues often provide problems for a project, it might be helpful to seek the assistance of specialists who can advise on the conduct of the process and train the planners who must interact with the publics.

The funds available for public participation are important. The U.S. Environmental Protection Agency (1976) discussed adequate funding as a critical element in maintaining an effective water quality planning program, recommending that at least 10% of the program budget might be allocated to public involvement. One firm's experience (Fusco 1980) has indicated that a controversial project could require allocation of as much as 15 to 30% of the total budget. The issue remains unclear with some claims of delays and time costs in excess of program benefits (Montanari 1978) and others claiming that such delays can be more than compensated by more rapid progress in design and construction stages after extensive participation in the planning stage (U.S. Environmental Protection Agency, 1979). What is clear is that many programs carry a federal mandate for public participation which must be met, and public opposition to projects because of limited involvement may be even more costly than the expenditure of funds to carry out public involvement programs.

7.4.4 Outreach

Identification and notification of appropriate groups or individuals in a timely fashion is a critical element of successful public participation. At least four "publics" should be involved in coordination, review, and input concerning the planning process:

- Public agencies and officials that have a legal mandate for consultation and/or approval of certain aspects of the project, or that have a planning function that overlaps with that of the sponsoring organization
- Organizations and individuals that have an economic interest in the project
- Public interest groups (civic, social, environmental, recreational, public health, educational, etc.) that have particular programs or points of view that bear on the project

- Other organizations and individuals with no financial gain or loss from the project, but who are interested in the project

Additionally, public information and education efforts should be undertaken to inform the general public, popularly known as the "man on the street."

Several methods have been described for identifying members of these publics. Willeke (1976) suggests three forms of identifying potential participants.

- Self-identification, where individuals come forward voluntarily to express concerns or opinions
- Third-party identification, where citizen committees or other organizations are used to identify groups and individuals who should be involved or who are affected
- Staff identification, where groups and individuals are identified by analyzing information on:
  —associations: available lists of organized groups
  —geographic data: photographs, maps, market, and economic areas
  —demographic data: census records, special surveys, or field work
  —historical information: reports, files, newspapers, and oral accounts
  —comparative information: studies of projects that are closely related to the proposed project
  —general lists of standard categories of public
  —user groups

The study design for the planning process or project should contain timetables for notification of the public arranged so that interested groups or persons will have adequate notice of opportunities to participate. The time and method of participation should be clearly stated and widely available to maximize ease of participation. Scheduling of planning and participation activities in an agency either in response to external requirements or deadlines or internal program needs should be well planned. Informed participation requires reading and thought. If too little time is available for proper review of agency materials or preparation of citizen comments, citizen input can be less informed and useful.

7.4.5 Effective Communication

Good planner/public communication during all phases of the planning process is essential. Timely and truthful information in plain language should be transmitted through individual, group, and media contacts. Suitable written materials, effective presentations with good graphics where feasible, and productive discussions all contribute to effective communication.

Written materials should be interesting and relatively easy to read. There are two formulas, developed by Robert Gunning (1952) and Rudolph Flesch (1960), which are frequently used to measure reading diffficulty. Gunning suggests a "fog index" formula, which deals with sentence length and number of syllables per word.

Flesch's method uses the same factors. He suggests that easily read material should contain a maximum of 200 syllables per 100 words, 18 to 20 words per sentence, and no more than five to seven sentences per paragraph. He also suggests the inclusion of human interest factors to increase the readability of the work.

Good graphics that include explanatory captions can be useful in illustrating problems and solutions. But overhead projector or slide material that has too much printed information or is poorly produced contributes little to citizen confidence or understanding. If visuals cannot be professionally produced, care should be taken that the "home" product is of good quality. Visuals should be previewed by staff and by citizens before taking any presentation to the public.

Good group discussion which is structured so that a variety of opinions are offered can be helpful. An understanding of group dynamics is essential to ensure that one set of opinions does not dominate and that the discussions are productive.

The individuals of a group may come from different professional backgrounds, have different ethical values, and behave in different ways. Deutsch (1960) has indicated that the activities of a group meet two kinds of needs: "task" roles and "group building and maintenance" roles. Task roles include initiating activity, seeking information, seeking opinion, giving information, giving opinion, elaborating, coordinating, and summarizing. Group building and maintenance roles relate to strengthening and maintaining group life and activities and are described by words such as "encouraging," "gatekeeping," "standard setting," "following," and "expressing group feeling." Some roles have both task and maintenance characteristics. These include evaluating, diagnosing, testing for consensus, mediating and relieving tension. Too much time spent on maintenance roles (over perhaps 40%) will typically reduce group effectiveness.

Deutsch also describes various types of "nonfunctional" behavior that may impede the work of the group. Spencer (1979) has suggested that each person is likely to interpret group behavior differently and "what appears to be nonfunctional behavior may not necessarily be so." A trained and sensitive moderator for groups is an asset to productive discussion. Efforts to involve persons with these skills or to acquire them through training should be explored.

7.4.6 Techniques

The techniques that are employed in the public information process should focus on the identification and resolving of problems, especially when they involve value judgments. They may also depend on a number of other factors, including:

- Applicable legal requirements
- Nature of the planning organization
- Regional institutions and other publics involved
- Desirable degree of delegation of authority to planning staff to speak for the organization and to make changes in the plans to reflect the input from the publics
- Physical location of the planning organization in relation to the planning area

A variety of public involvement techniques should be used in order to reach the affected publics. Use of only one technique may result in receiving the inputs of an unrepresentative group. Thus, in studying the public meetings held for several large Level B studies of the New England River Basins Commission, Ertel (1979) found that:

> Attendees at public meetings dealing with comprehensive water resource planning issues can be expected to be not a cross section of the general public, but those who are relatively affluent and well educated, public issue oriented, and have local governmental responsibility and a strong tendency toward major concern with environmental issues. Even so, their previous knowledge of the particular issues under consideration cannot be assumed.

Glasser et al. (1975) have classified 23 public participation and education techniques in five categories:

- Large group meetings
- Small group meetings
- Organizational approaches
- Media
- Community interaction

In Table 7.1 these techniques are defined and advantages and disadvantages of each are presented. Analyses of public involvement techniques have been made by many other investigators, including Bishop (1975), Brown (1980), Debo and Williams (1979), Dysart (1974, 1978), Finsterbusch (1977), Hanchey (1975), O'Riordan (1976), Ragan (1975), Silberman (1977), and Torrey and Mills (1977).

7.4.7 Responsiveness

During the planning process, citizens may contribute many opinions and ideas. These inputs may vary widely in values reflected and relevance to the planning alternatives or process. Some will be usable in formulating new alternatives or in restructuring existing work. All citizen comment should be reviewed and considered. Further, it is important to public relations and the credibility of the agency and the planning process that citizens are aware that their contributions did receive attention, and that their ideas and concerns were heard.

There are several ways to demonstrate responsiveness. One is by the use of a responsiveness summary (New 1979), which summarizes concerns expressed and describes:

- Nature of contact with the public
- Matters discussed
- Public's views, significant comments, and suggestions
- How public input was used or, if not used, why not

TABLE 7.1 PUBLIC PARTICIPATION AND EDUCATION TECHNIQUES

Technique	Description	Advantages	Disadvantages
Large Group Meetings			
Public hearing	*Definition*: Formal public meeting usually required by law *Purposes*: To certify proposed plans and discuss other related issues	Provides an opportunity for the public to ask questions and voice opinions. It is a traditional technique, familiar to many citizens.	Does not usually allow for two-way communication or continuity of interactions.
Public meeting	*Definition*: Informal public proceeding *Purposes*: To discuss issues	Same as above.	Same as above.
Small Group Meetings			
Presentation to community groups	*Definition*: Lecture and discussion with specialists *Purposes*: To identify community concerns and to inform citizens of the plans, issues, pollution control techniques, water quality agencies, etc.	Opportunity for informing the public and exchanging information.	Is not a decision-making meeting. Lack of good two-way communications may lead to citizen apathy.
Site visit	*Definition*: Field trip to sites of existing or potential impacts *Purposes*: To sensitize planners and citizens to project impacts	Provides opportunity to more clearly understand the many dimensions of a problem.	Time consuming and expensive, especially where sites are distant or inaccessible.
Citizen advisory body	*Definition*: Formally appointed representative citizen group *Purposes*: To sensitize planners and citizens to project impacts.	Provides opportunity for continuous two-way communications with a representative body and reduces the need for community meetings. Assists in gaining community support for a plan.	Role of body often mistakenly seen by the public as a decision-making body and by agencies as often reluctant to cooperate and use the body for superficial activities.
Citizen task force	*Definition*: Formally appointed citizens knowledgeable about a specific problem. *Purpose*: To study lay and professional concerns on a particular problem and make recommendations for action.	Provides in-depth information on issues. Often can cut across agency jurisdictional boundaries to seek solutions to problems.	Task force has no power to implement findings. It is usually disbanded after its work is completed, thus limiting its continued involvement with the problem.

TABLE 7.1 *(continued)*

Technique	Description	Advantages	Disadvantages
	Small Group Meetings		
Role playing	*Definition*: An educational and decision-making technique where real-world problems are simulated by individuals who act the part (play the roles) of decision makers or citizens. *Purpose*: To sensitize citizens and decision makers to the economic, political, social, and environmental aspects of resource decision making.	Provides an opportunity for citizens to experience decision-making problems and become sensitive to the complexities of economic, social, and environmental decision making.	Requires skilled group leader to be most effective.
Values clarification exercises	*Definition*: Carefully designed activities for people to examine conflicts between their behaviors (lifestyles) and their stated beliefs (values). *Purpose*: To clarify people's values and align their behaviors to these values.	Provides an opportunity for the public and agency persons to reexamine the basis for their opinions and decisions on water resource issues and potentially, to change their behaviors.	Requires careful preparation and well-trained leaders to be effective.
Workshops	*Definition*: Working sessions in which interested, affected public and government representatives discuss specific issues. *Purpose*: To identify and recommend solutions to problems.	Provides an opportunity for two-way communication and a good learning experience for both the public and government representatives.	Same as above.
Delphi exercises	*Definition*: An educational and decision-making tool in which citizens and decision makers can choose alternatives via pairwise comparisons.	Facilitates the processing of a large amount of information in a systematic manner. Immediate feedback and ranking by Delphi is a low-cost method of	Requires skilled group leader and participants who are committed to the objective of reaching a concensus.

TABLE 7.1 *(continued)*

Technique	Description	Advantages	Disadvantages
	Small Group Meetings		
Delphi exercises (*continued*)	*Purpose*: To reach consensus on the solutions to problems by jointly considering the opinions of a diverse group of expert witnesses.	assimilating expert opinions.	
	Organizational Approaches		
Regional and local offices	*Definition*: Public agency offices located close to projected areas to administer programs. *Purpose*: To provide better contact between agency and local citizenry.	Opportunity for agency personnel to become more sensitive to local issues. Increased services at the local level.	May be expensive to house. There may be some loss of central control.
Citizen representation on policy bodies	*Definition*: Lay citizen participation in the decision-making process. *Purpose*: To provide community interest groups with greater involvement in decision making.	Permits citizens to participate in decision making. Encourages commitment to support project implementation.	Appointed representative may not, in fact, represent their constituency. To be effective, representative must be forceful and articulate.
Ombudsman and community interest advocate	*Definition*: An agency appointee to serve as a liaison with the community. *Purpose*: To investigate and resolve community complaints and make policy recommendations to decision makers.	Provides a mechanism for two-way communication between public and agency. Cut through bureaucratic roadblocks.	Agency can abuse this mechanism by not giving the ombudsman access to vital information or by not considering citizen concerns.
Public interest center	*Definition*: An office which disseminates information and provides speakers for community meetings. *Purpose*: To serve the community as a source of information on environmental issues, citizen rights, and technical information	Provides a new institution devoted to assisting the citizen in improving two-way communication with government.	May easily be ignored by government which may see the center as a threat to their authority or merely as a public relations office.

TABLE 7.1 *(continued)*

Technique	Description	Advantages	Disadvantages
	Media		
Information pamphlets, brochures, and summary reports	*Definition*: Brief written materials on environmental issues. *Purpose*: To provide the public with general information and easily understood documents.	Can reach a large number of people at a low cost to the agency. Simplify complex information for easy consumption.	One-way communication with little feedback. Brevity may omit key information from being transmitted.
Slides and film presentation	*Definition*: Brief pictorial presentation showing water quality issues and solutions. *Purpose*: To create awareness of water quality problems, and methods of dealing with them (e.g., land use practices).	Can be inexpensive to develop. When used with local issues and opinion leaders it can be an effective change tool.	Distribution of films and projectors can be expensive.
Tape-recorded information network	*Definition*: Tape cassettes sent to citizen groups with discussion topics. Citizen responses are recorded and returned. *Purpose*: To inform citizens and obtain their opinions on issues quickly.	Allows information to be distributed to a wide audience. Promotes two-way communication.	Technique is expensive and requires time to prepare.
Radio and talk show	*Definition*: Program that provides experts a forum to respond to telephoned questions from citizens. *Purpose*: To provide a forum where many citizens can listen to a question and answer session with leaders or experts.	Citizens can have direct two-way communication with decision makers and a wide audience can be reached.	Agency administrators may be unwilling to commit the time to such a program. They may also not like the public scrutiny.
Press release, special feature articles, and newsletters	*Definition*: Easily understood articles that reach a wide audience. *Purpose*: To inform people of issues	Provides a forum for local issues and continuous communication.	Editorial subjectivity can distort issues and destroy credibility. Maintaining updated mailing lists may be expensive.

TABLE 7.1 *(continued)*

Technique	Description	Advantages	Disadvantages

Media

Press release, special feature articles, and newsletters (*continued*)		rapidly. To announce meeting dates, changes in technology, and changes in the law.	

Community Interaction

Response to public inquiries	*Definition:* Official response through letter, telephone, or other. *Purpose*: To maintain good communications with the public and to respond to questions.	Can provide honest and precise responses to concerns of citizens.	Requires open and knowledgeable persons in agencies to respond competently.
Formal attitude survey	*Definition*: A systematic assessment of a representative sample of a community. *Purpose*: To determine the values and positions of the public on specific issues.	Provides an objective view of popular values and preferences that are representative of the community.	Is expensive and requires experts to conduct accurately. Questions must be carefully worded so as to be interpreted correctly by respondents and analysts.

Legal Mechanisms

Citizen suits	*Definition:* Opportunities in the law for citizens to sue agencies and individuals for not enforcing water-related laws. *Purpose*: To ensure that the laws are enforced, that consideration is given to the impacts of projects, and that public information is available.	Provides direct line of citizen access to the policy process, and ensures equitable discharge of agency responsibility as defined by the judicial system. The threat of suit also acts as a restraint on agency action and is not expensive.	Is often expensive. Few citizens have the skills to use this technique effectively. It is often used to block agency actions, stopping them from fulfilling their public responsibilities.
Environmental impact statement	*Definition*: Legal document that must be filed by any agency spending federal funda on a project with potentially large impacts.	Is a source of information for proponents and opponents of the projects to support their viewpoints. Often, the statements are prepared by	Is usually highly technical and difficult to read and understand. They are prepared late in the planning process so that many decisions are already irreversible. They often cause

TABLE 7.1 *(continued)*

Technique	Description	Advantages	Disadvantages
Legal Mechanisms			
Environmental impact statement *(continued)*	*Purpose*: To provide the public and other agencies with technical data needed to understand the nature of the potential impacts from a project.	researchers not employed by the developer. This outside viewpoint can help the developer improve a project.	delays in the project planning, causing unnecessary expenses to the developer.

Source: Glasser et al. (1975).

This summary may be sent to participants or used in agency newsletters or publications.

Another responsiveness mechanism is personal contact. For small-scale programs or those which involve few persons or groups, this is an effective way to ensure citizens that they have been listened to. Citizens should be informed of how their opinions were used or why they were not used in this case.

7.4.8 Monitoring and Evaluation

Evaluation of all phases of a planning program is necessary to "investigate not only if a program meets its goals, but why it works or doesn't work [Weiss 1972]." This is particularly important in agency efforts in public involvement, since the credibility of the plan and the agency will be affected by its public image. If the agency has set goals for public involvement, criteria for ascertaining whether or not these goals have been met can be designed.

Program goals should be set with the recognition that four functions will be served:

1. Timely, truthful, and understandable information will be generated and disseminated.
2. Opportunities for citizen dialogue and discussion will be provided in a timely and productive manner.
3. Programs will be designed and conducted in a manner designed to establish and maintain credibility for the agency and the planning or review process.
4. Federal or other requirements will be met.

Informal evaluation using personal contacts and comments from participants on "how things are going" can provide excellent informal evaluation during the process and can serve as early warnings of problems to be solved. A more formal evaluation at the end of the program can be useful in designing future programs or in diagnosing weaknesses.

7.5 MATHEMATICAL MODELS
AND SPECIAL DISPLAY TECHNIQUES

Chapters 13, 15, and 16 discuss various anaytical and simulation models, graphical display techniques, and other formal techniques to analyze and take account of inputs from the public in the planning process.

REFERENCES

Bishop, A. B., "Structuring Communications Programs for Public Participation in Water Resources Planning," IWR Rep. 75-2, U.S. Army, Institute for Water Resources, 1975.

Brown, Levi A., "Political Aspects of Urban Stormwater Management," *J. Water Resources Plann. Manage., Div., Proc. Am. Soc. Civil Eng.*, vol. 106, no. WR1, March 1980.

Conservation Foundation, "Toward Clean Water: A Guide to Citizen Action," Washington, D.C., 1976.

Debo, Thomas N., and James T. Williams," Voter Reaction to Multiple-Use Drainage Projects," *J. Water Resources Plann. Manage. Div., Proc. Am. Soc. Civil Eng.*, vol. 105, no. WR2, September 1979.

Deutsch, A., "The Effects of Cooperation upon Group Process," in *Group Dynamics—Research and Theory*, D. Cartwright and A. Zander, eds., Row Peterson, Evanston, Ill., 1960.

Dysart, B. D., "Education of Planners and Managers for Effective Public Participation," *Proc. Conf. Public Particip. Water Resources Plann. Manage.*, Water Resources Institute, University of North Carolina, 1974.

Dysart, B. D., "Legal and Practical Requirements for Public Participation," Water Resources Research Institute, Clemson University, 1978.

Ertel, Madge O., "A Survey Research Evaluation of Citizen Participation Strategies," *Water Resources Res.*, vol. 15, no. 4, August 1979.

Finsterbusch, K., "Methods for Evaluating Non-market Impacts in Policy Decisions with Special Reference to Water Resources Projects," IWR Rep. 77-8, National Technical Information Service, 1977.

Flesch, R. *How to Write, Speak and Think More Effectively*, Signet, New York, 1960.

Fusco, Steven M., "Public Participation in Environmental Statements," *J. Water Resources Plann. Manage. Div., Proc. Am. Soc. Civil Eng.*, vol. 106, no. WR1, March 1980.

Glasser, Roslyn, Dale Manty, and Gerald Nehman, "Public Participation in Water Resources Planning," *Proc. Workshop Public Particip.*, International Joint Commission, Great Lakes Advisory Board, June 1975.

Gunning, Robert, *The Technique of Clear Writing*, McGraw-Hill, New York, 1952.

Hanchey, J. R., "Public Involvement in the Corps of Engineers Planning Process," IWR Rep. 75-R4, U.S. Army Institute for Water Resources, 1975.

MONTANARI, FRANCIS W., "Public Process Portion of Impacts Analysis," *J. Water Resources Plann. Manage. Div., Proc. Am. Soc. Civil Eng.*, vol. 104, no. WR1, November 1978.

NEW, LOIS, "Public Participation and the Facilities Planning Process," Short Course on Public Participation in Environmental Engineering Projects, University of Wisconsin—Madison Extension, December 13–14, 1979.

O'RIORDAN, T., "Policy Making and Environmental Management: Some Thoughts on Processes and Research Ideas," *Nat. Resources J.*, vol. 16, no. 1, The University of New Mexico School of Law, January 1976.

RAGAN, J. F., "Public Participation in Water Resources Planning: An Evaluation of the Programs of 15 Corps of Engineers Districts," IWR Rep. 75-6, U.S. Army Institute for Water Resources, 1975.

SALMON, ELIZABETH, "An Evaluation Model for Public Involvement Programs in Water Quality Planning," Ph.D. thesis, University of Wisconsin–Madison, 1979.

SILBERMAN, EDWARD, "Public Participation in Water Resource Development," *J. Water Resources Plann. Manage. Div., Proc. Am. Soc. Civil Eng.*, vol. 103, no. WR1, May 1977.

SPENCER, JUNE, "Factors That Impact Public Participation Progress," Short Course on Public Participation in Environmental Engineering Projects, University of Wisconsin—Madison Extension, December 13–14, 1979.

TORREY, W. R., and F. MILLS, "Selecting Effective Citizen Participation Techniques," Rep. FHWA-77/10, U.S. Department of Transportation, 1977.

U.S. ENVIRONMENTAL PROTECTION AGENCY, "Public Participation Handbook for Water Quality Management," January 1976.

U.S. ENVIRONMENTAL PROTECTION AGENCY, "Public Participation in Programs under the Resource Conservation and Recovery Act, the Safe Drinking Water Act and the Clean Water Act—Final Regulations," February 16, 1979.

U.S. WATER RESOURCES COUNCIL, "Principles and Standards for Planning Water and Related Land Resources," 1973; rev. December 14, 1975; rev. September 29, 1980.

U.S. WATER RESOURCES COUNCIL, "Economic and Environmental Principles and Guidelines for Water and Related Land Resources Implementation Studies," March 10, 1983.

WEISS, C., *Evaluation Research, Methods for Assessing Program Effectiveness*, Prentice-Hall, Englewood Cliffs, N.J., 1972.

WILLEKE, GENE E., "Identifying the Public in Water Resources Planning," *J. Water Resources Plann. Manage. Div., Proc. Am. Soc. Civil Eng.*, vol. 102, no. WR1, April 1976.

EIGHT

Economic Analyses

8.1 SCOPE

This chapter describes methodologies for the economic formulation and analysis of projects and the comparison of alternatives. Illustrations are included of benefit-cost evaluations of single-purpose projects for hydroelectric power, municipal water supply, irrigation, and urban flood control, from experience in both the United States and developing countries. A discussion of water quality management programs emphasizes costs.

Important topics of general interest in economic analyses are explored, including a comparison of the benefit-cost ratio with other indexes of economic efficiency to guide project formulation and to rank alternatives, the special characteristics of the internal rate of return, sensitivity analysis and the role of risk analysis, and the treatment of inflation. The final portions of the chapter treat the problems of multipurpose project analysis.

Chapter 10 deals with the determination of prices for estimating benefits and costs for a range of project purposes, including types not mentioned above. Material in other chapters on systems analyses, probability analyses, economic growth models, and multiobjective approaches provide further applications of economic analyses.

8.2 EVALUATIONS OF COSTS AND BENEFITS

Costs include those necessary to implement a project such as investment costs, operation and maintenance expenses, other direct costs, and any associated costs that are needed to make the products or services of the project available for use or sale.

Various methods for estimating benefits have previously been mentioned (Section 2.5). Willingness to pay is the basis for estimating benefits in the economic analysis of a municipal water supply development in Section 8.4. Change in net income is used for estimating benefits in the economic analysis of an irrigation development in Section 8.5. This method is also used to estimate benefits in the analysis of a flood control project in Section 8.6. Cost of most likely alternative is the basis for economic analyses of various hydroelectric power developments in Section 8.3. Another approach for valuing benefits is to use administratively established values; these are often applied to recreation developments, for which a person-day spent at a recreation site is valued for various types of recreation activity.

Economic analyses should also take account of external economies or diseconomies. Credits of benefits to a project for its use of unemployed or underemployed labor may also be considered in areas of surplus labor and/or when the prices for labor do not fully reflect the supply/demand relationship of a free market. When the value of goods and services entering into the estimates of benefits and costs cannot be determined from prevailing prices due to inadequate or nonexisting markets for certain commodities or services or distorted markets for others, it may be desirable to use adjusted *accounting* or *shadow prices*. Shadow prices are often determined for projects in developing countries. These adjusted prices are not generally applied in the United States, although otherwise unemployed labor adjustments have at times been used; a shadow pricing procedure for adjusting (reducing) prices involving unemployed or underemployed labor is equivalent to the separate credits for such benefits.

8.3 ECONOMIC ANALYSIS OF HYDROELECTRIC POWER DEVELOPMENTS

This section is based largely on procedures recommended by the U.S. Federal Energy Regulatory Commission (1979) and the U.S. Water Resources Council (1983).

Hydropower may be developed in a number of ways, including:

- Single-purpose hydroelectric power project
- Part of a new multipurpose water resources project
- Addition of power generating facilities to an existing dam
- Expansion of an existing hydroelectric plant

The results of benefit-cost analyses are in terms of net annual benefits (benefits minus costs) and benefit-cost ratio. The WRC "Principles and Guidelines" (1983, p. 42) established the following basis of benefit evaluation for federal projects:

The conceptual basis for evaluating the benefit from energy produced by hydroelectric power plants is society's willingness to pay for these outputs. If this is not possible or cost effective, benefit information may sometimes be obtained through examination of market prices. . . . In cases where it can be determined that market price to the final consumer is based on marginal production costs, this may be used as a measure of benefits. In the absence of such direct measures of marginal willingness to pay, the benefit from energy produced by the hydroelectric power plants is measured by the resource cost of the most likely alternative to be implemented in the absence of the alternatives under consideration.

For federal projects, the guidelines indicate that adjustments are needed when analyzing nonfederal investments with different financial conditions, insurance, and tax incentives.

The illustrations in this section will be limited to the method that values benefits as the equivalent cost of power from the most likely alternative. Costs of hydroelectric power are due to generating facilities, dam and other civil works, and externalities. For a new multipurpose project, the hydropower facilities should be assigned a portion of the cost of the works serving more than one purpose, using techniques described in Section 8.14. If the addition of hydropower facilities causes changes in the operation and output of existing activities, a new distribution of joint costs should be made among the new and existing activities.

8.3.1 Isolated Power Project

A power project may serve an isolated demand or may be integrated in a regional system. To illustrate the case of an isolated power demand, Table 8.1 shows the costs of a 400,000-kilowatt hydropower project for which the unit investment cost is $1000 per kilowatt. The annual fixed cost (annual capacity cost) is estimated to be $160.08 per kilowatt for private sponsorship or $76.68 per kilowatt for government sponsorship. The higher costs of private sponsorship are from higher interest rates for borrowing funds, higher costs of commercial insurance, and the need to pay taxes. Although unit costs vary with the amount of energy produced, the amount of variation is small for most conventional hydropower plants and Table 8.1 does not provide separately for energy-variable costs.

Table 8.2 shows the costs of an alternative power plant used to measure hydropower benefits. This alternative is a 1,500,000-kilowatt coal-fired thermal power plant sized for the isolated power demand previously mentioned. Thus, if the hydropower project were constructed, it would satisfy only a portion of the demand. The thermal power plant has an investment cost of $700 per kilowatt. The annual capacity cost is $127.37 per kilowatt for private financing and $70.59 per kilowatt for government sponsorship. The energy-variable costs, which are mostly from fuel consumption, are estimated to be 12.11 mills (1000 mills equal $1) for private or government operation.

In Tables 8.1 and 8.2, depreciation (amortization) is determined by sinking funds that accumulate over the *weighted* economic lives of the hydropower project and the thermal alternative. Separate calculations, not shown here, have established these lives as 50 years and 30 years, respectively. In an alternative procedure, a capital recovery factor could have been used to cover interest and amortization over the *overall* economic life (say 100 years for hydro) and a separate item could be added (by sinking fund calculations) for the interim replacements of major facilities that wear out in less than the overall economic life. Minor replacements are provided for in the operation and maintenance account. In these tables it is assumed that the

TABLE 8.1 EXAMPLE SHOWING ANNUAL COST OF ELECTRIC POWER AT STEP-UP SUBSTATION, TWO-UNIT, 400,000-KILOWATT, CONVENTIONAL HYDROELECTRIC PLANT (Average Annual Plant Factor of 55%)

	Percent	Dollars per Net Kilowatt
Private Sponsorship[a]		
I. Plant investment, excluding step-up substation		$1000.00
II. Annual capacity cost:		
A. Fixed charges		
1. Cost of money	10.50	
2. Depreciation (10.50% 50-year sinking fund)	0.07	
3. Insurance	0.10	
4. Taxes	5.00	
a. Federal income	2.25	
b. Federal miscellaneous	0.10	
c. State and local	2.65	
Total fixed charges	15.67	156.70
B. Fixed operating costs		
1. Operation and maintenance		2.50[b]
2. Administrative and general expense (35% of $2.50/kW-yr)		0.88
Total fixed operating costs		3.38
Total annual capacity cost (IIA + IIB)		160.08
		Mills per Net kWh
III. Energy-variable operating costs		
1. Energy fuel		0.00
2. Operation and maintenance		0.00[c]
Energy cost − total variable operating costs		0.00
Government Sponsorship		
I. Plant investment, excluding step-up substation		$1000.00
II. Annual capacity cost:		
A. Fixed charges		
1. Cost of money	7.50	
2. Depreciation (7.5% 50-year sinking fund)	0.25	
3. Insurance (equivalent)	0.08	
4. Taxes	—	
Total fixed charges	7.33	73.30
B. Fixed operating costs		
1. Operation and maintenance		2.50
2. Administrative and general expense		0.88
Total fixed operating costs		3.38
Total annual capacity cost (IIA + IIB)		76.68
		Mills per Net kWh
III. Energy-variable operating costs		0.00

[a]Federal Energy Regulatory Commission (1979), illustration only.
[a]Based on an estimated fixed operating and maintenance cost of 0.5 mills/kilowatt-hour.
[c]All operating and maintenance costs considered to be fixed.

TABLE 8.2 EXAMPLE SHOWING ANNUAL COST OF ELECTRIC POWER AT STEP-UP SUBSTATION, TWO-UNIT, 1,500,000-KILOWATT, COAL-FIRED PLANT (Average Annual Plant Factor of 55%; Fuel Cost of $1.10 per Million Btu; and Heat Rate of 9500 Btu/kWh)[a]

	Percent	Dollars per Net Kilowatt
Private Sponsorship[b]		
I. Plant investment, excluding step-up substation		$700.00
II. Annual capacity cost:		
A. Fixed charges		
1. Cost of money	10.50	
2. Depreciation (10.50% 30-year sinking fund)	0.55	
3. Insurance	0.25	
4. Taxes	5.00	
a. Federal income	2.25	
b. Federal miscellaneous	0.10	
c. State and local	2.65	
Total fixed charges	16.30	114.10
B. Annual carrying cost of fuel inventory		1.50[c]
C. Fixed operating costs		
1. Operation and maintenance		8.82[d]
2. Administrative and general expense (35% of $8.43/kW-yr)		2.95[e]
Total fixed operating costs		11.77
Total annual capacity cost (IIA + IIB + IIC)		127.37
		Mills per Net kWh
III. Energy-variable operating costs		
1. Energy fuel (9500 Btu/kWh at $1.10/$10^6$ Btu $\times 10^3$ mills/$)		10.45
2. Operation and maintenance		1.66
Energy cost-total variable operating cost		12.11
Government Sponsorship		
I. Plant investment, excluding step-up substation		$700.00
II. Annual capacity cost:		
A. Fixed charges		
1. Cost of money	7.00	
2. Depreciation (7% 30-year sinking fund)	1.06	
3. Insurance (equivalent)	0.20	
4. Taxes	—	
Total fixed charges	8.26	57.82
B. Fixed carrying cost of fuel inventory		1.00
C. Fixed operating costs		
1. Operation and maintenance		8.82
2. Administrative and general expense		2.95
Total fixed operating costs		11.77
Total annual capacity cost (IIA + IIB + IIC)		70.59

TABLE 8.2 *(continued)*

	Percent	*Dollars per Net Kilowatt*
Government Sponsorship		
III. Energy-variable operating costs		
1. Energy fuel		10.45
2. Operation and maintenance		1.66
Energy cost − total variable operating costs		12.11

[a]Includes fuel gas desulfurization.

[b]Federal Energy Regulatory Commission (1979), illustration only.

[c]75 days $\times$ 9500 Btu/kWh $\times$ 24 hours/day $\times$ 0.55 plant factor $\times$ \$1.10/10^6 Btu $\times$ 14.47% cost of money and applicable taxes. (10.50 cost of money + 2.25 federal income taxes + 0.65 $\times$ 2.65 state and local taxes).

[d]1.83 mills/kWh $\times$ 8760 hours/year $\times$ 0.55 plant factor $\times$ \$1.00/10^3 mills.

[e]1.75 mills/kWh $\times$ 8760 hours/year $\times$ 0.55 plant factor $\times$ \$1.00/10^3 mills $\times$ 35% administration and general factor.

hydro and thermal projects operate at an average plant factor (ratio of average output to rated capacity) of 0.55. This assumption could be quite approximate since the best use of the hydropower component of a reservoir project may change in the future and the "equivalent" thermal project may also be operated differently as it ages and becomes less efficient.

Perceptions of benefits and costs differ depending upon assumptions of ownership and evaluation procedure. Such perceptions can lead to widely varying results, as shown in Table 8.3. For this illustration, the hydropower project, although rated at 400,000 kilowatts, is credited with a dependable capacity of only 360,000 kilowatts. This lower value would be assumed for the evaluation of benefits if, for example, a less than normal head and/or flow were available for hydroelectric power production at the time of peak power demand. The average annual energy for a 55% annual plant factor would be 1927 million kilowatt-hours.

If private sponsorship were considered for both the hydroelectric power project and the most likely alternative, Table 8.3 shows a benefit-cost ratio of 1.08 and annual net benefits of \$5,159,592. If government sponsorship were considered for both the hydro and thermal alternative, the benefit-cost ratio would be 1.59 with annual net benefits of \$18,078,792.

In the United States, with the exception of the Tennessee Valley Authority, federal government agencies sponsor hydropower projects but do not construct commercial thermal power plants. As shown in Table 8.3, a benefit-cost evaluation oriented to the electric power consumer would indicate a benefit-cost ratio of 2.26 and annual net benefits of \$38,519,592, based on government hydro cost compared with benefits equivalent to private thermal cost. This is also similar to a situation when a regional or local government entity constructs a hydroplant but would be not empowered to construct a thermal plant.

Under the comparability test outlined in the Water Resources Council "Principles and Guidelines" (1983), the federal government discount rate is used for both federal and nonfederal alternatives, taxes are excluded, and other parallel

TABLE 8.3 BENEFIT-COST ANALYSIS OF 400,000-KILOWATT CONVENTIONAL ISOLATED HYDROELECTRIC PLANT (Plant Factor 0.55; Dependable Capacity 90% of Rated Capacity)

Project Data

Dependable capacity	
400,000 × 0.90	360,000 kW
Annual average energy	
400,000 × 0.55 × 8760	1,927,200,000 kWh

Annual Costs

Private sponsorship	
4000,000 × $160.08	$64,032,000
Government sponsorship	
400,000 × $76.68	$30,672,000

Annual Benefits

Private alternative:	
Capacity : 360,000 × 127.37	45,853,200
Energy : 1,927,200,000 × 0.01211	23,338,392
Total annual benefits	$69,191,592
Government alternative:	
Capacity : 360,000 × 70.50	25,412,400
Energy : 1,927,200 × 0.01211	23,338,392
Total annual benefits	$48,750,792

Benefit-Cost Results

Private hydro compared with private thermal

Benefit-cost ratio $\dfrac{69,191,592}{64,032,000} = 1.08$

Annual net benefits 69,191,592 − 64,032,000 = $5,159,592
Govt. hydro compared with govt. thermal

Benefit-cost ratio $\dfrac{48,750,792}{30,672,000} = 1.59$

Annual net benefits 48,750,792 − 30,672,000 = $18,078,792
Govt. hydro compared with private thermal

Benefit-cost ratio $\dfrac{69,191,592}{30,672,000} = 2.26$

Annual net benefits 69,191,592 − 30,672,000 = $38,519,592

---

assumptions are used. This is consistent with the omission of "transfer payments," as discussed in Section 2.5, for national economic development accounting. The results of this procedure would be to obtain values corresponding to the National Economic Development objective; such results, subject to minor procedural differences, should be close to the B/C of 1.59 and $(B - C)$ of $18 million stated previously.

In the United States, the Federal Energy Regulatory Commission provides estimates of costs of thermal alternatives when federal projects are being considered.

TABLE 8.4 MARGINAL POWER VALUES FOR HYDROELECTRIC ENERGY[a,b]

Plant Factor	Capacity Value ($/kW/yr)	Energy Value (mills/kWh)
Combustion Turbine Alternative		
0	33.30	—
10	33.30	56.5
20	33.30	56.3
Combined Cycle Alternative		
30	75.50	42.1
40	75.50	38.7
Nuclear Alternative		
0	215.80	1.4
60	215.80	5.8
70	215.80	8.6
80	215.80	10.9
90	215.80	12.7
100	215.80	14.1
Coal-Fired Alternatives		
50	183.70	15.1
60	183.70	17.0
70	183.70	18.4
80	183.70	19.4
90	183.70	20.3
100	183.70	20.9

[a]This table illustrates the marginal values for capacity and energy which would be sold to, or generated by, an existing electric utility.

[b]The capacity values shown here are based on the costs of new construction. A utility may not require additional capacity or may have significantly "paid down" the costs of existing equipment; in either case, the capacity value will be lower than those shown above, but the energy value may be higher for older less efficient units.

Source: New York State Regional Values; updated from estimates of U.S. Federal Energy Regulatory Commission (published June 23, 1978).

As shown in Table 8.4, such costs vary greatly with type of fuel, plant factor (capacity factor when plant capacity is utilized), and other assumptions.

8.3.2 Integrated Power Project

A hydroelectric power plant may be evaluated in terms of the isolated plant condition discussed in the preceding section for a remote location where a hydro development opportunity exists together with a single customer for the power produced (e.g., large hydro resource with a timber, aluminum, or oil shale resource), or where the hydro plant output will be absorbed by an electrical system that is almost completely dependent on this hydro output and is not expected to become a fully integrated regional system for many years. In the more usual condition, almost everywhere in the United States and other industrial countries and in many developing countries, the hydroelectric power would be fed into the electric power system of a regional utility.

This utility would operate various types of plants (hydro and thermal) of different capacities and, in many cases, the system would include interconnections for regular and/or emergency energy contributions from other systems.

For an integrated power project (and in some cases also for the isolated project) a number of adjustments should be made to the benefits to account for (U.S. Federal Energy Regulatory Commission, 1979):

1. Differences in transformation and transmission costs to market (load centers) due to different transmission distances for the hydroelectric power project and the alternative(s).

2. Greater reliability and operating flexibility of hydroelectric power generating equipment due to fewer outages for equipment failure and for normal maintenance and repair, ability to take on and shed power loads more quickly, need for less auxiliary equipment and power for shutdowns and restarts, and large rotating inertia to assist in system stability. An adjustment of 5 to 10% of the cost per kilowatt of the thermal-electric alternative to benefit hydro may be made for these characteristics.

3. Value of nondependable capacity. This depends on such factors as the time and duration of its availability, the market for interruptible power, its usefulness as reserve capacity for scheduled maintenances, and the savings in system costs when such capacity is utilized.

4. Expected future increases of thermal fuel costs in terms of constant dollars (real increases over and above general inflation).

5. Energy adjustment due to changing role of hydro or thermal alternative in the system in the future.

With respect to the last factor, the dependable capacity of a hydro plant having reservoir storage may change over its life due to changes in available storage and how it is used for hydroelectric energy production and for other purposes. The equivalent thermal powerplant may also have a changing role as to how its capacity and energy are employed in the electrical system. The Federal Energy Regulatory Commission (1979) has analyzed the growth of a system annual "load curve" and the changing position of a thermal power plant in the system. At first, the new efficient thermal plant serves "base" load at a high plant factor, and displaces older higher-cost thermal energy; this savings in energy cost reduces the benefits credited to the hydroelectric project. As time passes and the thermal plant grows older, it serves a portion of the load where it has the same capacity but produces less energy at a lower plant factor, and where the spread in energy costs between its production and the energy it displaces is less. The changing plant factor of the thermal alternative may be compared with an assumed constant plant factor of the hydro and the changing spread in system energy costs, to obtain an energy adjustment which reduces hydro benefits in the early years and increases hydro benefits for the later years.

The analyses presented above have been limited to the values normally utilized in economic analyses. There are other quantities which may in some cases be perceived to have economic value and are included in the analyses. These include additional benefits that are attributable to the conservation of fossil-fuel resources when hydro is employed, the lower air and water pollution compared with a thermal alternative, and the savings when the inclusion of hydro in a multipurpose development makes other development purposes more attractive economically. Particularly in a developing country, the savings in foreign exchange and improvement in its own security and self-reliance may be very important when hydro is used instead of thermal alternatives. This may be taken into account by "shadow pricing" the imported fuel when the thermal alternative is analyzed, where the foreign exchange rate is incorrect from the standpoint of the economic objective (Dasgupta et al. 1972), or by applying multiobjective weights for other objectives such as national security.

8.4 ECONOMIC ANALYSIS OF MUNICIPAL WATER SUPPLY DEVELOPMENT

The internal rate of return is the rate of interest for which the present value of a series of annual costs is equated to the present value of the associated series of annual benefits. If the internal rate is 10%, it is equivalent to a benefit-cost ratio of 1.0 at a stipulated discount rate of 10%.

The example presented here is based on the master plan for water supply of Kingston, Jamaica by Tippetts-Abbett-McCarthy-Stratton (TAMS, 1977). The analyses of alternative projects have been previously discussed in Chapters 5 and 6. The basic problem was to select a first priority scheme good for at least 7 years and a a longer range master plan to beyond year 2000. This section describes the detailed economic analysis for the recommended plan.

The economic analyses treated costs and benefits of each project on an incremental basis. Thus, the costs of implementing and operating a project were measured against the benefits derived from the project's capability to satisfy incremental needs for water supply. The benefits represent minimum amounts since they were limited to returns from water tariff revenue, a measure of "willingness to pay" by users of water. A more comprehensive economic analysis would be based on a less restricted evaluation of user benefits, and would consider the economic benefits of improved health standards, industrial benefits arising from a more reliable water supply, and the savings in water system costs in early years when project excess capacity may be used to replace more expensive pumping of domestic and irrigation water elsewhere in the system. Thus, the estimated internal rates of return presented here should not be compared, without substantial adjustment, with the "opportunity cost" for alternative investments in the nation's economic sectors.

Economic analyses were made at 1977 prices on the assumption that inflation would affect costs and benefits equally and therefore that the increases due to this effect would offset each other. The weighted average water rate in 1977 was estimated to be Jamaican J $1.16 per thousand imperial gallons sold (U.S. $0.93/1000 gallons). It was, however, expected that weighted average tariff per thousand gallons would increase to J $1.90 (U.S. $1.52) and this value was used in the economic analyses.

Table 8.5 shows the year-by-year minimum net incremental benefits obtained by subtracting annual costs from minimum annual benefits equivalent to revenues at U.S. $1.52 per imperial thousand gallons. The internal rate of return would be 8.9% since, as shown by the last column of Table 8.5, the sum of the present worths of each year's net incremental benefits discounted at this rate is zero. The internal rate of return was used to compare the recommended first priority scheme with other projects. This scheme would be adequate for 7 years, to about 1986.

Various alternatives were compared for a master plan which would be adequate to beyond year 2000. For this purpose, economic analyses were made using as economic indicators the internal rate of return and the discounted total costs at an interest rate of 10%. The calculations for the recommended master plan incorporating the first priority scheme as a first phase are given on Table 8.6. The net incremental benefits are obtained as the difference between the sum of costs for construction and operation (including operation, maintenance, renewals and replacements, water treatment, and distribution) and the revenue for incremental water sold that is attributable to the project. Table 8.6 shows that the discounted net benefits (revenue minus cost) equal zero at an interest rate of 7.6% and that the total discounted costs at 10% interest rate are $118,996,750; these values were compared with those for alternative master plans.

8.5 ECONOMIC ANALYSIS OF IRRIGATION DEVELOPMENT

Economic analyses were made by Tippetts-Abbett-McCarthy-Stratton (TAMS, 1963) for the Rio Ebro Right Bank Irrigation Project in Spain. The analyses were in terms of pesetas at a time when 60 pesetas were equivalent to U.S. $1.00. The project would involve the irrigation of 47,000 hectares of land using water pumped from the Rio Ebro. The project is described in Section 9.5, which also discusses the financial analyses.

For use in making the estimates of benefit-cost ratio and other economic indicators, the direct agricultural returns or benefits are those that result from the project before considering the cost of project works. The future market values of crops were estimated. The production costs for producing these crops were subtracted. These production costs included land rental; amortization of land conversion costs; expenses of machinery and animals; expenses of seed, fertilizers, and pesticides; and value of the farmers' own labor and hired labor. After subtracting future farm production costs from future market values, the figures obtained were adjusted for present agricultural returns. These net direct agricultural returns (or benefits) were compared with the costs of the project works, comprising both capital charges and operation and maintenance expenses.

When the full amount of irrigation is achieved in the project, the benefits would be approximately 31,200 pesetas per year per hectare in irrigated production. To take account of the somewhat smaller returns during the earlier years of development of irrigation before the most fertile lands are reached by the canals, a value of 30,000 pesetas per year per hectare in irrigated production was assumed.

The annual benefits and costs were determined for a 60-year project period with

TABLE 8.5 COMPARATIVE STUDY OF WATER SUPPLY PROJECTS, KINGSTON ECONOMIC ANALYSIS OF FIRST PRIORITY PHASE I PROJECT, CONSTANT 1977 PRICES ($1000 U.S.)[a]

Year	Project Investment	Operation Maintenance Replacement Treatment	Distribution Costs ($0.18 per thousand gallons)	Total Costs	Incremental Annual Revenue	Net Incremental Benefits	Discounted Net Benefits at 8.9%
1978	1,538.00	0.00	0.00	1,538.00	0.00	−1,538.00	−1,538.00
1979	20,228.00	0.00	0.00	20,228.00	0.00	−20,228.00	−18,571.95
1980	20,178.00	0.00	0.00	20,178.00	0.00	−20,178.00	−17,009.33
1981	0.00	723.00	151.19	874.20	1072.51	198.31	153.48
1982	0.00	723.00	322.01	1,045.02	2,284.19	1,239.17	880.54
1983	0.00	723.00	479.69	1,202.69	3,402.67	2,199.97	1,435.29
1984	0.00	723.00	656.99	1,380.00	4,660.31	3,280.31	1,964.91
1985	0.00	723.00	827.81	1,550.82	5,872.00	4,321.18	2,376.48
1986	0.00	723.00	1,005.29	1,728.29	7,130.92	5,402.62	2,727.98
1987	0.00	723.00	1,007.47	1,800.47	7,642.92	5,842.44	2,708.54
1988	0.00	723.00	1,077.47	1,800.47	7,642.92	5,842.44	2,486.79
1989	0.00	723.00	1,077.47	1,800.47	7,642.92	5,842.44	2,283.20
1990	0.00	723.00	1,077.47	1,800.47	7,642.92	5,842.44	2,096.28
1991	0.00	723.00	1,077.47	1,800.47	7,642.92	5,842.44	1,924.66
1992	0.00	723.00	1,077.47	1,800.47	7,642.92	5,842.44	1,767.09
1993	0.00	723.00	1,077.47	1,800.47	7,642.92	5,842.44	1,622.42
1994	0.00	723.00	1,077.47	1,800.47	7,642.92	5,842.44	1,489.59
1995	0.00	723.00	1,077.47	1,800.47	7,642.92	5,842.44	1,367.64
1996	0.00	723.00	1,077.47	1,800.47	7,642.92	5,842.44	1,255.67
1997	0.00	723.00	1,077.47	1,800.47	7,642.92	5,842.44	1,152.87
1998	0.00	723.00	1,077.47	1,800.47	7,642.92	5,842.44	1,058.49
1999	0.00	723.00	1,077.47	1,800.47	7,642.92	5,842.44	971.83
2000	0.00	723.00	1,077.47	1,800.47	7,642.92	5,842.44	892.26
2001	0.00	723.00	1,077.47	1,800.47	7,642.92	5,842.44	819.22
2002	0.00	723.00	1,077.47	1,800.47	7,642.92	5,842.44	752.15
2003	0.00	723.00	1,077.47	1,800.47	7,642.92	5,842.44	690.57
2004	0.00	723.00	1,077.47	1,800.47	7,642.92	5,842.44	634.03
2005	0.00	723.00	1,077.47	1,800.47	7,642.92	5,842.44	582.12
2006	0.00	723.00	1,077.47	1,800.47	7,642.92	5,842.44	534.47
2007	0.00	723.00	1,077.47	1,800.47	7,642.92	5,842.44	490.71

[a]Water tariff $1.52/1000 gal.
Source: TAMS (1977).

TABLE 8.6 COMPARATIVE STUDY OF WATER SUPPLY PROJECTS, KINGSTON ECONOMIC ANALYSIS OF RECOMMENDED MASTER PLAN, CONSTANT 1977 PRICES ($1000 U.S.)

Year	Construction Costs	Total Annual Operating Costs	Total Costs	Incremental Annual Revenue	Net Incremental Benefits	Discounted Net Benefits at 7.6%	Discounted Total Costs at 10.0%
1978	1,539.00	0.00	1,539.00	0.00	-1,539.00	-1,539.00	1,539.00
1979	20,226.00	0.00	20,226.00	0.00	-20,226.00	-18,781.00	18,387.27
1980	20,181.00	0.00	20,181.00	0.00	-20,181.00	-17,402.11	16,678.51
1981	0.00	874.20	874.20	1,072.51	198.31	158.79	656.79
1982	0.00	1,045.02	1,045.02	2,234.19	1,239.17	921.40	713.76
1983	2,074.00	1,202.69	3,276.70	3,402.67	125.97	86.97	2,034.57
1984	23,418.00	1,380.00	24,798.00	4,660.31	-20,137.67	-12,911.81	13,997.82
1985	25,954.00	1,550.82	27,504.82	5,872.00	-21,632.81	-12,880.14	14,114.32
1986	25,953.00	1,728.29	27,681.30	7,130.92	-20,550.37	-11,362.06	12,913.52
1987	0.00	3,021.60	3,021.60	8,388.57	5,366.97	2,755.47	1,281.45
1988	0.00	3,199.08	3,199.08	9,647.49	6,448.41	3,074.32	1,233.38
1989	0.00	3,389.51	3,389.51	10,998.35	7,608.83	3,368.56	1,188.00
1990	2,086.00	3,559.79	5,645.79	12,206.20	6,560.40	2,697.03	1,798.92
1991	28,122.00	3,757.43	31,879.44	13,608.13	-18,271.31	-6,975.18	9,234.33
1992	28,180.00	3,941.39	32,121.40	14,913.02	-17,208.38	-6,100.38	8,458.56
1993	0.00	4,884.50	4,884.50	16,311.11	11,426.61	3,761.51	1,169.31
1994	0.00	5,068.45	5,068.45	17,616.00	12,547.54	3,835.65	1,103.04
1995	0.00	5,278.70	5,278.70	19,107.30	13,828.60	3,925.39	1,044.36
1996	0.00	5,475.79	5,475.79	20,505.40	15,029.60	3,961.70	984.87
1997	0.00	5,679.55	5,679.55	21,950.73	16,271.17	3,982.74	928.65
1998	0.00	5,889.79	5,889.79	23,442.04	17,552.24	3,989.57	875.48
1999	0.00	6,106.51	6,106.51	24,979.30	18,872.78	3,983.45	825.17
2000	0.00	6,329.89	6,329.89	26,563.81	20,233.91	3,965.81	777.60
2001	0.00	6,329.89	6,329.89	26,563.81	20,233.91	3,682.66	706.91
2002	0.00	6,329.89	6,329.89	26,563.81	20,233.91	3,419.73	642.64
2003	0.00	6,329.89	6,329.89	26,563.81	20,233.91	3,175.57	584.22
2004	0.00	6,329.89	6,329.89	26,563.81	20,233.91	2,948.84	531.11
2005	0.00	6,329.89	6,329.89	26,563.81	20,233.91	2,738.30	482.82
2006	0.00	6,329.89	6,329.89	26,563.81	20,233.91	2,542.79	438.93
2007	0.00	6,329.89	6,329.89	26,563.81	20,233.91	2,361.24	399.03
2008	0.00	6,329.89	6,329.89	26,563.81	20,233.91	2,192.65	362.75
2009	0.00	6,329.89	6,329.89	26,563.81	20,233.91	2,036.10	329.77
2010	0.00	6,329.89	6,329.89	26,563.91	20,233.91	1,890.73	299.79
2011	0.00	6,329.89	6,329.89	26,563.81	20,233.91	1,755.73	272.54

TABLE 8.6 *(continued)*

Year	Construction Costs	Total Annual Operating Costs	Total Costs	Incremental Annual Revenue	Net Incremental Benefits	Discounted Net Benefits at 7.6%	Discounted Total Costs at 10.0%
2012	0.00	6,329.89	6,329.89	26,563.81	20,233.91	1,630.38	247.76
2013	0.00	6,329.89	6,329.89	26,563.81	20,233.91	1,513.97	225.24
2014	0.00	6,329.89	6,329.89	26,563.81	20,233.91	1,405.88	204.76
2015	0.00	6,329.89	6,329.89	26,563.81	20,233.91	1,305.50	186.15
2016	0.00	6,329.89	6,329.89	26,563.81	20,233.91	1,212.29	169.22
2017	0.00	6,329.89	6,329.89	26,563.81	20,233.91	1,125.73	153.84
2018	0.00	6,329.89	6,329.89	26,563.81	20,233.91	1,045.36	139.85
2019	0.00	6,329.89	6,329.89	26,563.81	20,233.91	970.72	127.14
2020	0.00	6,329.89	6,329.89	26,563.81	20,233.91	901.41	115.58
2021	0.00	6,329.89	6,329.89	26,563.81	20,233.91	837.05	105.07
2022	0.00	6,329.89	6,329.89	26,563.81	20,233.91	777.29	95.52
2023	0.00	6,239.89	6,329.89	26,563.81	20,233.91	721.79	86.84
2024	0.00	6,329.89	6,329.89	26,563.81	20,233.91	670.26	78.94
2025	0.00	6,329.89	6,329.89	26,563.81	20,233.91	622.40	71.76
							118,996.75

Source: TAMS (1977).

210

the assumptions of 3% interest rate and 0.4 peseta per kilowatt-hour power rate. These values for interest rate and power rate are much lower than some recent rates but were appropriate at the time of the analysis. The annual benefits were computed at the rate of 30,000 pesetas per hectare in irrigated production, as discussed above. Costs covered capital charges and operation and maintenance costs. The benefit-cost ratio based on a simple sum of all benefits and costs over the 60-year project period was estimated to be 5.3. The ratio of annual benefits and costs for each year after full development would be 5.5. A theoretically more precise value of the benefit-cost ratio was estimated by converting the benefits and costs for each year to present worth values; by this means, a ratio of benefits and costs of 5.2 was obtained. The annual costs of 248 million pesetas for full development amount to 0.92 peseta per cubic meter pumped, close to the cost of water which was used in the financial analysis (see Chapter 9).

The benefit-cost ratios and unit costs of water derived for 12 variations of criteria are shown on Table 8.7. For the economic criteria of 1963, all the benefit-cost ratios were very high (i.e. 4.0 to 5.6). The importance of the interest rate in the analysis is shown by the calculations in Table 8.8. For a discount rate of 10% rather than 3 or 4%, the benefit-cost ratio would be reduced to 2.1.

The ratio of net farm benefit to investment, expressed as a percentage, is a measure of the rate of return on the investment. For this analysis, the investment is made over a period of 20 years and then is assumed to be essentially constant, without significant depreciation. The net agricultural returns or benefits are reduced by the operation and maintenance for the project works.

Column (2) of Table 8.9 shows the annual direct agricultural returns or benefits. The annual operation and maintenance expenses shown in column (3) are subtracted, and the net farm benefits thus obtained are shown in column (4). Columns (6) and (7) show the average cumulative investment in construction charged to irrigation. The ratio of net farm benefits to the investment for each year of the project is shown as a percentage in column (8). The net benefits for year 12, just after completing construction, would be equivalent to a return of 23% on the investment. The rate of return would increase rapidly until, beginning with year 21, the net farm benefits would represent a net annual return of 46% of the investment in irrigation works.

An internal rate of return calculation is shown by Table 8.10. The present worth of benefits is equal to the present worth of costs with a discount rate of 19%. Note that in Table 8.8 the costs shown include capital costs for repaying construction costs, whereas in Table 8.10 the construction costs are shown separately as they are incurred; the latter approach is necessary because the interest rate is not known until the rate of return computation is completed.

In this study the analyses of economic feasibility were based primarily on estimates of direct agricultural benefits and costs. In view of the favorable results, additional detailed estimates of economic benefits were not needed to justify the project. However, there were additional impacts on the national and regional systems relevant to various accounts. The project would be expected to increase the supplies of labor and capital in the project area and would enable more intensive use of available land and water resources. The resources of state, provincial, and city governments would increase as the result of increased tax revenues. Foreign

TABLE 8.7 RIO EBRO PROJECT: BENEFIT-COST RATIOS AND UNIT COST OF WATER (Various Project Periods, Interest Rates, and Prices of Electric Energy)

	60-Year Period						50-Year Period					
	Interest at 3%			*Interest at 4%*			*Interest at 3%*			*Interest at 4%*		
	Power at 0.3 peseta/kWh	*Power at 0.4 peseta/kWh*	*Power at 0.5 peseta/kWh*	*Power at 0.3 peseta/kWh*	*Power at 0.4 peseta/kWh*	*Power at 0.5 peseta/kWh*	*Power at 0.3 peseta/kWh*	*Power at 0.4 peseta/kWh*	*Power at 0.5 peseta/kWh*	*Power at 0.3 peseta/kWh*	*Power at 0.4 peseta/kWh*	*Power at 0.5 peseta/kWh*
Benefit-Cost Ratios												
Simple sum of all annual values	5.8	5.3	4.9	5.1	4.7	4.4	5.4	5.0	4.6	4.8	4.4	4.2
Annual values for full development	6.0	5.5	5.1	5.3	4.9	4.5	5.7	5.2	4.8	5.0	4.7	4.4
Present worth of all annual values	5.6	5.2	4.8	4.9	4.5	4.2	5.3	4.9	4.5	4.6	4.3	4.0
Unit Cost of Water Pumped (peseta/cubic meter)												
Total period	0.84	0.92	0.99	0.96	1.04	1.11	0.89	0.96	1.04	1.01	1.09	1.16
Years after full development	0.84	0.92	0.99	0.96	1.04	1.11	0.89	0.96	1.04	1.01	1.08	1.16

Source: TAMS (1963).

TABLE 8.8 RIO EBRO PROJECT: BENEFIT-COST RATIO AT 10% INTEREST (Costs and Benefits in Million Pesetas)

Year	Costs	Discount Factor	Present Worth	Benefits	Discount Factor	Present Worth
1						
2						
3						
4	15.2	0.683 013	10.38	25.8	0.683 013	17.62
5	23.7	0.620 921	14.72	96.6	0.620 921	59.98
6	35.8	0.564 474	20.21	171.6	0.564 474	96.86
7	46.8	0.513 158	24.01	254.1	0.513 158	130.39
8	57.0	0.466 507	26.59	333.6	0.466 507	155.63
9	68.5	0.424 098	29.05	408.3	0.424 098	173.16
10	80.6	0.385 543	31.07	494.1	0.385 543	190.50
11	571.4	0.350 494	200.27	578.1	0.350 494	202.62
12	579.6	0.318 631	184.68	732.0	0.318 631	233.24
13	586.2	0.289 664	169.80	856.5	0.289 664	248.10
14	591.5	0.263 331	155.76	960.6	0.263 331	252.96
15	595.4	0.239 392	142.53	1038.4	0.239 392	248.58
16	598.2	0.217 629	130.19	1166.5	0.217 629	253.86
17	599.7	0.197 845	118.65	1263.7	0.197 845	250.02
18	600.4	0.179 859	107.99	1313.8	0.179 859	236.30
19	600.8	0.163 508	98.24	1346.7	0.163 508	220.20
20	601.0	0.148 644	89.34	1362.4	0.148 644	202.51
21	601.1	0.135 131	81.23	1373.8	0.135 131	185.64
22–60	601.1	1.266 120	761.06	1376.9	1.266 120	1743.32
			2395.77			5101.49

Benefit-cost ratio = 5101.49/2395.77 = 2.13
Net present worth = 5101.49 − 2395.77 = 2705.72
Average annual benefit = (5101.49 × 0.162745) − (2395.77 × 0.162745) = 440.35

TABLE 8.9 RIO EBRO PROJECT: COMPARISON OF ANNUAL FARM BENEFITS WITH INVESTMENT IN IRRIGATION WORKS (Million Pesetas)

Year	Benefits at 30,000 pesetas/hectare	Operation and Maintenance	Net Farm Benefits	Investment			Net Farm Benefits ÷ Investment (%)
				Annual	Cumulative End year.	Cumulative Mid-year.	
(1)	(2)	(3)	(4)	(5)	(6)	(7)	(8)
1		Pumping station		23.4	23.4	11.7	0
1		Main canal		230.8	254.2	138.8	0
2		Dist. system		234.0	488.2	371.2	0
3				318.3	806.5	647.3	0
4	25.8	15.2	10.6	230.6	1,037.1	921.8	1
5	96.6	23.7	72.9	255.7	1,292.8	1,164.9	6
6	171.6	35.8	135.8	215.5	1,508.3	1,400.6	10
7	254.1	46.8	207.3	378.4	1,886.7	1,697.5	12
8	333.6	57.0	276.6	317.3	2,204.0	2,045.3	13
9	408.3	68.5	339.8	310.2	2,514.2	2,359.1	14
10	494.1	80.6	413.5	200.6	2,714.8	2,614.5	16
11	578.1	93.3	484.8	19.3	2,734.1	2,724.5	18
12	732.0	101.5	630.5		2,734.1	2,734.1	23
13	856.5	108.1	748.4		2,734.1	2,734.1	27
14	960.6	113.4	847.2		2,734.1	2,734.1	31
15	1,038.4	117.3	921.1		2,734.1	2,734.1	34
16	1,166.5	120.1	1,046.4		2,734.1	2,734.1	38
17	1,263.7	121.3	1,142.4		2,734.1	2,734.1	42
18	1,313.8	122.3	1,191.5		2,734.1	2,734.1	44
19	1,346.7	122.7	1,224.0		2,734.1	2,734.1	45
20	1,362.4	122.9	1,239.5		2,734.1	2,734.1	45
21	1,373.8	123.0	1,250.8		2,734.1	2,734.1	46
22–60	1,376.9	123.0	1,253.9		2,734.1	2,734.1	46

Source: TAMS (1963).

TABLE 8.10 RIO EBRO PROJECT: ECONOMIC ANALYSIS FOR INTERNAL RATE OF RETURN (Million Pesetas)

Year	Construction Costs	O and M Costs	Total Costs	Net Benefits	Cash Flow	Discount Factor	Present Worth
-1	23.4		23.4		-23.4	1	-23.40
1	230.8		230.8		-230.8	0.840336	-193.95
2	234.0		234.0		-234.0	0.706165	-165.24
3	318.3		318.3		-318.3	0.593416	-188.88
4	240.6	15.2	255.8	25.8	-230.0	0.498669	-114.69
5	255.7	23.7	279.4	96.6	-182.8	0.419049	-76.60
6	215.5	35.8	251.3	171.6	-79.7	0.532142	-28.07
7	378.4	46.8	425.2	254.1	-171.1	0.295918	-50.63
8	317.3	57.0	374.3	333.6	-40.7	0.248671	-10.12
9	310.2	68.5	378.7	408.3	29.6	0.208967	6.18
10	200.6	80.6	281.2	494.1	212.9	0.175602	37.39
11	19.3	93.3	112.6	578.1	465.5	0.147565	68.69
12		101.5	101.5	732.0	630.5	0.124004	78.18
13		108.1	108.1	856.5	748.4	0.104205	77.99
14		113.4	113.4	960.6	847.2	0.087567	74.19
15		117.3	117.3	1038.4	921.1	0.073586	67.78
16		120.1	120.1	1166.5	1046.4	0.061837	64.71
17		121.6	121.6	1263.7	1142.1	0.051964	59.35
18		122.3	122.3	1313.8	1191.5	0.043667	52.03
19		122.7	122.7	1346.7	1224.0	0.036695	44.91
20		122.9	122.9	1362.4	1239.5	0.030835	38.22
21		123.0	123.0	1373.8	1250.8	0.025913	32.41
22–60		123.0	123.0	1376.9	1253.9	0.135504	169.91
							20.36

Internal rate of return = 19%

exchange earnings would be increased since a major portion of the crops would be exported. Other improvements in the regional economy may also occur (see Chapter 14).

8.6 ECONOMIC ANALYSIS OF FLOOD CONTROL PROJECT

This study was performed at the reconnaissance level and involved the comparison of costs and benefits for flood control works on the Hackensack River to reduce damages from inundation of structures in the Hackensack Meadowlands Area (TAMS, 1980).

The reduction of damages from floods was estimated for each of a number of nodes at locations subject to inundation (Figure 8.1a). All structures were inventoried within the floodplain limits for the 100-year flood. The structures were located on an aerial photo map, which was then overlaid with a map of the link and node system employed for the hydraulic analyses in order to define the structures related to each node. Based on a sample of these structures, estimates were made of the inundation stage (elevation) versus damage that would occur to the structures, contents, and property in each node area for current (1980) conditions; a typical stage-damage curve is shown in Figure 8.1b. Using projections based on the master plan of the Hackensack Development Commission, another set of stage-damage curves was estimated for "ultimate" development, which was assumed to be achieved by year 2000. The 1980 and 2000 values were both in terms of present prices. A growth was provided to project increases in residential damages in the future.

For various stages (elevations) at a node, values of damage were assumed to grow between 1980 and 2000 and to remain constant thereafter. The adjusted streams of damage values for each of 100 years of project operation were discounted to the date the project is completed, using the specified interest rate. These present worth values were converted into annual average values based on the same interest rate. This technique resulted in a set of curves, one for each node, showing the stage-damage relationships which were used for the estimates of benefits.

Complex hydrologic/hydraulic/statistical analyses were carried out to develop a stage-frequency curve for each node with the flood control project in place. Each ordinate (stage) of the stage-frequency curve corresponds to a value of damage from the stage-damage curve for the node. It was possible, therefore, to develop a damage-frequency curve for each node and for the entire area. The area under the latter curve was determined (units of dollars × probability) to obtain the average annual damages with the project.

The procedure described above was also carried out for each node for conditions without the project (Figure 8.1c and d). The difference in average annual benefits with- and without-project, gave the average annual benefits attributable to the flood control project. The costs of the project were determined on an annual basis, and compared with the benefits in terms of a benefit-cost ratio. A similar process was used to evaluate the principal alternative projects considered.

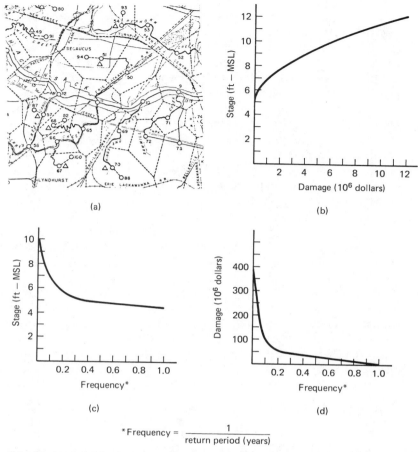

Figure 8.1 Hackensack Meadowlands: evaluation of benefits for flood control project. (a) Node system; (b) typical stage-damage curve for a node; (c) typical stage-frequency curve for a node without project; (d) damage-frequency curve for entire area without project. (From TAMS, 1980.)

8.7 ECONOMIC ANALYSES OF WATER QUALITY MANAGEMENT PROJECTS

Licensing activities are not covered in the Water Resources Council guidelines for planning. Thus, as discussed in Section 8.3, there are some differences in the analyses of hydroelectric projects between the methods of the Water Resources Council (which were designed for federal government projects) and the methods of the Federal Energy Regulatory Commission (which apply to private and nonfederal governmental projects). Similarly, the Water Resources Council guidelines do not apply to the Environmental Protection Agency, which is the principal federal agency involved in water quality management.

As a matter of national policy, it has been decided that plans for the attainment of satisfactory water quality goals for surface waterways and underground waters are in the national interest and need not be justified by benefit-cost analysis. The U.S. Environmental Protection Agency and counterpart state agencies are responsible for this program. Chapter 6 described various mandated programs for regional and local planning and discussed one example of an areawide planning effort.

The EPA is interested in the cost effectiveness of projects in terms of optimizing the cost of construction, operating efficiency, and attainment of standards for wastewater effluent quality and receiving water quality. Costs to achieve reductions in dangerous contaminants are very high and are subject to much study. As discussed in Chapter 6, however, the sponsor of a wastewater treatment plant or the planner of a regional program for water quality management is not required to determine benefit-cost relationships.

The benefits of water quality maintenance and enhancement are not fully measurable in economic terms. To some extent, values may be estimated for water-based recreation made possible by improved water quality, cost savings in water treatment due to improved quality at the intake, reductions in damages to structural facilities exposed to water, increased quantity and better quality of fish caught, and other effects. Evaluation of the benefits is very difficult and often becomes quite academic in view of the overall water pollution control policy of the United States, which comprehends both standards for minimum effluent quality and standards for minimum quality of water bodies. However, progress should be made in measuring water quality benefits in order to enable an informed judgment to be made about the merit of alternative policies.

With the background above, it is clear that most current solutions to problems in water quality management economics will tend to emphasize a minimum-cost plan which will, at the same time, be acceptable to the many parties having interests in the water and associated land resources of the project area. Such a plan may aim at a minimum cost from the standpoint of the responsible agency in overall charge or a minimum cost for the individual polluters who must consider wastewater treatment and disposal.

Bundgaard-Nielson and Hwang (1976) have made a comprehensive review of various models that have been proposed for economic analyses of regional water quality management. These analyses require information on: (1) the cost of wastewater treatment as a function of effluent quantity and quality; (2) the relationship of waste discharge to the quantity and quality of the receiving water systems; and (3) the benefits associated with particular receiving water qualities. As noted above, the information related to (3) is generally inadequate. The authors have classified the methods as "centralized," "decentralized," and "multiobjective" models. Centralized models assume that a "basin-wide firm" owns and operates all waste and water treatment plants and carries on all water-based activities within the region. The objective is to use treatment facilities and the assimilative capacities of the receiving water most efficiently. Thus, when regional water quality standards apply, the aim is for a minimum cost program or, if benefits can be measured, a minimum net cost program. Structural measures can include at-source treatment, regional waste treatment plants, and bypass piping (see Section 12.8 for a list of alternative approaches). Decentralized models optimize the plan based on letting each polluter determine his or her own actions using his or her own economic criteria. Each polluter may choose to build a wastewater treatment plant or pay an effluent charge imposed by a regional authority. Multiobjective models may include goals other than minimum cost relating to water quality, effluent charges, proportioning allowable discharges, and other factors. Some of the mathematical model approaches to determine the optimum regional system of treatment plants are described in Chapters 12 and 13.

The concept of the basin-wide firm and the role of effluent charges have been explored by Kneese and Bower (1968). Several types of incentives for managing environmental problems have been examined by Bower et al. (1977). Haimes et al. (1972) have defined a multilevel approach to determining charges. The cost allocation for a regional wastewater system has been considered by Loehman et al. (1979). Heggen (1980) has studied the savings in treatment plant cost that are possible when a portion of the reservoir volume and cost of a multipurpose reservoir is allocated to low-flow augmentation for water quality. Brill et al. (1979), have indicated that "although effluent charges are not currently central to water quality management practices in most countries, they continue to be considered in the search for more effective management programs"; they examine alternative effluent charges, waste removal costs, financial burdens, and punitive effects. Financial burden includes the total of waste removal costs and effluent charges paid. Punitive effects result when charges produce no significant waste removal yet increase the financial burden on the waste discharger.

8.8 PREFERRED SCALE OF DEVELOPMENT (CONSIDERING ONLY ECONOMIC EFFICIENCY)

Figure 8.2 (taken from the "Green Book," U.S. Inter-Agency Committee on Water Resources, 1958) shows in the upper chart how the benefits of a hypothetical project increase when the cost of the project increases with larger size. The lower chart shows how the benefit-cost ratio changes, both in terms of total benefits and costs and in terms of increments of benefits and costs. Several scales of development are significant.

The first point is the minimum scale for which the benefits are equal to or greater than the costs. This is at the point where the curve in the upper chart first cuts the 45-degree line, corresponding to a ratio of 1.0. The development must be at least this large to be justified economically.

When the scale of development is increased beyond this point, the benefits in the example are shown to increase at a faster rate than the costs, until a maximum benefit-cost ratio is reached at point 1. If the scale of development were established at point 1, maximum benefits would be received for each dollar expended. However, full economic development would not be realized because additional increments of development would be possible for which the incremental benefits exceed the incremental costs.

If the scale of development is further increased, point 2 is reached, at which the

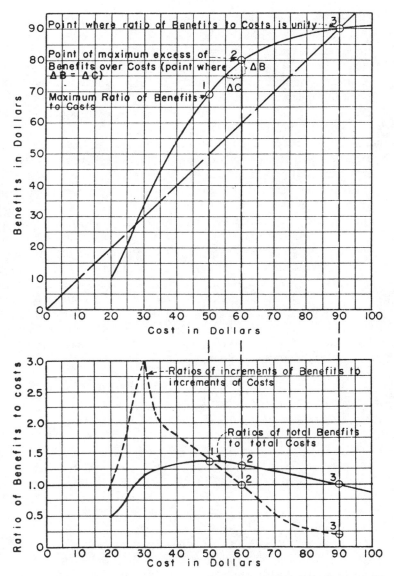

Figure 8.2 Relationships between benefits and costs for varying scales of development. (From U.S. Inter-Agency Committee, 1958.)

last increment of costs yielded benefits equal to those costs. At this point, maximization of net benefits is achieved. This is the preferred scale of development, according to the rules of federal agencies and economic theory.

Extension of the scale of development beyond point 2 would not be economically justified since such extension would result in increments of benefits which are less than the increments in cost. There will usually be some scale of development (point 3) for which the benefit-cost ratio is again unity, unless a physical limit is reached before this point.

8.9 BENEFIT-COST RATIO AND OTHER ECONOMIC MEASURES FOR RANKING PROJECTS

In order to provide information in a form that is useful for scheduling the implementation of projects and for other purposes, planning agencies often rank projects by some measure of merit based on economic considerations only. In comparing various federal projects, the measure that has been used most often is the benefit-cost ratio. If each project has been formulated to yield maximum net benefits, it is at the economic scale of development. Then, the project with the highest benefit-cost ratio results in the greatest benefits per dollar expended. Other methods of establishing the economic order include the net benefits (excess of benefits over costs, on a present-worth or annual basis); the rate of return on investment, that is, the (annual benefits − annual costs)/investment, expressed as a percentage; and the internal rate of return.

The methods described above have been widely used in water resources planning and have been justified as practical when time or planning funds are limited. In principle, however, the following is the theoretically correct economic approach. Individual projects should not be ranked, but projects and segments of projects should be designed as a whole for maximum discounted net benefits given all constraints, including the budget constraint (Maass and Major 1972; Major 1977); this may necessitate the redesign of projects when constraints (e.g., the budget constraint) change.

The examples in Tables 8.11 and 8.12 have been prepared to illustrate alternative measures of merit. Some simplifications have been made in order to permit comparison of projects with the four types of economic indicators mentioned above (B/C, $B - C$, rate of return on investment, internal rate of return).

Example 1 (Table 8.11) shows a project in column (1) with an investment cost of $2,500,000 compared with a project in column (2) having an investment cost of $5,000,000. Project 1 is the preferred project under the economic criterion of benefit-cost ratio since it has a B/C of 1.81, which is higher than the B/C of 1.53 for project 2. Project 1 is preferred even though its annual net benefits value $(B - C)$ of $178,700 is less than the $207,400 for project 2. For this example, the rate of return on the investment and the internal rate of return are also higher for project 1.

Example 2 (Table 8.12) shows a project in column (1) with an investment cost of $2,670,00 compared with a project in column (2) having an investment cost of $4,280,000. Project 1 with a B/C of 1.72 is preferred over project 2 with a B/C of 1.62, even though the $B - C$ and rate of return are smaller.

Column (3) in each example shows the B/C, $B - C$, and rate of return for the incremental investments between project 1 and project 2. In Example 1, the B/C ratio and the rate of return on investment both trend downward. In Example 2, the B/C ratio trends downward but the rate of return trends upward.

The B/C ratio defined at the marginal point where incremental benefits just

TABLE 8.11 COMPARISON OF ALTERNATIVES—EXAMPLE 1

Investment	(1) 2,500,000	(2) 5,000,000	(3) 2,500,000
Annual Costs			
1. Interest (5%)	125,000	250,000	125,000
2. Amortization ($A/F = 0.005$ for 50 years at 5%)	12,500	25,000	12,500
3. Operation and maintenance	65,000	80,000	15,000
4. Renewals and replacements ($A/F = 0.0075$ applied to inv., assuming 25% at 20-year average life at 5% interest)	18,800	37,600	18,800
5. Total annual costs $= (1) + (2)$ $+ (3) + (4)$	221,300	392,600	171,300
6. Annual benefits	400,000	600,000	200,000
7. $B/C = (6)/(5)$	1.81	1.53	1.17
8. $B - C = (6) - (5)$	178,700	207,400	28,700
9. Total costs without amortization $= (1) + (3) + (4)$	208,800	367,600	158,800
10. Rate of return on investment[a] $= \dfrac{(6) - (9)}{\text{inv.}} \times 100$	7.6%	4.7%	1.7%
11. Cash outlay for renewals and replacements 0.25 inv./20 $=$ 0.0125 inv.	31,200	62,400	31,200
12. Net annual benefits[b] $(6) - (3) - (11)$ B O&M R&R	303,800	457,600	153,800
13. Internal rate of return[c]	12%	9%	6%

[a]Assumes indefinite life of investment. Otherwise, reduce denominator by accumulated depreciation, and add annual amortization (depreciation) to numerator since it will now be out-of-pocket cost. Both (10) and this alternative are not entirely correct. See another approach (10A) below, based on partial amortization:

> 10A. Assume project constructed with sponsor's funds.
>
> | | |
> |---|---|
> | Annual O&M (3) | $65,000 |
> | R&R (4) | 18,800 |
> | Depreciation | |
>
> (assume that 50% of project is depreciated in 50 years)
> annual depreciation (straight line)
>
> | | |
> |---|---|
> | 1,250,000/50 = | 25,000 |
> | Annual costs | $108,800 |
> | Annual benefits | 400,000 |
> | Net benefits | 291,200 |
>
> Average book value over 50 years
> $(2,500,000 + 1,250,000)/2 = 1,875,000$
>
> Rate of return $\dfrac{291,200}{1,875,000} \times 100 = 16\%$
>
> This is rate of return on sponsor's funds.

[b]Before considering capital costs.

[c]$(P/A, i, 50) = \dfrac{\text{inv.}}{(12)}$

TABLE 8.12 COMPARISON OF ALTERNATIVES—EXAMPLE 2

Investment	(1) 2,670,000	(2) 4,280,000	(3) 1,610,000
Annual Costs			
1. Interest (5%)	133,500	214,000	80,500
2. Amortization ($A/F = 0.005$ for 50 years at 5%)	13,400	21,400	8,000
3. Operation and maintenance	140,000	380,000	240,000
4. Renewals and replacements ($A/F = 0.0075$ applied to inv., assuming 25% at 20-year average life at 5% interest.)	20,000	32,100	12,100
5. Total annual costs $= (1) + (2) + (3) + (4)$	306,900	647,500	340,600
6. Annual benefits	528,000	1,050,000	522,000
7. $B/C = (6)/(5)$	1.72	1.62	1.53
8. $B - C = (6) - (5)$	221,100	402,500	181,400
9. Total costs without amortization $= (1) + (3) + (4)$	293,500	626,100	332,600
10. Rate of return on investment $= \dfrac{(6) - (9)}{\text{inv.}} \times 100$	8.8%	9.9%	11.7%
11. Cash outlay for renewals and replacements 0.0125 inv.	33,400	53,600	20,200
12. Net annual benefits $(6) - (3) - (11)$	354,600	616,400	261,800
13. Internal rate of return	13.5%	14.5%	16.5%

equal incremental costs (for segments of projects and for projects as a whole) results in many projects being recommended by planning agencies that are too large or too small or improperly oriented, in the eyes of many economists, social scientists, and conservationists. As discussed above, economists recommend that, at a given time, with a given amount of available funds, projects or segments of projects should be sized so that, in combination, they yield the largest return (discounted net benefits) on these funds. Neely and North (1976) have developed a "portfolio" approach which maximizes the net present value with respect to both funds available and projects available for construction by relating all projects to each other and to expected budgets; this process assumes that the design and economic efficiency have already been established for each project considered. There are others who would have projects protect or develop certain natural fish and wildlife resources or scenic or historical sites at great cost, irrespective of measurable benefits. Some who are overly interested in water resource projects would have a basin developed as an end in itself.

A consistent approach to economic analysis is needed if projects are to be on a reasonably comparable basis for examination by higher authorities before the appropriation of funds for development. For example, basic recommendations could be: (1) establishing an initial scale of development for each project by marginal analysis, at the scale where the last increment of costs just pays for the last increment of tangible benefits; (2) computing the net benefits and the ratio of benefits to costs, using economic benefits; and (3) justifying separately any increases in the scale of development by reason of benefits for other objectives, or difficulties in measuring economic benefits, or special provisions. This approach is comparable to that utilized by many government agencies and by many other authorities in the United States and elsewhere. It emphasizes the objective of economic efficiency but also takes other needs and aspirations into account. It is emphasized that the criteria used by federal agencies to analyze projects from a national standpoint may be quite different from those that are appropriate for local governments and private interests. Various systems of objectives were discussed in Chapters 2 and 6.

8.10 INTERNAL RATE OF RETURN

The determination of the internal rate of return is often referred to as the *discounted cash flow* method in the analysis of private ventures. In this method, the costs and revenues (or benefits) are listed for each year of the project and they are discounted so that the present worth of all costs equals the present worth of all revenues (or benefits). Various interest rates are assumed until the desired result is obtained. The costs would include the costs incurred during the period of construction and all costs in subsequent years for operation and maintenance and for renewals and replacements.

The discounted cash flow analysis is used by the World Bank, the United Nations Development Programme, and many government agencies. The internal rate-of-return computation has several characteristics:

1. An interest rate does not have to be stated in advance, in order to proceed with the calculation.
2. The rate of return may be compared with the acceptable rate(s) of return for economic sectors established at a high policy level by the international bank or the country involved.
3. If a project is financed by funds on hand, or borrowed at a subsidized rate, the internal rate of return will permit the ranking of projects.

The internal rate of return is not, however, a fully correct method of evaluating projects, as noted in Section 8.9. It is theoretically correct only where projects are independent of one another and are compared one by one to a target rate of return. Moreover, the ranking given by the internal rate of return is not entirely insensitive to the discount rate. In the examples shown by Tables 8.11 and 8.12, it was necessary to calculate the renewals and replacements using a straight-line method of depreciation to avoid having to assume a discount rate. Section 8.14 discusses the problem of cost allocation for a multipurpose project. There are sometimes other difficulties in the calculations when benefit and cost streams are unusual (see Bierman and Smidt, 1966, for additional discussion of this issue).

8.11 SENSITIVITY ANALYSIS AND INTRODUCTION TO RISK ANALYSIS

Sensitivity Analysis. When the value of each design variable cannot be assumed with full confidence, it may be desirable to establish a range of values for each variable. In sensitivity analysis, ranges of results in economic terms (e.g., B/C, $B - C$) are determined corresponding to combinations of different values of variables. When only one variable has a range there would be two economic results corresponding to the high and low values of the range. When there are a number of variables, each with its range, the number of possible combinations can be very large and determinations should be made only for the more likely combinations.

A sensitivity analysis was shown in Section 8.5 for an irrigation project, in which the benefit-cost ratio and unit water cost were shown to vary with different combinations of project period, interest rate for discounting, and unit power cost.

Of the parameters considered in water resources project analysis, the interest rate for discounting is often the most sensitive because of the capital-intensive nature of water resources projects. As discussed by Nudds and Bottomley (1976) in connection with an irrigation project, the costs fall more heavily in the earlier years of a scheme, while benefits from the scheme (net increases in returns by producing new crops, by increasing yields of existing crops, etc.) usually are higher in later years of a scheme than they are in the earlier years. Thus, the effect of discounting the benefits from a scheme is normally more pronounced than the effect on the costs for a scheme. They illustrated the effect of the discount rate in analyzing an irrigation project for some 28,000 acres in southern Malawi, in which water supplies could be obtained by means of a canal scheme or a pumped scheme. Table 8.13 shows the cost stream over a 50-year period for each scheme and the corresponding present worths at discount rates of 5% and 8%. This table shows that at 5%, the pumped scheme was slightly more expensive than the canal scheme while at 8%, the order is reversed. If the present values of costs are plotted for varying discount rates, as in Figure 8.3, the cost curves for the two schemes intersect at 7.4%; this intersection is referred to by the authors as a "crossover interest rate."

The analysis was carried further by considering the benefits, which were projected to vary between B_1 and B_2 in terms of present-worth values. As noted earlier, the benefit curves, in terms of present value, fall more steeply with discount rate than the cost curves. Benefit curve B_1 intersects the pumped scheme cost curve at a discount rate of 6.3%, and the canal scheme cost curve at 6.9%; the conclusion is that for rates of return up to 6.9%, the preferred scheme is the canal scheme. If benefit curve B_2 is considered, it intersects the pumped costs curve at a discount rate of 10.4% and the canal cost curve at 7.9%; the conclusion is that both schemes are justified for rates of return of up to 7.9%, whereas only the pumped scheme should be constructed for interest rates between 7.9 and 10.4%. For this project, where the benefits to be

TABLE 8.13 KASINTHULA, CHOICE BETWEEN IRRIGATION SYSTEMS: ALTERNATIVES ILLUSTRATING CROSSOVER DISCOUNT RATE (Thousand Malawi Pounds)

Year	Canal Scheme			Pumped Scheme		
	Cost Stream	Present Worth 5%	Present Worth 8%	Cost Stream	Present Worth 5%	Present Worth 8%
1	143	136	132	143	136	132
2	594	538	509	354	321	303
3	1,882	1,626	1,494	1,042	900	827
4	1,733	1,428	1,274	1,266	1,043	931
5	724	568	493	843	661	574
6	229	171	274	691	516	435
7	226	160	132	708	501	413
8	241	163	130	293	199	158
9	229	149	114	294	191	147
10	145	90	67	216	133	100
11–50	148	1,536	817	229	2,375	1,264
Total	12,066	6,564	5,436	15,020	6,976	5,284

Source: Nudds and Bottomley (1976).

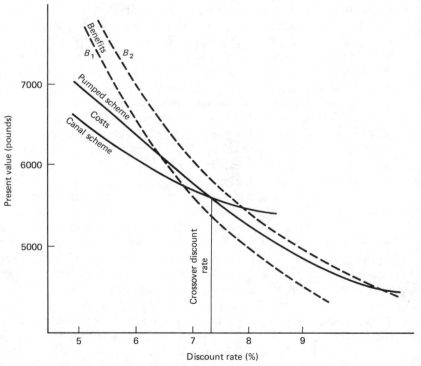

Figure 8.3 Kasinthula irrigation project: choice between irrigation supply alternatives. (From Nudds and Bottomley, 1976.)

Chap. 8 Economic Analyses

attained are not known with certainty but are expected to range between B_1 and B_2 for each scheme, the overall conclusions are that for interest rates up to 7.4% (the crossover rate), the canal scheme should be chosen. For interest rates between 7.4 and 10.4%, the pumped scheme is preferable. Above 10.4%, neither scheme is justified.

It should be noted that the points of intersection of benefits and costs are "internal rates of return" since they correspond to the equivalence of benefits and costs on a present-worth basis. Thus, the interest rates discussed above may be compared to an acceptable internal rate of return which may be established for project justification. The selection of an appropriate interest (discount) rate is discussed in Chapters 2 and 10.

Risk Analysis. With risk analysis, the values of key variables are expressed in the form of probability distributions. Results are then obtained in terms of various numerical values of B/C or other economic indicator, each paired with a probability estimate.

Strictly speaking, whenever it is possible to estimate a probability distribution for each variable, there are no *uncertainties*. Risk analysis can include probability distributions for variables that have known distributions (e.g., stream flows) and also ranges of distributions for variables that are basically uncertain (e.g., interest rate, inflation, construction contingencies, etc.), but for which judgment may be used to set optimistic, pessimistic, and most likely values or to establish variability in other ways.

The availability of economic results corresponding to sensitivity and risk analysis approaches assists the decision maker to make a more rational evaluation of options. An extended discussion of these subjects is presented in Chapter 11.

8.12 INFLATION EFFECTS

A survey of the benefit-cost literature by Hanke et al. (1975) indicated that the problems associated with project evaluation during inflation "have been largely neglected or incorrectly handled." They state that:

> For purposes of benefit-cost analysis, inflation can be handled in either of two ways. First, prices and interest rates, the two economic components used in computing the present value of expected net benefits, can be projected in real terms. That is, no inflationary components are included in either the prices or the interest rates. The second approach, which is equivalent to the first, includes inflation in both the price and the interest rate projections; nominal prices and interest rates are projected. In either approach it is important to note that the treatment of prices and interest rates must be the same. They must both be projected in either real or nominal terms.

When economic analyses are carried out for all values at constant dollars (when all costs and benefits escalate at the same rate as the devaluation rate of the dollar due to general inflation, and the interest rate for discounting is constant), the methodologies of the illustrations in the earlier sections of this chapter remain unchanged. If, however, it is forecast that inflation movements of individual components of the costs and/or benefits will be different, adjustments should be made in the calculations. Such adjustments should take account of the general inflation rate, R_a, the inflation rate of the individual component, R_b, and the discount rate, r. In the following it is assumed that the values of R_a, R_b, and r are on an annual basis and are constant for the period of analysis. The factor by which to multiply a benefit or cost in year N to obtain a value adjusted to constant dollars is the following:

$$\frac{(1 + R_b)^N}{(1 + R_a)^N} = \left(\frac{1 + R_b}{1 + R_a} \right)^N = (1 + R_c)^N$$

The factor $(1 + R_c)$ may be referred to as a "relative" inflation factor. If, for example, the planner is analyzing the economy of a hydroelectric plant, and the benefits are measured in terms of the costs of an equivalent thermal-electric plant, he may forecast the inflation rate of thermal fuel at 10% annually while holding the general inflation rate to 5%; for this, the relative inflation "factor" would be 1.10/ 1.05, or 1.048, and the relative inflation "rate" would be 4.8% annually. If the economic analysis is made on the basis of year-by-year projections which are then brought to a present-worth basis, every fuel component in year N in terms of present prices would be multiplied by 1.048^N.

If, however, the economic analysis is made on the basis of average annual values of benefits and costs, as in the examples of Table 8.3, another approach is needed. In the case where the energy component of power benefits is almost entirely due to thermal fuel utilization, a special factor is needed, as derived in Table 8.14. Assume that the following values apply for a 50-year period of analysis:

$$R_a = 0.05, \qquad R_b = 0.10, \qquad r = 0.07$$

Then

$$1 + R_c = \frac{1 + R_b}{1 + R_a} = \frac{1.10}{1.05} = 1.048$$

Table 8.14 requires the determination of a factor that depends on R_c and r. Thus,

$$1 + R_d = \frac{1 + r}{1 + R_c} = \frac{1.07}{1.048} = 1.02$$

The adjustment factor to be applied to the average annual benefits now becomes:

$$(P/A, 0.02, 50)(A/P, 0.07, 50) = 31.4 \times 0.072 = 2.26$$

The adjustment factor would be 2.26 for a 50-year period of analysis. It would be only 1.54 for a 20-year period of analysis.

The application of various test values of R_a, R_b, and r has indicated that for certain combinations, the factor must be computed to greater accuracy than obtained from the two component factors (P/A and A/P) in interest tables.

TABLE 8.14 DERIVATION OF FACTOR TO ADJUST AN AVERAGE ANNUAL VALUE FOR INFLATION EFFECTS

n = period of analysis
N = period through the year under consideration
X = unadjusted average annual value
R_b = inflation rate of the components in X
R_a = general inflation rate
r = discount rate

Adjustment factor due to general inflation in year $N = (1 + R_a)^N$
Adjustment factor due to inflation of components in X in year $N = (1 + R_b)^N$
Adjustment factor for X in year N in terms of

$$\text{constant dollars} = \left(\frac{1 + R_b}{1 + R_a}\right)^N = (1 + R_c)^N$$

Relative inflation factor $= (1 + R_c)$
Adjusted benefit stream $= X(1 + R_c)^1 + X(1 + R_c)^2 + \cdots + X(1 + R_c)^n$
Present value of benefit stream $=$

$$\frac{X(1 + R_c)^1}{(1 + r)^1} + \frac{X(1 + R_c)^2}{(1 + r)^2} + \cdots + \frac{X(1 + R_c)^n}{(1 + r)^n}$$

Let $(1 + r)/(1 + R_c) = (1 + R_d)$; then present value of benefit stream $=$

$$X\left[\frac{1}{(1 + R_d)^1} + \frac{1}{(1 + R_d)^2} + \cdots + \frac{1}{(1 + R_d)^n}\right] = X(P/A, R_d, n)$$

Average annual value of benefit stream $= X(P/A, R_d, n)(A/P, r, n)$
Adjustment factor $= (P/A, R_d, n)(A/P, r, n)$

8.13 ECONOMIC ANALYSIS OF MULTIPURPOSE PROJECTS

The economic analysis of multipurpose projects differs from that of single-purpose projects. Multipurpose projects should be analyzed both in terms of overall benefits and costs, and benefits and costs of each project purpose. For the latter it is necessary to have a means of allocating costs of facilities such as multipurpose reservoirs to the various projects and purposes it serves. The method used most often to make such allocations is the "separable cost-remaining benefits" (SCRB) method. This and other methods of cost allocation are discussed in the next sections.

The effects of cost allocation on benefit-cost analyses are illustrated for a multipurpose project. Several related topics are treated, including the analysis of a dual-purpose project, the economic ranking of alternative reservoirs serving several purposes, and the distribution of costs of projects when they serve more than one sponsor.

8.14 ALLOCATION OF COSTS OF MULTIPURPOSE PROJECT TO PURPOSES AND PROJECTS BY SCRB METHOD

A multipurpose project often includes a reservoir serving several purposes and projects. These may include purposes incorporated in the reservoir such as recreation and flood control, facilities attached to the reservoir such as a hydroelectric station, and facilities that are separated physically but depend on water supplies from the reservoir such as an irrigation project or a municipal and industrial water supply project. To allocate costs of multipurpose projects (i.e., reservoirs and other facilities serving several individual purposes and projects) the method used most often since the issuance of the "Green Book" (U.S. Inter-Agency Committee on Water Resources, 1950, 1958) has been the *separable cost-remaining benefits* method. In this and other examples of cost allocation, the allocation will be to "purposes," but such purposes could provide for more than one project of the same type (e.g., purpose A is irrigation project A and purpose B is irrigation project B).

The *separable costs* of a purpose are those costs that are identified with the purpose. They are computed as the difference between the cost of the multipurpose project when it serves the purpose and the cost of the project when the purpose is excluded. In the typical cost allocation procedure, each purpose is assigned at least its separable costs.

The purpose will also be assigned a portion of the total *joint costs* of the multipurpose project. The total joint costs are the difference between the total costs of the multipurpose project and the sum of the separable costs for all purposes.

There is an upper limit to the separable and joint costs allocated to any purpose. This maximum, known as the *adjusted benefits* or *justifiable costs*, is equal to the lesser of: (1) the benefits attributable to the purpose by the most preferred method of evaluating these benefits; or (2) the benefits evaluated as the costs of the most economic alternative (usually single-purpose) project that would likely be constructed.

In determining how to distribute the joint costs, attention is paid to the concept of an upper limit, as discussed above, and also to the *remaining benefits*. The remaining benefits for each purpose are equal to the adjusted benefits (justifiable costs) less the separable costs. After all the separable costs have been assigned, each purpose is allocated a portion of the joint costs in direct proportion to its remaining benefits.

The procedure is illustrated by the example in Table 8.15. This example distributes the $350 million cost of a reservoir serving four purposes (say, flood control, power, irrigation, and navigation). All costs and benefits considered in this example are present-worth values obtained by discounting annual values at a specified rate of interest. The cost allocation will be discussed for the irrigation purpose (purpose B). The irrigation benefits are estimated to be $100 million (for water supply from the reservoir and gravity canals), while the most likely alternative project would cost $120 million dollars (for a groundwater supply and spray irrigations). The lesser of the two amounts, $100 million, is, therefore, the adjusted benefits (justifiable costs). The adjusted benefits for all project purposes total $400 million.

The separable costs for purpose B are $50 million (this means that if the reservoir served the other purposes, but not irrigation, it would cost $50 million less). The calculation is carried out for each purpose, while retaining all other purposes, and the total of the separable costs becomes $150 million. The total joint costs are, therefore, $200 million ($350 − $150 million).

The remaining benefits for purpose B are $50 million ($100 million − $50 million), and total remaining benefits are $250 million. Irrigation (purpose B) is

TABLE 8.15 COST ALLOCATION FOR MULTIPURPOSE PROJECT USING SCRB METHOD
(All Value in Million Dollars; Total Costs Allocated $350 Million)

		Purpose				
Item	Description	A	B	C	D	Total
1	Benefits	140	100	150	100	490
2	Alternative costs	100	120	100	130	450
3	Justifiable costs[a] (lesser of 1 or 2)	100	100	100	100	400
4	Separable costs	80	50	20	0	150
5	Remaining benefits (3 − 4)	20	50	80	100	250
6	Allocated joint costs	16	40	64	80	200
7	Total allocated costs (4 + 6)	96	90	84	80	350

[a]Also referred to as "adjusted benefits."
Source: Loughlin (1977). Copyrighted by the American Geophysical Union.

assigned, in addition to its separable costs, the amount of $40 million, computed as follows:

$$\frac{\text{remaining benefits for purpose B}}{\text{total remaining benefits}} \times \text{total joint costs} = \frac{50}{250} \times 200 = \$40 \text{ million}$$

The allocated costs for purpose B are $90 million ($50 million for separable costs plus $40 million for joint costs). The allocated costs for all purposes are $350 million.

It is possible for the total separable costs of all purposes to exceed the total costs of the multipurpose facility. For this case, joint savings are distributed, instead of joint costs, and this procedure reduces the cost assigned to each purpose to less than its separable cost.

A variation of the SCRB method may be appropriate when a significant part of project cost is incurred for structures serving several but not all purposes. In such cases, the "Green Book" suggests that the separable costs be incremented by the specific costs assigned, and the remaining benefits be reduced accordingly, before allocating the remaining joint costs.

After all costs of all multipurpose features have been allocated, the benefit-cost analysis can be completed: (1) separately for each purpose; and (2) overall by summing up the benefits and costs for all purposes.

The SCRB method involves specifying an interest rate for discounting all benefits and costs or for obtaining equivalent average annual values. Thus, allocations obtained by the SCRB method cannot be used in subsequent calculations of internal rates of return without some inconsistency. There are other practical problems in applying the SCRB method; it may, for example, be very difficult to estimate for each purpose its alternative costs (line 2 of Table 8.15) and separable costs (line 4).

There are also conceptual problems with the methodology. According to

Loughlin (1977), a cost allocation method should satisfy the objectives of economic efficiency and equity. The SCRB method does meet the following criteria for *efficiency*: (1) the separable cost of adding each purpose as the last increment should not exceed the benefits derived therefrom; (2) the sum of the total costs allocated to each purpose should not exceed the sum of the total benefits allocated to that purpose; and (3) the total costs allocated to each purpose should not exceed the cost of a single-purpose alternative providing equivalent benefits. Several authorities (Stanford Research Institute, 1958; U.S. Inter-Agency Committee on Water Resources, 1958) have stated that an *equitable* cost allocation is one that permits all project purposes to share *fairly* in the savings from multipurpose rather than single-purpose construction. Loughlin (1977) claims that the fairness criterion is not satisfied by the SCRB method because when it subtracts either separable costs or specific costs from justifiable costs on a 1:1 basis, the project savings allocated to each purpose are not proportional to the savings from inclusion of that purpose in the project. Adjusted SCRB procedures have been proposed by Loughlin (1977) and Rossman (1978) to overcome this objection.

It should be noted that cost allocation methods all face a difficult conceptual problem. Costs that are truly joint costs cannot, from the economic standpoint, be allocated. Since, however, allocations are required for legal, administrative, or other reasons, the SCRB or some other method is ordinarily used. In a more sophisticated approach, the problem of cost allocation should be treated as part of the multi-objective problem of system design (and joint costs allocated according to, say, distributional objectives).

8.15 OTHER METHODS OF COST ALLOCATION FOR MULTIPURPOSE PROJECTS

The U.S. Water Resource Council "Principles and Guidelines" (1983, p. 14), provide alternatives to the SCRB procedures for allocation of joint costs. Thus, joint costs may be allocated in proportion to the use of facilities, provided that the sum of allocated joint cost and separable cost for any purpose does not exceed the lesser of the benefit or the alternative cost for that purpose. The WRC "Principles and Standards" considered National Economic Development (NED) and Environmental Quality (EQ) as coequal objectives. When purposes generate more than incidental or complementary EQ beneficial effects, this can result in a recommended project whose joint costs are greater than the sum of the remaining benefits. Under these conditions, the WRC guidelines stated that joint cost may be allocated by an alternative method that is "judged . . . to provide a more equitable distribution" (WRC, 1980 p. 64399).

The following is a summary of techniques for cost allocation, other than the SCRB method (Stanford Research Institute, 1958). Some of these have several variations. Also, certain methods may be more applicable to financial analysis (see Chapter 9) than to economic analysis. These techniques may be considered by planners of agencies that do not find the SCRB method to be satisfactory for economic analysis or to meet legislative requirements for distribution of financial costs.

The *benefits method* allocates costs among the various project purposes in proportion to the value of the benefits produced by each purpose.

In the *separate projects method*, costs are allocated in proportion to what the costs of obtaining equivalent benefits would have been if separate single-purpose projects had been built to serve each purpose. Barnea (1965) has described the use of this approach for allocating costs of a combined power and water desalination plant. The *net* annual marketable outputs of power and water are determined for the combined plant. The total annual costs of a single-purpose power plant and a single-purpose water conversion plant are estimated for these net outputs, and added. Suppose that combined costs are $50 million, and that single-purpose costs are $30 million for power and $45 million for water conversion, which gives a total of $75 million for the two single-purpose projects. Allocations are $20 million for power ($50 \times 30/75$) and $30 million for water conversion ($50 \times 45/75$).

The *alternative justifiable expenditure method* allocates the costs of joint facilities in direct proportion to the "remaining alternative justified investment" for each project purpose. This investment amount is defined as the smaller of either: (1) the cost of the most economical alternative single-purpose project that will produce equivalent benefits—less any direct costs; or (2) the total value of benefits ascribed to the purpose—less any direct costs. The method is sometimes referred to as the "specific costs–remaining benefits" method since it substitutes the specific costs of the various functions for their separable costs. Table 8.16 shows the allocation of $20,000 in specific costs and $60,000 in joint costs according to this method.

The *vendibility method* allocates costs in proportion to the market prices of the project commodities or services. To the extent that the market price can be considered equivalent to per unit benefits, the method and its variations are similar to methods that use benefits as the allocation determinant. By allocating costs in proportion to the market price of project commodities and services, the vendibility method attempts in general to follow private enterprise practices. It is applicable, however, only to those project purposes furnishing products or services that are commercially marketable and for which a market price can be determined.

The *use of facilities method* is based on the concept that the cost of joint facilities should be allocated among the various purposes in proportion to their respective "use" of those facilities. Use is measured either in terms of the storage capacity provided for the purpose, or in terms of the quantity of water flow, or both. Table 8.17 shows the allocation for a reservoir costing $520,000 and containing 10,000 acre-feet of storage. Loughlin points out that this procedure does not employ the concept of justifiable costs, which places an upper limit on the costs apportioned to a particular purpose. It is possible, therefore, for a purpose to be assigned a cost greater than the cost of a single-purpose alternative. The Stanford Research Institute also indicates that there is no assurance that separable costs will be covered and outlines other practical difficulties in using this method.

Four other methods listed by Stanford Research Institute are presented below. These have received less attention in the literature than the SCRB method and the methods discussed above.

The premise of the *priority of use method* is that the various purposes compete with each other to some extent for the use of water flow capacity or storage space.

TABLE 8.16 ALTERNATIVE JUSTIFIABLE EXPENDITURE METHOD
OF COST ALLOCATION (Thousands of Dollars)

Item	Description	Purpose A	B	C	Total
1	Benefits	50	70	30	150
2	Alternative costs	35	55	45	135
3	Justifiable costs (lesser of 1 or 2)	35	55	30	120
4	Specific costs	10	5	5	20
5	Remaining benefits (3 − 4)	25	50	25	100
6	Allocated joint costs[a]	15	30	15	60
7	Total allocated costs (4 + 6)	25	35	20	80

[a]Total joint costs of $60 (project costs of $80 − total specific costs of $20) are allocated to each purpose in the same ratio as that of the remaining benefits of each purpose to the total remaining benefits.
Source: Loughlin (1977). Copyrighted by the American Geophysical Union.

Some purposes are regarded as having priority over others, and the method is designed to give special attention to these priorities. The method identifies direct costs with their respective purposes and allocates the costs of joint facilities in a descending order of priority. The purpose with the highest priority is assigned only its direct costs plus a share of the costs of joint facilities equal to the lesser of either: (1) the benefits less direct costs; or (2) the cost of the most economic alternative project less the direct costs of the purpose.

The *incremental method* identifies separable costs with their respective purposes and allocates all joint costs to that single purpose, which is considered the primary function of the project.

The *direct costs method* is a variation of the incremental method, except that direct costs rather than separable costs are employed, and the costs of joint facilities, rather than joint costs, are allocated to the primary project purpose.

TABLE 8.17 USE OF FACILITIES METHOD OF COST ALLOCATION (Thousands of Dollars Except Where Otherwise Indicated)

Item	Description	Purpose A	B	C	Total
1	Benefits	300	250	150	700
2	Specific costs	60	40	20	120
3	Total storage (acre-feet)	5,000	3,000	2,000	10,000
4	Allocated joint costs[a]	200	120	80	400
5	Total allocated costs (2 + 4)	260	160	100	520

[a]Total joint costs of $400 (project costs of $520 − total specific cost of $120) are allocated to each purpose in the same ratio as that of the storage assigned to each purpose to the total storage.
Source: Loughlin (1977). Copyrighted by the American Geophysical Union.

In one variation of the *equal apportionment method*, separable costs are identified, and in the other variation direct costs are identified. Depending on the variation used, either joint costs or the costs of joint facilities are apportioned equally among the principal purposes of the project.

8.16 BENEFIT-COST ANALYSIS OF DUAL-PURPOSE PROJECT

In Section 8.4 an economic analysis was presented of the recommended master plan for water suppy to serve Kingston, Jamaica (TAMS, 1977). This master plan was selected after considering several alternative plans. All the alternatives considered, except one, were single-purpose water supply projects. One of these schemes (referred to as the Mahogany Vale scheme with power) would involve both power and water supply. This scheme was analyzed from an economic standpoint by comparing the costs for both power and water supply with their values. The combined power and water supply values (benefits) were estimated to be less than the combined power and water costs; thus, the scheme was not considered to be "economically" justified.

The water supply benefits, in accordance with generally accepted procedures, were equivalent to the costs of the alternative project that would most likely be undertaken in the absence of the Mahogany Vale scheme. In the case of this dual-purpose project the water supply benefits were taken to be equivalent to the costs of the recommended single-purpose master plan for water supply.

The differences between total project costs and the water supply benefits were resulting net costs chargeable to power. These were compared with the benefits for power, which were estimated as the costs of an equivalent thermal generating plant.

Estimates of energy production were based on the following characteristics of the hydroelectric plant. It was assumed that each of three 30-MW units would be installed consecutively.

Capacity	90 MW
Firm energy	211 GWh/yr
Average energy	252 GWh/yr
Firm power	24.1 MW
Average power	28.8 MW
Plant factor (firm power basis)	0.27
Plant factor (average power basis)	0.32

In comparing the hydro with the most likely alternative for peaking service, the latter was shown to be a gas turbine power plant using imported diesel fuel. The following values for power benefits were estimated at 1977 prices:

Investment cost, without interest during construction	180 U.S. $/kW
Fixed annual cost for operation, maintenance, insurance, and taxes	6.5 U.S. $/kW/yr
Energy cost	0.047 U.S. $/kWh
Hot spinning reserve cost	2.3 million U.S. $/yr

TABLE 8.18 COMPARATIVE STUDY OF WATER PROJECTS: KINGSTON ECONOMIC ANALYSIS MAHOGANY VALE
(Constant 1977 Prices, $1000 U.S.)

Year	Costs Charged to Power Function	Discounted Costs at 10%	Construction Cost	Operation and Maintenance Insurance Taxes	Energy, $0.047/kWh	Spinning Reserve	Total Cost of Benefits	Discounted Benefits at 10%	Net Benefits	Discounted Net Benefits at 5.4%
					Benefits of Power Equal to Costs of Thermal Alternative					
1973	6,014.00	6,014.00	0.00	0.00	0.00	0.00	0.00	0.00	−6,014.00	−6,014.00
1979	48,981.00	44,528.18	0.00	0.00	0.00	0.00	0.00	0.00	−48,981.00	−46,465.79
1980	62,833.00	51,928.10	0.00	0.00	0.00	0.00	0.00	0.00	−62,833.00	−56,545.63
1981	80,281.01	60,316.31	0.00	0.00	0.00	0.00	0.00	0.00	−80,281.01	−68,537.71
1982	50,700.82	34,629.34	10,800.00	0.00	0.00	0.00	10,800.00	7,376.54	−39,900.82	−32,315.00
1983	27,861.50	17,299.79	5,400.00	390.00	7,800.00	2,300.00	15,890.00	9,866.43	−11,971.49	−9,197.64
1984	−20,457.02	−11,547.45	0.00	585.00	11,844.00	2,300.00	14,729.00	8,314.17	35,186.02	25,645.06
1985	−20,560.20	−10,550.63	0.00	585.00	11,844.00	2,300.00	14,729.00	7,558.30	35,289.20	24,399.50
1986	−20,560.90	−9,591.81	0.00	585.00	11,844.00	2,300.00	14,729.00	6,871.13	35,289.90	23,147.02
1987	2,663.57	1,129.61	0.00	585.00	11,844.00	2,300.00	14,729.00	6,246.53	12,065.42	7,507.45
1988	2,663.87	1,027.04	0.00	585.00	11,844.00	2,300.00	14,729.00	5,678.66	12,065.12	7,121.76
1989	2,663.49	933.54	0.00	585.00	11,844.00	2,300.00	14,729.00	5,162.42	12,065.50	6,756.27
1990	1,251.79	398.86	0.00	585.00	11,844.00	2,300.00	14,729.00	4,693.11	13,447.20	7,159.24
1991	−16,457.58	−4,767.17	0.00	585.00	11,844.00	2,300.00	14,729.00	4,266.46	31,186.58	15,715.95
1992	−16,516.62	−4,349.34	0.00	585.00	11,844.00	2,300.00	14,729.00	3,878.60	31,245.62	14,937.15
1993	3,990.47	955.28	0.00	585.00	11,844.00	2,300.00	14,729.00	3,526.00	10,738.52	4,869.99
1994	3,984.77	867.20	0.00	585.00	11,844.00	2,300.00	14,729.00	3,205.45	10,744.22	4,622.37
1995	3,990.67	789.53	0.00	585.00	11,844.00	2,300.00	14,729.00	2,914.05	10,738.32	4,382.60
1996	3,990.77	717.77	0.00	585.00	11,844.00	2,300.00	14,729.00	2,649.13	10,738.22	4,157.50
1997	3,990.35	652.45	10,800.00	585.00	11,844.00	2,300.00	25,529.00	4,174.19	21,538.64	7,910.88

Year										
1998	3,990.59	593.17	5,400.00	585.00	11,844.00	2,300.00	20,129.00	2,992.04	16,138.40	5,623.06
1999	3,990.49	539.23	0.00	585.00	11,844.00	2,300.00	14,729.00	1,990.33	10,738.50	3,549.45
2000	3,990.87	490.26	0.00	585.00	11,844.00	2,300.00	14,729.00	1,809.39	10,738.12	3,367.06
2001	3,990.87	445.69	0.00	585.00	11,844.00	2,300.00	14,729.00	1,644.90	10,738.12	3,194.16
2002	3,990.87	405.17	0.00	585.00	11,844.00	2,300.00	14,729.00	1,495.37	10,738.12	3,030.14
2003	3,990.87	368.34	0.00	585.00	11,844.00	2,300.00	14,729.00	1,359.42	10,738.12	2,874.54
2004	3,990.87	334.85	0.00	585.00	11,844.00	2,300.00	14,729.00	1,235.84	10,738.12	2,726.93
2005	3,990.87	304.41	0.00	585.00	11,844.00	2,300.00	14,729.00	1,123.49	10,738.12	2,586.90
2006	3,990.87	276.74	0.00	585.00	11,844.00	2,300.00	14,729.00	1,021.35	10,738.12	2,454.06
2007	3,990.87	251.58	0.00	585.00	11,844.00	2,300.00	14,729.00	928.50	10,738.12	2,328.04
2008	3,990.87	228.71	0.00	585.00	11,844.00	2,300.00	14,729.00	844.09	10,738.12	2,208.49
2009	3,990.87	207.91	0.00	585.00	11,844.00	2,300.00	14,729.00	767.36	10,738.12	2,095.08
2010	3,990.87	189.01	0.00	585.00	11,844.00	2,300.00	14,729.00	697.60	10,738.12	1,987.50
2011	3,990.87	171.83	0.00	585.00	11,844.00	2,300.00	14,729.00	634.18	10,738.12	1,885.44
2012	3,990.87	156.21	10,800.00	585.00	11,844.00	2,300.00	25,529.00	999.26	21,538.12	3,587.55
2013	3,990.87	142.01	5,400.00	585.00	11,844.00	2,300.00	20,129.00	716.27	16,138.12	2,550.05
2014	3,990.87	129.10	0.00	585.00	11,844.00	2,300.00	14,729.00	476.47	10,738.12	1,609.64
2015	3,990.87	117.36	0.00	585.00	11,844.00	2,300.00	14,729.00	433.15	10,738.12	1,526.98
2016	3,990.87	106.69	0.00	585.00	11,844.00	2,300.00	14,729.00	393.77	10,738.12	1,448.57
2017	3,990.87	96.99	0.00	585.00	11,844.00	2,300.00	14,729.00	357.97	10,738.12	1,374.19
2018	3,990.87	88.17	0.00	585.00	11,844.00	2,300.00	14,729.00	325.43	10,738.12	1,303.62
2019	3,900.87	80.16	0.00	585.00	11,844.00	2,300.00	14,729.00	295.85	10,738.12	1,236.62
2020	3,990.87	72.87	0.00	585.00	11,844.00	2,300.00	14,729.00	268.95	10,738.12	1,173.17
2021	3,990.87	66.24	0.00	585.00	11,844.00	2,300.00	14,729.00	244.50	10,738.12	1,112.93
2022	3,990.87	60.22	0.00	585.00	11,844.00	2,300.00	14,729.00	222.27	10,738.12	1,055.78
2023	3,990.87	54.75	0.00	585.00	11,844.00	2,300.00	14,729.00	202.07	10,738.12	1,001.56
2024	3,990.87	49.77	0.00	585.00	11,844.00	2,300.00	14,729.00	183.70	10,738.12	950.13
2025	3,990.87	45.24	0.00	585.00	11,844.00	2,300.00	14,729.00	167.00	10,738.12	901.34
	187,453.28							110,211.69		

Source: TAMS (1977).

TABLE 8.19 RESERVOIR BENEFIT ALLOCATION EXAMPLE

Purpose	Costs (millions of dollars)			Benefits (millions of dollars)		Benefit Allocation Factor	Benefits (millions of dollars)	
	Reservoir Allocated	Project Facilities	Total	Project	Remaining		Reservoir Assigned Remaining	Reservoir Allocated
Irrigation project A	200	300	500	300	–(200)	0.5	–(100)	100
Irrigation project B	300	400	700	800	100	0.5	50	350
M&I project C	100	20	120	200	80	0.5	40	140
Hydro project D	400	500	900	1200	300	0.5	150	550
Flood control	100	0	100	150	50	1.0	50	150
Recreation	50	0	50	100	50	1.0	50	100
	1150	1220	2370	2750	380		240	1390

B/C ratio for reservoir $= \dfrac{1390}{1150} = 1.21$

B/C ratio for reservoir and projects $= \dfrac{2750}{2370} = 1.16$

Source: TAMS (1978).

TABLE 8.20 VARDAR/AXIOS PROJECT: RECOMMENDED COST SHARING BETWEEN TWO COUNTRIES FOR RESERVOIR PROJECT
(Based on Present Worth of Costs and Benefits in Millions of Equivalent 1977 U.S. Dollars)

Cost sharing for project(s): Kozjak
Conditions for year: 2000

Costs of project(s): 84.75[a]
Designation of project(s): K

Economic Component	Configuration D — Plan without Cebren, Galiste Jagmular, Babuna			Configuration E — Reduced Plan without Kozjak Cebren, Galiste Jagmular, Babuna			Differences in Benefits Attributable to Project(s)	
	Descrip.	Amount	Formula	Descrip.	Amount	Formula	Amount	Formula
Benefits in SRM								
Total benefits		4127.99			3737.91			
Total costs		1435.24			1295.88			
Net benefits		2692.75	e		2442.03	g		
Net benefits without costs of project(s)		2777.50	$e + K$		2442.03	g	335.47	$e + K - g$
Benefits in Greece[b]								
Total benefits		807.39			681.01			
Total costs		161.21			161.21			
Net benefits		646.18	f		519.80	h	126.38	$f - h$
Cost Sharing								
For SRM								
Amount		61.56	$\dfrac{e+K-g}{(e+K-g)+(f-h)} \times K$				461.85	
Percent		72.6						
For Greece								
Amount		23.19	$\dfrac{f-h}{(e-K-g)+(f-h)} \times K$					
Percent		27.4						

[a]Includes 55% of $32.77 million cost of Vardar/Treska diversion.
[b]Not including Florina Plain, which does not affect cost sharing.
Source: TAMS (1978).

Table 8.18 compares the discounted costs of the hydropower function with the power benefits (cost of thermal alternative). As explained above, the costs assigned to the power function, shown in the first column of this table, were obtained by subtracting the costs of the recommended master plan for water supply from the total costs for the dual-purpose plan for water supply and power. This table shows that the Mahogany Vale scheme would not meet a reasonable economic feasibility criterion, having an internal rate of return of only approximately 5%.

If the calculation were carried out with an upward adjustment for power benefits under the assumption that the cost of diesel fuel would increase at a faster rate than the general inflation, the internal rate of return would be more favorable.

8.17 ALLOCATION OF COSTS AND BENEFITS FOR SCREENING ALTERNATIVE RESERVOIRS

The usual cost allocation procedure involves the distribution of the costs of the reservoir among the various purposes it serves, and this is followed by the benefit-cost analysis of each project purpose. With this procedure, the entire cost of the reservoir is included in the costs of the various purposes.

If a screening study is made to rank alternative reservoirs, one way to compare them is to consider cost per unit of volume of reservoir. This, however, does not give a good measure of both benefits and costs attributable to the reservoir. One way of approaching this problem is to use the method of the preceding paragraph and compare the overall costs of all purposes (which already include the allocated costs of the reservoir) with the overall benefits of all purposes.

Another approach, which focuses on the reservoir itself, is to compare the costs of the reservoir with benefits that are allocated to the reservoir for the various purposes. This is based on the rationale that the purposes would not be feasible without the reservoir. One way to make the allocation is to assign a percentage of the net benefits of each purpose (benefits minus costs, not including reservoir cost allocation) to the reservoir. If it is assumed, for example, that the reservoir and the purpose are equally dependent on each other for justification, the allocation should be 50%.

Table 8.19 provides an example of this procedure. Note again that this procedure is for screening purposes only and not for final benefit-cost analysis.

8.18 ALLOCATION OF COSTS OF FACILITIES THAT BENEFIT TWO SPONSORS

In the studies made for the integrated development of the Vardar/Axios Basin to benefit Yugoslavia and Greece, a procedure was developed for allocating the costs of reservoirs situated in Yugoslavia (but benefiting both Yugoslavia and Greece) between the two countries. The method was based on net benefits attributable to the reservoir that accrued to each country (TAMS, 1978).

The procedure involved determining the total net benefits for all projects in each country *with* the operation of the reservoir (but not including the cost of the reservoir itself in this determination) and the total net benefits in each country *without* the reservoir. The difference in the net benefits for each country were then attributed to the reservoir, and the cost of the reservoir was divided between the countries in proportion to these differential net benefits. Table 8.20 shows an example of the cost allocation procedure.

Following the cost allocation between countries, it was necessary to allocate the respective costs to the separate irrigation and power projects in the countries. This was accomplished by a similar procedure.

8.19 ALLOCATION OF COSTS FOR ECONOMIC AND FINANCIAL ANALYSES

The methods outlined in this chapter are designed for economic analyses. The actual charges to beneficiaries for project costs may be guided somewhat by such methods but also often differ substantially for financial analyses. Beneficiaries of water resources projects pay for project services only as provided by law or as determined by the project sponsor. Also, the costs considered for financial analyses are based on the market costs of the enterprise (not shadow prices), do not include externalities, and may be based on different payout period, interest rate, and other financial arrangements.

REFERENCES

BARNEA, JOSEPH, "A Note on a New Method of Cost Allocation for Combined Power and Water Desalination Plants," *Water Resources Res.*, vol. 1, first quarter, 1965.

BIERMAN, HAROLD, JR., and SEYMOUR SMIDT, *The Capital Budgeting Decision*, 2nd ed., Macmillan, New York, 1966.

BOWER, B. T., C. N. EHLER, and A. V. KNEESE, "Incentives for Managing the Environment," *Environ. Sci. Technol.*, vol. 11, 1977.

BRILL, E. DOWNEY, JR., CHARLES S. REVELLE, and JON C. LIEBMAN, "An Effluent Charge Schedule, Cost, Financial Burden, and Punitive Effects," *Water Resources Res.*, vol. 15, no. 5, October 1979.

BUNDGAARD-NIELSEN, M., and C. L. HWANG, "A Review of Decision Models in Economics of Regional Water Quality Management," *Water Resources Bull.*, vol. 12, no. 3, June 1976.

DASGUPTA, P., A. SEN, AND S. MARGLIN: "Guidelines for Project Evaluation," United Nations Industrial Development Organization, Vienna, 1972.

HAIMES, Y. Y., M. A. KAPLAN, and M. A. HUSAR, JR., "A Multilevel Approach to Determining Optimal Taxation for the Abatement of Water Pollution," *Water Resources Res.*, vol. 8, no. 6, December 1972.

HANKE, STEVE H., PHILIP H. CARVER, and PAUL BUGG, "Project Evaluation during Inflation," *Water Resources Res.*, vol. 11, no. 4, August 1975.

HEGGEN, RICHARD J., "Water Quality Allocated Cost for Multipurpose Reservoirs," *Water Resources Bull.*, vol. 16, no. 1, February 1980.

KNEESE, A. V., and B. T. BOWER, *Managing Water Quality: Economics, Technology, Institutions*, Johns Hopkins University Press, Baltimore, Md., 1968.

LOEHMAN, E., J. ORLANDO, J. TSCHIRHART, and A. WHINSTON, "Cost Allocation for a Regional Wastewater Treatment System," *Water Resources Res.*, vol. 15, no. 2, April 1979.

LOUGHLIN, JAMES C., "The Efficiency and Equity of Cost Allocation Methods for Multipurpose Water Projects," *Water Resources Res.*, vol. 13, no. 1, February 1977.

MAASS, A., and D. C. MAJOR, "Budget Constraints and Multiobjective Planning," *Eng. Issues, Proc. Am. Soc. Civil Eng.*, vol. 98, 1972.

MAJOR, DAVID C., "Multiobjective Water Resource Planning," *Am. Geophys. Union Water Resources Monogr. 4*, 1977.

NEELY, W. P. and R. M. NORTH, "A Portfolio Approach to Public Water Project Decision Making," *Water Resources Res.*, vol. 12, no. 1, February 1976.

NUDDS, DONALD, and ANTHONY BOTTOMLEY, "The Use of Crossover Discount Rates in Irrigation Scheme Design," *Water Resources Bull.*, vol. 12, no. 2, April 1976.

ROSSMAN, LEWIS A., "Comment on the Efficiency and Equity of Cost Allocation Methods for Multipurpose Water Projects by James C. Loughlin," *Water Resources Res.*, vol. 14, no. 6, December 1978.

STANFORD RESEARCH INSTITUTE, "Economic Considerations in the Formulation and Repayment of California Water Plan Projects." Report supported by John Randolph Haynes and Dora Haynes Foundation, March 1958.

TAMS (Tippetts-Abbett-McCarthy-Stratton, New York, and Torán y Cia, Madrid), "Lower Ebro Right Bank Irrigation Project," 1963.

TAMS (Tippetts-Abbett-McCarthy-Stratton, New York, and Mattis Demain Beckford & Associates Ltd., Kingston), "Comparative Study of Water Supply Projects for Kingston and Surrounding Area," July 1977.

TAMS (Tippetts-Abbett-McCarthy-Stratton, New York, and Massachusetts Institute of Technology, Cambridge), "Integrated Development of the Vardar/Axios River Basin—Yugoslavia–Greece," December 1978.

TAMS (Tippetts-Abbett-McCarthy-Stratton), "Studies of the Hackensack Meadowlands Flood Control Project," 1980.

U.S. FEDERAL ENERGY REGULATORY COMMISSION, "Hydro-electric Power Evaluation," August 1979.

U.S. INTER-AGENCY COMMITTEE ON WATER RESOURCES, "Proposed Practices for Economic Analysis of River Basin Projects," May 1950; rev. May 1958.

U.S. WATER RESOURCES COUNCIL, "Principles and Standards for Planning Water and Related Land Resources," September 10, 1973; rev. December 14, 1979; rev. September 29, 1980.

U.S. WATER RESOURCES COUNCIL, "Economic and Environmental Principles and Guidelines for Water and Related Land Resources Implementation Studies," March 10, 1983.

NINE

Financial Analyses

9.1 SCOPE

A project is justified from a national economic viewpoint if it has positive net economic benefits, provided that the services of such a project are considered of high-enough priority for implementation compared with the use of valuable resources for other purposes. The results of an economic analysis do not, however provide sufficient information on financial viability during the course of each project's actual construction and operation.

The financial analyses presented in this chapter illustrate approaches for various types of projects and from the standpoint of different sponsors. Projects are discussed for the single purposes of hydroelectric power, municipal and industrial water supply, and irrigation, and for multipurpose development. The chapter also discusses the issues of cost allocation and subsidies and the problems of inflation in financial accounting.

When financial constraints do not obtain, the selection of a project from among the considered alternatives should generally follow the procedures to obtain the economically efficient (or multiobjective) optimum. Chapter 8 discusses these procedures for a variety of projects in the context of *economic analyses*; discussion of adjustments for inflation was also included. Once a project is selected on an economic basis, *financial analyses* such as those discussed in the following sections of this chapter are made to determine the needs for financing the project construction and handling the flows of costs, revenues, and subsidies after the project goes into operation. Although these financial analyses are important, they are seldom controlling in the case of central government agencies in the United States and other advanced countries that depend primarily on tax revenues and whose costs and revenues for a number of projects are pooled in a common treasury.

For other government entities at the regional or local level, for private sponsors, and for others who maintain strict accounting of costs and revenues on a project-by-project basis, however, the financial feasibility of a project and the ranking of alternatives on a financial basis may be as important as (or even more critical than) the results in economic terms.

9.2 COMPONENTS OF FINANCIAL ANALYSES

A schedule of year-by-year expenditures for construction, nonstructural measures, and associated costs should be developed and compared with the availability of capital funds. Capital funds should be considered in terms of their overall availability and the likelihood of their dedication to the project being analyzed.

If the project provides services for which there is a market, estimates of unit costs (e.g., per cubic meter of water or per kilowatt-hour of electric energy) should be compared with prevailing costs for such services and with the ability and willingness of beneficiaries to pay for such services. The cost of water or power from new projects may appear high when compared with existing projects because of inflation or other reasons. They may, however, still be justified because alternatives to provide the same services are more expensive.

Each project should also be examined to determine the extent to which, as a practical matter, revenues in each year would cover outlays. This requires assumptions to be made concerning the price schedules for marketable goods and services and the terms for repaying any loans obtained to construct the project. The loan repayment schedule can be complicated if more than one type of currency is needed or if several different creditors are involved. If revenues do not equal or exceed cost requirements, subsidies are needed; alternatively, the deficits in cash flows must be covered by bank-financed working funds, if temporary, or from the sponsor's surplus income from other operations.

In a financial analysis, the interest rate and term of financing may be different from the discount rate and period of analysis used in economic analysis. The length of time for capital recovery is often limited by law or preference to a shorter period than the life used in economic analysis. The financial interest rate will depend on the type of financing employed (general obligation bonds, revenue bonds, issuance of stock, bank loans, etc.), financial market conditions for the particular type considered, and the credit rating of the sponsor. When all revenues and costs move through a central account that merges all the activities of a government or private sponsor, bonds or stock may be sold periodically without identification with specific projects; in this case, a special study may be needed to determine the criteria that are appropriate for the financial analysis of a project.

Account should be taken of inflation in the prices used for the financial analysis even though assumptions of inflation rates are speculative, especially if projections are made for more than a few years into the future. For capital-intensive projects, this will properly distinguish the annual capital costs that are not subject to inflation (if the project is implemented immediately) from other annual costs and revenues that do change due to inflation.

In economic analyses, costs and benefits are usually considered on a constant-dollar basis. This means that increases in costs and benefits for the effects of inflation are not taken into account except when they are expected to increase relative to the general inflation rate. In financial analyses, however, increases due to inflation should be estimated and accounted for in a year-by-year analysis; to judge the effects of inaccurate forecasts, sensitivity analyses may be carried out with ranges of rates of inflation.

In addition to the analyses outlined above, financial institutions generally require other financial statements to be provided when judging the creditworthiness of the sponsor or its ability to run an enterprise in businesslike fashion.

9.3 FINANCIAL ANALYSES OF HYDROELECTRIC POWER PROJECTS

The financial analyses of hydroelectric power projects can differ substantially from the economic analyses discussed in Section 8.3. In economic analyses it is often possible to use weighting and discounting techniques to obtain annual average values of costs and benefits. In financial analyses, however, costs and revenues should be considered on a year-by-year-basis. In economic analyses, benefits are usually based on the cost of alternative capacity and energy that would be employed if the hydropower plant were not built. In financial analyses, the revenues should be based on the actual sales contracts that the sponsor expects to negotiate.

When a sales contract is negotiated for hydropower, the question of dependable capacity often becomes an important issue. The dependable capacity is also important for an industrial or municipal sponsor planning to use all or a portion of the hydroelectric energy and having to pay for standby capacity in the event of failure of the primary source. Some discussion of this has been included in economic analyses (Section 8.3). Actually, the dependable capacity can vary from month to month and year to year depending on the installed capacity and the amount of water available (U.S. Department of the Army, Corps of Engineers, 1979). Figure 9.1 shows one way of estimating the monthly and annual dependable capacity of a hydropower plant when it is considered in combination with other sources of power (hydro and thermal). Figure 9.2 shows an alternative way of estimating the annual dependable capacity of a small hydropower plant in the months of peak system demand.

Several examples will be presented to illustrate financial analyses of hydroelectric projects for different assumptions of sponsorship and use.

9.3.1 Government Sponsor—Comparison of Unit Cost and Unit Value

Table 9.1 derives the unit cost of service of a hydropower project sponsored by a municipal utility. The investment cost of the project is $6,000,000 and initial operation and maintenance costs are $135,000 per year. It is assumed that capital is repaid at 6% interest over 30 years; with these terms, the capital recovery factor is 0.07265 for an annual debt service of $435,900. Operation and maintenance costs

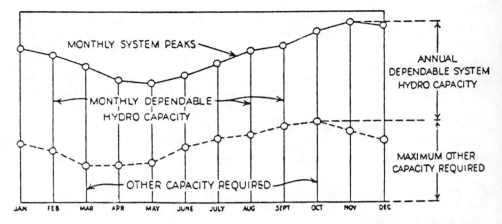

Figure 9.1 Monthly and annual dependable capacity of hydro plant. (From U.S. Department of the Army, Corps of Engineers 1979.)

are assumed to increase at the rate of 6% per year. The unit cost of service, given in the next-to-last column, varies from 2.537 cents per kilowatt-hour in the first year to 5.188 cents in the thirtieth year. The values in the last column may represent either: (1) the cost of alternative energy needed by the municipality (obtained by purchase or self-generation); or (2) the selling price if the energy is sold to a regional utility; capacity value is assumed to be included in the energy values. This example shows the costs would be met or exceeded by savings or revenue in each year except the first, and it can be concluded that the financial results are favorable.

9.3.2 Government or Industrial Sponsor— Internal Generation and Use

In this example, a municipal sponsor (or industrial sponsor with comparable terms for loans and taxes when income tax adjustments are accounted for) considers internal production and consumption of hydroelectric energy, where deficiencies are met by purchases from the regional utility. Table 9.2 shows the parameters for a small hydroelectric site. The sponsor's total annual energy demand is 9 million kWh, with a peak electrical demand of 5000 kW each month; the annual load factor for this requirement is 0.20, as follows:

$$\text{average power demand} = \frac{\text{annual energy in kWh}}{8760 \text{ hours per year}}$$

$$\text{annual load factor} = \frac{\text{average power demand in kW}}{\text{peak power demand in kW}}$$

Based on the tariff schedule of the regional utility applied to each month, the average cost when the utility supplies all the power needed by the sponsor would be

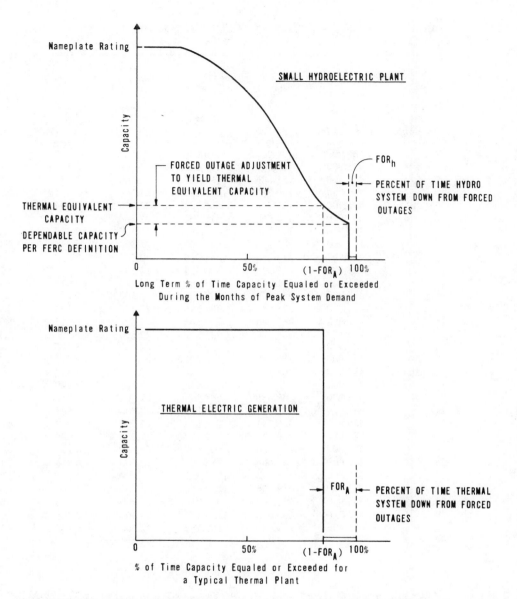

Figure 9.2 Dependable capacity of hydro plant in months of peak system demand. (From U.S. Department of the Army, Corps of Engineers, 1979.)

3.9 cents/kWh, or \$351,000 per year. After the sponsor has placed the hydropower facility on-line, it will still need to purchase 853,200 kWh of energy and this will be concentrated in the summer months, when stream flows are lowest. The cost of this supplemental power, using the same tariff schedule for capacity and energy as before, would be \$65,045. The gross savings of purchased energy would be \$285,955

TABLE 9.1 COMPARISON OF COST OF SERVICE OF HYDRO PLANT WITH VALUE OF ENERGY

Year of Operation	Bond Amortization	Operation and Maintenance	Total Annual Cost	Average Annual Energy Production (millions of kWh)	Cost of Service (cents/kWh)	Value of Energy (cents/kWh)
1	$435,900	$135,000	$570,900	22.500	2.537	2.500
2	435,900	143,100	579,000	22.500	2.573	2.650
3	435,900	151,686	587,586	22.500	2.611	2.809
4	435,900	160,787	596,687	22.500	2.651	2.977
5	435,900	170,434	606,334	22.500	2.694	3.156
6	435,900	180,660	616,560	22.500	2.740	3.345
7	435,900	191,500	627,400	22.500	2.788	3.546
8	435,900	202,990	638,890	22.500	2.839	3.759
9	435,900	215,169	651,069	22.500	2.893	3.984
10	435,900	228,079	663,979	22.500	2.951	4.223
11	435,900	241,764	677,664	22.500	3.011	4.477
12	435,900	256,270	692,170	22.500	3.076	4.745
13	435,900	271,646	707,546	22.500	3.144	5.030
14	435,900	287,945	723,845	22.500	3,217	5.332
15	435,900	305,222	741,122	22.500	3.293	5.652
16	435,900	323,535	759,435	22.500	3.375	5.991
17	435,900	342,947	778,847	22.500	3.461	6.350
18	435,900	363,524	799,424	22.500	3.552	6.731
19	435,900	385,335	821,235	22.500	3.649	7.135
20	435,900	408,455	844,355	22.500	3.752	7.563
21	435,900	432,963	868,863	22.500	3.861	8.017
22	435,900	458,941	894,841	22.500	3.977	8.498
23	435,900	486,477	922,377	22.500	4.099	9.008
24	435,900	515,666	951,566	22.500	4.229	9.549
25	435,900	546,606	982,506	22.500	4.366	10.122
26	435,900	579,402	1015,302	22.500	4.512	10.729
27	435,900	614,166	1050,066	22.500	4.666	11.373
28	435,900	651,016	1086,916	22.500	4.830	12.055
29	435,900	690,077	1125,977	22.500	5,004	12.779
30	435,900	731,482	1167,382	22.500	5.188	13.545

TABLE 9.2 PARAMETERS FOR A TYPICAL SMALL HYDROELECTRIC SITE

1. Installed capacity	1.50 mW
2. Dependable capacity	0.15 mW
3. Unit cost of construction	$800 per kW
4. Construction cost	$1,200,000
5. Investment cost	$1,411,100
6. Plant factor	0.62
7. Annual output	8,146,800 kWh
8. Annual costs	$176,389
	(12.5% of investment cost)

($351,000 − $65,045). This is more than the hydroelectric power costs, as shown in Table 9.2, of $176,389; thus, the financial results are favorable.

Adjustments of the financial analysis may be needed depending on the level of service required and the tariff details. If the sponsor had a need for power that could not be interrupted, a capacity charge would be incurred in every month, including those months in which there is adequate water to provide dependable capacity. If, however, year-round capacity is required only on a standby basis, the sponsor may be able to negotiate a lower capacity charge than considered in this example. If this example were to consider the effects of inflation, it is likely that (if present trends continue) the savings in purchased energy would increase at a faster rate than the costs of self-generated hydroelectric power, and these effects would improve the previous favorable results.

9.3.3 Government or Industrial Sponsor— Sale to Regional Utility

In this example, the hydroelectric plant whose parameters are indicated in Table 9.2 is considered to produce all its energy for sale to a regional electric utility. The annual costs of $176,389 in Table 9.2 are composed of $148,167 in fixed costs for capital recovery over a 20-year period and $28,222 in variable costs for operation and maintenance. These components are based on the charges of Table 9.3 applying to a public sponsor or a private sponsor having equivalent borrowing terms and tax concessions. As shown by Table 9.3, the costs for a private sponsor not having these advantages would be much higher.

TABLE 9.3 ANNUAL COSTS AS A PERCENTAGE OF INVESTMENT[a]

Cost Component	Private Project	Public Project
Fixed Charges		
Cost of money	14.00	7.00
Amortization	1.00	2.50
Property taxes	5.00	(not applicable)
Replacements	0.50	0.50
Insurance	0.50	0.50
Total fixed charges	21.00%	10.50%
Operating Costs		
Supplies and services	0.40	0.40
Maintenance	0.90	0.90
Salaries	0.45	0.45
Office expenses	0.15	0.15
Miscellaneous	0.10	0.10
Total operating costs	2.00%	2.00%
Total annual cost	23.00%	12.50%

[a]This table is based on a 20-year period of financing. Amortization is based on a sinking fund with interest at the cost of money. The format used is consistent with federal regulatory analysis of new hydroelectric capacity. See U.S. Federal Energy Regulatory Commission (1979).

Table 9.4 assumes that the variable costs (which are subject to inflation) increase at 7% per year and that the selling price for energy starts at 2 cents/kWh and escalates at 8.5% per year. For each year except the first, the total revenue exceeds the total costs and the net revenue (or "profit") is positive. In this example applying to a public project, the favorable financial results are obvious. In an example where unfavorable results persist for a number of years before net revenues are achieved, the overall financial results may be examimed in terms of present value. The computations are shown in the last two columns of Table 9.4.

The present values shown in the last column of Table 9.4 were obtained using a discount rate of 7%. It may be desirable to carry out the computation of net present value with higher discount rates, in order to recognize two problems in the estimates: (1) the uncertainties of the future net revenues, when inflation is included; and (2) the lower values of these escalated future net revenues in terms of constant dollars.

9.3.4 Management of Debt Service

The previous examples have assumed a constant debt service per year. When a project involves a long period of investment (e.g., when several hydropower plants are installed in sequence), the sponsor may not be able to manage the debt service with revenues in the early years. Figure 9.3 shows a plan for retiring the debt within a period of analysis of 50 years by using funds from the net operating income available for each year. The cumulative debt rises to year 2002 and then begins to fall, as the average rate for selling energy increases gradually to a level value of 12 cents/kWh. The plan assumes a 7% annual inflation rate and an interest rate on loans of 7%. In each year, only the portion of the available firm energy that meets new demand is credited as firm (dependable) energy, varying from 4 cents/kWh in 1985 to 5 cents/kWh in 1995. In the same period the undependable (or secondary) energy is assumed to vary from 1.0 cent/kWh to 1.5 cents/kWh.

9.3.5 Break-Even Points

The final illustrations in this section are in terms of break-even point. Tables 9.5 and 9.6 show the parameters and a portion of the calculations for a small hydroelectric plant sponsored by an investor-owned public utility whose interest rate, or desired earnings rate on capital, is 15% (corresponding to a capital recovery factor over 30 years of 0.15056 applied to the investment) and whose initial variable costs are 5.6% of the investment. In this problem it is assumed that the initial energy value, including an adjustment for capacity value, is 5 cents/kWh. The projected annual inflation rate both for variable costs and for energy value is 10%. In the calculations of Table 9.6, the interest rate for discounting is 15%. The annual costs and values are plotted on Figure 9.4. As shown on this chart and Table 9.6, values exceed costs starting by the end of the fourth year. The cumulative stream of values exceeds the cumulative stream of costs by the end of the eighth year. Another way of defining the break-even point is where the undiscounted accumulation of net operating income (values of energy minus variable costs) equals the original investment; this is known as the *payout method*. In this case this will occur by the end of the seventh year. This

TABLE 9.4 COMPARISON OF COSTS AND REVENUES AND PRESENT VALUE OF HYDROPLANT

Year	Fixed Costs[a]	Variable Costs[b]	Total Costs	Selling Price per kWh[c]	Gross Revenue	Net Revenue	Present-Value Factor[d]	Net Present Value
1	$148,167	$28,222	$176,389	0.020	$162,936	$(13,453)	0.935	$(12,579)
2	148,167	32,312	180,479	0.023	187,376	6,897	0.873	6,021
3	148,167	34,573	182,740	0.025	203,670	20,930	0.816	17,079
4	148,167	36,994	185,161	0.027	219,964	34,803	0.762	26,520
5	148,167	39,583	187,750	0.030	244,404	56,654	0.712	40,338
6	148,167	42,354	190,521	0.032	260,698	70,177	0.666	46,738
7	148,167	45,317	193,484	0.035	285,138	91,654	0.623	57,100
8	148,167	48,491	196,658	0.038	309,578	112,920	0.582	65,719
9	148,167	51,885	200,052	0.041	334,019	133,967	0.544	72,878
10	148,167	55,517	203,684	0.045	366,606	162,922	0.508	82,764
11	148,167	59,404	207,571	0.049	399,193	191,622	0.475	91,020
12	148,167	63,562	211,729	0.053	431,780	220,051	0.444	97,707
13	148,167	68,011	216,178	0.057	464,368	248,190	0.414	102,751
14	148,167	72,772	220,939	0.062	505,101	284,162	0.388	110,255
15	148,167	77,865	226,033	0.067	545,835	319,802	0.362	115,768
16	148,167	83,317	231,484	0.073	594,716	363,232	0.338	122,772
17	148,167	89,149	237,316	0.080	651,744	414,428	0.316	130,959
18	148,167	95,389	243,556	0.086	700,624	457,068	0.295	134,835
19	148,167	102,066	250,233	0.094	765,799	515,566	0.276	142,296
20	148,167	109,211	257,378	0.102	830,973	573,595	0.258	147,988

Net present value = $1,598,925

[a]Fixed costs are 10.5% of investment cost of $1,411,110.
[b]Variable costs are 2% of investment cost initially; escalation at 7%.
[c]Price escalation at 8.5%.
[d]Present value factors for 7% interest rate.

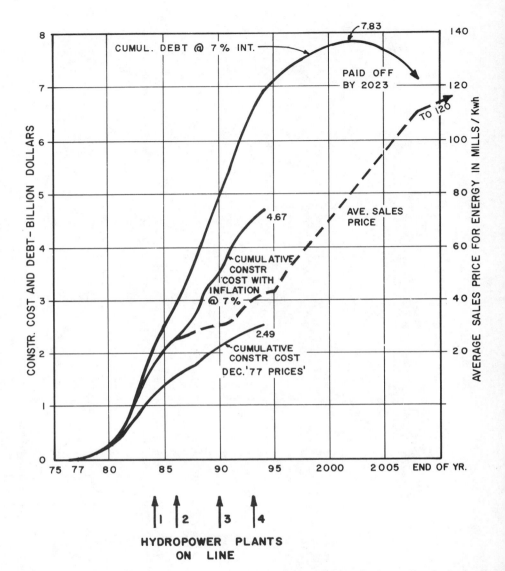

Figure 9.3 Example of financial plan involving varying debt repayment for four-project hydroelectric complex.

method is inexact because it does not involve the discounting process, but it is a rough method used by many businesses to judge profitability.

The break-even points discussed in the above paragraph are for an initial energy value of 5 cents/kWh, and inflation rates for variable costs and energy of 10%. For the break-even point determined as the year when the energy values exceed costs for that year, Figure 9.5 shows the results of a sensitivity analysis in which the initial

Financial Analyses   Chap. 9

TABLE 9.5 PARAMETERS FOR BREAK-EVEN PROBLEMS

1. Installed capacity (kW)	5,000
2. Capacity factor	0.55
3. Average annual energy (kWh)	24,090,000
4. Investment cost ($/kW)	1,500
5. Capital investment ($)	7,500,000
6. OMR (%)	0.5
7. Taxes (%)	5.0
8. Insurance (%)	0.1
9. Total OMR, taxes, and insurance (%)	5.6
10. Initial variable cost/year	420,000
11. Interest rate on capital (%)	15
12. Capital recovery period (years)	0.15056
14. Annual capital changes ($)	1,129,200
15. Annual cost first year	1,549,200
16. Initial energy value ($/kWh)	0.05
17. Initial energy value/year ($)	1,204,500
18. Inflation rate for OMR, taxes, and insurance (%)	10
19. Inflation rate for energy value (%)	10

energy value ranges from 2 to 5 cents/kWh and the annual inflation rates for energy and variable costs range from 5 to 15%.

9.4 FINANCIAL ANALYSES OF MUNICIPAL AND INDUSTRIAL WATER SUPPLY PROJECTS

Capital Investment Schedule. Table 9.7 shows the investment costs, not including interest during construction, for the recommended First Priority Phase I Project for water supply for Kingston, Jamaica. This schedule is broken down year by year, with separate accounts for domestic and foreign currency. The breakdown of these different currencies was based on the divisions shown in Table 9.8.

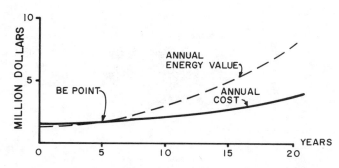

Figure 9.4 Comparison of annual costs and energy values for hydroelectric plant.

TABLE 9.6 ANALYSIS OF BREAK-EVEN POINT FOR HYDROPLANT

Year	Capital Charges	OMR, Taxes, and Interest (End of Year)	Annual Costs	Annual Energy Value	Net Value	Discounted Net Value (i = 15%)	Cumulative Discounted Net Value
1	$1,129,200	$462,000	$1,591,200	$1,325,000	$−266,200	$−231,500	$−231,500
2	1,129,200	508,200	1,637,400	1,457,500	−179,900	−136,000	−367,500
3	1,129,200	559,000	1,688,200	1,603,200	−85,000	−55,900	−423,400
4	1,129,200	614,900	1,744,100	1,763,400	19,300	11,000	−412,400
5	1,129,200	676,200	1,805,400	1,939,200	133,800	66,500	−345,900
6	1,129,200	774,100	1,903,300	2,133,200	229,900	99,400	−246,500
7	1,129,200	818,500	1,947,700	2,346,400	398,700	149,900	−96,600
8	1,129,200	900,300	2,029,500	2,581,200	551,700	180,400	83,800
9	1,129,200	990,300	2,119,500	2,839,000	719,500	204,500	288,300
10	1,129,200	1,089,400	2,218,600	3,123,300	904,700	223,600	511,900
11	1,129,200	1,198,300	2,327,500	3,436,400	1,108,900	238,400	750,300
12	1,129,200	1,318,100	2,447,300	3,780,200	1,332,900	249,100	999,400
13	1,129,200	1,449,800	2,579,000	4,157,900	1,578,900	256,600	1,256,000
14	1,129,200	1,594,700	2,723,900	4,573,500	1,849,600	261,400	1,517,400
15	1,129,200	1,754,300	2,883,500	5,031,200	2,147,700	263,900	1,781,300
16	1,129,200	1,929,800	3,059,000	5,533,500	2,474,500	264,400	2,045,700
17	1,129,200	2,122,700	3,251,900	6,088,100	2,836,200	263,600	2,309,300
18	1,129,200	2,334,800	3,464,000	6,696,900	3,232,900	261,200	2,570,500
19	1,129,200	2,568,300	3,697,500	7,365,500	3,668,000	257,700	2,828,200
20	1,129,200	2,825,300	3,954,500	8,102,700	4,148,200	253,500	3,081,700

TABLE 9.7 WATER SUPPLY PROJECT, KINGSTON: FIRST PRIORITY PHASE I INVESTMENT COSTS WITHOUT INTEREST ($1000 U.S.)

Construction	1978			1979			1980			Total		
	Domestic	Foreign	Total	Domestic	Foreign	Total	Domestic	Foreign	Total	Domestic	Foreign	Total
Land rights & relocation	39	0	39	44	0	44	0	0	0	84	0	84
Diversion dam	0	0	0	861	548	1,410	947	586	1,533	1,809	1,135	2,944
Conveyance tunnels	0	0	0	2,572	2,456	5,029	2,828	2,627	5,455	5,400	5,084	10,485
Conveyance pipelines	0	0	0	2,753	6,135	8,889	3,028	6,564	9,592	5,781	12,699	18,481
Treatment facilities	0	0	0	1,576	1,505	3,082	1,732	1,609	3,342	3,309	3,115	6,425
Compensation wells	0	0	0	375	358	733	412	383	795	787	741	1,529
Contingencies, 15%	5	0	5	1,228	1,650	2,878	1,342	1,765	3,108	2,576	3,415	5,992
Engineering and administration, 12%	660	966	1,626	724	1,038	1,763	797	1,110	1,907	2,182	3,115	5,297
Subtotal direct costs	705	966	1,671	10,137	13,694	23,831	11,089	14,647	25,737	21,932	29,308	51,240

Source: TAMS (1977).

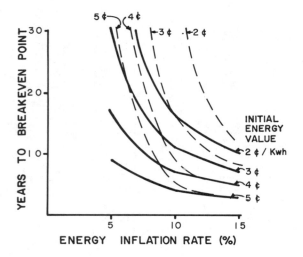

Figure 9.5 Sensitivity analysis for break-even point of hydro plant as function of initial energy value and inflation rates for energy value and OMR cost. Solid and broken lines are for OMR inflation rates of 5% and 10%, respectively.

For financial analyses, schedules were prepared with inflation taken into account. It was assumed that the domestic inflation rate would be 10 percent per year and that the foreign inflation rate would be 7.5 percent up to 1979 and 7.0 percent thereafter. It was determined that the estimated cost of the first phase would increase with these assumptions from $41,944,000 without inflation to $51,240,000 as shown in Table 9.7.

Cash Flow Analysis. Cash flow analyses for Kingston, Jamaica, were based on the schedule of investment costs for the first priority scheme as shown in Table 9.7. The water supply demands were based on population projections and unit demands, which are discussed in Chapter 4. The supply from other sources was estimated to be 58.8 million imperial gallons per day in 1980. The analysis for the first priority scheme estimated that of the total capacity of 5.98 billion imperial gallons per year, 0.84 billion would be needed to meet incremental demand in 1981 and that 6 additional years would be needed before the full capability of the scheme is realized.

Financial analyses were made for constant prices and for prices with inflation. Only the latter are shown in this section. Various assumptions made in the financial analysis are reviewed below.

TABLE 9.8 WATER SUPPLY PROJECT, KINGSTON: DOMESTIC AND FOREIGN EXCHANGE COMPONENTS OF PHASE I CONSTRUCTION COSTS

First Priority Scheme	Domestic (%)	Foreign (%)
Diversion dam	60	40
Conveyance tunnels	50	50
Conveyance pipelines	30	70
Treatment facilities	50	50
Compensation wells	50	50

Source: TAMS (1977).

Financial Analyses   Chap. 9

Water Sales As Related to Production.   The percentage of unaccounted for water was assumed to decline from 25% of total water production in 1976, to 16% in 1980, and thereafter to remain constant. This should result from leak detection and repair programs as well as improving billing operations.

Exchange Rate.   The exchange rate was assumed to be J $1,25 to U.S. $1.00, or J $1.00 to U.S. $0.80.

Loans.   The terms differed for foreign and domestic components as follows:

Foreign component: 9% interest
              15-year repayment
              5-year grace period
Domestic component: 11% interest
              20-year repayment
              5-year grace period

It was assumed that all money needed for expenditures in a given year was available at the beginning of that year. Full interest would be paid on loans from the beginning of each year in which such funds are available. Money that is is not used until later in the year might earn interest which could partially offset loan charges, but this adjustment was not considered substantive and was not made.

Water Rates.   The existing weighted average water rate was estimated to be J $1.16 per 1000 gallons sold (U.S. $0.93 per 1000 gallons). A 64% rate increase was contemplated, however, which would bring the weighted average tariff per thousand gallons sold up to J $1.90 (U.S. $1.52); this value was used in the economic and financial analyses based on 1977 market prices. For financial analyses based on prices with inflation, a rate of increase of water tariffs was assumed, based on historical trends and projections by the World Bank, as shown in Figure 9.6. The suitability of these tariff rates would have to be determined during analyses of the water utility's consolidated operations.

Distribution Costs.   In this analysis, distribution costs for 1976 were computed as a cost per thousand gallons and as a percentage of the tariff. Total direct distribution costs for 1976 were J $1.59 million, and total distribution costs, including overhead, were J $2.91 million. This gives a cost per 1000 gallons of J $0.22 (U.S. $0.18), which is 19% of the weighted average tariff in 1976 (J $1.16). In the financial and economic analyses at constant prices, a figure of J $0.22 or U.S. $0.18 per 1000 gallons produced was charged to the project as distribution costs. Using prices with inflation, the distribution costs were assumed at 20% of the current tariff applied to the water produced.

Inflation.   As mentioned above, the domestic inflation rate was assumed to be 10% per year and the foreign inflation rate was assumed to be 7.5% up to 1979, and 7.0% thereafter. It was considered that all analyses at current prices after the year

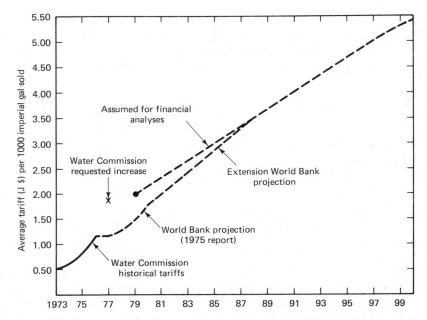

Figure 9.6 Kingston, Jamaica: historical and projected water rates. (From TAMS, 1977.)

1987 were highly speculative, since rates of inflation cannot be accurately forecast far into the future.

Forecast of Net Operating Income. Table 9.9 shows the year-by-year operating income attributable to the project's water production after revenues are reduced by operation, maintenance, replacement, and treatment costs, and by distribution costs.

Financial Analysis. Table 9.10 shows the schedules of year by year borrowings (disbursements) to meet investment costs and the annual loan repayments based on amounts owed including interest accumulated during grace periods. The net operating income each year is used to meet the loan payment due, to the extent possible; if this is inadequate, the difference was assumed to be derived from surpluses in the water utility's income from other sources.

Economic and Financial Comparisons of First Phase Alternatives. These analyses are summarized in Table 9.11. Economic analyses were discussed in Chapter 8. In the financial analyses, each alternative was examined to determine the extent to which, as a practical matter, revenues in each year would cover outlays. Required subsidies were estimated for years when revenues would not meet or exceed costs. The results of these analyses at 1977 prices and at assumed inflation rates indicated the clear advantage of the first priority scheme.

Financial Analyses   Chap. 9

TABLE 9.9 WATER SUPPLY PROJECT, KINGSTON: FIRST PRIORITY PHASE I FORECAST OF NET OPERATING INCOME ($1000 U.S.)

Year	Operation Maintenance Replacement Treatment	Distribution Costs 20% Water Tariff	Incremental Production (Billion Gallons/Yr)	Incremental Water Sold (Billion Gallons/Yr)	Incremental Annual Revenue	Net Operating Project Income	Water Tariff per Thousand Gallons
1981	1,058.54	315.83	0.84	0.70	1,326.52	−47.85	1.88
1982	1,164.39	715.59	1.78	1.50	3,005.51	1,125.52	2.00
1983	1,280.83	1,129.95	2.66	2.23	4,745.83	2,335.03	2.12
1984	1,408.92	1,664.39	3.65	3.06	6,990.47	3,917.15	2.28
1985	1,549.81	2,207.51	4.59	3.86	9,271.58	5,514.24	2.40
1986	1,704.79	2,814.83	5.58	4.69	11,822.32	7,302.69	2.52
1987	1,875.27	3,208.49	5.98	5.02	13,475.67	8,391.90	2.68
1988	2,062.80	3,352.15	5.98	5.02	14,079.06	8,664.10	2.80
1989	2,269.08	3,495.82	5.98	5.02	14,682.45	8,917.55	2.92
1990	2,495.98	3,687.37	5.98	5.02	15,486.97	9,303.60	3.08
1991	2,745.58	3,831.03	5.98	5.02	16,090.36	9,513.73	3.20
1992	3,020.14	3,974.70	5.98	5.02	16,693.75	9,693.89	3.32
1993	3,322.16	4,166.25	5.98	5.02	17,498.26	10,009.85	3.48
1994	3,654.37	4,309.91	5.98	5.02	18,101.66	10,137.36	3.60
1995	4,019.81	4,453.58	5.98	5.02	18,705.04	10,231.64	3.72
1996	4,421.79	4,645.13	5.98	5.02	19,509.56	10,442.63	3.88
1997	4,863.97	4,788.79	5.98	5.02	20,112.95	10,460.18	4.00
1998	5,350.37	4,932.46	5.98	5.02	20,716.34	10,433.50	4.12
1999	5,885.41	5,076.12	5.98	5.02	21,319.73	10,358.19	4.24
2000	6,473.95	5,171.90	5.98	5.02	21,721.98	10,076.13	4.32
2001	7,121.34	5,267.67	5.98	5.02	22,124.25	9,735.22	4.40
2002	7,833.47	5,315.56	5.98	5.02	22,325.37	9,176.33	4.44
2003	8,616.82	5,363.45	5.98	5.02	22,526.50	8,546.22	4.48
2004	9,478.50	5,411.34	5.98	5.02	22,727.63	7,837.78	4.52
2005	10,426.35	5,459.23	5.98	5.02	22,928.76	7,043.17	4.56
2006	11,468.99	5,507.11	5.98	5.02	23,129.89	6,153.78	4.60
2007	12,615.89	5,555.00	5.98	5.02	23,331.02	5,160.12	4.64

Source: TAMS (1977).

TABLE 9.10 WATER SUPPLY PROJECT, KINGSTON: FIRST PRIORITY PHASE I FINANCIAL ANALYSIS ($1000 U.S.)

Year	Loan Disbursement at Beginning of Year			Total Loan Repayment at End of Year			Net Operating Project Income	Project Balance	Percent Water Commission Income Other Sources to Finance Project Deficit	Water Commission Income from Other Sources
	Domestic	Foreign	Total	Domestic	Foreign	Total				
1978	705	966	1,671	0	0	0	0	0	0	0
1979	10,137	13,694	23,831	0	0	0	0	0	0	0
1980	11,089	14,647	25,737	0	0	0	0	0	0	0
1981	0	0	0	0	0	0	-47	-47	0	40,349
1982	0	0	0	149	184	333	1,125	791	0	42,924
1983	0	0	0	2,294	2,798	5,092	2,335	-2,757	6	45,499
1984	0	0	0	4,641	5,594	10,235	3,917	-6,318	12	48,933
1985	0	0	0	4,641	5,594	10,235	5,514	-4,721	9	51,509
1986	0	0	0	4,641	5,594	10,235	7,302	-2,932	5	54,084
1987	0	0	0	4,641	5,594	10,235	8,391	-1,843	3	57,518
1988	0	0	0	4,641	5,594	10,235	8,664	-1,571	2	60,094

1989	0	0	4,641	5,594	10,235	8,917	−1,318	2	62,669
1990	0	0	4,641	5,594	10,235	9,303	−931	1	66,103
1991	0	0	4,641	5,594	10,235	9,513	−721	1	68,678
1992	0	0	4,641	5,594	10,235	9,698	−536	0	71,254
1993	0	0	4,461	5,594	10,235	10,009	−225	0	74,688
1994	0	0	4,641	5,594	10,235	10,137	−98	0	78,980
1995	0	0	4,641	5,594	10,235	10,231	−3	0	79,839
1996	0	0	4,641	5,594	10,235	10,442	207	0	83,273
1997	0	0	4,641	5,409	10,051	10,460	409	0	85,848
1998	0	0	4,641	2,795	7,437	10,433	2,996	0	88,423
1999	0	0	4,641	0	4,641	10,358	5,716	0	90,999
2000	0	0	4,641	0	4,641	10,076	5,434	0	92,716
2001	0	0	4,641	0	4,641	9,735	5,094	0	94,433
2002	0	0	4,492	0	4,492	9,176	4,684	0	95,291
2003	0	0	2,346	0	2,346	8,546	6,199	0	96,150
2004	0	0	0	0	0	7,837	7,837	0	97,008
2005	0	0	0	0	0	7,043	7,043	0	97,867
2006	0	0	0	0	0	6,153	6,153	0	98,725
2007	0	0	0	0	0	5,160	5,160	0	99,584

Source: TAMS (1977).

TABLE 9.11   KINGSTON WATER SUPPLY: ALTERNATIVE FIRST PHASE PROJECTS
ECONOMIC AND FINANCIAL COMPARISONS

1	2	3	4	5	6	7	8	9	10	11
	Production				Cost of Project (1977 Prices)				Economic Analysis (1977 Prices)	
Scheme	Million Imperial Gallons per Day	Billion Imperial Gallons per Year	On-Line Year	Subsequent Years to Capacity	Construction Cost ($1000)	Investment Cost^a ($1000)	Investment Cost per imgd ($1000) with Full Production	Cost per 1000 ig with Full Production	Assumed Water Tariff ($)	Minimum Internal Rate of Return (%)
First priority scheme	16.4	5.986	1981	7	32,567	49,502	3,018	1.14	1.52	8.9
Blue Mountain— Southern route, phase I	16.4	5.986	1982	7	41,226	66,787	4,072	1.44	1.52	6.8
Blue Mountain— Northern route, phase I	12.0	4.380	1983	5	30,805	51,445	4,287	1.50	1.52	6.9
Mahogany Vale scheme (without hydropower)	27.2	9.928	1982	11	7,967.8	129,078	4,746	1.77	1.52	3.5

^{a}Includes contingencies, engineering and administration, and interest.
^{b}Analysis covers 30 years, 1978–2007.
^{c}Assumption is that Water Commission sells 61.1 imgd or 22.302 ibgy from other projects in 1981 and 58.7 imgd or 21.426 ibgy in 1980.
Source: TAMS (1977).

Economic and Financial Comparisons of Master Plan Alternatives.   The recommended master plan incorporated the first priority scheme as its first phase. Table 9.12 shows the financial results for this plan in terms of net incremental "benefits" (revenues minus costs) for each year from 1978 to 2025. Some years have deficits that would have to be made up by subsidies from other operations of the water utility. Table 9.12 also shows the total discounted costs at 10% for this plan. Three alternative master plans are compared in Table 9.13 in terms of internal rate of return

Financial Analyses   Chap. 9

12	13	14	15	16	17	18	19	20	21	22
Financial Analysis at 1977 Prices and Assumed Tariff $1.52/1000 I.G.				*Financial Analysis at Current Prices with Inflation and Tariff Range of $1.88–$4.64 (1981–2007)*						
No. of Years of Deficit[b]	Range of Deficit ($1000)	Average Annual Deficit ($1000)	Average Annual Deficit as Percent of Water Commission Income Other Sources[c]	Construction Cost ($1000)	Investment Cost ($1000)	Investment Cost per imgd	No. of Years of Deficit[b]	Range of Deficit ($1000)	Average Annual Deficit ($1000)	Average Annual Deficit as Percent of Water Commission Income Other Sources[c]
16	90-5,085	2,619	7.4	39,951	60,726	3,703	14	3-6,318	1,716	2.7
17	1,062-7,067	4,400	12.4	5,300	85,860	5,235	15	1,711-9,025	4,022	5.8
18	211-4,371	3,131	8.3	42,999	71,808	5,984	17	229-6,035	3,127	4.2
21	1,570-18,449	10,306	30.0	102,503	166,055	6,105	25	1,086-24,825	22,649	15

(economic analysis) and discounted total costs (financial analysis), again, confirming the superiority of the recommended master plan.

Sensitivity Analyses. The analyses described above were made for "most likely" water demand projections based on an extension of historical trends. Economic and financial analyses were also carried out for "high" and "low" projections of demand, for an early unforeseen increment of demand, and for higher

TABLE 9.12 KINGSTON WATER SUPPLY: RECOMMENDED MASTER PLAN FINANCIAL ANALYSIS
($1000 U.S.)

Year	Construction Costs	Total Annual Operating Costs	Total Costs	Incremental Annual Revenue	Net Incremental Benefits	Discounted Total Costs at 10%
1978	1,669.81	0.00	1,669.81	0.00	−1,669.81	1,669.81
1979	23,810.53	0.00	23,810.53	0.00	−23,810.53	21,645.94
1980	25,776.95	0.00	25,776.95	0.00	−25,776.95	21,303.26
1981	0.00	1,374.38	1,374.38	1,326.52	−47.85	1,032.59
1982	0.00	1,879.99	1,879.99	3,005.51	1,125.52	1,284.06
1983	3,383.66	2,410.79	5,794.45	4,745.83	−1,048.62	3,597.90
1984	41,453.13	3,073.32	44,526.45	6,990.47	−37,535.97	25,134.01
1985	49,847.28	3,757.33	53,604.61	9,271.58	−44,333.03	27,507.64
1986	54,082.21	4,519.63	58,601.84	11,822.32	−46,779.51	27,338.18
1987	0.00	8,291.40	8,291.40	14,790.38	6,498.97	3,516.36
1988	0.00	9,475.23	9,478.23	17,771.70	8,293.47	3,654.26
1989	0.00	10,802.13	10,802.13	21,128.41	10,326.27	3,786.08
1990	6,024.20	12,237.67	18,261.88	24,733.62	6,471.73	5,818.79
1991	88,117.32	13,804.71	101,922.03	28,648.69	−73,273.32	29,523.17
1992	95,804.46	15,437.46	111,241.92	32,573.17	−78,668.75	29,293.46
1993	0.00	20,769.39	20,769.39	37,343.86	16,574.47	4,972.02
1994	0.00	22,999.62	22,999.62	41,722.12	18,722.49	5,005.38
1995	0.00	25,506.32	25,506.32	46,762.61	21,256.28	5,046.29
1996	0.00	28,272.16	28,272.16	52,342.73	24,070.57	5,084.99
1997	0.00	31,144.15	31,144.15	57,765.10	26,620.94	5,092.31
1998	0.00	34,258.25	34,258.25	63,540.27	29,282.02	5,092.26
1999	0.00	37,632.84	37,632.84	69,679.12	32,046.27	5,085.34
2000	0.00	41,122.35	41,122.35	75,497.15	34,374.80	5,051.71
2001	0.00	43,769.90	43,769.90	76,895.25	33,125.34	4,888.13
2002	0.00	46,482.50	46,482.50	77,594.29	31,111.79	4,719.16
2003	0.00	49,449.70	49,449.70	78,293.34	28,843.63	4,564.00
2004	0.00	52,696.98	52,696.98	78,992.39	26,295.40	4,421.56
2005	0.00	56,252.34	56,252.34	79,691.43	23,439.08	4,290.79
2006	0.00	60,146.60	60,146.60	80,390.48	20,243.87	4,170.76
2007	0.00	64,413.64	64,413.64	81,089.53	16,675.88	4,060.59
2008	0.00	72,211.48	72,211.48	94,895.71	22,684.23	4,138.33
2009	0.00	80,460.40	80,460.40	108,701.90	28,241.50	4,191.87
2010	0.00	89,205.48	89,205.48	122,508.10	33,302.63	4,224.98
2011	0.00	98,496.34	98,496.34	136,314.31	37,817.96	4,240.93
2012	0.00	108,387.59	108,387.59	150,120.46	41,732.86	4,242.56
2013	0.00	118,939.23	118,939.23	163,926.68	44,987.44	4,232.34
2014	0.00	130,217.32	130,217.32	177,732.87	47,515.53	4,212.42
2015	0.00	142,294.50	142,294.50	191,539.08	49,244.57	4,184.64
2016	0.00	155,250.68	155,250.68	205,345.28	50,094.60	4,150.60
2017	0.00	169,173.78	169,173.78	219,151.43	49,977.66	4,111.66
2018	0.00	184,160.43	184,160.43	232,957.65	48,797.22	4,069.00
2019	0.00	200,317.03	200,317.03	246,763.84	46,446.82	4,023.62
2020	0.00	217,760.56	217,760.56	260,570.03	42,809.47	3,976.36
2021	0.00	236,619.75	236,619.75	274,376.25	37,756.47	3,927.94
2022	0.00	257,036.12	257,036.12	288,182.43	31,146.28	3,878.96
2023	0.00	279,165.43	279,165.43	301,988.62	22,823.19	3,829.92
2024	0.00	303,179.00	303,179.00	315,794.81	12,615.81	3,781.24
2025	0.00	329,847.68	329,847.68	332,047.68	2,200.00	3,739.87
						350,808.04

Source: TAMS (1977).

TABLE 9.13   MASTER PLANS: ECONOMIC AND FINANCIAL COMPARISONS

Scheme	Internal Rate of Return (%)	Discounted Total Costs at 10% Interest	
		Without Inflation ($1000 U.S.)	With Inflation ($1000 U.S.)
Recommended master plan	7.6	118,997	350,807
Blue Mountain—Southern Route	6.4	122,618	407,624
Blue Mountain—combined Northern Route and Yallahs River diversion	7.0	126,311	371.738

and lower inflation rates. These analyses further confirmed the merit of the recommended plans.

9.5 FINANCIAL ANALYSIS OF IRRIGATION PROJECT

Various standard financial analyses are shown in this section for the Lower Ebro Right Bank Project in Spain (TAMS, 1963). Economic analyses for this project were described in Section 8.5. The arrangement of the project is shown schematically in Figure 9.7. In 1963, when the financial analyses were made, allowances for inflation were not made. Year-by-year estimates of construction cost were made for three major components: pumping facilities, main canal system, and distribution systems for the irrigation zones. In addition, there are costs for land conversion. These are for land leveling, terracing, and other measures to make farms suitable for irrigation.

Scheme Assumed for Financing. The project works were planned to be adequate not only for the Lower Ebro Right Bank irrigation area of 47,000 hectares but also to provide water supply for irrigation in Castellon de la Plana, downstream of the project area, and for municipal water supplies. In order to focus on the financial and economic analyses for the project area, the cost for these additional provisions were subtracted and the remainder of the analyses discussed below were based on the adjusted costs.

The total adjusted investments of the three major components of project works—(1) pumping station; (2) main canal system, including Murs reservoir; and (3) distribution systems for the irrigation zones, including secondary and tertiary canals and other local works—together with (4) land conversion costs for individual farms, would be as shown on Table 9.14.

Various assumptions were made with respect to financing of the project works. The government would construct the pumping station and arrange for its financing by means of loans at current borrowing terms from foreign development banks. These loans would cover the major portion of the foreign exchange requirements for the project. An interest rate of 6% and amortization over 25 years were assumed,

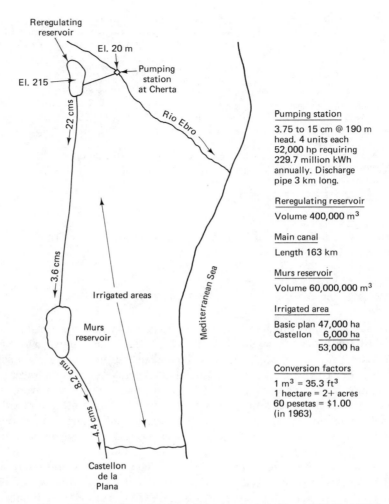

Pumping station

3.75 to 15 cm @ 190 m head. 4 units each 52,000 hp requiring 229.7 million kWh annually. Discharge pipe 3 km long.

Reregulating reservoir

Volume 400,000 m³

Main canal

Length 163 km

Murs reservoir

Volume 60,000,000 m³

Irrigated area

Basic plan 47,000 ha
Castellon   6,000 ha
            53,000 ha

Conversion factors

1 m³ = 35.3 ft³
1 hectare = 2+ acres
60 pesetas = $1.00
(in 1963)

Figure 9.7   Rio Ebro right-bank irrigation project. (From TAMS, 1963.)

TABLE 9.14 ALLOCATION OF INVESTMENTS IN RIO EBRO PROJECT AREA

	Investments (million pesetas)	Percentage
1. Pumping station	597.5	16.4
2. Main canal system	1208.8	33.1
3. Irrigation zone distribution systems	927.8	25.5
4. Land conversion	910.4	25.0
Total	3644.5	100.0

comparable to the terms of the International Bank for Reconstruction and Development. The resulting capital charges would be reimbursed from revenues of the project. The government would also construct the main canal system, using appropriated funds. Computations showed that, if no subsidies were granted, the government could expect to receive return of cost within 60 years. The government, in financing or arranging for financing, and constructing the pumping station and the main canal system to serve all the irrigation zones in common, would cover approximately 49% of the capital investment cost of the project.

The irrigation zone distribution systems and other local works would be the responsibility of the proprietors of land that would be benefited by irrigation. The financial terms would be representative of reasonable mortgages on the land to be improved by irrigation and raised in value thereby. It was assumed that the works in the irrigation zones would be financed by means of 4% 35-year loans. The land conversion requirements would also be the responsibility of the proprietors of land, either directly or with the aid of Spanish credits. With the foregoing assumptions, the farmers would assume responsibility for financing approximately 51% of the overall cost of the project. For the financial analysis, it was assumed that the capital charges for the irrigation zones would be paid out of revenues of the project while the land conversion costs would be reflected in the crop production expenses.

An overall project period of 60 years was assumed. Most of the construction would be completed in the first 10 years, and in the next 10 years virtually the full amount of irrigation would be achieved. Repayment of all construction costs would be completed within the 60-year period. A lag period was assumed between the time each phase of construction is completed and the time repayment of costs begins. Interest charges are accumulated during these lag periods and are reflected in the annual capital charges during the repayment periods.

Capital charges derived from the foregoing assumptions were combined with operation and maintenance expenses to estimate a schedule of annual costs for the purpose of estimating a unit cost of water. It was found that the financial program outlined above would be equivalent to deriving capital charges for all project works at 3% interest over the 60-year period.

Estimates of Annual Project Costs. Table 9.15 shows the annual operation and maintenance costs at various levels of energy prices and with the projected growth of pumping requirements. Table 9.16 shows the annual costs of the pumping station, which grow with the four phases of the construction program and the volume of water pumped. A similar table, not shown here, was prepared for the annual costs of the irrigation systems in the various irrigation zones as they are completed and progressively utilized over the years of development.

Repayment of Main Canal Costs. The investment cost of the main canal would be repaid when surplus revenues permit this to be done. The projected schedule for main canal repayment is shown in Table 9.17. Annual revenue was based on water pumped and a tariff rate averaging 0.95 peseta per cubic meter. Priority charges before main canal repayment include all the pumping station costs, all the irrigation zone costs except amortization of land conversion, and operation and maintenance

TABLE 9.15 RIO EBRO PROJECT: OPERATION AND MAINTENANCE EXPENSES (Million Pesetas)

Year	Water Pumped (Million Cubic Meters)	Without Power				Power at 0.3 pesetas per kWh	Total	With Power			
		Pump Station	Main Canal System	Distribution System	Total			Power at 0.4 pesetas per kWh	Total	Power at 0.5 pesetas per kWh	Total
−1											
1											
2											
3											
4	6.0	4.0	8.0	1.4	13.4	1.4	14.8	1.8	15.2	2.3	15.7
5	21.2	4.0	9.0	4.2	17.2	4.9	22.1	6.5	23.7	8.1	25.3
6	41.4	6.0	10.0	7.2	23.2	9.5	32.7	12.6	35.8	15.8	39.0
7	65.1	6.0	11.0	9.9	26.9	14.9	41.8	19.9	46.8	24.8	51.7
8	88.6	6.0	12.0	12.0	30.0	20.3	50.3	27.0	57.0	33.8	63.8
9	115.5	7.0	13.0	13.3	33.3	26.4	59.7	35.2	68.5	44.0	77.3
10	144.6	7.0	14.0	15.5	36.5	33.1	69.6	44.1	80.6	55.1	91.6
11	175.7	8.0	15.0	16.7	39.7	40.2	79.9	53.6	93.3	66.9	106.6
12	201.6	8.0	15.0	17.0	40.0	46.2	86.2	61.5	101.5	76.8	116.8
13	223.4	8.0	15.0	17.0	40.0	51.2	91.2	68.1	108.1	85.1	125.1
14	240.6	8.0	15.0	17.0	40.0	55.1	95.1	73.4	113.4	91.7	131.7
15	253.5	8.0	15.0	17.0	40.0	58.1	98.1	77.3	117.3	96.6	136.6
16	262.5	8.0	15.0	17.0	40.0	60.1	100.1	80.1	120.1	100.0	140.0
17	267.4	8.0	15.0	17.0	40.0	60.2	101.2	81.6	121.6	101.9	141.9
18	269.9	8.0	15.0	17.0	40.0	61.8	101.8	82.3	122.3	102.8	142.8
19	271.0	8.0	15.0	17.0	40.0	62.1	102.1	82.7	122.7	103.3	143.3
20	271.9	8.0	15.0	17.0	40.0	62.2	102.2	82.9	122.9	103.5	143.5
21	272.0	8.0	15.0	17.0	40.0	62.3	102.3	83.0	123.0	103.6	143.6
22−	272.0	8.0	15.0	17.0	40.0	62.3	102.3	83.0	123.0	103.6	143.6

Source: TAMS (1963).

costs of the main canal. The difference between annual revenue and annual priority costs constitute the annual operating surplus which can be considered for main canal repayments. It was assumed that such repayments would begin when surpluses accumulate to 200 million pesetas, approximately equal to one year's total operating costs at full development; this scheme was designed to reduce dependence on revolving credits from the banking institutions for working funds to accommodate variations in cash flows, which result from lower and higher water requirements than the amounts estimated for years of average rainfall.

With the repayment schedule shown in the last column of Table 9.17, it was possible to estimate the financial return for the monies to build the main canal. It was determined that, at the end of 60 years, the future value of all canal repayments would equal the future value of canal investments, when both repayments and investments were compounded at 2% interest.

Farm Payment Capacity.   The capacities of various types of farming operations to pay for the irrigation project can be estimated from model farm budgets. A summary farm budget for a single farm in Table 9.18 shows a capacity of 69,936 pesetas, and a net of 46,973 pesetas after payment for water at 0.95 peseta per cubic meter. The farm payment capacity expressed as a ratio of such capacity to project cost is over 3. Note that the ability to pay for water takes account of the value of crops grown on the farm that are consumed by the farm family and a basic living allowance. The farm capacity per hectare was determined to be 27,974 pesetas per hectare. The farm payment capacity was compared with cost of water for 12 different types of farms; the resulting ratios ranged from 1.1 to 29.7.

9.6 FINANCIAL ANALYSIS OF A MULTIUNIT, MULTIPURPOSE PROJECT

Capital Investment Schedule.   A summary capital investment schedule, including annual values for each project and totals for all developments, is shown for the Greek portion of the Vardar/Axios project in Table 9.19, modified for historical inflation of prices to 1977 but with no adjustments for subsequent inflation.

Cost of Services.   A useful financial indicator of water resources projects is the unit cost of their services. Estimates of unit costs are obtained by dividing total annual costs by total annual volume of products or services provided (dollars per cubic foot of water, cents per kilowatt-hour, etc.). For multipurpose projects, such costs should include allocations of reservoirs and other features serving more than one purpose.

If the output of a project is not fully utilized, the cost of services is needed in terms of the output utilized, as well as in terms of total production capability. Low output may occur in the initial years of operation due to partial construction or inadequate market growth.

TABLE 9.16   RIO EBRO PROJECT: PUMPING STATION, ANNUAL COSTS (Million Pesetas)

Year	Water Pumped (million cubic meters)	Cumul. Const. Costs without Interest	Phase I — Const. Costs with Interest at 6%	Phase I — Annual Capital Costs	Phase 2 — Cumul. Const. Costs without Interest	Phase 2 — Const. Costs with Interest at 6%	Phase 2 — Annual Capital Costs	Phase 3 — Cumul. Const. Costs without Interest	Phase 3 — Const. Costs with Interest at 6%	Phase 3 — Annual Capital Costs
−1		12.6								
1		102.8								
2		193.1								
3		283.4								
4	6.0				36.6					
5	21.2				77.1					
6	41.4									
7	65.1							59.2		
8	88.6		428.8					118.5		
9	115.5			33.5						
10	144.6			33.5		112.6				
11	175.7			33.5			8.8			
12	201.6			33.5			8.8			
13	223.4			33.5			8.8		173.1	
14	240.6			33.5			8.8			13.5
15	253.5			33.5			8.8			13.5
16	262.5			33.5			8.8			13.5
17	267.4			33.5			8.8			13.5
18	269.9			33.5			8.8			13.5
19	271.0			33.5			8.8			13.5
20	271.9			33.5			8.8			13.5
21	272.0			33.5			8.8			13.5
22	272.0			33.5			8.8			13.5
23	272.0			33.5			8.8			13.5
24	272.0			33.5			8.8			13.5
25	272.0			33.5			8.8			13.5
26	272.0			33.5			8.8			13.5
27	272.0			33.5			8.8			13.5
28	272.0			33.5			8.8			13.5
29	272.0			33.5			8.8			13.5
30	272.0			33.5			8.8			13.5
31	272.0			33.5			8.8			13.5
32	272.0			33.5			8.8			13.5
33	272.0			33.5			8.8			13.5
34	272.0						8.8			13.5
35	272.0						8.8			13.5
36	272.0									13.5
37	272.0									13.5
38	272.0									13.5
39	272.0									
40	272.0									
41	272.0									
42–60	272.0									

Phase 4		Total				
Cumul. Const. Costs without Interest	Const. Costs with Interest at 6%	Annual Capital Costs	Capital Costs	Operation and Maintenance	Power at 0.4 pesetas/kWh	Total Cost
				4.0	1.8	5.8
				4.0	6.5	10.5
				6.0	12.6	18.6
				6.0	19.9	25.9
				6.0	27.0	33.0
59.2			33.5	7.0	35.2	75.7
118.5			33.5	7.0	44.1	84.6
			42.3	8.0	53.6	103.9
			42.3	8.0	61.5	111.8
			42.3	8.0	68.1	118.4
			55.8	8.0	73.4	137.2
	173.1		55.8	8.0	77.3	141.1
		13.5	69.3	8.0	80.1	157.4
		13.5	69.3	8.0	81.6	158.9
		13.5	69.3	8.0	82.3	159.6
		13.5	69.3	8.0	82.7	160.0
		13.5	69.3	8.0	82.9	160.2
		13.5	69.3	8.0	83.0	160.3
		13.5	69.3	8.0	83.0	160.3
		13.5	69.3	8.0	83.0	160.3
		13.5	69.3	8.0	83.0	160.3
		13.5	69.3	8.0	83.0	160.3
		13.5	69.3	8.0	83.0	160.3
		13.5	69.3	8.0	83.0	160.3
		13.5	69.3	8.0	83.0	160.3
		13.5	69.3	8.0	83.0	160.3
		13.5	69.3	8.0	83.0	160.3
		13.5	69.3	8.0	83.0	160.3
		13.5	35.8	8.0	83.0	126.8
		13.5	35.8	8.0	83.0	126.8
		13.5	27.0	8.0	83.0	118.0
		13.5	27.0	8.0	83.0	118.0
		13.5	27.0	8.0	83.0	118.0
		13.5	13.5	8.0	83.0	104.5
		13.5	13.5	8.0	83.0	104.5
				8.0	83.0	91.0
				8.0	83.0	91.0

Source: TAMS (1963).

TABLE 9.17 RIO EBRO RIGHT BANK IRRIGATION PROJECT: ANALYSIS OF ANNUAL REVENUES AND COSTS (Million Pesetas)

			Annual Charges and Costs						Working Fund			
Year (1)	Water Pumped (Million Cubic Meters) (2)	Revenue at 0.95 Pesetas/ Cubic Meters (3)	Pump Station (4)	Main Canal System (5)	Irrigation Zones (6)	Total (7)	Operating Surplus (8)	Interest Credit at 4% (9)	Before Main Canal Payment (10)	After Main Canal Payment (11)	Main Canal Payment (12)
1											
2											
3											
4	6.0	5.7	5.8	8.0	1.4	15.2	−9.5		−9.5	−9.5	
5	21.2	20.1	10.5	9.0	4.2	23.7	−3.6	−0.4	−13.5	−13.5	
6	41.4	39.3	18.6	10.0	7.2	35.8	3.5	−0.5	−10.5	−10.5	
7	65.1	61.8	25.9	11.0	9.9	46.8	15.0	−0.4	4.1	4.1	
8	88.6	84.2	33.0	12.0	12.0	57.0	27.2	0.1	31.4	31.4	
9	115.5	109.7	75.7	13.0	13.3	102.0	7.7	1.3	40.3	40.3	
10	144.6	137.4	84.6	14.0	23.5	122.1	15.3	1.6	57.2	57.2	
11	175.7	166.9	103.9	15.0	36.2	155.1	11.8	2.3	71.3	71.3	
12	201.6	191.5	111.8	15.0	47.7	174.5	17.0	2.9	91.2	91.2	
13	223.4	212.2	118.4	15.0	57.3	190.7	21.5	3.6	116.3	116.3	
14	240.6	228.6	137.2	15.0	64.5	216.7	11.9	4.7	132.9	132.9	
15	253.5	240.8	141.1	15.0	68.9	225.0	15.8	5.3	152.4	152.4	
16	262.5	249.4	157.4	15.0	78.5	250.9	1.5	6.1	157.0	157.0	
17	267.4	254.0	158.9	15.0	81.2	255.1	1.1	6.3	162.2	162.2	
18	269.9	256.4	159.6	15.0	81.2	255.8	0.6	6.5	169.3	169.3	
19	271.0	257.5	160.0	15.0	81.2	256.2	1.3	6.8	177.3	177.3	
20	271.9	258.3	160.2	15.0	81.2	256.4	1.9	7.1	186.3	186.3	
21	272.0	258.4	160.3	15.0	81.2	256.5	1.9	7.4	195.6	195.6	
22	272.0	258.4	160.3	15.0	81.2	256.5	1.9	7.8	205.3	200.0	5.3
23	272.0	258.4	160.3	15.0	81.2	256.5	1.9	8.0	209.9	200.0	9.9
24	272.0	258.4	160.3	15.0	81.2	256.5	1.9	8.0	209.9	200.0	9.9
25	272.0	258.4	160.3	15.0	81.2	256.5	1.9	8.0	209.9	200.0	9.9
26	272.0	258.4	160.3	15.0	81.2	256.5	1.9	8.0	209.9	200.0	9.9
27	272.0	258.4	160.3	15.0	81.2	256.5	1.9	8.0	209.9	200.0	9.9

272

28	272.0	258.4	160.3	15.0	81.2	256.5	1.9	8.0	209.9	200.0	9.9
29	272.0	258.4	160.3	15.0	81.2	256.5	1.9	8.0	209.9	200.0	9.9
30	272.0	258.4	160.3	15.0	81.2	256.5	1.9	8.0	209.9	200.0	9.9
31	272.0	258.4	160.3	15.0	81.2	256.5	1.9	8.0	209.9	200.0	9.9
32	272.0	258.4	160.3	15.0	81.2	256.5	1.9	8.0	209.9	200.0	9.9
33	272.0	258.4	160.3	15.0	81.2	256.5	1.9	8.0	209.9	200.0	9.9
34	272.0	258.4	126.8	15.0	81.2	223.0	35.4	8.0	243.4	200.0	43.4
35	272.0	258.4	126.8	15.0	81.2	223.0	35.4	8.0	243.4	200.0	43.4
36	272.0	258.4	118.0	15.0	81.2	214.2	44.2	8.0	252.2	200.0	52.2
37	272.0	258.4	118.0	15.0	81.2	214.2	44.2	8.0	252.2	200.0	52.2
38	272.0	258.4	118.0	15.0	81.2	200.7	57.7	8.0	265.7	200.0	52.2
39	272.0	258.4	104.5	15.0	81.2	200.7	57.7	8.0	265.7	200.0	65.7
40	272.0	258.4	104.5	15.0	81.2	187.2	71.2	8.0	279.2	200.0	65.7
41	272.0	258.4	91.0	15.0	81.2	187.2	71.2	8.0	279.2	200.0	79.2
42	272.0	258.4	91.0	15.0	81.2	187.2	71.2	8.0	279.2	200.0	79.2
43	272.0	258.4	91.0	15.0	81.2	187.2	71.2	8.0	279.2	200.0	79.2
44	272.0	258.4	91.0	15.0	81.2	187.2	71.2	8.0	279.2	200.0	79.2
45	272.0	258.4	91.0	15.0	73.2	179.2	79.2	8.0	287.2	200.0	87.2
46	272.0	258.4	91.0	15.0	61.7	167.7	90.7	8.0	298.7	200.0	98.7
47	271.0	258.4	91.0	15.0	50.5	156.5	101.9	8.0	309.9	200.0	109.9
48	272.0	258.4	91.0	15.0	40.9	146.9	111.5	8.0	319.5	200.0	119.5
49	272.0	258.4	91.0	15.0	33.7	139.7	118.7	8.0	326.7	200.0	126.7
50	272.0	258.4	91.0	15.0	29.3	135.3	123.1	8.0	331.1	200.0	131.1
51	272.0	258.4	91.0	15.0	19.7	125.7	132.7	8.0	340.7	200.0	140.7
52	272.0	258.4	91.0	15.0	17.0	123.0	135.4	8.0	343.4	200.0	143.4
53	272.0	258.4	91.0	15.0	17.0	123.0	135.4	8.0	343.4	200.0	143.4
54	272.0	258.4	91.0	15.0	17.0	123.0	135.4	8.0	343.4	200.0	143.4
55	272.0	258.4	91.0	15.0	17.0	123.0	135.4	8.0	343.4	200.0	143.4
56	272.0	258.4	91.0	15.0	17.0	123.0	135.4	8.0	343.4	200.0	143.4
57	272.0	258.4	91.0	15.0	17.0	123.0	135.4	8.0	343.4	200.0	143.4
58	272.0	258.4	91.0	15.0	17.0	123.0	135.4	8.0	343.4	200.0	143.4
59	272.0	258.4	91.0	15.0	17.0	123.0	135.4	8.0	343.4	200.0	143.4
60	272.0	258.4	91.0	15.0	17.0	123.0	135.4	8.0	343.4	200.0	143.4

Source: TAMS (1963).

TABLE 9.18 RIO EBRO PROJECT: MODEL FARM BUDGET, SUMMARY PRODUCTS AND EXPENSES

Type of farming: Vegetables
Class of soil: II 1 C 1
Total area: 2.50 hectares
Useful area: 2.43 hectares
Financial summary:

Revenues from sales		174,676 pesetas
Value of family consumption		20,656
		195,332
Expenses of production		65,396
	Difference	129,936
Family living allowance		60,000
Farm capacity to pay for irrigation project		69,936
	per hectare	27,974
Estimate of cost of water		22,963
	Difference (net return)	46,973 pesetas
	Ratio	$\dfrac{69,936}{22,963} = 3+$

Source: TAMS (1963).

The cost may also vary from year to year, to reflect terms of financing resulting in uneven annual capital charges and the variation in operation and maintenance costs (e.g., pumping cost varies with volume pumped) and inflation effects. When loans are finally amortized, the unit cost of services may be substantially lowered.

Table 9.20 shows benefit-cost and financial results of analyses for the hydroelectric projects of the Vardar/Axios master plan. All of these projects are in the Yugoslavian (SRM) portion of the basin. The benefit-cost (economic) results are based on shadow-priced values, while the financial results (capital expenditures and unit costs) are based on market values. In this case, the hydro production was expected to be fully utilized as soon as it was made available, and no adjustment was needed to accommodate the growth of demand.

9.7 COST ALLOCATIONS AND SUBSIDIES

9.7.1 General

Most of the examples discussed in the preceding sections applied to single-purpose projects. In these examples, the projections accounted for fully satisfying the costs from revenues or identified the deficits that would have to be covered by surpluses from other activities and/or sales of the enterprise.

In the case of multipurpose projects, the "separable costs-remaining benefits" method was discussed in Chapter 8 for cost allocation needed for economic analyses of the component project purposes. The cost allocations for a financial analysis need not necessarily follow the same rules as for economic analysis. They may depend on legal requirements, payment capacities, availability of money for subsidies, and other agency policies concerning project beneficiaries.

Policies of the U.S. government concerning cost allocation, reimbursement, and cost sharing with respect to federal and nonfederal interests are expressed in federal guidelines such as those of the Water Resources Council (1983) and the regulations of individual agencies. Nonfederal contributions to project cost may include subsidies by local or regional government agencies or purchases of water, power, or other products and services by utilities and subsequent recovery of these costs from customers and other beneficiaries.

9.7.2 Apportionment of Costs for Federal Projects

The reimbursement and subsidy policies of the federal government are shown by the example of the Water Resources Survey of the Appalachian region by the Corps of Engineers (1969). The following summarizes the principles of apportionment applying in 1969 to the sharing of the costs of flood control, water quality control, power, water supply, recreation, fish and wildlife, and economic expansion by the federal government and beneficiaries:

> *Flood Control.* For local protection projects and upstream flood control structures, nonfederal interests are apportioned the costs of lands, easements, rights-of-way, alterations (with the exception of railroad bridges and approaches) and relocations; in addition, nonfederal interests must operate and maintain the project. For major reservoir projects, all costs associated with flood control providing widespread flood control benefits are apportioned to the federal government.
>
> *Water Quality Control.* Where benefits are widespread, the costs associated with reservoir storage of dilution water, for water quality purposes, are apportioned to the federal government.
>
> *Power.* All costs allocated to power are reimbursed by the appropriate marketing agency or firm.
>
> *Water Supply.* The costs allocated for the provision of reservoir storage to provide water supply are apportioned to nonfederal interests.
>
> *Recreation.* The separable costs of providing water-based recreation lands and facilities in reservoir projects are divided equally between federal and nonfederal interests. Nonfederal interests must agree to operate and maintain all recreation facilities and lands.
>
> *Economic Expansion.* The portion of the joint costs of federal multiple-purpose projects allocated to the purpose of regional income expansion is apportioned to the federal government.

Although not applicable to the Appalachian Water Resources Survey, the federal government also subsidized navigation and irrigation costs in 1969. Construction and maintenance and operation costs of *commercial* navigation projects have been borne almost entirely by the federal government. Local interests are required to provide terminal facilities, dredging in berthing areas, and the necessary lands, easements, rights-of-way and spoil disposal areas, and the alteration of

TABLE 9.19 VARDAR/AXIOS PROJECT: CAPITAL EXPENDITURES SCHEDULE AXIOS AND FLORINA PLAINS, GREECE (Millions of Equivalent 1977 U.S. Dollars)

Projects	1985	1986	1987	1988	1989	1990	1991	1992	1993	1994	1995	1996	1997	1998	1999	Total
								Year								
Dams																
AXIOS																
Polikastron diversion[a]																19.63
Ayak[a]																5.66
Kotza Dere[a]																19.63
Subtotal																44.92
FLORINA																
Florina								2.10	4.77	6.66	6.26					19.79
Trapeouhos				2.91	6.60	9.20	8.66									27.37
Hydroussa							3.37	7.08	11.16	14.81	12.93					49.35
Papadia	5.02	10.54	16.61	22.03	19.22											73.42
Subtotal	5.02	10.54	16.61	24.94	25.82	9.20	12.03	9.18	15.93	21.47	19.19					169.93
Total, dams	5.02	10.54	16.61	24.94	25.82	9.20	12.03	9.18	15.93	21.47	19.19					214.85

Irrigation Projects

Projects	Hectares	1985	1986	1987	1988	1989	1990	1991	1992	1993	1994	1995	1996	1997	1998	1999	Total
AXIOS																	
West Bank A	5,300			6.04	8.65	7.51											22.20

	Area (ha)											Total
West Bank B	8,800		9.67	15.47	17.02	13.88						56.04
East Bank[a]	24,800											146.50
Ayak[a]	5,400	6.04	18.32	22.98	17.02	13.88						39.15
Subtotal												263.89
FLORINA												
Florina											3.70	3.70
Trapeouhos	2,320						7.07					7.07
Hydroussa	2,310										7.28	7.28
Diversions	1,250										3.55	3.55
Papadia	10,400			3.87	7.01	7.71	8.49	6.57				33.65
Subtotal				3.87	7.01	7.71	15.56	6.57			14.53	55.25
Total, irrigation		6.04	18.32	26.85	24.03	21.59	15.56	6.57			14.53	319.14
Total, all projects (1977 prices)		5.02	10.54	22.65	43.26	52.67	33.23	33.62	24.74	22.50	21.47	33.72	533.99

[a]Projects are recommended for implementation after 2000. Costs are included in totals but annual amounts, which would occur after 2000, are not shown. Ayak project is recommended for further study.

Source: TAMS (1978).

TABLE 9.20 VARDAR/AXIOS PROJECT: ANALYSIS OF HYDROELECTRIC PROJECTS

Project	Region	Construction Period	Considered		Model Results				Benefit-Cost Results[a] 1977 Basis[b]				
			Installed Capacity (MW)	Estimated Production (GWh)	Installed Capacity (MW)	Estimated Production (GWh)	Capacity Factor	Dependable Capacity (MW)	Estimated Cost (Million U.S.$)	Estimated Benefits (Million U.S.$)	B/C Ratio	Capital Expend. (Million U.S.$)	Unit Costs U.S.$/kWh
Major Hydroelectric Projects—2025													
Kozjak	1	1982, 1986	75	255	75	208.3	0.32	47.0	92.84[c]	175.12	1.9	85.95	0.080
Matka II	1	1986–1987	60	208	60	165.6	0.32	43.1	80.11[c]	147.18	1.8	73.07	0.068
Titov Veles	2	1997–1998	50	252	50	232.2	0.53	19.5	102.84	151.85	1.4	97.71	0.079
Cebren	10	1984–1986	167	342	167	179.1	0.16	56.0	167.47	171.14	1.0	150.12	0.149
Galiste	10	1988–1990	116	176	116	159.9	0.16	55.9	153.05	160.31	1.0	147.13	0.172
Gradec	4	1984–1985	54	301	54	203.4	0.43	14.3	106.71	127.63	1.2	49.65	0.092
Total			522	1534	522	1146.3		235.8	701.03	933.23	1.3	653.63	0.103 (average)
Minor Hydroelectric Projects—2025													
Paligrad	1	1981	11.2	63.1	11.2	58.3	0.60	2.1	24.61	32.49	1.3	21.91	0.060
Konjsko	4	1982–1983	13.6	15.0	13.6	29.4	0.25	4.1	10.94	17.31	1.6	9.50	0.064
Vakuf	6	1989	14.8	28.7	9.4	14.3	0.17	0.4	11.22	7.84	0.7	9.67	0.128
Razlovci	7	1988	6.3	9.3	3.7	11.1	0.34	0.4	6.84	6.11	0.9	6.38	0.089
Jagmular	8	1991	14.2	34.5	14.2	26.1	0.21	0.4	17.77	14.25	0.8	16.38	0.120
Strezevo	10	1982	2.5	5.5	2.5	5.3	0.24	0.0	1.40	2.91	2.1	1.78	0.033
Total			62.5	156.1	49.3	144.5		7.4	72.78	80.91	1.1	65.62	0.083 (average)
Major Hydroelectric Projects—1985													
Kozjak	1	1982	75	255	37.5	142.8	0.44	31.0	57.64	117.78	2.0	52.22	0.068
Gradec	4	1984–1985	54	301	54	240.1	0.51	19.0	106.72	153.05	1.4	99.65	0.078

[a] Present-worth basis. Costs include reservoir allocations.
[b] 1973 values from computer runs converted to 1977 values by factor of 1.863.
[c] Includes allocated cost of Vardar/Treska diversion.
Source: TAMS (1978).

pipelines and sewer outlets. Federal government participation in general navigation facilities serving *recreational* traffic is limited to about 50%.

In federal projects, interest has been waived on costs allocated to the *irrigation* water supply purpose. This amounts to a subsidy of over 50% of the long-term cost of a project. Costs allocated to irrigation are further limited to an amount determined to be within the user's "ability to pay," with the remaining costs paid for out of power or other revenues.

Projects under the jurisdiction of the Soil Conservation Service of the Department of Agriculture may include a variety of multipurpose benefits (flood control, water supply, recreation, land treatment). Reservoir installations under their PL 566 program are limited to 25,000 acre-feet, of which no more than 5000 acre-feet can be devoted to flood protection.

Other subsidy programs are for *beach and shore protection* works (Corps of Engineers), *water pollution control* works (Environmental Protection Agency), *and water distribution and sewerage systems* (Department of Housing and Urban Development).

It is clear from the above that the charges to beneficiaries for project costs may differ substantially from the allocations of costs for the purposes of economic analysis. Beneficiaries of water resources projects pay for project services only as provided for by law. The length of payout period, interest rate, relationships of value or costs of services, and so on, may be quite different for economic and financial analysis.

9.7.3 Recent Federal and Nonfederal Cost Shares

Federal cost sharing policy has resulted from approximately 185 separate rules that have been developed over the years by congressional acts and amendments and administrative decisions. Factors influencing cost sharing policies in the United States have included the federal interest in encouraging regional development, federal efforts to achieve changing national goals, and results of political bargaining. Once procedures are enacted, the beneficiaries have a vested interest in resisting change. A number of study commissions have recommended reform in this area.

Cost-sharing arrangements by the federal government in the United States were analyzed by the U.S. Water Resources Council (1975) for fiscal year 1974. According to Wheeler et al. (1980), the results of that study were generally applicable to the situation in 1980. The Water Resources Council utilized the concept of "effective composite" to estimate actual cost shares, which could be different from cost shares stated in the legislation. This composite refers to the combined total of implementation costs plus capitalized value (present value) of operation and maintenance costs. It was found that large differences exist not only among the various water resource purposes, but also among agencies serving similar purposes. Detailed arrangements for repayment of the nonfederal share also differ for different programs and agencies. (North and Neely 1977). For the four principal federal planning and construction agencies—Soil Conservation Service, Corps of Engineers, Bureau of Reclamation, and the Tennessee Valley Authority—the average federal subsidies ranged from 26 to 80%.

9.7.4 Changes in Cost-Sharing Policies

Many articles and reports have commented on the deficiencies of cost-sharing policies, including their inefficiencies, inequities, nonuniformity of application, and inappropriateness when they no longer serve their original purpose. Sellers and North (1979) have discussed the issues that should be considered when analyzing proposals to make significant changes in cost-sharing arrangements. They recommend that such proposals be viewed in terms of their impacts in an assessment process comprised of four levels, beginning with the "most accessible and easily identifiable (program impact) and proceeding sequentially to more complex levels of impact analysis (comprehensive impact assessment)." Dobbs and Huff (1974) developed an impact matrix and a reimbursement matrix for a proposed water transfer project and utilized efficiency, equity, revenue-raising ability, and administrative criteria in conjunction with these matrices to assess the reimbursement mechanisms. Marshall (1970, 1973) considered the problems that arise when cost-sharing rules induce local interests to select projects and scales of development that are not socially efficient (not optimal from a national standpoint) and suggested an approach to such problems using local cost shares involving project cost percentages with ceiling (100%) and floor (20%) percentages for traditional purposes and constant percentages for costs allocated to environmental quality (50%) and regional development (100%). Loughlin (1970) analyzed this issue in case studies pertaining to flood control and proposed a cost-sharing policy under which existing occupants in the floodplain would be assessed a smaller percentage of allocated costs than future occupants. In any reimbursement scheme, the nonapplication or application of interest charges and, in the case of the latter, the rates charged are of particular significance in the financial feasibility of projects; the different treatment of interest rates in agency regulations were discussed by Hoggan (1970), who urged a more consistent policy.

Mathematical models to determine project impacts and provide guidance for cost-sharing policies for both economic and financial analyses are described in later chapters. Particular attention is paid to water quality management projects. Such projects in the United States, except when involved with federal multipurpose reservoirs, need not generally follow planning guidelines such as those of the U.S. Water Resources Council.

9.8 OTHER FINANCIAL STATEMENTS

When a financial institution reviews an application for a loan for a water resources project, it often requires financial statements that are in the forms commonly prepared by public accountants. These statements are often for the consolidated operations of the enterprise, in which the proposed project represents an increment to the already existing operations. For example, the World Bank requires the following (Krombach 1970):

● Financing plan during construction period
● Balance sheet

Financial Analyses Chap. 9

- Income statement
- Cash flow

These exhibits are prepared to show historical performance and projected for a number of years to include the effects of the proposed project.

9.9 EFFECTS OF INFLATION

Koenig (1975) considered the deficiencies of present-worth analyses that fail to take inflation effects into account. Since the present value of a future expense stated in present dollars is less than the present value of the same expense in escalated dollars, analyses that do not consider inflation (other things being equal) will incorrectly favor projects with high operating costs (relative to initial capital investment) over those with low operating costs. Furthermore, they will incorrectly favor projects with components subject to high escalation rates over those with components having low escalation rates. He showed that for the period 1948–1968, when the escalation rate for labor was higher than the escalation rate for energy, an analysis that did not account for inflation would incorrectly favor a labor-intensive alternative over an energy-intensive alternative. In 1980, when recent experience indicated a high energy inflation rate, this interpretation might be revised.

Financial analyses use the interest rates that are arranged by the sponsor of a project. These interest rates may be higher or lower than the prevailing market rates. Miller and Erickson (1975) have shown the effect of high interest rates in modifying the least-cost system design for urban drainage systems when water quality is a critical parameter.

REFERENCES

DOBBS, THOMAS L., and CHARLES E. HUFF, "Analyzing Reimbursement Mechanisms for Resource Development Projects," *Water Resources Res.*, vol. 10, no. 6, December 1974.

HOGGAN, DANIEL H., "Repayment Interest Rates for Water Projects," *Water Resources Res.*, vol. 6, no. 3, June 1970.

KOENIG, LOUIS, "Modeling of Future Expenditures for Planning and Economic Evaluation of Alternatives," *Water Resources Bull.*, vol. 11, no. 5, October 1975.

KROMBACH, JURGEN, "Financing of Water Supply and Sewerage Projects in Developing Countries," *Proc. Columbia Univ. Semin. Pollut. Water Resources*, September 1970.

LOUGHLIN, JAMES C., "Cost-Sharing for Federal Water Resource Programs with Emphasis on Flood Protection," *Water Resources Res.*, vol. 6, no. 2, April 1970.

MARSHALL, HAROLD EMORY, "Economic Efficiency Implications of Federal–Local Cost Sharing in Water Resource Development," *Water Resources Res.*, vol. 6, no. 3, June 1970.

MARSHALL, HAROLD EMORY, "Cost Sharing and Multi-objectives in Water Resource Development," *Water Resources Res.*, vol. 9, no. 1, February 1973.

MILLER, W. L., and S. P. ERICKSON, "The Impact of High Interest Rates on Optimum Multiple Objective Design of Surface Runoff Drainage Systems," *Water Resources Bull.*, vol. 11, no. 1, February 1975.

NORTH, RONALD M., and WALTER P. NEELY, "A Model for Achieving Consistency for Cost Sharing, in Water Resource Programs," *Water Resources Bull.*, vol. 13, no. 5, October 1977.

SELLERS, JACKIE, and R. M. NORTH, "A Descriptive Model for Analyzing Proposed Cost Sharing Rate Changes," *Water Resources Bull.*, vol. 15, no. 6, December 1979.

TAMS (Tippetts-Abbett-McCarthy-Stratton, New York, and Torán y Cía, Madrid), "Lower Ebro Right Bank Irrigation Project," 1963.

TAMS (Tippetts-Abbett-McCarthy-Stratton, New York, and Mattis Demain Beckford & Associates Ltd., Kingston), "Comparative Study of Water Supply Projects for Kingston and Surrounding Area," July 1977.

TAMS (Tippetts-Abbett-McCarthy-Stratton, New York, and Massachusetts Institute of Technology, Cambridge), "Integrated Development of the Vardar/Axios River Basin—Yugoslavia–Greece," December 1978.

U.S. DEPARTMENT OF THE ARMY, Corps of Engineers, Office of Appalachian Studies, "Development of Water Resources in Appalachia," Main Report, Part IV, Planning Concepts and Methods, September 1969.

U.S. DEPARTMENT OF THE ARMY, Corps of Engineers, Institute for Water Resources, "Feasibility Studies for Small Scale Hydropower Additions—A Guide Manual," July 1979.

U.S. FEDERAL ENERGY REGULATORY COMMISSION, "Hydroelectric Power Evaluation," August 1979.

U.S. WATER RESOURCES COUNCIL, "Section 80(C) Study, Planning and Cost Sharing Policy Options for Water and Related Land Programs," 1975.

U.S. WATER RESOURCES COUNCIL, "Economic and Environmental Principles and Guidelines for Water and Related Land Resources Implementation Studies," March 10, 1983.

WHEELER, RICHARD, M., JR., LEO M. EISEL, and GERALD D. SEINWILL, "Financing Federal Water Development Projects and Sharing the Costs," *Water Resources Bull.*, vol. 16, no. 2, April 1980.

TEN

Prices for Financial and Economic Analysis

10.1 SCOPE

This chapter contains additional information on the techniques for estimating the components of financial and economic analyses, to supplement the presentations in Chapters 2, 8, and 9. Sections 10.2 to 10.4 deal with the problems of estimating costs for financial analyses; these sections also include comments concerning economic analyses. Sections 10.5 to 10.9 treat the costs and benefits for economic analyses. Sections 10.10 to 10.12 contain a discussion of shadow pricing techniques for economic analysis. The final section discusses costs for infrastructure needs (social overhead costs).

10.2 BASIS OF COSTS FOR FINANCIAL ANALYSES

Financial analyses determine how a project would fare as a private venture, or its equivalent as a public enterprise. Thus, they provide measures of the capability of a sponsor to construct and operate a project, while repaying loans and/or providing returns on the capital invested in the project. Financial entities participating in the project may be one or more of the following: public agencies, investor-owned utilities, private firms, individual entrepreneurs, and users of project outputs of goods and services.

Financial analyses account for all cash flow outputs (costs) and inputs (principally sales revenues and subsidies but also including other income of the enterprise). Costs should be based on prevailing market prices for labor, materials, and equipment unless the project is large or specialized enough to exert an appreciable effect on market prices. The project may cause an increase in prices if the resources it demands for implementation are in short supply, or it may lower costs if it results in more efficient production and/or distribution of goods and services.

The following sections deal with techniques for pricing various components of investment costs and annual costs, for purposes of financial analyses. Adjustments to these components for economic analyses are also described.

10.3 COMPONENTS OF PROJECT CONSTRUCTION AND INVESTMENT COSTS

10.3.1 Direct Construction Costs

This and the next three subsections discuss the components of a project investment cost estimate such as that for the Bridge Canyon Project in Table 2.1. Table 10.1 shows a portion of the details of the estimate of direct construction cost. The quantities of construction and installed equipment are estimated from formal and sketch-type arrangement and design drawings and from experience with similar projects. Both unit cost and lump sum items are based on estimates of amounts of work. Preliminary estimates may be based on experience with overall costs of finished work (e.g., $80 per square foot of finished office space or $950 per kilowatt of installed power generating machinery).

The best construction and installation cost estimates are based on "contractor-type" estimates of:

- Cost of purchased materials
- Equipment rental or ownership costs
- Wages or salaries paid to construction and/or installation personnel
- Cost of management and supervision
- Other overhead costs and profit

When the cost estimates are prepared primarily for the budgeting process, or to provide guidance to those who examine bids made by contractors and equipment suppliers, the large effort and cost to prepare contractor-type estimates may not be warranted for all project components. Estimates may then be based on unit prices experienced on other jobs, adjusted for actual job conditions and inflation. Cost indexes such as those shown in Figure 10.1 may be useful for such adjustments. In the United States, such indexes are published for different locations and for different types of projects; these include the *Engineering News-Record* building cost and construction cost indexes, the Environmental Protection Agency wastewater treat-

TABLE 10.1 BRIDGE CANYON PROJECT: DETAILS OF PORTION OF ESTIMATE OF DIRECT CONSTRUCTION COST (Dollars)

Description Production Plant	Unit	Quantity	Unit Cost	Amount
Land and Land Rights	Job	L.S.	—	200,000
Power Plant Structures and Improvements				
Powerhouse				
Foundation exploration	Job	L.S.	—	50,000
Excavation, common	Cu. Yd.	54,000	1.50	81,000
Excavation, rock	Cu. Yd.	160,000	4.00	640,000
Foundation treatment	Job	L.S.	—	100,000
Substructure				
Concrete	Cu. Yd.	88,300	35.00	3,091,000
Reinforcing steel	Lb	3,500,000	0.18	630,000
Superstructure				
Structural steel	Ton	1,070	500.00	535,000
Concrete	Cu. Yd.	10,300	75.00	772,000
Reinforcing steel	Lb	1,460,000	0.18	263,000
Architectural treatment	Job	L.S.	—	450,000
Plumbing	Job	L.S.	—	30,000
Lighting	Job	L.S.	—	86,000
Miscellaneous metal	Job	L.S.	—	48,000
Permanent townsite				
Permanent residences	Job	L.S.	—	525,000
Streets and utilities	Job	L.S.	—	175,000
Community building	Job	L.S.	—	50,000
Water supply, water and sewage treatment facilities	Job	L.S.	—	200,000
Electrical service and distribution	Job	L.S.	—	75,000
Subtotal Power Plant Structures and Improvements				7,801,000
Reservoirs, Dams, and Waterways				
Dams, concrete				
Diversion and care of water				
Cofferdams	Cu. Yd.	260,000	1.80	468,000
Cutoff wall	Job	L.S.	—	140,000
Excavation, diversion tunnel				
Common	Cu. Yd.	6,000	1.50	9,000
Rock, dry	Cu. Yd.	30,000	3.25	98,000

Source: TAMS (1960).

ment facility and sewer system cost indexes, and the Bureau of Reclamation water and power construction cost indexes. Such indexes should be applied only to the construction and equipment supply portions (the "field costs") of the investment cost estimate. The costs of lands and relocations as well as interest during construction and the other additions made to field costs to reach the "bottom line" of the investment cost estimate in Table 2.1 may be subject to market effects other than inflation of construction and equipment costs.

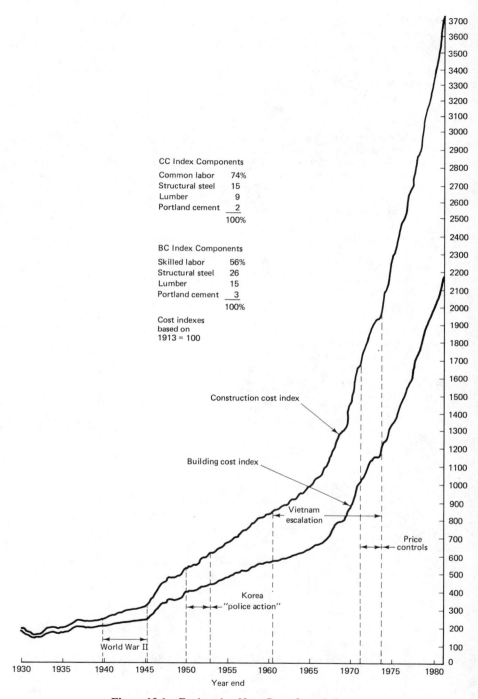

CC Index Components

Common labor   74%
Structural steel 15
Lumber   9
Portland cement   2
                 100%

BC Index Components

Skilled labor   56%
Structural steel 26
Lumber   15
Portland cement   3
                 100%

Cost indexes
based on
1913 = 100

Construction cost index

Building cost index

Vietnam
escalation

Price
controls

Korea
"police action"

World War II

Year end

Figure 10.1 *Engineering News-Record* cost indexes.

For either contractor-type or budget-type estimates, the field costs should be recognized as being dependent on such variables as the geographical location of the work; seasonal weather conditions; problems of care of water during construction; unusual or special geotechnical conditions (foundations, construction materials); accessibility of the work; accomodations for housing and transportation; materials handling and storage facilities; sources of construction power; availability of labor and material required; wage rates; construction plant and equipment; terms of financing available; taxes, insurance, and risks.

The bid items for which contractors offer prices, as they appear in the contract documents, are selected to distribute the construction work among various types of contractors and to facilitate the measurement and payment for work during construction; they may, therefore, be arranged differently and with greater detail than those used for an investment cost estimate. The prices bid by various contractors for individual items may be quite different due to their: (1) construction methods; (2) ways of spreading overhead; (3) interpretations of the drawings and specifications; and (4) mistakes. They may also be due to "unbalancing," by which the contractor leaves his total price bid unchanged while modifying component prices to: (1) obtain payments early in the job to assist in financing; and (2) attempt to make extra profits if the contractor suspects that actual field quantities for certain items of work (e.g., rock and earth excavation) will be substantially different from those listed in the bid documents as the basis for bids. The planner must use caution in using published bid prices because of the reasons given above and the specific field conditions that may exist for the project being studied.

10.3.2 Contingencies

Contingencies cover differences between estimated and actual quantities, omissions of work incidental to items included in the estimate, difficulties unforeseen at the site, changes in plans, and other uncertainties. Some guidance as to appropriate contingency percentages to apply to direct construction cost estimates may be drawn from Table 10.2. It is clear that the appropriate contingency percentage depends on the type of project or component and the quality of data available.

Some planners increase the quantities of construction or the unit prices to allow for all or a portion of the contingencies. This is not, however, considered a candid professional practice. The allowance for contingencies is not a cover-up for errors or inadequate engineering and is actually expected to be spent for the project.

10.3.3 Land and Land Rights

These should include all costs for land, water, and mineral rights connected with project features. Among these costs are the purchase price or easement costs minus salvage value of improvements, the cost of surveys incident to a sale, legal fees and transfer costs, and severance payments. Allowances should also be included for buffer areas, relocation, access, and other needs. Special estimates may be required for agricultural land and other land whose producing capability may be lost or modified by the project.

TABLE 10.2 TYPICAL CONTINGENCY FACTORS (Percent to be Applied to Field Cost to Cover Contingencies)

Class		Better-than-Average Data[a]	Average Data[b]	Meager Data[c]
01	Reservoir and dams (concrete)	10	15	25
01	Reservoir and dams (earth)	15	20	25
02	Diversion works	10	15	25
03	Pumping plants	10	15	25
04	Deep wells	10	15	25
05	Canals and conduits	10	15	25
06	Laterals	10	15	25
07	Drains	10	15	25
08	Farm unit development	15	25	40
09	Channels, levees, and floodworks	15	20	25
10, 11, 12	Power plants	10	15	25
13	Switchyards and substations	10	15	25
13	Transmission lines	10	15	15
14	Distribution lines and substations	10	15	25
15	General property	10	15	25
20	Construction facilities	15	25	40

[a]Better-than-average data: Final investigations and surveys complete and sufficient for preparation of final designs and specifications; types and locations of all structures definitely established; tentative designs prepared and approved; design requirements definitely established; land classification complete; foundation exploration for all structures complete; and materials investigations complete.

[b]Average data: Preliminary investigations and surveys sufficient for preparation of preliminary designs; types and locations of structures tentatively established; tentative designs prepared; design requirements tentatively established; land classification partially complete; foundation exploration for major structures complete; suitable construction materials located and tested; etc.

[c]Meager data: Reconnaissance investigations and surveys sufficient for preparation of rough preliminary designs; types and locations of major structures roughly determined by use of USGS maps or other means; design requirements roughly determined; reconnaissance land classification; materials deposits not explored and tested; and superficial structure foundation exploration.

Source: U.S. Department of the Interior, Bureau of Reclamation (1950).

10.3.4 Engineering, Supervision of Construction, and Sponsor Overhead

Among the costs to be included for a financial analysis are the costs incurred in the development of final design, specifications, and construction drawings; the cost of inspection for construction, installation, and/or maintenance activities; the cost of administering contracts; and other sponsor overhead costs.

For an economic analysis, this cost item should include the additional costs attributable to the project but not a financial responsibility of the project sponsor, such as: cost of relocation assistance advisory services, educational costs, and other costs of governmental entities.

10.3.5 Timing of Project Construction and Investment Costs

The project investment cost includes interest during construction. This may be based on a detailed breakdown of the various items of construction and installed equipment in a construction schedule and the application of interest charges for each item for a period reckoned to the end of construction, or on a simplified method. An example of the latter approach is to apply the full interest rate to all the construction cost, including contingencies, for one-half of the total construction period.

10.4 ANNUAL COSTS

In the analyses presented in earlier chapters, two methods were used to estimate annual costs. One approach was to estimate the costs for each separate year of construction and then for each year of operation after the completion of construction. Another approach was to estimate all costs as annual costs extending from the date when construction is completed; this requires spreading of all costs, including construction costs, during the period of operation. Table 2.2 showed the annual Bridge Canyon costs on the latter basis. Table 10.3 shows the details of these costs.

Like the contractor-type estimates for construction, the operation and maintenance cost estimates may be based on detailed estimates of personnel costs, office supplies, gasoline, oil, depreciation and repair of automobiles and short-lived replacement parts, and other expendables. Alternatively, the estimates may be based on experience on other projects adjusted for inflation and different project conditions. Additional allowances are included for general administrative expenses, to spread sponsor costs that are not identified with specific projects. Estimates for operation and maintenance do not generally include costs for replacement of major structural or machine elements, which are more properly included in the renewals and replacements (or interim replacements). Such costs may be estimated by developing a schedule for major replacements, estimating their costs, and then averaging such costs over the period of analysis of the project, using appropriate discounting or depreciation techniques. A procedure often used is to depreciate each major item to be replaced by means of a sinking fund; this is equivalent to placing an equal annual amount at compound interest in order to accumulate the required replacement amount at the end of the item's useful life.

If all the money to build the project is borrowed, the annual debt service depends on the terms of the loans applying to the investment cost of each project component. For Table 10.3, it is assumed that equal annual amounts over a 45-year period will be used to pay off the loans. This is equivalent to paying only interest each year and making a single payment to cover the entire principal at the end. Other schedules could have been developed to provide for an increasing payment each year to reflect the growth of demand for project services. This is not appropriate in this case because all power produced would find a ready market at the beginning of operation.

TABLE 10.3 BRIDGE CANYON PROJECT: DETAILS OF ESTIMATE OF ANNUAL CHARGES

Description	Amount
Operation and Maintenance	
A. Generation	
Operation	
Supervision and engineering	$22,300
Station labor	85,200
Supplies and expense	25,800
Maintenance	
Supervision and engineering	27,100
Structures and improvements	36,000
Generating and electric equipment	76,900
Reservoirs, dams, and waterways	75,000
Subtotal	348,300
B. Transformation and switching	
Operation	57,000
Maintenance	67,300
Subtotal	124,300
Subtotal Acct. A & B	472,600
C. Transmission line	
Operation and maintenance	212,700
Subtotal acct. A, B, C—operation and maintenance	685,300
General Administrative Expenses	
27% of total operation and maintenance	185,000
Renewals and Replacements	
Structures and improvements	9,700
Reservoirs, dams, waterways	59,800
Turbines and generators	245,500
Accessory electrical equipment	21,500
Miscellaneous power plant equipment	100,400
Switching station equipment Bridge Canyon	131,000
Switching station equipment beyond Bridge Canyon	349,200
Transmission line, towers and footings	32,600
Transmission overhead conductors and devices	54,200
General Plant	3,400
Subtotal acct.—renewals and replacements	1,007,300
Debt Service on Investment	
(3½% bonds for a period of 45 years, 4.44534% of 193,515,000)	8,602,400
F.P.C. License Fees	
1,680,000 hp at $0.01 per hp	16,800
3.39 billion kWh at 0.025 mill/kWh	84,800
Subtotal acct.—F.P.C. license fees	101,600

Source: TAMS (1960).

Prices for Financial and Economic Analysis   Chap. 10

In updating annual costs, inflation should be taken into account. For this purpose, the construction cost indexes are not directly applicable, but may be used for guidance together with consumer and other more general indexes.

10.5 BASIS OF COSTS AND BENEFITS FOR ECONOMIC ANALYSES

Economic analyses take a broader social viewpoint than do financial analyses. As stated by Gittinger (1972, p. 5), economic analyses determine "the total return or productivity or profitability to the whole society or economy of all the resources committed to the project regardless of who in the society contributes them and regardless of who in the society receives the benefits." There are three important distinctions between economic and financial analysis:

1. In economic analysis, certain prices may be changed to reflect true social or economic values. In financial analysis, market prices including taxes and subsidies are *always* used.
2. In economic analysis, taxes and subsidies are not included since they are treated as transfer payments of society as a whole. In financial analysis such adjustments are unnecessary; taxes are treated quite simply as a cost and subsidies as a return.
3. In economic analysis, interest on capital is not separated out and deducted from gross returns since it is a part of the total return to capital available to the society as a whole and it is that total return, including interest, which our economic analysis is designed to estimate for us. In financial analysis, interest paid to *outside* suppliers of money is treated as a cost, and repayment of money borrowed from *outside* suppliers is deducted before arriving at the net revenue (benefit) stream.

In the examples of economic analyses presented in Chapter 8, results were expressed in terms of benefit-cost ratio, internal rate of return, and other measures of economy. Both market value and shadow price-based benefits and costs were used in these examples. Sections 10.6 to 10.9 deal with the estimates of benefits based on prices that are not adjusted by "shadow" or "accounting" pricing techniques. Shadow pricing is then discussed in Sections 10.10 to 10.12 for both costs and benefits.

The cost procedures for financial analyses presented in earlier sections apply generally for economic analyses. The principal differences are the inclusion in economic costs of associated costs (measures needed over and above project measures to achieve the benefits claimed), external diseconomies, other direct costs other than associated costs required for a project or plan but not included in financial costs, and shadow pricing adjustments if appropriate. Also economic analyses do not include the effects of taxes and subsidies.

10.6 GENERAL MEASUREMENT CONCEPTS FOR BENEFITS

Tangible benefits in a national perspective may be measured by the value of contributions to the national economic development (NED) objective, which, as stated in the U.S. Water Resources Council "Principles and Guidelines" (1983, p. iv) are increases in the net value of the national output of goods and services. A water resources project accomplishes this by utilizing additional resources and/or by making more efficient use of existing resources.

The following sections provide summaries of procedures for evaluating benefits for various project purposes. These summaries are based largely on the Water Resources Council (WRC) "Principles and Guidelines" of 1983. Earlier WRC documents have also been considered, including especially the "Procedures" (1979, 1980). Although these summaries should provide guidance on the basic procedures and additional important elements, the latest full documents and publications of individual agencies should be consulted for some of the fine points of analyses.

In each case, benefits are evaluated on a year-by-year basis or at specific points in the period of analysis. Benefits are always evaluated on a with- minus without-project basis. The benefits are discounted to the beginning of the period of analysis using the applicable project interest rate. These benefits are compared to the costs estimated in the same manner. Benefits and costs may also be compared on an annual basis by appropriate conversions of the present-worth values.

The period of analysis begins at the start of expenditures or at the end of the installation period. The latter requires that the installation expenditures be brought forward to the end of construction by charging compound interest at the discount rate. This is consistent with the concepts of the investment and annual cost estimates presented in Tables 2.1 and 2.2 and further explained earlier in this chapter. For internal rate-of-return estimates, the period of analysis begins with the first year of expenditures, and compound interest is involved in the general discounting procedure of this method.

The benefits discussed in the next sections are determined starting with a conceptual preference of a measure of "willingness to pay" by the users of a project's output of goods and services. Such benefits are "direct" benefits in older terminology, although not so characterized in the WRC guidelines. The guidelines allow additional credits for the use of unemployed and underemployed labor resources and for "other direct benefits" (external economies).

The NED approach of the WRC restricts the evaluation of benefits to those that are significant at a national level and, therefore, as is proper, do not specifically recognize in the NED account a project's potential value as an instrument for regional economic development or its contribution to other national and regional goals and objectives. These effects may be considered in other accounts. For example, when using water in an irrigation project to produce more crops, a farmer may purchase more goods and services to produce and market these crops. Also, the farmer's improved economic condition as a result of the project enables the purchase of more goods and services from others in pursuance of an increased standard of living. These indirect effects of the irrigation project are not accounted for in the guidelines for evaluation of NED benefits for agricultural water supply. Under superseded

Prices for Financial and Economic Analysis   Chap. 10

categorizations, such benefits could be labeled as "indirect" benefits and added to the "direct" (user) benefits in a regional analysis. In this book, such benefits are considered (sometimes implicitly) under the concepts of multiobjective planning (in Chapters 2 and 6 as well as mentioned briefly in other contexts in other chapters), in the example of an irrigation project in Chapter 8, in economic growth studies (Chapter 14), and in social impact assessments (Chapter 16).

10.7 BENEFITS FOR PROJECT PURPOSES

10.7.1 Benefits for Municipal and Industrial Water Supply

In this discussion of a water supply plan, it is assumed that costs and benefits are analyzed for water provided at the raw water or wholesale level. Future uses should be projected separately by sector (residential, commercial, industrial, and public, including unaccounted-for losses) and aggregated. Costs and benefits are evaluated for each alternative that closes the gap between projected future demands and available supplies. Such evaluations consider seasonal and daily variations. Each alternative should consider the management of deficits, if any. Available supplies include existing supplies and all new supplies under construction or already authorized. The impact of nonstructural measures should be considered in the projections of future uses. The evaluation of available supplies should include all nonstructural and conservation measures that are reasonably expected in the absence of the alternative (WRC, 1983, pp. 20–25).

Direct measures of benefits would require demand curves for the various classes of users throughout their expected ranges of supply, and that show true willingness to pay for water used. Historical data are inadequate to identify demand curves as historical price/quantity points do not necessarily or probably lie on a single demand curve. Careful data gathering would be required to estimate demand curves either for producer's or consumer's demands for water system outputs.

In the absence of direct measures of willingness to pay, indirect measures must be used. The alternative cost approach assumes the community's willingness to pay for alternative levels of supply or reductions of demand as the basis for benefits. The alternative selected for the estimate of benefits must be a realistic alternative that could and likely would be undertaken in the absence of the considered project. The selection should be based on cost but should also consider reliability, water quality, environmental quality, and other policy factors, and should consider not only those integrated plans that close the entire gap between supply and demand but also plans that would reasonably be attempted by the various water users in the absence of any other alternative (WRC, 1983, pp. 20–25).

10.7.2 Benefits for Agricultural Projects

Agricultural projects include: (1) irrigation; (2) drainage; and (3) flood protection and erosion and sediment control features. Plans consider the benefits of solving three types of economic problems associated with water and the use of land and water resources in agricultural production (WRC Procedures, 1979, pp. 72921-30):

- The cost of damage to crops, pasture, and range by water inundation, drought, sedimentation, and erosion
- Costs associated with using water and land resources that are subject to variation with the application of various water management practices or the installation of water control measures
- Impaired productivity or use of the land resource

Benefits for a plan are the increased value of agricultural output from a national standpoint, or the reduced cost of maintaining a given level of output. Benefits include reductions in production costs and in associated costs; reduction in damage costs from floods, erosion, sedimentation, inadequate drainage, or inadequate water supply; the value of increased production of crops; and the economic efficiency of increasing the production of crops in the project area (WRC Principles and Guidelines, 1983, p. 25).

Cropping patterns, prices, production costs, crop yields, and livestock production, and land values are key evaluation components in crop budget procedures and in other aspects of evaluating the three economic problem categories and the impact of water management practices or control measures. The most probable cropping patterns, crop yields, and production costs expected to exist with and without the project are the projected with- and without-project conditions. The difference in net agricultural income between each alternative project and the without-project condition, estimated by means of farm budget analysis, is the benefit.

If project measures are designed to reduce damage or associated cost problems without changing crop patterns, the current crop pattern is determined and projected in the future for both with- and without-project conditions. If project measures are designed to change the cropping pattern in a project area by alleviating impaired productivity, the current cropping pattern is determined and projected as a constant for the without-project condition; for the with-project condition, the expected cropping pattern is projected.

For changed cropping patterns, two types of crops are considered in the United States depending on their presumed benefits with respect to national economic development. For "basic" crops (in the WRC guidelines of 1983, these would usually be limited to rice, cotton, pasture, corn, oats, soybeans, wheat, milo, barley, and hay), benefits from reduced production cost or intensification of production attributable to a project are fully credited to the project. For other crops (neither existing nor "basic" crops), benefits are limited to these from the increased production efficiency in the project area over that which could be carried on in another comparable area.

In connection with the 10 crops in the list above, a version of the procedures prior to 1979 included only the low-net-income crops and specifically excluded rice and cotton. The justification of different evaluation procedures for the "basic" and "other" crop categories is based on the rationale that the output of basic crops is seldom restricted by factors other than the availability of suitable land, whereas the variability of output of other crops is limited primarily by other factors, such as market demand, availability and cost of risk capital, specialized labor or management, and government programs or other institutional restraints. It is claimed, therefore, that since the returns from such generally higher-value crops would primarily reflect factors other than land and water, they could be realized in the future (on a national basis) without the project. For the calculations of improved efficiency of such crops, information is needed on areas that can be used for comparison.

Estimates of market prices are needed for determinations of value for crops. Such estimates are probably the most difficult and uncertain aspect of agricultural economics. Agricultural prices at the time of plan formulation may diverge from long-term normal prices. A review of this subject has been made by Miller (1980).

The approach by the Water Resources Council (WRC) deemphasizing the benefits attributable to crops that are not land-constrained has not been generally applied to projects in developing countries. For these countries the without-project condition is usually taken as the returns of existing agriculture on project lands as they may be modified and improved by changes in farming practices that could reasonably be instituted without the project. The with-project condition is taken to be the returns from project lands based on a future cropping pattern judged to be reasonable and made practical by the availability of water supply, project facilities, and supporting infrastructure. Cropping patterns and yields for the with- and without-project conditions are based on a consideration of factors such as soils, water, climate, labor, equipment, and markets. Market studies, taking account of present and future demands and prices as they may be modified by the project, are carried out to determine appropriate prices to use for the with- and without-project conditions.

For developing countries, matters of increasing importance are the determination of who pays and who benefits from a project, and the income redistribution effects of a project. The World Bank and other international financing agencies focus on these matters in their individual project studies and have made a number of exploratory research studies.

The WRC Principles and Guidelines of 1983 encourage separate evaluation of the effects of flood damage reduction, drainage, irrigation, erosion control, and sediment reduction but provide much less detailed information focused on these physical components than the Procedures of 1979. The following discussion is, therefore, based on the Procedures (1979, pp. 72921-9) with some adjustments for the Principles and Guidelines (1983, pp. 25–32).

Irrigation. The chart in Figure 10.2 shows an approach for calculating reduced production cost benefits and intensification benefits in a project area. As discussed above, the procedures treat the three types of crops: existing (current) crops, additional generally low-value "basic" crops, and other generally high-value crops. Net income is evaluated for conditions with and without the project for acreages of these crops, with the limitations on credits to the NED account for the third class of crops. For the second and third types of crops, the WRC Principles and Guidelines (1983, pp. 26–28) allow the use of increased market values of land, as an alternative to farm budget analysis. Benefits on a per crop and per acre basis should be adjusted for the effect of short supply years and the value of excess project water in wet years. The calculations should also take account of projected maintenance of existing on-farm drainage and irrigation systems and installation of new systems

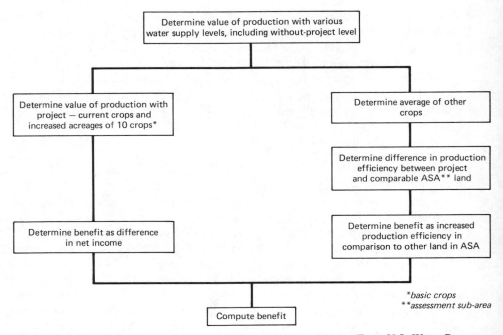

```
┌─────────────────────────────────────────────┐
│ Determine value of production with various   │
│ water supply levels, including without-project level │
└─────────────────────────────────────────────┘
```

Determine value of production with project — current crops and increased acreages of 10 crops*

Determine average of other crops

Determine difference in production efficiency between project and comparable ASA** land

Determine benefit as difference in net income

Determine benefit as increased production efficiency in comparison to other land in ASA

*basic crops
**assessment sub-area

Compute benefit

Figure 10.2 Flowchart of agricultural irrigation evaluation procedures. (From U.S. Water Resources Council, 1979.)

without and with the project, unless the benefits for drainage are evaluated as a separate project purpose. Physical constraints to yields other than the lack of irrigation water should also be taken into account. If the irrigated area develops over a long period of time (e.g., 15 years) it is necessary to adjust for this growth pattern in the discounting process.

Flood Prevention and Control. Benefits can be considered for structural measures that reduce inundation damages to crops that would be grown without the project and for nonstructural measures that remove a given land use from the floodplain. The following procedures apply largely to these benefits. In addition, intensification benefits are also evaluated where they are made possible by a floodplain hazard reduction plan.

Current and projected land use and cropping patterns are identified for various floodplain reaches. Based on interviews with floodplain farmers and other experts, estimates are prepared of the current and projected yields in the floodplain in years in in which no flood occurs; such yields should reflect other factors that may affect production including the *threat* of floods. Gross values corresponding to these yields represent the *damageable* values. Crop damage estimates are prepared for each crop for various flood depths and/or durations, as follows: value of yield reduction and quality reduction of flooded crop plus added expenses of flooded crop, minus production costs saved on flood crop and minus net returns from substitute crop. Dividing a crop damage estimate by the corresponding flood-free (damageable) value provides a *flood damage factor* for that crop subjected to inundation of given depth and/or duration. The flood damage factor multiplied by the product of yield and price gives the flood damages for a given flood depth or duration for that crop. Weighted flood damages can be determined for an area containing several crops.

The procedure described above should preferably be carried out for historical floods whose frequencies have been estimated and floods of other magnitudes needed to define the damage-frequency relationship. These damage estimates are now integrated with data on flood frequency, acres flooded, and flood depth or duration, to determine average annual damages. The damages for a probable flood event are determined and converted to the damages for an average year by considering the frequency (return period) of the flood. This procedure is repeated for all probable flood events, the values are aggregated, and adjustments are made to avoid double counting for recurrent flooding in a given year. This process is equivalent to developing a curve of damage (ordinate) versus frequency (abscissa as probability of occurence, the inverse of return interval) for all possible floods, and integrating the area under the curve (see Figure 8.1). The overall estimates may have to be carried out for the with- and without-project conditions for several points in time over the period of analysis, and weighted by a discounting procedure to allow for the progressive economic growth of the area.

For a structural measure, the benefit is the reduction of damage as described above. For a nonstructural measure that removes a given land use from the floodplain, the benefit is the cost savings to other economic sectors (e.g., local services) plus the net returns to the new use of the land.

For existing crops or increased acreages of the "basic" crops, intensification benefits are computed as the difference in net income with the project and net income from flood-free yields without the project. For other crops, the limitations for credits to the NED account apply as for irrigation.

Additional benefits may be considered for flood prevention and control to other agricultural properties, including the physical floodplain improvements associated with various farm enterprises and the agricultural community. Benefits are measured for the reductions in inundation damages attributable to the project.

Erosion Reduction Benefits. These may result from projects to reduce gully, stream bank, floodplain scour, and sheet erosion and are measured as net income maintenance or recovery on agricultural lands and damage reduction to other agricultural properties.

Reductions in gully and stream bank erosion may be realized through reduced land voiding, reduced production losses on adjacent areas, and efficiency gains on interdependent areas. Voiding refers to the destruction of the productivity of the land for agricultural use. Production losses on adjacent areas may be caused by a lowering of water tables, increased cost of production due to irregular field patterns, and less intensive land use. Efficiency gains on interdependent areas occur when elimination of a gully erosion problem provides a stable outlet for land treatment measures upstream, thereby allowing for a more intensive farming operation. Benefits in each of these cases are determined by the difference in the annualized projected net income flows over the evaluation period without and with the project.

The potential for scour erosion is related to the depth and velocity of floodwater and the resistance of the soil material to erosion. Benefits are determined in the same manner as for gully and stream bank erosion except that an allowance is made in projecting the net income flow with project to account for recoverable productivity. Benefits are calculated for reduced sheet erosion in a similar fashion as for gully and stream bank erosion reduction benefits on an interdependent area. Erosion benefits may also be allowed for damages prevented to roads, bridges, fences, buildings, and so on.

Sediment Reduction Benefits. These result from reduced damages from overbank deposition of infertile soils, impairment of drainage systems resulting in raised water tables (swamping), channel filling, and increased maintenance costs of other properties (i.e., roads, bridges, reservoirs, buildings, etc.). Benefits are measured as increased net income for agricultural crops and reduced damage to other agricultural properties.

Agricultural Drainage. Benefits are computed as the increased net returns resulting from reduced production costs or intensification benefits of increased production. The evaluations (including limitations on benefits to non-basic crops) follow approaches that are similar to those described in the preceding subsections. Drainage problems on flatland areas are generally interrelated with inundation damages; for this case, benefits are evaluated jointly and then assigned to specific project purposes. If damages due to direct precipitation are reduced by drainage, drainage and flood prevention benefits are evaluated jointly and then allocated.

10.7.3 Benefits for Urban Flood Damage Reduction

The general categories are the same as for agricultural flood damages: inundation reduction benefits, intensification benefits, and location benefits. The first category assumes that floodplain use is the same with and without the plan; if an activity is removed from the floodplain, a benefit may be credited if this results in the reduction of emergency costs or subsidized reimbursement for flood damages. The second category assumes that a commercial or industrial activity in the floodplain modifies its operation because the reduction in the flood hazard makes it profitable to do so. The third category assumes that an activity will use the floodplain with the plan but not without the plan. For each category, the benefits are measured by the increase in net income with and without the plan.

Flood damages can be classified as physical damages or losses, income losses, and emergency costs. Physical damages include damages to or loss of buildings or parts thereof; loss of contents; cost of cleanup; and loss of roads, sewers, bridges, power lines, and so on. Income losses are in addition to physical damages and include losses of wages or of net profits to business; from a national standpoint, such losses occur only when activities cannot be postponed or transferred. Emergency costs are for evacuation and reoccupation, flood fighting, disaster relief, increased expense of normal operations during the flood; and increased costs of police, fire, or military patrol.

In the United States, federal flood control project evaluation must take account of the extensive floodplain management and flood insurance programs likely to occur under existing improvements, laws, and policies; these, in particular, affect assumptions for the without-project condition. Thus, existing and authorized flood hazard reduction plans normally will be considered in-place and careful consideration will be given to the actual remaining economic life of existing structures. Land use regulations pursuant to the Flood Disaster Protection Act of 1973 (PL 93-234) are assumed, which requires new activities locating in the floodplain to undergo flood proofing for protection against the 100-year flood level. The without-project condition also assumes the adoption and enforcement of federal floodplain management guidelines. In addition, the without-project condition should also assume that individuals will undertake certain additional flood hazard reduction measures such as flood proofing when it is rational to do so.

The evaluation procedures of the Water Resources Council (WRC, 1983, pp. 32–41) involve 10 key steps, as shown in Figure 10.3 and summarized as follows:

1. Delineate area affected by a proposed plan, including the floodplain and all other nearby areas likely to serve as alternative sites for any major activity type (e.g., commercial) that might use the floodplain if it were protected.

2. Inventory the floodplain characteristics that make it attractive or unattractive for various land uses. These characteristics include inherent characteristics such as flooding; floodway and natural storage; natural and beneficial values, including open space, recreation, wildlife, and wetlands; transportation; and other. They also include physical characteristics (slope, soil types, water table); available services (transportation, power, sewerage, water, labor, access to markets); and existing activities. The description of the flooding situation includes the characteristics of the flooding, such as depths, velocity, duration, debris content, area flooded by floods of selected frequencies (including 100-year frequency), historical floods, and where applicable Standard Project Flood; and designation of high-hazard areas. This step will estimate the available floodplain acres for use by the activities of step 3, including the characteristics thereof.

3. Forecast activities in the affected area. Economic and demographic projections should consider such factors as population, personal income, recreation demand, and manufacturing, employment, and output.

4. Estimate potential land use by converting the projections of step 3 into quantities of area.

5. Project land use, allocating land based on a comparison of floodplain characteristics, characteristics sought by potential occupants, and the availability of sought-after characteristics in the nonfloodplain portions of the affected area. Land use is allocated for the with- and without-project condition and to floodplain and nonfloodplain lands. This analysis should not allocate activities to the floodplain unless it is superior to other available sites within the

affected area, taking into account potential flood losses, flood-proofing costs, and the costs of related hazards.

6. Estimate existing flood damages, in terms of average annual damages. This is based on estimates of the losses actually sustained in historical floods, estimates of damages under existing conditions for floods of magnitude that have not historically occurred, and the use of standard damage-frequency integration techniques. The output will consist of unit and total flood damages for existing land uses for the various types of activity.

7. Estimate future flood damages to economic activities that might use the floodplain in the future in the *absence* of a plan and *with* a plan. This considers the activities from step 3 in the absence of a plan and projected land uses from step 5 with a plan. Future flood damages include losses borne by the floodplain occupant (internalized losses) and those borne by others, through insurance subsidies, tax deductions for casualty losses, disaster relief, and so on (externalized losses). In discounting such damages to the base year, account should be taken of hydrologic changes that result from changed basin land use and changed economic activities that would affect the level of flood losses.

8. Estimate other costs of using the floodplain. These include flood-proofing costs, national flood insurance costs, and costs when structures are used less efficiently with a project.

9. Collect land market value and related data, where land use is different with and without the project, in order to compute the difference in income. Significant externalities may be involved, when open space use of flood land renders adjacent lands more attractive and valuable.

10. Compute average annual benefits for inundation reduction, intensification, and location benefits. These will generally be obtained from the estimates of step 6, with adjustments for steps 7 and 9. Table 10.4 provides a guide to the types of benefits attributable to types of structural measures and nonstructural measures, principally flood-proofing and evacuation programs.

The WRC procedures include an extensive discussion of problems of analysis and of the format for display of results. Grigg and Helweg (1975) have reviewed the state of the art of estimating flood damages in urban areas.

10.7.4 Benefits for Hydropower

In the case of benefits of hydropower projects, alternative cost has generally been applied as the measure of willingness to pay. In the United States, federal hydropower projects have been evaluated on the assumption that the most likely alternative would be a thermal alternative constructed by the private sector. The following adjustments are made for the privately constructed alternative when evaluating federal projects according to the Water Resource Council guidelines (WRC, 1983, pp. 41–48): (1) all interest and amortization charges are based on the federal discount rate; (2) no costs for taxes of any kind or insurance are charged; (3) credit is given for use of unemployed labor as for a federal project; and (4) all other assumptions and

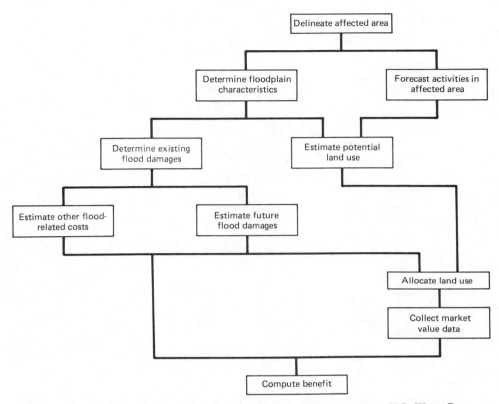

Figure 10.3 Flowchart of urban flood damage evaluation procedures. (From U.S. Water Resources Council, 1983.)

procedures are exactly parallel to those employed in calculating the costs for the proposed federal project. This differs from the procedure followed by the Federal Energy Regulatory Commission, which computes power values on a private financial basis (1979) when reviewing license applications from nonfederal public agencies and private entities.

The benefits for a hydropower project are normally divided into two components. The fixed or "capacity" costs of the thermal alternative are used as a measure of the value of the hydropower project's generating capacity and the variable or "energy" costs are used as the measure of the energy production. The capacity costs include amortized investment costs, transmission costs, interim replacement costs, and fixed operation and maintenance costs. Energy costs consist primarily of variable operation and maintenance costs and fuel costs. Effects on system energy and capacity costs must be taken into account when computing the value of hydroelectric energy.

The evaluation of benefits has been discussed in some detail in Chapter 8. In the case of power projects, it may not be realistic to assume that current relative price relationships of hydro and thermal alternatives will hold generally for the future. In

TABLE 10.4 ASSIGNMENT OF FLOOD CONTROL BENEFITS

Type of Benefit and Step	Structural	Flood Proofing	Evacuation
Inundation:			
Incidental flood damages (step 6)	Claimable	Claimable	Claimable
Primary flood damages (step 6)	Claimable	Claimable	Not claimable
Flood-proofing costs reduced (step 7)	Claimable	Not claimable	Not claimable
Reduction in insurance overhead (step 7)	Claimable	Claimable	Claimable
Restoration of land value (step 9)	Claimable	Claimable	Not claimable
Intensification (steps 7 and 9)	Claimable	Claimable	Not claimable
Location:			
Difference in use (step 9)	Claimable	Claimable	Not claimable
New use (step 9)	Not claimable	Not claimable	Not claimable
Encumbered title (step 9)	Not claimable	Not claimable	Not claimable
Open space (step 9)	Not claimable	Not claimable	Claimable

Source: U.S. Water Resources Council (1983).

particular, the costs may advance at a greater rate due to real fuel cost escalation to reflect increasing scarcity or due to increasing capital costs to accommodate increased environmental or safety criteria.

A market study is necessary to determine whether the power available can be used from the time it is put on line. In a developing country or area, in particular, progressive growth of demand must be taken into account. If either demand or price is expected to vary, the benefits are calculated for sequential periods before discounting.

10.7.5 Benefits for Navigation

The basic economic benefit for the *inland navigation* features of water resources development projects is the reduction in the value of resources required to transport commodities (WRC, 1983, pp. 49–58). All of the following four benefit components require projections of commodity movements:

1. For traffic that uses the waterway with the project, with the same origin–destination, the benefit is the reduction in economic cost of using the waterway.
2. For traffic that uses a waterway with the project, but without the project uses a

different mode, with the same origin–destination, the benefit is the difference in costs.

3. If implementation of a project would result in a shift in the origin of a commodity, the benefit is taken as the difference in total cost of getting the commodity to its place of use with and without the project. If implementation of a project would result in a shift in the destination of a commodity, the benefit is taken as the difference in net revenue to the producer with and without the project.

4. For new movements that result when a commodity would be transported only because of the lowered transportation charge with the project, the benefit can be measured as the delivered price of the commodity less all associated economic costs, including all the costs of barge transportation other than the navigation project.

For existing waterways, prevailing competitive rates are used to determine distribution of traffic among modes of transportation (such as different waterways, and railroad, highway, and air routes) and for benefit values. For new waterways, these rates may not represent the best estimate of long-run marginal rates.

The benefits of *deep draft navigation* (i.e., harbor improvements) include transportation savings and other benefits (WRC, 1983, pp. 58–67). The methodology is similar to that for inland navigation benefits.

10.7.6 Benefits for Recreation

Outdoor recreational activities for which benefits are considered include water-dependent activities such as swimming, boating, water skiing and fishing and water-enhanced activities such as camping, hiking, picnicking, hunting, birdwatching, photography, sightseeing, and other activities. Conceptually, benefits in terms of willingness to pay include entry and use fees actually paid for site use plus any unpaid value (surplus) enjoyed by consumers. It is not appropriate to include payment for equipment, food, transportation, or lodging since these payments are not specifically for site use.

The demand curve for recreation varies with availability and cost of alternative opportunities, characteristics of project recreation facilities, and user population location, income, and other socioeconomic characteristics. Because most recreation is publicly provided, however, it is usually not possible to estimate demand directly from observed price–consumption data. Demand may be approximated, however, by means of surveys, travel behavior, and other quantifiable measures.

Many projects involve both recreation gains and recreation losses. Reservoir-related recreation may be provided while stream and associated terrestrial recreation may be lost.

Three methods of valuation are described in the Water Resources Council guidelines: travel cost, contingency valuation (or survey), and unit-day value (WRC, 1983, pp. 67–87). A brief outline of important features is given below. All methods start with estimates of the recreation resource, forecasts of potential recreation use unconstrained by supply, and forecasts of the without- and with-project use. These estimates should recognize that the average intensity of use of a recreation site is usually substantially lower than the peak intensity of use.

The *travel cost method* (TCM) makes the basic premise that per capita use of a recreation site will decrease as the out-of-pocket and time costs of traveling from place of origin to the site increase. With this method such costs include variable costs to operate an automobile (not including such fixed costs as depreciation, insurance, and registration) and a time allowance (one-third the average wage rate in the county of origin; one-twelfth for children).

The procedure starts with the proportioning of the total estimated visitor-days among the various places of origin (e.g., counties in the project's service area). Regression curves for similar projects are obtained which relate per capita rate of use to travel distance, and an adjusted curve is formulated to account for factors other than travel distance, which are judged to affect demand. The visitor-days from each place of origin are determined by multiplying population by the per capita value from the adjusted curve. Additional adjustments are made so that the additions correspond to the total estimated visitor-days. This will give one point on the demand curve, assumed to be at zero price, such as the following:

Origin	Population	Distance	Capita	Visitation
A	10,000	10	3	30,000
B	1,000	20	2	2,000
C	3,000	30	1	3,000
				35,000

If an additional travel distance is assumed for each place of origin, the new estimate of use might be:

Origin	Population	Distance	Capita	Visitation
A	10,000	20	2	20,000
B	1,000	30	1	1,000
C	3,000	40	0	0
				21,000

This operation can be continued to obtain several points on the demand site of the relationship. On the price side, the previously mentioned variable costs for automobile operation and opportunity costs for time are applied as proxies for price to the incremental distances. Adjustments are made for round-trip mileage and for number of passengers per car. A demand curve can now be defined.

The final computational step in the travel cost approach is to measure the area under the demand curve. This area is equal to the amount users would be willing to pay (but do not have to pay) for the opportunity to participate in recreation at the resource being evaluated. Any user charges or entrance fees should be added to this value. The TCM procedure is applicable for any type of activity or groups of activities for which use can be described by a use-estimating equation or a per capita use curve.

Contingent valuation methods (CVMs) obtain estimates of changes in benefits as a result of changes in the quantity of recreation assumed by directly asking individual recreationists. The CVM procedures are particularly appropriate for: (1) evaluating projects likely to be one of several destinations visited on a single trip; and (2) a project that results in a relatively small change in quality of recreation at a site. Results may be adversely affected unless questions are carefully designed and pretested to avoid several possible kinds of responsive bias. Several approaches are described below.

Iterative bidding techniques are most effectively applied in personal interview surveys. Following establishment of the market and a complete description of the recreational good, service, or amenity to be valued, the respondent reacts to a series of values posed by the enumerator. The respondent answers "yes" or "no" to questions asking if he or she is willing to pay the stated amount of money to obtain the desired increment in the recreational good. The enumerator iteratively varies the value posed until the highest amount that the respondent is willing to pay is identified. This amount is treated as the respondent's bid for the specified increment in the recreational good.

Noniterative bidding formats are adaptable to implementation with mail surveys. There are two kinds of formats: (1) closed-ended formats, which ask respondents to react ("yes" or "no") to a single stated value; and (2) open-ended formats, which ask the respondent to write down the maximum amount he or she would be willing to pay. According to the Water Resources Council procedures, noniterative bidding formats are not likely to be as reliable as iterative formats and are considered permissible only for recreation benefit analyses of small projects.

Contingent valuation methods can be used to develop value estimator models, which are statistical models of the relationships between the bid and selected characteristics of the sites and user populations, or to estimate recreation benefits for a specific project.

The *unit-day value (UDV) method* relies on expert or informed opinion and judgment to approximate the average willingness to pay by users of recreational developments. It is used when the TCM or CVM estimates are either not feasible or not justified for the particular project under study. For the UDV method, planners select a specified value from the range of values in the most current published schedule. Two classes of outdoor recreation days, general or specialized, may be differentiated for evaluation purposes.

"General" refers to a recreation day involving primarily those activities which are attractive to the majority of outdoor recreationists and which generally require the development and maintenance of convenient access and adequate facilities. Such activities include picnicking, camping, hiking, riding, cycling, fishing, and hunting, which would be of normal quality. The range of maximum unit-day values for federal projects as of July 1, 1982 was $1.60 to $4.80. The appropriate value may be based on a point system that takes account of the recreation experience, availability of opportunity, carrying capacity, accessibility, and environmental quality. It may also be adjusted by using the Consumer Price Index.

"Specialized" refers to a recreation day involving those activities for which opportunities are limited, intensity of use is low, and a high degree of skill, knowledge, and appreciation of the activity by the user may be involved. The range of unit-day values in 1982 was $6.50 to $19.00. The higher end of the range includes activities such as big game hunting, wilderness pack trips, inland and marine fishing for salmon and steelhead, white water boating and canoeing, and long-range boat cruises in areas of outstanding scenic value. Values at the lower end include upland bird hunting and specialized nature photography.

10.7.7 Benefits for Commercial Fishing

The benefits of commercial fishing are the change in income due to increased output and changes in harvesting costs (WRC, 1983, pp. 87–91).

10.8 BENEFITS FOR UTILIZATION OF UNEMPLOYED OR UNDEREMPLOYED LABOR RESOURCES

The use of shadow pricing for adjusting costs and benefits for economic analysis is discussed subsequently in this chapter, but these adjustments are not generally used in the United States. A procedure covering only labor is outlined in the Water Resources Council Principles and Guidelines (WRC, 1983, pp. 93–96).

The basic premise is that the opportunity cost of employing otherwise unemployed labor resources is zero because society does not give up any alternative production of goods and services by virtue of their employment in the project. Similarly, the opportunity cost of employing otherwise underemployed labor resources equals their without-project earnings, which, by virtue of their under-employment, are less than their market cost. There is a difference, therefore, between the social cost of labor and the market cost. The difference is considered as a project benefit rather than as a decrease in project costs.

In the WRC guidelines "primarily because of identification and measurement problems and because unemployment is regarded as a temporary phenomenon" (WRC, 1983, p. 93), benefits are limited to those arising from construction and installation of a project or a nonstructural measure. It is further restricted to the portion of the project construction located in an area of substantial and persistent unemployment. The following percentages of total wages have been estimated as benefits for case 1 (no "local hire" rule) and case 2 (80% "local hire" rule):

	Case 1	Case 2
Skilled	30	43
Unskilled	47	58
Other	35	35

10.9 EXTERNAL ECONOMIES AND DISECONOMIES

Economic analyses should take account of external economies on the benefits side and external diseconomies on the cost side. Such adjustments do not apply to financial analyses. External economies are the beneficial effects to individuals, groups, or industries that occur as an indirect result of the project or plan. The Water Resources Council "Principles and Guidelines" refer to these as "other direct benefits" due to "incidental effects of a project that increase economic efficiency by increasing the output of intermediate or final consumer goods over and above the direct outputs for which the plan is being formulated" (WRC, 1983, pp. 91–93).

The WRC Procedures (WRC, 1979, pp. 72965-7) distinguished between "technological external economies" and "pecuniary external economies." The first type occurs when the output of firms and/or individuals becomes more efficient through the use of new or improved technology made possible by the direct output of the project. The second type refers to the financial effects of one project or plan on others, as encompassed in price changes for outputs or inputs; this type of externality is not taken as a benefit in benefit-cost analysis from a national standpoint because they only represent transfers between economic sectors. Several examples of "other direct benefits" are provided in the Principles and Guidelines (WRC, 1983, p. 92). A flood control plan would, as a result of regulating flows to obtain direct outputs of flood control, also increase the recreational potential of land and water in the lower reaches of the river system, improve the fish and wildlife on this area, lower water treatment costs for firms and households, and increase groundwater recharge. See Marglin (1967) for additional discussion of externalities.

External diseconomies are the uncompensated net economic losses of a project. These costs should be included with the NED costs. The WRC "Principles and Guidelines" refer to these as "other direct costs" (WRC, 1983, p. 99) and provide the following examples: increased downstream flood damages caused by channel modifications, dikes, or the drainage of wetlands; increased water supply treatment costs caused by irrigation return flows; erosion of land along streambanks caused by dams that prevent the replenishment of bedload material; loss of land and water recreation values through channel modifications, reduced instream flow due to consumptive use of water by irrigated agriculture, or inundation by reservoirs; increased transportation costs caused by rerouting traffic around a reservoir; new or increased vector control costs caused by the creation of wetlands; and decreased output or increased cost per unit of private firms caused by project-induced decreases in raw materials.

10.10 RATIONALE FOR SHADOW (ACCOUNTING) PRICES

Although distortions in market price occur due to violations of the conditions of perfect competition, such effects are not taken account of in the evaluation of federal projects in the United States (in the Water Resources Council "Principles and Guidelines"), except in the case of unemployed or underemployed labor resources for which rather limited downward adjustments of project cost are included as a benefit addition.

Although shadow pricing may not be important in the economic analyses of public projects in the United States and other highly developed countries (where markets are in reasonable equilibrium and water resource projects are not used as a major means of boosting economic development), this may not be the case elsewhere. In fact, the "Guidelines for Project Evaluation" of the United Nations Industrial Development Organization (Dasgupta et al. 1972, p. 2) state that:

> [The] raison-d'etre of this volume is the clear recognition that the prices that obtain in the market in developing countries are not necessarily the prices that ought to be used in public-sector evaluation. . . . [The] problem then is to obtain notional prices that the Government ought to use instead. These prices, which we shall call "shadow prices" are the values we would want to attach to specific commodities (e.g., steel, bulldozers, fertilizers and machine tools); or to services (e.g., unskilled labor); or to the "act of waiting" (the rate of discount).

The need for adjustment of market prices in developing countries results not only from the distortion caused by the actions of those participating in the market, but also from the effect of instruments of government policy such as taxes, tariffs, quotas, licenses, and public investment.

The implementation of shadow prices in project analysis is difficult because of the technical problems of interpreting market prices and the central government economic policies. A further difficulty is their variation from country to country and with time.

These difficulties should not result in a decision to prepare economic analyses in a developing country without shadow pricing. The possible distortions and inaccurate benefit-cost results that are obtained without such adjustments of market prices and other parameters are too serious to ignore. For best results, cooperative studies should be carried out, with participation of project analysts and central government planners and economists.

10.11 SHADOW PRICES FOR VARIOUS PROJECT FACTORS

10.11.1 Shadow Price of Labor

The following discussion on shadow pricing unskilled labor is based on the unpublished "Appraisal Guidelines for Development" of the Agency for International Development (1971). The basic concept of this approach has been discussed by Little and Mirrlees (1969).

In principle, the accounting price should be based on the net cost, to the national economy, of the input of unskilled labor into the project under review. The net cost will be composed of essentially two elements (AID, 1971, p. 90):

1. The output of the worker in his or her present employment, from which it is assumed he or she would transfer to the project

2. The additional consumption and other demands on output attributable to employment in the particular project

For the first of these components, totally unemployed workers would have a marginal opportunity cost of zero. For underemployed, unskilled workers, the marginal opportunity cost will be something more than zero, but probably less than the going market wage rate for the type of labor. For the underemployed worker, the first component can be estimated as the total reduction in value of output if the worker were withdrawn from his or her present (under)employment.

Where data exist, a rough estimate of the second component of the marginal opportunity cost of unskilled labor may be made by comparing consumption levels of unemployed and underemployed unskilled workers with consumption of fully employed unskilled workers, and treating the difference as the *additional* cost of utilization of unskilled labor in the project.

The *incremental* real economic cost of employment versus unemployment or substantial underemployment may include such elements as the resources required to provide training; additional requirements for food, clothing and medical care; the costs of social infrastructure that may be necessary as the rural unemployed shift to urban jobs; and transportation to and from the place of employment. It is only to the extent that the output of the worker exceeds these increments in the costs of maintenance (plus any loss in real output in present employment) that employment of the worker will yield any positive return on the capital employed in the project.

In "less developed countries" (LDCs), large numbers of unemployed and underemployed members of the labor force usually reflect the constraints of capital shortages and the lack of foreign exchange, as well as imperfections in the labor markets. Money wage rates established in the urban industrial sectors (or in modern plantation agricultural schemes) tend to become the "norm" that employers are expected to pay for additional workers from the urban unemployed or the rural underemployed. These norms are often supported by unionized workers and by government regulations. In fact, the productivity of workers may well exceed their wages, but from the standpoint of project evaluation the relevant real cost of labor is the marginal opportunity cost of its employment on the project in question, not the money wage necessary to put the worker in productive employment.

As pointed out by Gittinger (1972), the shadow price should be adjusted if there is a pattern of seasonal employment. In the case of agricultural employment, there may actually be a shortage of labor during harvesting (and during transplanting of rice) and the marginal value of labor is not zero during such periods. He also notes that although labor in a country or project area is presently unemployed or underemployed, this may not be the case in a number of years when development has had a chance to proceed. For a hypothetical case, therefore, he suggests the following (p. 43):

> [F]rom the first to the tenth year your shadow price would be zero; from the eleventh through the twentieth years labor would be thought to be fully employed at the peak season so you shadow price agricultural labor at, say, one-half the annual money wage;

and from the twenty-first year to the end of the project analysis period you use the going wage rate as the best indicator of the value of agricultural labor.

Gittinger also discusses the matter of skilled labor, stating that in most cases such labor should not be shadow priced below the going wage rate. In fact, he suggests that a case may even be made for shadow pricing certain kinds of skilled labor above its wage to reflect its scarcity.

10.11.2 Shadow Price of Foreign Exchange

The following is based on the aforementioned "Appraisal Guidelines" of the Agency for International Development (AID, 1971, pp. 92–3). In many less developed countries, the domestic monetary unit tends to be substantially overvalued. Thus, imported inputs tend to be too cheap relative to domestic inputs; and the values of exported outputs, expressed in the domestic monetary unit, are also understated. These distortions can give rise to serious bias in project appraisal. The capital–labor relationship is especially sensitive to the foreign exchange rate. Under these circumstances, the evaluation of projects involving substantial imported inputs and/or exports of output will be improved by the use of an accounting exchange rate.

One approach to the estimation of an accounting rate of exchange is through comparisons between the wholesale prices of imported and domestically produced goods considered to be perfect substitutes, disregarding the import duties and internal excise taxes. Thus, if the price of domestically produced portland cement, for example, is 25% above world market prices (cost, insurance, and freight [c.i.f.], plus local handling costs), the presumption is that the ratio of the accounting exchange rate to the official rate is 1.25:1.00 for this good. If similar comparisons can be made for a large number of goods, or in terms of a broadly based, representative wholesale price index, the resulting ratio can be used as a correction factor to estimate an accounting exchange rate (U.S. Agency for International Development, 1971).

Alternatively, where there is a substantial volume of foreign trade, "effective rates" of exchange for imports and exports may be of use in estimating the accounting or shadow rate of exchange. However, if import licenses are denied for significant quantities of important commodities, the effective rate will be below the appropriate level for the accounting of shadow rate of exchange. An effective rate of exchange on imports may be computed by dividing the sum of domestic c.i.f. cost of imports plus all duties, port charges, customs clearance and import license fees, and penalty interest on deposits required to obtain import licenses, by the c.i.f. value of imports expressed in foreign currency. A similar computation may be made to arrive at an effective rate of exchange for exports. To the official exchange receipts from exports all subsidies—direct and indirect—would be added, and the total divided by the freight-on-board (f.o.b.) value of the export stated in foreign currency. In this computation it is important to include all indirect forms of subsidy, including loans at preferential interest rates, the profits from sales of privileged imports available only to exporters, lower transport and electric rates for exporters, and so on, as well as direct subsidies. In many countries, central monetary authorities compute more or less continuously what is generally called the "effective rate of exchange," generally following these procedures.

For some developing countries, independent market rates of foreign exchange may be available from published (or easily obtainable) quotations in free markets outside the country. However, such market quotations should be used with extreme caution, as they often reflect illicit transactions or very limited volumes of exchange. Similarly, black-market rates within a country are not generally an appropriate base for an accounting exchange rate. These rates are generally set in very thin markets in which both buyers and sellers are frequently engaged in illicit transactions involving high risks.

10.11.3 Shadow Price of Commodities That Have World Markets

As stated in the AID guidelines (1971, p. 94), markets for many products in less developed countries:

> are highly imperfect, with prices set by few buyers and sellers, price determination by administrative action, the compartmentalization of markets because of inadequate transport and communication, etc. Prices in such markets are an imperfect guide, at best, to the estimation of the national economic value of output from prospective projects.

The AID guidelines and Gittinger (1972) suggest that world prices be used in place of domestic prices for commodities that have world markets. As noted by the latter (p. 39):

> [T]he reasoning here is that world markets—whatever their drawbacks—are more nearly perfect markets than protected markets. Thus the world market price for wheat is more nearly a true measure of the "value" of wheat than a domestic price. In the last resort, you could always choose to import wheat rather than to increase domestic production. If your shadow price for foreign exchange is right, this would not introduce a bias into your analysis.

Where output will consist of marketable products (i.e., divisible goods that can be sold for a price) and such goods are traded in world markets, the c.i.f., price (exclusive of duties) provides a satisfactory base for valuation of domestic output—if a "correct" exchange rate is employed in converting the foreign to the domestic currency value. If both nonlabor inputs and outputs consist largely of goods traded in world markets, it may be useful to use world prices, with domestic labor inputs converted to world prices by use of the accounting rate of foreign exchange.

10.11.4 Discount Rate

The calculations to arrive at the economic results of a project in terms of a benefit-cost ratio or in terms of present worth of net benefits involve the use of a discount rate.

Furthermore, it may be desirable not only to compare the internal rates of return of various alternative water resource projects, but also to compare this value with the opportunity cost of capital, instead of the actual borrowing rate, which would amount to considering a shadow price for capital.

Of various parameters in economic analysis, the discount rate is often the most important as well as being very sensitive. A movement of two or three percentage points in the discount rate may be enough to change the benefit-cost ratio to a satisfactory or unacceptable value. Despite its importance, however, there appears to be more disagreement among economists as to the proper rate of discount than for any other economic parameter (James and Rogers 1979). The most fundamental controversy is between those who would utilize a rate taken from theoretically approximated or actual market rates, and those who would utilize a social rate of discount together with a shadow price on capital to incorporate opportunity costs correctly. The latter approach treats the choice of interest rate as an explicit social choice, whereas the former approach does not.

For many projects, the planner will find that the discount rate for economic analyses has already been established by a central planning authority. If this is not the case, the planner may ascertain that a general consensus exists on the appropriate rate among the professional economists in the decision-making hierarchy that reviews water resources projects. The planner may find that the ranking of alternative projects and scales is not affected significantly when a sensitivity analysis is carried out with a range of interest rates. Finally, if a definite selection of an interest rate for discounting must be made by the planner, he may refer to the AID document, to the Little and Mirrlees reference mentioned previously, and to a number of other literature sources, including: Schmedtje (1965), Baumol (1968), Marglin (1963, 1967), Sen (1967), Dasgupta, Sen, and Marglin (1972), Squire and Van der Tak (1975), Hirschleifer, DeHaven, and Milliman (1960), Maass et al. (1962), Arrow (1965), English (1972), Haveman (1969), Whipple (1975), Gittinger (1972), and James and Lee (1971).

The AID document recommends the use of the marginal opportunity cost of capital as the basis for the discount rate, with a minimum value of at least 10%. It defines the marginal opportunity cost of capital as the probable or projected return on the alternative investments superseded or substituted by the contemplated project investment.

Squire and van der Tak (1975) distinguish among the opportunity cost of capital, the consumption rate of interest, and the accounting rate of interest. The "consumption rate of interest" measures the discount attached to having additional consumption next year rather than this year and is thus a way of introducing government fiscal policy into the discount rate. They state (pp. 27–29) that:

> In shaping its investment and fiscal policies the government will have to choose between encouraging savings and investment and thus future growth and immediate increases in consumption and living standards. The government—in the absence of policy constraints arising from political feasibility, administrative costs and repercussions on incentives— could ensure through its fiscal policy that at the margin additional savings to promote growth and future consumption are in its view as valuable as additional present consumption. In that case project analysis need not concern itself with the impact of a project on consumption or savings, but should concentrate on the impact on income, irrespective of its use for consumption or savings, since both are worth the same. . . . The traditional procedure used by the World Bank and most other project-financing agencies essentially implies a judgment that there is no significant imbalance between the value

attached to current consumption and future growth (current savings). . . . This approach may not always be appropriate. In cases in which growth rates are considered too low because of insufficient savings rather than inefficient use of resources, and greater fiscal efforts are ruled out by overriding constraints, project appraisals should take account of the greater value that then attaches to savings than to consumption. A further breakdown of consumption may be warranted if the government wishes to use project selection to influence the current distribution of consumption.

The concepts in the latter part of this quotation are embodied in the approach recommended by Squire and van der Tak to determine the accounting rate of interest based on "uncommitted public income measured in convertible currency," which they refer to as "free foreign exchange." Their rationale derives from the earlier work by Little and Mirrlees (1969), which concerned a new approach to benefit-cost analysis in which every input and output is priced in terms of foreign exchange or a foreign exchange–based accounting (shadow) price, and which allows planners as they determine these shadow prices to make a value judgment that a dollar's worth of savings may be worth more than a dollar's worth of consumption, and which implicitly allows for the value judgment that consumption by lower-income people has a greater social worth than consumption by those whose incomes are higher (see Gittinger, 1972).

10.12 EXAMPLE OF APPLICATION OF SHADOW PRICES

It is particularly important in the formulation and analyses of plans that affect more than one country to resort to shadow pricing in order to reduce the distortions in planning that might otherwise occur due to different foreign exchange rates, market imperfections, and other factors.

For the economic analyses of the Vardar/Axios project in Yugoslavia–Greece (TAMS, 1978), shadow prices reflected adjustments to financial prices where market prices did not indicate the true costs to the national economy. Shadow price adjustments were made to project costs, to benefits of hydroelectric power and municipal and industrial water when evaluated by the method of most likely alternative cost, and in the case of agricultural benefits, to all sensitive items of the farm budgets.

The principal assumptions were that the social rate of discount should be 10%; foreign exchange costs should be increased by 50%; and unskilled labor costs should be valued at 50% of the market rate except for irrigation labor, which was valued at 65%. The interest rate is within the range usually cited for these studies. The adjustments for foreign exchange and unskilled labor were considered appropriate for developing countries with inadequate foreign exchange and a surplus of labor, and have the effect of favoring projects that are more intensive in terms of local capital and labor resources. In the case of agricultural estimates, farmgate prices of crops that can be exported or substituted for imports were adjusted to reflect internal prices. Selections of cropping patterns were based on practical considerations, including

TABLE 10.5 BENEFIT-COST RATIO FOR HYDROPOWER PROJECT, WITH AND WITHOUT SHADOW PRICING

B/C based on shadow prices (from results for 2025)	$= \dfrac{107.25}{102.88} = 1.04$
Ratio of economic costs to financial costs	$=\quad 0.93$
Ratio of economic benefits to financial benefits	$=\quad 1.31$
Factor to adjust shadow prices	$= \dfrac{0.93}{1.31} = 0.71$
B/C based on financial prices	$=\quad 1.04 \ \times 0.71$
	$=\quad 0.74$

Source: TAMS (1978).

values without shadow pricing; however, the farm budget analyses for basin studies were based on economic values after shadow pricing.

Table 10.5 provides an example of benefit-cost ratios calculated with and without shadow pricing. For a hydropower project, shadow pricing increased the benefits by about 30% when they were based on the cost of alternative thermal power with imported fuel. Shadow pricing reduced the costs but only by about 7%. Thus, the net effect was that the benefit-cost ratio with shadow pricing (the economic B/C) was determined to be 1.04, whereas the benefit-cost ratio without shadow pricing (the financial B/C) was estimated to be approximately 0.7.

For an irrigation project, the farming operations, not including payments for the irrigation project, are reflected in the numerator of the B/C ratio. Thus, the benefits are equal to crop prices minus farm costs. The effects of shadow prices were taken into account by using adjusted unit values of crop prices and unit values of each of the components of farm costs. The economic analysis was run only with shadow-priced unit values; therefore, an estimate of the net effect of shadow pricing on benefits is not available. However, it is possible to generalize by noting that shadow pricing adjustments usually raise crop prices and lower the farm costs due to the important effect of labor. Both of these actions increase benefits. The denominator of the B/C ratio, applying to irrigation project costs, is reduced by shadow pricing but only by a modest amount (e.g., approximately 8% for one irrigation project studied). Therefore, the net effect of shadow pricing, by increasing benefits and reducing costs, was to increase the benefit-cost ratios for irrigation projects in the Vardar/Axios river basin.

10.13 INFRASTRUCTURE COSTS

Whittlesey et al. (1978), in analyzing irrigation project areas in the eastern part of the state of Washington, refer to infrastructure costs as "social overhead capital costs." They point out that the growth in population induced by additional irrigation requires new roads, water and sewage facilities, schools, fire and police protection, and other facilities and services. The increased energy demands due to irrigation and growth in economic activity must also be met. They estimated that capital investments required to service the needs of new development can reach $2000 per acre irrigated or $70,000 per job created. On an annual basis, these amounts are equivalent to $180 per acre or $6700 per job.

In the United States and other economically advanced countries, the social overhead capital costs must be paid locally through increased taxes, utility rates, or costs for services. The capital is provided by local governments and through private enterprise.

In developing countries, there may be inadequate financial capability in the local public and private sectors to implement the facilities and services required. In any event, a project sponsor should make adequate provision for these aspects in the financial plan. If this is not done, the economic and financial returns of the project (which depend on adequate infrastructure) will not be attained.

It is difficult to determine the extent to which infrastructure (social overhead) costs should be taken into account in an economic analysis. In the United States, only the more obvious "externalities" are included in the economic analyses by federal agencies. Some infrastructure costs are needed for the determination of benefits (e.g., in evaluating the production factors for irrigation) if they are established as costs in the market. Most of the other infrastructure costs are not included, on the implicit assumption that they are equaled or exceeded by other benefits similarly omitted. This assumption has not been fully tested. In developing countries, where the project sponsor may also provide the supporting infrastructure, a portion or all of its cost may be accounted for in the economic analyses.

In economic analyses, the inclusion of such costs (and corresponding benefits) also depends on whether the analysis is made from a national or regional standpoint. For the national analysis, many of the costs and benefits may be transfer payments that do not result in net national effects.

REFERENCES

ARROW, K. J., "Criteria for Social Investment," *Water Resources Res.*, vol. 1, no. 1, 1965.

BAUMOL, W. J., "On the Social Rate of Discount," *Am. Econ. Rev.*, vol. 63, 1968.

DASGUPTA, P., A. SEN, and S. MARGLIN, "Guidelines for Project Evaluation," United Nations Industrial Development Organization, Vienna, 1972.

ENGINEERING NEWS RECORD, chart based on information on pages 118 and 119, March 18, 1982.

ENGLISH, J. M., ed., *Economics of Engineering and Social Systems*, Wiley, New York, 1972.

GITTINGER, J. PRICE, *Economic Analysis of Agricultural Projects*, Johns Hopkins University Press, Baltimore, Md., 1972.

GRIGG, NEIL S., and OTTO J. HELWEG, "State-of-the-Art of Estimating Flood Damage in Urban Areas," *Water Resources Bull.*, vol. 11, no. 2, April 1975.

HAVEMAN, ROBERT H., "The Opportunity Cost of Displaced Private Spending and the Social Discount Rate," *Water Resources Res.*, vol. 5, no. 5, October 1969.

HIRSCHLEIFER, J., J. C. DEHAVEN, and J. W. MILLIMAN, *Water Supply: Economics, Technology and Policy*, University of Chicago Press, Chicago, 1960.

JAMES, L.D., and R. R. LEE, *Economics of Water Resources Planning*, McGraw-Hill, New York, 1971.

JAMES, L. DOUGLAS, and JERRY R. ROGERS, "Economics and Water Resources Planning in America," *J. Water Resources Plann. Manage. Div., Proc. Am. Soc. Civil Eng.*, vol. 105, no. WR1, March 1979.

LITTLE, J. M. D., and J. A. MIRRLEES, "Manual of Industrial Project Analysis in Developing Countries," vol. II, Social Cost Benefit Analysis, OECD, Paris, 1969.

MAASS, A. et al., *Design of Water-Resource Systems*, Harvard University Press, Cambridge, Mass., 1962.

MARGLIN, S. A., "The Social Rate of Discount and the Optimal Rate of Investment," *Q. J. Econ.*, vol. 77, no. 1, 1963.

MARGLIN, S. A., *"Public Investment Criteria*, MIT Press, Cambridge, Mass., 1967.

MILLER, JOHN R., "Normalized Agricultural Prices and Water Resources Planning, *Water Resources Bull.*, vol. 16, no. 3, June 1980.

SCHMEDTJE, J. K., "On Estimating the Economic Cost of Capital," IBRD-IDA, Rep. EC-138, 1965.

SEN, A. K., "Isolation, Assurance and the Social Rate of Discount," *Q. J. Econ.*, vol. 81, no. 1, 1967.

SQUIRE, LYN, and HERMAN G. VAN DER TAK, *Economic Analysis of Projects*, Johns Hopkins University Press, Baltimore, Md., 1975.

TAMS (Tippetts-Abbett-McCarthy-Stratton, New York), "Bridge Canyon Project, Application for License before Federal Power Commission," amended September 1960.

TAMS (Tippetts-Abbett-McCarthy-Stratton, New York, and Mattis Demain Beckford & Associates Ltd., Kingston) "Comparative Study of Water Supply Projects for Kingston and Surrounding Area," July 1977.

TAMS (Tippetts-Abbett-McCarthy-Stratton, New York, and Massachusetts Institute of Technology, Cambridge), "Integrated Development of the Vardar/Axios River Basin—Yugoslavia–Greece," December 1978.

U.S. AGENCY FOR INTERNATIONAL DEVELOPMENT, "Appraisal Guidelines for Development," prepared by Charles Nathan Associates, September 1971.

U.S. DEPARTMENT OF ENERGY, Federal Energy Regulatory Commission, "Hydroelectric Power Evaluation," August 1979.

U.S. DEPARTMENT OF THE INTERIOR, BUREAU OF RECLAMATION, "Reclamation Manual, " vol. X: Design and Construction, Part 8: Construction Cost Estimates, August 28, 1950.

U.S. WATER RESOURCES COUNCIL, "Procedures for Evaluation of National Economic Development (NED) Benefits and Costs in Water Resources Planning (Level C)," December 14, 1979; rev. September 29, 1980.

U.S. WATER RESOURCES COUNCIL," Economic and Environmental Principles and Guidelines for Water and Related Land Resources Implementation Studies," March 10, 1983.

WHIPPLE, WILLIAM, JR., "Principles of Determining a Social Discount Rate," *Water Resources Bull.*, vol. 11, no. 4, August 1975.

WHITTLESEY, NORMAN K., KENNETH C. GIBBS, and WALTER R. BUTCHER, "Social Overhead Capital Cost of Irrigation Development in Washington State," *Water Resources Bull.*, vol. 11, no. 3, June 1978.

ELEVEN

Analyses of Risk and Uncertainty and Other Studies Involving Probabilities

11.1 APPROACHES TO RISK AND UNCERTAINTY

Projects are planned to meet future (therefore, uncertain) needs, using water and related land resources that are themselves uncertain. Problems of uncertainty have received increased attention from planners as: (1) the differences between predicted and actual project outcomes have been recognized; (2) available water and land resources have become scarce and must be used more intensively; and (3) issues of uncertainty have been faced in the review and public involvement process. Thus, the planner should have a thorough grounding in the ways to assess uncertainty and its ramifications. This chapter focuses on two principal approaches to considering uncertainty: determining the probability of occurrence of an event, and translating that probability into an evaluation of risk by determining the consequence of the event occurring (or not occurring).

In its simplest form, the planner deals intuitively with risk. For example, when a water resources project includes structural components, construction quantities and costs cannot be predicted with certainty. This can be allowed for by increasing the cost estimate for *contingencies*. The allowances for contingencies may be reduced as more is learned about foundation conditions, availability of construction materials, and the problems of diverting water during construction, but some uncertainty always remains until the project is completed. If further investigations reveal serious problems that were previously unforeseen, the allowances for contingencies may have to be increased.

Benefit-cost analyses require the specification of a discount rate and project period, and estimates of the annual costs and benefits, including their variation with time. The planner must often use his or her best judgment when estimating or assuming values for a few or many of the variables that determine the benefit-cost ratio or other indicator of the economy. Once the project is implemented, the available water supplies, demands for services, and other factors affecting economic outcomes may be quite different from the "most likely" or "expected" values. The planner may adopt a very conservative approach and select pessimistic values of the variables that lead to a lower benefit-cost ratio. Or, he or she may select a very optimistic set of values, resulting in a higher benefit-cost ratio. Such determinations of most likely, pessimistic, and optimistic benefit-cost ratios may be included in *sensitivity analyses.*

Another, and increasingly favored method of analysis is *risk analysis.* When the variables or parameters affecting the potential outcome of a project are described in terms of probability distributions, the outcome is also expressed in a form that permits more rational consideration of the project by planners and decision makers. For example, suppose that the risk analysis for a project produces the following estimates of the outcome:

- 90% probability that the B/C will be greater than 1.0
- 80% probability that the B/C will be greater than 1.5
- 70% probability that the B/C will be greater than 2.5

Say that a B/C of 1.0 just meets the minimum standard for project implementation, while a B/C of 1.5 is good and a B/C of 2.5 is very attractive. Although the probability of a good or very attractive B/C is high, an inexperienced and underfinanced sponsor may be unwilling to accept the 10% possibility that the project will fail. A sponsor that is already involved in many successful projects may, however, consider the risk of failure to be acceptable when compared to the likelihood of very desirable outcomes.

The planner's approach may, therefore, reflect not only his or her degree of confidence in the values selected for the study variables but also the organization's financial strength. A large organization that pools many risks can accept the risk of failure of a project, whereas an organization completely dependent on a single project should be quite "risk averse." Another point to consider is that the consistent use of values of variables having low probabilities of occurrence (i.e., always pessimistic or optimistic), can lead to unreasonable results because the joint probabilities of the values in combination may be inconceivably low.

Attitudes toward uncertainty vary not only with the sponsor organization but also with the individual and the type of risk. Members of society may be more willing to accept a higher but known risk (e.g., everyday risk of automobile accident) than the unknown risk of a catastrophic event (e.g., earthquake, great flood, or nuclear incident). Risk probabilities do not fully conform with the value scales perceived by society, which may be "risk neutral" in the case of automobile accidents and "risk averse" with respect to the large and sudden changes in wealth and psychic damage from an earthquake. The planner should recognize that these seemingly irrational attitudes exist, in considering alternative plans and especially in conducting the public involvement process.

Authorities (Hirschman 1967; Howe 1971; Kaynor 1978; Lindblom 1968; Mack 1971; U.S. General Accounting Office, 1978) are not in agreement on what to do about uncertainty—reduce it, ignore it, avoid it, or analyze it in mathematical terms for planning purposes. The "Principles and Guidelines" of the U.S. Water Resources Council (1983, p. 17) state that "The assessment of risk and uncertainty in project evaluation should be reported and displayed in a manner that makes clear to the decisionmaker the types and degrees of risk and uncertainty believed to characterize the benefits and costs of the alternative plans considered." This document also lists (pp. 5–6) the following methods of dealing with risk and uncertainty and provides additional guidance on project evaluation (pp. 15–17):

- Collecting more detailed data to reduce measurement error
- Using more refined analytic techniques
- Increasing safety margins in design
- Selecting measures with better known performance characteristics
- Reducing the irreversible or irretrievable commitments of resources
- Performing a sensitivity analysis of the estimated benefits and costs of alternative plans

Major (1977) recommends airing the problems of uncertainty in an "open" planning process involving governmental and nongovernmental organizations and individuals with different points of view (degree of conservatism, biases, organizational policies, degree of reliance on planning organization, etc.). He also states that when general adjustments are applied to all projects and programs [such as those suggested by the U.S. Inter-Agency Committee on Water Resources (1958)—a factor added to the interest rate, overestimation of costs and underestimation of benefits, or limitation of the period of analysis], they tend to obscure the differences in uncertainty that characterize different parts of a program or project. Major prefers instead to make explicit assessments of the degrees of uncertainty prevailing for different aspects of programs and projects, and to present these to participants in the political process.

Finally, the following comments by Wiener (1972, p. 167) are believed to be cogent:

> Attention is drawn to a type of optical illusion to which most of us are prone, namely *underestimating the extent of uncertainty*. When reviewing possible outcomes, we are not usually in a position to list all factors that may modify our future assumptions or to identify all unpredictable future developments; furthermore, we also tend to neglect influence from outside the system that may bear upon outcomes within the system. As a consequence we tend to underestimate the importance of low sensitivity of outcomes and the value of decision or action liquidity. In arriving at our final conclusion, we should compensate for this built-in bias and grant to decision liquidity and low sensitivity a higher utility and value than we can directly prove.

Traces (sequences) of stream flow values are needed for many water resources planning studies, ranging from the development and testing of the operation rules for a single purpose reservoir to the application of optimizing techniques to a multiunit, multipurpose river basin system. Many individual project and systems studies are made using historical records. Often, however, these historical records of stream flow may be of inadequate length, not sufficiently representative of long term conditions, or both. In these cases, the available records may be considered to be a sample of a longer hydrologic period, for the purpose of obtaining a *synthetic record* of stream flows. This procedure is often referred to as *operational hydrology* because of its application to operations studies. Most synthetic records are derived for annual, seasonal, or monthly time intervals.

The following is a widely used mathematical formulation for a synthetic flow model for a single site (Thomas and Fiering 1962). This model preserves the means, standard deviations, and first-order correlation coefficients of the historical record. Descriptors for this model include "Markov series," "multiseason," and "lag-one."

$$Q_{ij} = \bar{Q}_j + m_j(Q_{i-1,j-1} - \bar{Q}_{j-1}) + t_i s_j (1 - r_j^2)^{1/2}$$

where

i = month in series, $i = 1, 2, \ldots, n$ measured from the beginning

j = month in the year, $j = 1, 2, \ldots, 12$ for January, February, $\ldots$, December

Q_{ij} = flow during ith month from the beginning, in the jth month of the year

$\bar{Q}_j$ = mean flow in the jth month of the year

s_j = standard deviation of the flows in the jth month of the year

m_j = regression coefficient of jth month on flows of $(j-1)$st month = $r_j s_j / s_{j-1}$

r_j = correlation coefficient between flows for jth and $(j-1)$st months.

t_i = random normal deviate

There are 12 values of each of $\bar{Q}_j$, s_j, m_j, and r_j calculated from the historical record (sample). The random normal deviate, t_i, is obtained from a sequence of random numbers having a normal distribution with a mean of zero and with a standard deviation of 1.

If the last term were omitted from this model, this equation could be written as

$$(Q_{ij} - \bar{Q}_j) = m_j(Q_{i-j,j-1} - \bar{Q}_{j-1})$$

In this case the process for developing a synthetic series would be completely deterministic (i.e., with a specified initial flow, the entire series would be fully predictable). With the addition of the last term, the process becomes stochastic and the resulting series depends on the random numbers that are used. The random numbers may be selected from a table of random numbers or generated by a computer. The random numbers, instead of being from a normal distribution, may follow another distribution (e.g., gamma) if a better representation of a long hydrologic period is thereby obtained.

The development and use of models having the structure described above has been discussed by Hufschmidt and Fiering (1968), Fiering (1967), and Fiering and Jackson (1971). Such Markovian models make "stationary stochastic" or "short memory" assumptions. More recently, "long memory" processes have been investigated which recognize the persistence effects that have been identified in long historical records. "Fractional noise," "broken-line," "autoregressive integrated–moving average (ARIMA)," and "range and run" are examples of non-Markovian models. Markovian and non-Markovian models have been described and compared by a number of investigators (e.g., Matalas and Wallis 1976; Jackson 1975; Domokos et al. 1976; Lettenmaier and Burges 1976; Hipel et al. 1979; Chow 1964, 1978; Haan 1977; and Yevjevich 1972).

Seasonal, monthly, weekly, or daily events can be generated from values for larger time intervals, using methods of disaggregation (e.g., Valencia and Schaake 1973). Daily flows have also been generated by other techniques using steam flow records (Beard 1967; Payne et al. 1969; Quimpo 1968) and by river basin simulation models involving rainfall–runoff relationships (Linsley et al. 1975; Jettmar et al. 1979; Young et al. 1980).

Special problems must be solved for multisite models (concurrent records at various locations). Also, as discussed by Matalas and Wallis (1976), historical flow sequences may be of unequal length, may span different periods of time, or may be discontinuous over time. The Vardar/Axios River Basin master planning studies (see Chapter 13) considered such issues, as well as the need to transfer and adjust flow sequences to locations where no historical flow data existed.

11.3 DURATION ANALYSES

11.3.1 Hydroelectric Power Project without Storage for Stream Flow Regulation (Run of River)

For this type of hydroelectric power plant, the outflow from the reservoir utilized by the plant essentially equals the inflow. The water has been raised behind the dam to create a head, but there is no storage to provide hourly, daily, or seasonal regulation of stream flows. The head H, which is the vertical distance between the reservoir surface and the tailwater of the plant less hydraulic losses, and the flow Q define the power in kilowatts (kW) which the plant is capable of producing. The energy in kilowatt-hours (kWh) is determined by the time T over which the power is produced. The output is also affected by the efficiency of generation e. Thus,

$kW = QHe/11.8$ where Q is in cubic feet per second (cfs) and H is in feet (ft)
$kWh = QHeT/11.8$, where T is in hours

In the equations, the efficiency is the ratio between the actual and theoretical values of output, and is derived from mechanical and electrical losses in the turbines, generators, and transformers.

The variability of flows and hydroelectric power plant output may be studied by means of "duration curves." The duration curves on Figure 11.1 are based on a record of daily flows. The ordinate is the flow (Q) in cfs and the abscissa is the percent of time each Q is equaled or exceeded. The values of Q may be transformed by means of the equation above to values of kW, and the percentages may be converted to number of hours in the year (8760 hours). A grid may be imagined defined by horizontal lines having an interval of 1 kW and vertical lines having an interval of 1 hour, for which each box is equal to 1 kWh of energy. The area under the redefined duration curve is the annual energy output of the plant provided that the plant can pass all values of Q from the minimum to the maximum. In the more usual case, the installed capacity is lower, and the energy is limited to that defined by the area below a horizontal line corresponding to the largest flow carried through the turbines and may have to be further reduced for plant shutdowns during very low flows; the excess is wasted as "spillage" via the spillway and other outlet facilities. Because of the nature of turbine operation, depending on the magnitude and variability of flow utilized by the power plant, one or more generating units are used to obtain the installed capacity.

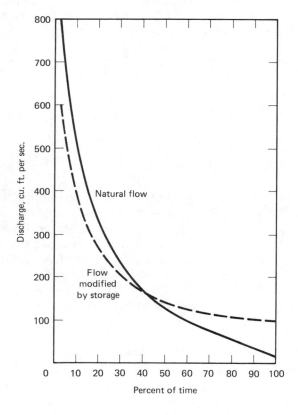

Figure 11.1 Duration curve based on daily flows.

Analyses of Risk and Uncertainty   Chap. 11

If the hydroelectric plant is constructed solely to serve an industrial plant or a single community, the "dependable capacity" and the dependable or "prime energy" of this "isolated" plant are determined at or near the minimum flow (which is equaled or exceeded 100% of the time). The "secondary energy" is the remaining energy produced up to the capability of the turbines. The secondary energy is less valuable than the prime energy since it is interruptible and cannot be guaranteed. When the plant is connected via transmission facilities to the regional electric system, its appropriate installed capacity and the energy utilized may be quite different because the problems of the plant's variable output are compensated for by the operation of the other power generating plants in the electric system. In this service, the hydro plant may have a higher installed capacity and produce more energy than an isolated plant, with less spillage of water. As an integrated plant, the dependable capacity of the hydroelectric plant is determined by the amount of alternative (usually thermal) capacity whose construction can be substituted for or deferred.

11.3.2 Hydroelectric Power Project with Pondage
(Run of River)

If a relatively small amount of reservoir storage is available to accommodate operational requirements throughout the week, it is referred to as "pondage." The availability of pondage permits the installation of a higher capacity than without it. To illustrate, suppose that the flow to be utilized by the plant is available at a rate of Q_1. Without pondage the capacity would be determined by Q_1 and H and the plant would operate for all 168 hours in a week. With pondage, the plant could be operated for 8 hours a day for 5 days per week or for a total of 40 hours, with a discharge Q_2 equal to $(168/40)Q_1$, or 4.2 Q_1. The appropriate installed capacity would therefore be 4.2 times as much. Such a plant could be more valuable either as an isolated plant serving an industrial firm operating 40 hours per week or as a plant that is integrated into a regional electric system.

The illustration above is somewhat oversimplified because it does not take account of the effect of varying head on plant capacity, nor does it consider the possible adverse effects of closing down the plant and shutting off flow downstream.

11.3.3 Hydroelectric Power Project with Seasonal Storage
as Well as Pondage (Storage Plant)

The availability of substantial storage permits the regulation of inflows and modification of the duration curves of daily outflows. The principal effects are to increase the lowest flows and decrease the highest flows. Not only can a more valuable hydroelectric plant be constructed (larger capacity, more dependability, more operating flexibility), but the reservoir can be operated for additional purposes such as flood control and low-flow augmentation. On the other hand, large drawdowns of the reservoir may interfere with recreation facilities (e.g., by curtailing operation of boat launching pads when the reservoir falls too low), may expose mud flats, or cause other adverse effects.

11.3.4 Pumped-Storage Hydroelectric Power Project

A pumped-storage plant has an upper reservoir and a lower reservoir, separated by a large vertical distance. Power is generated by releasing water from the upper to lower reservoir through the plant. The water released from the upper reservoir is then replaced by pumping water from the lower to the upper reservoir. The plant is usually equipped with units that operate as turbine/generators during hydroelectric power generation and as pump/motors during the pumping phase of the cycle. The overall efficiency of the combined generating/pumping cycle is less than for a generating plant alone, but the pumped-storage plant can be justified when a unit of energy generated is more valuable than a unit of energy needed to operate the pumps.

This and the three preceding subsections have shown how the variability of stream flow and the storage available to regulate the stream flow, on a daily and/or seasonal basis, are taken into account when establishing the capacity of a hydroelectric plant and operating the plant either in an isolated mode or as part of a large electric power system. For all these studies, the probabilities of the stream flows are determined by a statistical study of historic stream flows and defined by a duration curve (or its equivalent in tables or computerized analysis).

11.3.5 Other Types of Projects

Recreation Project. If a reservoir serves only recreation, a fairly constant level should be maintained during the recreation season. If the recreation overlaps with flood periods or if minimum flows must be released downstream to satisfy other requirements, the level may undergo substantial variations, and this may result in a loss of recreation values. A duration curve, or its analytical equivalent, of reservoir elevation versus percent of time equaled or exceeded during the recreation season may assist in determining recreation values.

Navigation Project. A duration curve, or its equivalent, showing flow, depth, or stage (elevation) of water surface versus percent of time equaled or exceeded during the navigation season can assist in determining when drafts must be limited or nagivation curtailed entirely.

Water Quality Management Project. A duration curve of flow versus percent of time equaled or exceeded, especially for the warm months when water quality problems are most serious, when considered with the prevailing water temperatures, can assist in the assessment of water quality problems and help to define the water available for dilution of wastewaters after treatment.

Irrigation Project. Duration curves of flow available for diversion to irrigation versus percent of time equaled or exceeded, for the irrigation season as a whole or for portions thereof, may be helpful for irrigation project studies.

11.3.6 Limitations of Duration Curves

The duration curve cannot provide good definition of flows at the lowest and highest values plotted at the extremes of the curve. Thus, it can be used only in a limited way for studies of low (drought) flows and of high (flood) flows. Furthermore, the duration curve does not account for sequences of flows that may occur (i.e., during the low-flow periods when flows are critical for, say, irrigation, or during high flow periods when a continuous history of a flood is important for determining reservoir operation procedures).

Better analyses of rare occurrences (floods and droughts) and of the sequences of flows during normal- and high-, and low-flow periods, require other techniques. Two methods that are commonly used for such purposes are frequency analyses and simulation analyses.

11.4 FREQUENCY ANALYSES

11.4.1 Normal Distribution—Water Supply Reservoir Project

A reservoir serving the single purpose of a water supply may be sized by determining the required volume of storage each year, based on the water supply demand and the variations in stream flow for that year. Such analyses over a period of record of n years would provide n values of required storage. These values of storage may be arrayed in order of magnitude $S_1 \cdots S_i \cdots S_n$ with the largest storage S_1 having an order number $m = 1$, the second largest with $m = 2$, and so forth, with the smallest storage having $m = n$.

If it is assumed that the record is a perfect representative sample of a long period of stream flows, the largest S_1 will be equaled or exceeded once in n years and will, therefore, have an "exceedence probability" in any year of $1/n$. The second largest will have an exceedence probability of $2/n$, and the general estimates for $S \geq S_m$ in terms of annual probability of occurrence p and return period T are as follows:

$$p = \frac{m}{n}$$

$$T = \frac{n}{m}$$

These formulas provide values of p or T that can be plotted on a graph against values of S_m. Other "plotting formulas" favored by some analysts take account of the size n and sometimes other characteristics of the sample (Haan 1977; Chow 1964).

Figure 11.2 is based on an analysis of a water supply reservoir (Fair et al., 1971). In this case it is desired to provide a continuous water supply, or draft on the reservoir, of 750,000 gallons per day (gpd) per square mile. A year-by-year analysis,

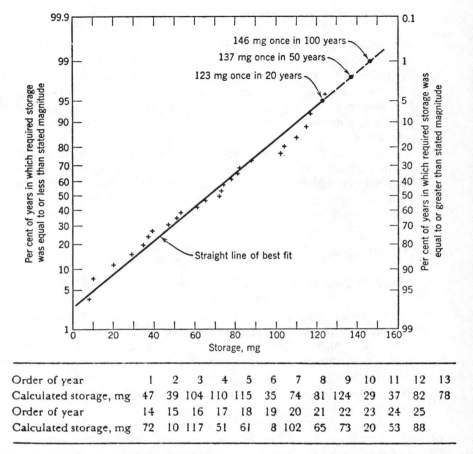

Order of year	1	2	3	4	5	6	7	8	9	10	11	12	13
Calculated storage, mg	47	39	104	110	115	35	74	81	124	29	37	82	78
Order of year		14	15	16	17	18	19	20	21	22	23	24	25
Calculated storage, mg		72	10	117	51	61	8	102	65	73	20	53	88

Figure 11.2 Frequency distribution of required storage plotted on arithmetic-probability paper. (From Fair et al., 1971.)

over the record of 25 years of flow, provides 25 values (n) of required storage (S). These are arrayed in order of size, $m = 1, 2, \ldots$, n, and each value of required storage is plotted on the figure at a position corresponding to its return period. The arrangement of the grid on the figure follows the "normal probability distribution" by ensuring that if the set of storage values has a perfect normal distribution, the points will plot in a straight line. The "line of best fit" in this case corresponds to the normal distribution, which is fully defined by the values of the *mean* $\bar{x}$ and *standard deviation s* of the sample set of storage values.

For this problem, the computation of the plotting position for each value of S_m was done by means of the formula

$$P(S \le S_m) = \frac{n + 1 - m}{n + 1}$$

On the special "normal probability paper," the straight line was defined by plotting $\bar{x}$ at 50% and $\bar{x} + s$ at 84.1%. The position of every point on the straight line is established by the number of standard deviations above or below the mean, with the percentage obtained from a table of normal probability values. Such tables and the formulas for computing $\bar{x}$ and s are found in any general textbook or reference on statistics (e.g., Haan 1977).

The required reservoir size for any specified level of service can be determined by reference to the figure. For example, if the reservoir is to provide for full service requirements in 19 of 20 years, the return period for reservoir failure is 20 years and the probability of failure in any one year is 0.05. In this case the required S is 123 million gallons (mg). In years when a reservoir having an S of 123 mg is not adequate, special conservation measures would be needed to reduce the draft on the reservoir below the normal design value of 750,000 million gallons per day (mgd) per square mile.

The preceding analysis of a water supply reservoir was based on the use of a frequency curve of annual storage values. The frequency curve was based on the assumption of a normal probability distribution. The normal probability distribution is a symmetrical distribution about the mean value; and in this case the mean and the median (50% value) coincide. For this problem the assumption of the normal distribution appears reasonable from a visual comparison of plotted points for the actual distribution and the line drawn for the theoretical distribution. The determination of the "goodness of fit" of a theoretical distribution using statistical tests (e.g., chi-square or Komalgorov-Smirnov methods) is beyond the scope of this brief presentation of frequency distributions. The selection of an appropriate theoretical distribution depends on the nature of the variability of the historical data.

11.4.2 Other Types of Frequency Distributions

Instead of the normal distribution for water supply storage, a log-normal distribution could have been considered. This is a distribution in which every piece of data (in this case a storage value) is processed in terms of its logarithmic value instead of original value (e.g., a storage of 10,000 acre-feet becomes 4.0 in logarithmic terms). The transformation can have the effect of changing a "skewed" distribution to a symmetrical or "normal" distribution.

Skewed distributions are often found to be suitable for the study of floods and droughts. Figure 11.3 compares five different distributions for flood discharges in the St. Mary's River at Stillwater, Nova Scotia (Kite 1977).

For both symmetrical and skewed distributions, a principal advantage of the theoretical distribution is that the use of a statistical method permits the estimation of rare occurrences that is not possible by simple interpretation of raw data. For example, the highest flow in a 20-year record can be stated to roughly have a probability of 0.05 and a return period of 20 years, but these values are very questionable. The highest value, while imagined to be the highest in a 20-year period, may actually be the highest value in the last 100 years but cannot be so determined because of inadequate record length. Also, the approach cannot be used to estimate the 200- or 500-year floods.

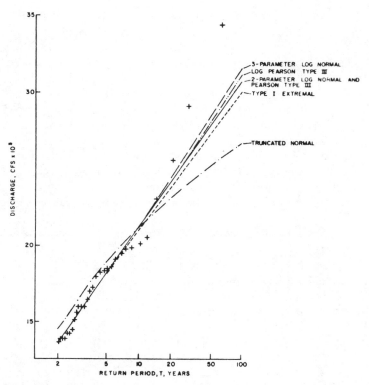

Figure 11.3 Comparison of frequency curves for various distributions—St. Mary's River, Nova Scotia. (From G. W. Kite, *Frequency and Risk Analysis in Hydrology*, Water Resources Publications, P. O. Box 2841, Littleton, Colorado 80161, USA.)

The various frequency distributions, as used in hydrologic analyses of water resources developments with an emphasis on flood flows, have been described by Kite (1977), Chow (1964), Haan (1977), and Yevjevich (1972). McCuen and Rawls (1979) analyzed a number of flood frequency estimates for ungaged watersheds in terms of accuracy, reproductivity, and probability. Dracup et al. (1980a; 1980b) performed statistical tests to analyze multiyear drought events. They state that time series involving droughts should be considered in terms of their duration, magnitude (water deficiency in case of drought), and severity (cumulative water deficiency).

11.4.3 Pollution Control Project

When stream flows are used to dilute wastewater discharges after treatment, the criterion often used for wastewater treatment plant design is the 10-year 7-day low flow. This refers to the annual minimum 7-day average flow that is equaled or exceeded with a return period or interval of 10 years. This corresponds to an annual exceedence probability of 0.1. A frequency analysis based on annual 7-day low-flow values can be used to determine the value for a 10-year return period. Actually, the

Analyses of Risk and Uncertainty   Chap. 11

flow and temperature of the receiving water are both important in determining the level of treatment required. If high temperature does not coincide with low flow, the design criteria for receiving waters as described above may have to be modified.

11.4.4 Flood Control Project

A reservoir designed for flood control purposes stores all or a portion of an inflow flood, with the result that the outflows are nondamaging values or produce less damage than if the dam were not in place. Depending on the reservoir volume used for flood control and the spillway capacity, the reservoir may range from full effectiveness for small floods to very little regulation effect for large floods (e.g., the spillway design flood).

A flood control program utilizing local protection works such as walls, levees, and other structural and nonstructural features is often designed for the flood of record, or a 25% greater value, or similar approach. Alternatively, the program may be based on the use of a flood with a specified frequency. From the standpoint of economic efficiency only, the design flood should be selected to maximize project net benefits. The flood insurance program sponsored by the U.S. federal government is based on the inundation resulting from the 100-year flood.

As discussed in Chapters 8 and 10, the benefit-cost analyses depend on the development of damage-frequency curves. These curves result from analyses of stage-discharge, stage-damage, and discharge-frequency relationships. The discharge-frequency analyses are carried out most often for log-Pearson type III, log-normal, or Gumbel distributions.

11.5 JOINT PROBABILITIES

Figure 11.4 shows the frequency curves for streams A and B and the sum of their simultaneous flows (E). Since the two streams are in the same general area and are affected by the same set of storms and other hydrologic/meteorological events, one would expect a frequency distribution for combined flows, in which the flow for each probability or return period would be close to the sum of the flows for streams A and B for the same probability. This logical approach is confirmed by a comparison of the frequency curve on this basis (C) with the actual frequency curve (E).

The joint frequencies for this and other selected problems may be determined by logical application of probability concepts, but this is generally an intractable problem for very complex interrelationships. One approach to this problem, in a river basin context, is to employ "brute force" solutions such as simulation methods using concurrent series of stream flows for each of the locations of interest. When the problem can be structured to fit programming solutions for stochastic inputs, chance-constraint methods can be considered. These approaches are discussed in Chapters 12 and 13.

An alternative approach is to adopt a method of sampling. This approach can be introduced by considering the analysis of any type of occurrence that can be described

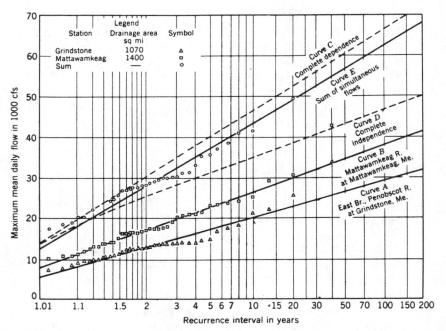

Figure 11.4 Example of joint frequency analysis. (From *Water Resources Engineering*, Third Edition, by Ray K. Linsley and Joseph B. Franzini. Copyright 1979 by McGraw-Hill Book Company. Used with the permission of McGraw-Hill Book Company.)

by a probability distribution. A probability distribution can be displayed in various forms: histogram, probability density function, and cumulative frequency curve.

The histogram shows the actual frequency or relative frequency (ordinate) for each value of, or interval of, variable (abscissa). The probability density function plots as a curve in which the area under the curve is equal to unity; the area under the curve bounded by an interval of variable is the relative frequency of the midpoint value in that interval. The cumulative frequency curve shows the actual or relative frequency of all values of variable up to a specified value.

Probability distributions provide the basis of a Monte Carlo sampling procedure. This may be introduced by considering the damage-frequency curve for a flood control project. Imagine that 1000 values of annual damages based on the frequency curve are written on pieces of paper and placed in a container. The container will now have more values for more frequent (lower) floods than for rarer (higher) floods. Proceed now to pull one of the papers from the container, record the value, and return the paper to the container. If this is done 100 times, the 100 values may be averaged to obtain the average annual flood damages. If this is done 500 or more times, the result will be more precise.

Now assume that five variables are studied for a more complex project or a system of projects, each of which can be defined by a probability distribution but

Analyses of Risk and Uncertainty   Chap. 11

where the joint probabilities are unknown. The procedure is to sample each variable once and obtain one overall result by applying these five values. Repeat the operation using another set of five values, one for each variable. Continue this until 100, 500, or 1000 overall results are obtained. These results may then be characterized by statistical parameters such as the mean and standard deviation or may be cast into a frequency distribution or frequency curve of overall results. The method assumes that the variables are independent of each other. It may be necessary to combine variables or make other adjustments where this is not the case.

11.6 COFFERDAM DESIGN FLOOD

An important problem of construction planning is that of protecting an area, within which a hydraulic structure will be built, against water damage. The construction may include the full or partial encircling of the work area with a low dam that diverts water away from the work area. The height of this "cofferdam" is established to protect against its overtopping by any flood less than a specified design discharge Q_D. If a flood discharge is greater than Q_D, the resulting overtopping of the cofferdam and damage within the work area is accepted by the sponsor. The sponsor thus accepts the risk of failure (overtopping) in lieu of paying a greater "premium on an insurance policy" (cost of the cofferdam) for a more costly (higher) cofferdam.

Analysis of the record of discharges in the affected river provides an estimate of the frequency of exceeding Q_D. This may be expressed as the "return period" or "return interval" T. The probability that Q_D will be exceeded in any year is p, and $p = 1/T$. The probability that Q_D will not be exceeded in any year is q. Since the combined probability of all possible outcomes is unity, $q = 1 - p$. The "design period" for the cofferdam is the number of years of its use, n.

The probability of nonoccurrence of cofferdam failure in n years is q^n. Again, since the total probability of all possible outcomes is unity, the probability of cofferdam failure is $1 - q^n$. All of the foregoing assumes the independence of annual events, which is reasonable for most problems of this type. Summarizing the formulation in various forms:

$$\text{Risk of failure } (Q > Q_D) = 1 - q^n = 1 - (1 - p)^n = 1 - \left(1 - \frac{1}{T}\right)^n$$

If the permissible risk of failure and the design period are specified, the value of p or T may be determined by the formula. Table 11.1 shows values of T for various levels of permissible risk and design period. For example, suppose that a cofferdam is to be in service for 5 years. If the cofferdam is designed to be high enough to protect against overtopping by a flood having a probability of occurrence in any one year of 0.1; this corresponds to a design return period of 10 years. Interpolating in the table, the probability that the cofferdam will be overtopped over the 5-year period of operation is about 0.4. This would not be acceptable unless the actual damage from overtopping is low. The 5-year risk of failure (0.4) is thus much greater than the 1-year risk (0.1).

TABLE 11.1 PROBABILITY THAT EVENT OF GIVEN RECURRENCE INTERVAL (T) WILL BE EQUALED OR EXCEEDED DURING PERIODS OF VARIOUS LENGTHS

T (yr)	Period (yr)							
	1	5	10	25	50	100	200	500
1	1.0	1.0	1.0	1.0	1.0	1.0	1.0	1.0
2	0.5	0.97	0.999	a	a	a	a	a
5	0.2	0.67	0.89	0.996	a	a	a	a
10	0.1	0.41	0.65	0.93	0.995	a	a	a
50	0.02	0.10	0.18	0.40	0.64	0.87	0.98	a
100	0.01	0.05	0.10	0.22	0.40	0.63	0.87	0.993
200	0.005	0.02	0.05	0.12	0.22	0.39	0.63	0.92

[a]In these cases the probability can never be exactly 1, but for all practical purposes its value may be taken as unity.

Source: From *Water Resources Engineering*, Third Edition, by Ray K. Linsley and Joseph B. Franzini. Copyright 1979 by McGraw-Hill Book Company. Used with the permission of McGraw-Hill Book Company.

11.7 SPILLWAY DESIGN FLOOD

A dam is designed so that it will not fail when the "spillway design flood" is routed through the reservoir and discharged downstream via the spillway and possibly other outlet works. For a major project, the conservative practice in the United States is to base the spillway design flood on the determination of the probable maximum precipitation (PMP) and the conversion of this precipitation pattern to flood flows by means of a "unit hydrograph" analysis. The PMP is based on the maximum conceivable combination of unfavorable meteorological events and the resulting flood is not normally assigned a frequency (return period). A committee of the American Society of Civil Engineers (according to Benson, 1962) has suggested that the PMP is perhaps equivalent to a return period of 10,000 years. For smaller projects, whose failure would not result in disastrous property damage or loss of life, planners often select the spillway flood on the basis of a frequency analysis. Such analyses provide estimates of peak discharge, but a full hydrograph must be also derived for design. Biswas (1971) has surveyed the return periods "commonly used" for different types of structures as follows: major dams with probable loss of life—earth, 1000 years, masonry or concrete, 500 years, costly dams with no likelihood of loss of life, 500 years; moderately costly dams, 100 years; and minor dams, 20 years. The return periods cited by Biswas are not believed to be typical of American practice, which tends to be more conservative. Designs based on return periods of 100 years and 20 years would have a very high probability of failure, based on the compounding of probabilities. For example, it can be shown from Table 11.1 that a 100-year flood has a 40% chance of occurring within 50 years.

The spillway design flood is different from the selected project design flood for flood hazard reduction. The latter concept relates either to a flood control reservoir to reduce downstream damages or to a local protection project involving levees, walls, and other structural and nonstructural measures.

It is possible, however, to consider the "flood control project" approach to the design of any type of dam. Kite (1977) has described a procedure in which the spillway design flood and floods of lower magnitude are assessed in terms of return period and damages incurred. The results of this approach are shown on Figure 11.5. The use of a larger design flood may require a larger spillway, a higher dam, and other measures that increase cost. The method considers the construction cost and the "risk cost" derived from estimates of damages caused by floods of various magnitudes. Kite identifies the damages as upstream damages (in the event of overtopping and subsequent failure of the dam) to recreation, piers, boats, and buildings, loss of power, and loss of water supply; to the structure itself, including dam fill eroded, repair time, powerhouse losses, and switchyard losses; and damage downstream from the dam, including deaths, injuries, property damage, and compensation for loss of water supply, power supply, telephone, road access, and lost employment. The property damages should be determined by carrying out a stage-damage analysis using estimated flood profiles. The stage-damage analysis involves integration of a damage-frequency curve (as discussed in Chapters 8 and 10). Balloffet (1979) and others (Katopodes and Strelkoff 1978; Strelkoff, Schamber, and Katopodes 1977; Xanthopoulos and Koutitas 1976) have developed methods to determine the water surface elevations downstream from a dam in the event of a dam break.

In past years, water resource project planners were not willing to admit that dams could fail, although such events occur every year, sometimes with grave consequences. Recently, the possibility that any dam will fail is being recognized not only in deciding whether a project will be undertaken with unfavorable geological and hydrologic conditions, but also in explicit accounting procedures that are adopted when making an economic analysis of the project. As noted in Chow (1954), there are now approximately 10,000 large dams in the world, 1000 of which are in independent basins. Kite (1977) indicates that the use of an average return period for design of 1000 years would give an estimate of at least one major dam failure each year. A study of spillway design practice by the American Water Works Association has shown that in Japan, where there are about 1700 dams, the average design return period for spillway floods is on the order of 200 years, which leads to an expected rate of failure of eight or nine dams annually.

11.8 ECONOMIC ALLOWANCE FOR CATASTROPHY RISK— DAM FAILURE

This section considers not only the possibility of a catastrophy but also the economic consequences of the event. In order to perform an analysis for a dam failure, it is necessary to estimate the probability of failure and the economic damages that ensue. This procedure should account for changes over the period of analysis in both the failure probability and the resulting damages.

Biswas and Chatterju (1971) have identified the following causes of failure, based on a study of over 1600 dams:

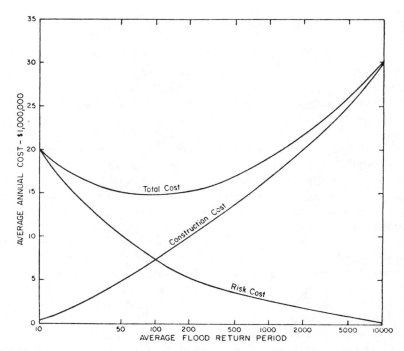

Figure 11.5 Average annual costs for different designs. (From G. W. Kite, *Frequency and Risk Analysis in Hydrology*, Water Resources Publications, P.O. Box 2841, Littleton, Colorado 80161, USA.)

Foundation problems	40%
Inadequate spillway	23%
Poor construction	12%
Uneven settlement	10%
High pore pressure	5%
Acts of war	3%
Embankment slips	2%
Defective materials	2%
Incorrect operation	2%
Earthquakes	1%

They cite another study in which it was found that 35% of over 300 dam disasters were due to inadequate spillway design. Other surveys of dam failure have been cited by Baecher et al. (1980), who estimated failure rates from 2×10^{-4} to 7×10^{-4} per dam-year based on these surveys. They estimated a failure rate of 2×10^{-4} per dam-year for dams built in the United States between 1940 and 1972. Also, based on these surveys, they estimated that about half of all failures occurred during the first 5 years after completion, and the remaining failures seemed to be distributed uniformly over the age of the dam. They note that although, overall, failures must be expected, the failure of a single dam will almost always occur for reasons that cannot be foreseen. They refer to Flint et al. (1976) in stating that recent studies of the historical occurrence of structural failures seem to indicate that possibly as few as 10% are attributable to mechanisms within the scope of either present or prospective methods of engineering analysis.

The foregoing provides a background for the procedure for evaluating dam failure, which was considered by the Water Resources Council in a *draft* "Manual of Procedures" (1979). The approach started with the premise that, on the average, there is 1 chance in 10,000 that a dam will fail in any year. It further assumed that half the failures occur during the initial filling of a reservoir, and the remainder are spread over the life of the structure. These concepts are shown in Figure 11.6. The "default" value of 10^{-4} per dam-year is about half the statistical failure rate of failures of dams constructed in the United States after 1940, but it was stated that the higher rate "primarily reflects failures of smaller, private sector dams that might be expected not to benefit from the same high degree of design conservation of dams designed and constructed by U.S. Government agencies."

The WRC draft manual made an important point with respect to the economic analysis concerning "sunk costs," which was not to account for the cost of replacement of the dam; rebuilding a new dam at the same place (which is seldom done) is a new project with its own costs and benefits. This view is consistent with the "with and without" assumptions adopted for the evaluation of costs and benefits. Under the draft procedure, the following four major components of the failure losses were to be estimated: (1) the direct physical damage due to the flooding after rupture of the dam; (2) the costs of emergency and rescue; (3) the loss of economic activity due to the unavailability of the land, of the facilities and equipment, and more generally to the loss of capital (a secondary economic loss might occur in economic sectors linked by supply and demand to those that have been affected by flooding; economic activity claimed for direct users in determining benefits would not be included here); and (4) the loss of foregone future benefits (all benefits evaluated in the cost-benefit analysis from the time the dam breaks).

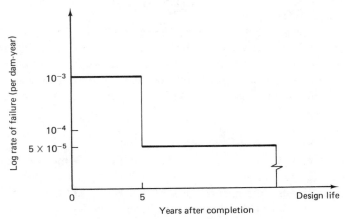

Figure 11.6 Failure rate distribution for time after completion, used for evaluation procedure. (From U.S. Water Resources Council, 1979.)

Under the draft procedure the failure, or risk, costs would be computed in terms of their expected value for the life of a dam, taking account of: (1) the potential losses in case of failure for the initial year and for each subsequent year of the design life; (2) the annual probabilities of failure that relate to these losses; (3) the annual loss (1) $\times$ (2); and (4) the discounting of all annual losses to a present-worth basis. The losses obtained as described above could be considered as reductions in the project benefits for purposes of benefit-cost evaluations. Baecher et al. (1980) suggest that preliminary estimates of the losses can be compared with the unadjusted benefits and costs to determine whether a more detailed risk-benefit analysis is justified.

Following the receipt of comments on the draft procedures, which revealed a wide disparity of opinion on rationale for risk-benefit analysis as well as disagreement on methodological details, the WRC determined that although studies of the consequences of failure were important and should be included in project studies and reports, the calculation of an adjusted B/C ratio based on the above-described procedure would not be required (U.S. Water Resources Council Procedures, 1980, pp. 64464-6).

11.9 STATISTICAL DECISION THEORY

A conceptual basis for statistical decision theory is often attributed to Bayes (1763), and this subject is, therefore, also referred to as Bayesian decision theory or analysis. The following brief introduction is based primarily on work by Benjamin and Cornell (1970) and Davis et al. (1972).

Problems in this field deal with factors that are not known with certainty; such factors can be referred to as "states of nature." In the case of dams, major uncertainties can include hydrology, soil and rock properties, grouting, earthquake occurrence and response to that ground motion, hydrodynamics, failure modes, and consequences of failure. For a number of these factors, the probabilities can be described by probability statements, ranging from probability (or return interval) for a single state of nature to a probability distribution for various states of nature (e.g., flood discharges).

Approaches may be developed to deal with three principal types of situations: (1) to make a decision based on the available information about nature; (2) to decide whether more information should be obtained; and (3) to decide how the new information should be processed. Davis et al. (1972) suggest that decision analysis is not a rigid method but a series of "signposts" and offer the following outline for an investigation:

A. Define the goal.
B. Define the decision to be made and identify the alternatives.
C. Analyze the project.
   1. Define the goal function.
      a. Select the state and decision variables.
      b. Set a time preference.
      c. Include a risk aversion.

2. Make a sensitivity analysis.
3. Develop the stochastic properties of the knowledge of the values of the state variables as a probability density function.
4. Calculate the outcomes of the various alternatives and determine the stochastic properties of the outcomes.
5. Eliminate the dominated alternatives.

D. Make the decision.
1. Calculate the expected value of the goal function for each alternative.
2. Choose an alternative to minimize the expected value of the goal function.

E. Evaluate the decision.
1. Determine the expected opportunity loss due to uncertain parameters in the problem.
2. Evaluate information-gathering programs.
   a. Determine the expected reduction in the expected opportunity loss with further information.
   b. Determine the full cost of obtaining further information.
   c. Obtain further information if warranted and repeat the process.

It is often helpful to visualize the process as a "decision tree" such as that shown in Figure 11.7 for a cofferdam for which four alternative cofferdam designs are analyzed (a_1, a_2, a_3, a_4). The performance of each cofferdam design will depend on the magnitude of the flood to which it is subjected. That flood (θ) will be from a range of values whose probability distribution can be determined by an analysis of the

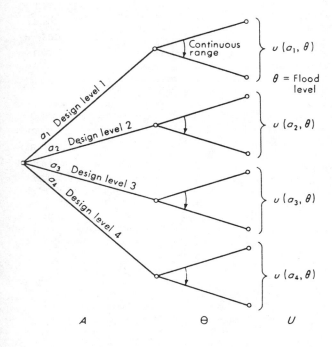

Figure 11.7 Decision tree for cofferdam. (From *Probability, Statistics and Decision for Civil Engineers*, by Jack R. Benjamin and C. Allin Cornell. Copyright 1970 by McGraw-Hill Book Company. Used with the permission of McGraw-Hill Book Company.)

historic record discharges. The performance of the cofferdam would have a value $u(a, \theta)$. In this case the state of nature is from a continuous range of values. In other cases, the state of nature may be a discrete number of possible values.

A decision rule is desired by which the optimal decision is identified. The rational decision can often be based on the "minimax" or "expected value" decision rules. The minimax decision rule, the simplest, is to choose the action with the *smallest possible loss*. This requires determining the maximum possible loss for each action and selecting the minimum of these values. The expected value rule may be illustrated for a simple case (see Figure 11.8).

The problem involves a construction engineer who must decide between a_1, paying for insurance (B) against work stoppage due to rain during a critical 1-day erection operation, and a_2, buying no insurance. If the true state of nature is θ_1, good weather, the consequences are A, which includes no insurance costs. If the state of nature is θ_2, bad weather, the consequences include monetary losses (C). The optimal decision depends on the likelihood of θ_2 and the *relative* degrees of seriousness of these various consequences. In this problem it is obvious that the engineer prefers A to B and B to C; the theory also formally requires that he or she prefer A to C. Numerical values need to be assigned to A, B, and C such that

$$u(A) > u(B) > u(C)$$

It is now necessary to determine the engineer's preferences in numerical terms. Typically, $u(A)$, the most preferable outcome, could be assigned the value 100, and $u(C)$, the least preferable outcome, could be assigned the value 0. The engineer's judgment is now brought into play by some means of interrogation to find a "crossover value" p^*, between 0 and 1, such that the engineer is "indifferent" between choosing a_1 with its certain consequence B and choosing a_2, the "lottery" with chance p^* of receiving A and $1 - p^*$ of receiving C. If in this case p^* is 0.3, we choose to assign $u(B)$ the value

$$u(B) = p^*u(A) + (1 - p^*)u(C)$$
$$= 0.3 \times 100 + (0.7) \times 0 = 30$$

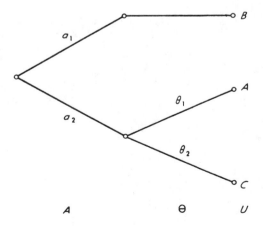

Figure 11.8 Decision tree for simple cofferdam evaluation. (From *Probability, Statistics and Decision for Civil Engineers*, by Jack R. Benjamin and C. Aklin Cornell. Copyright 1970 by McGraw-Hill Book Company. Used with the permission of McGraw-Hill Book Company.)

Analyses of Risk and Uncertainty   Chap. 11

This result is the expected value of the utility of action a_1. The expected value of the utility of action a_2 is related to the probability p that θ_1 is the true state. The decision maker should choose a_1 if and only if the expected utility given this action choice, $E[u|a_1]$, is greater than $E[u|a_2]$.

If the probability of θ_1 is $p = 0.4$,

$$E[u|a_1] = u(B) = 30$$
$$E[u|a_2] = pu(A) + (1-p)u(C)$$
$$= 0.4 \times 100 + 0.6 \times 0 = 40$$

and the engineer should choose a_2 since $40 > 30$.

Benjamin (n.d.) describes the use of both the minimax rule and the expected value rule, using the decision tree in Figure 11.9. The problem involves the potential damages of the overtopping of a dam by floods. The alternative actions are AA, do nothing except to install a warning system to be activated in the event of a "probable maximum flood" (PMF); AB, reconstruct the spillway at a cost of $1,486,000; or AC, change the reservoir operation to provide adequate reservoir storage in the event of the PMF.

The possible consequences of AA are discussed first. The PMF is estimated to have a return period of 10,000 years. The probability of the PMF not occurring in a 50-year period is 0.995, and in this case the outcome would be the value of agriculture served by the project. The probability of the PMF in a 50-year period is 0.005. If the dam fails, the economic loss would be $9,808,000. If the dam were then reconstructed at a cost of $3,766,000, the outcome would be the value of agriculture minus $13,574,000. If the dam were not reconstructed, the outcome would be a lower value of agriculture minus $9,808,000. Failure of the dam might involve the loss of up to 200 to 400 lives depending on the warning system and associated evacuation.

If the spillway were reconstructed (action AB), it is assumed that the dam cannot fail, and the outcome of failure is not valued. The outcome of action AB is therefore the value of agriculture minus the cost of reconstructing the spillway, $1,486,000. For the changed reservoir operation (action AC) it is again assumed that the dam cannot fail and this outcome is not valued. The outcome of action AC is, however, a loss in the value of agriculture.

For the minimax rule (minimum possible loss) the decision should be to select the action AB. The loss in agriculture with AC has not been determined, but could be very large.

If the expected value rule is implemented, action AA is optimal. The expected value depends on the probability of failure. For AA, the expected value of the outcome is $0.005 \times 13,574,000$, or $67,870. For AB, the expected value of the outcome is $1.000 \times 1,486,000$, or $1,486,000.

The discussion above is oversimplified, because it does not quantify the agricultural values nor take account of the time value of money (i.e., interest rate for discounting) or the time of failure. Earlier studies for this project had also indicated that the dam had performed adequately for 46 years without failure. The Bayesian approach can be used to provide better estimates of the probability of failure and its consequences based on this information.

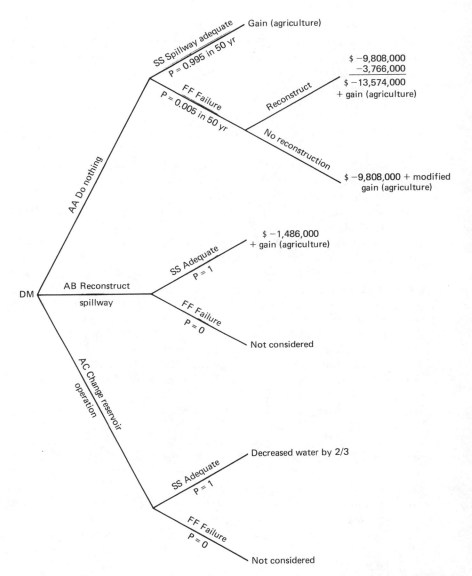

Figure 11.9 Decision tree for illustrating minimax and expected value rules. (From Benjamin, no date.)

The following is a list of some of the subjects that have been studied in recent years using the methods of statistical decision theory.

- Selection of crop rotations based on late season stream flows from reservoir releases and snow pack runoff (Anderson et al. 1971)
- Determination of number of interviews to secure information concerning recreation visitations (McCuen 1973)

- Optimal design of flood level, as affected by uncertainties in yearly flood peak stage (Duckstein et al. 1975)
- Optimal size of local flood protection, considering natural uncertainty of flood discharges and uncertainty of flood frequency model and its parameters (Wood and Rodriguez-Iturbe 1975)
- Economic uncertainties and their effect on flood-level planning (Szidarovszky et al. 1976)
- Selection of flood frequency model (Bodo and Unny 1976)
- Flood level reliability (Wood 1977)
- Worth of hydrologic data for nonoptimal decision making (Davis et al. 1979)
- Decision making under conditions of multiple objectives and uncertainty aspects (Goicoechea et al. 1979)
- Preference criterion for real-time flood control with a multipurpose reservoir, considering uncertainties of inflows, trade-offs between purposes, and subjective valuational inputs from the decision maker (Krzysztofowicz and Duckstein 1979)
- Statistical forecasting of mine water in rushes (Bogardi et al. 1979)
- Worth of additional data in setting premiums for flood damages (Attanasi and Karlinger 1979)
- Analysis of energy prices on determination of type of irrigation system (McAniff et al. 1980)

11.10 RISK ANALYSIS USING MONTE CARLO SIMULATION AND TRIANGULAR DISTRIBUTIONS

This method is based on work by Taylor et al. (1979) and requires a minimum of subjective estimation. It was recommended by the investigators after examination of the beta, triangular, adjusted triangular, Weibull, and normal distributions. It is based on selecting three estimates for each project *benefit* and *cost*: a most likely, an optimistic, and a pessimistic.

The "optimistic" estimate is the maximum benefit value (or minimum cost value) that can result from a particular benefit type (i.e., flood control) which can be obtained only if unusually good luck is experienced and everything "goes right"; call this a. The "pessimistic" estimate is the minimum benefit (or maximum cost) that will result only if unusually bad luck is experienced; call this c. The "most likely" estimate is the normal benefit or cost value which should be expected to occur most often if the activity could be repeated many times under similar circumstances; call this b.

The three estimates (a, b, c) define a triangular distribution. Symmetry is not required. The probability density function $f(x)$ for a benefit is described by Figure 11.10.

The interpretation of the function in Figure 11.10 is as follows:

$$f(x) = \frac{2(x - a)}{(b - a)(c - a)} \quad \text{for } a \leq x \leq b$$

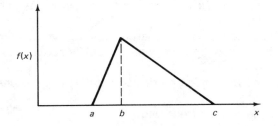

Figure 11.10 Triangular distribution.

$$= \frac{2(c - x)}{(c - b)(c - a)} \qquad \text{for } b \le x \le c$$

$$= \qquad 0 \qquad\qquad \text{elsewhere}$$

The cumulative probability density function $F(x)$ is the following:

$$F(x) = \int_0^x f_x(x)\, dx$$

$$= \frac{(x - a)^2}{(b - a)(c - a)} \qquad\qquad \text{for } a \le x \le b$$

$$= \frac{b - a}{c - a} + \frac{(c - b)^2 + (c - x)^2}{(c - b)(c - a)} \qquad \text{for } b \le x \le c$$

In order to use the technique in a simulation model, a random number U is obtained from a table or computer subroutine for a uniform distribution. For this the value of U is between 0 and 1 and has an equal probability of being selected. The value of U is transformed into a value of x as follows:

$$x = a + \sqrt{(b - a)(c - a)U} \qquad \text{for } 0 \le U \le \frac{b - a}{c - a}$$

$$= c - \sqrt{(c - b)(c - a)(1 - U)} \quad \text{for } \frac{b - a}{c - a} \le U \le 1$$

The value of x is one value of benefit, say for flood control. One value of cost for flood control is obtained by a similar procedure. Similarly, a value of benefit and a value of cost is obtained for each of the other other project purposes. They are all used to obtain a single value of net present value or B/C for the project.

Repeating the process a large number of times results in a frequency distribution of net present value or B/C values. An interpretation may now be made in terms of the risk analysis results. The following is an example of one determination of annual benefit for a navigation project:

$$a = \$30{,}000$$
$$b = \$40{,}000$$
$$c = \$60{,}000$$

$$x = 30{,}000 + \sqrt{(40{,}000 - 30{,}000)(60{,}000 - 30{,}000)U} \qquad \text{for } 0 \leq U \leq 0.33$$
$$= 60{,}000 - \sqrt{(60{,}000 - 40{,}000)(60{,}000 - 30{,}000)(1 - U)} \qquad \text{for } 0.33 \leq U \leq 1$$

A value of U equals 0.20 is drawn from a table of random numbers and gives a value of x equal to \$37,746. The same procedure would be repeated for all benefit values, and these summarized for total project benefits. The same procedure gives a value of total project costs. These could be applied with a designated discount rate and project life to yield *one* net benefit or benefit-cost value. By repeating the same process many times (100 to 1000), the many outcomes form a probability distribution from which a mean and standard deviation (or coefficient of variation) are calculated. For many trials, the procedure should be computerized.

Suppose that the procedure described above gives the following results:

$$\bar{x} = \text{mean } B/C \text{ ratio} \qquad = 1.5$$
$$s = \text{standard deviation} \qquad = 0.3$$
$$v = \text{coefficient of variation} = 0.3/1.5 = 0.2$$

Three interpretations may be made. The value of v may reflect too much uncertainty (as a percentage of the mean) or may be within the acceptable limit of the evaluating agency. A second interpretation is based on confidence limits. For example, for a 95% confidence interval based on a normal distribution of errors,

$$SL = 1.5 \pm (1.96) \times 0.3$$
$$= 1.5 \pm 0.6$$

Thus,

$$0.9 \leq x \leq 2.1$$

Therefore, one could be 95% confident that the B/C would fall within the range indicated (or there is a probability of 95% that the B/C will be within the range above).

A third interpretation could be based on determining the probability that the B/C would be higher than a designated value. The probability can be calculated by using the 100 to 1000 results of the simulation, or calculated from the mean and standard deviation.

11.11 RISK ANALYSIS USING MONTE CARLO SIMULATION AND STEP RECTANGULAR AND OTHER DISTRIBUTIONS

This approach has been recommended by staff of the World Bank (Reutlinger 1970; Pouliquen 1970). Each of the variables in the project analysis is given a probability distribution. As shown on Figure 11.11 for the analysis of the Mogadiscio Project (Pouliquen 1970), distributions were selected for seven variables. With the step

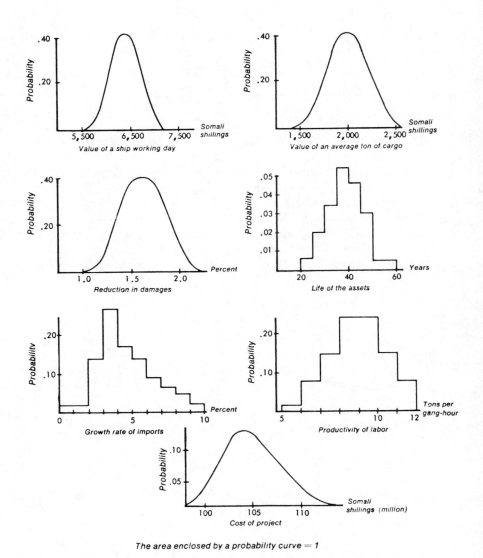

The area enclosed by a probability curve = 1

Figure 11.11 Probability distributions used in the simulation of Mogadiscio Port project. (From Pouliquen, 1970.)

rectangular distribution, probabilities were selected for intervals of values of the variable in steps from minimum to maximum.

One value of B/C, net benefit or return, was determined based on combining one value from each of the seven distributions. The value for each distribution was selected based on the nature of the distribution. For example, for the step distribution for productivity of labor, the following was obtained:

Probability	Tons per Gang-Hour	Cumulative Probability	Value Used
0.02	5–6	0.02	6
0.09	6–7	0.11	7
0.15	7–8	0.26	8
0.25	8–9	0.51	9
0.25	9–10	0.76	10
0.15	10–11	0.91	11
0.09	11–12	1.00	12
1.00			

The same procedure was followed for each of the other variables. For one simulation, a value was selected from a table of random numbers fitting a uniform distribution, say 7685. This value of 0.77 corresponds to a productivity of 10.1. For the *same* simulation, a random number of 6254 was selected, and for this a value was obtained for the growth rate of imports. Continuing, one value was obtained for each of the seven variables, and the simulation was run using these values to obtain *one* value of B/C, net benefit or rate of return.

The process is repeated, say 100 times, to obtain 100 values of B/C, net benefit or rate of return. These can be arranged in order of magnitude and a curve can be drawn of B/C versus the percent of time this B/C is equaled or exceeded.

11.12 SENSITIVITY ANALYSIS

Sensitivity analysis is, as discussed in earlier chapters, another way of dealing with problems of uncertainty. Other examples of sensitivity analysis are those of James et al. (1969), O'Laoghaire and Himmelblau (1972), Moore and Yeh (1980), Hansen et al. (1980), Dudley et al. (1976), and Byer (1979).

REFERENCES

ANDERSON, JAY C., HAROLD H. HISKEY, and SUWAPHOT KACKAWATHANA, "Application of Statistical Decision Theory to Water Use Analysis in Sevier County, Utah," *Water Resources Res.*, vol. 7, no. 3, June 1971.

ATTANASI, E. D., and M. R. KARLINGER, "Worth of Data and Natural Disaster Insurance," *Water Resources Res.*, vol. 15, no. 6, December 1979.

BAECHER, GREGORY B., M. ELISABETH PATE, and RICHARD DE NEUFVILLE, "Risk of Dam Failure in Benefit-Cost Analysis," *Water Resources Res.*, vol. 16, no. 3, June 1980.

BALLOFFET, A., "Dam Break Flood Routing. Two Cases," *MIT Semin. New Perspect. Safety Dams*, June 1979.

BAYES, T., "Essay towards Solving a Problem in the Doctrine of Chances," *Biometrika*, vol. 45, 1958 (reproduction of 1763 paper).

BEARD, L. R., "A Simulation of Daily Streamflow," *Proc. Int. Hydrol. Symp.*, Ft. Collins, Colo., 1967.

BENJAMIN, JACK, R., "Statistical Decision Theory Applied to Dams," n.d.

BENJAMIN, JACK R., and C. ALLIN CORNELL, *Probability, Statistics and Decision for Civil Engineers*, McGraw-Hill, New York, 1970.

BENSON, M. A., "Plotting Positions and the Economics of Engineering Planning," *J. Hydraul. Div., Proc. Am. Soc. Civil Eng.*, vol. 88, no. HY6, 1962.

BISWAS, A. K., "Some Thoughts on Estimating Spillway Design Flood," *Bull. Int. Assoc. Sci. Hydrol.*, vol. 26, no. 4, 1971.

BISWAS, A. K., and S. CHATTERJU, "Dam Disasters: An Assessment," *J. Eng. Inst. Can.*, vol. 54, no. 3, 1971.

BODO, BYRON, and T. E. UNNY, "Model Uncertainty in Flood Frequency Analysis and Frequency-Based Design," *Water Resources Res.*, vol. 12, no. 6, December 1976.

BOGARDI, I. L. DUCKSTEIN, A. SCHMIEDER, and F. SZIDAROVSZKY, "Stochastic Forecasting of Mine Water Inrushes," in *Advances in Water Resources*, Pergamon Press, Elmsford, N.Y., 1979.

BYER, PHILIP H., "Screening Objectives and Uncertainties in Water Resources Planning," *Water Resources Res.*, vol. 15, no. 4, August 1979.

CHOW, V. T., "The Log-Probability Law and Its Engineering Applications," *Proc. Am. Soc. Civil Eng.*, vol. 80, 1954.

CHOW, VEN T., ed., *Handbook of Applied Hydrology*, McGraw-Hill, New York, 1964.

CHOW, VEN T., "Evolution of Stochastic Hydrology," *Am. Geographical Union Conf., Appl. Kalman Filtering Theory Tech. Hydrol., Hydraul. Water Resources*, Pittsburgh, Pa. 1978.

DAVIS, DONALD R., CHESTER C. KISIEL, and LUCIEN DUCKSTEIN, "Bayesian Decision Theory Applied to Design in Hydrology," *Water Resources Res.*, vol. 8, no. 1, February 1972.

DAVIS, DONALD R., LUCIEN DUCKSTEIN, and ROMAN KRZYSZTOFOWICZ, "The Worth of Hydrologic Data for Non-optimal Decision Making," *Water Resources Res.*, vol. 15, no. 6, December 1979.

DOMOKOS, MIKLOS, JEAN WEBER, and LUCIEN DUCKSTEIN, "Problems in Forecasting Water Requirements," *Water Resources Bull.*, vol. 12, no. 2, April 1976.

DRACUP, JOHN A., KIL SEONG LEE, and EDWIN G. PAULSEN, JR., "On the Statistical Characteristics of Drought Events," *Water Resources Res.*, vol. 16, no. 2, April 1980a.

DRACUP, JOHN A., KIL SEONG LEE, and EDWIN G. PAULSEN, JR., "On the Definition of Droughts," *Water Resources Res.*, vol. 16, no. 2, April 1980b.

DUCKSTEIN, L., I. BOGARDI, F. SZIDAROVSZKY, and D. R. DAVIS, "Sample Uncertainty in Flood Levee Design: Bayesian vs. Non-Bayesian Methods," *Water Resources Bull.*, vol. 11, no. 3, June 1975.

DUDLEY, NORMAN J., DIANE M. REKLIS, and OSCAR R. BURT, "Reliability, Trade-offs, and Water Resources Development Modelling with Multiple Crops," *Water Resources Res.*, vol. 12, no. 6, December 1976.

FAIR, GORDON M., JOHN C. GEYER, and DANIEL C. OKUN, *Elements of Water Supply and Waste Water Disposal*, Wiley, New York, 1971.

FIERING, M. B., *Streamflow Synthesis*, Harvard University Press, Cambridge, Mass., 1967.

FIERING, M. B., and B. JACKSON, "Synthetic Streamflows," *Am. Geophys. Union Water Resources Monogr. 1*, 1971.

Analyses of Risk and Uncertainty   Chap. 11

FLINT A. R., et al., "Rationalization of Safety and Serviceability Factors in Structural Codes," Rep. 63, Construction Industry Research and Information Association, London, 1976.

GOICOECHEA, AMBROSE, LUCIEN DUCKSTEIN, and MARTIN M. FOGEL, "Multiple Objectives under Uncertainty, an Illustrative Example of Protrade," *Water Resources Res.*, vol. 15, no. 2, April 1979.

HAAN, CHARLES T., *Statistical Methods in Hydrology*, Iowa State University Press, Ames, Iowa, 1977.

HANSEN ROGER D., A. BRUCE BISHOP, and RANGESAN NARAYANAN, "Stochastic Approach to Waste Treatment Planning," *J. Water Resources Plann. Manage. Div., Proc. Am. Soc. Civil Eng.*, vol. 106, no. WR1, March 1980.

HIPEL, KEITH W., E. A. McBEAN, and A. I. MacLEOD, "Hydrologic Generating Model Selection," *J. Water Resources Plann. Manage. Div., Proc. Am. Soc. Civil Eng.*, vol. 105, no. WR2, September 1979.

HIRSCHMAN, ALBERT O., "Development Projects Observed," Brookings Institution, Washington, D.C., 1967.

HOWE, CHARLES W., "Benefit–Cost Analysis for Water System Planning." *Am. Geophys. Union Water Resources Monogr. 2*, 1971.

HUFSCHMIDT, M. M., and M. B. FIERING, *Simulation Techniques for Design of Water Resources Systems*, Harvard University Press, Cambridge, Mass., 1968.

JACKSON, BARBARA B., "The Use of Streamflow Models in Planning," *Water Resources Res.*, vol. 11, no. 1, February 1975.

JAMES, I. C., III, B. T. BOWER, and N. C. MATALAS, "Relative Importance of Variables in Water Resources Planning," *Water Resources Res.*, vol. 5, no. 6, December 1969.

JETTMAR, R. U., G. K. YOUNG, R. K. FARNSWORTH, and J. C. SCHAAKE, JR., "Design of Operational Precipitation and Streamflow Networks for River Forecasting," *Water Resources Res.*, vol. 15, no. 6, December 1979.

KATOPODES, N., and T. STRELKOFF, "Computing Two-Dimensional Dam-Break Flood Waves," *J Hydraul. Div., Proc. Am. Soc. Civil Eng.*, vol. 104, no HY9, September 1978.

KAYNOR, EDWARD R., "Uncertainty in Water Resources Planning in the Connecticut River Basin," *Water Resources Bull.*, vol. 14, no. 6, December 1978.

KITE, G. W., *Frequency and Risk Analysis in Hydrology*, Water Resources Publications, Fort Collins, Colo., 1977.

KRZYSZTOFOWICZ, ROMAN, and LUCIEN DUCKSTEIN, "Preference Criterion for Flood Control under Uncertainty," *Water Resources Res.*, vol. 15, no. 3, June 1979.

LETTENMAIER, DENNIS P., and STEPHEN J. BURGES, "Use of State Estimation Techniques in Water Resources System Modelling," *Water Resources Bull.*, vol. 12, no. 1, February 1976.

LINDBLOM, CHARLES E., *The Policy-Making Process*, Prentice-Hall, Englewood Cliffs, N.J., 1968.

LINSLEY, R. K., and I. R. FRANZINI, *Water Resources Engineering*, 3rd ed., McGraw-Hill, New York, 1979.

LINSLEY, RAY K., MAX A. KOHLER, and JOSEPH L. H. PAULHUS, *Hydrology for Engineers*, 2nd ed., McGraw-Hill, New York, 1975, Chap. 10.

McANIFF, RICHARD J., MARSHALL FLUG, and JAMES WADE, "Bayesian Analysis of Energy Prices on Inflation," *J. Water Resources Plann. Manage. Div., Proc. Am. Soc. Civil Eng.*, vol. 106, no. WR2, July 1980.

McCUEN, RICHARD H., "A Sequential Division Approach in Recreational Analysis," *Water Resources Bull.*, vol. 9, no. 2, April 1973.

McCUEN, RICHARD H., and WALTER J. RAWLS, "Classification of Evaluation of Flood Flow Frequency Estimation Techniques," *Water Resources Bull.*, vol. 15, no. 1, February 1979.

MACK, RUTH P., *Planning on Uncertainty: Decision-Making in Business and Government Administration*, Wiley, New York, 1971.

MAJOR, DAVID C., "Multi-objective Water Resource Planning," *Am. Geophys. Union Water Resources Monogr.* 4, 1977.

MATALAS, N. C., and J. R. WALLIS: "Generation of Synthetic Flow Sequences," in *Systems Approach to Water Management*, A. K. Biswas, ed., McGraw-Hill, New York, 1976.

MOORE, NANCY N., and WILLIAM W. G. YEH, "Economic Model for Reservoir Planning." *J. Water Resources Plann. Manage. Div., Proc. Am. Soc. Civil Eng.*, vol. 106, no. WR2, July 1980.

O'LAOGHAIRE, D. T., and D. M. HIMMELBLAU, "Modeling and Sensitivity Analysis for Planning Decisions in Water Resources Expansion," *Water Resources Bull.*, vol. 8, no. 4, August 1972.

PAYNE, K., W. R. NEUMAN, and K. D. KERRI, "Daily Streamflow Simulation," *J. Hydraul. Div., Proc. Am. Soc. Civil Eng.,* vol. 95, no. HY4, July 1969.

POULIQUEN, LOUIS Y., "Risk Analysis in Project Appraisal," *World Bank Staff Occas. Paper 11*, 1970.

QUIMPO, R. G., "Stochastic Analysis of Daily River Flows," *J. Hydraul. Div., Proc. Am. Soc. Civil Eng.*, vol. 94, no. HY1, January 1968.

REUTLINGER, SHLOMO, "Techniques for Project Appraisal under Uncertainty," *World Bank Staff Occas. Paper 10*, 1970.

STRELKOFF, T., D. SCHAMBER, and N. KATOPODES, "Comparative Analysis of Routing Techniques for the Floodwave from a Ruptured Dam," Dam-Break Flood Routing Model Workshop, Hydrology Committee, U.S. Water Resources Council, Bethesda, Md., October 1977.

SZIDAROVSZKY, F., I. BOGARDI, L. DUCKSTEIN, and D. DAVIS, *Water Resources Res.*, vol. 12, no. 4, August 1976.

TAYLOR, B. W., K. R. DAVIS, and R. M. NORTH, "Risk, Uncertainty, and Sensitivity Analyses for Federal Water Resources Project Evaluation," U. S. Water Resources Council, March 1979.

THOMAS, H. A., and M. B. FIERING, "Mathematical Synthesis of Streamflow Sequences for the Analysis of River Basins by Simulation," in *Design of Water-Resource Systems*, A. Maass et al., Harvard University Press, Cambridge, Mass., 1962.

U.S. GENERAL ACCOUNTING OFFICE, "Better Analysis of Uncertainty Needed for Water Resource Projects," June 2, 1978.

U.S. INTER-AGENCY COMMITTEE ON WATER RESOURCES, "Proposed Practices for Economic Analysis of River Basin Project," May 1950; rev. May 1958.

U.S. WATER RESOURCES COUNCIL, "Principles and Standards for Planning Water and Related Land Resources," September 10, 1973; rev. December 14, 1979; rev. September 29, 1980.

U.S. WATER RESOURCES COUNCIL, "Manual of Procedures for Evaluating Benefits and Costs of Federal Water Resources Projects," Review Draft, 1979.

U.S. WATER RESOURCES COUNCIL, "Procedures for Evaluation of National Economic Development (NED) Benefits and Costs and Other Social Effects in Water Resources Planning (Level C)," September 29, 1980.

U.S. WATER RESOURCES COUNCIL, "Economic and Environmental Principles and Guidelines for Water and Related Land Resources Implementation Studies," March 10, 1983.

VENCIA, D., and J. C. SCHAAKE, JR., "Disaggregation Processed in Stochastic Hydrology," *Water Resources Res.*, vol. 9, no. 3, June 1973.

WIENER, AARON, *The Role of Water in Development*, McGraw-Hill, New York, 1972.

WOOD, ERIC, "An Analysis of Flood Levee Reliability," *Water Resources Res.*, vol. 13, no. 3, June 1977.

WOOD, ERIC F., and IGNACIO RODRIGUEZ-ITURBE, "Bayesian Inference and Decision Making for Extreme Hydrologic Events," *Water Resources Res.*, vol. 11, no. 4, August 1975.

XANTHOPOULOS, T., and C. KOUTITAS, "Numerical Simulation of a Two-Dimensional Flood Wave Propogation Due to a Dam Failure," *J. Hydraul. Res.*, IAHR, vol. 14, no. 4, 1976.

YEVJEVICH, V., *Stochastic Processes in Hydrology*, Water Resources Publications, Ft. Collins, Colo., 1972.

YOUNG, G. K., T. R. BONDELID, and S. A. DALEY, "Methods of Water Supply Forecasting," *Water Resources Res.*, vol. 16, no. 3, June 1980.

TWELVE

Mathematical Models for the Development of Planning Alternatives

12.1 INTRODUCTION

The next two chapters discuss how mathematical tools can be used in generating alternatives for the planning process (Chapter 12), and how mathematical and other approaches can be used to evaluate competing alternatives in multiobjective planning (Chapter 13). In Chapter 12 an introduction is provided to a set of powerful, usually computer based, tools for helping to sort out from among the numerous possible plans those that most deserve further study and examination. Techniques such as linear programming, dynamic programming, integer programming, network analysis, and simulation have an important role in this process. Evaluating candidates when multiobjectives are considered (in Chapter 13) requires a much greater integration of public preference decision making. While such mathematical techniques as those presented in Chapter 12 can be used, many other less quantitative procedures are also turned to in complex problem solving with multiobjectives. Thus, the structure of these two chapters is to focus on the basic mathematical building blocks for planning here and to continue on to the more difficult integration methods in the next chapter.

The *mathematical model* is an essential tool in modern water resources planning and management. Broadly, such a model consists of one or more statements, expressed in mathematical terms, which describe interrelationships among variables.

The analysis of mathematical models has been greatly facilitated by the availability of modern electronic computers, principally of the digital type. Such computers often permit the solution of problems that would otherwise be impossible to analyze, except crudely, by other means.

The problems stressed in this chapter focus on planning and management issues such as the allocation of scarce resources (particularly water and money) and the determination of the appropriate scales (sizes) and operation policies of projects that are economically efficient. This chapter cannot, for lack of space, deal with the full range of mathematical models, computer codes, and applications. Thus, engineering problems that have a large design content are not discussed; such problems for water resources facilities, for which computer applications are common, include structural analyses (stability, stresses in structural elements, foundation stresses); hydrologic analyses (quantity, occurrence, and movement of water); hydraulic analyses (depths, velocities, and water pressure; sediment movement); water and waste treatment analyses (selection of treatment methods, layouts of elements); and many other areas in the practice of civil, mechanical, and electrical engineering and of other technical specialities.

12.2 USE OF COMPUTERS AND MATHEMATICAL BACKGROUND

Bugliarello and Gunther (1974) have described various types of electronic computers and considered their status and future role in water resources technology.

The digital computer is generally found to be the most efficient, flexible, and cost-effective type for handling large amounts of data and carrying out the analysis of mathematical models in water resources planning. The digital computer is composed of three major elements: the central processing unit (CPU), the memory, and the input–output (I/O) devices. Technological improvements, particularly since the mid-1960s, have resulted in several generations of digital computers and marked reductions in the unit cost of automatic data processing (ADP).

Most important water resource analyses require computers with substantial memory and I/O capabilities. When this is not the case, minicomputers may be useful. These inexpensive computers have found wide application in process control, data management, and data communications.

Analog computers are used at most in 1 or 2% of water resources planning applications. The early analog computers were special-purpose machines. In the 1950s, general-purpose machines were developed and became popular. They are most effectively used to solve problems stated as integral/differential equations. The analog computer is composed of amplifiers—integrators, adders, and multipliers—that are patched or wired together to represent a problem. Whereas the digital computer generally performs operations sequentially and can store a complete record of any operation, the analog computer performs simultaneous operations and has essentially no memory facilities. The digital computer must use a numerical approximation method (e.g., finite differences or finite elements) to solve differential equations, whereas the analog computer produces a continuous exact solution.

Hybrid computer systems are composed of both a digital and an analog computer, linked by a mating interface, and incorporating the best features of both. The accuracy, memory, and capacity of digital is combined with the speed of analog.

Basic mathematical concepts for systems analyses emphasizing optimization techniques are briefly reviewed in the next several sections. Methods of the calculus are covered in any college textbook on the subject and in textbooks on systems analysis (see Section 12.4.4).

12.3 SYSTEMS ANALYSIS AND OPERATIONS RESEARCH

12.3.1 Systems Analysis

Systems Analysis, in a generic sense, can refer to any orderly and scientific approach to problem solving. It includes traditional engineering methods and the more recently developed mathematical methods of the field of *operations research*. A systems approach applying to both traditional and new methodologies includes at least the following:

- Problem definition, including objectives and constraints
- System modeling—description of the elements of the system and definition of their interrelationships and interactions
- Generation of alternatives
- Evaluation of competing alternatives
- Implementation

Flow sheets or other charts and word descriptions may be used to define the boundaries of the system and its elements. Tables, charts, mathematical equations, logic statements, and word descriptions are means of describing the system elements and their relationships, the inputs and outputs of the system, and any feedback between outputs and inputs.

A simple *objective* statement would be: "Develop and operate water resources project at minimum cost consistent with meeting service requirements and legal, public health, and aesthetic specifications." The latter portion of this statement may be taken as a set of *constraints*, and these requirements may be stated separately from the principal objective of minimum cost. A more complex objective statement may involve more than one objective, which would require some means of weighting them or considering trade-offs.

Traditional approaches for analyzing systems are based on studying a limited number of projects and combinations of projects that are judged most likely to be suitable in achieving the objectives. These are formulated by screening methods and other techniques (such as those discussed in Chapter 5) that depend for their effectiveness on engineering experience and intuition. Such traditional methods are difficult to implement for multiunit, multipurpose systems, particular when there are many options for employing limited resources (natural, economic, etc.). The newer methods of systems analysis, the operations research techniques, include a number of well-ordered approaches to problem solving which are particularly flexible in being able to value many possible combinations.

If a minimum-cost objective is firm and exclusive, it may be possible to develop a single solution to present to decision makers. In many cases, however, the objective(s) is not as clear cut, and several alternatives may be worthy of presentation to the decision makers because they contribute in effective ways to the components of the objective(s).

12.3.2 Operations Research

The roots of *operations research* (OR) can be traced back many decades when early attempts were made to use the scientific approach in the management of organizations. The beginning of the activities called operations research, however, is generally attributed to the military services of the allied powers early in World War II, in allocating scarce resources to various military operations and to activities within each operation in an effective manner (Hillier and Lieberman, 1980). Since the war, OR has had extensive growth in industry, business, and government. This growth has been attributed to the improvement in OR techniques and to the availability of powerful electronic computers.

In the water resources field, progress in the employment of OR techniques has often followed their development in industry and business. A number of papers on OR applications in water resources planning were published in the 1960s (three are discussed in a later section on water quality management applications). Work in the Harvard Water Program had great impact (Maass et al. 1962; Hufschmidt and Fiering 1966), and mathematical methods became important in the planning and operation of the Columbia River System (Shoemaker 1963). The first major book on the subject appeared in 1970 (Hall and Dracup 1970), and the body of literature grew so extensively that a selected annotated bibliography on the analysis of water resource systems appeared in 1969 (Gysi and Loucks 1969).

A common approach applies to most OR methods. The *system* is described by means of a *mathematical model*. This model consists of equations, logic statements, and other instructions for processing available data and/or generating and processing synthetic data.

The controllable and partially controllable inputs are the *decision variables*. A *policy*, or set of decisions, results for each set of values for the decision variables. Restrictions applied to the model, or *constraints*, may include physical, economic, or any other quantities expressible in mathematical terms. A policy that does not violate any constraints is a *feasible policy*, and the set of all feasible policies constitutes the *feasible policy space*.

The *state variables* represent the condition of the system at any time or place. The state variables are affected by *system parameters* which may be constant or which may vary in a prescribed manner.

In an OR technique, the *objective function* is a means for expressing the concepts of *optimality* or *best*. In more general terms, the objective function is a statement by means of which the consequences or output of the system can be judged. For example, in a water resources context, an objective function can define the cost as a function of various magnitudes of resources used or developed.

For almost all problems, the computer is used as an aid to the solution. Because of this, OR applications require a complete and explicit definition of the system and explicit statements that anticipate intermediate results and determine alternative paths of processing information. The ordered procedure for directing the solution of a programming problem is referred to as an *algorithm*. To apply OR techniques, approximations, simplifying assumptions, and transformations into mathematical forms that are tractable are often necessary. It is important that, after such procedures are applied, the model remains a valid representation of the system.

12.3.3 Types of Mathematical Models

There are various types of mathematical models. One classification is related to the kinds of mathematical functions involved. The following is based largely on the definitions by Haimes (1977).

In a *linear* model, the objective function and the constraints are in linear form. In a *nonlinear* model, part or all of the constraints and/or the objective function are nonlinear.

In *deterministic* models, or elements of models, each variable and parameter is assigned a definite fixed number or a series of fixed numbers for any set of conditions. In the *probabilistic* (or *stochastic*) model, the variables and parameters and the structure of the model may be more difficult to define.

Static models do not explicitly take the variable time into account, whereas *dynamic* models do. This distinction is not always limiting in the *linear programming* (LP), *dynamic programming* (DP), and other named operations research techniques, as most can be used for both static and dynamic problems.

In a *lumped parameter* model, the various parameters and dependent variables are homogeneous throughout the system. A *distributed parameter* model takes account of variations in behavior from point to point throughout the system.

The principal modeling techniques have been classified by Meta Systems (1975) as: (1) analytical optimization models and techniques; (2) probabilistic models and techniques; (3) statistical techniques; and (4) simulation and search or sampling techniques.

The *analytical optimization* models include the methods that use the classical calculus and Lagrange multipliers as well as the mathematical programming techniques: linear, nonlinear, and dynamic. Network models such as PERT are also briefly mentioned in this chapter and are disucssed for the critical path method (CPM) version in Chapter 18.

Probabilistic techniques are used to describe stochastic system elements by means of appropriate statistical parameters. Techniques of queuing and inventory theory are of this type. Queuing models that predict such characteristics as waiting-time means and variances may provide input to optimization models that utilize either analytical techniques or simulation and search approaches. Discussion of these methods is included later in this chapter.

Statistical techniques include such methods as multivariate analysis, statistical inference, and decision theory. These techniques have wide application to the analysis of hydrologic data, and the interested reader may find them elaborated in other texts (e.g., Yevjevich 1972a, b; Haan 1977). Some aspects of hydrologic data analysis and decision theory are presented in Chapter 11.

Simulation and *search* or sampling techniques are widely used in water resources planning. Simulation is a descriptive technique that incorporates the quantifiable relationships among variables and describes the outcome of operating a system under a given set of inputs and operating conditions. If an objective function is defined, the values of the objective for several runs generate a "response surface." The model then becomes prescriptive by combining it with sampling or search techniques that explore the response surface and seek near-optimal or optimal solutions. Examples of simulation models are given in this chapter.

A complex water resource system may have to be analyzed in terms of multiunit operation, multipurpose outputs, and multiobjectives. Simulation models that have been developed for such systems are discussed in Chapter 13. That chapter also contains a description of decomposition and multilevel approaches and other special methods to deal with trade-offs among various purposes and objectives.

12.4 APPROACHES TO OPTIMIZATION

At the heart of optimization is the desire to solve the following problem:

Find $x_1, x_2, \ldots, x_n$, such that

Min or Max $f(x_1, x_2, \ldots, x_n)$

subject to: $\quad g_1(x_1, x_2, \ldots, x_n) \leq b_1$

$\qquad\qquad g_2(x_1, x_2, \ldots, x_n) \leq b_2$

$$\vdots \qquad\qquad \vdots$$

$\qquad\qquad g_m(x_1, x_2, \ldots, x_n) \leq b_m$

The function $f(x_1, x_2, \ldots, x_n)$ is the objective function; $x_1, x_2, \ldots, x_n$ are decision variables; and $g_i(x_1, x_2, \ldots, x_n) \leq b_i$ are constraints.

There are many methods for solving this problem. For simple problems, graphic functions can lead to solutions, or methods of calculus such as Lagrange multipliers may be helpful. However, for large problems, different solution techniques are needed, each requiring a special structure for the objective function and constraints. Major classes of these techniques are described next.

12.4.1 Linear Programming

Linear programming and its offshoots are probably the most widely used methods of operations research in industry and business and are often applied in certain areas of water resource planning (e.g., agricultural studies). They are suitable for problems in which it is desired to allocate scarce resources among various activities in an optimal manner. This section describes the basic version of linear programming (LP), in which all functions are in linear form. Other methods that have a structure similar to that of LP but that can handle nonlinear and other special forms of the functions are discussed in a later subsection.

The following *objective function* is to be optimized (maximized or minimized):

$$Z_x = c_1 x_1 + c_2 x_2 + \cdots + c_n x_n$$

subject to the following *constraints*:

$$a_{11} x_1 + a_{12} x_2 + \cdots + a_{1n} x_n \leq b_1 \quad (\text{or} \geq b_1, \text{or} = b_1)$$
$$a_{21} x_1 + a_{22} x_2 + \cdots + a_{2n} x_n \leq b_2 \quad (\text{or} \geq b_2, \text{or} = b_2)$$
$$\vdots \qquad\qquad \vdots$$
$$a_{m1} x_1 + a_{m2} x_2 + \cdots + a_{mn} x_n \leq b_m \quad (\text{or} \geq b_m, \text{or} = b_m)$$

for all $x_j \geq 0$.

The input data include all the constants a_{ij} and c_j and amounts of the resources b_i, and the problem is to find $x_1, x_2, \ldots, x_n$.

The solution of relatively simple LP problems can be demonstrated graphically as shown by the following example, which is adapted from a problem formulated by Hillier and Lieberman (1980, pp. 17–21).

An irrigation project is to be developed. There is 1800 acre-feet of water available annually. Two high-value specialty crops, A and B, are considered for which water consumption requirements are 3 acre-feet per acre and 2 acre-feet per acre, respectively. It has also been determined that the planting of more than 400 acres to crop A or 600 acres to crop B would cause an adverse effect on the market for these special crops. It has been estimated that each acre devoted to crop A will result in $300 profit, while an acre of crop B will net $500. From this description, the *decision variables* will be the acres of crop A, x_a, and the acres of crop B, x_b, and the problem may be formulated as:

$$\text{Maximize } Z = 300 x_a + 500 x_b$$

subject to:

$$x_a \leq 400$$
$$x_b \leq 600$$
$$3 x_a + 2 x_b \leq 1800$$

and

$$x_a \geq 0, \quad x_b \geq 0$$

A *feasible solution* is a value of (x_a, x_b) for which all the constraints are satisfied. The feasible solutions are shown by the shaded area in Figure 12.1. It is now desired to select the point in the shaded area that maximizes the objective function. Lines are drawn as shown on Figure 12.2 for the objective function with different values of Z (100,000; 200,000, etc.) and it is found that the maximum is

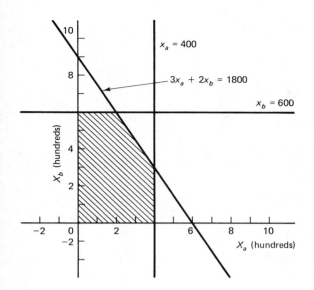

Figure 12.1 Shaded area shows permissible values of (x_a, x_b). (From Hillier and Lieberman, 1980.)

reached at an extreme point where $Z = \$360,000$ at $x_a = 200$ acres and $x_b = 600$ acres.

In most LP problems in water resources planning, there are too many decision variables to permit a simple graphical solution. Fortunately, most computers are fitted with software to solve LP problems using the *simplex algorithm* developed by Dantzig (1963).

A fundamental property of linear programming upon which the simplex method is based is that the optimal solution is a "corner-point feasible solution" (Hillier and Lieberman 1980). The simplex method does not examine all the feasible solutions. The procedure starts at a corner-point feasible solution and moves from this extreme point along an "edge" to an adjacent extreme point having a larger value of Z. The procedure is continued. When no adjacent extreme point has a larger value of Z, an optimal solution has been reached and the procedure stops. Computer codes are widely available (e.g., IBM's MPS System) for solving LP problems of extremely large size (thousands of constraints and variables).

12.4.2 Dynamic Programming

Dynamic programming (DP) is a mathematical technique that is often useful for making a sequence of interrelated decisions where nonlinearities in the objective function or constraints are present. It provides a systematic procedure for determining the combination of decisions which maximizes overall effectiveness (Hillier and Lieberman 1980). There is no standard mathematical formulation for dynamic programming, and general DP computer codes are usually not available. The procedures are not difficult, however, and a computational code can be written for each application. Although there are similarities in the construction of various DP

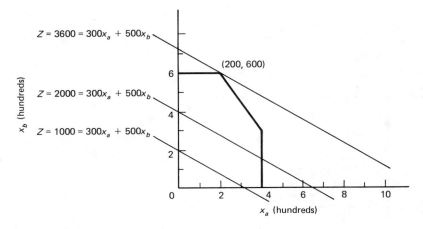

Figure 12.2 Values of (x_a, x_b) that maximize $3x_a + 5x_b$. (From Hillier and Lieberman, 1980.)

problems, the specific approach and the necessary equations are tailored to suit the actual conditions.

The following problem will illustrate the features of dynamic programming. This water resources problem has been adapted from the "stagecoach problem" developed by Wagner and presented by Hillier and Lieberman (1980, pp. 266–70).

It is desired to build an aqueduct to convey water from point 1 to point 10. From point 1, the route may extend to points 2, 3, or 4. From one of these points, the route proceeds to 5, 6, or 7, then to 8 or 9, and finally to point 10. The schematic arrangement is shown on Figure 12.3, which also shows the cost of the route between any two points considered in millions of dollars. There are 18 possible permutations in the route from point 1 to point 10 ($3 \times 3 \times 2 \times 1$); each could be valued and the least-cost solution selected. Dynamic programming reduces the valuation process by an ordered procedure.

For this problem there are four *stages* of the route from *state* 1 to *state* 10. The route selected will be $1 \rightarrow x_4 \rightarrow x_3 \rightarrow x_2 \rightarrow x_1$, where $x_1 = 10$. With this subscripting convention, x_n ($n = 1, 2, 3, 4$) is the decision variable (state number) to be selected when there are $n - 1$ more stages to go. For the route between state s and immediate destination x_n, the cost is $f_n(s, x_n)$. The x_n that minimizes $f_n(s_1, x_n)$ is denoted by x_n^*, and the corresponding minimum cost is $f_n^*(s)$. The solution proceeds as shown in the four tableaus in Figure 12.4.

The first tableau refers to the final stage. In this case, the route is between state 8 or 9 and immediate destination x_1, which is also x_1^*. The cost $f_1(s, x_1)$ between 8 and 10 is \$3 million, which is also $f_1^*(s)$ for this route, while the cost between 9 and 10 is \$4 million [also $f_1^*(s)$].

The second tableau refers to the next-to-last stage. For this case, the route is between state 5, 6, or 7 and the immediate destination x_2, either 8 or 9. The cost to the final destination is the cost to the immediate destination (C_{sx_2}) plus the minimum cost from there to the final destination $f_1^*(s)$. For route 5–8–10, it is \$1 million plus \$3

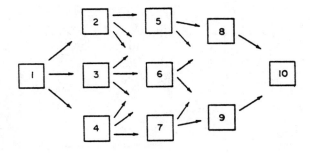

Figure 12.3 Dynamic programming. (From Hillier and Lieberman, 1980.)

	2	3	4
1	2	4	3

	5	6	7
2	7	4	6
3	3	2	4
4	4	1	5

	8	9
5	1	4
6	6	3
7	3	3

	10
8	3
9	4

million, for a total of $4 million. For route 5–9–10, it is $4 million plus $4 million, for a total of $8 million. Between these two routes the least cost is $4 million $[f_2^*(s)]$, corresponding to an immediate least-cost destination $x_2^* = 8$. The procedure is repeated to determine the $f_2^*(s)$ and x_2^* for the route between state 6 and state 10, and between state 7 and state 10.

When the third and fourth tableaus are completed, the overall least-cost solution is shown in the fourth tableau to be $11 million for the alternatives $1-x_4-x_3-x_2-x_1$, which are identified in the first and last columns of tableaus 4, 3, 2, and 1. Three alternatives add up to a cost of $11 million, as shown below:

$$\text{Route} = 1\text{–}3\text{–}5\text{–}8\text{–}10; \ \text{cost} = 4 + 3 + 1 + 3 = 11$$

$$\text{Route} = 1\text{–}4\text{–}5\text{–}8\text{–}10; \ \text{cost} = 3 + 4 + 1 + 3 = 11$$

$$\text{Route} = 1\text{–}4\text{–}6\text{–}9\text{–}10; \ \text{cost} = 3 + 1 + 3 + 4 = 11$$

The basic features that characterize dynamic programming are outlined below (Hillier and Lieberman 1980, p. 270):

1. The problem can be divided up into stages, with a policy decision required at each stage.
2. Each stage has a number of states associated with it.
3. The effect of the policy decision at each stage is to transform the current state into a state associated with the next stage (possibly according to a probability distribution).
4. Given the current stage, an optimal policy for the remaining stages is independent of the policy adopted in preceding stages. Knowledge of the current state of the system conveys all the information about its previous behavior necessary for determining the optimal policy henceforth. (This is a Markovian property.)

s	$f_1^*(s)$	x_1^*
8	3	10
9	4	10

	$f_2(s, x_2) = c_{sx_2} + f_1^*(x_2)$			
s \ x_2	8	9	$f_2^*(s)$	x_2^*
5	4	8	4	8
6	9	7	7	9
7	6	7	6	8

	$f_3(s, x_3) = c_{sx_3} + f_2^*(x_3)$				
s \ x_3	5	6	7	$f_3^*(s)$	x_3^*
2	11	11	12	11	5 or 6
3	7	9	10	7	5
4	8	8	11	8	5 or 6

	$f_4(s, x_4) = c_{sx_4} + f_3^*(x_4)$				
s \ x_4	2	3	4	$f_4^*(s)$	x_4^*
1	13	11	11	11	3 or 4

Figure 12.4 Tableaus for DP problem. (From Hillier and Lieberman, 1980.)

5. The solution procedure begins by finding the optimal policy for each state of the last stage. The solution of this one-stage problem is usually trivial.

6. A recursive relationship that identifies the optimal policy for each state at stage n given the optimal policy for each state at stage $(n + 1)$ is available. In the example shown above this relationship was

$$f_n^*(s) = \min_{x_n}[C_{sx_n} + f_{n-1}^*(x_n)]$$

7. Using this recursive relationship, the solution procedure moves backward stage by stage, each time finding the optimal policy for each state of that stage, until it finds the optimal policy when starting at the initial stage.

For water resources planning studies, it may be convenient to recursively work forward from the start, rather than backward from a given end condition as described above. A DP program by Young (1967) illustrates this approach.

12.4.3 Other Optimization Techniques

Although LP and DP are the most popular optimization tools in water resources planning, other special techniques are also used in problem specific areas. Some of these are discussed below.

Transportation Problems. In the transportation problem, there are m origin points and n destination points. Quantities may be transferred from any origin to any destination, and the unit cost for this is known. If the quantity needed at each destination is specified, the pattern of shipment is determined that minimizes total transportation cost. This is a special application of linear programming (Hillier and Lieberman 1980; Gillett 1976; Haimes 1977) for which special network (transportation) codes are readily available.

Integer Linear Programming and Other Discrete Programming Applications. The values of one or more of the resources to be allocated may have integer values. Thus, the number of workers or machines may be indivisible. The schedule of expenditures may be established in annual amounts. In practice, only several different types of sewage treatment may be considered in which case intermediate values of efficiency (BOD removal) may not have physical significance. There is another class of problems in which a choice is to be made between two constraints so that one must hold but not necessarily both. In still other problems, some of the decision variables may have a limited finite number of values, whereas others are of a continuous nature. When any of these restrictions apply, the unmodified linear programming approach can lead to results in which the values of the decision variables either make no sense or, if they are adjusted by rounding or by moving to the nearest practical value, can be a nonoptimal solution. The issues described above can be treated by various modifications of the simplex method and by other algorithms applying to integer programming and to mixed-integer problems. Some of these methods are described in Hillier and Lieberman (1980), Gillett (1976), and Haimes (1977). Dynamic programming may also be found applicable to problems of this type. The branch-and-bound technique described in the next subsection is another procedure that can be considered.

Branch-and-Bound Technique. This technique involves a "well-structured systematic search of the space of all feasible solutions of constrained optimization problems that have a finite number of feasible solutions" (Gillett 1976). The enumeration procedure for finding an optimum solution must be organized to reduce the number of combinations that might otherwise have to be examined. For example, 10 variables having 10 feasible values can lead to 10^{10} feasible solutions.

The basic idea of the branch-and-bound technique has been described by Hillier and Lieberman (1980, p. 716):

> Suppose . . . that the objective function is to be minimized. Assume that an upper bound on the optimal value of the objective function is available (this usually is the value of the objective function for the best feasible solution identified so far). The first step is to

partition the set of all feasible solutions into several subsets, and, for each one, a *lower bound* is obtained for the value of the objective function of the solutions within that subset. Those subsets whose lower bounds exceed the current upper bound on the objective function are then excluded from further consideration. . . . One of the remaining subsets, say, the one with the smallest lower bound, is then partitioned further into several subsets. Their lower bounds are obtained in turn and used as before to exclude some of these subsets from further consideration. From all of the remaining subsets, another one is selected for further partitioning, and so on. This process is repeated again and again until a feasible solution is found such that the corresponding value of the objective function is no greater than the lower bound for any subset.

As Gillett (1976) points out, the general principle is the same for any algorithm of the branch-and-bound technique. The algorithms vary with respect to the procedure for branching, bounding, and pruning. He discusses procedures to find solutions to three problems entitled "assignment problem," "traveling salesman problem," and "back-pack loading problem." The examples discussed have counterparts in water resource planning.

Duality Concept in Linear Programming. The duality concept provides an interesting economic interpretation at the point of optimality with respect to the allocation of resources. The *primal* problem has been described for linear programming in Section 12.4.1.

The *dual* version of the LP problem is:

Find $y_i \geq 0$ $(i = 1, 2, \ldots, m)$ in order to

minimize $Z_y = b_1 y_1 + b_2 y_2 + \cdots + b_m y_m$

subject to the constraints:

$$a_{11} y_1 + a_{21} y_2 + \cdots + a_{m1} y_m \geq c_1$$

$$a_{12} y_1 + a_{22} y_2 + \cdots + a_{m2} y_m \geq c_2$$

$$\vdots \qquad \qquad \vdots \qquad \qquad \vdots$$

$$a_{1n} y_1 + a_{2n} y_2 + \cdots + a_{mn} y_m \geq c_n$$

In this form, the limited resources have become the coefficients of the objective function, and the row coefficients in the constraints have become the column coefficients. Take the example previously outlined, for which it was shown that $Z_{max} = 360,000$ for $x_a = 200$ and $x_b = 600$, where x_a and x_b are the acreages for crop A and crop B respectively. For the dual:

Minimize $Z_y = 400 y_1 + 600 y_2 + 1800 y_3$

subject to: $y_1 + 3 y_3 \geq 300$

$$y_2 + 2 y_3 \geq 500$$

and

$$y_1 \geq 0, \quad y_2 \geq 0, \quad y_3 \geq 0$$

Each primal problem has a dual version. When the dual problem is solved (a graphical solution is not easily obtained here because of the three-dimensional problem in y), the value of y_1 would indicate the marginal value of 1 acre of crop A at the point of maximum profit with respect to all resources (acreage of crop A, acreage of crop B, and total water availability). If one more acre of crop A is made available, the resulting increase in profit would be y_1 provided that the original optimal basis does not change.

The coefficients in the dual version of linear programming are similar to the Lagrange multipliers in the classical method of optimization for a constrained function of multiple variables. The Lagrange multiplier λ is equal to the negative of the marginal change of the objective function for a unit change in the value of the constraint (scarce resource). The coefficient in LP or the λ represents a concept of shadow prices on the "binding" resources.

Parametric Linear Programming. The parameters of the model in the objective and constraint functions (c_j, a_{ij}, b_i) are usually not known with complete certainty. *Sensitivity analyses* can be carried out to determine the effect on the optimal solution if particular parameters take on other possible values. Hillier and Lieberman (1980) discuss several approaches that can be applied when (1) a single change is made in the model (c_j, or a_{ij}, or b_i) and where a new constraint or variable is added; and (2) *parametric linear programming* approaches in which simultaneous changes are considered in c_j, and b_i; in the case of water resources planning these are often the unit costs and resources, respectively, applying to a problem.

Linear Programming under Uncertainty. This includes chance constraint programming and stochastic linear programming. The techniques involve reducing the problems to ordinary linear programming problems that can be solved by the simplex method.

In dealing with uncertainty the two methods take different approaches. The chance constraint replaces an uncertain value with a certainty equivalent, say the value that would be exceeded 95% of the time. This is a one-for-one substitution and does not increase computational difficulty. This method then assumes that the resulting solution will be valid 95 times out of 100. It is equivalent to specifying a zero penalty for oversupply up to the 95% level and an infinite amount afterward. Stochastic programming assumes a loss function and essentially solves for the reliability level. Thus, penalties could lead to a solution that was acceptable only, say 50 or 60% of the time. Generally, chance constraint is a more conservative technique and is used when loss functions are not known or produce nonlinear objective functions that are difficult to solve. Concepts of mathematical programming under uncertainty are not very advanced theoretically or computationally.

Other Nonlinear Programming Methods. *Quadratic programming* refers to the problem of maximizing (or minimizing) a quadratic objective function subject to linear constraints. Thus, the objective function may contain x_i^2 and $x_i x_j$ terms. Several solution procedures based on linear programming have been developed for the special case where the objective function is a concave function (Hillier and Lieberman 1980).

Separable convex programming applies where the objective function can be written in the form

$$f(x_1, x_2, \ldots, x_n) = f_1(x_1) + f_2(x_2) + \cdots + f_n(x_n)$$

where $f_j(x_j)$ is a specified function of x_j only for $j = 1, 2, \ldots, n$. The linear programming objective is separable, whereas the quadratic is not because it contains $x_j x_k$ terms. A technique widely used for this problem reduces the problem to a linear programming problem by approximating each $f_j(x_j)$ by a piecewise linear function. All the $f_j(x_j)$ must be concave functions when the objective function is to be maximized, whereas all the $f_j(x_j)$ must be convex functions when the objective function is to be minimized.

General convex programming applies where $f(x_1, x_2, \ldots, x_n)$ is a concave function and all the $g_i(x_1, x_2, \ldots, x_n)$ are convex functions. Hillier and Lieberman (1980) discuss various algorithms for the convex programming problem which involve iterative procedures (gradient search procedure and the sequential unconstrained maximization technique).

Quasilinearization is an algorithm that solves nonlinear systems of ordinary and partial differential equations by iteratively solving a series of related linear initial-value problems. When the sequence of linear initial-value problems converges to the solution of the original nonlinear problem, it converges quadratically (Haimes 1977; Bellman and Kalaba 1965). The *Newton–Raphson* method is used in connection with this method; it can also be used to solve systems of simultaneous nonlinear equations (Haimes 1977).

Other methods of solution for nonlinear programming problems involve *searches* and include grid searches and Fibonacci or Golden section searches. Searches are also used for simulation problems, as discussed later in this section.

Generalized Software for Nonlinear Optimization Problems. A number of algorithms are computer coded and available to the public for general application to problems in which the objective function and/or the constraint functions are nonlinear. These have been compared by various investigators in terms of their characteristics and reliability in obtaining optimal results (Waren and Lasdon 1979; Lasdon and Waren 1980; Lasdon et al. 1978; Schittkowski 1980; Sandgren and Ragsdell 1977). In a survey of 26 of the codes, Waren and Lasdon (1979) have categorized these algorithms as: reduced gradient or generalized reduced gradient; penalty and augmented Lagrangian; gradient projection; successive linear programming or method of approximation programming; successively linearly constrained programming; and other feasible direction methods and search methods.

Network Analyses. Figure 12.5 is an example of a *graph*. The junction points are called *nodes* and the lines connecting them are called *branches* (or arcs, links, or edges). If there is flow in the branches, the graph is called a *network*. A node is a *source* if the flow moves away from the node in every branch and a *sink* if each of its

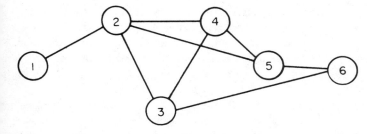

Figure 12.5 Example of a graph for network analysis. (From Hillier and Lieberman, 1980.)

branches is oriented toward that node. A number of problems that fit into this scheme are described and solved by Hillier and Lieberman (1980, pp. 235–8):

1. The maximal flow problem, in which there is a single source and a single sink, and a flow capacity in each branch. The problem is to maximize the total flow from the source to the sink.

2. The shortest route problem is concerned with finding the shortest route from origin to destination through a connecting network, given the distance along each branch.

3. The minimum spanning tree problem specifies the nodes and the distances between them, but does not specify the branches. The problem is to choose the branches for the network that have the shortest total length while providing a route between each pair of nodes.

4. The program evaluation and review technique (PERT) and the critical path method (CPM). Here the problem involves activities (branches) and events (nodes). An event is the completion of all activities leading into that node, and this event must precede the initiation of activities leading out of that node. There is a *critical path* through the system flow plan, which is the longest route through the network. PERT and CPM are used to schedule activities and evaluate the current status of project, in order to improve management. (This methodology is discussed in Chapter 18.)

The dynamic programming method is also applicable to many network-type problems.

Queuing Models. Queuing theory is used in many problems in industry and transportation but has found less application in water resource work. It refers to the study of queues or waiting lines. Some studies have involved the random inflows to reservoirs (Moran 1959) and the random pattern of ship arrivals at a group of piers (Fratar, Goodman, and Brant 1960). Thomas and Burden (1963) have discussed their applicability to wastewater treatment problems. Most models assume a theoretical distribution to apply to the queuing pattern, usually the Poisson distribution.

Search Techniques. In a general sense, the term "search technique" applies to any trial-and-error or enumeration procedure. Many of the algorithms used for solving analytical programming problems are constrained gradient techniques (Hadley 1964; Wilde 1963); the simplex method of linear programming and the quadratic and convex programming methods for solving nonlinear programming problems are examples.

For example, the specifications of the general convex programming problem are that the objective function $f(x_1, x_2, \ldots, x_n)$ be concave and the constraint functions $g_i(x_1, x_2, \ldots, x_n)$ convex. These specifications ensure that if a local optimum is found for the objective function, it will at the same time be the global optimum. The concept of "gradient" or "steepest ascent or descent" techniques is that in iterative solutions, changes should be made in $(x_1, x_2, \ldots, x_n)$ that maximize the rate at which $f(x_1, x_2, \ldots, x_n)$ is increasing or decreasing, and this will be the case when these changes are proportional to the elements of the vector obtained by differentiating the objective function with respect to each of the decision variables:

$$\frac{df}{dx_1}, \frac{df}{dx_2}, \ldots, \frac{df}{dx_n} \quad \text{at } (x_1, x_2, \ldots, x_n)$$

The search methods generally have in common a method of determining the direction in which to proceed and a step size for the next trial.

Search techniques are widely used for *simulation models.* Some concepts applying to these models were introduced in Section 6.5. For practical large and complex water resource systems, the approach is often largely experimental since the variables may not be related by smooth functions that permit techniques based on a differentiation concept (e.g., gradient techniques), or may not have a regular structure in other respects. There may be problems of more than one local minimum or maximum, flat spots, or straight portions without curvature. Also, instead of a clear-cut objective function, components of the objective(s) may be reflected in the operating rules for the facilities, in the constraints, or in noneconomic elements of performance (e.g., hydrologic reliability).

When a simulation model is run a number of times with different values of the decision variables, the resulting values of the objective function define a "response surface." Schaake (1974) has shown the response surface (Figure 12.6) for a small simulation problem in which the decision variables were reservoir volume and irrigation area and performance was measured in terms of present value. The simulation was carried out using the MITSIM program developed at the Massachusetts Institute of Technology. Economic performance is measured by the present value of expected net benefits over a period of analysis, for which the runs are carried out using historical or synthetic flow data:

present value of expected net benefit	=	present value of expected long-run benefits	−	present value of investment and OMR costs	−	present value of expected value of shortage costs

This expression for the objective function was found to lend itself to searches based on marginal value estimation (McBean and Schaake 1973; Schaake 1974). The expression shown above may be written as

$$\Pi = B_L(x) - C_I(x) - C_S(x)$$

where x is the vector of decision variables. The marginal value of x_1, an element of x, is

$$\frac{\partial \Pi}{\partial x_1} = \frac{\partial B_L}{\partial x_1} - \frac{\partial C_I}{\partial x_1} - \frac{\partial C_S}{\partial x_1}$$

The first two terms on the right-hand side can be evaluated directly from the benefit and cost data input to the program relating to decision variable x_1. The third term is evaluated by simulation. In a complex system of interrelated activities a change in x_1 may affect not only the activity it represents but also activities downstream, and even activities upstream if these are affected by the operating policy of x_1. Methods of determining marginal values for reservoir nodes, irrigation nodes,

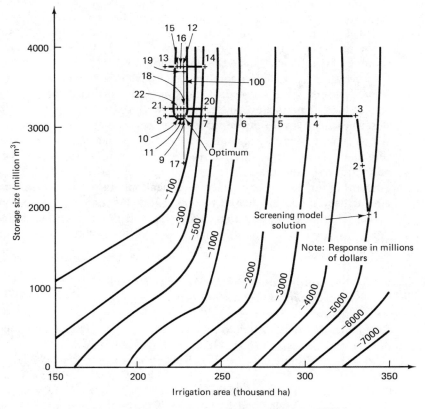

Figure 12.6 Example of search path. (From Schaake, 1974.)

diversion nodes, junction nodes and confluence nodes, and municipal and industrial demand nodes are presented by Schaake and Facet (1974), and Leytham has developed a package of search techniques (in Schaake, 1974). Leytham evaluated the *steepest ascent* method, particularly in connection with the problems of errors in calculating gradients and searching near the optimum point (at the "ridge" of a response surface). He also evaluated the *parallel tangent* (partan) search method (Shah, Beuhler, and Kempthorne 1964) and the *pattern* search method that was proposed by Hooke and Jeeves (1961) and reviewed by Wilde and Beightler (1967), and he refers to other methods.

Leytham combined his search package with the simulation model MITSIM in order to find the optimum for the response surface on Figure 12.6. This is shown for a search starting at reservoir volume 1949 and irrigation area 337940. The same optimum point was reached with experiments starting at 4000, 337940 and at 4000, 150000.

Meta Systems (1975) discusses various search techniques for simulation problems that use sampling methods. It is indicated that except in the simplest situations, the use of *systematic sampling* procedures is highly inefficient. Such a method would subdivide the range for each decision variable into a number of steps or increments. A coarse mesh or a finer grid would be selected depending on the number of variables, the speed of computation, and the sensitivity of system response to changes in the variable. If there are 4 variables and 10 intervals for each variable, there are over a million combinations (4^{10}). With *random sampling*, a smaller number of combinations is tested in order to find an optimum which is then subject to statistical tests. Finally, a combination of systematic and random techniques called *hybrid sampling* is discussed. A random sample is investigated and the outcomes are ranked and the first few are selected for further investigation. As Meta Systems describes the hybrid scheme, it "utilizes derivatives in the multi-dimensional space which characterizes the response surface, and design changes or steps are made in the direction of the largest derivative. A more general technique blends the several derivatives so that the step occurs along the gradient and is, consequently, more efficient in terms of convergence to a local optimum." In several respects, there are similarities among the search techniques in this method, the search techniques for solving nonlinear programming problems and those described above developed at MIT, and the less formal procedures applied to simulation that are discussed later in this chapter.

12.4.4 Recommendations for Further Reading on Optimization Techniques

Recommended texts in operations research include Hillier and Lieberman (1980), Ackoff and Sasieni (1968), Gillett (1976), Bellman and Dreyfus (1962), Hadley (1964), and Himmelblau (1972). Books that deal specifically with water resource systems include Maass et al. (1962), Hall and Dracup (1970), Haimes (1977), Buras (1972), Meta Systems (1975), Dracup et al. (1970), Bugliarello and Gunther (1974), Biswas (1976), Major and Lenton (1979), Loucks et al. (1981), and Goicoechea, Hansen, and Duckstein (1982).

12.4.5 Applications of Systems Analysis in Reservoir Studies

Many water resources systems analyses include the studies of reservoirs. In a study of methods for optimizing reservoir operations for planning and design purposes, Yeh et al. (1979) made an extensive search of the literature, identifying papers on the subjects of simulation, linear programming, chance-constraint programming, non-linear programming, dynamic programming, queuing and storage theories, combinations of techniques, and real-time techniques. They found no general algorithm that covered all types of problems. The choice of techniques usually depends on the characteristics of the reservoir system, on the availability of data, and on the objective and constraints specified.

Of the various methods, the techniques of *simulation* are applied the most often. Applications of simulation to reservoir studies and other problems will be described later in this chapter. As a foundation for reservoir applications, the following section on operation principles is given.

12.5 RESERVOIR OPERATION PRINCIPLES

Stream flow regulation by a reservoir refers to the use of the reservoir's storage volume and physical appurtenances to modify stream flows. Inflows to the reservoir are stored, evaporated, diverted from the reservoir, and released downstream. Schedules for diversion and release, and detailed operating procedures, provide for beneficial purposes (i.e., hydroelectric power, flood control, recreation, water supplies for irrigation and for municipal and industrial needs, and water quality management) while maintaining the integrity of the dam and other structures. The reservoir project is operated to handle extreme flows (flood and drought) as well as more normal flows.

Operating rules are based on an analysis of stream flows. Sequences of stream flow (inflows in successive intervals of time) are available from historical records if the stream has a flow gaging station, or may be estimated by analyses of records for other streams. If the records are short or otherwise inadequate, sequences may be synthesized using methods of mathematical statistics (see Section 11.2). Outflows depend on the hydraulic characteristics of the release facilities (spillways, penstocks, and other outlet works), the way in which these facilities are operated, and the height of water behind the dam. The time interval may be in terms of hours for flood control, navigation, or hydropower studies. For hydropower or water quality studies, hourly or weekly intervals may be important. For water supply studies (public water supplies, irrigation), monthly or seasonal time intervals may be suitable.

When a dam is placed on a stream, it receives the inflows that originate in the drainage area upstream of the dam. The reservoir usually occupies only a small portion of the drainage area. If the reservoir is very large, it may be used to regulate the inflows to achieve outflows according to any desired pattern. Because of topographic and economic limitations, however, it is not usual for a reservoir to be constructed large enough to provide full regulation. To take advantage of a good site for construction, the dam and reservoir are often located upstream in a basin and the reservoir controls the flows originating in only a portion of the drainage area. The regulated flow may be estimated based on studies of reservoir operation, and considering the flows from the controlled and uncontrolled areas.

If a stream has more than one dam, the downstream reservoir operation considers the releases from the upstream reservoir and the flows from the uncontrolled intermediate area.

A set of operating rules established for the reservoir takes account of inflows, needs for water withdrawals and releases, storage volumes, and reservoir elevations. The designs of the spillway and other outlet works are dependent on these rules. The ability to provide releases for water supplies and other conservation uses requires that water be held in storage at certain times to augment low inflows when they occur. In addition to the releases of water that are desirable, the maintenance of reservoir (or pool) elevations within defined limits may be important. Thus, if the reservoir is used for navigation, a minimum pool may be needed for lockage facilities. A minimum pool may also be necessary to gain access to the reservoir for recreation. Also, if the reservoir is drawn down too far, there may be a serious reduction of hydroelectric power. For flood control, on the other hand, the pool elevation must be kept low enough to provide space for containing flood flows during periods of high inflows.

The operating rules may be simple, as for a single-purpose reservoir designed to provide a constant rate of withdrawal for water supply purposes, and to waste any flows in excess of the reservoir capacity. In the case of a multipurpose reservoir, however, the allocations of storage and desirable reservoir elevations may vary from one month to the next, and very detailed operating instructions may be required to handle flood flows.

The rules are initially assumed and may be tested with historical or synthetic inflow records to determine their effectiveness. By successive simulations with modified rules, a set of acceptable rules is derived. In other cases, the optimal operating rules may be established using mathematical programming techniques.

The operating rules obtained in this manner are considered tentative, particularly if they are based on a short period of record. Once actual operation of the project begins, it is possible to improve the rules based on experience. The desirable reservoir elevations at various times of the year may be shown by *rule curve* elevations. Rule curves are usually based on "hindsight" analyses of past stream flows (or synthetic flows) and are only guides; the elevations reached in actual operation depend on the actual inflows and needs for the various project purposes.

A continuous trace of flow rate is referred to as a *hydrograph*. The available storage volume and appurtenances can be utilized to modify an inflow flood hydrograph in order to obtain an outflow hydrograph having a different pattern of flows, including a reduced instantaneous peak discharge. The storage volume needed to accommodate any specified inflow flood hydrograph is determined by a *reservoir routing* procedure, which involves comparing inflow volumes for successive intervals of time with outflow volumes for the same intervals and adding differences until a maximum storage value is obtained. The outflow volumes are determined from the release rates of the spillways and outlet works; these facilities may be uncontrolled or controlled by gates, and their capacities depend on the headwater elevation and the extent to which the gates are opened.

The outflow hydrograph from the reservoir will be different for each different inflow hydrograph, and the operation rules must be properly formulated to cope with any pattern of inflow that may occur. Important dams are designed to withstand the outflow from the largest potential flood, known as the *probable maximum flood* (see Section 11.7). This hypothetical flood is used as the basis for designing the spillway and estimating the maximum reservoir elevation reached. It would result from the most critical heavy rainfall, or a combination of snowmelt and rainfall.

The operating rules for the reservoir and other water supply and water using facilities constituting a water resources system are determined, in modern engineering practice, by *systems studies* with the assistance of a computerized mathematical model. The inflows to any reservoir are the natural flows adjusted for the regulation effects of any upstream reservoirs or other water facilities. The outflows from the reservoir are the result of these inflows and the rules for operating the reservoir, and (after modification by intervening natural valley storage, surface runoff, and water facilities) constitute the inflows to a reservoir downstream.

To analyze a complex system of projects, a detailed study may be carried out with flows and assumed operation rules. When a system requirement can be achieved by operating more than one reservoir, it is necessary to establish priorities for releasing water from the conservation spaces of single and multipurpose reservoirs. If the historical record of stream flow is short (say, less than about 20 years) or if these stream flows are not representative of a longer hydrologic period, a synthetic record should be created of adequate length for simulation to determine the hydrologic reliabilities and economic consequences.

The system studies may seek to maximize firm water supplies, to optimize power production, or to maximize stream flows in the dry season of the year for water quality management. A compromise may be sought that achieves maximum net benefits while meeting specified system constraints. If the study is carried out for a system in which some or all of the units are already existing, it is necessary to accept their reservoir volumes and release capacities as given unless they can be changed.

12.6 SIMULATION AND OTHER APPROACHES THAT EMPLOY STOCHASTIC TIME SERIES

12.6.1 Simulation Methods

In a complex system involving many projects and purposes of development in a river system, assumptions concerning the scale and operation rules of each project may be tested with the aid of simulation models. Depending on the results from the computer runs, the planner can adjust the scales and operating rules. By a number of iterations, satisfactory selections are established. Theoretically (as explained in Section 12.4.3), the number of combinations of variables is very large and the computational burden can easily become excessive. The efficiency by which the scales and operation rules are determined depends to a large extent on the experience and judgment of the planners.

Simulation requires the availability of a long sequence of flows, either reproducing the historical record or derived synthetically. Flows for monthly intervals are appropriate for many simulations. Hourly intervals may be needed for flood flow routings and for certain detailed power operation and benefit studies. The record of flows used for testing must be established so that the concurrent flows at all points of interest are consistent with each other.

In the HYPO model used for studying power operations in the Upper Hudson River Basin in New York discussed in Section 12.7, simulation was used to determine the optimal power installations and operating rules. Hourly intervals were used for these studies.

In the MITTAMS model used for the Vardar/Axios project in Yugoslavia and Greece (Chapters 6 and 13), the hydrologic reliabilities and economic performances of some 150 projects and purposes were determined. In that study, carried out with monthly time intervals, each computer run provided estimates of the percentage of time that water requirements (targets) were met. Such results, together with economic results, were analyzed in order to develop the optimal scale and operating rules for the various facilities.

12.6.2 Programming Methods

Chance constraint programming and several other techniques adapt the methods of programming to obtain optimal solutions to water resource problems that involve stochastic hydrology. Once the objective functions and constraints are established, the solution can proceed provided that a suitable algorithm for optimization is available.

ReVelle et al. (1969) developed linear decision rules that permitted them to structure chance-constrained linear programming models for determining optimal reservoir capacity. The optimal reservoir capacity was defined as the minimum size that would meet constraints at the end of each interval that are expressed in probabilistic form. Loucks and Dorfman (1975) evaluated alternative linear decision rules by using optimization and simulation techniques. Developments by other investigators have adapted dynamic programming, nonlinear programming, and special algorithms, and have considered penalties for failure to meet constraints.

Mathematical models of the programming type should be used only for preliminary investigations. Simulation analyses are recommended to confirm and/or "fine tune" capacities and operating policies.

12.7 APPLICATION OF SIMULATION TO RESERVOIR SYSTEM

Simulation of a water resource system requires a mathematical model in which: (1) equations, logic statements, and other functional relationships describe the interrelationships among the variables; and (2) the mathematical statements are listed in an appropriate sequence in time and/or space that follows the order of occurrence in the system being reproduced.

Typically, a system consists of facilities that control and utilize water, and that handle surface water, groundwater, or both. A trial design specifies the capacity of each facility, and operating rules. For example, for a river basin having reservoirs, and in which only surface waters are considered, the release for each reservoir may be specified for each time interval as a function of starting reservoir elevation, anticipated reservoir inflow, and a target discharge. The inflows to the most upstream reservoirs may be determined as historical or synthetic sequences of stochastic values, the latter based on a statistical analysis of the available stream flow records. The inflows to downstream reservoirs depend on the releases from upstream reservoirs and any overland flow contributions and regulating effects in the intervening reaches of stream.

The flows are routed through the facilities and the stream reaches using the instructions embodied in the mathematical statements. The physical and/or economic consequences of the simulation are displayed according to a preset format. When the run is concluded, the results are examined and the next trial design (i.e., reservoir capacities and operating rules) is selected. This trial design is determined by an algorithm included in the computer program, or by external rules followed by the analyst, or may be established by judgment. One approach is to "exercise" the model by considering various combinations of input variables; this constitutes a form of sensitivity analysis. By successive examinations of results, modifications of input, and repeated iterations, a set of results is obtained that is judged to be nearly optimal.

A simulation program called HYPO was developed by Tippetts-Abbett-McCarthy-Stratton (Balloffet et al. 1980) for the study of a system of reservoirs and power plants in the upper Hudson River System in New York state. The system is shown schematically in Figure 12.7. Starting with an assumed set of operation policies, the operation policies were modified in successive computer runs to maximize the value of the energy output of the hydroelectric power stations. The studies investigated the operation policies that were appropriate and the economy of adding additional reservoir and/or power facilities in the system.

HYPO simulated the releases from reservoirs and power plants and the transit of discharges in the river system, including its first- and second-order tributaries. For the study of power operations, a time interval of 1 hour was selected. For the study of flood control responses to power operations, flow hydrographs were generated at selected locations in the network, and statistics were calculated for reservoir and powerhouse headwater elevations. The cascade operation of reservoirs and power plants was simulated based on specified constraints and operation rules. For system optimization, the program provided quantitative parameters to guide the analyst in successive revisions of rules and evaluations of responses.

The system consisted of nodes and connecting links. Inflow nodes were boundary condition nodes, where inflow (input) hydrographs were defined. Terminal nodes were also boundary nodes, where outflow hydrographs were computed. River nodes divide each routing reach into a number of links. Diversion nodes were used to simulate diversions where the flow in each branch was given as a fraction of the total

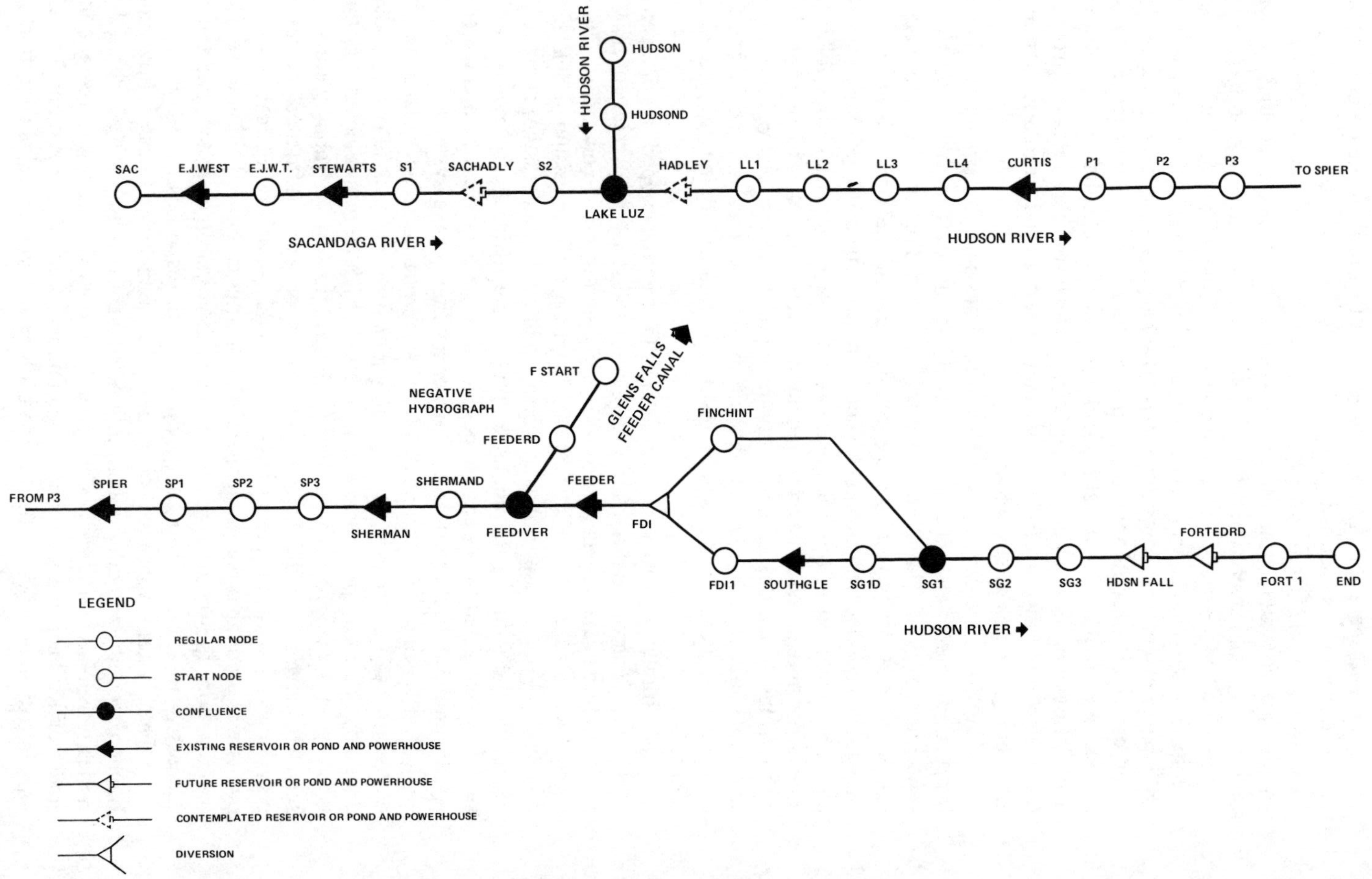

Figure 12.7 Map of the hypo model. (From Balloffet et al., 1980.)

inflow to the node. Junction nodes were used to model confluences. Reservoir nodes represented reservoirs with or without associated power plants. The operation of these nodes was predicated on tables of target hourly discharges. Pond nodes were used to model run-of-river power plants having a modest reservoir capacity used mainly for peaking purposes. The operation of reservoir nodes was predicated on tables of target hourly *discharges*, while the operation of pond nodes was based on target hourly *power generation* values.

Routing procedures were used to propagate hourly discharges through the channels, reservoirs, and ponds of the system. The Muskingum procedure was used for channel routing.

The reservoir routing procedure started by subtracting the powerhouse discharge from the reservoir inflow, to obtain a net inflow for routing through the reservoir and the spillway. Simulation of several possible flashboard and gate configurations for spillway operation was performed assuming a set of minimum target elevations for each month as input according to power, storage, or recreation requirements. For reservoir elevations below the target elevation, the outflow from the reservoir was set to zero. A maximum operating pool was also established for each month as an upper bound for normal reservoir elevations, to allow for flood control operation.

Pond routing used the same concepts as for a reservoir, including the flashboard and gated spillway operation options. The main difference was that instead of a target elevation curve, there were minimum and maximum operating pool elevations. When the pool elevation was below minimum, the discharge through the powerhouse and the spillway was set to zero. When the pool was above maximum, the routing procedure used all available spillway capacity, including fully open gates.

The value of energy produced varied with the time of day and the day of the week. The program established an hourly discharge schedule for each day to maximize the energy value for the day. This schedule divided the expected daily volume of discharge for that day into optimal hourly amounts. Different operation schedules were established for weekdays and weekends.

The daily volume of discharge from a reservoir was related to an index discharge calculated at hour zero of any day as a function of reservoir volume and inflow for the preceding day.

$$D^{\text{IDAY}} = \frac{\text{RES VOL}^{(\text{IDAY-1})}}{86,400} + Q^{(\text{IDAY-1})}$$

where

$$D^{\text{IDAY}} = \text{index discharge for a given day IDAY}$$

$$\text{RES VOL}^{(\text{IDAY-1})} = \text{reservoir volume above target or minimum level at end of preceding day}$$

$$Q^{(\text{IDAY-1})} = \text{mean reservoir inflow for preceding day, used as an index for inflow during given day}$$

For a run-of-river plant, the program started with a vector of hourly target discharges as a function of target power and head. The target power depended on the index discharge. As the day proceeded, the target discharge was maintained (case II), downgraded (case I), or upgraded (case III) as the availability of water changed. As shown in Figure 12.8, the availability of water depended on the pond volume at the end of the preceding hour and the expected inflow, which was known for this hour from the node just upstream of the pond. The program for a reservoir plant followed a similar procedure, except that it started with a vector of hourly power outputs as a function of target discharge and head.

$S(I - 1)$ = pond (or reservoir) volume at the end of the preceding hour

INFLOW (I) = inflow discharge during "this" hour, which will be known from the outflow from the node located just upstream of the pond (or reservoir)

PERIOD = time increment in hours (usually equal to 1)

The program computed the power benefits by multiplying hourly generated output by a rate given by the marginal value of each kWh in the electric utility's system. The efficiency of energy production was judged from information generated by the program on the power (kW) and energy (kWh) for each power plant and for the total of all plants.

12.8 APPLICATIONS OF SYSTEMS ANALYSIS IN WATER QUALITY MANAGEMENT STUDIES

12.8.1 Classification of Problems

Applications of LP, DP, and simulation analyses may be considered for the problem of designing the least-cost wastewater treatment system, for which the locations of point sources and the water quality standards in all river reaches are specified. This and other types of water quality management problems have been classified by Loucks (1976), Bundgaard-Nielsen and Hwang (1976), U.S. Water Resources Council (1980), and Loucks et al. (1981). Many of these problems include consideration of stream, lake, or estuary dynamics (see review in Biswas, 1976). Models that trace the physical and quality characteristics of such water bodies may be combined with economic optimization models that utilize operations research techniques.

The following list of alternative methods in water quality management, which may be considered singly or in combination, is attributable to Loucks (1976) and others: (1) remove a portion of the BOD and other pollutants prior to discharge to receiving waters; (2) change the quantity and/or strength of wastewaters by process changes by the producers of waste or by pretreatment; (3) store a portion of treated wastewater and discharge it when the assimilative capacity of the receiving water body is more favorable; (4) use pumping and piping to move wastewaters, either prior

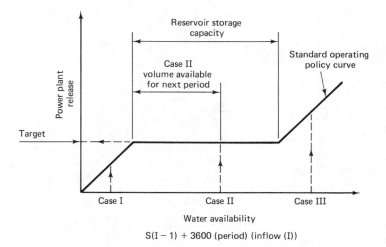

Figure 12.8 Standard operating policy for reservoir or pond. (From Balloffet et al., 1980.)

to or subsequent to some treatment, to other locations for additional treatment and/or disposal at sites having greater waste assimilative capacities; (5) reduce the cost of treatment by taking advantage of the larger scale of regional treatment plants, even though the costs of wastewater collection may be increased thereby; (6) use flow augmentation from reservoirs to increase dilution and assimilative capacities of receiving waters; (7) use artificial aeration devices to increase assimilative capacity of receiving waters; (8) control pollution from storm water discharges, through storage, treatment, and other measures; (9) control pollutants from nonpoint sources (e.g., agricultural, land, organic wastes from animals, pesticides); (10) land management that affects erosion and sedimentation, dredging and filling operations, etc.; (11) control contamination of aquifers from oil and other polluting materials, seepage from land fills and septic tanks, etc.; (12) consider modifications of water body use classifications and water quality standards; and (13) develop institutional methods for sharing costs, taxes, effluent charges, etc.

12.8.2 Comparison of LP, DP, and Simulation for a Class of Water Quality Management Problems

Water Quality Dynamics for Stream. The application of systems analysis (operations research) techniques in water resources planning may be illustrated for a class of problems in the field of water quality management. These problems involve the selection of a set of wastewater treatment plants in a region so that the cost of treatment is minimized while satisfying water quality criteria for receiving waters. Figure 12.9 shows the general arrangement to be considered. Three treatment plants (TPA, TPB, and TPC) are specified as to their locations and flow rates to be handled. The flow rate and quality of the stream above point 1 are also specified. The flow

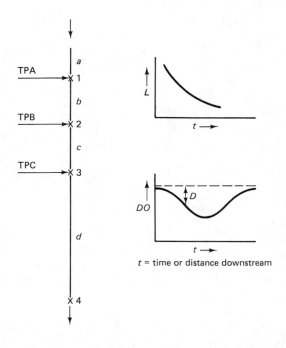

Figure 12.9 Arrangement of waste-water treatment plants, and variations of water quality.

t = time or distance downstream

rates of the subsequent reaches are incremented by the treatment plant effluents but are not affected by any overland flows. The stream temperatures are specified. A water quality criterion for each of the stream reaches is specified in terms of a standard for minimum dissolved oxygen (DO) concentration. The minimum DO refers to a critical period for design—typically an average flow over 7 days, having a return period of 10 years, and which occurs at a time of unfavorably high water temperature.

The quality of the stream may be characterized by its concentrations of dissolved oxygen (DO) and biochemical oxygen demand (BOD). The DO can range from zero to a saturation value DO_S. The actual DO condition and the DO standard can be expressed in terms of the DO deficit (D) with respect to DO_s. The BOD is a measure of the degradable organic material.

As the water moves downstream, its DO and BOD change due to the following:

- The BOD material in suspension tends to deplete the DO.
- The DO tends to be replenished by reaeration from the ambient air above the stream.
- There are movements of BOD material suspension to bottom deposits and resuspension from bottom deposits.
- The DO may be affected by photosynthesis due to the presence of algae and water plants.

The various effects are combined in equations for BOD and for "oxygen sag" developed by Streeter and Phelps (1925) and modified by Camp (1963) and Dobbins

(1964). The equations estimate the BOD (L_y) and the DO deficit (D_y) at the downstream point y in a reach of stream when the upstream point x has a DO deficit D_x and a BOD equal to L_x. It is also necessary to account for the combination of flows and resulting quality characteristics at each junction of a treatment plant effluent with the stream. Values of BOD and DO deficit are in terms of milligrams per liter (identical with parts per million by weight). The equations for BOD and D are as follows:

$$L_y = \left[L_x - \frac{p}{2.3(k_1 + k_3)} \right] 10^{-(k_1+k_3)t} + \frac{p}{2.3(k_1 + k_3)}$$

in which

L_x and L_y = upstream and downstream BODs (ppm), respectively

t = time of flows (days)

k_1 = deoxygenation rate constant (days^{-1})

k_3 = rate constant for settling out of BOD to bottom deposits (days^{-1})

p = rate of addition of BOD to the overlying water from bottom deposits (ppm/day)

$$D_y = \frac{k_1}{k_2 - k_1 - k_3} \left[L_x - \frac{p}{2.3(k_1 + k_3)} \right] \left[10^{-(k_1+k_3)t} - 10^{-k_2t} \right]$$
$$- \frac{k_1}{k_2} \left[\frac{p}{2.3(k_1 + k_3)} - \frac{a}{2.3k_1} \right] (1 - 10^{-k_2t}) + D_x \times 10^{-k_2t}$$

in which

D_x and D_y = upstream and downstream DO deficits (ppm), respectively

k_2 = atmospheric reaeration rate constant (days^{-1})

a = rate of production of DO by algae through photosynthesis (ppm/day)

If k_3, p, and a are eliminated from the equations above (assuming that the effects of bottom deposits and algae are either negligible or included with the other stream parameters), the equations that result are the original Streeter–Phelps formulations:

$$L_y = L_x \times 10^{-k_1t}$$

$$D_y = \frac{k_1}{k_2 - k_1} L_x (10^{-k_1t} - 10^{-k_2t}) + D_x \times 10^{-k_2t}$$

All of the equations above are written in terms of base 10. Many investigators prefer to work with the equations in terms of natural base e. The studies described below have been limited to steady-state problems (all characteristics at a point remain unvarying with time), in which the stream reaches are not affected by estuarial action or regulation effects of reservoirs.

As implied by the name of the equation, the DO is reduced at first (oxygen "sag"). Subsequently, the DO increases. If the reach is long enough, the critical (largest) value of DO deficit (D_c) is obtained before the downstream end of the reach; if not, the largest value of D is less. The modeling procedure must obtain the largest value of D in a reach for comparison with the specified water quality criterion for DO deficit.

At a junction, say at point 1 in Figure 12.9, the following weighting equations apply when the upstream flow Q_a, and effluent Q_A combine to form the downstream flow Q_b.

$$Q_b = Q_a + Q_A$$
$$L_b = \frac{L_a Q_a + L_A Q_A}{Q_b}$$

$$\text{DO}_b = \frac{\text{DO}_a Q_a + DO_A Q_A}{Q_b}$$
$$D_b = D_s - \text{DO}_b$$

Three approaches to the problem of minimizing treatment plant cost while satisfying water quality criteria are outlined below. They are based on linear programming (Loucks et al. 1967), dynamic programming (Liebman and Lynn 1966), and simulation (Goodman and Dobbins 1966).

Linear Programming.   To solve this problem using LP, Loucks et al. (1967) wrote a series of linear equations.

For a particular stream flow, the time of travel to the end of the reach, t, and the parameters k_1, k_2, k_3, a, and p are known for the reach. These constraints were combined into two coefficients λ_r and μ_r applying to the reach (r). The equation for determining the BOD at the end of the reach was written as

$$L_y = \lambda_r L_x + \mu_r$$

By combining the same constants into three coefficients, the equation for determining the D at the end of the reach was written as

$$D_y = \alpha_r D_x + \gamma_r L_x + \rho_r$$

Then the DO at the end of the reach was, as before,

$$\text{DO}_y = \text{DO}_s - D_y$$

Constraints defining the minimum allowable DO within each reach limit the amount of BOD that can be released into each reach. The BOD that can exist at the beginning of each reach L_x and not violate the standard may be expressed as a function of the initial dissolved oxygen deficit D_x. The equation required two additional constants as follows:

$$L_x \leq \sigma_r + \phi_r D_x$$

The investigators found that a plot of maximum allowable initial BOD, L_x, as the ordinate versus initial dissolved oxygen deficit, D_x, gave a reasonably straight line with negative slope ϕ_r and intercept with the ordinate σ_r.

Their methodology required an additional constraint which stated that an effluent BOD, W_r, could not exceed the total amount of BOD available for release, W_r max.

The cost of removing all the BOD from an effluent is ψ_r. There is a cost saving for the portion of the effluent BOD, W_r, which is not removed, equal to CW_r if the unit cost of removal is constant. The cost of wastewater treatment for each reach is $\psi_r - CW_r$. The objective function minimized the total cost of wastewater treatment for all reaches:

$$\text{Minimize } \sum_r (\psi_r - CW_r)$$

Equations were written using weighting equations for the combined values of Q_x, L_x, DO_x, and D_x entering each reach at a treatment plant junction point. Other equations were included for the downstream L_y, DO_y, and D_y for each reach, involving λ, μ, α, γ, ρ, and DO_s. Additional constraint equations were provided for each L_x in terms of σ_r, ϕ_r, and D_x, and for each W_r as limited by W_r max. The linear programming solution yielded the required values of W_r (which gives the required BOD removals) which met the stream quality standard at a minimum total cost. The paper presents an application of the technique and discusses some problems of nonlinearity.

Dynamic Programming. The general description of the problem by Liebman and Lynn (1966) is the same as presented above. A stream in which there are N waste discharges is divided into N reaches, the ith reach being the stretch of stream between the ith and $(i+1)$st discharge. The amount of flow from each discharge, the DO concentrations, and the raw BOD loadings are known. The stream flow in each reach is known. Standards for minimum DO in each reach are given. The treatment cost for each plant is a function of BOD removal. It is desired to find the required BOD removal at each discharge such that the treatment cost is minimized and the standards are not violated.

The objective function and constraints are expressed differently from those specified for LP but have the same effect:

$$\text{Minimize: } \sum_{i=1}^{N} C_i(P_i)$$
$$\text{subject to: } O_i^m \geq S_i \text{ (all } i; \ i = 1, 2, 3, \ldots, N)$$

where

P_i = percent BOD removal at the ith discharge

O_i^m = minimum DO actually obtained in each reach i

S_i = minimum allowable DO in each reach i

$C_i(P_i) =$ function giving the cost for providing an amount of BOD removal P_i at the ith discharge

The value of O_i^m in reach i results from the effects of the ith discharge of waste and *all preceding* waste discharges. The function $C_i(P_i)$ may be given in any convenient mathematical form or in tabular form. Liebman and Lynn used the original Streeter-Phelps equations, which are the formulations shown at the beginning of this section, but without explicit inclusion of BOD settling and resuspension and photosynthesis (k_3, p, and a omitted).

Water quality was treated as a discrete variable. The range of possible water quality values at the top of each reach was divided into a number of increments. In the uppermost reach, there is one and only one way of obtaining each "level" of quality; thus, a table of quality level and the cost of obtaining it was made. The cost is attributable to wastewater treatment in plant 1 at the head of the uppermost reach. In the second reach, many different ways of obtaining each quality level are possible, as various combinations of quality in the first reach and treatment at the second plant will give the same quality in the second reach. For each quality level in the second reach, however, some combination of quality in the first reach and treatment at the second plant will have a lower cost than any other combination that gives the same quality level. A table was constructed of quality in the second reach and minimum cost of obtaining that quality, and a record was kept of the combinations of treatment at plants 1 and 2 that provided the minimum cost.

Similarly, in the third reach, there are a large number of ways of reaching a given quality level. Each of these ways involves a particular quality level in reach 2 and a particular amount of treatment at plant 3. Since the best (least costly) way of reaching each quality level in reach 2 had already been tabulated, it was unnecessary to investigate again the various combinations of treatment at plants 1 and 2.

Thus, at each "stage" a new table was made listing the least costly way of reaching each level of quality. The entries in this table were found by combining the entries in the preceding table with the required treatment at the last plant to find the minimum cost.

A problem in which there are 10 plants and 10 levels of quality at each reach may be solved by investigating 910 combinations, instead of the 10^{10} combinations that would be required for complete enumeration of all treatment plant possibilities. For the uppermost reach, 10 levels of quality correspond to 10 levels of treatment (each of which involves a BOD discharge and cost). For the second reach, 10 levels of quality just above the reach are considered with 10 levels of treatment; the 100 combinations are investigated to give 10 levels of quality at the bottom of the reach at minimum cost to achieve each level. This process is continued for the third through tenth reaches.

The accuracy of results depends on the size of the increment of quality used. The paper discusses the applications of DP to a simplified representation of the Williamette River in Oregon.

Simulation. Goodman and Dobbins (1966) analyzed a "community and river model" (CARM) based on the geographical and population configurations and other

TABLE 12.1 CHARACTERISTICS EVALUATED FOR EACH RIVER SECTION, FOR EACH COMMUNITY, AND FOR STUDY AREA AS A WHOLE

Characteristics Evaluated for Each River Section
(I = number designating river section)

$Q(I)$	=	river flow, in million gallons per day
$T(I)$	=	river travel time, in days
$E(I)$	=	BOD of river water, in parts per million
$F(I)$	=	DO deficit of river water, in parts per million
$H(I)$	=	coliforms in river water, most probable number per 100 milliliters
$V(I)$	=	chlorides in river water, in parts per million
WI(I)	=	river water quality rating for water supply
WR(I)	=	river water quality rating for recreation

Characteristics Evaluated for Each Community
(J = number designating community)

QO(J)	=	average municipal water supply demand, in million gallons per day
QB(J)	=	average off-river municipal water supply, in million gallons per day
QH(J)	=	average on-river municipal water supply, in million gallons per day
QI(J)	=	maximum weekly on-river municipal water supply, in million gallons per day
SI(J)	=	investment cost for on-river water treatment plant, in dollars
CI(J)	=	annual cost for on-river water treatment plant, in dollars
BI(J)	=	annual benefits for on-river water supply, in dollars
QS(J)	=	average sewage discharge, in million gallons per day
QD(J)	=	maximum daily sewage discharge, in million gallons per day
ES(J)	=	BOD of raw sewage, in parts per million
FS(J)	=	DO deficit of raw sewage, in parts per million
HS(J)	=	coliforms in raw sewage, most probable number per 100 milliliters
VS(J)	=	chlorides in raw sewage, in parts per million
ED(J)	=	BOD of treated sewage, in parts per million
FD(J)	=	DO deficit of treated sewage, in parts per million
HD(J)	=	coliforms in treated sewage, most probable number per 100 milliliters
VD(J)	=	chlorides in treated sewage, in parts per million
SD(J)	=	investment cost for sewage treatment plant, in dollars
CD(J)	=	annual cost for sewage treatment plant, in dollars
BD(J)	=	annual benefits for sewage treatment, in dollars [more properly should be designated "other pollution control benefits" since these are in addition to those included in BI(J) and BR(J)]
$R0(J)$	=	total annual participation in water-oriented recreation activities—on-river and elsewhere—, in activity-days
$R1(J)$	=	annual participation in community-sponsored swimming, in activity days
$R2(J)$	=	annual participation in community-sponsored boating, in activity days
$R3(J)$	=	annual participation in community-sponsored fishing, in activity days
$R4(J)$	=	total annual participation in community-sponsored water-oriented recreation, in activity days
SR(J)	=	investment cost for recreation facilities, in dollars
CR(J)	=	annual cost for recreation facilities, in dollars
BR(J)	=	annual benefits for on-river recreation, in dollars
$S(J)$	=	total investment cost for facilities, in dollars
$C(J)$	=	total annual cost for facilities, in dollars
$B(J)$	=	total annual benefits for facilities, in dollars

Characteristics Evaluated for Community and River Model as a Whole

---

SIT	=	total investment costs for on-river water treatment plants, in dollars
SDT	=	total investment costs for sewage treatment plants, in dollars

TABLE 12.1 *(continued)*

Characteristics Evaluated for Community and River Model as a Whole

SRT	= total investment costs for recreation facilities, in dollars
CIT	= total annual costs for on-river water treatment plants, in dollars
CDT	= total annual costs for sewage treatment plants, in dollars
CRT	= total annual costs for recreation facilities, in dollars
BIT	= total annual benefits for on-river water supply, in dollars
BDT	= total annual benefits for sewage treatment, in dollars [see note under BD(J)]
BRT	= total annual benefits for on-river recreation, in dollars
ST	= total of SIT, SDT, and SRT
CT	= total of CIT, CDT, and CRT
BT	= total of BIT, BDT, and BRT

Source: Goodman and Dobbins (1966).

river and community data for the Merrimack River Basin in northeastern Massachusetts. The model utilized the equations shown in the first part of this section and a number of other formulations to estimate relationships for water quality, wastewater treatment, water treatment, and recreation. Table 12.1 is a list of the characteristics evaluated for each river section, for each community, and for the study area as a whole.

The number given to the river station under study was the current value of I. The "control" section at the most upperstream point had a value of 1 for I. Other stations were numbered consecutively in the downstream direction. Stream characteristics included flow rate, travel time, BOD, DO, DO deficit, coliforms, and chlorides. Two indexes of water quality, WI for municipal water supply and WR for recreation, were introduced to indicate how weightings of quality properties could be used in a practical way to assist in decisions, and to estimate costs and benefits.

The number of the community under study was the value of J. The numbers of communities were established in the order that their pollution discharge locations appear when moving downstream. This convention facilitated the computation of coliform bacteria quantities. If a community does not have a sewage discharge, a location and dummy number were established and appropriate input data screened out this activity by giving a zero sewage discharge value.

Total investment costs S, total annual costs C, and total annual benefits B were computed for each community. These, together with the components making up these totals, defined the community's overall participation in the water pollution control program for a basin. Total investment costs (SIT, SDT, SRT), total annual costs (CIT, CDT, CRT), and total annual benefits (BIT, BDT, BRT) for each of the three major types of facilities—water supply, sewage treatment, and recreation—and grand totals (ST, CT, BT) were computed.

One method for achieving a reasonably satisfactory plan for water pollution control for a river basin is to make computer runs for a substantial number of input sets. The first sets might be "all primary treatment" and "all secondary treatment," to enable the planner to gain a preliminary understanding of the interactions that occur among the communities and the river sections. By successive trials and modifications of the input data, the planner may direct the plans toward specified (or desirable) objectives with respect to water qualities, costs, benefits, and other policy considerations.

An optimizing routine was developed and included in the computer program, based on the concept of "path of steepest ascent." In this procedure, changes leading to a set of quality objectives were made by means of a series of efficient steps (i.e., exhibiting a maximum gradient in the direction of an objective of minimum cost).

The optimizing routine made successive improvements to the quality of water (in terms of DO deficit) at one river station at a time. The objective quality was reached for the most upstream station for which a quality was specified, before proceeding to adjust the quality at the next station downstream with a specification. The water quality at a river station was adjusted by raising the level of treatment at one or more upstream sewage treatment plants. Up to nine "levels" of treatment were considered with the routine, ranging from a minimum of comminution and chlorination (with 10% BOD removal) to a maximum of tertiary treatment (with 99% BOD removal).

Starting with an initial state of performance levels for the treatment plants, one increment of level was examined for each plant and the *most efficient* of these increments was selected. Proceeding from the new state of performance levels, one increment was again examined for each plant and the most efficient selected. The process was repeated until the objective quality specified for the river station was reached. The routine then went on to make adjustments for the next station.

The "efficiency," or "effectiveness," of an increment (increase in level of treatment) required a definition by the planner. Three alternative measures of effectiveness were accepted by the routine and could be specified by the planner as part of the input data. Each was based on a ratio of "CDELTA" to "FDELTA." In this expression, FDELTA was the reduction of DO deficit at station I and CDELTA was the increase of cost associated with this improvement of water quality. CDELTA could be: (1) the increase in annual cost of sewage treatment; (2) the increase in annual cost of sewage treatment less the annual savings of water treatment at downstream plants; or (3) the increase in all annual costs less the increase in all annual benefits.

The results for input sets 5-2 and 6-3 were obtained by using the optimizing procedure. Input set 5-2 obtains from the assumption that a minimum of 30% BOD removal would be required, whereas input set 6-3 comprehended a minimum of 5% BOD removal. Table 12.2 shows the results, both physical and economic, of various treatment plans, all based on a specified flow (650 mgd) and DO deficit [3 parts per million (ppm)] at the control section. The central portion of the table shows the maximum DO deficit for each reach of stream.

The optimizing procedure discussed above obtained water pollution control plans for an objective of 3 ppm DO deficit in each river reach. A similar procedure could be used to obtain the most economic water pollution control plan for another objective quality, say, 4 ppm DO deficit. A comparison of the dollar values of costs and benefits for the two plans would reveal the economic effects of adopting a more or less stringent water quality objective in terms of DO deficit. Other procedures could be developed to study the economic effects implied by other water quality objectives,

TABLE 12.2   SELECTED RESULTS FROM COMPUTER RUNS—WATER POLLUTION CONTROL PROGRAMS FOR CARM-1

	All Plants: Best Primary Treatment	All Plants: Secondary Treatment	Practical Optimal Plans	
			Minimum BOD Removal 30%	Minimum BOD Removal 5%
	Input Set 2-1	*Input Set 3-1*	*Input Set 5-2*	*Input Set 6-3*
Percentage BOD removal—plant 1	38	90	30	5
2	38	90	80	80
3	38	90	80	80
4	38	90	30	30
5	38	90	80	80
6	38	90	30	5
7	38	90	30	5
8	38	90	30	5
9	38	90	30	5
Maximum DO deficit, in parts per million—station 1–6	3.00	3.00	3.00	3.00
7–16	2.82	2.79	2.82	2.83
17–23	2.97	2.60	2.70	2.72
24–26	3.21	2.46	2.65	2.68
27–32	3.78	2.29	2.91	2.94
33–43	4.84	1.47	2.71	2.75
44–47	4.87	0.97	2.49	2.56
48–57	4.96	0.84	2.64	2.33
58–59	4.14	0.07	2.10	2.46
60–62	4.16	0.05	2.20	2.60
Investment—water treatment, in dollars	16,831,888	13,209,498	16,831,888	16,831,888
Investment—sewage treatment, in dollars	30,512,824	61,025,649	34,555,492	21,951,277
Investment—water and sewage treatment, in dollars	47,344,712	74,235,147	51,387,380	38,783,165
Annual cost—water treatment, in dollars	3,189,172	1,674,344	2,505,762	2,551,326
Annual cost—sewage treatment, in dollars	3,303,979	5,781,273	3,580,302	2,721,287
Annual cost—water and sewage treatment, in dollars	6,493,151	7,455,617	6,086,064	5,272,613
Total annual benefits, in dollars	14,669,985	16,983,131	16,599,975	16,599,975
Total annual costs, in dollars	7,426,352	8,936,533	7,499,505	6,686,054
Total annual benefits less costs, in dollars	7,243,633	8,046,598	9,100,470	9,913,921

Source: Goodman and Dobbins (1966).

for example, in terms of an index for coliforms or an index defining recreation class.

The paper by Goodman and Dobbins (1966) discussed certain limitations of the optimizing routine and methods of overcoming them by a modified optimizing procedure.

Goodman and Tucker (1969) utilized the same simulation model as discussed above for a sensitivity analysis of the parameters of the BOD and DO equations in terms of required treatment levels and overall sewage treatment costs. The results showed the substantial variation of designs and costs resulting from the assumption of different values of parameters.

REFERENCES

ACKOFF, RUSSELL L., and MAURICE W. SASIENI, *Fundamentals of Operations Research*, Wiley, New York, 1968.

BALLOFFET, ARMANDO, ALVIN S. GOODMAN, and THOMAS F. SERGI, "Intermediate Time Step Simulation of Hydroelectric Power Systems," *Int. Symp. Water Resources Syst.*, University of Roorkee, India, December 20–22, 1980.

BELLMAN, R., and R. KALABA, *Dynamic Programming and Modern Control Theory*, Academic Press, New York, 1965.

BELLMAN, R. E. and S. E. DREYFUS, *Applied Dynamic Programming*, Princeton University Press, Princeton, N.J. 1962.

BISWAS, ASIT K., ed., *Systems Approach to Water Management*, McGraw-Hill, New York, 1976.

BUGLIARELLO, G., and F. J. GUNTHER, *Computer Systems and Water Resources*, Elsevier, Amsterdam, 1974.

BUNDGAARD-NIELSEN, M., and C. L. HWANG, "A Review on Decision Models in Economics of Regional Water Quality Management," *Water Resources Bull.*, vol. 12, no. 3, June 1976.

BURAS, NATHAN, *Scientific Allocation of Water Resources*, Elsevier, Amsterdam, 1972.

CAMP, T. R., *Water and Its Impurities*, Reinhold, New York, 1963.

DANTZIG, GEORGE, *Linear Programming and Extensions*, Princeton University Press, Princeton, N.J., 1963.

DOBBINS, W. E., "BOD and Oxygen Relationships in Streams," *J. Sanit. Eng. Div., Proc. Am. Soc. Civil Eng.*, vol. 90, no. SA3, June 1964.

DRACUP, J. A., et al., "An Assessment of Optimization Techniques as Applied to Water Resource Systems," U.S. Department of the Interior, Office of Water Resources Research, August 1970.

FRATAR, THOMAS J., ALVIN S. GOODMAN, and AUSTIN E. BRANT, JR., "Prediction of Maximum Practical Berth Occupancy," *Proc. Am. Soc. Civil Eng.*, paper 2517, June 1960.

GILLETT, BILLY E., *Introduction to Operations Research*, McGraw-Hill, New York, 1976.

GOICOECHEA, AMBROSE, DON R. HANSEN, and LUCIEN DUCKSTEIN, *Multiobjective Decision Analysis with Engineering and Business Applications*, Wiley, New York, 1982.

GOODMAN, ALVIN S., and WILLIAM E. DOBBINS, "Mathematical Model for Water Pollution Control Studies," *J. Sanit. Eng. Div., Proc. Am. Soc. Civil Eng.*, vol. 88, no. SA6, paper 5031, December 1966.

GOODMAN A. S. and R. J. TUCKER, "Use of Mathematical Models in Water Quality Control Studies," Res. Rep. ORD-6, U.S. Department of Interior, FWPCA, July 1969.

GYSI, MARSHALL, and DANIEL P. LOUCKS, "A Selected Annotated Bibliography on the Analysis of Water Resource Systems," Cornell University Water Resources and Marine Sciences Center, Ithaca, N.Y., August 1969.

HAAN, CHARLES T., *Statistical Methods in Hydrology*, Iowa State University Press, Ames, Iowa, 1977.

HADLEY, G., *Non-linear and Dynamic Programming*, Addison-Wesley, Reading, Mass., 1964.

HAIMES, YACOV Y., *Hierarchical Analyses of Water Resources Systems: Modeling and Optimization of Large-Scale Systems*, McGraw-Hill, New York, 1977.

HALL, WARREN A., and JOHN A. DRACUP, *Water Resources Systems Analysis*, McGraw-Hill, New York, 1970.

HILLIER, FREDERICK S., and GERALD J. LIEBERMAN, *Introduction to Operations Research*, 3rd ed. Holden-Day, San Francisco, Calif., 1980.

HIMMELBLAU, DAVID M., *Applied Non-linear Programming*, McGraw-Hill, New York, 1972.

HOOKE, R., and T. A. JEEVES, "Direct Search Solution of Numerical and Statistical Problems," *J. Assoc. Comput. Mach.*, vol. 8, no. 2, 1961.

HUFSCHMIDT, M. M., and M. F. FIERING, *Simulation Techniques for Design of Water Resources Systems*, Harvard University Press, Cambridge, Mass., 1966.

LASDON, L. S., and A. D. WARREN, "A Survey of Nonlinear Programming Applications," *Oper. Res.*, September–October 1980.

LASDON, L. S., A. D. WARREN, A. JAIN, and M. RATNER, "Design and Testing of a Generalized Reduced Gradient Code for Nonlinear Programming," *ACM Trans. Math. Softw.*, vol. 4, no. 10, March 1978.

LIEBMAN, JOHN C., and WALTER R. LYNN, "The Optimum Allocation of Stream Dissolved Oxygen," *Water Resources Res.*, 3rd quarter, 1966.

LOUCKS, D. P., "Surface-Water Quality Management Models," in *Systems Approach to Water Management*, A. K. Biswas, ed., McGraw-Hill, New York, 1976.

LOUCKS, DANIEL P., and PHILIP J. DORFMAN, "An Evaluation of Some Linear Decision Rules in Chance-Constrained Models for Reservoir Planning and Operation," *Water Resources Res.*, vol. 11, no. 6, December 1975.

LOUCKS, D. P., CHARLES S. REVELLE, and WALTER R. LYNN, "Linear Programming Models for Water Pollution Control," *Manage. Sci.*, December 1967.

LOUCKS, D. P., JERRY R. STEDINGER, and DOUGLAS A. HAITH, *Water Resource Systems Planning and Analysis*, Prentice-Hall, Englewood Cliffs, N.J., 1981.

MAASS, A., M. HUFSCHMIDT, R. DORFMAN, H. THOMAS, JR., S. MARGLIN, and G. M. FAIR, eds., *Design of Water-Resource Systems*, Harvard University Press, Cambridge, Mass., 1962.

MCBEAN, E., and J. C. SCHAAKE, "A Marginal Analysis—Systems Simulation Technique to Formulate Improved Water Resources Configurations to Meet Multiple Objectives," Rep. 166, Ralph M. Parsons Laboratory for Water Resources and Hydrodynamics, Massachusetts Institute of Technology, 1973.

MAJOR, DAVID C., and ROBERTO L. LENTON, *Applied Water Resource Systems Planning*, Prentice-Hall, Englewood Cliffs, N.J., 1979.

META SYSTEMS, INC., "Systems Analysis in Water Resources Planning," Water Information Center, Port Washington, N.Y., 1975.

MORAN, P. A. P., *The Theory of Storage*, Methuen, London, 1959.

REVELLE, C. S., E. JOERES, and W. KIRBY, "The Linear Decision Rule in Reservoir Management and Design: I. Development of the Stochastic Model," *Water Resources Res.*, vol. 5, no. 4, 1969.

SCHAAKE JOHN C., JR., ed., "Systematic Approach to Water Resources Plan Formulation," Rep. 187, Ralph M. Parsons Laboratory for Water Resources and Hydrodynamics, Massachusetts Institute of Technology, July 1974.

SCHAAKE, J. C., JR., and T. B. FACET, "Role of Partial Gradient Equation," in "Systematic Approach to Water Resources Plan Formulation," Rep. 187, John C. Schaake, Jr., ed., Massachusetts Institute of Technology, July 1974.

SCHITTKOWSKI, K., "Nonlinear Programming Codes—Information, Tests, Performance," Institut für Angewandte Mathematik und Statistik, Universität Wurzburg, West Germany, 1980.

SHAH, B. V., R. J. BUEHLER, and O. KEMPTHORNE, "Some Algorithms for Minimizing a Function of Several Variables," *J. Soc. Ind. Appl. Math.*, vol. 12, no. 1, 1964.

SHOEMAKER, L. A., "Mathematical Methods in Water Resources Development Planning and Operations," *Trans. Am. Soc. Civil Eng.*, vol. 128, 1963.

STREETER, H. W., and PHELPS, E. B., "A Study of the Pollution and Natural Purification of the Ohio River," *Public Health Bull. 146*, U.S. Public Health Service, Washington, D.C., February 1925.

THOMAS, H. A., JR., and R. P. BURDEN, "Operations Research in Water Quality Management," Final Report of Harvard Water Program, 1963.

U.S. WATER RESOURCES COUNCIL, "State of the States: Water Resources Planning and Management," April 1980.

WAREN, ALLAN D., and LEON S. LASDON, "The Status of Nonlinear Programming Software," *Oper. Res.*, vol. 27, no. 3, May–June 1979.

WILDE, DOUGLASS J., *Optimum Seeking Methods*, Prentice-Hall, Englewood Cliffs, N.J., 1963.

WILDE, D. J., and C. S. BEIGHTLER, *Foundations of Optimization*, Prentice-Hall, Englewood Cliffs, N.J., 1967.

YEH, WILLIAM W.-G., LEONARD BECKER, and WEN-SEN CHU, "Real-Time Hourly Reservoir Operation," *J. Water Resources Plann. Manage. Div., Proc. Am. Soc. Civil Eng.*, vol. 105, no. WR2, September 1979.

YEVJEVICH, VUJICA, *Stochastic Processes in Hydrology*, Water Resources Publications, Fort Collins, Colo., 1972a.

YEVJEVICH, VUJICA, *Probability and Statistics in Hydrology*, Water Resources Publications, Fort Collins, Colo., 1972b.

YOUNG, G. K., "Finding Reservoir Operation Rules," *J. Hydraul. Div., Proc. Am. Soc. Civil Eng.*, vol. 93, no. HY6, paper 5600, June 1967.

THIRTEEN

Models for Optimization:
Multiobjective
and Multipurpose

13.1 INTRODUCTION

In this chapter techniques are described for obtaining an optimal water resources plan in which trade-offs must be considered between two or more objectives. These techniques often also apply to problems in which trade-offs are made among various purposes. While purposes can take on the character of objectives in the social decision process, the analysis must take care to distinguish between purposes and objectives. When selecting a set of decision variables and operation rules, the optimal plan for one objective or purpose must be considered, and usually altered, so that the overall set of objective and purpose elements is optimized.

Three different approaches are discussed for analyzing multiobjective/purpose problems. These are mathematical programming techniques, simulation modeling, and nonmathematical methods. Various case studies are described encompassing each of these types and, in some cases, a combination of them.

13.2 MATHEMATICAL PROGRAMMING TECHNIQUES

Much of the material in this section is based on two papers on multiobjective optimization by Cohon and Marks (1973, 1975). It is an extension of some concepts

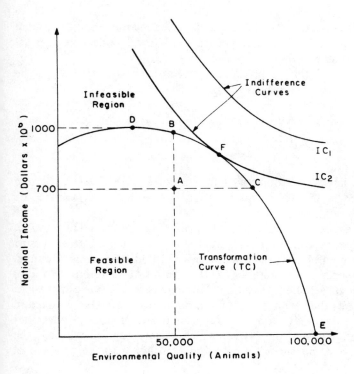

Figure 13.1 Graphical representation of multiobjective analysis. (From Cohon and Marks, 1973. Copyrighted by the American Geophysical Union.)

of multiobjective analyses that were introduced in Chapter 2. The review will start by treating the subject in only a few dimensions so that graphical illustrations are possible.

Figure 13.1 shows the basic problem of trade-offs between two objectives. Conceptually, this figure is similar to the representation by Major (1977), which was discussed in Section 2.13. The two objectives in this case are maximization of national economic development (NED) measured in dollars of income, and maximization of a component of environmental quality (EQ) measured in appropriate units. Note that although both have been quantified, they are not in commensurate units. The quantities of NED and EQ are in terms of net discounted values for the planning period, and a different discount rate could have been used for each objective. The figure derives from a study of a water resources system for which a number of alternatives have been found to be feasible. Point A, for example, corresponds to a feasible alternative with 700 NED units and 50,000 EQ units. The transformation curve (TC) represents the boundary of the set of feasible alternatives. Point D represents the achievement of maximum NED and point E the maximum EQ, but neither corresponds to multiobjective optimization.

The preferences of society are represented by a family of "social indifference" curves, such as IC_1 and IC_2. The optimal alternative will be at point F, at the tangency of the highest attainable indifference curve with the feasible set. At this point the negative slope is equal to $10,000/EQ unit, indicating the relative marginal social values of NED and EQ. This marginal trade-off toward one objective for another can be referred to as a *weight*.

In mathematical terms, this approach to "vector optimization" can be formulated as follows (Cohon and Marks 1975):

$$\text{Max } \bar{Z}(\bar{x}) = \text{Max } [Z_1(\bar{x}), Z_2(\bar{x}), \ldots, Z_k(\bar{x})]$$
$$\text{subject to: } \bar{g}_i(\bar{x}) \leq 0 \quad i = 1, \ldots, m$$
$$x_j \geq 0 \quad j = 1, \ldots, n$$

in which $\bar{Z}(\bar{x})$ is the k-dimensional objective function for k objectives. A *feasible region* in *decision space* is the set of nonnegative x_j that does not violate the constraint set $\bar{g}_i(\bar{x})$.

Strictly speaking, a vector cannot be optimized (Haimes and Hall 1974). Information about preferences, which provides a rule for combining the objectives or otherwise makes them comparable, is required in order to find an optimal solution.

In general, one chooses a "noninferior" (NI) solution, also referred to as a "Pareto optimal" solution or "efficient" solution. This extension of a basic concept of classical economics ensures that, with this solution, no increase may be obtained in any objective without causing a simultaneous decrease in at least one of the other objectives. A solution belonging to the NI set which society considers best is the "preferred," "best," "best compromise," or "optimal" solution to the problem of *vector optimization*.

Figures 13.2 and 13.3 apply to a problem involving two decision variables (x_1 and x_2), two objectives $Z_1(x_1, x_2)$ and $Z_2(x_1, x_2)$, and five constraints [$g_i(x_1, x_2)$, $i = 1, \ldots, 5$]. The feasible region in decision space and the set of noninferior

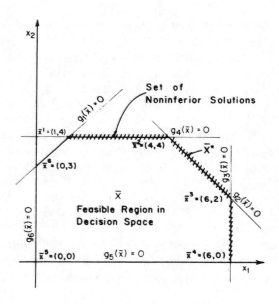

Figure 13.2 Feasible region in decision space X and the set of noninferior solutions X^*. (From Cohon and Marks, 1975. Copyrighted by the American Geophysical Union.)

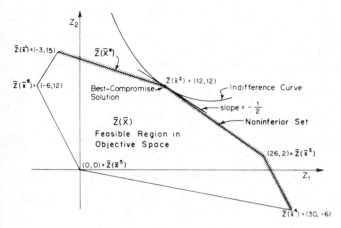

Figure 13.3 Feasible region in objective space $Z(X)$, the noninferior set $Z(X^*)$, and the best-compromise solution. (From Cohon and Marks, 1975. Copyrighted by the American Geophysical Union.)

solutions are shown in Figure 13.2. The decision variables are valued at each corner to obtain values of Z_1, Z_2, and plotted on Figure 13.3, which now shows the feasible region and the noninferior set in objective space. If the preferences of the decision maker(s) are expressed by an "indifference curve," one of the NI solutions can be identified as the "best."

It is obvious that when the objectives are increased beyond two dimensions, the simple graphics shown in Figures 13.1, 13.2, and 13.3 will no longer suffice and a more general approach must be taken to the problem of vector optimization. Multiobjective programming techniques have been classified and evaluated by a number of investigators, including Cohon and Marks (1975), Haimes, Hall, and Freedman (1975), Taylor et al. (1975), Loucks (1975), Krzysztofowicz et al. (1977), Bishop et al. (1976), Haith and Loucks (1976), and Loucks et al. (1981). These assessments have compared the utilities of the techniques using different criteria. Improvements since the earlier critiques have overcome some of the deficiencies perceived in these reviews. The following will be limited to a summary description of the techniques themselves, using the classification by Cohon and Marks (1975). References given are in addition to those cited in later sections when discussing specific studies.

Generating Techniques That Identify Only the Noninferior Set. These techniques identify the set of noninferior solutions in the decision space as well as the noninferior solutions in objective space within which the best-compromise solution will lie. One technique is to transform the various components of the objective function into a single scalar-valued function by *weighting* each of the components. The noninferior solutions are obtained for:

$$\text{Max} \sum_{k=1}^{p} W_k Z_k(\bar{x})$$

subject to: $W_k \geq 0$ for all k
and all $\bar{x}$ in decision space

The parameters (W_k) may be varied systematically to yield points that are noninferior solutions. If all the functions are linear, or can be converted to linear form, linear programming packages can be used.

The *constraint* method is similar to the dual of the weighting method. Thus, the problem is:

$$\text{Max } Z_r(\bar{x})$$

$$\text{subject to: } Z_k(\bar{x}) \geq L_k, \qquad \text{all } k \neq r$$
$$\text{and all } \bar{x} \text{ in feasible decision space}$$
$$\text{and } L_k \text{ is a lower bound on objective } k$$

This formulation also leads to a scalar function, so that the problem can be solved with existing techniques (varying L_k and using linear programming packages).

Descriptions of the use of generating techniques for multiobjective water resource problems are given by Cohon and Marks (1973), McKusick et al. (1973), Thampapillai and Sinden (1979), and McBean et al. (1979) for linear programming; Tauxe et al. (1979a,b, 1980), and Szidarovsky (1979) for dynamic programming; and Vemuri (1974), Croley and Rao (1979), and Cohon et al. (1979, 1980) for other algorithmic approaches. Various concepts of trade-off functions for multiple objectives have been explored by Miller and Byers (1973), Croley (1974), Lynne (1976), Passy (1978), and Pendse and Wyckoff (1976). Another approach used in both mathematical programming and simulation models is the use of penalty functions for failure to meet target values (Falkson 1976).

Techniques That Rely on Prior Articulation of Preferences: Noniterative Methods: These techniques reduce the computational burden (compared to generating techniques) by an ordering of preferences prior to the solution of the multiobjective problem. One such technique is *goal programming,* whose general formulation is as follows:

$$\text{Min } \sum_{k=1}^{P} |d_k|$$

$$\text{subject to: } Z_k(\bar{x}) - d_k = T_k, \qquad k = 1, 2, \ldots, p$$
$$\text{and all } \bar{x} \text{ in feasible decision space}$$

where d_k is the deviation from the target for the kth objective and is unrestricted in sign and T_k is the target for the kth objective. Here a target serves as a surrogate for preference articulation.

The aim of a *utility function* is to formulate an expression for the social indifference curve. If this is available, the best-compromise solution is found at the point at which the noninferior set (or transformation curve) and the social indifference curve are tangent. The application of this method usually requires the development of the noninferior set using generating techniques. Certain types of problems do not require the generation of the entire noninferior set. Utility functions are very difficult to formulate and their development for water resources development has been meager.

The line that passes through the point of tangency of the noninferior set and the social indifference curve is a surrogate for preferences. The slope of this line is proportional to the ratio of the weights on the objectives. This is the basis of the *optimal weights* method, which has the following formulation:

$$\text{Max } Z(\bar{x}W^*) = \sum_{k=1}^{P} W_k^* Z_k(\bar{x})$$

subject to all $\bar{x}$ in feasible decision space and where the optimal weights W^* are known. Dean and Shih (1975) have utilized the method in the analyses of alternatives for a water-oriented recreation project. Byer (1979) has considered it in the planning of a hypothetical multipurpose dam and reservoir system.

The distinguishing feature of the *surrogate worth trade-off method* is the generation of "trade-off functions," which show the relationship between a weight on one objective (when another objective is the numéraire) and the values of that objective (Haimes and Hall 1974). A set of trade-off functions may be interpreted as a disaggregated noninferior set, in which the objectives are considered in pairs. This method may also be considered in the next category.

Techniques That Rely on Progressive Articulation of Preferences. These methods can be characterized by the following general algorithmic approach: (1) find a noninferior solution; (2) get decision makers' reactions to this solution and modify the problem accordingly; and (3) repeat steps (1) and (2) until satisfaction is obtained or some other termination rule is applicable. Cohon and Marks (1975) consider the step method, or STEM, proposed by Benayoun et al. (1971) as being representative of this class of techniques. The method has also been discussed by Haith and Loucks (1976) and Loucks (1978). The method begins with the construction of a "payoff table" (Table 13.1). In row k of this table, the maximum value for the kth objective is M_k and the associated values of the other objectives in feasible decision space are Z_i^k. An ideal solution consisting of the values of the objectives in the diagonal cells M_k, $k = 1, 2, \ldots, p$ in the payoff table does not exist, since otherwise the objectives would not conflict. Step 1 in the general algorithm is accomplished by finding a

TABLE 13.1 PAYOFF TABLE FOR THE STEP METHOD

Solution That Optimizes kth Objective	Value of kth Objective					
	Z_1	Z_2	$\cdots$	Z_k	$\cdots$	Z_p
x^1	M_1			Z_k^1		
x^2		M_2		Z_k^2		
$\vdots$				$\vdots$		
x^k	Z_1^k	Z_2^k	$\cdots$	M_k	$\cdots$	Z_p^k
$\vdots$				$\vdots$		
x^p				Z_k^p		M_p

Source: Cohon and Marks (1975). Copyrighted by the American Geophysical Union

noninferior solution that is nearest in a minimax sense to the ideal solution. Step 2 of the general algorithm consists of asking the decision makers to indicate which objectives in the solution can be decreased so that unsatisfactory levels of objectives may be increased. The minimax solution is repeated, and the decision makers are again approached. The iterations continue until the decision makers are satisfied with the results.

13.3 SIMULATION TECHNIQUES

Simulation models provide results (outcomes) for an assumed set of decision variables and operating rules for water resources facilities. These results may be in terms of hydrologic performance, economic indicators (such as net benefits), project outputs of goods and services, or all of these. Objectives may be related to each of these three types of outputs. Other objectives may be embedded in constraints limiting the scale of facilities that are tested, omitting or including certain facilities, and defining the operating rules.

Simulation is usually an iterative process in which the results for a set of assumptions for decision variables and operating rules are examined by the planner, who then determines the composition of a rival set of assumptions for optimization.

Efforts at optimization are made, even if they are not based on explicit rules, when planners use conventional (nonmodeling) approaches to select a set of decision variables and operating rules to be tested by simulation. In other cases, the selection of these variables (particularly scales) and operating rules (e.g., setting priorities) is made with the assistance of preliminary models (simulation or mathematical programming). A *set* of models may be needed for complex river basin studies.

13.4 TECHNIQUES THAT EMPHASIZE OBJECTIVES THAT ARE NOT QUANTIFIABLE IN MONETARY TERMS

The methods outlined in the preceding sections stress mathematical models and other procedures that lead to a multiobjective optimum. Most of these techniques provide measures for equivalence of objectives by comparing them in terms of an economic indicator (e.g., present value of net benefits), by weightings, or by other expressions that facilitate trade-offs of amounts of the objectives.

Other methods have been developed that stress objectives in nonmonetary terms, or are designed to account for the preferences of the public, experts, and political decision makers. These methods are often useful in modern water resources planning since few projects can be implemented unless they recognize "nonmarket" impacts and the perceptions of those affected by or interested in the projects. The planning approaches and applications presented in various chapters of this book utilize techniques for considering noneconomic objectives, many of which are classified and described in this section. In practice, the methods are often not identified with the specific nomenclature presented in this section.

Finsterbusch (1977) reviewed alternative evaluation frameworks for comparing nonmarket values and identified two generic sets of techniques. The first set includes methods such as common-metric or weighting-scheme techniques, which derive a cumulative number for each option under consideration as a basis for selecting the "best" option. The techniques in the second set do not obtain cumulative numbers; rather, they provide information—in itself insufficient to make a decision—to be utilized within a decision process. The next five headings and much of the accompanying discussions are based on the Finsterbusch paper.

Common Metrics. The ideal valuation technique is one that can account for all the consequences of each alternative on a common *objective metric.* This is an unrealizable ideal. *Subjective metrics* also cannot scale all impacts of complex policies and therefore cannot provide a complete evaluation framework.

Weighting Schemes. Weighting schemes are both feasible and widely practiced. They provide procedures for aggregating scores on separate dimensions into a total score for each policy alternative. *Consensual weights* represent a consensus among experts or an official decision of an authoritative group, which are constructed from empirically established trade-off curves for the affected parties and subjective judgments of the relative importance of each group's trade-off curve. *Formula weights* provide, for example, a weight for an impact obtained by the product of people affected, intensity of impact, and probability of impact. Ortolano (1976) has reviewed a number of studies dealing with weighting of objectives and component parts of objectives (factors). *Justified subjective weights* imply that the criteria for assigning weights are explicitly identified. Procedures using *subjective weights* are quite prevalent. They may be assigned to objectives, dimensions, impacts, or alternatives and by decision makers, expert judges, representatives of interested parties, or samples of the relevant general public. Subjective weights may be assigned by simple score assignment process, a trade-off matrix, paired comparison trade-offs, indifference curves, or Delphi procedures.

When a certain type of judgment is made repeatedly, the judges' subjective weights may be inferred from past choices using linear regression. Subjective weights can also be inferred from data other than previous choices. One of the easiest weighting schemes includes *ranking.* It is easy to judge whether one item is preferable to another and to establish a ranking on a particular dimension. When several dimensions are involved, however, rankings on individual dimensions are less likely to sum to the best choice than are ratio-scaled subjective weights. *Equal weights* are the simplest but are the least accurate. Frequently, projects combine several of these techniques in the evaluation of alternatives. Also, more than one method may be used for the same evaluations, and the results compared and combined into a compromise set of scores.

Various matrix approaches for multiobjective planning that combine technical engineering and citizen preferences into a matrix decision-making tool have been used. Klee (1970) has developed a system called DARE (for "decision alternative ratio evaluation"). This involves a dual evaluation system. First, a series of technical evaluations by planners describe how each alternative satisfies each objective. Next, a second set of weights by citizens describes the importance of each objective in the overall project. Various methods are available to minimize inconsistencies. Other matrices were developed and tested by Phillips (1978) and Phillips and DeFilippi (1976).

The techniques of goal programming, the surrogate-worth trade-off (SWT) method, and ELECTRE are mathematical programming methods that utilize the concepts of metrics, weighting, and matrices. Scores on a scale, say −10 to +10 or −1 to 1, are used in the SWT method, and in several environmental assessment schemes. An elaborate paired comparison technique is the outranking method in ELECTRE (David and Duckstein 1976). Fuzzy set theory has also been proposed as a suitable framework for evaluating qualitative information (Zadeh 1973); applications to water resources planning have been investigated by Znotinas and Hipel (1979), Ragade et al. (1976a; 1976b), and Kempf et al. (1979). Bishop (1972) has described the "factor profile" method of comparing the indirect, environmental, social, and community effects with the economic effects of a water resources plan.

Discrete Dimensions Evaluation. This term refers to a decision-making framework that does not have a set of weights or a total score. In the *balance sheet* approach, all important costs and benefits are presented in summary form. The system of accounts described by the Water Resources Council in its planning guidelines for showing the beneficial and adverse effects of a recommended project and considered alternatives is an example of this approach. *Lexicographic pruning* is a method proposed by Finsterbusch which provides for immediately eliminating from consideration alternatives that are rated low with respect to dimensions of overriding importance. A *minimum criteria analysis* provides minimum standards for all dimensions and for eliminations of alternatives that violate any of these standards. Minimum wastewater treatment criteria to meet effluent or water quality standards is an example.

Methods That Utilize Public or Political Evaluations. These methods link a public participation program with technical planning. Finsterbusch identifies three target groups for external evaluation of alternatives: *public choice, advisory committee choice,* and the *political process.*

Methods That Obviate Evaluation. Finally, Finsterbusch indicates that there are several ways to take nonmarket impacts into account. If it is possible to *standardize costs or benefits* of a project for all alternatives, the evaluation process is greatly simplified. A second procedure for making the evaluation of nonmarket impacts unnecessary is to *minimize negative effects* from the start. A third procedure is *compensation and mitigation* of adverse effects.

Another approach to classifying techniques has been to use the term "forecasting techniques," for which three categories have been proposed: time series and projections, models and simulations, and qualitative and holistic techniques. These were analyzed for their suitability for water resources planning in three publications prepared at the Stanford Research Institute (Mitchell et al. 1975, 1977). The descriptions of techniques under the next five headings are based on this work and have been selected for their applicability to the mathematical models discussed later in this chapter and also to the nonmarket evaluations discussed above.

Expert-Opinion Methods (Panels and Delphi). When panels are used, experts are brought together in open discussion to reach a consensus judgment concerning the future of a specified trend or project. Panels may be informal, ad hoc, one-time-only groups meeting face to face to hammer out a consensus. Many other variations are possible, including extremely formal, continuing groups which—as in Delphi panels—may never meet face to face. The Delphi technique differs from most panel techniques in usually maintaining anonymity of panel members, iteration of results with controlled feedback, and statistical group response. With Delphi, a panel of experts is asked to give their judgment on the future of specified trends or events. Responses are summarized and returned to the panel for reassessment of previous judgments. Usually, three iterations are involved. Expertise may be equated with special knowledge about a topic, informed opinions about the attitudes and intents of some population, or both.

Singg and Webb (1979) have described the use of Delphi methodology to assess goals and social impacts of the Cooper Dam and Reservoir Project in Texas. A Delphi poll on the future of American water resource utilization and development was conducted for the Institute for Water Resources of the Corps of Engineers (University of Minnesota, 1973).

Scenarios and Paradigms. Scenarios are literary, numerical, and/or graphic narratives which describe and explore the implications of future sequences of events and states of affairs, given some specified topic and some set of explicit or implicit premises. It is basically an outline of one conceivable state of affairs, given certain assumptions about the present and the course of events in the intervening period. It is important to note that scenarios usually are "portraits of *possible* futures" rather than predictions of what will come to pass.

The development of scenarios requires a large fund of data, information, and ideas pertinent to the topic. It also requires writers who can devise relatively smooth and plausible accounts in rich detail dependent on scattered, disparate, discontinuous individual forecasts. Four scenarios were generated by the Omaha district of the U.S. Corps of Engineers (1975) for exploring alternative patterns of future growth in the region in connection with the Urban Studies Program of the Corps.

Paradigms are similar to scenarios. A paradigm is different in that it shows side by side the characteristics and implications of various futures, such as those which might be developed in a scenario. They can be used to analyze various sets of ideas on a comparative basis. A paradigm may have a special structure and functional notation that enables new concepts to be logically derived from a previous part and that provides for systematic cross-tabulation of concepts.

Decision Trees and Matrices. Decision (or issue) trees, described in Chapter 11, represent the structure of all possible sequences of decisions and outcomes and provides for cost, value, and probability inputs. Trees are used mainly to evaluate alternatives and determine the sequences of decisions that should be used to pursue planning goals. Probabilities of occurrence and values are assigned to each of the possible outcomes. The optimum decision is usually found by selecting the alternative of highest expected value, but other bases (e.g., minimax) are also possible.

Another use of trees is in relevance trees. This is a systematic decision-making aid in which weighted indexes based on consensus expert judgment are used to indicate how closely related (relevant) given technological capabilities are to specified needs. Needs may be specified generally (e.g., nationally) or at one or more levels of successive detail, with relevance index numbers assigned at each level. The output is a relevance tree diagram, showing the technological capabilities analyzed, together with the names of the levels or sectors for which relevance index numbers have been estimated, and the index numbers themselves.

Decision matrices are conceptually an extension of decision trees. When two basic kinds of factors (e.g., resources versus requirements) are crucial, a two-dimensional decision table is used. When three kinds of factors are crucial, a three-dimensional cube is employed. A variety of quantitative and qualitative procedures are used to specify each interrelationship among all the factors considered.

Games. A simulation game is an activity involving two or more decision makers playing assigned roles seeking to achieve role-related objectives in some limiting concept. They facilitate learning about the subtle consequences of actions, the development of scenarios, and the assessment of policy options. Good decision-making games combine the analytical, rational, technical point of view with the intuitive, artistic, "seat-of-the-pants" experience of decision making in the real world.

Through multiple iterations of a particular game, alternative scenarios can be devised for the situation under study (e.g., initial assumptions, timing, roles, etc.). The game may be based on historical or hypothetical case studies. Policymaking in a particular situation usually calls for a unique game to be designed. Ideally, the participants in a game will be those directly involved in the decisions to be made. Several rounds of play may be involved (e.g., one round equals one year). There are three main results:

- Learning of the participants
- Alternative scenarios of development (forecasts of alternative outcomes that incorporate the softer, nonquantifiable variables)
- Evaluation of alternative actions

There is a whole field of operations research, called "game theory," that deals with competitive situations in a formal, abstract way, and which places particular emphasis on the decision-making process of the adversaries. The bulk of the research on game theory has been on problems involving only two adversaries or players (armies, teams, firms, etc.). In this respect, game theory is different from the simulation games described above, which involve an average of 10 to 30 players with different personal and institutional points of view.

Concepts of game theory have been investigated for their applicability to water resources planning problems in which tangible and intangible effects are viewed differently by various interest groups. Approaches using the theory of "metarationality" and "metagames" have been presented by Hipel et al. (1976), Ragade et al. (1976), Fronza et al. (1977), and Hipel and Fraser (1980).

Cross-Impact Analysis and KSIM. Cross-impact analysis has some similarities with decision matrices. Participants in scenario writing, Delphi forecasting, and other techniques also intuitively make use of cross-impact analysis. The procedure compares individual forecasts on a pairwise basis to determine whether there are any interactions among several forecasts. It is judgmental, but the use of experts and probabilities provides for extensive feedback and review. The technique provides insight into trade-off options and is useful in testing the consequences of various policy actions.

With a typical cross-impact matrix, initial probabilities of occurrence are estimated for various events (e.g., project impacts such as lower population, more leisure, more urban, more households). Assuming that each event were to occur in turn, participants are asked to estimate conditional probabilities of all the other events. The initial and conditional probabilities can be used in a simulation procedure involving random numbers (Gordon and Hayward 1965) to arrive at a final probability estimate of each event in a new scenario.

KSIM is a cross-impact simulation technique developed by Kane et al. (1973) which combines a small group workshop procedure with a mathematical forecasting model and a computer program to generate changes over time for significant planning variables.

Social Welfare Goal Evaluation—Techcom (Strawman). A technical committee of the Water Resources Research Centers of 13 western states developed the TECHCOM (earlier called STRAWMAN) model, which relates water resources development and use to social goals (Brown et al. 1974; Technical Committee of the Water Resources Centers, 1971, 1974; Gum, Roefs, and Kimball 1976; Roefs 1976). The model is characterized by a hierarchy of goals, all subsumed under the general goal "social welfare." Nine phrases were selected to describe goals of all human endeavor in this model: individual security, collective security, environmental security, economic opportunity, recreational opportunity, aesthetic opportunity, individual freedom and variety, educational opportunity, and cultural and community opportunity. These phrases were intended to be collectively exhaustive but not mutually exclusive (Roefs 1976). These primary goals were further defined by various levels of subgoals. At the lowest level of subgoals, a set of "social indicators" was determined.

An aggregation process used by TECHCOM is based on the use of a power function to model peoples' satisfaction with subgoals. Gum et al. (1976) describe a procedure for determined preference weights for the various goals by utilizing public input to questions.

13.5 NESTED MODELS AND HIERARCHICAL ANALYSES

It has been found that the systems studies for complex river basins can be carried out comprehensively and efficiently when a set of linked models is used in which the outputs of one model are inputs to another. This is particularly true when the river basins have multiunit, multipurpose, multiobjective characteristics and/or when the investigations involve interrelationships of water user units and groundwater and surface water supplies. Meta Systems (1971) suggested the term "nested models" to describe such a set of models. The choice of models and their linkages are usually problem specific. The output from one model need not be fed automatically into other models. Substantial review and possible adjustments may be made by the planners before the results are used. The process need not always be in a forward direction, since there may be feedback links and also reiteration.

Many features of this approach were used for the river basin master planning in the Vardar/Axios Basin, discussed in Chapter 6 and again in this chapter, and the Rio Colorado Basin, also discussed in this chapter. Planning by the Texas Water Development Board (1974) included the development of a variety of models for use in studies of the large multibasin, multipurpose water resource system of the Texas Water System; the emphasis in this planning was on irrigation and on minimizing cost (or maximizing benefits).

Haimes (1977) has developed a formal approach for hierarchical analyses for studies of complex water resource systems, which involves mathematical procedures for decomposition and multilevel optimization. The reader is referred to Haimes's book (1977) for his extensive mathematical formulation and numerous examples. One component of the package of models is discussed in a later subsection of this chapter (the surrogate worth trade-off method).

13.6 GOAL PROGRAMMING—CROSS FLORIDA BARGE CANAL

Goal programming methods are adaptations of linear programming and its extensions (e.g., integer programming). General references are Charnes and Cooper (1961), who are usually credited with the development of goal programming, Mao (1969), and Lee (1972). It has been discussed in a water resources planning context by Taylor et al. (1975), Neely et al. (1976), and Sellers and North (1979).

The objective function with goal programming is formulated to consider more than one objective. The priorities among the objectives are defined by a scalar procedure involving weights. Policy decisions are required to define a desired level for each goal and a relative penalty weight for failure to achieve the goal. Goal programming can also permit an ordinal weighting of objectives (Keown and Martin 1976) or an absolute ranking system (Krouse 1974). Sellers and North (1979) have outlined the following formulation for considering multiple objectives:

$$\text{Minimize } Z = \sum_{i=1}^{n} |W_i^+ Y_i^+ + W_i^- Y_i^-|$$

$$\text{subject to: } \sum_{i=1}^{n} \sum_{j=1}^{m} GC_{ij}X_j - W_i^+ Y_i^+ + W_i^- Y_i^- \gtrless GL_i$$

$$\text{for all } X_j \geq 0$$

where

GC_{ij} = amount of any goal i contributed by any alternative j
X_j = a decision variable corresponding to any alternative j
W_i^+ = penalty weight for overattainment of GL_i
W_i^- = penalty weight for underattainment of GL_i
Y_i^+ = positive deviation from a goal, GL_i
Y_i^- = negative deviation from a goal, GL_i
GL_i = a goal level specified which may be underachieved, overachieved, or exactly achieved.

North et al. (1976) adapted the goal programming methodology to an analysis of the Cross Florida Barge Canal, with specific reference to the Oklawaha River Valley. The study has been described by Sellers and North (1979). The work involved the consideration of fourteen alternatives, each with different contributions to 12 components of national economic development (NED) and 11 components of environmental quality (EQ) values. The alternative plans were developed and evaluated with NED and EQ as coequal objectives. The procedure consisted of the following steps:

1. All viable alternatives were determined, subject to resource constraints.
2. The positive and negative effects on desirable outcomes of each operational alternative were estimated.
3. Estimates were made of desired goal levels (second column of Table 13.2), subject to physical capacity constraints, demand estimates, or other parameters.
4. The relationship of goal levels to resource capacities was estimated for each operational alternative.
5. Goal weights and acceptable penalties for under- or overachievement were established.
6. These relationships and the GP technique were used to determine the "highest and best use" alternative and preference ordering of other alternatives (see Table 13.2).

In the approach employed by Sellers and North (1979), the preferred solution ("highest and best solution") was obtained as the combination of operational alternatives that minimized the sum of the weighted deviations. They also modified the programming algorithm to delete the "highest and best use solution" and produce a "second best" solution that optimizes the specified goals "ex" the preferred highest and best-use solution. For the goal levels specified in the Cross Florida Barge Canal restudy, the successively less desirable alternatives were outlined with a general indication of the sensitivity of various goals. In earlier goal programming formulations the "second best" solutions would have been obtained by varying either goal levels or goal weights to indicate the consequences of different sets of priorities.

TABLE 13.2 SUMMARY OF GOAL ACHIEVEMENTS FOR THE "PREFERRED" AND SELECTED ALTERNATIVE SOLUTIONS, CROSS FLORIDA BARGE CANAL STUDY AREA

Objectives/Goals (Units)	Goal Levels	Restore Tourism, Rodman, Eureka, West End, Scenic River Park, Upper River	Restore National Recreation Area, Rodman, Eureka, Upper River, W&S River, West End[a]	Construct CFBC with Upland R 18 Routing[b]
ECONOMIC				
Commercial navigation (mil. $, PV)	390.537	0.000	0.000	390.537
General recreation (mil. days, AA)	6.800	6.765	4.637	2.112
Flood damage reduction (mil. $, AA)	0.002	0.000	0.000	0.002
Developed land (000 acres)	15.710	13.191	13.125	12.143
Agricultural development (mil. $, PV)	6.873	6.073	6.110	6.417
Wildlife development (000 days)	254.091	249.370	252.715	210.128
Forestry development (mil. $, PV)	75.344	57.285	4.924	50.883
Fishery development (000 days)	424.172	98.393	98.393	211.927
Tourism development (mil. days, AA)	7.340	7.340	0.480	0.050
Facilities area (000 acres)	1.290	0.614	0.548	1.290
Capital cost (mil. $, PV)	16.700	61.811	60.567	306.133
OMR cost (mil. $, AA)	0.140	1.191	0.758	3.062
ENVIRONMENTAL				
Reservoir area (000 acres)	3.501	3.501	3.501	14.366
River length (miles)	78.000	78.000	78.000	55.400
Wetlands area (000 acres)	3.254	3.254	3.254	2.812
Reservoir shoreline (miles)	213.800	26.300	26.300	118.300
Aquatic habitat, others (000 acres)	4.068	4.068	4.068	3.209
Water quality (yes/no)	4.000	4.000	4.000	2.000
Game habitat (000 acres)	110.414	109.300	109.868	94.624
Rare species effects (no. species)	+7.000	+7.000	+7.000	−24.000
Cultural features (no sites)	5.000	5.000	5.000	5.000
Natural features (no. sites)	13.000	13.000	13.000	10.000
Aquifer effects (yes/no)	4.000	4.000	4.000	3.000

[a]The Tourism Development and Scenic River Park operational alternatives were deleted from consideration.
[b]The Tourism Development, National Recreation Area (Restore and Preserve), Scenic River Park, Wild and Scenic River, Abandon and Preserve, and Maintain operational alternatives were deleted from consideration.
Source: Sellers and North (1979).

13.7 MULTICRITERION RANKING (ELECTRE) AND MULTIATTRIBUTE UTILITY THEORY— TISZA RIVER BASIN

Several studies have been made of alternative systems for water resources development in the 30,000-square kilometer Tisza River Basin in Hungary (David and Duckstein 1976; Keeney and Wood 1977; Duckstein 1978; Duckstein and

Opricovic 1980). The analyses considered five principal systems, each of which was an optimal selection within its own constraints: (1) Danube–Tisza Interbasin Transfer using a multipurpose canal-reservoir system; (2) Pumped Reservoir System in the northeastern part of the region; (3) Flat Land Reservoir System; (4) Mountain Reservoir System in Upper Tisza River Basin; and (5) Groundwater Storage System.

In the David and Duckstein "cost-effectiveness" approach (1976), sets of goals (objectives) for development over a 55-year planning horizon were established for: (1) water requirements; (2) flood protection; (3) drainage and used water disposal; (4) utilization of resources; (5) environmental impact; and (6) flexibility. Specifications or "criterion functions" were used to define ideal quantities of the goal components and "opportunity losses" when plans departed from these values. When monetary values could not be assigned, other "measures of effectiveness" (MOE) were used (e.g., very good, good, fair, and bad). Table 13.3 charts the results for each system for 12 criteria.

The multicriterion algorithm ELECTRE (Benayoun et al. 1972) was selected for further comparisons. This method is based on "outranking" relationships in which a "concord index" and a "discord index" are calculated to express a comparison between any two alternative systems. Two systems, i and j, were compared according to 12 criteria. For each criterion, the relationship between i and j may be expressed as $i < j$ (j preferred to i), $i > j$ (i preferred to j), or $i = j$. Criterion weights used by David and Duckstein for computing the concord index are shown on Table 13.4; for ties, one-half of the weight was used.

The concord index between systems i and j with a hypothesis $i < j$ is defined as

$$c(i, j) = \frac{\text{sum of weights where } i < j}{\text{total sum of weights}}$$

The concord index between systems III and IV was as follows:

$$C(\text{III, IV}) = \frac{2 + 1 + 2 + 2 + 0 + 2 + 1 + 0 + 2 + 0 + 0 + 1}{20} = 0.65$$

A discord coefficient was calculated for each of the criteria where $i > j$, using values on Table 13.4, and the largest for each i, j was selected as the discord index, as follows:

$$d(i, j) = \frac{\text{maximum interval where } i > j}{\text{total range of scale}}$$

For the discord index between systems III and IV, the largest interval was for criterion 10, for which the numerator is $20/4 = 5$, and the index is, accordingly,

$$d(\text{III, IV}) = \frac{5}{20} = 0.250$$

TABLE 13.3 SYSTEM VERSUS CRITERIA ARRAY

Number	Criteria	Alternative System				
		I	II	III	IV	V
1	Yearly Costs on Optimal Level					
	Construction and operation:	83.5	66.0	54.0	62.4	47.0
	Expected Losses:	16.1	19.7	47.1	32.7	54.8
	Total (10^9 ft/yr):	99.6	85.7	101.1	95.1	101.8
2	Probability of water shortage	4	19	50	50	50
3	Water quality	Very good	Good	Bad	Very good	Fair
4	Energy (reuse factor)	0.7	0.5	0.01	0.1	0.01
5	Recreation	Very good	Good	Fair	Bad	Bad
6	Flood protection (%)	Good	Excellent	Fair	Excellent	Bad
		(1)	(0.5)	(1.5)	(0.5)	(2)
7	Land and forest use (1000 hectares)	90	80	80	60	70
8	Manpower impact	Very good	Very good	Good	Fair	Fair
9	Environmental architecture	Very good	Good	Bad	Good	Fair
10	International cooperation	Very easy	Easy	Fairly difficult	Difficult	Fairly difficult
11	Development possibility	Very good	Good	Fair	Bad	Fair
12	Sensitivity	Not sensitive	Not sensitive	Very sensitive	Sensitive	Very sensitive

Source: David and Duckstein (1976).

TABLE 13.4 DATA FOR COMPUTING DISCORD AND CONCORD INDICES

Number	Criteria	Maximum Scale Intervals (for Discord Index)	Criterion Weight (for Concord Index)
1	Costs	20	2
2	Water shortage	19	2
3	Water quality	18	2
4	Energy	17	2
5	Recreation	16	2
6	Flood protection	18	2
7	Land and forest use	10	1
8	Manpower	10	1
9	Environmental architecture	16	2
10	International cooperation	20	2
11	Development possibility	10	1
12	Sensitivity	10	1
			20

Source: David and Duckstein (1976).

As shown above, where descriptions such as excellent, very good, good, fair, and poor are used, the total interval is proportioned accordingly (in this case, into five intervals).

The concord and discord indexes are shown for the five systems in two matrices with rows i and columns j in Table 13.5. The values in the discord index were limited to those for concord index greater or equal to 0.45. The systems were further compared using "composite graphs" to indicate preferences for limiting values of concord index ($\geq p$) and discord index ($\leq q$).

Keeney and Wood (1977) reviewed some of the more important characteristics of *multiattribute utility theory* and made a preliminary evaluation of the five development alternatives for the Tisza River Basin using the same information on project characteristics and outputs. Multiattribute utility theory involves concepts that go beyond the representation of multiple objectives as a weighted linear function or as modified by constraints, as discussed in earlier sections. Keeney and Wood state that the multiattribute utility approach, "which requires an explicit consideration of the trade-offs among attributes, is a cardinal evaluation of the alternatives. This indicates how much better, given the assumptions, one alternative is than another and permits as well a sensitivity analysis of the trade-offs used." Keeney and Wood discuss the reasonableness of utility theory in aiding decision making (Raiffa 1968), theorems stating conditions under which the utility function can be expressed in simple form (Fishburn 1970; Keeney 1974; Raiffa 1969), and applications to decision problems (Keeney and Raiffa 1976). Kryzysztofowicz and Duckstein (1979) have made a study of assessment errors that can occur in multiattribute utility functions.

The first step in the utility assessment was to obtain a set of attributes and their ranges to be used in evaluating alternatives. For this study, attributes $x_1 \cdots x_{12}$ are

TABLE 13.5 MATRICES OF CONCORD AND DISCORD INDEXES

$$[C] - [c(i, j)] = \begin{bmatrix} - & 0.30 & 0.05 & 0.30 & 0.05 \\ 0.70 & - & 0.02 & 0.25 & 0.05 \\ 0.95 & 0.98 & - & 0.65 & 0.45 \\ 0.70 & 0.75 & 0.35 & - & 0.27 \\ 0.95 & 0.95 & 0.55 & 0.73 & - \end{bmatrix}$$

$$[D] = [d(i, j)] = \begin{bmatrix} - & - & - & - & - \\ 0.875 & - & - & - & - \\ 0.125 & 0.00 & - & 0.25 & 0.225 \\ 0.500 & 0.250 & - & - & - \\ 0.375 & 0.125 & 0.250 & 0.250 & - \end{bmatrix}$$

shown in Table 13.6. Subjective indices were put on a 0 to 100 scale based on the David and Duckstein work, for the purpose of quantifying the utility functions; for example, for recreation, 100 was assigned for an "excellent" rating, 80 for very good, 60 for good, 40 for fair, 20 for bad, and 0 for no recreation potential. In the next step, Keeney and Wood investigated the appropriateness of various preferential and utility independence assumptions. Three types of tests indicated the proper type of utility function as the multiplicative form

$$1 + ku(x_1, x_2, \ldots, x_{12}) = \prod_{i=1}^{12} [1 + kk_i u_i(x_i)]$$

where u is scaled from 0 to 1; the component utility functions u_i, $i = 1, \ldots, 12$, are scaled from 0 to 1; the scaling constants k_i, $i = 1, \ldots, 12$, are positive and less than 1, and k is a constant calculated from the k_i. The Keeney and Wood (1977) paper describes the assessment of the u_i and k_i values that define the utility function. For the

TABLE 13.6 ATTRIBUTES FOR THE TISZA PROBLEM

Attribute	Measure	Worst	Best
$X_1 \equiv$ costs[a]	10^9 ft/yr	110	80
$X_2 \equiv$ water shortage	Percent	60	0
$X_3 \equiv$ water quality	Subjective	0	100
$X_4 \equiv$ energy[b]	$\alpha \equiv$ energy produced/energy used	0	1
$X_5 \equiv$ recreation	Subjective	0	100
$X_6 \equiv$ flood protection	Recurrence interval	40	500
$X_7 \equiv$ land and forest use	1000 hectares	100	50
$X_8 \equiv$ social impact	Subjective	0	100
$X_9 \equiv$ environment	Subjective	0	100
$X_{10} \equiv$ international cooperation	Subjective	0	100
$X_{11} \equiv$ development possibility	Subjective	0	100
$X_{12} \equiv$ flexibility	Subjective	0	100

[a]Twenty forints are equal to $1.
[b]Reuse factor.
Source: Keeney and Wood (1977). Copyrighted by the American Geophysical Union.

five alternative systems, Keeney and Wood found the utilities to be as follows:

System	Utility Value
I	0.832
II	0.831
III	0.503
IV	0.648
V	0.521

These results implied that system I is a little better than II, which is much better than IV, which in turn is much better than V. System III is the least desirable. Various tests were then carried out to determine the sensitivity of the utilities to different values of attributes, uncertainties in achieving levels of attributes, and changes in the k_i weights (i.e., the trade-offs) of the utility function.

A number of methods are available for multiobjective decision making studies such as those for the Tisza River Basin, in addition to the ELECTRE cost-effectiveness approach and multiattribute utility theory, which were discussed earlier in this section. Compromise programming has been compared with the first two methods by Duckstein (1978) and Duckstein and Opricovic (1980). Armijo et al. (1978) have discussed the applicability of Q-analysis (polyhedral dynamics) to multicriterion ranking that involves both quantitative and qualitative measures. A number of other methods involve active participation in the decision-making process, including SEMOPS (Monarchi et al. 1973), TRADE (Goicoechea et al. 1976), and PROTRADE (Goicoechea et al. 1979); the latter utilizes chance constraints for noneconomic factors. The surrogate worth trade-off method (Haimes and Hall, 1974) and STEM (Benayoun et al. 1971; Haith and Loucks 1976; Loucks 1978) are other examples of mathematical programming approaches. Other methods include metagame theory (Hipel et al. 1976) and special versions of ELECTRE and concordance analysis (Duckstein 1978). These and other methods for multiobjective decision analysis have been reviewed by Goicoechea et al. (1982).

13.8 SURROGATE WORTH TRADE-OFF METHOD— KSC RIVER BASIN

The surrogate worth trade-off (SWT) method was developed by Haimes and Hall. References describing the methodology are Haimes and Hall (1974), Hall and Haimes (1976), Haimes, Hall, and Freedman (1975), and Haimes (1977). It has been applied to problems involving multiple-purpose reservoir use (Haimes and Hall 1974; Ahmed 1978); water quality management as affected by non–point- and point-source pollution (Das and Haimes 1979); comprehensive river basin planning (Haimes, Das, and Sung 1979); and interior drainage systems behind levees (Haimes et al. 1980).

The SWT approach to the multiobjective planning problem emphasizes the relative value of the trade-off of a marginal increase or decrease between any two objectives. With this method, it is not necessary to assess the absolute values of the objectives, and they may be in noncommensurate units. The process involves the generation of noninferior sets and "surrogate worth trade-off" functions. The decision maker participates in the evaluation of the surrogate worth trade-off function by expressing his preferences on an ordinal scale. Some solutions are obtained in which the procedure leads to a point where all worth functions are zero. In other cases, the noninferior solution whose worth functions are closest to zero is accepted as the maximum utility solution.

Ahmed (1978) analyzed the water resources in the K-S-C river basin in Pakistan by means of the SWT method. The analyses focused on maximizing firm power, maximizing firm irrigation water, and minimizing cost. Firm power, firm irrigation water, and cost were, therefore, the three objectives. The general formulation is:

$$\text{Max } Z_1 (\underline{X})$$
$$\text{subject to: } Z_j(\underline{X}) \geq \varepsilon_j; \quad j = 1, 2$$
$$g_k(\underline{X}) \leq 0; \quad k = 1, 2, \ldots, m$$

The general Lagrangian for the above is

$$L = Z_1(\underline{X}) + \sum_{k=1}^{m} \mu_k g_k(\underline{X}) + \sum_{j=1}^{2} \lambda_{ij}[Z_j(\underline{X}) - \varepsilon_j]$$

The μ_k values and the λ values are Lagrange multipliers, which are either zero or nonzero. It has been shown (Haimes and Hall 1974) that the nonzero Lagrange multipliers correspond to the noninferior set of solutions, whereas the zero Lagrange multipliers correspond to the inferior set of solutions. Therefore, only $\lambda_{ij} > 0$ have to be considered in the analysis, and

$$\lambda_{ij} = -\frac{\partial Z_i(\underline{X})}{\partial Z_j(\underline{X})} \qquad \text{holds for all } \lambda_{ij} > 0$$

If T_{ij} represents the trade-off function between $Z_i(\underline{X})$ and $Z_j(\underline{X})$, then

$$T_{ij} = \lambda_{ij} = -\frac{\partial Z_i(\underline{X})}{\partial Z_j(\underline{X})} \qquad \text{and can be approximated by}$$

$$T_{ij} = \left. \frac{\Delta Z_i(\underline{X})}{\Delta Z_j(\underline{X})} \right| \begin{array}{l} Z_n(\underline{X}) \text{ where } Z_n(\underline{X}) \text{ is held constant for} \\ \text{all } n \neq i, j \end{array}$$

Extensive computations were made of the possible trade-offs between firm irrigation water and firm power; these relationships were charted on three figures. Thus, Figure 13.4 shows firm water versus firm power for various storage capacities and total costs. The negative of the slope of a storage capacity isoquant is the marginal rate at which firm water and firm power can be substituted for each other while the storage capacity is held constant. This figure also includes isocost transformation curves showing trade-offs between firm water and firm power while total cost is held constant. A horizontal curve shows no possibility of substitution

TABLE 13.7   RESULTS OF MULTIOBJECTIVE ANALYSIS FOR K-S-C RIVER BASIN

	Simulation-Optimization Model and Transformation Functions					Decision Maker	
Trial	E_f^* (MW/yr)	W_f (MAF/yr)[a]	C (million $ per year)	$\lambda_{C.E._f}$ ($/kW)	$\lambda_{C.W._f}$ ($/AF)[a]	$\omega_{C.W._f}$	$\omega_{C.E._f}$
1	122	2.5	12.5	98	1.562	+5	+8
2	150	2.7	15.55	99.5	.94	+3	+5
3	175	3.0	18.05	101	1.25	+2	+3
4	263	3.6	29.55	160	5.32	−5	+1
5	298	3.17	33.9	333	5.0	+2	−2
6[b]	275	3.295	31.1	145	4.17	0	0

[a]AF = acre-feet; MAF = million acre-feet

[b]Trial 6 provides the most preferred solution, with $E_f^{**} = 275$ MW/yr, $W_f^{**} = 3.295$ MAF/yr, and $C^{**} = 31.1$ million $/yr.

Source: Ahmed (1978).

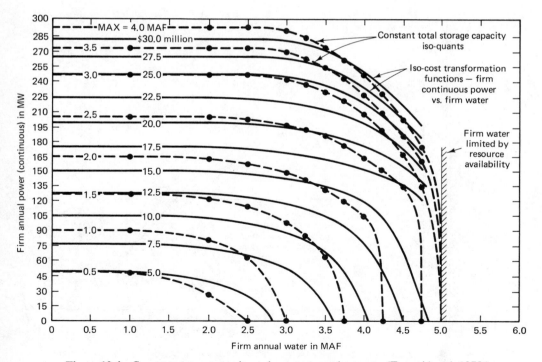

Figure 13.4   Constant storage capacity and constant cost isoquants. (From Ahmed, 1978.)

between firm water and firm power. Other figures (not shown here) were prepared for the cost of firm water at various levels of firm power and for the cost of firm power at various levels of firm water.

To apply the SWT method, the decision maker (DM) must rate his or her willingness to make substitutions. The DM expresses preferences at each trade-off point on a scale of -10 to $+10$, with minus values signifying disfavor, plus values signifying favor, and zero signifying indifference. As long as the ratings are favorable (surrogate worth ratios are positive) the solution proceeds to higher combined costs. The surrogate worth ratios are based on annual cost C, annual firm power E_f, and annual firm water W_f. The process for the K-S-C River Basin involved SWT values obtained from Figure 13.4 and the two figures not shown; the results of the process are shown on Table 13.7 and Figures 13.5 and 13.6.

The following solution set E_f, W_f, and C was assumed to start the analysis procedure:

$$E_f = 122 \text{ MW}$$
$$W_f = 2.5 \text{ MAF}$$
$$C = 12.5 \text{ million \$/year}$$

The following trade-off ratio between firm water and annual cost corresponding to this solution set was estimated:

$$\lambda C, W_f = \frac{\Delta C}{\Delta W_f} \ \bigg|\ E_{f=122} = 1.56 \text{ \$/AF}$$

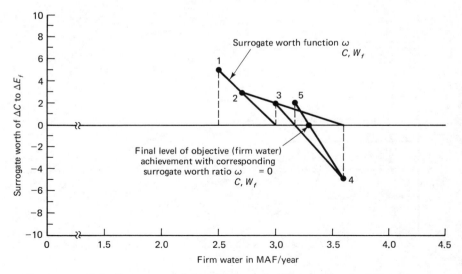

Figure 13.5 Surrogate worth function for trade-off between cost and firm water. (From Ahmed, 1978.)

Models for Optimization: Multiobjective and Multipurpose   Chap. 13

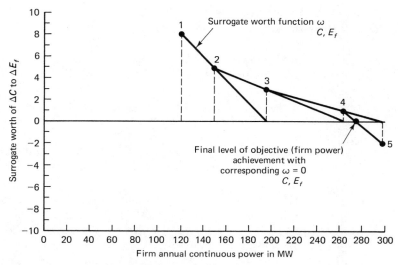

Figure 13.6 Surrogate worth function for trade-off between cost and firm power. (From Ahmed, 1978.)

The following trade-off ratio between firm power and annual cost was estimated:

$$\lambda C,\, E_f = \frac{\Delta C}{\Delta E_f} \;\Bigg|\; W_{f=2.5} = 98 \; \$/kW$$

At this point, the DM was asked the following question:

With a magnitude of 2.5 MAF/year of firm water and 122 MW of continuous firm annual power achieved at a total annual cost of 12.5 million dollars per year, would you be willing to pay an additional $1.56 per year in order to have 1.0 AF more of water availability? Please rate your willingness on a scale of −10—if totally unwilling—to +10 if totally willing—and with zero signifying indifference. Similarly, please rate your willingness to pay an additional $98 per year to raise the firm continuous power by 1 kW.

Based on information on the potential value of more water and power, the DM responded with a rating of +5 to the first question and of +8 to the second. The surrogate-worth functions of +5 and +8 justified moving to a higher level of W_f and E_f and a reevaluation of functions for evaluating λ's and W's. The results of these trials 1 and 2 were plotted on Figures 13.5 and 13.6. Straight-line extrapolations were made to obtain trial 3 values for W_f and E_f. The process was continued through trial 6, at which point ($W_f = 3.295$ and $E_f = 275$) the surrogate-worth functions were zero.

13.9 SCREENING AND SEQUENCING MODELS— RIO COLORADO BASIN

A number of mathematical models were developed for studies of the Rio Colorado, Argentina, under a cooperative effort of the Ralph M. Parsons Laboratory for Water Resources and Hydrodynamics of the Massachusetts Institute of Technology and State Subsecretariat for Water Resources of Argentina. These models and other aspects of the planning efforts are fully discussed in a book by Major and Lenton 1979) with contributions by other key investigators.* For the development of basin configurations of projects and their scheduling for implementation, principal reliance was on three planning models, which, in general, were used sequentially:

- Steady-state mathematical programming model, using a mixed-integer programming algorithm, to *screen* initial configurations of plan elements
- Simulation model, to *evaluate further* configurations selected by the screening process in terms of net benefits and of hydrologic reliability, and to test operating policies
- Sequencing model to *schedule* the projects in the configurations that remained after the simulation process

A fourth model was used for detailed hydrologic studies and included modules for the hydrologic cycle, for the operation of hydraulic works, and for generating synthetic stream flow series.

In the planning process, a range of objectives was considered. Among these were: increasing Argentine national income, increasing income to each of the five riverine provinces, emphasizing irrigation rather than power production, achieving an equitable allocation of water among the riverine provinces, controlling interbasin transfers, and achieving "territorial integration" an Argentine goal involving the development of underpopulated areas of the nation.

Screening Model.   In this mathematical programming screening model, all the projects were assumed to be implemented in the first year of a 50-year planning period. Each year was the same hydrologically and was composed of three 4-month seasons. In addition to the objective function, there were seven groups of constraint formulations (to define water balances; to define physical relationships for reservoirs, irrigation, hydroelectric energy, and for imports and exports; to ensure that projects that depended on each other were both constructed; and to define certain planning objectives). Integer variables were used to permit the inclusion or omission of a project (by a variable valued at 1 or 0) and for certain other purposes. A number of complex relationships were represented by simplified versions. Nonlinear functions were converted to linear expressions, sometimes by piecewise linear approximations.

*In "The Mathematical Programming Screening Model" and "The Mathematical Programming Sequencing Model" by Cohon, Facet, Marks, in *Applied Water Resources Systems Planning* by David C. Major and Roberto L. Lenton, © 1979. Adapted by permission of Prentice-Hall, Inc., Englewood Cliffs, N.J.

The general form of the objective function was the maximization of the weighted sum of net benefits from each planning objective:

$$\text{Max } Z = \lambda_{\text{NI}}(\text{NIB}) + \sum_{i=1}^{P} \lambda_i(\text{RIB}_i)$$

where λ_{NI} is the weight on discounted net national income benefits, λ_i is the weight on discounted net regional income benefits to the ith region, NIB is discounted net national income benefits, and RIB_i is discounted net regional income to region i.

Net benefits were calculated as the difference between discounted benefits and costs. Benefits were evaluated by linear functions. Capital cost functions were typically nonlinear and were handled by piecewise linear approximations or, in the case of reservoirs, by applying the 0–1 variable to its fixed cost.

For most runs the objective function included only one objective, the maximization of net discounted national income benefits. These were, however, actually multiobjective runs, in which the other objectives were represented by constraint formulations.

Simulation Model. The basic simulation model used in the Rio Colorado planning was a forerunner of the MITTAMS model used for the Vardar/Axios Basin studies (discussed in the next section). In both the Rio Colorado and the Vardar/Axios studies, the discounted net benefits were considered together with other objectives that were not explicit in the objective function to formulate optimal plans.

Sequencing Model. This mathematical programming sequencing model took the projects that were included, after the screening and simulation models studies, and determined the time periods during which they should be constructed. The model took into account in the scheduling decision: benefits over time, budget constraints, constraints on the number of farmers available to work new irrigation areas, and project interrelationships such as the necessity to ensure that an irrigation area is not built before the construction of a dam to supply it.

The model was a mixed-integer programming model. Unlike the screening model, where most of the variables are continuous (irrigation areas, power plant sizes, dam heights), all the variables in the sequencing model were integer variables except for the flow variable, representing flow downstream of a site. This is because the model dealt only with decisions as to whether to construct a particular project within a given time period. The sequencing model assumed that projects are constructed during four time periods, each of equal length (10 years), and that each project has a life of 40 years from the time of construction. The flow equations within each planning period were written for "critical" season flows. Each year is the same only within each planning period, and flows change between time periods because of the construction of the projects. There were five groups of constraints and an objective function.

A number of the constraints were of similar form to those utilized in the screening model. In addition, special constraints were needed. Continuity constraints ensure that when a project is built, the water it will use will be available during the critical season of every year from construction onward. On the other hand, in the periods preceding that in which a project is built the water will be available for any other use. Other constraints ensure that a project will be constructed at most once and incorporates the effect of a decision made in any one period in the remaining periods. An additional continuity constraint takes account of the need to include part of the critical flow during the construction period to fill the reservoir, after which the yield from the reservoir can be made available. Irrigation constraints take account of volumes of water diverted from the stream and corresponding return flows. Hydroelectric energy constraints take account of effects of power plants on stream flow.

The 0–1 variables that apply to every proposed project were used to define conditionality constraints for hydroelectric production, irrigation, and exports to or imports from other basins. One project may depend on another project being constructed earlier or at the same time. For example, PPV_{si} is defined as a 0–1 integer variable that represents the construction or not of a variable-head power plant at site s in period i. Because the reservoir R_s at site s must be built by the time the power plant begins operation,

$$PPV_{si} \leq \sum_{j=1}^{i} R_{sj} \qquad \text{for all } s, i$$

If PPV_{si} takes on a value of 0, representing no construction of a power plant, the constraint shows that this has no impact on whether or not the reservoir is built. If, however, PPV_{si} takes a value of 1, representing construction of the power plant, the sum at the right must be at least equal to 1, indicating that the reservoir is built either in the same or previous period. Since another constraint prevents the reservoir from being built more than once, the right-hand side will be either 0 or 1.

Budget and population restrictions were treated as constraints, with upper bounds in every planning period. Each integer decision variable representing the construction (or not) of a project is multiplied by a coefficient that represents the total expenditures or people required for construction or operation of a project, and the expenditures and people for all projects in a period are limited by the upper bounds.

The mathematical form of the objective function for national income Z is as follows:

$$\text{Max } Z = \sum_{s} \sum_{i} [(\beta_{si}^{PPV} - \alpha_{si}^{PPV})PPV_{si} + (\beta_{si}^{P} - \alpha_{si}^{P})P_{si}$$

$$+ (\beta_{si}^{x} - \alpha_{si}^{x})X_{si} + (\beta_{si}^{M} - \alpha_{si}^{M})M_{si} + (\beta_{si}^{IA} - \alpha_{si}^{IA})IA_{si}$$

$$+ (\beta_{si}^{IB} - \alpha_{si}^{IB})IB_{si} - \alpha_{si}^{R}R_{si}]$$

where α_{si}^{k} is the present value of capital and operation and maintenance costs for a project of type k at site s constructed in period i, and β_{si}^{k} is the present value of the stream of benefits for a project of type k at site s constructed in period i. In this analysis the benefits may vary from period to period. The other terms stand for integer variables (0 or 1) applied to a site for a variable-head power plant (PPV), fixed-head power plant (P), export (X), import (M), irrigation areas A(IA) and B(IB), and reservoir R.

13.10 SIMULATION MODEL FOR INTEGRATED RIVER BASIN STUDIES—VARDAR/AXIOS BASIN

Master plan studies for the integrated development of the Vardar/Axios River Basin in Yugoslavia and Greece relied on computer models for data processing and testing of plans (TAMS, 1978). Section 6.5 provides a summary description of each of the 12 models used.

As discussed in Chapter 6, the principal planning considerations that influenced plan formulation and the scheduling of projects were: economic sector development (agricultural, industrial, electric power); balanced regional development; engineering and economic feasibility; and financial implications. These considerations motivated the arrangements of projects, their controlling dimensions, and operating requirements. Thus, to a large extent, the considerations (which were similar to "objectives") were embedded in the procedures that led to the plans that were tested in an overall systems context.

The MITTAMS simulation model (and its extension, EXTGW1, which was applied in the Axios portion of the basin to encompass surface/groundwater relationships) was used to confirm and "fine tune" the master plans. The largest portion of the study's manpower, perhaps 80%, was used to prepare and evaluate plans and organize input data, with the remaining 20% for final processing with MITTAMS and EXTGW1.

The general approach used for MITTAMS was to prepare a set of input for specified project arrangements and operation rules as the basis for a computer run. The run provided output in terms of hydrologic and economic performance of each reservoir and each water-using project. Some 150 reservoirs and projects were analyzed in a single run. The results were examined by the planners who made adjustments in the input designed to improve hydrologic reliability and/or economic performance of the projects, and this revised input was the basis for another run. The large number of projects and their complex and often nonlinear relationships made it impractical to develop an algorithm to analyze output automatically and revise the input for successive runs.

Hydrologic reliability was determined as the percentage of time that water quantity targets were met for each project. All runs were made for 1-month intervals and reliability computations for all projects were in terms of percent of months except for irrigation projects, where annual failure means an inadequate water supply for any month in the irrigation season.

In the definition of reliability above, no account is taken of the magnitude of the shortages. The seriousness of a shortage was reflected in a penalty that reduces benefits, computed by means of a "loss function" defined for each type of water use. Economic indicators valued by the model were benefit-cost ratio, discounted net benefits (benefits minus costs) for 50 years of operation, and internal rate of return (for power and irrigation projects only).

MITTAMS can simulate the operation of the system for the period of hydrologic record or for any period of a synthetically generated hydrologic series, evaluating the response of the system from the standpoints of hydrologic reliability and economic performance.

A schematic diagram was presented in Chapter 6 showing the types of projects and hydraulic connections between projects that were the basis for the final basin simulation studies. The system was represented as a network of "nodes" and "arcs." *Nodes* in MITTAMS can either represent elements of the system that use water for consumptive or nonconsumptive purposes; or locations in the basin where flows are added, subtracted, or simply recorded, and the statistics of the resulting stream flow series computed. Nodes for water use are: reservoir/power plant, irrigation, and municipal and industrial diversion. Nodes for stream flow are: start, confluence, diversion, terminal, and low-flow. In EXTGW1, nodes are also provided for groundwater cells and for groundwater recharge. *Arcs* represent conveyances linking the nodes of the network. In some cases, fictitious diversion, terminal, and confluence nodes were included to achieve a more accurate representation of real conditions in the system.

Responses to hydrologic inputs, and the performance of individual projects and the system as a whole, were programmed using algebraic and logic statements. Operating procedures included all of the practical operational policies likely to occur in the system. The model was structured basically in three sections: input and initialization routines, hydroeconomic simulation routines, and output routines.

When reservoir storage is defined, its cost is allocated internally by the model to projects that are served, according to a modified version of the "separable cost-remaining benefits" method (see Section 8.14) or according to percentages that are specified in the input.

The program performs the monthly operation of the system by first reading the monthly flows at all the start nodes and then routing these flows, one month at a time, through the network of nodes and arcs, following the rules and operating policies specified for each node and the node connectivities (characteristics of the interconnections). The routing routine computes the hydrologic performance statistics for all development project nodes and this information is subsequently used by another routine to evaluate the economic responses of these nodes. At the end of the period of recorded or synthetic stream flow, the hydrologic and economic results generated by the operation of the system are combined with other costs and benefit input data in the final output. Measures of annual hydrologic and economic performance for the period of record were averaged and assumed to apply over a 50-year period for purposes of the economic analyses.

The computation of original flows (those that apply in the absence of water resource facilities) was one of the most important components of the data preparation process, as they constituted the principal hydrologic input for river basin simulation. For the Vardar/Axios Basin, most runs were based on monthly flow values for a 19-year period of record. The HIMP program, based on hydrologic (statistical and water balance) techniques, was used to analyze flows available for 19 years at "characteristic" gaging stations, and to estimate concurrent flows at start nodes and certain downstream nodes affected by these flows and intervening flows.

The input data for each water use node depends on the type of project. For an irrigation node, the following items were included:

1. Maximum size of the irrigable land, in hectares.
2. Size of the irrigation area, in hectares.
3. Capital investment cost at the end of construction period for up to six sizes of development.
4. Present worth of the annual OMR cost for up to six sizes of development.
5. Average annual irrigation water requirement, in thousand cubic meters.
6. Monthly distribution of the annual requirement expressed as percent of this requirement.
7. Return flow coefficient, canal conveyance efficiency, and coefficients to establish the portion of return flow lost to groundwater. Only the return flow coefficient was used as it was judged to be sufficient for the purposes of this study.
8. Annual benefit coefficient, expressed as the monetary benefit per hectare under full water supply.
9. Build-up coefficients.
10. Coefficients of a quadratic equation to evaluate the short-term losses that occur when less than full water supply is provided in any given year.

The operating policy programmed in the model states that the water available at an irrigation node in a given month can be diverted for irrigation until the target for the month is met or until the water supply source is exhausted. Refinements of this rule for a month of shortage could apply in practice.

The output for one of the irrigation projects is shown in Figure 13.7, first for the hydrologic performance evaluation and then for the benefit-cost analysis. Potential benefits are the long-term expected benefits if the irrigation target is met every year. They are computed as the present worth of a uniform series of annual values equal to the unit benefit per hectare times the irrigation area in hectares, as modified by build-up coefficients. These coefficients adjust for the progressive growth of irrigation, water use, costs, and benefits during a period of years after water is first made available to the project. The short-term loss is computed by applying the quadratic equation to the water shortages for any year. All losses over the period of operation are first converted to an annual average, then to present worth, and subtracted from the potential benefits.

The detailed simulation procedures for municipal and industrial water supply and power plant nodes will not be discussed. The evaluation of recreation and flood control benefits and of water quality and navigation flows are also omitted. The description of the simulation techniques will conclude with the process for the reservoir nodes.

Three types of reservoirs were included: (1) a storage site that can be operated to regulate stream flow; (2) a storage reservoir with an associated hydroelectric power plant; or (3) a run-of-river hydropower plant. Physical, economic, and operational characteristics of the reservoirs or hydroelectric power plants or both are specified as

PERFORMANCE EVALUATION FOR IRRIGATION AREA IR8.4.4C

General Characteristics

Maximum potential area	20528.00 HA
Target area	20528.00 HA
Application efficiency	100.00 %
Return flow coef.	11.00 %
Return to stream	100.00 %
Percolation to groundwater	0.0 %

Monthly Use Parameters

Parameter	Jan.	Feb.	Mar.	Apr.	May	Jun.	Jul.	Aug.	Sep.	Oct.	Nov.	Dec.	Year
Diversion target (MCM)				1.5	4.5	12.0	31.5	37.0	13.2	2.0	0.2		102.7

Performance Results

Index	Jan.	Feb.	Mar.	Apr.	May	Jun.	Jul.	Aug.	Sep.	Oct.	Nov.	Dec.	Year
Reliability %				100.0	100.0	100.0	100.0	89.0	83.0	94.0	100.0		78.0
Mean diversion (MCM)				1.5	4.5	12.0	31.5	36.5	12.1	1.9	0.2		100.4
Standard dev.				0.0	0.0	0.0	0.1	5.1	2.9	0.0	0.0		6.6
Coef. of var.				0.0	0.0	0.0	0.0	0.1	0.2	0.0	0.0		0.1

Benefit and Cost Analysis for Irrigation Area IR8.4.4C

Target area	20528.00 HA
Irrigation capital costs	32.33 $
Irrigation OMR costs	13.63 $
Total irrigation costs	45.96 $
Total allocated costs (see below)	18.07 $
+ Total costs	64.03 $

Reservoir, Groundwater or Diversion Costs Attributed to This Irrigation Area

Project type	Name	Total cost	% Attributed to irrigation area	Attributed costs
		$	%	$
Reserv.	VAKUF	20.00	90.0	18.07
Total	IR8.4.4C		100.0	18.07

Economic Results

*Potential irrigation benefits	233.19 $
**Shortage losses	5.63 $
++ Actual irrigation benefits	227.56 $
Total remaining benefits	163.53 $
Total benefit-cost ratio	3.55 $
Internal rate of return	32.00 %

+ Include attributable reservoir, diversion, and/or pumping costs where applicable.

*Present value of annual benefits, if no shortfalls from the specified supply target occur.

**Present value of annual losses due to shortfalls from specified supply target.

++ Potential benefits minus shortage losses.

Figure 13.7 Hydrologic and economic performance of irrigation area. (From TAMS, 1978.)

TABLE 13.8. ALTERNATIVE RESERVOIR OPERATING RULES FOR MITTAMS

Operating Rule	Reservoir Conditions	Release Targets Designed to Meet
1	No power plant	Irrigation, municipal and industrial, low-flow requirements
2	Power plant, but power production subject to downstream releases for other uses	Same as number 1; MITTAMS computes energy generation
3	Power plant, power production with priority over other users	Monthly energy production targets
4	Power plant and two outlets: one for backwater withdrawals for irrigation or other purposes, and another for power or other downstream requirements	Irrigation requirements through first-priority backwater outlet for irrigation and other purposes, and downstream requirements for power production or other uses

PERFORMANCE EVALUATION FOR RESERVOIR PROHOR

General Characteristics

Normal water surface elevation M.S.L.	565.3 M
Maximum potential storage capacity	164.0 MCM
Total storage capacity	164.0 MCM
Minimum irrigation storage	35.0 MCM
Maximum storage	164.0 MCM
Minimum storage	35.0 MCM
Operating policy	4

Monthly Performance

	Jan.	Feb.	Mar.	Apr.	May	Jun.	Jul.	Aug.	Sep.	Oct.	Nov.	Dec.	Year
Max. stor. target (MCM)	164.0	164.0	164.0	164.0	164.0	164.0	164.0	164.0	164.0	164.0	164.0	164.0	
Min. stor. target (MCM)	35.0	35.0	35.0	35.0	35.0	35.0	35.0	35.0	35.0	35.0	35.0	35.0	
% at maximum	21.1	21.1	36.8	42.1	47.4	21.1	0.0	0.0	0.0	0.0	5.3	5.3	16.7
% at minimum	0.0	0.0	0.0	0.0	0.0	0.0	0.0	0.0	5.3	5.3	0.0	0.0	0.9
Mean storage	121.1	129.2	139.8	145.8	147.0	140.8	120.8	96.1	89.1	91.6	99.4	106.6	118.9
Standard dev.	27.9	24.3	22.4	22.2	22.8	22.9	22.0	21.2	20.7	24.6	30.0	30.8	32.2
Coef. of var.	0.2	0.2	0.2	0.2	0.2	0.2	0.2	0.2	0.2	0.3	0.3	0.3	0.3
Ave. spill (MCM)	4.1	6.6	6.4	8.2	4.3	0.0	0.0	0.0	0.0	0.0	0.8	2.9	33.2
Ave. release 1 (MCM)	2.7	2.7	2.7	4.4	8.9	15.4	26.1	28.1	10.0	4.5	3.1	2.7	111.3
Ave. release 2 (MCM)	0.0	0.0	0.0	0.0	0.0	0.0	0.0	0.0	0.0	0.0	0.0	0.0	0.0

Note: Spills may include water passed through the turbines that otherwise would have been spilled.

Figure 13.8 Hydrologic performance of reservoir. (From TAMS, 1978.)

input to MITTAMS. The model is programmed for a "standard operating policy," which simulates three alternative cases for reservoir release. In case I, as water availability is insufficient to meet the target release requirements, all available water is released from the reservoir. In case II, there is more than sufficient water to satisfy the target release and all excess water is saved. In case III, the water available after target demand has been satisfied exceeds the storage capacity and excess water must be released from the reservoir. Operating limitations such as minimum and maximum storage levels, target releases, and initial reservoir level are specified as reservoir node inputs.

A reservoir node can be operated according to the four operating rules programmed in MITTAMS, depending on whether or not a power plant is included. These rules are described in Table 13.8.

The hydrologic performance evaluation of a reservoir is shown on Figure 13.8. As described in Section 8.17, a reservoir benefit-cost analysis method is also included in MITTAMS, in which the reservoir costs are compared with a portion of the benefits that are generated for each of the projects it serves, according to a procedure called the "allocated cost-remaining benefits" method. This is only for relative comparison of the various reservoirs in the basin; the principal economic evaluations are those for the projects and purposes served by the reservoir and not for the reservoirs themselves.

The performances of individual projects and the overall basin were shown in several summary tables included in the computer output applying to the different types of projects. Key output values were also entered manually in summary tables.

REFERENCES

AHMED, SAJJAD, "Multiobjective Optimization of Water and Power in the K-S-C River Basin, Pakistan," Ph.D. thesis, Colorado State University, 1978.

ARMIJO, R., J. CASTI, and L. DUCKSTEIN, "Multi-criterion Water Resources System Design by Q-Analysis," University of Arizona Department of Systems and Industrial Engineering, 1978.

BENAYOUN, R., O. LARICHER, J. DE MONTGOLFIER, and J. TERGNY, "Linear Programming with Multiple Objective Functions, the Method of Constraints," *Autom. Remote Control,* January 1972.

BENAYOUN, R. J., et al., "Linear Programming with Multiple Objective Functions: Step Method (STEM)," *Math. Program.* vol. 1, no. 3, 1971.

BISHOP, A. BRUCE, "An Approach to Evaluating Environmental, Social and Economic Factors in Water Resources Planning," *Water Resources Bull.*, vol. 8, no. 4, August 1972.

BISHOP, A. BRUCE, M. McKEE, T. W. MORGAN, and R. NARAYANAN, "Multiobjective Planning Concepts and Methods," *J. Water Resources Plann. Manage. Div., Am. Soc. Civil Eng.,* vol. 102, no. WR2, November 1976.

BROWN, JERRY W., et al., "Models and Methods Applicable to Corps of Engineers Urban Studies," U.S. Army Engineer Waterways Experiment Station, Vicksburg, Miss., August 1974.

BYER, PHILIP H., "Screening Objectives and Uncertainties in Water Resources Planning," *Water Resources Res.,* vol. 15, no. 4, August 1979.

CHARNES, A., and W. W. COOPER, *Management Models and Industrial Applications of Linear Programming,* Vol. 1, Wiley, New York, 1961.

COHON, JARED L., and DAVID H. MARKS, "Multiobjective Screening Models and Water Resources Investment," *Water Resources Res.,* vol. 9, no. 4, August 1973.

COHON, JARED, L., and DAVID H. MARKS, "A Review and Evaluation of Multiobjective Programming Techniques," *Water Resources Res.,* vol. 11, no. 2, April 1975.

COHON, JARED L., RICHARD L. CHURCH, and DANIEL P. SHEER, "Generating Multiobjective Trade-offs: An Algorithm for Bicriterion Problems," *Water Resources Res.,* vol. 15, no. 5, October 1979.

COHON, JARED L, CHARLES S. REVELLE, and RICHARD N. PALMER, "Multiobjective Generating Techniques for Risk/Benefit Analysis," *Eng. Found. Conf. Risk/Benefit Anal. Water Resources Plann. Manage.,* Asilomar, Pacific Grove, Calif., September 1980.

CROLEY, THOMAS E, II, "Reservoir Operation through Objective Trade-offs," *Water Resources Bull.,* vol. 10, no. 6, December 1974.

CROLEY, THOMAS E, JR., and KUCHIBHOTLA N. RAJO RAO, "Multiobjective Risks in Reservoir Operation," *Water Resources Res.,* vol. 15, no. 4, August 1979.

DAS, PRASANTA, and YACOV Y. HAIMES, "Multiobjective Optimization in Water Quality and Land Management," *Water Resources Res.,* vol. 15, no. 6, December 1979.

DAVID, L., and L. DUCKSTEIN, "Multi-criterion Ranking of Alternative Long-Range Water Resources Systems," *Water Resources Bull.,* August 1976.

DEAN, JOE H., and C. S. SHIH, "Decision Analysis for the River Walk Expansion in San Antonio, Texas," *Water Resources Bull.,* vol. 11, no. 2, April 1975.

DUCKSTEIN, LUCIEN, "Imbedding Uncertainties into Multiobjective Decision Models in Water Resources," *Int. Symp. Risk Reliab. Water Resources,* University of Waterloo, Canada, June 1978.

DUCKSTEIN, LUCIEN, and SERAFIM OPRICOVIC, "Multiobjective Optimization in River Basin Development," *Water Resources Res.,* vol. 16, no. 1, February 1980.

FALKSON, LOUIS M., "Discussion of 'Approaches to Multi-objective Planning in Water Resources Projects,' by B. W. Taylor III et al.," *Water Resources Bull.,* vol. 12, no. 5, October 1976.

FINSTERBUSCH, KURT, "Methods for Evaluating Non-market Impacts in Policy Decisions with Special Reference to Water Resources Development Projects," U.S. Army Corps of Engineers, Institute for Water Resources, December 1977.

FISHBURN, P. C., *Utility Theory for Decision Making,* Wiley, New York, 1970.

FRONZA, G., A. KARLIN, and S. RINALDI, "Reservoir Operation under Conflicting Objectives," *Water Resources Res.,* vol. 13, no. 2, April 1977.

GOICOECHEA, A., L. DUCKSTEIN, and M. M. FOGEL, "Multiobjective Programming in Watershed Management: A Study of the Charleston Watershed," *Water Resources Res.,* vol. 12, no. 6, December 1976.

GOICOECHEA, A., L. DUCKSTEIN, and M. M. FOGEL, "Multiple Objectives under Uncertainty: An Illustrative Application of Protrade," *Water Resources Res.,* vol. 15, no. 2, April 1979.

GOICOECHEA, AMBROSE, DON R. HANSEN, and LUCIEN DUCKSTEIN, *Multiobjective Decision Analysis with Engineering and Business Applications,* Wiley, New York, 1982.

GORDON, THEODORE J., and H. HAYWARD, "Initial Experiments with the Cross-Impact Matrix Method of Forecasting," *Futures,* vol. 1, no. 2, December 1965.

GUM, RUSSELL L., THEODORE G. ROEFS, and DAN B. KIMBALL, "Quantifying Societal Goals: Development of a Weighting Methodology," *Water Resources Res.,* vol. 12, no. 4, August 1976.

HAIMES YACOV Y., *Hierarchical Analyses of Water Resource Systems: Modeling and Optimization of Large-Scale Systems,* McGraw-Hill, New York, 1977.

HAIMES, Y. Y., and W. A. HALL, "Multiobjectives in Water Resources Systems Analysis: The Surrogate Worth Trade-off Method," *Water Resources Res.,* vol. 10, no. 4, 1974.

HAIMES, Y. Y., W. A. HALL, and H. T. FREEDMAN, *Multiobjective Optimization in Water Resources Systems,* Elsevier, Amsterdam, 1975.

HAIMES, YACOV Y., PRASANTA DAS, and KAI SUNG, "Level-B Multi-objective Planning for Water and Land," *J. Water Resources Plann. Manage. Div., Proc. Am. Soc. Civil Eng.,* vol. 105, no. WR2, September 1979.

HAIMES, Y. Y., K. A. LOPARO, S. C. OLENIK, and S. K. NANDA, "Multiobjective Statistical Method for Interior Drainage Systems," *Water Resources Res.,* vol. 16, no. 3, June 1980.

HAITH, DOUGLAS A., and DANIEL P. LOUCKS, "Multiobjective Water Resources Planning," in *Systems Approach to Water Management,* A. K. Biswas, ed., McGraw-Hill, New York, 1976.

HALL, W. A., and Y. Y. HAIMES, "The Surrogate Worth Trade-off Method with Multiple Decision-Makers" in *Multiple Criteria Decision Making: Kyoto, 1975,* M. Zeleny, ed., Springer-Verlag, New York, 1976.

HIPEL, KEITH W., and NIALL M. FRASER, "Metagame Analysis of the Garrison Conflict," *Water Resources Res.,* vol. 16, no. 4, August 1980.

HIPEL, KEITH W., R. K. RAGADE, and T. E. UNNY, "Metagame Theory and Its Application to Water Resources," *Water Resources Res.,* vol. 12, no. 3, June 1976.

KANE, S., I. VERTUNSKI, and N. THOMSON, "KSIM: A Methodology for Interactive Resource Policy Simulation," *Water Resources Res.,* February 1973.

KEENEY, R. L., "Multiplicative Utility Functions," *Oper. Res.,* vol. 22, 1974.

KEENEY, R. L., and H. RAIFFA, *Decisions with Multiple Objectives,* Wiley, New York, 1976.

KEENEY, RALPH L., and ERIC F. WOOD, "An Illustrative Example of the Use of Multiattribute Utility Theory for Water Resources Planning," *Water Resources Res.,* vol. 13, no. 4, August 1977.

KEMPF, JAMES, LUCIEN DUCKSTEIN, and JOHN CASTI, "Polyhyedral Dynamics and Fuzzy Sets as a Multicriteria Decision-Making Aid," Joint TIMS/ORSA Meet., New Orleans, May 1979.

KEOWN, A. J., and J. D. MARTIN, "An Integer Goal Programming Model for Capital Budgeting in Hospitals," *Financ. Manage.,* vol. 5, no. 3, 1976.

KLEE, A. J., "Let Dare Make Your Solid Waste Decisions," *Am. City,* February 1970.

KROUSE, C. G., "Programming Working Capital Management," in *Management of Working Capital,* K. V. Smith, ed., West Publishing Company, St. Paul, Minn., 1974.

KRZYSZTOFOWICZ, ROMAN, and LUCIEN DUCKSTEIN, "Assessment Errors in Multiattribute Utility Functions," *Int. Meet. Inst. Manage. Serv.,* Honolulu, June 18–22, 1979.

KRZYSZTOFOWICZ, ROMAN, EUGENIO CASTANO, and ROBERT L. FIKE, "Comment on 'A Review and Evaluation of Multiobjective Programming Techniques', by Jared L. Cohon and David H. Marks," *Water Resources Res.,* vol. 13, no. 3, June 1977. A Reply by Cohon and Marks, same issue.

LEE, S. M., *Goal Programming for Decision Analysis,* Auerbach, Philadelphia, 1972.

LOUCKS, D. P., "Conflict and Choice," in *Planning for Multiple Objectives in Economy with Models and Development Planning,* C. Blitzer et al., eds., Oxford University Press, New York, 1975.

LOUCKS, D. P., "Interactive Multiobjective Water Resources Planning—An Application and Some Extensions," *Proc. Int. Symp. Risk Reliab. Water Resources,* University of Waterloo, Canada, June 1978.

LOUCKS, DANIEL P., J. R. STEDINGER, and D. A. HAITH, *Water Resource Systems Planning and Analysis,* Prentice-Hall, Englewood Cliffs, N.J., 1981.

LYNNE, GARY D., "Incommensurables and Tradeoffs in Water Resources Planning," *Water Resources Bull.,* vol. 12, no. 6, December 1976.

McKUSICK, R. B., J. M. KRESS, P. G. ASHTON, and W. A. BUNTER, JR., "The Development of a Plan of Study—An Interagency Approach to Multiobjective Planning and Evaluation of Water and Land Resource Use," *Water Resources Bull.,* vol. 9, no. 3, June 1973.

MAJOR, DAVID C., "Multiobjective Water Resource Planning," *Am. Geophy. Union Water Resources Monogr. 4,* 1977.

MAJOR, DAVID C., and ROBERTO L. LENTON, *Applied Water Resource Systems Planning,* Prentice-Hall, Englewood Cliffs, N. J., 1979.

MAO, J. C. T., *Quantitative Analysis of Financial Decisions,* Macmillan, New York, 1969.

MILLER, W. L., and D. M. BYERS, "Development and Display of Multiobjective Project Inputs," *Water Resources Res.,* vol. 9, no. 1, February 1973.

MITCHELL, ARNOLD, et al., "Handbook of Forecasting Techniques," Stanford Research Institute, December 1975; List of 73 Techniques, August 1977; Description of 31 Techniques, August 1977.

MONARCHI, D., C. KISIEL, and L. DUCKSTEIN, "Interactive Multiobjective Programming in Water Resources: A Case Study," *Water Resources Res.,* vol. 9, no. 4, August 1973.

NEELY, WALTER P., RONALD M. NORTH, and JAMES C. FORTSON, "Planning and Selecting Multiobjectives by Goal Programming," *Water Resources Bull.,* vol. 12, no. 1, February 1976.

NORTH, R. M., W. P. NEELY, and ROBERT CARLTON, "The Highest and Best Uses of the Oklawaha River Basin and Lake Rousseeau for the Economy and the Environment," U.S. Department of the Army, Corps of Engineers, Jacksonville District, 1976.

ORTOLANO, LEONARD, "Water Plan Ranking and the Public Interest," *J. Water Resources Plann. Manage. Div., Proc. Am. Soc. Civil Eng.,* vol. 102, no. WR1, April 1976.

PASSY, URY, "On the Cobb–Douglas Functions in Multiobjective Optimization," *Water Resources Res.,* vol. 14, no. 4, August 1978.

PENDSE, DILIP, and J. B. WYCKOFF, "Measurement of Environmental Trade-offs and Public Policy: A Case Study," *Water Resources Bull.,* vol. 12, no. 5, October 1976.

PHILLIPS, KEVIN J., "Multi-objective Analysis Applied to Areawide Wastewater Management," Ph.D. thesis, Polytechnic Institute of New York, 1978.

PHILLIPS, K. J., and J. A. DEFILIPPI, "A Matrix Approach for Determining Wastewater Management Impacts," *J. Water Pollut. Control. Fed.,* vol. 48, no. 7, July 1976.

RAGADE, R. K., KEITH W. HIPEL, and E. T. UNNY, "Metarationality in Benefit–Cost Analyses," *Water Resources Res.,* vol 12, no. 5, October 1976a.

RAGADE, R. K., K. W. HIPEL, and T. E. UNNY, "Nonquantitative Methods in Water Resources Management," *J. Water Resources Plann. Manage. Div., Proc. Am. Soc. Civil Eng.,* vol. 102, no. WR2, November 1976b.

RAIFFA, H., *Decision Analysis,* Addison-Wesley, Reading, Mass., 1968.

RAIFFA, H., "Preferences for Multi-attributed Alternatives," Rand Corporation, Santa Monica, Calif., April 1969.

ROEFS, T. G., "Two Methods of Adding Information to the Resources Management Process," in *Economic Modeling for Water Policy Evaluation,* R. M. Thrall et al., eds., North-Holland/American Elsevier, Amsterdam, 1976.

SELLERS, JACKIE, and RONALD M. NORTH, "A Viable Methodology to Implement the Principles and Standards," *Water Resources Bull.,* vol. 15, no. 1, February 1979.

SINGG, R. N., and B. R. WEBB, "Use of Delphi Methodology to Assess Goals and Social

Impacts of a Watershed Project," *Water Resources Bull.,* vol. 15, no. 1, February 1979.

SZIDAROVSKY, FERANC, "Some Notes on Multiobjective Dynamic Programming," Department of Systems and Industrial Engineering, University of Arizona, Tucson, Pub. 79-1, 1979.

TAMS (Tippetts-Abbett-McCarthy-Stratton, New York, and Massachusetts Institute of Technology, Cambridge), "Integrated Development of the Vardar/Axios River Basin— Yugoslavia–Greece," United Nations, December 1978.

TAUXE, GEORGE W., ROBERT R. INMAN, and DEAN M. MADES, "Multiple Dynamic Programming with Application to a Reservoir," *Water Resources Res.,* vol. 15, no. 6, December 1979a.

TAUXE, GEORGE W., ROBERT R. INMAN, and DEAN M. MADES, "Multiobjective Dynamic Programming: A Classic Problem Redressed," *Water Resources Res.,* vol. 15, no. 6, December 1979b.

TAUXE, GEORGE W., DEAN M. MADES, and ROBERT R. INMAN, "Multiple Objectives in Reservoir Operation," *J. Water Resources Plann. Manage. Div., Proc. Am. Soc. Civil Eng.,* vol. 106, no. WR1, March 1980.

TAYLOR, B. W., K. ROSCOE DAVIS, and RONALD M. NORTH, "Approaches to Multiobjective Planning in Water Resources Projects," *Water Resources Bull.,* vol. 11, no. 5, October 1975.

TECHNICAL COMMITTEE OF THE WATER RESOURCE CENTERS OF THE THIRTEEN WESTERN STATES, "Water Resources Planning, and Social Goals: Conceptualization toward a New Methodology," Utah Water Resources Laboratory, Utah State University, 1971.

TECHNICAL COMMITTEE OF THE WATER RESOURCE CENTERS OF THE THIRTEEN WESTERN STATES, "Water Resources Planning, Social Goals and Indicators: Methodological Development and Empirical Test," Utah Water Resources Laboratory, Utah State University, 1974.

TEXAS WATER DEVELOPMENT BOARD, "Economic Optimization and Simulation Techniques for Management of Regional Water Resource System," February 1974.

THAMPAPILLAI, DODO J., and J. A. SINDEN, "Trade-offs for Multiple Objective Planning through Linear Programming," *Water Resources Res.,* vol. 15, no. 5, October 1979.

UNIVERSITY OF MINNESOTA, Minneapolis, Office for Applied Social Science and the Future, "Report of Delphi Inquiry into the Future of American Water Resource Utilization and Development," January 15, 1973.

U.S. DEPARTMENT OF THE ARMY, Corps of Engineers, Omaha District, "This Land Is Your Land: Water Resources Management Alternatives for the Omaha–Council Bluffs Area," 1975.

VEMURI, V., "Multiple-objective Optimization in Water Resource Systems," *Water Resources Res.,* vol. 10, no. 1, February 1974.

ZADEH, L. A., "Outline of a New Approach to the Analysis of Complex Systems and Decision Processes," *IEEE Trans. Syst. Man Cybern.,* vol. SMC-3, no. 1, 1973.

ZNOTINAS, NORA M., and KEITH W. HIPEL, "Comparison of Alternative Engineering Designs," *Water Resources Bull.,* vol. 15, no. 1, February 1979.

FOURTEEN

Economic Growth Studies

14.1 INTRODUCTION

This chapter discusses various concepts and techniques for evaluating the economic impacts of investments in water resource developments, including: econometric models, export/economic base models, multipliers, accelerator effect/location theory, simulation/dynamic models, input–output models, and comprehensive economic planning models. Some of these methods are more successful than others in capturing the income effects of a project. The methods generally consider the impacts of public investments on the existing economic structure; linkages may, however, occur in both the forward and backward directions.

The methods provide information for improving the estimates of demands for products and services of water resources projects. They are also useful in estimating the direct and indirect economic effects of projects. Such analyses can be used together with the more customary estimates of population and water needs (Chapter 4) and economic and financial analyses (Chapters 8, 9 and 10) to formulate and justify projects. Evaluations of economic impacts are considered together with other assessments (financial, environmental, social, legal, political, etc.) in the complex process of decision making.

Chapter 4 introduced the subject of economic growth as a component of demographic studies. That chapter focused on population projections, however, and considered economic impacts in only a fairly limited way. The export-base method was mentioned as a way of jointly projecting population and economic growth.

The presentations in this chapter, to a varying extent, recognize that public investments can create economic and physical conditions that *induce additional economic growth*. The National Planning Association study for the Chesapeake Basin, discussed in Chapter 4, makes mention of this effect.

Extensive studies of such economic impacts for water resources projects were carried out by the Office of Appalachian Studies (OAS) of the Corps of Engineers in its Appalachian Water Resources Survey (U.S. Department of the Army, 1969) which emphasized this concept in its "comprehensive economic planning" and also sponsored a number of research projects pertaining to induced economic growth. The investigations for Appalachia drew upon theoretical economic concepts developed earlier by pioneering work, and systematic procedures developed by OAS staff and outside consultants. Previous investigators who were referenced in the AWRS included Kahn (1931), Keynes (1936), members of a Panel of Consultants of the Department of the Interior (1952), Krutilla (1955), Eckstein (1958), Hirschman (1958), Isard (1960), Maass et al. (1962), Meyer (1963), Leven (1964), Isard and Czamanski (1965), Maass (1966), and Marglin (1967). Special studies were made for the OAS by Cecil B. Haver and Associates (1965), R. Nathan and Associates (1966), Spindletop Research (1967a,b), The Fantus Company (1966), and Research and Development Corporation (1968). Leven (1969), Tolley (1970), and other investigators cited in this chapter have carried out additional studies for the Institute for Water Resources of the Corps of Engineers.

In its studies, the OAS sought to evaluate what it then referred to as "expansion benefits"; this term is not now in general use. The Water Resources Council "Principles and Standards" (1973, 1979, 1980) do not apply special distinctions to direct and indirect effects. The literature of water resource planning does, however, often use descriptors such as "primary and secondary" and "direct and indirect."

Expansion benefits were defined by the OAS as the total change in income brought about by a project. Such benefits tend to be equal to the user benefits when a project is built in a fully employed economy and where no externalities are brought about by the project. When a major reason for a water resource project is to stimulate economic growth (as in Appalachia or in a developing country), however, it is anticipated that the economic benefits will include not only user benefits, but will also include indirect effects *induced* by or *stemming* from the project.

Income and employment analyses do not always distinguish between net national accounting and regional accounting, which can include regional transfers. Differentiations are sometimes not made for analyses in developing countries but are usually required by government planning agencies in industrialized countries such as the United States.

This chapter is based largely on research studies, since the applications of economic growth models to water resources projects are limited, and this is a developing field. Further details and applications are contained in the publications of professional planners and economists. For more advanced treatment of some of the methods, the reader is referred to a comprehensive survey of economy-wide planning models for developing countries sponsored by the World Bank (Blitzer et al. 1975). 1975).

14.2 ECONOMETRIC MODELS

An econometric model is composed of equations that are used to forecast economic indicators, such as population, employment, income, or capacity of a specific industry that will locate in a specific area. The equations are "best fit" equations that relate a dependent variable to one or more independent variables, by statistical techniques. The equations are derived by *regression* analysis and are studied in terms of their reliability by *correlation* analysis. Their suitability for forecasting depends on the amount and quality of data on which they are based. Furthermore, if the relationships are not expected to hold in the future because of substantial changes anticipated in the structure of the economy, this introduces additional complications. The econometric model may be most useful for short-range forecasts.

The equations are determined by "calibrating" or "fitting" them to historical data. Projections can then be made about the effects of new developments in the region by assessing these effects on the variables in the equations.

A number of studies (Howe 1968; Cox et al. 1971; Attanasi 1975; Lewis 1973; Cicchetti et al. 1975) have applied regression analysis to indicators of economic growth. The study by Cicchetti et al. estimated the effects on regional economic growth in five states in the southwestern United States of the water resource projects of the U.S. Bureau of Reclamation over the period 1940–1970. The empirical results of their analysis indicated that water investments have an impact on regional economic growth and that the extent of the effect depends on the nature of the investment, the state of the regional economy, and the amount and nature of other investments in the region. For example, the following equations were obtained to describe the effects of Bureau investments in terms of constant (depreciated) dollars of farm output V_{FP} and subregional income A_{RV}.

$$\ln(V_{FP}) = 2.260 + 0.816 \ln(F_{EM}) + 0.023 \ln(K_{IR}) + 0.084 \ln(K_{HP})$$

$$\ln(A_{RY}) = 2.052 + 0.957 \ln(N_{FE}) + 0.030 \ln(K_{HP}) + 0.011 \ln(K_{FC})$$

where

F_{EM} = farm employment

K_{IR} = capital stock measure (undepreciated simple aggregate) for Bureau irrigation investments

K_{HP} = capital stock measure for Bureau hydropower investments

N_{FE} = nonfarm employment

K_{FC} = capital stock measure for Bureau flood control investments

Other equations were developed that took account not only of the foregoing variables but also of non-Bureau public expenditures for education, health, fire and public services, and highways.

Most of the techniques discussed in the following sections of this chapter involve econometric models or similar procedures. For some techniques, sophisticated statistical analyses are necessary, whereas for others, ratios or other simple relationships may be adequate.

14.3 EXPORT/ECONOMIC BASE MODELS

Chapter 4 described certain elements of the BREAM model prepared by Mountain West Research, Inc. (1978) for the U.S. Bureau of Reclamation. That chapter also referred to economic projections by the National Planning Association (1967) for the Chesapeake Basin. The methodologies in both cases used economic models of the *export-base* type. As used in urban and regional studies (Meyer 1963), export-base theory assumes that the economic growth of an area occurs principally as the result of industrial and commercial activities that produce, transfer, and distribute goods and services that are exported outside the area itself. A broader use of the concept (Chalmers and Anderson 1977) refers to *basic* activity as activity determined by forces external to the area in which it occurs. The relevant distinction is not the location of the purchaser (as is connotated by the term "exports"), but whether the purchase decision is motivated by forces internal or external to the local economy. Thus, basic activities would include not only activity associated with exported commodities (agriculture, mining, and manufacturing), but would also include tourist-related activity, some federal or state government activities, and employment at universities attended largely by nonlocal students. Activities that service basic industries can be categorized as basic if the level of activity is largely determined outside the area. Activities can also be classified as partly basic and partly nonbasic.

The methodology consists of quantitative division of activities into basic (export, exogenous) activities and nonbasic (service, endogenous) activities in terms of their respective employees; estimating future growth of the basic activities and employees; estimating total future employment by applying a ratio of total to basic employment; and estimating total future population by applying a ratio of population to employment. Existing and future income can be computed in a parallel way by applying appropriate unit income per employee in basic and nonbasic activities.

The foregoing employment and income pictures are somewhat oversimplified. Existing ratios of total to basic employees and of population to employment should be adjusted for future conditions if they are expected to change. Further refinements may be made in estimating income effects (Chalmers and Anderson 1977). The structure of the economic submodel for BREAM is shown in Figure 14.1.

Chalmers and Anderson (1977) assess the impact of a project as the change in basic activity associated directly with the proposed action plus the indirect or induced effects caused by the change in basic activity. The most common method used to estimate the relationship between direct and indirect effects is a simple multiplier approach that uses the ratio of total activity to basic (export) activity and applies this to the change in basic activity associated with the project. The result measures the total employment impact expected, which can then be used to generate estimates of changes in other variables. For assessments they surveyed, simple employment multipliers of this type varied from 1.2 to 3.9. The more employment that is identified as basic, the lower the multiple will be. The impacts analyzed by BREAM are based to a large extent on census data related to population and industry, to the impact of projects in terms of their construction activities, and to the normally expected growths of basic activities.

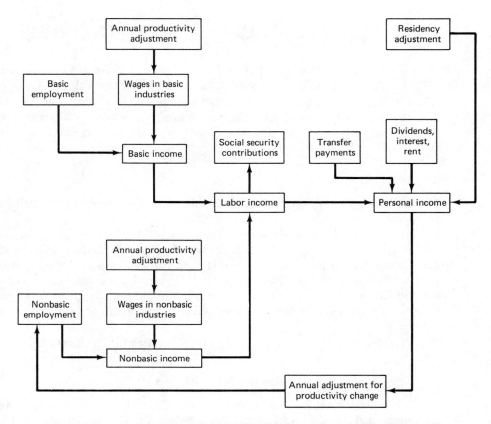

Figure 14.1 Economic submodel for BREAM. (From Mountain West Research, Inc., 1978.)

BREAM and other economic base methods require estimates of basic (export) activities. A popular approach to such estimates is the use of *location quotients*, based on relationships between two economies. If the study area is a region (r) of a nation (n) and employment (E) is a measure of economy activity, the location quotient for industry i (LQ_i) may be expressed in either of the following forms:

$$LQ_i = \frac{E_{ir}}{E_r} \bigg/ \frac{E_{in}}{E_n} \qquad \text{or} \qquad LQ_i = \frac{E_{ir}}{E_{in}} \bigg/ \frac{E_r}{E_n}$$

The first form compares the relative concentrations of the region's and nation's employment in industry i. The second form compares the region's share of the nation's employment in industry i to the total employment. If the LQ for an industry is greater than 1, the region exports the products of that industry and it should be included in the export base. The export activity (X_{ir}) of regional employment in industry i (E_{ir}) is estimated by either of the following:

$$X_{ir} = \left(1 - \frac{1}{LQ_i}\right) E_{ir} \quad \text{or} \quad X_{ir} = \left(\frac{E_{ir}}{E_r} - \frac{E_{in}}{E_n}\right) E_r$$

If T is total activity and X is export activity, the employment multiplier is $T/\Sigma\, X_i$ where $\Sigma\, X_i$ is the total employment of all industries with LQ_i greater than 1. With the second equation, only industries having a larger share of the region than of the nation need be considered. The methodology is described in greater detail by Isserman (1977), who also discusses other work with location quotients.

14.4 MULTIPLIERS

Multipliers are used by themselves and as elements of mathematical models based on input–output and other concepts. An illustration of the multiplier effect on an expenditure of $1.00 is shown in Table 14.1. When a consumer receives an additional income (Y) of $1.00, he or she will allocate this money to consumption (C) and savings (S). If his or her "marginal propensity to consume" (mpc) is 0.9, the person will spend $0.90 and save $0.10. The $0.90 the consumer spends will be regarded as income by the receivee, who then will proceed to spend $0.81 and save $0.09. This process will continue until total savings equals the original injection of income.

The multiplier (k) is equal to $1/(1 - \text{mpc})$, which for this illustration is equal to 10. Thus,

$$\Delta Y = 10(\$1.00) = \$10.00$$

This illustration is an oversimplification. A portion of the new income in the area may "leak" out; if this is 50%, the ΔY becomes $5. Furthermore, although $5 may be a fair value for the region, the nation will benefit only from the productivity of nationally underemployed resources and not from income transfers, and could be much lower.

The multiplier is a shortcut to the successive-period analysis of Table 14.1. It demonstrates the manner in which a change in investment, working through consumption, will produce a multiplied change in income. In more general terms, the

TABLE 14.1 ILLUSTRATION OF MULTIPLIER EFFECT OF AN EXPENDITURE OF $1.00

Period	Y (dollars)	C (dollars)	S (dollars)
0	1.00	.90	.10
1	.90	.81	.09
2	.81	.729	.081
	.729	.	.
.	.	.	.
.	.	.	.
n	.	.	.
Total	10.00	9.00	1.00

multiplier may be stated as a technique for demonstrating how a change in a component of a time series, by working through another variable, will produce changes in that time series.

The multiplier concept was mentioned in Section 14.3 in connection with the BREAM model of the U.S. Bureau of Reclamation. Its use in the AWRS may also be illustrated.

Employment and income multipliers varying from 1.4 to over 2.0 were estimated for each county in the study area. The purpose of the employment multiplier was to estimate the regional employment resulting from local employment engaged in a basic (export, exogenous) activity. The multipliers were based on the following relationships:

$$E_r = E_{rc} + E_{rI} + E_{rg} + E_{rx}$$

$$E_r = (E_{rI} + E_{rg} + E_{rx}) \frac{1}{1 - E_{rc}/E_r}$$

$$\frac{\partial E_r}{\partial E_{rI}} = \frac{\partial E_r}{\partial E_{rg}} = \frac{\partial E_r}{\partial E_{rx}} = \frac{1}{1 - E_{rc}/E_r}$$

where

E_r = regional employment

E_{rc} = local employment servicing local household consumption expenditures

E_{rI} = local employment servicing exogenous investment activity

E_{rg} = local employment servicing local, state, and national government activities

E_{rx} = local employment engaged in regional exports

The multipliers were used to estimate expansion benefits for recreation. The total number of visitors and their daily expenditures were estimated. The portion of these expenditures flowing to unemployed and underemployed labor was determined and this amount was multiplied by the county multiplier to obtain the expansion benefits.

14.5 ACCELERATOR EFFECT/LOCATION THEORY

Multiplier, input–output, and export base analyses are concerned largely with the impact of public investment on the existing economic structure. As such, they may not recognize the full potential for increased income throughout a region. This can be conceptually achieved by the assumption of a multiplier/accelerator effect.

The accelerator concept assumes that the change in income of the beneficiaries of public investment will cause existing private investment to be used more intensively or, more significantly, will cause the demand to rise for new private investment. Public investments may either change the comparative advantages that a

TABLE 14.2 SELECTED MEASURES OF ECONOMIC IMPACT

Report No.	Industry	Interindustry Impact[a]	Annual Wage Impact (millions)[b]	Purchases from Leading Supplier[c]	Major Supplying Industry[d]	Potential Satellite Industries[e]
1.	Paper and allied products	46.3(4)/18.9(3)	$ 8.1	189–432	Paper	Chlor-alkalies, sodium silicate, rosins, resins, tree farming
2.	Textile mill products	39.8(2)/34.6(11)	4.1	165–347	Textiles	Mill supplies, machinery repair, chemical distributors
3.	Apparel	44.2(1)/17.2(1)	1.2	273	Textiles	Machinery repair, distribution warehousing
4.	Printing and allied industries	49.8(3)/13.0(1)	3.5	172	Paper	Platemaking, repair services, paper merchants
5.	Electrical component parts	53.8(8)/2.2(1)	4.7	72	Nonferrous metals	Industrial gas distributors, tool and die, electroplating
6.	Textile machinery/pumps and valves	51.4(6)/4.9(1)	5.6	193	Iron and steel	Machine shops, tool and die, mill suppliers, foundries
7.	Office machinery	34.6(6)/9.1(2)	20.8	91	Office machinery	Tool and die, die casting, mill and electrical suppliers, metal stampings
8.	Motor vehicle parts	41.5(5)/29.5(9)	4.4	295	Motor vehicle parts	Tool and die, metal stampings, rubber and plastic parts
9.	Chlor-alkali industry	42.0(7)/19.4(6)	3.4	194	Chemical	Organic chemicals, herbicides, plastics, contract motor carriers
10.	Materials handling equipment	59.3(5)/4.0(2)	2.6	107	Iron and steel	Foundries, mill suppliers, tool and die
11.	Mobile homes	41.5(5)/29.5(9)	2.2	110	Lumber	Sheet metal, wheel and axle assembly, unitized fixtures
12.	Instruments and controls	47.8(8)/6.7(2)	10.5	67	Instruments	Metal distributors, electroplating, tool and die
13.	Noncellulosic synthetic fibers	57.8(1)/2.7(1)	21.5	341	Chemicals	Corrugated containers, chemicals

		A(C)/B(D)		D		
14.	Metal stampings	52.0(2)/4.0(1)	1.9	199	Iron and steel	Mill supplies, machine shops, tool and die, electroplating, steel distribution centers
15.	Aircraft and aerospace parts	33.9(6)/19.2(7)	10.1	190	Aircraft parts	Machine shops, tool and die, research and development
16.	Primary aluminum industry	41.2(4)/30.4(11)	19.3	304	Nonferrous metals	Electrical repair, machine shops, cookware, auto parts
17.	Nonferrous castings	41.2(4)/30.4(11)	2.6	304	Nonferrous metals	Patternmaking, electroplating, tool and die
18.	Malleable and ductile castings	37.8(7)/22.7(11)	6.1	227	Iron and steel	Patternmaking, machine shops, tool and die
19.	Foamed plastic products	51.4(3)/3.1(1)	1.4	143	Plastics	Contract motor carriers, chemical distributors
20.	Rolling, drawing and extruding of nonferrous metals	41.2(4)/30.4(11)	6.4	304	Nonferrous metals	Wire product fabricators, tool and die, metal treating chemicals
21.	Meats, dried, and frozen produce	57.7(2)/16.7(1)	5.6	161	Livestock	Fertilizer, eggs, hatcheries, feed lots, truck farming
22.	Plastic and powder metal products	51.4(3)/3.1(1)	1.4	143	Plastics	Tool and die
23.	Refractory metals	41.2(4)/30.4(11)	8.8	175	Nonferrous ores	Aircraft parts, fabricated products, ore dressing
24.	Primary steel and steel mill products	37.8(7)/22.7(11)	21.8	227	Iron and steel	Machine shops, refractories, cookware, kitchenware
25.	Plastic resins	57.8(1)/2.7(1)	1.0	341	Chemicals	Chemical suppliers, contract motor carriers

[a]Interindustry Impact is a four-factor numerical expression, A(C)/B(D), based on the 1958 OBE input–output study of the interindustry structure of the United States: (A) input of direct requirements from other industries per dollar output in the named industry; (B) input of direct requirements from the named industry itself; (C) number of other industries providing 50% of the other industries indirect input; (D) number of other industries needed to approximate the direct input of the named industry.

[b]Annual direct wage impact based on the 1965 average annual wage for production workers, typical employment size, and an economic velocity of 3.

[c]Dollars (1958) per $1000 gross output going to purchases from the leading supplier (data from the 1958 Interindustry Relations Study).

[d]Per the 1958 Interindustry Relations Study.

[e]Industries most likely to be attracted by new manufacturing facilities.

Source: The Fantus Company (1966).

435

TABLE 14.3 COMPARATIVE SUMMARY OF LOCATIONAL FACTORS[a]

Report No.	Industry	Manpower Training Assistance	Labor Supply	Labor Cost Advantage	Unique Site Requirements	Transportation Costs	Transportation Services	Utilities[b]	Urban Orientation	Proximity to Customers	Proximity to Raw Materials	Other[c] (see footnote)
1.	Paper and allied products		P		C	I	P	$E_pF_iS_cW_c$	P(7)	C(7)	C	1,2,5
2.	Textile mill products	P	C	C	P	P	P	$E_iF_iS_pW_p$				1
3.	Apparel	C	C	C		I	P					
4.	Printing and allied industries	I	P	I		I	P		P	C		
5.	Electrical component parts	P	C	P		I	C			C		6
6.	Textile machinery/ pumps and valves	C	P	I			I	E_i	I	P		3
7.	Office machinery	P	P				P		C			3,4,6
8.	Motor vehicle parts	P	P	P		I	C		I	P		1
9.	Chlor-alkali industry				C	C	C	E_cW_p		C		1
10.	Materials handling	P	C	I	I	P	I			P		6
11.	Mobile homes	I	P	P		C	I			C		
12.	Instruments and controls	P	P	I			I		P	I		4,6
13.	Noncellulosic synthetic	I	C	I	C	P	I	$E_pF_iW_p$	I	I		1,4
14.	Metal stampings	P	I	P		I	C			P	I	
15.	Aircraft and aerospace parts	P	C	I	I		P		I	I		3,4,6

436

No.	Industry				Utility Codes[b]			Other[c]
16.	Primary aluminum industry	I		C	$E_cF_pS_iW_i$		I	1,3,4
17.	Nonferrous castings	P	I	C		P	P	1,3
18.	Malleable and ductile castings	P	C	C	E_p	C	C	1,4
19.	Foamed plastic products			P		P(8)	C(8)	
20.	Rolling, drawing, and extruding of nonferrous metals	P	I	C	$E_pF_pW_p$	P	P	1,3
21.	Meats, dried and frozen produce	C	I	C	$E_pS_cW_p$	I	C	3,5
22.	Plastic and powder metal products	I	P	P	E_i	P	P	
23.	Refractory metals	P	C	P	E_p	I	I	1
24.	Primary steel and steel mill products	I	C	C	$E_pF_iS_cW_c$	C	P	1,3
25.	Plastic resins	I		P	$E_iS_pW_p$	P	P	4

[a] Key to locational factor evaluations: C(c)—critical, inflexible factors required for locational consideration; P(p)—primary, relatively inflexible factors weighing heavily in the locational decision; I(i)—important factors that must be considered in determining new locations but may be subject to trade-off against other elements of the locational equation; Blank—space indicates factors that generally are of minor or no importance in locational decisions.

[b] Utility Codes: E—electric power; F—fuel (gas, oil, or coal); S—sewage treatment and disposal; W—water for processing; W_p—subscript denotes locational evaluation of utility requirements.

[c] Codes to "other" column: 1—highly sensitive to state and local taxation; 2—requires woodland ownership; 3—requires supporting services; 4—prefers proximity to community colleges; 5—desires active program of soil and land development; 6—desires community services and improvements; 7—applies only to corrugated container manufacturing; 8—applies primarily to producers of foam packaging.

Source: The Fantus Company (1966).

region has, or create a means to use an existing comparative advantage by removing inhibiting costs (e.g., due to flooded land). The two aspects of induced investment are: (1) the provision of a source of employment and income now; and (2) the establishment of an institutional framework which will, in the future, be the basis for sustained growth and a more extensive use of economic resources.

Although the OAS did not obtain values of multiplier/accelerator that could be applied to a change in public investment to estimate the full magnitude of change in the economic structure, they did sponsor studies of location criteria to indicate what aspects of infrastructure are important to selected industries, reasoning that such information can be of value for making projections of industrial growth and location which can then be used to estimate economic impact. The Fantus Company (1966) analyzed the location requirements of 25 industries believed to have significant potential for location in Appalachia. Table 14.2 presents selected measures of interindustry impact derived from input–output and other analyses (explanations are contained in the footnotes to the table). Table 14.3 shows the relative importance of those factors that recur most often in the location decision, using a scale of values—critical, primary, or important, labeled C, P, or I, as explained in the footnotes.

14.6 SIMULATION/DYNAMIC MODELS

Chapters 12 and 13 have described the use of simulation models in planning constructed facilities, including their operation. Mitchell et al. (1975) include the following techniques in their review of forecasting models for economic growth studies: dynamic models, cross-impact analysis, KSIM, input–output analysis, and policy capture. They refer to these techniques as "structural models" because they demonstrate the interactions of the separate elements of a system or problem as well as their combined overall effect. As discussed in earlier chapters, modeling begins with a conceptualization of the system which can be accomplished by means of a diagram of "links" (flow paths) and "nodes" (reservoirs, levels). In the context of a socioeconomic model, the nodes represent population, income and other demographic and economic characteristics, and physical variables with which they may be related. The links represent the relationships between the nodes, which are usually expressed in mathematical terms. "Feedbacks" may also be shown in the representation, due to the cause-and-effect relationships from a given variable back to itself, as shown in Figure 14.2 for population growth. The exercise of identifying the elements and graphically tracing out the relationship is useful for shedding light on the issues involved and highlighting problems.

The simulation approach may be illustrated by the dynamic modeling technique known as system dynamics (Forrester 1961, 1969, 1971; Meadows et al. 1972; Mesarovic and Pestel 1974). The New England Water Model is discussed by Mitchell et al. (1975). The graphical representation is called the "feedback loop diagram." It is shown for the overall model on Figure 14.3. As shown on the diagram, there are two types of loops: positive and negative. Positive loops amplify whereas negative loops attenuate any change in the system.

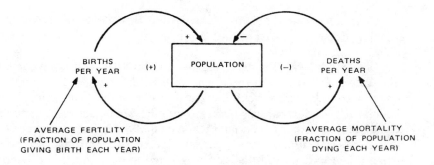

Figure 14.2 Feedback loops for population growth. (From Mitchell et al., 1975.)

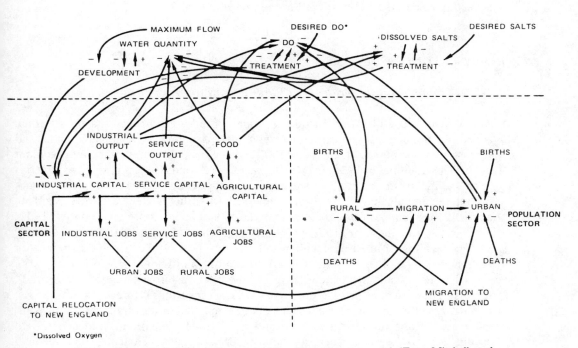

Figure 14.3 Feedback loop diagram for New England water model. (From Mitchell et al., 1975.)

The important problems studied were the effects of urban–rural migration, changes in the economy toward services, allocation of water to recreation, and pollution control policies.

The model was first disaggregated into three main sectors: capital, population, and water. The capital sector was further disaggregated into three subsectors: industry, services, and agriculture. The demands of these subsectors for water and the associated pollution burdens were fed into the water sector, which then affected the capital allocations for water quality and quantity. The population sector was divided into rural and urban subpopulations which are sensitive to both intra- and interregional migration. Migration was taken to be a function of employment. The water availability loop attempts to develop new water sources to meet stream flow demands of industry and urban municipalities. The water quality loop is a negative feedback loop as any change in required treatment will ultimately result in a change in the opposite direction in required dissolved oxygen.

As an example of the output derived, the model determined the effect of different planning periods on water treatment costs and on dissolved oxygen. With alternative A, planning was based on biological oxygen demand (BOD) loads (pollution quantities) two years into the future, while alternative B was based on a 10-year planning horizon. The importance of an extended planning horizon was shown by the ineffectiveness of alternative A in meeting the desired dissolved oxygen (DO). It also demonstrated, however, that the costs of A rise less rapidly than B because fewer future costs are internalized in the present.

14.7 INPUT–OUTPUT MODELS

14.7.1 Input–Output Model—General Description

The input–output (I/O) technique is widely used for impact studies in which economic projections and structural relationships among disaggregated industrial sectors are to be pursued (Kim et al. 1977). Since the publication of the input–output analysis by Leontief in 1936, the development of interindustry economic analysis has been significant in both theory and empirical applications. The concepts of input–output techniques have also been employed for other water resources planning applications. Some selected references in the economic literature are Leontief (1941, 1966), Bourque and Cox (1970), Chenery and Clark (1967), and Miernyk (1965). The following simplified explanation is based on the Corps of Engineers report on Appalachia (U.S. Department of the Army, 1969) and Kim et al. (1977).

The input–output technique displays the relationships among the "industrial" sectors. These sectors include producing sectors (agriculture, forestry and fisheries, mining; construction; nondurable and durable manufacturing; transportation, communications, and utilities; wholesale and retail trade; finance, insurance, and real estate; various services such as hotels, research establishments, and medical organizations and government enterprises) and other sectors.

The input–output structure of the U.S. economy is shown on Figure 14.4. A matrix shows the sectors as column and row titles. The table is read so that vertical readings indicate purchases of a given sector from all other sectors (both direct and indirect) and horizontal readings across the rows indicate the sales to other sectors. To the right of the basic matrix are displayed the "final demand" sectors of investment, government, consumers, and foreign trade. At the base of the table are displayed the "value-added" components of each column, corresponding to the sum of factor payments at each level of production or income generated in that vertical sector.

As outlined by Kim et al. (1977), there are several alternative I/O models: national, regional, interregional, and international. Depending on the extent of impact to be measured, the model can also be classified into open and closed categories. An open model provides only the direct and indirect impact of a given investment. With a closed model, one can extend the measurement of the impact induced by the increase in consumption expenditures resulting from the increase in an output.

Coefficients describe the relationships between sectors. These relationships are further discussed in the following subsections.

14.7.2 I/O Model for Appalachian Water Resources Survey

Three regions and 28 subareas of Appalachia were employed in the AWRS. The I/O model was built up from national input–output coefficients and estimates of interregional trade. The national coefficients were disaggregated for Appalachia on the basis of estimates of interregional trade in the Appalachian region for which surveys and statistical models were used.

As stated in the OAS report:

> This model of Appalachia, when confronted with a change in final demand, will enable estimation of the resulting changes in industrial output by input–output sectors in each region of Appalachia. Additionally, because of the built-in relationships between income and expenditures, estimates can be made of the increases in personal consumption expenditures and income. Therefore, the model enables estimation of the direct and indirect incomes which result from changes in final demand. For example, the model can be used to estimate the economic impacts of such changes in final demand as construction of water development projects or changes in government expenditures, and the impact of the production from a new manufacturing plant.

14.7.3 I/O Model for McClellan–Kerr Arkansas River Multiple-Purpose Project

A study by Kim et al. (1977) analyzed the economic impact on local and national economies, in terms of output and income resulting from construction expenditures of MKARMPP. The principal elements involved were: (1) construction of an inter-regional I/O model; (2) conversion of MKARMPP cost into regional final demand sectors; (3) estimate of direct and indirect and induced construction impact of the

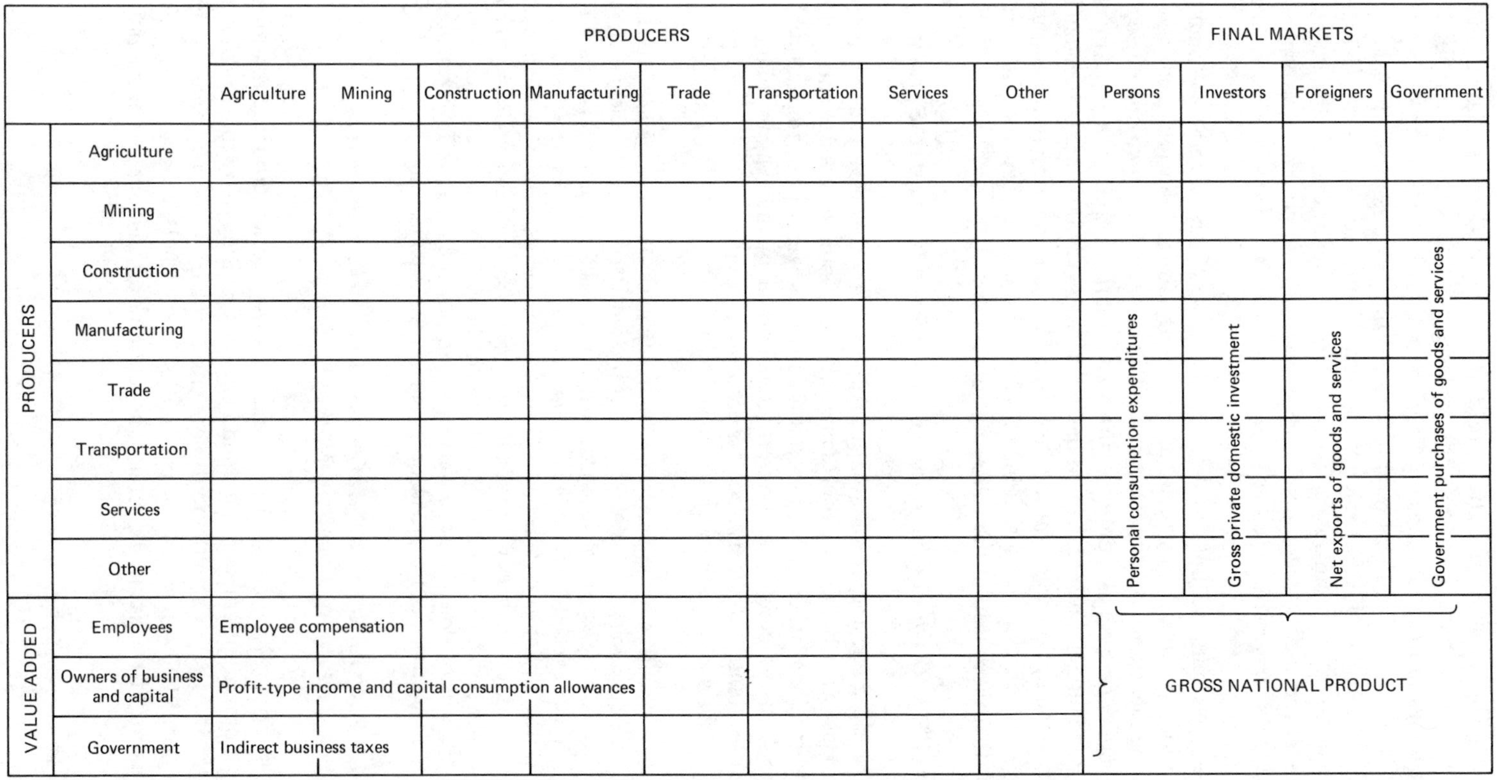

	PRODUCERS								FINAL MARKETS			
	Agriculture	Mining	Construction	Manufacturing	Trade	Transportation	Services	Other	Persons	Investors	Foreigners	Government
PRODUCERS Agriculture									Personal consumption expenditures	Gross private domestic investment	Net exports of goods and services	Government purchases of goods and services
Mining												
Construction												
Manufacturing												
Trade												
Transportation												
Services												
Other												
VALUE ADDED Employees — Employee compensation									GROSS NATIONAL PRODUCT			
Owners of business and capital — Profit-type income and capital consumption allowances												
Government — Indirect business taxes												

Figure 14.4 Input–output structure of U.S. economy. (From U.S. Department of Commerce, 1974.)

MKARMPP in terms of output and income; and (4) sensitivity analysis of the model. Basic data required for the model included: (1) regional technical coefficients; (2) trade coefficients; (3) regional household income and expenditure coefficients; and (4) regional final demands.

A closed interregional I/O model with fixed column coefficients was selected based on earlier research (Kim 1972). This model was developed first by Chenery and Clark (1959) and Moses (1955). In the typical model, structural coefficients are expressed (Isard 1951) as a_{ij}^{rs}, where an amount of commodity i from region r is required to produce \$1 of output j in region s. In the model used here, two sets of structural relationships, interindustrial and interregional, were considered in combination. The following is based on the report by Kim et al. (1977).

Economic activities are analyzed in terms of both input–output among industries and trades among regions. The interregional I/O coefficient is estimated by two separate coefficients. A regional technical coefficient a_{ij}^{s} represents the ith input (amount of commodity input) required for producing \$1 of jth output commodity in region s, disregarding the region of its origin. t_i^{rs} represents the fixed portion of total receipts (consumption) of the ith commodity by region s from region r. The trade coefficients are derived by ratios of a region's purchase of a commodity from various regions including its own, and are derived from the base-year trade flow estimates. Thus, the sum of the coefficients equals 1.

The trade pattern described above does not specify the interindustry relationship between trading regions. It is assumed that each purchasing industry in region s purchases the same portion of the ith input from the region r. Thus in the fixed column coefficients model, $a_{ij}^{rs} = a_{ij}^{s} \cdot t_i^{rs}$. Having estimated the two structural coefficients a_{ij}^{s} and t_i^{rs}, the solution of the interregional I/O model may be obtained by the following procedure. In the definition of the matrices, mn, 1 means a column with dimensions $mn \times 1$; mn, mn means a matrix with dimensions $mn \times mn$. The enormous sizes of the matrices should be noted.

n = number of regions

m = number of industries

X = column vector $(mn, 1)$ giving production. Each element describes the output of commodity i produced in region r

Y = column vector $(mn, 1)$ giving final demand, in which each element describes the total amount of commodity i consumed by final users in region r regardless of the place where the good was produced

A = block diagonal matrix (mn, mn) with n square matrices (m, m) of input coefficients along the diagonal describing the structure of production in each region

T = square matrix (nm, nm) filled with diagonal matrices (m, m). Each element t_i^{rs} describes the fraction of total consumption of commodity i in region s that is imported from region r. The sum of each column of this matrix must equal unity, since the coefficients are proportions of the total consumption. It is assumed that

$$t_i^{rs} = t_{i1}^{rs} = t_{i2}^{rs} = \cdots = t_{im}^{rs}$$

If the technical coefficients (A), trade coefficients (T), and final demands (Y) are given, X can be solved as follows:

$$X = (1 - TA)^{-1} TY \quad \text{or} \quad X = (T^{-1} - A)^{-1} Y$$

For this study, the model used four internal regions closed within the national boundaries: the impact region (I), Arkansas River Valley; Southern and Northern regions (II and III); and the rest of the United States (IV). Each model had 83 industrial sectors, of which 79 were producing sectors. The model also includes household column and row coefficients in order to estimate income multiplier effects resulting from the induced household expenditures from the project construction. The basic data sources for the model were from the multiregional (51 U.S. states) I/O study for the year 1963 by the Harvard Economic Research Project (Polenske 1970) and Trade Flow Analysis for the same year of 44 U.S. Regions by Jack Faucett Associates (1968) for the Harvard Study. The details of construction and operation of the I/O model are reviewed by Kim et al. (1977).

To construct the final demand vectors for the impact study through the I/O model, the MKARMPP cost was converted into 1963 dollars and classified into contract costs and noncontract costs. The investment costs were distributed among the various industrial sectors by applying the demand patterns for input by 12 different types of water resources investments. Four different types of projects were included: multipurpose (48%), locks and dams (37%), revetments (11%), and flood control (4%). The demand pattern showed that the single largest demand for input is labor (50.7%), followed by manufactured goods (29%), stone and clay mining products (7.2%), trade and services (6.2%), and transportation and communications (5.3%). Of the national final demand, the project region (Region I) shares about 73% of its demand.

Two types of multipliers were used. The type I multiplier was derived from the open model and is suited for evaluating the direct and indirect impact of a given investment. The type II multiplier is derived from the closed model and shows the added induced impact resulting from the spending of the household income that is earned during the production process.

The output multiplier is suited for evaluating interindustry linkages and size of transaction for a $1 change in final demand, while the income multiplier is suited for evaluating the magnitude of income changes induced by a $1 change in household income. Type I output multipliers by industry in region I ranged from 1.35 to 2.25. Type II output multipliers for the same region by industry sector ranged from 3.76 to 6.55. Type I income multipliers ranged from 1.23 to 3.04, while the type II income multipliers ranged from 2.82 to 6.76.

Table 14.4 shows that $1000 of project cost is estimated to bring $5780 of output. Table 14.5 shows the sensitivity of impacts by project type and region. In this table the numbers in parentheses show the corresponding amount of income due to the investment. The direct, indirect, and induced impact per $1000 MKARMPP project

TABLE 14.4 OUTPUT RESULTING FROM THE McCLELLAN–KERR ARKANSAS RIVER MULTIPLE-PURPOSE PROJECT COST (PER $1000) BY INDUSTRY AND REGION (1963 Dollars)

Industry	Region I	Region II	Region III	Region IV	Nation	
1	12.41	29.56	14.91	114.32	171.20	
	(7.2)[a]	(17.3)	(8.7)	(66.8)	(100)	3.0
2	18.84	106.71	5.96	37.33	168.85	
	(11.2)	(63.2)	(3.5)	(22.1)	(100)	2.9
3	20.96	14.96	2.41	24.50	62.83	
	(33.4)	(23.8)	(3.8)	(39.0)	(100)	1.1
4	93.33	199.17	51.57	536.98	881.05	
	(10.6)	(22.6)	(5.6)	(60.9)	(100)	15.2
5	72.77	106.55	55.88	511.24	746.44	
	(9.7)	(14.3)	(7.5)	(68.5)	(100)	12.9
6	170.87	49.81	12.02	125.39	358.09	
	(47.7)	(13.9)	(3.4)	(35.0)	(100)	6.2
7	286.60	66.26	18.00	188.71	559.56	
	(51.2)	(11.8)	(3.2)	(33.7)	(100)	9.7
8	189.93	116.14	19.00	205.89	530.96	
	(35.8)	(21.9)	(3.6)	(38.8)	(100)	9.2
9	133.67	73.30	14.28	205.66	426.90	
	(31.3)	(17.2)	(3.3)	(48.2)	(100)	7.4
10	8.89	3.57	0.83	9.53	22.82	
	(39.0)	(15.6)	(3.6)	(41.8)	(100)	0.4
11	923.15	229.86	60.09	638.18	1851.27	
	(49.9)	(12.4)	(3.2)	(34.5)	(100)	32.0
Total	1931.43	995.88	254.94	2597.73	5779.97	
	(33.4)	(17.2)	(4.5)	(44.9)	(100)	100

[a]Except for the last column, each figure in parentheses shows the percentage of national output by each industry by region. The figures in parentheses in the last row are the regional shares of total national industrial output by each region.
Source: Kim et al. (1977).

cost was estimated to bring $5780 of output or $1851 income on the national economy. The construction impact of the MKARMPP ($1.1 billion) on the national economy was estimated to increase approximately $6.4 billion in terms of output or $2.1 billion in household income in 1963 prices. Of this amount about one-third of the output and one-half of the income were estimated to be shared by project region I. These values cannot be directly applied to other projects.

This analysis was based essentially on the short term. The time impact of the MKARMPP investment must be the long-term economic development of the Arkansas River Basin Area induced by the main output of the investment. The main outputs of the investment are improvement of the water transportation system, supply of water and electric power, and recreation sites and flood control for the region. The assessment of the long-term economic impact was beyond the scope of this research project.

TABLE 14.5 SENSITIVITY OF IMPACTS BY PROJECT TYPE AND REGION[a]

Project Type/Region	Region I	Region II	Region III	Region IV
1. Multipurpose project, including power	5808.41 (1849.96)	5509.32 (1745.31)	5791.51 (1833.23)	5713.28 (1817.08)
2. Dredge	5860.71 (1892.74)	5557.62 (1787.72)	5858.08 (1880.73)	5787.62 (1868.70)
3. Large earth fill dam	5816.61 (1832.97)	5505.03- (1724.19)	5803.93 (1817.19)	5732.63 (1804.57)
4. Small earth fill dam	5756.57 (1764.08)	5453.01 (1658.01)	5749.43 (1750.63)	5673.03 (1735.78)
5. Local flood protection	5798.86 (1857.55)	5496.62 (1748.12)	5779.02 (1839.61)	5700.29 (1823.41)
6. Pile dikes	5650.84 (1781.84)	5325.43 (1667.81)	5645.33 (1769.87)	5549.39 (1746.75)
7. Levees	5771.06 (1908.42)	5437.55 (1792.08)	5761.11 (1894.21)	5676.27 (1876.05)
8. Revetment	5329.35 (1557.03)	4998.68 (1439.21)	5330.90 (1548.95)	5198.72 (1509.79)
9. Powerhouse	5766.01 (1611.03)	5540.14 (1531.92)	5762.21 (1599.31)	5691.85 (1585.52)
10. Medium concrete dam	5848.40 (1848.35)	5548.66 (1743.19)	5823.61 (1828.44)	5750.16 (1814.39)
11. Lock and concrete dam	5696.50 (1665.00)	5424.27 (1569.03)	5682.71 (1649.88)	5598.46 (1630.59)
12. Miscellaneous	5752.85 (1762.19)	5450.04 (1656.73)	5753.13 (1751.45)	5676.44 (1736.76)

[a]The first row of each project type shows the total amount of output due to $1000 contract cost investment for each region. The numbers in parentheses under the output show the total amount of income due to the investment.
Source: Kim et al. (1977).

14.7.4 Other I/O Models

Gantle (1979) applied recreational expenditures in the MKARMPP to an inter-regional I/O model based on the work by Kim et al. (1977). In 1976, there were 23 million visitor-days. Average expenditure in 1975 was $9.54 per visitor-day, of which about $5 was applied to lodging, food, transportation and recreation activities, and $4.5 was used to operate and maintain equipment for boating, fishing, skiing, and camping. Preliminary estimates of the gross direct and indirect impacts of the recreational expenditures amounted to $390,000,000.

Gray and McKean (1976) used an extension of the I/O model to assess the adequacy of a water resource base to support economic growth in four counties in Colorado. This paper also refers to other applications of I/O models to water uses.

Table 14.6 shows intake and consumptive use requirements in 1970 for 15 economic sectors in terms of gallons per dollar of output. The I/O model was used to estimate the increases in both direct and indirect water withdrawals resulting from projected increases in final demand in all sectors; Table 14.7 shows these values in

TABLE 14.6 WATER INTAKE AND CONSUMPTIVE USE REQUIREMENTS BY SECTOR, BOULDER, LARIMER, AND WELD COUNTIES, COLORADO, 1970

Sector	Intake (gal/$)	Consumptive Use (gal/$)
Livestock	10.15	9.03
Irrigated agriculture	6246.93	3682.22
Dryland agriculture	0.00	0.00
Food processing	3.02	0.29
Mining and extraction	37.60	9.66
Metals and electronic components	1.22	0.22
Paper and allied products	100.00	19.00
Printing and publishing	1.27	0.13
Chemicals, petroleum, and rubber	6.27	0.98
Lumber and wood products	1.04	0.21
Miscellaneous manufacture	15.00	2.01
Utilities, transportation, and communication	24.80	6.45
Services	6.25	0.63
Trade	2.30	0.23
Education	5.90	0.59

Source: Gray and McKean (1976). Copyrighted by the American Geophysical Union.

TABLE 14.7 DIRECT PLUS INDIRECT WATER INTAKE AND CONSUMPTIVE USE REQUIREMENT, DELIVERED TO FINAL DEMAND BY SECTOR, BOULDER, LARIMER, AND WELD COUNTIES, COLORADO, 1970

Sector	Intake Requirements (gal/$)	Consumptive Use Requirements (gal/$)
Livestock	806.7326	478.5846
Irrigated agriculture	6282.0533	3701.6967
Dryland agriculture	32.0570	17.8496
Food processing	593.1280	349.6294
Mining and extraction	51.3737	13.2732
Metals and electronic components	3.7421	0.8586
Printing and publishing	2.0403	0.3268
Chemicals, petroleum, and rubber	7.1824	1.2129
Miscellaneous manufacture	16.7948	2.4533
Utilities, transportation, and communication	26.7588	6.9639
Services	9.2818	1.6392
Trade	8.1952	3.0022
Education	13.9389	5.0406

Source: Gray and McKean (1976). Copyrighted by the American Geophysical Union.

1970, which are quite different from the direct withdrawals of Table 14.6. Using projected changes in final demand for each of the sectors for the period 1970–1980, the authors obtained the following types of results for water resource requirements:

- Aggregate increases in water withdrawals in the whole economy given exogenous increases in final demands
- Direct and indirect water withdrawals in each sector as a result of projected increases in all sectors
- Sector-by-sector direct plus indirect water requirements, as a single sector expands its deliveries to final demands

When an I/O model is coupled with linear programming, a dynamic resource model is created with capability for optimization. The planning process using the LP-I/O is iterative. In order to reduce the time and effort required by each model setup, Liang and Huang (1975) incorporated matrix generators for converting impact data into the basic form required by the model. Liang (1976) applied the LP-I/O model to a county in Hawaii. This involved maximizing the gross regional product subject to a number of linear constraint equations relating to industry outputs, final demands, and size; water supplies; pollutants; land resources; population; energy; and shipping capacity. The model provided information on industry size, location, resource utilization, population distribution, and other effects.

14.8 COMPREHENSIVE ECONOMIC PLANNING MODELS

Comprehensive planning models may employ a variety of export economic-base, multiplier, input–output, and accelerator concepts. The Upper Licking River (Salyersville–Royalton area in Kentucky) was subjected to a case study by Spindletop Research (1967a) for the AWRS, which involved development planning and estimates of expansion (total income) benefits. There were five principal features in this model for estimating expansion benefits.

1. Identifying preliminary development opportunities available in study area
2. Providing development framework areas where development is most likely to occur, and the water-related and other bottlenecks that have hindered or prevented development in the past
3. Providing service employment multiplier
4. Computation of wage expansion benefits
5. Computation of induced investment

A list was developed of 63 industries most likely to locate in the study area based on industrial location studies by Spindletop Research, Fantus (Section 14.5), and others. Growth projections for the study area were made and disaggregated. The disaggregation procedure considered the capacity of the land to support economic growth in an area with a chronic shortage of developable land due to topography, flooding, and other reasons. Projected manufacturing employment was multiplied by 0.74, derived at the University of Kentucky, to obtain an estimate of service and commercial employment. Employment was classified in various categories and total wages and salaries determined and assigned to national and regional accounts. The regional account reflected all increased wages and salaries, whereas the national account reflected only the wages of persons who would be expected to be under- and unemployed without the project.

Another approach to comprehensive planning involved the development of a model for sequencing public investment. This was developed for OAS by Spindletop Research and partially tested in a fairly well developed area in northeast Tennessee and an undeveloped area in northern West Virginia. Since the AWRS goals were expressed in terms of income flows, the planning process aimed to supply information on the public investments necessary to achieve the specific levels of activities needed and to indicate bottlenecks that may limit the required flow of goods and services. In this context "needs" referred to the steps that must be taken to overcome the bottlenecks for development; these include the absence of flat, flood-free land for industrial expansion, lack of access, shortage of skilled labor, inadequate capacity of public facilities or absence of needed public infrastructure, and tax base. The model involved the formulation of "state matrices." The methodology began with the construction of a set of incomplete historical input–output tables for the region under study. These were called "incomplete" because they contained only those elements describing annual flows from the public sectors to one another and to the private sectors. The future state matrices were estimated for each 5-year period after consideration of the relationships between economic sectors and public sectors as affected by public investments.

REFERENCES

ATTANASI, EMIL, "Regional Impact of Water Resource Investments in Developing Area," *Water Resources Bull.*, vol. 11, no. 1, February 1975.

BLITZER, CHARLES A., PETER B. CLARK, and LANCE TAYLOR, eds., *Economy-Wide Models and Development Planning*, published for the World Bank by Oxford University Press, New York, 1975.

BOURQUE, PHILIP, and MILLICENT COX, "An Inventory of Regional Input–Output Studies in the United States," Graduate School of Business Administration, University of Washington, Seattle, 1970.

CHALMERS, J. A., and E. J. ANDERSON, "Economic/Demographic Assessment Manual," Mountain West Research, Inc., November 1977.

CHENERY, HOLLIS B., and PAUL G. CLARK, *Interindustry Economics*, Wiley, New York, 1959.

CICCHETTI, CHARLES J., V. KERRY SMITH, and JOHN CARSON, "An Economic Analysis of Water Resource Investments and Regional Economic Growth," *Water Resources Res.*, vol. 11, no. 1, February 1975.

Cox, P. T., W. Grover, and B. Seskin, "Effect of Water Resources Investment on Economic Growth," *Water Resources Res.*, vol. 8, no. 1, February 1971.

Eckstein, Otto, *Water Resource Development, the Economics of Project Evaluation*, Harvard University Press, Cambridge, Mass., 1958.

The Fantus Company "The Appalachian Location Research Studies Program," Appalachian Regional Commission, 1966.

Jack Faucett Associates, Inc., "1963 Output Measures for Input–Output Sectors by County," Office of Civil Defense, Washington, D.C., 1968.

Forrester, Jay W., *Industrial Dynamics*, MIT Press, Cambridge, Mass., 1961.

Forrester, Jay W., *Urban Dynamics*, MIT Press, Cambridge, Mass., 1969.

Forrester, Jay W., *World Dynamics*, Wright-Allen Press, Cambridge, Mass., 1971.

Gantle, Lloyd, "Recreation at the McClellan–Kerr Arkansas River Navigation System" *Water Resources Bull.*, vol. 15, no. 5, October 1979.

Gray, S. L., and J. R. McKean, "The Development of Water Multiplier Impacts from Input– Output Analysis: An Empirical Example from Boulder, Larimer and Weld Counties, Colorado," *Water Resources Res.*, vol. 12, no. 2, April 1976.

Cecil B. Haver and Associates, "The Economic Analysis and Role of Water Resource Projects in Regional Development," U.S. Department of the Army, Corps of Engineers, Office of Appalachian Studies, August 1965.

Hirschman, Albert, *The Strategy of Economic Development*, Yale University Press, New Haven, Conn., 1958.

Howe, C. W., "Water and Regional Economic Growth in the United States, 1950–1960," *South Econ. J.*, 34, 1968.

Isard, Walter, "Interregional and Regional Input–Output Analysis: A Model of a Space-Economy", *Review of Economic Statistics*, vol. XXXIII, November 1951.

Isard, W., *Methods of Regional Analysis: An Introduction to Regional Science*, MIT Press, Cambridge, Mass., 1960.

Isard, W., and S. Czamanski, "Techniques for Estimating Local and Regional Multiplier Effects of Changes in the Level of Major Government Programs," *Peace Res. Soc. Papers*, vol. III, 1965.

Isserman, Andrew M., "The Location Quotient Approach to Estimating Regional Economic Impacts," *J. Inst. Plann.*, January 1977.

Kahn, R. F., "The Relation of Home Investment to Unemployment," *Econ. J.*, vol. 41, 1931.

Keynes, J. M., *The General Theory of Employment, Interest and Money*, Harcourt Brace & World, New York, 1936

Kim, Ungsoo, et al., "An application of the Interregional I/O Model for the Study of the Impact of the McClellan–Kerr Arkansas River Multiple Purpose Project," Institute of Social and Behavioral Research, Catholic University of America, Washington, D.C., March 1977.

Krutilla, John V., "Criteria for Evaluating Regional Development Programs," *Am. Econ. Rev.*, vol. 45, 1955.

Leontief, Wasily, *The Structure of the American Economy 1919–1929*, Harvard University Press, Cambridge, Mass., 1941.

Leontief, Wasily, *Input–Output Economics*, Oxford University Press, Fair Lawn, N.J., 1966.

Leven, Charles, "Establishing Goals for Economic Development," in *Regional Development and Planning*, John Fieldman and William Alonso, eds., Cambridge, 1964.

Leven, Charles L., ed., "Development Benefits of Water Resources Investments," Institute for Urban and Regional Studies, Washington University, St. Louis, November 1969.

Lewis, W. C., "Public Investment Impacts and Regional Economic Growth," *Water Resources Res.*, vol. 9, no. 4, August 1973.

Liang, Tung, "An LP-I/O Model for Coordinating Multi-group Inputs in Resource Planning," *Water Resources Bull.*, vol. 12, no. 3, June 1976.

Liang, T., and W. Y. Huang, "A Dynamic Model for Water and Related Land Resource Planning," *Water Resources Bull.*, vol. 11, no. 1, 1975.

Maass, Arthur, "Benefit–Cost Analysis: Its Relevance to Public Investment Decisions," *Q. J. Econ.*, May 1966.

Maass, A., M. Hufschmidt, et al., *Design of Water Resource Systems*, Harvard University Press, Cambridge, Mass., 1962.

Marglin, S., *Public Investment Criteria*, Allen & Unwin, London, 1967.

Meadows, Donella H., et al., *The Limits to Growth*, a report for the Club of Rome's project on the Predicament of Mankind, Potomac Associates Books, Washington, D.C., 1972.

Mesarovic, Mihajlo, and Edward Pestel, *Mankind at the Turning Point*, E. P. Dutton, New York, 1974.

Meyer, John, "Regional Economics—A Survey," *Am. Econ. Rev.*, March 1963.

Miernyk, William H., *The Elements of Input–Output Analysis*, Random House, New York, 1965.

Mitchell, Arnold, et al., "Handbook of Forecasting Techniques," Stanford Research Institute, December 1975; "List of 73 Techniques," August 1977; "Description of 31 Techniques," August 1977.

Moses, Leon N., "The Stability of Interregional Trading Patterns and Input–Output Analysis", *American Economic Review*, pp. 803–32, 1955.

Mountain West Research, Inc., "Bureau of Reclamation Economic Assessment Model (BREAM) Technical Description," January 1978.

R. Nathan and Associates, "Recreation as an Industry," Appalachian Regional Commission, Washington, D.C., 1966.

National Planning Association, "Economic Base Study for Chesapeake Basin," February 1967.

Polenske, Karen R., "Multiregional Input–Output Model for the United States," Harvard Economic Research Project, Rep. 21, prepared for EDA, Harvard University, Cambridge, Mass., 1970.

Research and Development Corporation, "An Input–Output Model of Appalachia," Silver Springs, Md., February 1968.

Spindeltop Research, Inc., "Expansion Benefits Analysis for the Salyersville-Royalton Area Pilot Project," U.S. Army Corps of Engineers, Office of Appalachian Studies, March 1967a.

Spindeltop Research, Inc., "A Model for Sequencing Public Investment Programs and Allocating Multi-program Benefits," U.S. Army Corps of Engineers, Office of Appalachian Studies, September 1967b.

Tolley, George S., ed., "Estimation of First Round and Selected Subsequent Income Effects of Water Resources Investment," Department of Economics, University of Chicago, February 1970.

U.S. Department of the Army, Corps of Engineers, Office of Appalachian Studies, "Development of Water Resources in Appalachia," Main Report, Part IV, Planning Concepts and Methods, September 1969.

U.S. Department of Commerce, Bureau of Economic Analysis, "The Input–Output Structure of the U.S. Economy: 1967, *Survey of Current Business*, February 1974.

U.S. Department of the Interior, "Report of the Panel of Consultants on Secondary or Indirect Benefits of Water Use Projects," June 26, 1952.

U.S. Water Resources Council, "Principles and Standards for Planning Water and Related Land Resources," September 10, 1973; rev. December 14, 1979; rev. September 29, 1980.

FIFTEEN

Environmental Impact Assessment

15.1 INTRODUCTION

Preceding chapters (in particular, Sections 2.10, 5.5, 5.8 to 5.12, and 6.7) have identified many types of environmental and social impacts, and have shown how they should be considered (together with engineering, economic, and other factors) in water resources planning problems such as site selection; establishment of development purposes; arrangement and sizing of project features; comparison of alternative projects; and determination of construction, operation, and maintenance methods. The incorporation of environmental quality and beneficial social effects as formal objectives in the planning process has also been discussed (Sections 2.10 to 2.13).

The role of environmental assessments is still undergoing development. A major problem with some assessments (particularly those by federal agencies) is that they have been too long and complex. The planner should, therefore, seek ways to discriminate among the data, and to focus on what is important and useful in the planning process. Since there is no general agreement on the details of these assessments, this chapter provides information on various ways to quantify environmental effects, on display techniques for the comprehensive comparison of alternatives, and on methods to satisfy formal requirements of federal and state laws and regulations requiring evaluation of environmental impacts. Some of these methods include the consideration of social impacts; other methods of social impact assessment are described in Chapter 16. The procedures described in this chapter (or briefer versions of the procedures) may be used in any phase of planning, but are especially applicable in the final stages of planning and justifying a project.

15.2 ENVIRONMENTAL LAWS AND REGULATIONS

United States. Despite an increasing interest by individuals and groups in the preservation and conservation of water resources and an awareness of the short- and long-range effects of water resources development on the environment, both beneficial and adverse, it is only relatively recently that such an interest and awareness has been translated into legislative directives and agency planning procedures. The National Environmental Policy Act of 1969 (NEPA) requires the preparation of an environmental impact statement (EIS) for every major federal action (program, project, or licensing action) "significantly" affecting the quality of the human environment.

The historical development of national objectives for water resources planning has been discussed in Section 2.10. This led in 1973 to the establishment by the Water Resources Council of "Principles and Standards" in which Environmental Quality was designated as a coequal objective with National Economic Development. In its 1983 "Principles and Guidelines" the WRC made NED the single federal planning objective but emphasized that planning must be "consistent with protecting the Nation's environment, pursuant to national environmental statutes, applicable executive orders, and other federal planning requirements." Environmental quality procedures for Level C planning (implementation studies), published in 1980, and "Principles and Guidelines," issued in 1983, are useful references for water resources planning.

The Council of Environmental Quality created by NEPA developed regulations in 1973 and 1978 for implementing the act. Federal (e.g., Department of the Army, 1978, 1979; Department of the Interior, 1979) and state agencies have also prepared guidelines for complying with NEPA, WRC "Principles and Guidelines" and the extensive federal and state legislation dealing with many specific aspects of protection, conservation, and enhancement of environmental quality. Experience with these documents has indicated that public involvement (see Chapter 7) is essential in environmental and social assessments. It is of particular importance in "scoping" when the planner determines what should be studied and what is most important to analyze.

Other Countries. Although economic development and meeting identified water needs will undoubtedly continue to be the principal motivations for projects in developing countries, there has been an increasing interest in and awareness of the environment even in these countries. The U.S. State Department in the overseas programs of its Agency for International Development now seeks to consider more fully the environmental impacts of projects it assists.

In 1972, the United Nations held a Conference on the Human Environment in Stockholm, which led to the development of a UN Action Plan and to the establishment of the UN Environmental Fund. In 1970, the World Bank Group established the post of Environmental Advisor and an Office of Environmental and Health Affairs. The Bank has no formal environment standards and does not require impact statements (World Bank, 1973). It does, however, have checklists for analyzing projects in terms of environmental, health, and human ecological considerations (World Bank, 1974). Guidelines are developed for assessing impacts for various types of projects by joint committees of the United Nations Environment Programme, United Nations Development Programme, and the World Bank (United Nations, 1980).

15.3 WATER RESOURCES COUNCIL GUIDELINES FOR PROJECT PLANNING AND ASSESSMENT

WRC guidelines issued in 1980 in "Principles and Standards" and "Procedures" and in 1983 in "Principles and Guidelines" provided for four accounts for displaying the effects of each plan or project on national economic development (NED), environmental quality (EQ), regional economic development (RED), and other social effects (OSE). The four accounts are intended to cover all effects on the "human environment," a term mentioned in the National Environmental Policy Act and regulations for the implementation of the act. The EQ account is limited to effects on the "ecological, cultural, and aesthetic properties of natural and cultural resources that sustain and enrich human life" (WRC, 1983, p. 103). The net effects of a plan on EQ are determined by estimating conditions with and without the plan.

Significant EQ resources and attributes and significant effects are based on institutional, public, and technical recognition. Institutional recognition means that the importance of an EQ resource is acknowledged by the laws, adopted plans, and other policy statements of public agencies or private groups. Public recognition means that some segment of the general public recognizes the importance of an EQ resource or attribute. Technical recognition means that the importance of an EQ resource or attribute is based on scientific or technical knowledge or judgment of critical resource characteristics (WRC, 1983, pp. 110–112).

The EQ account is developed using concepts for EQ attributes and EQ resources, mentioned above, and on guidelines and indicators. The WRC "Principles and Guidelines" define these terms as follows (WRC, 1983, pp. 103–104):

EQ attributes. EQ attributes are the ecological, cultural, and aesthetic properties of natural and cultural resources that sustain and enrich human life.

1. *Ecological attributes* are components of the environment and the interactions among all its living (including people) and nonliving components that directly or indirectly sustain dynamic, diverse, viable ecosystems. In this category are functional and structural aspects of the environment, including aspects that require special consideration because of their unusual characteristics.
   a. Functional aspects of the environment include production, nutrient cycling, succession, assimilative capacity, erosion, and other dynamic, interactive processes and systems. Examples are the role of wetlands as a potential sink

for nutrients and pollutants; the high productivity of marshes, which is often exported to other systems; and prime and unique farmlands.

b. Structural aspects of the environment include plant and animal species, populations and communities; habitats; and the chemical and physical properties of air, water (surface and ground), and soil and other geophysical resources. Examples are water quality factors that support or are indicative of trout fisheries; the substrate characteristics and the aggregation of plants and animals that support a rookery; the pH of the rainfall; pristine wilderness areas; endangered, threatened, and other unique or scarce plant and animal species; and rock strata with scientific or educational uses.

2. *Cultural attributes* are evidence of past and present habitation that can be used to reconstruct or preserve human lifeways. Included in this category are structures, sites, artifacts, environments, and other relevant information, and the contexts in which these occur. Cultural attributes are found in archeological remains of prehistoric and historic aboriginal occupations; historic European and American areas of occupation and activities; and objects and places related to the beliefs, practices, and products of existing folk or traditional communities and native American groups. Examples are campsites of prehistoric mammoth hunters, a nineteenth-century farmstead, and a stream crossing in long-standing use by an Appalachian community for baptizing church members.

3. *Aesthetic attributes* are perceptual stimuli that provide diverse and pleasant surroundings for human enjoyment and appreciation. Included in this category are sights, sounds, scents, tastes, and tactile impressions, and the interactions of these sensations, of natural and cultural resources. Examples are the sight of a pristine landscape, the view of a historic fortress, the sound of a waterfall or brook, the scent of a hedgerow of honeysuckle or a pine forest, and the taste of mineral water.

EQ resource. An EQ resource is a natural or cultural form, process, system, or other phenomenon that: (1) is related to land, water, atmosphere, plants, animals, or historic or cultural objects, sites, buildings, structures, or districts; and (2) has one or more EQ attributes (ecological, cultural, aesthetic).

Guidelines. A guideline is a standard, criterion, threshold, optimum, or other desirable level for an indicator that provides a basis for judging whether an effect is beneficial or adverse. Guidelines are to be based on institutional, public, or technical recognition.

Indicator. An indicator is a characteristic of an EQ resource that serves as a direct or indirect means of measuring or otherwise describing changes in the quantity and/or quality of an EQ attribute.

1. Quantity indicators describe how much of a resource attribute is present in terms of physical size, magnitude, or dimension. They are usually measurable in numeric units (example: The indicator "depth" is measurable in meters, feet,

etc.); but they may be described in nonnumeric terms (example: The indicator "amount" could be described on a scale of "abundant/adequate/scarce/unique"). The diversity or stability of an ecosystem or natural community may be a numeric or nonnumeric indicator.

2. Quality indicators are characteristics that describe the degree or grade of an attribute's desirability (how good or how bad). Some quality indicators are measurable in numeric units (example: The indicator "landscape beauty" measured by an ordinal ranking of landscapes); some represent composites of numeric measurements (example: The indicator "class 'A' water quality" is a composite of measurements of concentrations of dissolved oxygen, suspended solids, etc.); some are described in nonnumeric units (example: The indicator "desirability of scent" described on a scale of "offensive/neutral/pleasant").

Section 6.8 summarizes the plan formulation procedure described in the WRC "Principles and Guidelines." The EQ evaluation procedures are integrated in the plan formulation and evaluation process and consist of four stages (WRC, 1983, p. 109):

1. *Preliminary identify/inventory stage*
   Identify EQ resources.
   Collect available data.
   Identify information needs.
2. *Preliminary assess/appraise stage*
   Identify EQ resources likely to be significantly affected.
3. *Detailed identify/inventory stage*
   Develop adequate information base.
4. *Detailed assess/appraise stage*
   Assess and appraise significant effects.
   Judge net EQ effects.

Figure 15.1 and Table 15.1 (WRC, 1983, pp. 126–136) illustrate for a hypothetical plan the results of the EQ evaluation recorded in a table format.

15.4 ENVIRONMENTAL IMPACT STATEMENT (CEQ GUIDELINES)

The National Environmental Policy Act of 1969 (NEPA) requires that the environmental impact statement (EIS) be prepared by the "responsible official." In practice, such EISs by federal agencies are often based largely on environmental impact assessments (EIA) prepared by state and local governmental agencies, consulting firms, and other entities. The EIS is submitted to the Council on Environmental Quality (CEQ) and is made available to the public. The document does not require formal approval by the CEQ as a prerequisite to project

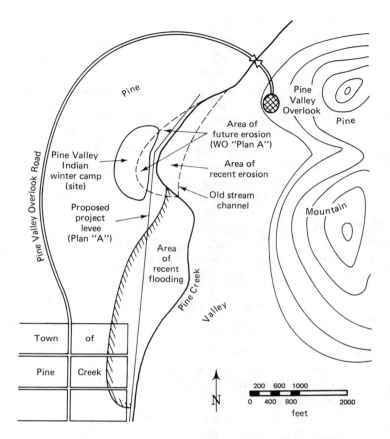

Figure 15.1 Area used as basis for Table 15.1 (From U.S. Water Resources Council, 1983.)

authorization. It is, however, an important relevant information document that can be considered by federal legislators and agency officials in the process of reviewing legislation and specific plans. Nonfederal agencies, public interest groups, or individuals may also influence, delay, or otherwise affect project implementation by raising questions (at public hearings and in the legislative and judicial processes) concerning the adequacy and correctness of the statements.

The following points that must be covered in the EIS are elaborated on in the CEQ guidelines (1973 and 1978):

1. A description of the proposed action, a statement of its purposes, and a description of the environment affected
2. The relationship of the proposed action to land use plans, policies, and controls for the affected area
3. The probable impact of the proposed action on the environment

TABLE 15.1a   TABLE FORMAT FOR EQ EFFECTS: IDENTIFICATION OF EQ RESOURCES TO BE EVALUATED

Resources	EQ Attributes			Institutional Recognition	Significance		Likely to Be Affected (yes/no)	Resource to Be Evaluated (yes/no)	Notes
	Ecological	Cultural	Aesthetic		Public Recognition	Technical Recognition			
R_1: Pine Valley meadow	Deer fawning area	—	—	—	—	Major fawning area for Pine Mt. deer herd	Yes	Yes	
	—	Indian winter camp (site)	—	Included in state list of historic sites	—	—	Yes	Yes	
	—	—	View of meadow and winter camp	—	Public acknowledged desirability of meadow and winter camp	—	Yes	Yes	
R_2: Pine Creek (river miles 169–171)	Trout spawning habitat	—	—	—	—	40% of suitable spawning gravels located in this reach of Pine Creek	Yes	Yes	
R_3: Pine Valley overlook area	—	—	View site for Pine Valley	—	—	—	No	No	
R_4: Town of Pine Creek (area of flooding)	—	—	—	—	Acknowledged as a problem that needs resolution	—	Yes	No	To be evaluated in NED account

Source: U.S. Water Resources Council (1983).

459

TABLE 15.1b TABLE FORMAT FOR EQ EFFECTS: EVALUATION FRAMEWORK

| Resources | EQ Attributes | Indicators | Units | Guidelines | Techniques | | Notes |
					Names	Documentation References	
R₁: Pine Valley meadow	Ecological	Terrestrial habitat (quality and quantity aspects)	Habitat units	Not less than 19 habitat units	HEP	Habitat evaluation procedures (FWS-ESM 102)	
		Deer fawns	Number of fawns	75 or more fawns per year	State annual deer census (Pine V. Herd)	See Bibliography #1	
		Area of site	Acres	Preservation of entire site	Map planimeter	See Bibliography #2	
	Cultural	Representativeness	Importance ranking	Preservation (high ranking)	Importance ranking technique	See Bibliography #3	
		Research value	Importance ranking	Preservation (high ranking)	Importance ranking technique	See Bibliography #4	
	Aesthetic	Landscape priority	Landscape priority ranking	H^9	PEPLA	Procedures to establish priorities in landscape architecture (SCS TR #65)	
R₂: Pine Creek (etc.)							

Source: U.S. Water Resources Council (1983).

460

TABLE 15.1c TABLE FORMAT FOR EQ EFFECTS: TREND AND EXISTING CONDITIONS

Resources	EQ Attributes	Indicators	Trend Conditions			Existing Condition (Units/Date)	Notes
			Trend (Units/Date)	Trend (Units/Date)	Trend (Units/Date)		
R₁: Pine Valley meadow	Ecological	Habitat	22 (1950)	20 (1970)	19 (1978)	19 (1980)	Trend conditions estimated from 1950, 1970, and 1978 surveys (photos)
		Fawns	50 (1950)	58 (1970)	60 (1975)	65 (1980)	Information from annual census (Pine Mt. deer herd)
	Cultural	Area of site	6 ac. (1942)	6 ac. (1950)	6 ac. (1970)	6 ac. (1979)	Indian winter camp discovered in 1942
		Representative-ness	Unknown	Unknown	Unknown	High	
		Research value	Unknown	Unknown	High	High	
	Aesthetic	Landscape priority	Unknown	Unknown	H^8 ranking (1978)	H^8 ranking (1980)	
R₂: Pine Creek							

Source: U.S. Water Resources Council (1983).

TABLE 15.1d TABLE FORMAT FOR EQ EFFECTS: WITHOUT-PLANS CONDITIONS

Resources	EQ Attributes	Indicators	Without-Plans Conditions						Forecast Techniques		Notes
			Start Implementation Date (1990)	End Implementation Date (1995)	Forecast Date 1 (2006)	Forecast Date 2 (2025)	Forecast Date 3 (2045)	Locational Changes	Names	Documentation References	
R₁: Pine Valley meadow	Ecological	Habitat	22	24	27	29	30	None	Extrapolation	See Bibliography #5	Local wildlife group is very active in wildlife management program
		Deer fawns	68	69	75	78	80	None	Extrapolation	See Bibliography #6	
	Cultural	Area of site	5.9 ac.	5.6 ac.	5.3 ac.	3.0 ac.	2.9 ac.	Loss along eastern side of winter camp due to erosion loss of some artifacts and part of site	Extrapolation	See Bibliography #7	
		Representativeness	High	High	High	High	High		Scenarios	See Bibliography #8	
		Research value	High	High	Moderate	Low	Low		Extrapolation	See Bibliography #9	
	Aesthetic	Landscape priority	H^8	H^8	H^7	H^6	H^7	None	Scenarios	Pine County Planning Dept. report: Future Landscapes for Pine Valley 1978–2028, Vol I	
R₂: Pine Creek											

Source: U.S. Water Resources Council (1983).

TABLE 15.1e TABLE FORMAT FOR EQ EFFECTS: WITH-PLAN CONDITIONS FOR PLAN A

Resources	EQ Attributes	Indicators	With-Plan Conditions						Forecast Techniques		Notes
			Start Implementation Date (1990)	End Implementation Date (1995)	Forecast Date 1 (2005)	Forecast Date 2 (2025)	Forecast Date 3 (2045)	Locational Changes	Names	Documentation References	
R₁: Pine Valley meadow	Ecological	Habitat	19	8	10	14	19	None	Model	See Bibliography #10	Riparian vegetation slowly returned after construction
		Dear fawns	65	20	32	47	65	None	Model	See Bibliography #11	
	Cultural	Area of site	5.9 ac.	5.9 ac.	5.9 ac.	5.9 ac.	5.9 ac.	0.1 ac. of camp site and artifacts lost due to erosion	Model	See Bibliography #12	
		Representativeness	High	High	High	High	High	None	Scenario	See Bibliography #13	
		Research value	High	High	High	High	High	None	Scenario	See Bibliography #14	
	Aesthetic	Landscape priority	H[8]	L[4]	L[4]	M[5]	M[6]	None	Scenario	See Bibliography #15	
R₂: Pine Creek											

Source: U.S. Water Resources Council (1983).

TABLE 15.1f TABLE FORMAT FOR EQ EFFECTS: IDENTIFICATION OF EFFECTS FOR PLAN A

Resources	EQ Attributes	Indicators	Difference Between Without-Plans and With-Plan Conditions (yes/no)						Notes
			Start Implementation Date (1990)	End Implementation Date (1995)	Forecast Date 1 (2005)	Forecast Date 2 (2025)	Forecast Date 3 (2045)	Effect (yes/no)	
R₁: Pine Valley meadow	Ecological	Habitat	Yes	Yes	Yes	Yes	Yes	Yes	
		Deer fawns	Yes	Yes	Yes	Yes	Yes	Yes	
	Cultural	Area of site	No	Yes	Yes	No	No	No	
		Representativeness	No	No	No	No	No		
		Research value	No	No	Yes	Yes	Yes	Yes	
	Aesthetic	Landscape priority	No	Yes	Yes	Yes	Yes	Yes	
R₂: Pine Creek									

Source: U.S. Water Resources Council (1983).

TABLE 15.1g TABLE FORMAT FOR EQ EFFECTS: DESCRIPTIONS OF EFFECTS FOR PLAN A

| | | | Effect Characteristics | | | | | | | | |
| | | | Magnitude | | | | | | | | |
Resources	EQ Attributes	Indicators	Start Implementation Date (1990)	End Implementation Date (1995)	Forecast Date 1 (2005)	Forecast Date 2 (2025)	Forecast Date 3 (2045)	Duration	Location	Other Effects Characteristics	Notes
R_1: Pine Valley meadow	Ecological	Habitat	−3	−16	−17	−15	−11	55 years and long term (starting 1990)	—	—	
		Deer fawns	−3	−49	−43	−31	−15	55 years and long term (starting 1990)	—	—	
	Cultural	Area of site	0	+0.3	+0.6	+1.4	+2.9	55 years and long term (starting 1990)	—	—	
		Representativeness	No change	No change	No change	No change	No change	—	—	—	
		Research value	No change	No change	No change	Slight increase	Great increase	20 years and long term (starting 2025)	—	—	

TABLE 15.1g *(continued)*

| | | | Effect Characteristics | | | | | | | |
| | | | Magnitude | | | | | | | |
Resources	*EQ Attributes*	*Indicators*	*Start Implementation Date (1990)*	*End Implementation Date (1995)*	*Forecast Date 1 (2005)*	*Forecast Date 2 (2025)*	*Forecast Date 3 (2045)*	*Duration*	*Location*	*Other Effects Characteristics*	*Notes*
R₂: Pine Creek	Aesthetic	Landscape priority	No change	Great decrease	Moderate decrease	Slight decrease	Slight decrease	45 years and long term (starting 1995)	—	The levee would detract from the "natural" look of the meadow even after revegetation	

Source: U.S. Water Resources Council (1983).

TABLE 15.h TABLE FORMAT FOR EQ EFFECTS: DETERMINATIONS OF EFFECTS SIGNIFICANCE FOR PLAN A

			Significant			
Resources	EQ Attributes	Indicators	Institutional Recognition	Public Recognition	Technical Recognition	Significant Effect (yes/no)	Notes
R₁: Pine Valley meadow	Ecological	Habitat			State and federal wildlife biologists recognize that the project will decrease habitat below threshold levels	Yes	
		Deer fawns	40 CFR 1508.27(b)(3) (ecologically critical areas)	Pine-Creek Wildlife Club states the deer population will decrease		Yes	
	Cultural	Area of site Representa- tiveness	40 CFR 1508.27(b)(8) & (10) (loss of historic resource and loss of historic site)	State historic preservation officer supports protecting the site	Site and associated characteristics saved	Yes No	
		Research value				Yes	
	Aesthetic	Landscape priority	None	Community groups support saving the area from erosion, but want plantings made on the levee to compensate for loss of aesthetic values	None	Yes	
R₂: Pine Creek							

Source: U.S. Water Resources Council (1983).

467

TABLE 15.1i TABLE FORMAT FOR EQ EFFECTS: APPRAISALS OF EFFECTS (INDICATORS) FOR PLAN A

Resources	EQ Attributes	Indicators	Appraisals (beneficial/adverse)					Notes
			Start Implementation Date (1990)	End Implementation Date (1995)	Forecast Date 1 (2005)	Forecast Date 2 (2025)	Forecast Date 3 (2045)	
R_1: Pine Valley meadow	Ecological	Habitat	Adverse	Adverse	Adverse	Adverse	Adverse	
	Cultural	Deer fawns	Adverse	Adverse	Adverse	Adverse	Adverse	
		Area of site	No change	Beneficial	Beneficial	Beneficial	Beneficial	
		Representative-ness	No change	No change	No change	No change	No change	
		Research value	No change	No change	No change	Beneficial	Beneficial	
	Aesthetic	Landscape priority	No change	Adverse	Adverse	Adverse	Adverse	
R_2: Pine Creek								

Source: U.S. Water Resources Council (1983).

468

TABLE 15.1j   TABLE FORMAT FOR EQ EFFECTS: APPRAISALS OF EFFECTS (EQ ATTRIBUTES) FOR PLAN A

Resources	EQ Attributes	Description (magnitude, duration, location; see Table g)	Appraisal (Beneficial/ Adverse; see Table i)	Appraisal Considerations					Appraisal judgment (also enter in significant EQ Effects table 714, 441)	Notes
				Quantity/ Quality Factors	Institutional Factors (see Table h)	Public Factors (see Table h)	Technical Factors (see Table h)	Other Factors		
R₁: Pine Valley meadow	Ecological	Major loss of fawning area	Adverse for all indicators	Quantity and quality of habitat and deer population decreased	Destruction of critical ecological areas	Opposed by Pine Creek Wildlife Club	Habitat and population will drop below threshold levels	—	Adverse: major loss of deer fawning area	Mitigation recommended
	Cultural	Site saved from loss due to erosion which would have been irretrievable	Beneficial because long term losses from erosion are prevented	The quantity of the site (ac.) is saved; therefore, the quality is saved	State historic site saved	State historic preservation officer supports plan A	Area, representativeness and research value saved	—	Beneficial: site saved from potential loss due to erosion	
	Aesthetic	Site mapped by construction of levee, but major erosion is curtailed	A long-term adverse effect on aesthetics occurs, but decreases as vegetation covers levee	Views are degraded	None	Community groups want restrictions placed on the project	None	—	Adverse: because view of meadow as a whole is marred	
R₂: Pine Creek										

Source: U.S. Water Resources Council (1983).

4. Alternatives to the proposed action
5. Any probable adverse environmental effects that cannot be avoided
6. The relationship between local short-term uses of the environment and the maintenance and enhancement of long-term productivity
7. Any irreversible and irretrievable commitments of resources that would be involved in the proposed action should it be implemented
8. An indication of what other interests a consideration of federal policy are thought to offset the adverse environmental effects of the proposed action identified pursuant to paragraphs 3 and 5

Table 15.2 is a table of contents corresponding to the eight points above for either an environmental impact assessment (EIA) or a statement (EIS). Note that the EIA/EIS does not cover the same issues as the Water Resources Council guidelines for environmental quality planning, described in Section 15.3. The EIA would precede the EIS and provide a basis for intraagency review of project impacts. It would have adequate information for judging whether a more formal (and perhaps more complete) EIS should be prepared. A draft EIS is prepared first and is subjected to review by federal agencies (in particular the Environmental Protection Agency), state and local agencies, and the public. Suitable responses and/or revisions are made based on the questions raised by those entities before a final EIS is issued. The following discusses some of the eight points of the EIS that may not be self-evident from the list above and Table 15.2.

Issue III covers both primary and secondary effects. The latter term refers also to indirect effects. As noted in CEQ's guidelines (1973, Sec. 1500.8)

> Many major Federal Actions, in particular those that involve the construction or licensing of infrastructure investments (e.g., . . . water resource projects . . .) stimulate or induce secondary effects in the form of associated investments and changed patterns of social and economic activities. Such secondary effects, through their impacts on existing community facilities and activities, or through changes in natural conditions, may often be even more substantial than the primary effects of the original action itself. For example, the effects of the proposed action on population and growth . . . should be estimated if expected to be significant . . . and an assessment made of the effect . . . upon the resource base, including land use, water, and public services.

In considering alternatives to the proposed action, issue IV, the analysis should contain a "comparative evaluation of the environmental benefits, costs and risks of the proposed action and each reasonable alternative." The terms "comparative" and "reasonable" imply a degree of detail that is less than the full treatment of the recommended plan.

In issue VI concerning trade-offs between "short-term" and "long-term" effects, these terms "do not refer to any fixed time periods, but should be viewed in terms of the environmentally significant consequences of the proposed action."

In considering issue VII, CEQ cautions that the term "resources" does not mean only the labor and materials devoted to an action, but also means the natural and cultural resources committed to loss or destruction by the action.

Environmental Impact Assessment   Chap. 15

TABLE 15.2 OUTLINE FOR CEQ-PRESCRIBED EIA/EIS CONTENT

  I. Project Description
     A. Purpose of action
     B. Description of action
        1. Name
        2. Summary of activities
     C. Environmental setting
        1. Environment prior to proposed action
        2. Related federal activities
 II. Land Use Relationships
     A. Conformity or conflict with other land use plans, policies, and controls
        1. Federal, state, and local
        2. Clean Air Act and Federal Water Pollution Control Act
     B. Conflicts and/or inconsistent land use plans
        1. Extent of reconciliation
        2. Reasons for proceeding with action
III. Probable Impact of the Proposed Action on the Environment
     A. Positive and negative effects
        1. National and international environment
        2. Environmental factors
        3. Impact of proposed action
     B. Direct and indirect consequences
        1. Primary effects
        2. Secondary effects
 IV. Alternatives to the Proposed Action
     A. Reasonable alternative actions
        1. Those that might enhance environmental quality
        2. Those that avoid some or all adverse effects
     B. Analysis of alternatives
        1. Benefits
        2. Costs
        3. Risks
  V. Probable Adverse Environmental Effects That Cannot be Avoided
     A. Adverse and unavoidable impacts
     B. How avoidable adverse impacts will be mitigated
 VI. Relationship between Local Short-Term Uses of the Environment and the Maintenance and Enhancement of Long-Term Productivity
     A. Trade-off between short-term environmental gains at expense of long-term losses
     B. Trade-off between long-term environmental gains at expense of short-term losses
     C. Extent to which proposed action forecloses future options
VII. Irreversible and Irretrievable Commitments of Resources
     A. Unavoidable impacts irreversibly curtailing the range of potential uses of the environment
        1. Labor
        2. Materials
        3. Natural
        4. Cultural
VIII. Other Interests and Considerations of Federal Policy That Offset the Adverse Environmental Effects of the Proposed Action
     A. Countervailing benefits of proposed action
     B. Countervailing benefits of alternatives

Source: Jain et al. (1974).

Finally, for issue VIII, it is stated that agencies that prepare benefit-cost analyses of proposed actions should "attach such analyses, or summaries thereof, to the environmental impact statement, and should clearly indicate the extent to which environmental costs have not been reflected in such analyses."

15.5 ENVIRONMENTAL PROTECTION AGENCY GUIDELINES

The EPA prepares environmental assessments for wastewater facilities, making federal grants for this purpose under the Federal Water Pollution Control Act Amendments of 1972. EPA regional agencies have provided aid grantees with guidance in the preparation of environmental assessments (e.g., "Environmental Assessment Manual" by Region 1, EPA, applying to the New England States, n.d.) and the EPA Office of Program Operations has also prepared a pamphlet of instructions for construction grants projects (1979). The latter document indicates that:

> [The environmental assessment is] the part of the facility plan that examines and analyzes the environmental impacts of the alternative plans being considered for the treatment works. It serves two purposes: it protects the environment by ensuring that all environmental impacts are taken into account in selecting a plan for the facility, and it serves as a basis for deciding if an Environmental Impact Statement (EIS) is required. If an EIS is required the environmental assessment serves as a starting point. For some projects, a joint EIS/Assessment (piggy backing) can be prepared.

The document also indicates that many of the items investigated as part of the development of areawide water quality management plans ("208" plans) must also be addressed in doing an environmental assessment for an implementation project.

The guidelines include a table of contents/checklist for the environmental assessment, a table listing the required and suggested features to be evaluated by overlay systems (see Section 5.13.5), and a format for a summary matrix for environmental impacts to be used in the final stage of selecting a plan.

15.6 ENERGY IMPACT ANALYSIS

Energy is expected to become increasingly important in impact analyses as its cost increases and as the side economic effects of its use and development become more pronounced (American Society of Civil Engineers, 1978). The U.S. Water Resources Council in its "Principles and Guidelines" includes energy requirements and energy conservation in its Other Social Effects account.

The California Environmental Quality Act (1976) states that the environmental impacts of energy may include:

- The project's energy requirements and its energy use efficiencies by amount and fuel type for each stage of the project's life cycle, including construction, operation, maintenance and/or removal. If appropriate, the energy intensiveness of materials may be discussed.
- The effects of the project on local and regional energy supplies and on requirements for additional capacity.
- The effects of the project on peak- and base-period demands for electricity and other forms of energy.
- The degree to which the project complies with existing energy standards.
- The effects of the project on energy resources.

The same act requires that a proposed project be compared with alternatives with respect to their energy consumptions and that energy terms be used to describe unavoidable adverse effects, irreversible commitment of resources, short-term gains versus long-term impacts, and growth-inducing effects.

Chapter 4 discusses water and energy relationships that can provide information for energy assessments. Chapter 14 describes input–output models and other mathematical models that can be useful for estimating water and energy requirements resulting from economic growth.

Another approach to energy analysis (which, however, cannot substitute for the energy and environmental assessments and the rules of regulatory agencies) has an ecological basis and employs "energy flow" to study interrelationships between people and nature. This approach has been researched since about 1960 by Odum and his co-workers at the University of Georgia (Wang, Odum, and Kangas 1980; Wang, Odum, and Costanza 1980).

15.7 ENVIRONMENTAL IMPACT ASSESSMENT METHODOLOGIES

A review and analysis of environmental impact assessment methodologies was prepared by Jain and Urban (1975) based on updating earlier work by Warner and Preston (1974). Henderson (1982) has identified a large number of methodologies that are available.

The comprehensiveness and extent of detail for an EIA/EIS may be quite different from what is suitable for preliminary identification and analysis of alternative plans; in preliminary "screening" studies, as discussed in Section 5.5, environmental studies must be limited to those required to eliminate unattractive projects and focus on the alternatives warranting the expenditure of substantial personnel and other resources. Furthermore, the methodologies, while providing useful environmental and related information for comparison of projects, would also not satisfy a formal procedure for plan evaluation with respect to the EQ account, such as the Water Resources Council guidelines discussed in Section 15.3.

Jain and Urban summarized the considerations for determining which methodology is most appropriate for a project as: (1) use to which the analysis will be put; (2) extent to which alternatives differ; (3) involvement of the public; (4) study resources available; (5) familiarity with project site and contemplated actions; (6) importance of issues to be studied; and (7) procedure or format requirements of the sponsoring agency. They also recommend that the adequacy of a methodology be determined from the standpoints of their capabilities for impact identification, measurement, interpretation, and communication.

The reviewers classified EIA/EIS methodologies into six types, based on the way impacts are identified: ad hoc, overlays, checklists, matrices, networks, and combination computer-aided. Examples of these types, although not formally classified, have been shown previously (Chapters 5, 6, and 13) for analyzing both market and nonmarket effects. Other selected methodologies are presented in the following sections. It will be evident that all the procedures require a substantial amount of judgment even when there is a strong information base; such judgment will be reliable only with an interdisciplinary team of professional experts who can properly establish ratings with respect to particular environmental or resource characteristics, or implement a procedure in which environmental and other resource factors are combined, or both.

15.8 DESCRIPTION OF SELECTED IMPACT ASSESSMENT METHODOLOGIES

15.8.1 Checklists

In the Environmental Evaluation System (EES), developed and tested for the U.S. Bureau of Reclamation by Battelle–Columbus Laboratories, Dee et al. (1972) prepared a generalized approach to evaluating the "without" and "with" environmental quality in terms of scores that can be used for comparative evaluations of alternatives for one project or for comparing different projects. The evaluations are in terms of Environmental Impact Units (EIUs). A hierarchical structure considers the environmental impacts in four categories: ecology, environmental pollution, aesthetics, and human interest, as shown in Figure 15.2. These categories are subdivided into 18 environmental components and further subdivided into 78 environmental parameters. Each parameter is assigned a number in the system, which does not vary from project to project, indicating its relative importance; the parameter importance units (PIUs) total 1000.

Based on the environmental examinations, a score is assigned to each environmental parameter expressing its environmental quality (EQ); this is on a scale of 0 to 1, with a higher value indicating better quality. Methods are suggested to determine the EQ by "value functions."

The assessment of each environmental parameter in terms of EIUs is obtained by multiplying its fixed value of parameter importance by the selected value of environmental quality:

Environmental impact = parameter importance × environmental quality

(EIU) (PIU) (EQ)

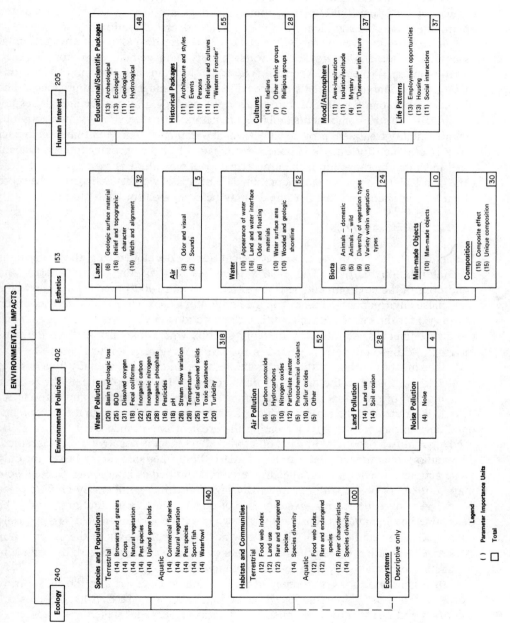

ENVIRONMENTAL IMPACTS

Ecology 240

Species and Populations 140
Terrestrial
(14) Browsers and grazers
(14) Crops
(14) Natural vegetation
(14) Pest species
(14) Upland game birds
Aquatic
(14) Commercial fisheries
(14) Natural vegetation
(14) Pest species
(14) Sport fish
(14) Waterfowl

Habitats and Communities 100
Terrestrial
(12) Food web index
(12) Land use
(12) Rare and endangered species
(14) Species diversity
Aquatic
(12) Food web index
(12) Rare and endangered species
(12) River characteristics
(14) Species diversity

Ecosystems
Descriptive only

Environmental Pollution 402

Water Pollution 318
(20) Basin hydrologic loss
(25) BOD
(31) Dissolved oxygen
(18) Fecal coliforms
(22) Inorganic carbon
(25) Inorganic nitrogen
(28) Inorganic phosphate
(16) Pesticides
(18) pH
(28) Stream flow variation
(28) Temperature
(25) Total dissolved solids
(14) Toxic substances
(20) Turbidity

Air Pollution 52
(5) Carbon monoxide
(5) Hydrocarbons
(10) Nitrogen oxides
(12) Particulate matter
(5) Photochemical oxidants
(10) Sulfur oxides
(5) Other

Land Pollution 28
(14) Land use
(14) Soil erosion

Noise Pollution 4
(4) Noise

Esthetics 153

Land 32
(6) Geologic surface material
(16) Relief and topographic character
(10) Width and alignment

Air 5
(3) Odor and visual
(2) Sounds

Water 52
(10) Appearance of water
(16) Land and water interface
(6) Odor and floating materials
(10) Water surface area
(10) Wooded and geologic shoreline

Biota 24
(5) Animals – domestic
(5) Animals – wild
(9) Diversity of vegetation types
(5) Variety within vegetation types

Man-made Objects 10
(10) Man-made objects

Composition 30
(15) Composite effect
(15) Unique composition

Human Interest 205

Educational/Scientific Packages 48
(13) Archeological
(13) Ecological
(11) Geological
(11) Hydrological

Historical Packages 55
(11) Architecture and styles
(11) Events
(11) Persons
(11) Religions and cultures
(11) "Western Frontier"

Cultures 28
(14) Indians
(7) Other ethnic groups
(7) Religious groups

Mood/Atmosphere 37
(11) Awe-inspiration
(11) Isolation/solitude
(4) Mystery
(11) "Oneness" with nature

Life Patterns 37
(13) Employment opportunities
(13) Housing
(11) Social interactions

Legend
( ) Parameter Importance Units
☐ Total

Figure 15.2 Environmental evaluation system. (Numbers in parentheses are parameter importance units. Numbers enclosed in boxes represent the total.) (From Dee et al., 1972.)

The overall environmental assessment for a project is obtained by summing the EIUs for all the parameters.

Problem areas and data gaps in any considered project are keyed in the EES by the use of "red flags." Major and minor red flags are used when elements of the environment may be significantly changed in an adverse direction by the project.

The Battelle investigators (Dee et al. 1973) also developed an environmental assessment approach for review of water quality management plans for the U.S. Environmental Protection Agency. According to Jain and Urban (1975), this methodology contains elements of checklist, matrix, and network approaches. The hierarchical system consists of four categories—ecology, physical/chemical, aesthetic, social—with 19 components and 64 parameters. A matrix shows which activities in water quality treatment projects affect which parameters. An environmental impact score is obtained for each component by means of an "environmental assessment tree" in which the range for each parameter impact magnitude is expressed on a scale from 0 to 1. The components are combined by means of weights assigned to the score of each component and this net impact may be compared for each alternative.

15.8.2 Matrix Analysis

Leopold et al. (1971) of the U.S. Geological Survey developed what they refer to as an "information matrix." This matrix identifies 88 "existing characteristics and conditions of the environment" on the vertical axis and 100 "proposed actions which may cause environmental impact" on the horizontal axis. Figure 15.3 shows a portion of the grid for the matrix. Each significant interaction between a proposed action and the environment is identified by marking the box where lines drawn from the axes intersect. A diagonal slash is placed in the box from upper right to lower left.

The most important of these interactions are evaluated individually by a number from 1 to 10 placed in the upper left-hand corner of the box to indicate the relative "magnitude" of the impact, 10 representing the greatest magnitude and 1 the least. The "importance" of the impact is shown by a number from 1 to 10 in the lower right-hand corner, again with a 10 indicating the greatest importance. A + sign may be used to identify a beneficial impact; otherwise, the impact is negative or not classified. The authors recommend that a reduced matrix be formed containing boxes for only those actions and environmental characteristics identified as interacting. Special note may be taken of boxes with exceptionally high individual numbers by circling these boxes. An overall scoring system is not given, but "computations" may be determined by the analyst. Ordinarily, no two boxes on any one matrix are precisely equatable. The significance of high or low numbers applies only to the specific box considered. If, however, alternative projects or actions are considered, the values in the same boxes may provide a means of comparison.

In a handbook for environmental impact analysis prepared at the U.S. Army Corps of Engineers Construction Engineering Laboratory (CERL), attributes are identified and characterized by means of descriptor packages which are made up of "attributes" (Jain et al. 1974). These are further refined and incorporated in a computer-aided methodology (Jain and Webster 1977). The CERL system consists of an Environmental Impact Computer System (EICS), an Environmental Impact

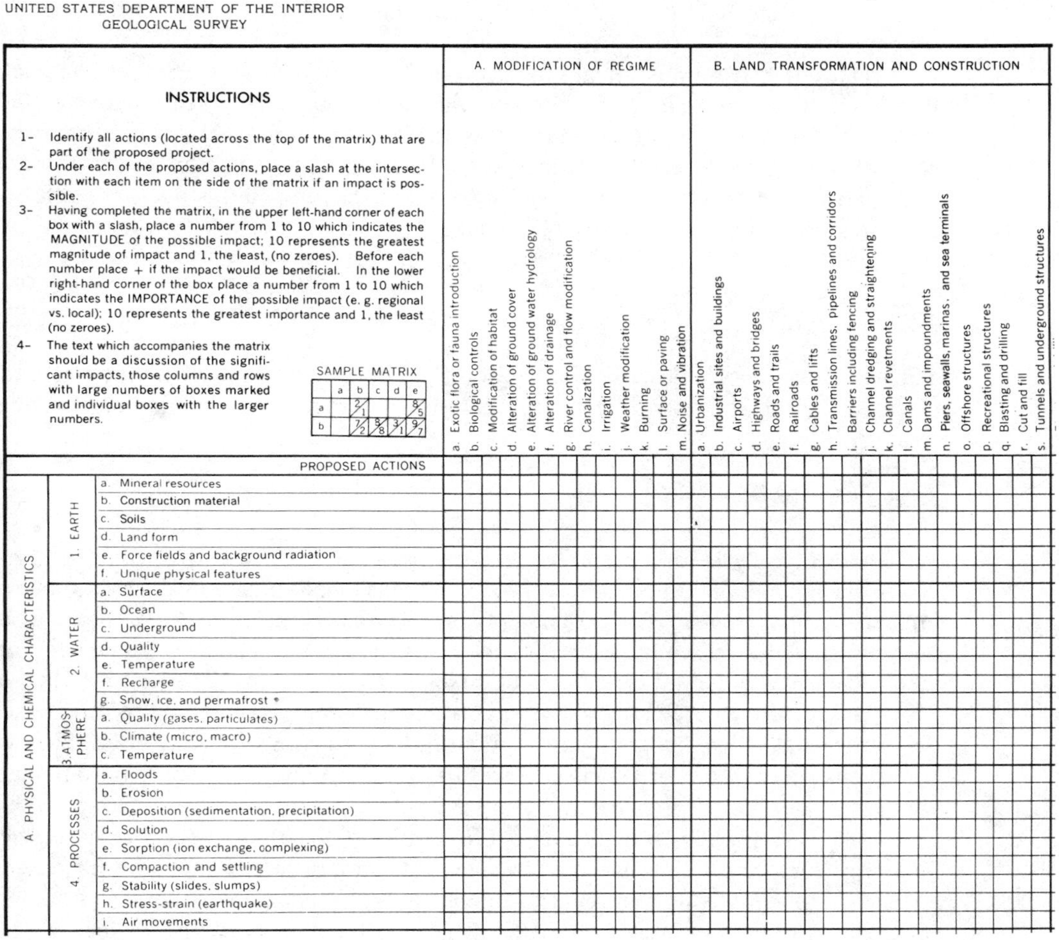

A. MODIFICATION OF REGIME   **B. LAND TRANSFORMATION AND CONSTRUCTION**

INSTRUCTIONS

1– Identify all actions (located across the top of the matrix) that are part of the proposed project.

2– Under each of the proposed actions, place a slash at the intersection with each item on the side of the matrix if an impact is possible.

3– Having completed the matrix, in the upper left-hand corner of each box with a slash, place a number from 1 to 10 which indicates the MAGNITUDE of the possible impact; 10 represents the greatest magnitude of impact and 1, the least, (no zeroes).   Before each number place a + if the impact would be beneficial.   In the lower right-hand corner of the box place a number from 1 to 10 which indicates the IMPORTANCE of the possible impact (e. g. regional vs. local); 10 represents the greatest importance and 1, the least (no zeroes).

4– The text which accompanies the matrix should be a discussion of the significant impacts, those columns and rows with large numbers of boxes marked and individual boxes with the larger numbers.

SAMPLE MATRIX

	a	b	c	d	e
a		2/			6/
b	1/2	3/8	1/3		9/7

Columns under A. MODIFICATION OF REGIME:
a. Exotic flora or fauna introduction
b. Biological controls
c. Modification of habitat
d. Alteration of ground cover
e. Alteration of ground water hydrology
f. Alteration of drainage
g. River control and flow modification
h. Canalization
i. Irrigation
j. Weather modification
k. Burning
l. Surface or paving
m. Noise and vibration

Columns under B. LAND TRANSFORMATION AND CONSTRUCTION:
a. Urbanization
b. Industrial sites and buildings
c. Airports
d. Highways and bridges
e. Roads and trails
f. Railroads
g. Cables and lifts
h. Transmission lines, pipelines and corridors
i. Barriers including fencing
j. Channel dredging and straightening
k. Channel revetments
l. Canals
m. Dams and impoundments
n. Piers, seawalls, marinas, and sea terminals
o. Offshore structures
p. Recreational structures
q. Blasting and drilling
r. Cut and fill
s. Tunnels and underground structures

PROPOSED ACTIONS

A PHYSICAL AND CHEMICAL CHARACTERISTICS

1. EARTH
 a. Mineral resources
 b. Construction material
 c. Soils
 d. Land form
 e. Force fields and background radiation
 f. Unique physical features

2. WATER
 a. Surface
 b. Ocean
 c. Underground
 d. Quality
 e. Temperature
 f. Recharge
 g. Snow, ice, and permafrost *

3. ATMOSPHERE
 a. Quality (gases, particulates)
 b. Climate (micro, macro)
 c. Temperature

4. PROCESSES
 a. Floods
 b. Erosion
 c. Deposition (sedimentation, precipitation)
 d. Solution
 e. Sorption (ion exchange, complexing)
 f. Compaction and settling
 g. Stability (slides, slumps)
 h. Stress-strain (earthquake)
 i. Air movements

Figure 15.3 Portion of information matrix. (From Leopold et al., 1971.)

Forecast System (EIFS), and a Computer-Aided Legislative Data System (CELDS).

Attributes are considered for ecology, environmental health, air quality, surface water, groundwater, economics, sociology, earth science, land use, noise, transportation, aesthetics, and energy and resources conservation. To use the EICS, the user provides information regarding the type of project undertaken, the level of detail for the analysis required, and the environmental setting at the site where the project is to be implemented. The output shows the impacts in matrix format, supplemented with technical information. "Ramification remarks" clarify the importance of the impacts. "Mitigation statements" specify common methods and procedures to reduce the magnitude of impacts. User manuals for different functional areas assist the user in providing the required input and in describing how the output can be used for preparing an EIS.

The EIFS is an analytical model for consideration of socioeconomic impacts; this model employs export-base, location-quotient techniques (see Chapter 14 for further discussion of this type of model). Other analytical models can use the output of the EICS for specialized analyses. The CELDS summarizes and stores informative abstracts of pertinent environmental legislation and is operational for all 50 states as well as the federal government.

15.8.3 Overlays

The use of overlays is described in Section 5.13. Overlays are used more often in the process of siting and arranging project features than in making environmental ratings of alternatives.

15.8.4 Network Analysis

A network analysis approach to environmental assessment was developed by Travelers Research Corporation (1969). It was used to identify environmental impacts for marine resource planning in Long Island, New York. As a basis for the network analysis, three matrices were constructed to function as guides for the identification of potential cause–condition–effect relationships. The first matrix lists 35 causal factors on the vertical axis against 39 environmental conditions affected on the horizontal. The second matrix identifies interactions among environmental conditions, and the third matrix identifies interactions between environmental conditions and human activities.

Sorenson (1970) extended the TRC method to study the adverse impacts resulting from conflicting uses and resource degradation in the California coastal zone, but the procedure is general enough to be applicable to any environment (Ortolano 1973). The major strength of the approach is its ability to identify the pathways by which both primary and secondary environmental impacts are produced (Jain et al. 1974). Sorenson added an additional factor, "uses," in front of the TRC cause–condition–effect relationships, and devised a new format for organizing and displaying the relationships. In another application of the method by Sorenson and Pepper (1973) for the purpose of reviewing environmental impact statements, they identified data types for each resource degradation element, and suggested some general criteria for identifying projects of regional significance based on project size and types of impacts generated.

15.8.5 Some Other EIA/EIS Methodologies

Whitlatch (1976) reviewed the methodologies discussed above (checklists, matrices, overlays, networks) and also described two other methods: linear vector approaches and nonlinear evaluation systems. For the linear vector approach, the impact index I

for any project alternative is found as a linear sum of *component* values (X) multiplied by appropriate *scaling* (S) and *weighting* (W) factors:

$$I = \sum_{i=1}^{n} W_i S_i X_i$$

The impact index is a dimensionless number representing the overall desirability of a project alternative, and the relative worths of alternatives are compared by means of these indexes. Several other methodologies may also be considered to be versions of the linear vector (Stover 1972); Krauskopf and Bunde 1972) or nonlinear evaluation system (Dee et al. 1972, 1973) types.

15.9 APPLICATIONS

Various cases involving environmental studies have been presented in previous chapters (Sections 5.5, 5.12, and 6.7). The illustrations given earlier in this chapter are hypothetical, but their methodologies are straightforward and may be adapted by the planner for suitable projects. Three more case studies are presented in this section (one with more detail than the others) that incorporate some additional approaches. One is an assessment prepared by a nongovernmental entity and two were prepared by federal governmental agencies (Bureau of Reclamation and Corps of Engineers).

The materials in various sections of this book emphasize a range of displays for comparing alternatives. The environmental reports that accompany these displays should contain much more extensive analyses of environmental and other impacts for the alternatives, particularly for the project proposed in each case. The reader should consult full reports (and their guidelines in the case of government agencies) for a perspective of the detail typical of practice in the United States.

15.9.1 Environmental Evaluation of Electric Power System in the Connecticut River Basin

A framework for environmental impact evaluation was prepared for the Federal Power Commission (now Federal Energy Regulatory Commission) by the Center for the Environment & Man, Inc. (CEM) (Northrop et al. 1975). The Environmental Impact Evaluation Model (EIEM) is composed of "models and modules in a comprehensive, interconnected arrangement." It is "viewed as a framework within which models and modules (i.e., systematic procedures) can be added, improved, or deleted appropriate to the particular application." The EIEM can consider various scenarios involving different assumptions for growth of population and electrical demand, electrical supply plans, and environmental and recreational requirements. Five models cover electrical demand, the physical system (water, air, land, electrical system), ecology (specifically anadromous fish), human activities, and socioeconomic effects. As shown on Figure 15.4, the models are interrelated. The approach was tested for the Connecticut River Basin, an area of about 11,250 square

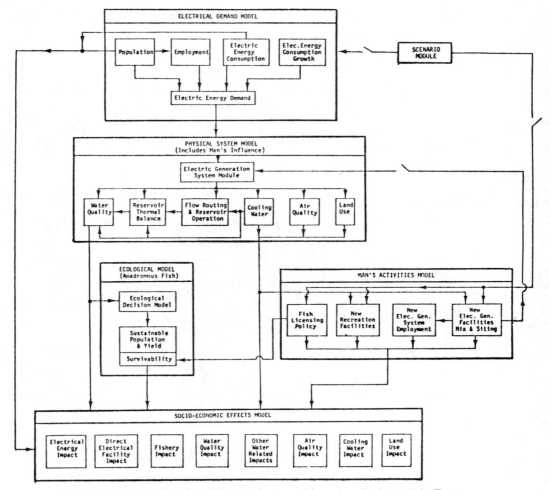

Figure 15.4 Connecticut River Basin environmental impact evaluation model. (From Northrop et al., 1975.)

miles, which extends into four states plus a small area in Canada, and which had a 1970 population of 1,923,000.

15.9.2 Environmental Impact Statement for the Salmon Falls Irrigation and Wildlife Enhancement Project in Upper Snake River Basin (Idaho–Wyoming)

This draft statement was prepared by the U.S. Bureau of Reclamation (at the time, the U.S. Department of the Interior, Water and Power Resources Service, 1979). This statement analyzes the environmental consequences of a supplemental water supply for approximately 57,210 acres of farmland (with new irrigation facilities, including pumping plants, a well field, a canal, and drainage facilities) and an upgrading of wildlife habitat on about 1570 acres of land and 20 watering ponds. A comparative impact analysis of the proposed action and alternatives was accomplished by numerical evaluations of the effects according to the National Economic Development (NED) and Environmental Quality (EQ) accounts, and limited consideration of Regional Development (RD) and Social Well-Being (SWB).

Table 15.3 compares the environmental quality effects of the proposed action and alternatives. In this table, plan A represents the proposed action, plan B is construction of the Salmon Falls Division with development of a well field at Hawley, and plan C is construction of the division with development of a well field at Lava. The table was developed in the following manner.

"Category rank scores" were assigned to each of the various environmental categories by adding five values ranging from 0 to 1 given for: (a) the uniqueness of category in the project area; (b) the vulnerability of the category to impact; (c) the ease of mitigating impacts to the category; (d) the value of the category to regional society; and (e) the contribution of the existing condition to diversity within the category, and then using these values to assign each category a rank score ranging from 1 to 4.

The "category rank scores" are an attempt to equate the differing values of the environmental categories in the project area to the overall impact of the proposed project, that is, the categories are not equally valuable in the planning area and the same degrees of impact on different categories would not necessarily mean the same degree of overall impact. For example, a significant adverse impact on sagebrush–grassland in the planning area would not be as serious as a significant adverse impact on wetlands, because wetlands are a much more scarce resource in the project area. The "category rank scores" were derived by consultation among planning team members with expertise in various environmental fields and in consultation with biologists of the Fish and Wildlife Service and Idaho Department of Fish and Game.

"Impact statements" for the various alternatives were developed by ranking on a +3 to −3 scale the impact of an alternative on the specific environmental category being evaluated. The numerical assignments in many cases take into account several positive and negative impacts on the category.

An "effect of plan" value was developed for each alternative and environmental category by multiplying the "impact statement" by the "category rank score." The "effect of plan" value represents the overall impact of the alternative, taking into account the degree of impact and the relative value of the environmental category being affected. The "effect of plan" values used in the table represent the professional judgment of persons involved in planning the Salmon Falls Division; while it is likely that a different group of individuals would come up with different scores, the ranking among the alternatives would probably remain about the same.

15.9.3 Environmental Impact Statement for the Green Brook Basin, New Jersey, Flood Control Project

This draft statement was prepared by the New York District of the U.S. Corps of Engineers (1978). This project was designed principally for flood damage reduction,

TABLE 15.3 COMPARISON OF ENVIRONMENTAL QUALITY IMPACTS OF PROPOSED
ACTION AND ALTERNATIVES SALMON FALLS PROJECT

Environmental Category	Remarks	Effect of Plan[1]			
		Plan A	Plan B	Plan C	No Action
Air quality	Positive effect of irrigation cancels short-term adverse effects during construction.	0	0	0	0
Sound quality					
Division area	Minor impact from construction and increased activity during operations.	−2	−2	−2	0
Well field areas	Impact increases from Coltman to Hawley to Lava because value of present sound quality is low at Coltman, moderate at Hawley, and high at Lava.	−2	−4	−6 ⬏	0
Visual quality					
Division area	Visual quality in division area would remain unchanged.	0	0	0	0
Well field areas	Wells would be compatible with present development at Coltman, a minor intrusion at Hawley, and a significant intrusion on the pristine landscape at Lava.	0	−3	−6 ⬏	0
Open space and greenbelts					
Division area	The project would not affect present open space values in the division area.	0	0	0	0
Well field areas	Wells would not affect open space values at Coltman but would be a significant intrusion at Hawley and more of an intrusion at Lava.	0	−4	−6 ⬏	0
Other natural beauty areas	No unique or protected beauty areas would be affected by the project.	0	0	0	0
Wilderness, primitive, and natural areas	No such areas are found in the project vicinity.	NA	NA	NA	NA
Geological resources	Geological values would not be affected by the project.	0	0	0	0
Water quantity					
Surface waters	Minor reduction in existing excess supplies.	−3	−3	−3	0
Ground water	Localized, minor impacts on water table.	−2	−2	−2	0
Water quality					
Surface waters	Minor adverse effects from construction, irrigation return flows, and the addition of well water to the Snake River.	−2	−2	−2	0

TABLE 15.3 *(continued)*

Environmental Category	Remarks	Effect of Plan[1]			
		Plan A	Plan B	Plan C	No Action
Ground water	Slight adverse effect on the aquifer beneath the Milner-Cottonwood Unit.	−2	−2	−2	0
Streams and stream ecosystems					
Snake River	Beneficial effect from additional streamflows outweighs minor adverse impacts on quantity and quality.	+3	0	+3	0
Rock Creek	Loss of 1 mile of stream and diversion of spring runoff water would be minor adverse effects.	−3	−3	−3	0
Lakes and reservoirs	Drawdowns at Palisades and Ririe would have a minor adverse effect on present ecosystems.	−3	−3	−3	0
Beaches and shores	Drawdowns at Palisades and Ririe would have minor effects on human enjoyment of resources.	−2	−2	−2	0
Land quality	Irrigation and plowing would improve soil quality.	+1	+1	+1	0
Estuaries and wetlands					
Division area	Creation of 40 pounds would significantly improve wetland resources in project area.	+8	+8 ▸	+8 ▸	0
Well field areas	Creation of ponds would be beneficial at Hawley and slightly beneficial at Lava.	0	+8 ▸	+4	0
Biological resources					
Flora					
Division area	Loss of natural vegetation on 12,880 acres would outweigh plantings on wildlife areas.	−2	−2	−2	0
Well field areas	Little natural vegetation at Coltman; vegetation is more lush at Lava than Hawley.	0	−2	−4	0
Fauna					
Division area	Wildlife tracts would significantly benefit wildlife.	+6 ▸	+6 ▸	+6 ▸	−3
Well field areas	Development at Lava could have highly significant adverse effects on wildlife; potential effects can be mitigated at the other sites.	0	0	−12 ▸	0
Ecological systems					
Division area	Loss of 12,880 acres of natural vegetation would have minor adverse effects on area ecosystem.	−2	−2	−2	0

TABLE 15.3 *(continued)*

Environmental Category	Remarks	Plan A	Plan B	Plan C	No Action

Environmental Category	Remarks	Effect of Plan[1]			
		Plan A	Plan B	Plan C	No Action
Well field areas	Natural ecosystems would not be affected at Coltman; ecosystem at Lava more complex than that at Hawley.	0	−2	−4	0
Historical resources	Project would not affect any resource of value.	0	0	0	0
Archeological resources Division area	Disturbance of low value resources would be minor adverse effect.	−2	−2	−2	0
Well field areas	No sites would be affected by project.	0	0	0	0
SUMMARY Impact ranking of plans (Plans are ranked from 1 to 4 in order of increasing adverse environmental impact.)	No Action and Plan A would have little overall environmental impact. Plan B would have minor adverse environmental impacts. Plan C would have significant adverse environmental impacts.	2	3	4	1

[1]Effects are rated on a scale from −12 to +12. ➤ = highly significant effect
Source: U.S. Department of Interior, Water and Power Resources Service (1979).

with stream environment preservation and open-space preservation as other planning objectives. The proposed plan of protection consists of a combination of levees, flood walls, channel modifications, concrete flumes, and dry detention reservoirs.

A number of plans were initially formulated which met the planning objectives at different levels (plans I, II, III, IV, II-A, III-A, IV-A) as well as a primarily nonstructural plan. Table 15.4 shows contributions of these plans and a no-action alternative toward the three planning objectives, nine evaluation criteria, and four other formulation criteria, by means of five symbols indicating the approximate level of the contribution for each factor. To facilitate further analysis and comparisons, the following plans were formulated and compared in the same table: *plan A* (NED plan); *plan B* (EQ-oriented NED plan); and *plan C* (plan favored by local interests).

These plans were compared by means of a comparison analysis which "consists of a trade-off analysis of the contributions to the planning objectives, the beneficial and adverse impacts of each alternative, and the responses to specific evaluation criteria such as tests of acceptability, effectiveness, efficiency, and completeness. This type of comparison categorizes the various impacts and displays each plan in terms of components of the system of accounts." At the completion of this final iteration, and based primarily on this comparative analysis, the selected plan was

TABLE 15.4 RESPONSE TO PLANNING OBJECTIVES AND EVALUATION AND FORMULATION CRITERIA, GREEN BROOK BASIN PROJECT[a]

	Plan I	Plan II	Plan III	Plan IV	Plan II-A	Plan III-A	Plan IV-A	Nonstruct.	No Action	Plan A	Plan B	Plan C
Planning Objectives												
Flood damage reduction	+	+	+	+	+	+	+	+	−	+	+	+
Stream environment preservation	−	−	−−	−	−	−−	−	++	0	−	0	−
Open-space preservation	−−	−	−	−	−	−	−	++	0	−	−	−−
Evaluation Criteria												
Acceptability	−−	−	0	0	−	0	+	−−	−	+	0	++
Certainty	+	+	++	+	+	++	+	0	−	+	+	+
Completeness	+	+	+	+	+	+	+	+	−	+	+	+
Effectiveness	+	+	++	+	+	++	+	+	−	+	+	+
Efficiency	+	+	++	+	+	++	+	++	−	+	+	+
Geographic scope	+	+	+	+	+	+	+	+	0	+	+	+
NED *B/C*	−−	−	−	−	−	−	−	−	−−	−	−	−
Reversibility	+	+	+	+	+	+	+	+	++	+	+	+
Stability	+	+	+	+	+	−	+	0	0	+	+	+
Other Formulation Criteria												
Implementibility	0	0	++	++	0	++	++	−	++	++	++	++
Adequacy of level of protection	+	+	++	++	+	++	++	0	−	+	++	+
Public health and safety	+	+	+	+	+	+	+	0	−	+	+	+
Cultural resources	−	−−	−−	−−	−−	−−	−	−	0	−	−	−

[a] ++, most positive contribution; +, positive contribution; 0, neutral; −, negative contribution; −−, most negative contribution.
Source: U.S. Department of the Army, Corps of Engineers (1978).

chosen as plan A, the NED plan, on the basis "that it maximizes net positive economic benefits while addressing the array of planning objectives for the Green Brook Basin study area."

REFERENCES

AMERICAN SOCIETY OF CIVIL ENGINEERS, "The Civil Engineer's Responsibility in Impact Analysis," Committee on Impact Analysis, *J. Water Resources Plann. Manage. Div., Proc. Am. Soc. Civil Eng.*, vol. 104, no. WR1, November 1978.

CALIFORNIA ENVIRONMENT QUALITY ACT, "Guidelines for State Environmental Impact Reports," September 1976.

DEE, NORBERT, et al., "Final Report on Environmental Evaluation System for Water Resource Planning," Battelle–Columbus Laboratories, Columbus, Ohio, January 31, 1972.

DEE, NORBERT, et al.,"Planning Methodology for Water Quality Management: Environmental Evaluation System," Battelle Memorial Institute, Columbus, Ohio, July 1973.

HENDERSON, JAMES E., "Handbook of Environmental Quality Measurement and Assessment: Methods and Techniques," Publ. IR-E-82-2, Environmental Laboratory, U.S. Army Engineer Waterways Experiment Station, Vicksburg, Miss., 1982.

JAIN, R. K., and L. V. URBAN, "A Review and Analysis of Environmental Impact Assessment Methodologies," Construction Engineering Research Laboratory, Champaign, Ill., Tech. Rep. E-69, June 1975.

JAIN, RAVINDER K., and RONALD D. WEBSTER, "Computer-Aided Environmental Impact Analysis," *J. Water Resources Plann. Manage. Div., Proc. Am. Soc. Civil Eng.*, vol. 103, no. WR2, November 1977.

JAIN, R. K., et al., "Handbook for Environmental Impact Analysis," Construction Engineering Research Laboratory, Champaign, Ill., Tech. Rep. E-59, September 1974.

KRAUSKOPF, THOMAS M., and DENNIS C. BUNDE, "Evaluation of Environmental Impact through a Computer Modeling Program, in *Environmental Impact Analysis: Philosophy and Methods*, Robert Ditton and Thomas Goodale, eds., University of Wisconsin Sea Grant Program, 1972.

LEOPOLD, LUNA B., et al., " A Procedure for Evaluating Environmental Impact," *U.S. Geol. Surv. Circ. 655*, 1971.

NORTHROP, GAYLORD, et al., "A Framework for Environmental Impact Evaluation for Electric Power Systems in a River Basin," Center for the Environment & Man, Inc., Hartford, Conn., December 1975.

ORTOLANO, LEONARD, ed., "Analyzing the Environmental Impacts of Water Projects," Stanford University, Dept. of Civil Engineering, March 1973.

SORENSEN, JENS, "A Framework for Identification and Control of Resource Degradation and Conflict in the Multiple Use of the Coastal Zone," University of California, Dept. of Landscape Architecture, 1970.

SORENSEN, JENS, and JAMES E. PEPPER, "Procedures for Clearinghouse Review of Environmental Impact Statements—Phase Two," Association of Bay Area Governments, April 1973.

STOVER, LLOYD V., "Environmental Impact Statement: A Procedure," Sanders and Thomas, Inc., 1972.

TRAVELERS RESEARCH CORPORATION, "The Development of a Procedure and Knowledge

Requirements for Marine Resource Planning," Hartford, Conn., 1969.

UNITED NATIONS ENVIRONMENT PROGRAMME, "Guidelines for Assessing Industrial Environmental Impact and Environmental Criteria for the Siting of Industry," Draft, April 1979 (and oral communication, New York, 1980).

U.S. COUNCIL ON ENVIRONMENTAL QUALITY, "Preparation of Environmental Impact Statements: Guidelines," Federal Register, vol. 38, pp. 20550-62, August 1, 1973; "Regulations for Implementing the Procedural Provisions of the National Environmental Policy Act," Federal Register, vol. 43, pp. 55978-56007, November 29, 1978.

U.S. DEPARTMENT OF THE ARMY, Corps of Engineers, "Water Resources Council (WRC) Principles and Standards, National Environmental Policy Act (NEPA) and Related Policies—Guidelines for Conducting Feasibility Studies for Water and Related Land Resources, Final Rules," July 13, 1978.

U.S. DEPARTMENT OF THE ARMY, New York Engineer District, "Draft Environmental Impact Statement—Flood Control Project for the Green Brook Basin," September 1978.

U.S. DEPARTMENT OF THE ARMY, Office of the Chief of Engineers, "Environmental Quality, Policy and Procedures for Implementing NEPA," Regulation No. 200-2-2, Draft, June 22, 1979.

U.S. DEPARTMENT OF THE INTERIOR, Bureau of Reclamation, "Reclamation Instructions, Series 110, Planning, Part 117, Environmental Investigations," Draft, July 17, 1979.

U.S. DEPARTMENT OF THE INTERIOR, Water and Power Resources Service, "Draft Environmental Statement—Salmon Falls Division, Upper Snake River Project, Idaho–Wyoming," December 14, 1979.

U.S. ENVIRONMENTAL PROTECTION AGENCY, Region 1, "Environmental Assessment Manual," n.d.

U.S. ENVIRONMENTAL PROTECTION AGENCY, "Environmental Assessment of Construction Grants Projects," January 1979.

U.S. WATER RESOURCES COUNCIL, "Principles and Standards for Planning Water and Related Land Resources," September 10, 1973; rev. December 14, 1979; rev. September 29, 1980.

U.S. WATER RESOURCES COUNCIL, "Environmental Quality Evaluation Procedures for Level C Water Resources Planning," September 29, 1980.

U.S. WATER RESOURCES COUNCIL, "Economic and Environmental Principles and Guidelines for Water and Related Land Resources Implementation Studies," March 10, 1983.

WANG, FLORA C., HOWARD T. ODUM, and ROBERT COSTANZA, "Energy Criteria for Water Use," J. Water Resources Plann. Manage. Div., Proc. Am. Soc. Civil. Eng., vol. 106, no. WR1, March 1980.

WANG, FLORA C., HOWARD T. ODUM, and PATRICK D. KANGUS, "Energy Analysis for Environmental Impact Assessment," J. Water Resources Plann. Manage. Div., Proc. Am. Soc. Civil Eng., vol. 106, no. WR2, July 1980.

WARNER, M. L., and E. A. PRESTON, "A Review of Environmental Impact Assessment Methodologies," Battelle–Columbus Laboratories, Columbus, Ohio, April 1974.

WHITLATCH, ELBERT E., JR., "Systematic Approaches to Environmental Impact Assessment: An Evaluation," Water Resources Bull., vol. 12, no. 1, February 1976.

WORLD BANK, "Environmental Aspects of World Bank Group Projects— Some Questions and Answers," September 1973.

WORLD BANK, Environmental, Health and Human Ecological Considerations in Economic Development Projects," May 1974.

SIXTEEN

Social Impact Assessment

16.1 SCOPE OF SOCIAL IMPACT ASSESSMENT

Social impact assessments have become an integral part of the water resources planning and evaluation process in the United States. They are needed for virtually every federal water resources project and for many nonfederal projects. The scope for such assessments has been defined in legislation, rules published by government agencies, and manuals and special reports prepared for the agencies. In many studies, social impacts are assessed together with, or even as part of, the environmental impact assessment.

Social impact assessments are the basis for completing most of the Other Social Effects (OSE) account specified in the Water Resources Council "Principles and Guidelines" issued in 1983. They also provide essential information for the Regional Economic Development (RED) account and, to a lesser extent, for the Environmental Quality (EQ) account. The OSE and RED accounts were so named in 1980 revisions of the "Principles and Standards." Earlier (1973, 1979) versions of the "Principles and Standards" had organized the RED and OSE effects in accounts named Regional Development (RD) and Social Well-Being (SWB). Much of both Chapter 14 (Economic Growth Studies) and this chapter is suitable for the RED and OSE accounts. Impacts on the "human environment" must be included in the Environmental Impact Statement (EIS) prepared for every significant federal action under the National Environmental Protection Act of 1969.

Social impact analysis, which has flourished in the United States since the National Environmental Policy Act of 1969, inherited an image of negative assessment, project delay, or bearer of bad news. This image is being changed as social scientists employ the tools of their disciplines to help planners understand the social impacts of projects.

Multiobjective planning often results in projects that have benefits that are distributed across geographical and social class boundaries, while causing highly concentrated local community effects. Under such conditions, people in local communities may perceive that they are either bearing unduly high costs or assuming disproportionate risks. This may lead to coalitions opposing projects that form from local community and national interest groups. Such coalitions are more likely to form than are coalitions (pro- or anti-project) of the widely distributed and marginally affected beneficiaries. The success of a large water resources project often hinges on an effective balance of local costs and distributed benefits. Social assessment techniques are useful in suggesting appropriate trade-offs of these costs and benefits.

Social impact assessments have contributed to the planning process in many other ways, such as:

- To assist in handling the difficult methodological problems of assessing benefits and costs which are both monetary and nonmonetary and are thus not directly commensurate.
- To assist in the identification and estimation of water-based needs and the formulation of alternatives
- To improve ability to project the acceptability and costs of alternatives
- To reduce the number of alternatives considered in planning, and to make them more representative
- To assist public involvement programs
- To enhance ability to project conditions both with and without the project
- To assist the environmental evaluation of alternatives
- To complete the other social effects account
- To define human and other non–property-based flood damages for the national economic development account
- To better project national economic development benefits for previously unemployed or underemployed labor
- To project construction phase impact and to suggest means of mitigation

Figure 16.1 briefly outlines the social assessment process. This figure shows that a water resources project is more than a physical phenomenon—it is an intervention into a social system. The baseline social conditions are not static but are a dynamic system of interactions that must be somehow described. Technology can be applied by a project to increase the resilience of the social system or to mitigate the effects of natural events on that system. The dynamic system should be projected both with and without the proposed water project. Social assessment assists the planning process to profile this dynamic system, project future states with and without the project, and identify and evaluate the impact of the project.

The central concept throughout social assessment is "values," that is, people's sense of how things "ought to be." Such values are held and brought to the project by

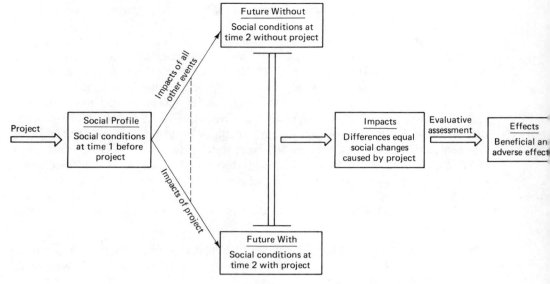

Figure 16.1 Social assessment process.

the professional planners, as well as held by the people the projects affect. Understanding, projecting, and coping with such values is the focus of social impact assessment. Social impact assessment, to be effective, must rely on the public involvement activities outlined in Chapter 7.

Fitzsimmons et al. (1979, p. 64) have stated:

> All of these types of impacts involve a phenomenon quite familiar to the economist, that of "trade-offs"; i.e., certain social concerns may be operating in a contradictory manner, thus complicating the decision-making process. Implementation of a water development plan may simultaneously generate good and bad social effects. For example, implementation of a plan may simultaneously enhance recreational opportunities for local residents (generally perceived as "good") and also attract many outside tourists who inundate the area for weekends (seen as both "good" and "bad" depending upon the perspective). Similarly, increases in employment opportunities for youth may also produce an increase in high school dropout rates. Preservation of natural environment under strict federal codes may also result in a plant closing, with a consequent drop in employment and income security for local residents. A sound social assessment must take into account that a combination of good and bad effects will arise from the implementation of a plan or the decision to not implement any plan. Frequently, these tradeoffs do not affect the same people; some people will benefit while others will lose.

16.2 STATE OF DEVELOPMENT OF SOCIAL IMPACT ASSESSMENT

Hitchcock (1977) prepared an analytical review of research reports on social impacts of water resources development projects issued after 1961. Thirty-eight studies were

Social Impact Assessment   Chap. 16

selected for review from over 90 studies identified in bibliographies. He considered impacts separately in the preconstruction, postconstruction, and construction phases and classified impacts as to their distribution, opportunity, local service delivery, and community cohesion effects. The Hitchcock study and other recent critiques in the literature have indicated some of the shortcomings of social impact analysis. However, as experience with social assessment increases, some consensus over both the major issues that social assessment should address and the best tools to use is emerging. Social assessments have proved most useful in designing nonstructural flood control alternatives, identification of stress on community infrastructure services and designing measures to mitigate such stress, interpretation of public involvement information, design of relocation measures, improvement of projections, and improvement of techniques for estimating benefits.

Twelve generic social science tools, old and new, are increasingly favored by various water resources agencies. These are:

- Institutional analysis
- Policy profiling
- Value mapping
- Social profiling
- Content analysis
- Small group processes techniques
- Human cost accounting
- Community impact assessment
- Ethnographic field analysis
- Questionnaire and nonparametric statistical analysis
- Population projections
- Trend and cross impact analysis

Although many of these tools have long been available, their applicability to water resources projects has been more relevant in recent years. Their application by social scientists from disciplines other than traditional economics has permitted the broadening and improvement of social evaluations.

Institutional analysis, policy profiling, and value mapping are methods, not utilizing a questionnaire, for assessing social acceptability of project proposals. Taken together, the procedures can yield information on implementation outlay costs, on cost-sharing arrangements, and on the special institutional agreements that are necessary for each alternative (Taylor 1982).

Policy profiling is a technique for assessing the opinions of various individuals, groups, and organizations of decisions that affect a project. It is most useful in situations where a small group of professionals must either reach a decision or assess the impacts of decisions on an external political–social environment (O'Leary et al. 1982). Based on common sense and political science principles, the technique simply guides individuals through a systematic thought process, records their perceptions at crucial steps in the process, and produces a net political assessment number that reflects the group's subjective judgment of the feasibility of actions. Among other uses, it has been a quick way to "red-flag" controversial water quality permit problems from among several potential decisions.

Value mapping is a generic term for value identification, display, and trade-off analysis. Improved techniques in these areas are the key to understanding relative deprivation perceived by those affected by water projects, facilitating trade-offs, and increasing planning efficiency by focusing on measures of high probable acceptance (Creighton 1982a).

Social profiling has been the most visible social impact assessment activity. Agencies have sought to move beyond traditional census data "dumps," to focus on the social data gathered. Flynn and Schmidt (1977) have inventoried the sources of information for social profiling. Since information on public values is rarely organized in ways that are compatible for water resources planning, much of it has not been fully utilized. For example, an organization may receive hundreds or even thousands of letters and comments from the public, and yet much of the depth and richness of this information is never captured and used. The content analysis technique allows planners to routinely and cheaply analyze these data. Simple basic coding is needed in order to produce machine-readable outputs (Dunning 1982).

Information needed for social assessment is not readily available in standard statistical formats. Much of it must be generated by the planner primarily through various forms of public involvement such as public workshops mentioned in Chapter 7. Small group techniques offer alternatives to questionnaires for generating value, opinion, and attitude data (Creighton 1982b).

In the drive to quantify social effects, new techniques of human cost accounting have emerged. Based on observations that property-based values are only a partial measure of flood damage prevention, human cost accounting quantifies psychological trauma damages prevented and behavioral damages prevented. For the first type of damages, victims of flooding are positioned on a value trauma scale, levels of impairment are related to American Medical Association values, and degrees of impairment are translated into dollars paid by the Veterans Administration for comparable disabilities. For the second type, descriptions of behavior are examined through questionnaires and translated into economic disruption costs (Institute for Water Resources, 1979).

Community impact assessment has evolved as a clearly defined subset of more general impact assessment areas. Chapters 4 and 14 have mentioned the use of the BREAM model in such assessment. Briefly, it focuses on the influx of construction workers before, during and after peak construction of the water project. The planner estimates the construction worker phasing, translates that into population increase in local communities, and estimates whether this influx will exceed the capacity of basic community services. Estimates depend on a number of subjective locational preferences and subcounty population statistics. Data bases have also been built on surveys of construction workers at actual sites. These data bases, together with before, during, and after case studies, and community impact techniques, provide a guide for planners to make initial estimates and to manage the fear of the "boom–bust" syndrome (Chalmers and Anderson 1977; Dunning 1981; Harnisch 1980; Dietz and Dunning 1982).

An old social science technique that is frequently used in water resources planning is ethnographic field analysis. In this method, a planner "walks the study area." He or she can sometimes observe seemingly little items that can translate into larger effects (e.g., project stoppages). These techniques are essentially sensing mechanisms to provide "early warning" of the impacts on the social environment. It is difficult to train people in the sensitivity techniques employed in this method.

Questionnaires are the most frequently overused of social science techniques. Since questionnaire data provide only a snapshot, their best use is as a good comparative static picture. Data from questionnaires and other sources are often stated in nominal or ordinal terms. Such data cannot be analyzed by typical engineering methods such as regression analysis. The social scientist employs less familiar statistics, such as contingency table inferences, more appropriate to social values data.

Population projections are discussed in Chapter 4. In the United States, the water resources planner usually starts with federal population projections. However, in special regions or in cases of subregional data needs, the planners may have to adjust these projections. Although projections may appear unbiased, they are assumption based and value driven. Trend and cross-impact techniques (discussed in Chapter 13) are useful tools to help planners make projections, and several computer-assisted packages are available to use these techniques in planning (Mitchell et al. 1975, 1977).

16.3 APPLICATION OF SOCIAL ASSESSMENT TO PLANNING PROCESS

As mentioned in Section 16.1, important references for social assessment in water resources planning include the Water Resources Council "Principles and Standards" (1980) and "Principles and Guidelines" (1983). Table 16.1 suggests where social science techniques can be effective for the planning process steps described in these documents. A decision to use any tool or technique depends on manpower and other resources, the availability of data, and the stage of planning.

16.4 OTHER SOCIAL EFFECTS ACCOUNT

Although social assessment is useful across the planning process, its major focus has been on the superseded Social Well-Being (SWB) and on the Other Social Effects (OSE) accounts described in the Water Resources Council guidelines for planning. Considerable debate continues among social scientists over what should be included in the OSE account. A Water Resources Council review (1981) listed the principal (baseline) variables used by major water resources studies in the 1970s to fill out these accounts. Table 16.2 lists these variables and relates them to principal components of the OSE account. These variables are not the only possible ones, but they do reflect experience in applying social assessment to water resources projects.

TABLE 16.1 APPLICATION OF SOCIAL SCIENCE TOOLS TO WATER RESOURCES PLANNING

| | *Planning Process* | | | | | | |
| | | | | *Evaluate* | | | |
Techniques	*Specify Problems*	*Inventory Conditions*	*Formulate Alternatives*	*Assess*	*Appraise*	*Compare Plans*	*Selection*
Social profiling	X	X					
Content analysis	X	X			X		
Community impact assessment		X		X	X		
Institutional analysis		X			X	X	X
Small-group processes	X		X	X	X	X	
Human cost accounting	X	X		X			
Policy profiling			X			X	X
Population projections		X					
Field analysis		X		X			
Questionnaire and nonparametric	X	X				X	
Values analysis			X	X	X	X	X
Trend and cross-impact				X		X	

Source: Delli Priscoli (1981).

16.5 FORECASTING METHODS

Although the reliability of estimates will differ with the effort and methods employed, existing conditions can usually be determined in a straightforward manner. The projection of future conditions is much more difficult and becomes rather speculative when carried far in the future. Social forecasts are not merely descriptive statements of what the world will be. Forecasts are assumption based, value driven, and rarely neutral. They may thus be normative statements reflecting what the forecasters feel the world "ought to be." Methods have been developed for social forecasting which are sensitive to this situation. They range from the extrapolation of past trends by simple mathematical methods to the formulation of future scenarios through a combination of objective analyses and experienced judgment in which many interrelated factors are taken into account.

Fitzsimmons et al. (1977) have identified a variety of parameters that are important in making such forecasts. "Direct" impacts are the effects of disruption, demographic impacts, and economic impacts. Disruption impacts take place at an early stage, with different opinions on the project, anxieties, contingency plans, and so on. "Indirect" impacts are due to changes in population and economic characteristics and may include effects on health, education, attitudes, family life, and the social structure of communities. Impacts may be "short-term" or "long-term." Other characteristics of impacts relate to "geographic location" of the impacts and the "recipients" of the impacts.

TABLE 16.2   RELATIONS OF SOCIAL SCIENCE VARIABLES USED IN REPORTS
AND OSE COMPONENTS

OSE Components	*Baseline Variables*

A. Urban and Community Impacts
 1. Income distribution
   a. General
   b. Low-income households
 	
 2. Employment distribution
   a. General
   b. Minorities
 	
 3. Population
   a. Distribution
   b. Composition
 	
 4. Fiscal condition of government
   a. State
   b. Local
 5. Quality of community life
   a. General community quality elements; these may include a broad perspective of elements such as: attitudes, infrastructure, disorganization, facilities
	A. Socioeconomic and Social Differentiation
	 1. Income
	   a. General income
	   b. Income levels
	   c. Income distribution
	 2. Employment
	   a. Employed
	   b. Unemployed
	   c. Minority employment
	   d. Employment availability
	B. Population
	 1. General
	 2. Number
	 3. Change
	 4. Characteristics
	 5. Mobility and migration
	 6. Housing
	 7. Occupation
	 8. Projections
	C. Government Fiscal Conditions
	 1. Taxes
	 2. Community finances
	D. Quality of Life or Life-Style
	 1. General community quality elements
	   a. Subjective aspects
	     (1) Attitudes toward community: satisfaction, feelings, etc.
	     (2) Perceptions of effects of the project on the community
	   b. Community viability and cohesion
	 2. General life-style patterns of an area
	 3. Community disorganization: crime, displacement, poverty, breakdown of informal systems
	 4. Mass communication
	 5. Transportation facilities
	 6. General individual quality elements
	   a. Subjective aspects
	     (1) Perceptions of the effects of the project on the individual
	E. Community Institutional Infrastructure
	 1. Health care
	 2. Safety services
	 3. Sanitation services
	 4. Public utilities
	 5. Schools
	 6. Government
	 7. Welfare and social services
	 8. Religious institutions
	 9. Recreation opportunities

TABLE 16.2 *(continued)*

OSE Components	*Baseline Variables*
	10. Cultural opportunities
	11. General or others
	F. Other Subjective Components
	1. Attitudes toward the project
	2. Perceptions of the environment
	3. Aesthetic elements
	4. Other attitudes
	5. Level of knowledge about the project
	G. Background and Historical Factors that Affect Planning
	H. Land Use Patterns: rural–urban, etc.
	I. Special Groups Affecting Planning
	1. Ethnic groups
	2. Interest groups
	J. Economic Resources of the Area That Affect the Community and Planning: lumber, mining, agriculture, etc.
B. Life, Health, and Safety	
1. Risk of flood	(Also related to safety services of
2. Risk of drought	police and fire protection and
3. Other disaster	health and sanitation services.)
C. Displacement	
1. People	(Related to attitudes and perceptions
2. Business	toward the project, and community
3. Farms	disorganization components.)

Source: U.S. Water Resources Council (1981).

Fitzsimmons et al. (1977) discuss the following principal forecasting techniques available for dealing with some of the variables: trend extrapolation, discussion with expert informants, contingency trees, surveys, Delphi techniques, and scenario generation. Forecasting techniques have also been surveyed and analyzed by Vlachos et al. (1975), Mitchell et al. (1975, 1977), and Brown et al. (1974). A review of methods for evaluating nonmarket impacts of policy decisions with special reference to water resources development projects has been prepared by Finsterbusch (1977). A number of methods for forecasting or evaluating market and nonmarket impacts are described in Chapters 13, 14, and 15. Legal and institutional aspects (Chapter 17) and public involvement (Chapter 7) are also involved in the social assessment process.

16.6 OTHER COMMENTS CONCERNING SOCIAL ASSESSMENT METHODOLOGIES

A very important aspect of socioeconomic effects (particularly in developing countries but also in economically advanced countries) is income distribution, especially as this may be affected by project alternatives. This subject is briefly discussed in Chapters 6, 8, and 10, but an extensive treatment is too specialized for the scope of this book. Krouse (1972) has analyzed social well-being in terms of income redistribution concepts. It is also important to examine other ways that a project affects different social classes. For example, does a project produce effects that cause people to feel they have lost or gained relative to other classes with whom they associate? This phenomenon is called relative deprivation and is important in projecting social behavior.

Social impacts may be examined at various levels: (1) at the individual and family level; (2) from the perspective of groups and the community; (3) with respect to the larger picture of socioeconomic effects in the area and contributions to the national good; and (4) in terms of aggregate social effects.

In considering the *family* and *individual* levels, Maslow (1954) has formulated a hierarchy of fundamental human needs in which a person must first satisfy fundamental needs before satisfying higher needs. This hierarchy is: (1) basic survival and physiological needs; (2) security and self-sufficiency needs; (3) social and belongingness needs; (4) esteem; and (5) growth or self-actualization. Fitzsimmons et al. (1977, pp. 33–4) discuss the significance of this heirarchy:

> This approach emphasizes several concepts about human behavior. First, when an individual experiences a need, especially at the lower end of the continuum, this may block concern over resolution of higher order needs. Second, the achievement of higher economic standards may motivate behavior up to a point, but beyond that point, quality of life may require non-monetary improvement. In short, a higher standard of living does not necessarily mean that people will be happier. As standards of living rise, the needs of levels three through five may become more important, and demand for various amenities (e.g., cultural, aesthetic, and environmental) may arise. Third, it is important to identify individuals and families in the planning area whose standard of living is below the general poverty line and whose need levels are at the lower end of the hierarchy, both because they are most in need and because helping these individuals may be an especially significant social contribution. Conversely, harming them may be an especially serious matter, for they have the least capacity to bear additional costs.

Fitzsimmons et al. (1977) also discuss the social concerns associated with family life which are focused on the qualities and services found in a community that directly facilitate family structure. A similar impact can have different meaning to the individual, depending on one's family role, particularly if associated with displacement from one's home. Another area of special concern has to do with the attitudes held by individuals and how the plans are related to them. Finally, the planner must consider the fundamental concern of the relationship of the individual to his or her natural environment. Many families are especially concerned that they are able to live in a clean, accessible, and attractive area.

At the *community* level of social concern, the focus is on institutions and values that tie people together and encourage cooperation efforts and the development of collective action for the general community good. Three concerns identified by Merton (1957) are particularly relevant here: (1) the opportunities available to people enabling them to participate in their communities; (2) the stability and enhancement of community values and norms; and (3) the nature of social organization and control in the community. Various questions may be raised with these concerns. For example, how is a predominantly rural community affected by the emergence of a whole new set of values associated with the increase of urban-dominated, economic activities and with very different types of people coming into the area? How is the capacity of the community affected in its ability to respond to legitimate needs in education, social services, cultural expression, and many government services?

The larger picture of *socioeconomic effects in the area* is concerned with the nature of the economic base of the area and its implications in employment, basic communications and transportation characteristics of the area, and with the effects of the planning process and construction in the area, all of which cause important social changes in communities and services of the area.

The national good may be affected in a variety of ways by a plan that has social significance (e.g., in contributing to national viability by expanded crop production, enhanced electric power supplies, reduction of fossil-fuel use). Plans that comply with national laws and international treaties pertaining to water utilization are also important from the national perspective.

Aggregate social effects include three types of effects: (1) effects on the general quality of life of the people; (2) effects on the relative social position of groups of people; and (3) effects on the social well-being of communities and their social institutions.

Quality of life refers to the overall nature of impacts on the individual and his or her family and to the effects that such changes, in turn, may have on the individual's perception of the opportunities for personal and family development. Quality of life may include good health, opportunity for a reasonable income and a reasonable standard of living, healthy development of children, happy family life, decent home and neighborhood, peace of mind and emotional maturity, recreation, community stability, and so forth. Concepts differ with the individual, as shown by the following findings by Burdge (1973), who also developed a Quality of Life Index:

- Quality of life impacts will be different if one is displaced versus not displaced.
- Quality of life impacts will be different depending on who is involved and what they value (e.g., younger people may value recreation, farmers the certainty of crop development, the elderly a sense of security).
- Quality of life impacts will be different if one is in a position of strength (e.g., economically, in terms of age, legally) rather than a position of weakness (e.g., poor, elderly, unable to secure legal help).
- Quality of life impacts will be different if one is able to maintain one's sense of community and have neighbors who share one's beliefs, compared with a situation where one is thrust into a new community, especially if that community has a new life-style (e.g., rural to urban, comfortable economic circumstances to marginal existence).
- Quality of life impacts will be different if one is leaving a situation with which one has only marginal attachment rather than leaving a place where one has strong roots and deep attachments.

- Quality of life impacts will be different depending on whether one is anticipating a favorable future in his or her new circumstances or whether one is anticipating a personal family crisis in a new situation.

The effects of a plan in terms of "relative social position" require assessing the equity of the distribution of plan effects. This involves determining the distribution of beneficial and adverse social effects of a plan and the capacity of different groups of people to bear economic and social costs. Measures are in terms of such indices as income distribution, job opportunities, and housing availability.

A distinction is made between "quality of life" and "social well-being" by Fitzsimmons et al. (1977, pp. 46–7):

> While quality of life is an expression of the degree to which individuals and families enjoy their lives in good health, in economic security, and in general peace of mind about the present and future, *social well-being* can be evaluated at a higher level of aggregation; i.e., the level of the community and its constituent groups. Social well-being *contributes* to the quality of life. The effects of impacts are assessed on formal institutions (such as school, churches, and local government) and informal groups of people (such as farmers, fraternal orders, local leisure groups, and special interest groups) that collectively reflect the values, goals, and life activities of people in the community. Most important, the future capacity of the community to sustain itself in a character consistent with the desires of its residents and institutions must be assessed.

The following are some of the further evaluation categories that water resources planners have found useful in assessing the social effects of projects:

- The viability and stability of organizations and institutions such as schools, churches, clubs, colleges, and the like, especially as they contribute to the quality of life of individuals
- Improvement of conditions associated with the achievement of economic stability and improved personal income
- Achievement of a desirable population distribution in terms of male/female balance in various age groups, reasonable dependency ratios of elderly to work-age population, continuity of values such as rural or urban orientation, and avoidance of severe problems associated with high density
- Enhancement of security of life and health through a reduction in the risk of floods, drought, or other water-related disasters by better water management and control
- Improved stability of local government operations
- Improvements in national, emergency preparedness which make a contribution to the nation's collective security

In summary, social assessment is a process by which the water resources planner can define the dynamic social trends currently existing and likely to exist in communities affected by a water resources project, describe the impact of the project on those trends, and evaluate the impacts. Social assessment describes how physical engineering projects intervene into and change those social systems they seek to assist. As such, social assessment is concerned with the differentials created among classes, people, and communities by water projects, the implementability of various alternatives, and the representativeness of those alternatives. Since social assessment is focused on values, it must be closely aligned to the project's public involvement efforts. Social assessment is as much an art as a technical procedure.

16.7 FORMATS FOR SOCIAL IMPACT ASSESSMENT

Chapter 15 has presented several formats for environmental impact assessment that may be adopted for social impact assessment. Others are shown by Fitzsimmons et al. (1977) and in other studies discussed above. There are no consistent agency rules for such formats, nor does there appear to be a consensus concerning this matter, judging by the diversity of methods in use. Table 16.3 presents a comparative summary analysis of social impacts that follows the same format as for the environmental assessment of the Salmon Falls Project in Chapter 15.

TABLE 16.3 COMPARISON OF SOCIAL WELL-BEING IMPACTS OF PROPOSED ACTION AND ALTERNATIVES SALMON FALLS PROJECT.

Component	Impact	Effect of Plan[1]			
		Plan A	Plan B	Plan C	No Action
Area, Socioeconomic Agricultural production	Division lands would experience a considerable increase in agricultural production.	+2	+2	+2	0
Business expansion	Some business expansion would occur in the Twin Falls area.	+1	+1	+1	0
Economic stability	The economic swings related to long and short water years in the Salmon Tract would be greatly reduced.	+2	+2	+2	0
Income	The greater Twin Falls area would experience a considerable income increase.	+2	+2	+2	0
Employment	A few more farm jobs would be created in the division area, and farm employment would be stabilized considerably. An average of about 160 construction jobs would be available over a 7-year period (with a peak of 344 in the sixth year).	+1	+1	+1	0
Energy costs	The power used and relatively large amount of power foregone would contribute to the trend in the Northwest toward	−1	−1	−1	0

TABLE 16.3 *(continued)*

Component	Impact	Effect of Plan[1]			
		Plan A	*Plan B*	*Plan C*	*No Action*
	increased thermal generation and higher rates.				
Community, institutional					
Population	Construction workers and their families would account for an an increase of 200-300 persons in the Twin Falls-Kimberly-Hansen area during the peak year of construction. Small population increases (200-400 people) would be experienced in the greater Twin Falls area including minor increases in the Salmon Tract during operations.	0	0	0	0
Services and facilities	Only minor problems would be experienced in absorbing increased population, and some improvements would be likely in both quantity and quality of services.	+1	+1	+1	0
Recreation	Hunting, nature study, and bird-watching would be enhanced in the division area.	+1	+1	+1	0
Cohesion	The loss of common water problems and feelings of "toughness" in the face of adversity accompanied by a small inmigration of new people would lead to a decrease in cohesion on the Salmon Tract.	−2	−2	−2	0
Attitudes	Opposition to the project is high in both the Coltman (Plan A) and Lava (Plan C) areas. Residents in these areas are opposed to sending "their water" downstream.	−3▸	−1	−3▸	0
Individual, personal					
Economic stability	The economic stability of families who are hurt badly during dry years would be improved considerably.	+3	+3	+3	0
Family income	Family incomes in the division area would increase.	+2	+2	+2	0
Family stability	Increased opportunities would keep more young people in the area and provide support for continuance of family farms.	+2	+2	+2	0
Standard of living	The standard of living would increase, with people who currently have the least water	+2	+2	+2	0

TABLE 16.3 *(continued)*

Component	Impact	Effect of Plan[1]			
		Plan A	*Plan B*	*Plan C*	*No Action*
	experiencing the greatest improvements.				
Anxiety reduction	Reduced anxiety of water supply and related financial problems would lead to increased peace of mind.	+2	+2	+2	0
Life style	No significant changes in life style are anticipated.	0	0	0	0
Attitudes	A sizable minority of Salmon Tract residents are opposed to the wildlife areas.	−2	−2	−2	0
National, emergency preparedness					
Water supplies	New well fields would be available under emergency conditions.	+1	+1	+1	0
Food production	Irrigated acreage in Twin Falls County would increase by 10 to 15 percent.	+1	+1	+1	0
Power supplies					
Power foregone	About 150,000 Mwh of generation would be lost annually in the Snake-Columbia system (enough power for more than 10,700 homes).	−3	−3	−3	0
Power use	In a dry year Plan A would use 106,770 MWh; Plan B would use 139,470 MWh; and Plan C would use 94,170 MWh.	−2	−3	−2	0
Aggregate					
Quality of life	Some minor improvements in quality of life would occur in the project area, largely as a result of increased income and economic stability. With Plan C (Lava) these gains would be partly offset by initial concerns over loss of water and the perceived threat of lowering ground water tables.	+1	+1	+1	0
Relative social position	People who have a large amount of land and little water will benefit the most from the project.	+1	+1	+1	0
	Well area people (especially in the Lava and Coltman areas) perceive that they are giving up water, suffering increased power bills, and helping their	−3	−1	−3	0

TABLE 16.3 *(continued)*

Component	Impact	Effect of Plan[1]			
		Plan A	Plan B	Plan C	No Action
Community viability	competition while receiving nothing in return. Some increase in viability would be expected for Hollister and Murtaugh and a decrease in the Salmon Tract.	+1	+1	+1	0

[1]Effects are rated on a scale ranging from −5 to +5.   ► = highly significant impact
Source: U.S. Department of Interior, Water and Power Resources Service (1979).

REFERENCES

BROWN, JERRY W., et al., "Models and Methods Applicable to Corps of Engineers Urban Studies," U.S. Army Corps of Engineers, Waterways Experiment Station, 1974.

BURDGE, R. J., "A Summary of Sociological Studies of Water Resources Dealing with Social Goals and the 'Quality of Life'," University of Kentucky, 1973.

CHALMERS, J. A., and E. J. Anderson, "Economic/Demographic Assessment Manual," Mountain West Research Inc., November 1977.

CREIGHTON, JAMES L., "Review of Values Display Techniques and Their Application to Public Involvement," U.S. Army Corps of Engineers, Institute for Water Resources, 1982a.

CREIGHTON, JAMES L., "Public Involvement: A Ten Year Reader," U.S. Army Corps of Engineers, Institute for Water Resources, 1982b.

DELLI PRISCOLI, JERRY, "People and Water: Social Impact Assessment Research," *Water Spectrum*, Summer 1981.

DIETZ, THOMAS, and C. M. DUNNING, "Assessing Demographic Change in Impacted Communities," in "Methods of Social Impact Assessment," K. Finsterbusch, ed., U.S. Army Corps of Engineers, Institute for Water Resources, 1982.

DUNNING, C. M., "Content Analysis," in *Social Impact Assessments Training Manual*, U.S. Army Corps of Engineers, Institute for Water Resources, 1982.

DUNNING, C. M., "Construction Workforce Profile," U.S. Army Corps of Engineers, Institute for Water Resources, June 1981.

FINSTERBUSCH, KURT, "Methods for Evaluating Non-market Impacts in Policy Decisions with Special Reference to Water Resources Development Projects," U.S. Army Corps of Engineers, Institute for Water Resources, Fort Belvoir, Va., December 1977.

FITZSIMMONS, STEPHEN J., et al., *Social Assessment Manual*, Abt Associates, Westview Press, Boulder, Colo., 1977.

FLYNN, CYNTHIA B., and ROSEMARY T. SCHMIDT, "Sources of Information for Social Profiling," U.S. Army Corps of Engineers, Institute for Water Resources, December 1977.

HARNISCH, ARTHUR, "Chief Joseph Community Impact Assessment," U.S. Army Corps of Engineers, Institute for Water Resources, 1980.

HITCHCOCK, HENRY, "Analytical Review of Research Reports on Social Impacts of Water Resources Development Projects," Program of Policy Studies in Science and Technology, George Washington University, Washington, D.C., March 1977.

INSTITUTE FOR WATER RESOURCES, *Human Costs of Flooding: Tug Fork*, U.S. Army Corps of Engineers, 1979.

KROUSE, MICHAEL R., "Quality of Life and Income Redistribution: Objectives for Water Resources Planning," U.S. Army Corps of Engineers, Institute for Water Resources, Fort Belvoir, Va., July 1972.

LOVE, RUTH, "Doing Social Effects Assessment: Two Cases from a Corps Field District," U.S. Army Corps of Engineers, Institute for Water Resources, November 1978.

MASLOW, ABRAHAM H., *Motivation and Personality*, Harper, New York, 1954.

MERTON, R. K., *Social Theory and Social Structure*, The Free Press, Glencoe, Ill., 1957.

MITCHELL, ARNOLD et al., "Handbook of Forecasting Techniques," Stanford Research Institute, December 1975; "List of 73 Techniques," August 1977; "Description of 31 Techniques," U.S. Army Corps of Engineers, Institute for Water Resources, August 1977.

O'LEARY, MICHAEL, et al., "Policy Profiling Handbook," U.S. Army Corps of Engineers, Institute for Water Resources, Spring 1982.

TAYLOR, SARAH, "Institutional Analysis Handbook," U.S. Army Corps of Engineers, Institute for Water Resources, Spring 1982.

U.S. DEPARTMENT OF THE INTERIOR, Water and Power Resources Service, "Draft Environmental Statement—Salmon Falls Division, Upper Snake River Project, Idaho–Wyoming," December 14, 1979.

U.S. WATER RESOURCES COUNCIL, "Principles and Standards for Planning Water and Related Land Resources," 1973; rev. December 14, 1979; rev. September 29, 1980.

U.S. WATER RESOURCES COUNCIL, "Evaluating Social Effects in Water Resources Planning: First Steps," Washington, D.C., September 1981.

U.S. WATER RESOURCES COUNCIL, "Economic and Environmental Principles and Guidelines for Water and Related Land Resources Implementation Studies," March 10, 1983.

VLACHOS, EVAN, et al., "Social Impact Assessment, an Overview," U.S. Army Corps of Engineers, Institute for Water Resources, Fort Belvoir, Va., December 1975.

SEVENTEEN

Legal and Institutional Aspects

17.1 INTRODUCTION

Water resources planning, to be effective, must be done with a clear understanding of the "real world" in which projects are implemented. Chapter 7 has discussed the need for public involvement in the various stages of planning. This chapter discusses the legal and institutional aspects, which, like public involvement, must be considered not as a final step in the planning process but rather as essential ingredients in all stages of a plan's development. Ignoring this fundamental truism will greatly increase the chances that a planning document will be relegated to the archives, where it will gather dust and die unceremoniously.

The following sections provide basic information about the legal framework within which any planning for water resources must be fitted, based on U.S. experience. The water laws also circumscribe the institutional arrangements that must be accommodated in implementing any water resource project. These sections are designed to sensitize readers to the issues and their interrelationships, and to establish a basis for awareness of the legal and institutional problems that must be addressed.

Any treatment of the legal issues of water resources must also recognize the interrelationships of land and water. Many of these interrelationships are described in Section 5.9.

17.2 THE LAW RELATED TO WATER

The law that governs the allocation and use of water depends on whether the water under consideration is: (1) surface water with bed and banks; (2) water beneath the surface of the ground; or (3) diffused water flowing over the surface of the ground. Thus, disputes over water necessarily involve a factual determination as to the state of the water in question. When, for example, does diffused water develop sufficient concentration and regularity of flow to constitute water with bed and banks? Is water flowing beneath the surface to be litigated the same as water with bed and banks, or does it represent a "pool" of water beneath the surface?

In the physical world, the interconnections and other interrelationships between water in its various forms are now well understood. Legal concepts, however, had to be developed when the underlying basic hydrologic principles were not known. The hydrologic cycle, which is driven by solar energy and the force of gravity, is a continuous circulation of water from precipitation to surface and ground water drainage, which then is taken up through evaporation and transpiration for recycling as precipitation again. Current water law, in dealing separately with the three states mentioned above, is not consistent with the physical laws that clearly connect water in all its forms. The dichotomy that exists between the actual hydrologic cycle and water rights created on unsound hydrologic principles make these water rights insecure. As more complete utilization of our water resources becomes a necessity, more complex problems will arise that will require water law to conform to physical reality. Only recently have attempts been made to reconcile these differences. Those who plan for the use of water nevertheless must recognize the different rules that currently are applied to the management of this resource. Each "form" of water law will be discussed in detail in later sections of this chapter.

To understand the law as it relates to water, it is essential to have some appreciation of the property rights in water. Property under the law is not an absolute right, since society's perception of the common need—upon which property concepts are based—changes with time (Lauer 1958, p. 131).

In property law, a distinction is made between real property and personal property. A water right generally is considered to be real property. However, when the corpus of the water has been captured, the water may become personal property. Thus, water taken from such natural surroundings as a stream and a reservoir then may become personal property.

Another principle is that water in its natural state generally cannot be owned absolutely as specific tangible property. The property interest in water is *usufructuary* in character; that is, it consists of a right *to the use* of the water, not private ownership of the corpus of the water.

The source of the law related to water is found in the *common law* and in *statutory law*. Statutory modifications in the common law can be made by legislation from all three levels of government: federal, state, and local. The constraints on each of these levels of government trying to effectuate change in water law are discussed in detail in later sections.

The common law can be viewed simply as "judge-made law." It is a record of judicial decisions in cases and controversies involving water. The common law is rooted in judicial recognition of precedent, which is the use of decisions made in the past in similar types of situations to examine current fact situations. Exceptions, modifications, or extensions to these previous decisions or statutory modifications may be used to allow the common law to accommodate changing times, values, and morals. This provides stability and predictability in the law while providing a mechanism for change. The common law has played a significant part in establishing both surface water and groundwater rights in the states east of the 98th meridian (a line following the eastern borders of North Dakota, South Dakota, Nebraska, Kansas, Oklahoma, and Texas). While the common law must be well understood by planners concerned with water and related land issues, it must also be recognized that the judiciary is not well suited to the needs of the planning process. First, judicial decisions are always made after disputes have arisen. Second, the judiciary has no jurisdiction beyond the actual litigants involved in the cases directly before the court. Planners cannot rely on the common law as a mechanism to effect change in the future or to forestall general problems that have been resolved by the courts only with respect to a specific fact situation.

17.3 FEDERAL JURISDICTION

The legal basis of all actions by the federal government is the power delegated to it in the federal Constitution. Those powers not specifically delegated to the federal government are reserved for the states. Although no expressed power to manage water resources is found in the U.S. Constitution, the federal government has nevertheless played a significant role in the resource's development. Actions of the federal government have been confirmed by the courts through interpretations of the constitutional provisions relating to commerce, public lands, general welfare, and war.

During the early development of the country, water resources legislation was central to the implementation of many important congressional policies. For example, water for transportation was a matter of national concern not only in terms of the settlement of the western United States, but also for the promotion of commerce between areas. The jurisdictional base of the federal government for water policies with respect to navigation was the commerce clause of the federal Constitution. An 1824 decision of the U.S. Supreme Court involving the right to navigate coastal waters was the first time federal supremacy in the area of navigation was clearly enunciated (Gibbons v. *Ogden*, 22 U.S. 1).

Since then a series of cases have expanded the breadth of the commerce clause base to include navigation, the potential for navigation, and activities that substantially interfere with navigation, even if such interference occurs on nonnavigable reaches of steams. It is recognized that states can exercise control over navigable waters, but they are always subject to the paramount authority of the federal government. This has given rise to what is known as the "navigation-servitude principles." Since the interest of the federal government in navigation is superior to all others, these other interests are not compensable ones when they are displaced by the federal government. The courts have consistently held that such action does not amount to a taking of property under the provisions of the Fifth Amendment.

During the period from 1890 to 1917, Congress made appropriations for broad navigational purposes and some of these contained incidental benefits for flood control. Flood control took on greater significance after some very bad flooding which began in 1915. Later, the constitutional base for the federal government to act with respect to flood control activities was firmly established by authority of the general welfare provision of the Constitution in the Flood Control Act of 1936 (Act of June 22, 1936, Ch. 688). Later decisions by the Supreme Court indicated that the power to legislate with respect to flood control could be found in the commerce clause (*United States* v. *Appalachian Electric Power Co.*, 311 U.S. 37,426, 1940). In 1941 the Supreme Court held in another case that there was no constitutional barrier to congressional power to "treat the watersheds as a key to flood control on navigable streams and their tributaries" (*Oklahoma ex rel Phillips* v. *Guy F. Atkinson Co.*, 313 U.S. 508, 525).

The federal government has also used the property clause of the federal Constitution to sustain certain activities, including water-related activity. The Homestead Act, for example, was used as a device to encourage the settlement of the western United States. It was soon found, however, that the ultimate success of this endeavor would be contingent on the ability to provide water for the settlers to sustain themselves. The power of the federal government to reclaim arid lands was questioned in a 1907 case. The Supreme Court, in this case relying on the property clause, said that the power to reclaim arid lands owned by the United States was within the legislative power of Congress (*Kansas* v. *Colorado*, 206 U.S. 46).

Even the war powers contained in the Constitution have been used to sustain the right of the federal government to act with respect to waters of the United States. The best example is a case in which the Supreme Court took judicial notice of the international situation and concluded that a water project was intended to be adapted to the processes of national defense (*Ashwander* v. *Tennessee Valley Authority*, 297 U.S. 288).

Although Congress gave recognition to state water rights in legislation such as the Desert Land Act of 1977 and the Reclamation Act of 1902, it also passed legislation to promote the orderly development of water power on major rivers apart from any state action. The power of Congress to regulate power development on navigable streams had its early beginnings in 1879, when the Missouri River Commission was given authority to lease water power to private companies "if the same can be done with the interest of the government of the United States" (Act of March 3, 1879, Ch. 182). Beginning in 1884, Congress passed a series of acts that authorized the construction of private power development on navigable streams. An outgrowth of these activities was the passage of the Federal Water Power Act of 1920, which created the Federal Power Commission.

17.4 THE RIPARIAN DOCTRINE

The word "riparian" is derived from the Latin word "ripa," meaning bank. Under the *riparian doctrine*, the right to use stream water is restricted to the owners of land

Legal and Institutional Aspects   Chap. 17

contiguous or riparian to the stream. The riparian owner may divert water from the stream only on his or her riparian land, which must, by definition, be contiguous to a stream at some point, although the length of the stream frontage is not material to its status as riparian land.

The amount of water a riparian owner may use and the purpose for which he or she may use it are not subject to exact determination. Some courts at times enforce a "natural flow" rule, which permits each riparian owner to divert water to the extent of the owner's domestic needs and to demand that the natural flow of the stream reach his or her land materially unaltered except for the domestic uses of upstream riparians. However, most important nondomestic uses have some material effect on the quality and quantity of flow, so most courts have rejected this nonutilitarian rule in favor of the "reasonable use" rule. This rule allows each riparian owner to satisfy domestic needs and then, subject to the domestic needs of other riparians, to use water for other purposes and in such amounts as is reasonable in the light of all the surrounding circumstances. The natural flow of the stream is not preserved necessarily under the "reasonable use" rule, as it must be under the "natural flow" rule. The two rules have been confused sometimes, particularly in statements that a riparian is entitled to the natural flow of the stream, except as diminished by the reasonable use of other riparians. The right of "reasonable use" for nondomestic purposes is limited by the similar rights of all other riparians along the stream. Priority of use by one riparian is either immaterial or only one factor to be weighted in judging the reasonableness of the use, and reasonableness is determined when, and only when, a court is called upon to weigh the relative reasonableness of conflicting uses. The courts' determination is limited to each case accordingly. Nonuse of water by riparians does not result in the loss of water rights unless coupled with someone's adverse use for a prescriptive period (Fischer 1958, pp. 75, 77–78).

In theory, the standard of relative reasonableness under the riparian doctrine facilitates an adjustment of conflicts between uses in accordance with the needs of each user and the dictates of the general public interest. "The advantages of this 'reasonable use' theory are that it is entirely utilitarian and tends to promote the fullest beneficial use of water resources" (4 Restatement, Torts, pp. 345–46). It allows each riparian a certain amount of flexibility in beginning a new use or in expanding or altering an existing one, especially in the light of changing conditions of water use and supply. In theory this flexibility enhances the public interest in the optimum use of water, and it rewards the enterprising and efficient user.

At the same time, it is not clear how much advantage this flexibility actually contributes to the operation of the riparian system. In many cases, facts disclosed in the court's opinion do not permit an appraisal of the decision's impact on the parties' uses. At other times, the court's discussion of the case does not clearly disclose the grounds for favoring or disfavoring a particular use in a given situation. Moreover, the weighing process in some cases may be distorted by factors not relevant to the issue of relative reasonableness, such as the frequent reluctance of courts to issue decrees that would involve them too closely in the actual supervision of uses. Despite the lack of data on this question, however, the flexible standard of reasonable use under the riparian theory is generally commented on favorably.

The riparian system also is criticized on several grounds. Some criticisms are leveled at its restriction of use of stream water to riparian owners and its requirement that they use the water only on their riparian lands. In particular, it is said that a better use of water frequently may be made in other places, whether it is made by riparians or nonriparian owners (Fischer 1958, p. 79).

The major criticism of the riparian system relates to the elements of uncertainty associated with the right of reasonable use for nondomestic purposes. It is argued that in the attempted exercise of this right the riparian owner has no adequate way of determining for what types of activities the water may be used, how much may be used, and when it may be used. Because the reasonableness of a particular use of water by one riparian varies with the needs of other riparians, the best estimate of this right under prevailing and foreseeable conditions may be upset by the unpredictable activities of other riparians, who are free to commence or enlarge uses, despite long nonuse of their rights.

Critics assert that this uncertainty results, on the one hand, in needless loss of resources invested in water-using enterprises whose supplies are subsequently reduced by competing projects and, on the other hand, in the waste of water that goes unused or that is devoted to less valuable uses because extensive investment is discouraged by the risk of such laws. For example, the riparian system may discourage investment in the increasingly necessary "seasonable" storage of excess water for use during drier periods (Fischer 1958, p. 81).

Another criticism of the riparian system concerns the judicial review by which it is administered, which only seems to aggravate the uncertainty inherent in the riparian theory. The extent of the riparian's right of reasonable use can be determined only by litigation. It is thought that generally a court decree provides an insufficient degree of flexiblity to meet changing conditions that may alter the relative standing of the parties, and the outcome of such litigation does not enable the parties themselves to judge the reasonableness of their uses under changing conditions. The litigated uses may still be upset by the uses of riparians not parties to the decree. In addition, the cost and time-consuming nature of the judicial procedure is said to nullify much of the protection sought by the litigants.

17.5 THE APPROPRIATION DOCTRINE

The *prior appropriation doctrine* evolved out of usage and custom in the mid-1800s to become the predominant water policy for the 17 states located west of the 98th meridian. In considering this doctrine, it is essential to put it into historical perspective. First, it developed in a frontier society out of necessities that existed at the time. It was never conceived as a broad, public policy objective that would guide water resources development over time. Second, because of the arid climate of the West, water rights developed as property rights, and the basic principles governing prior appropriation provided security for this property right. The priority system that was adopted dictated that the first user in time had the superior right. Thus, factors such as the public interest or maximum use of the resource were always subservient to the fundamental concept that a water right as property must be allocated on a time basis.

This method of establishing water rights and the general rules that evolved for settling disputes became known as the appropriation doctrine. Its application was primarily on the public domain where miners were trespassers. The rules governing the acquisition, holding, and forfeiture of individual mining claims were based on priority of discovery and diligence in working them. Thus, the same rules controlled the acquisition and exercise of water rights as those which applied to mining claims. Although there was no state or federal law respecting water, the courts nevertheless began to recognize the miners' claims as possessory rights which could be preempted only by the federal government. During the period 1850–1875, the appropriation doctrine was formally adopted by the states and the territories in the western United States. The passage by Congress of the Act of 1866 confirmed both the mineral and water rights of the miners and accepted the elements that defined the prior appropriation doctrine (Wiel 1911).

Since much has been written about the prior appropriation doctrine as it was applied in the West, it may be thought that this doctrine is well defined and uniformly applied. It is, in fact, nothing more than a guiding philosophy that each state has modified to reflect its needs and preferences. Nevertheless, certain general characteristics describe the appropriative right.

The superiority of a water right is based solely on time and not affected by such factors as purpose, place, or amount of use. Thus, the person acquiring the first water right on a stream has the superior right to all others. This allows the person to divert water as needed, up to the full amount covered by his or her right, before any water can be diverted under rights acquired subsequently.

The water right acquired under the appropriation doctrine requires diversion of water at the same point for use at the same place, for the same purpose, and at the same time of year as stated in the permit. The maximum amount of water beneficially used during that period in which the use was first begun is the maximum amount that may be used under it at any subsequent time. The amount of water available under a water right can be specified in terms of maximum rate of flow and/or maximum volume of water to be used over a given period of time.

The water right can be lost through nonuse, either by abandonment or loss in forfeiture proceedings for nonuse exceeding a statutory limit. The water right also can be lost by prescription, which is similar to the concept of adverse possession in real property.

The major advantages of the appropriation doctrine, when contrasted with the riparian doctrine, are primarily four: flexibility regarding place of use, certainty as to the amount of use, elimination of unused water rights, and greater certainty in administration. The absence of riparian land restrictions under the appropriation doctrine makes it possible for water to be used where it will be most beneficial, both to the individual users and the general public. More significant is the advantage claimed for the priority relationships established by appropriation rights which allow much greater certainty than the reasonable use relationships of riparian rights. In addition, the appropriation doctrine emphasizes the actual beneficial use of water, and unused rights are not allowed to persist as threats to the stability of existing ones. It is claimed also that the inherent certainty of the appropriation theory is translated into reality through the acquisition, adjudication, and distribution procedures of the administrative system (Fischer 1958, p. 86).

Most problems with the appropriation doctrine as experienced by the West are related to wasted water, and result from the priority system of rights where uses are frozen in terms of the original amount, place, and purpose of use. Other problems occur because certainty under appropriation rights is far from absolute. The certainty attached to a water right of a junior appropriator can be no greater than the dependability of the water supply. Priorities are almost impossible to enforce in some physical circumstances. For example, when the most senior appropriation right is located below all other users on a stream (the earliest settlements of the western villages frequently occurred in downstream areas) and the existing supply in the most senior's stretch of the stream is not adequate to meet his or her need, the reduction or stopping of use upstream by junior appropriators may not make the necessary water available in time because of evaporation and seepage losses. In addition, there are questions relating to the right to use return flows.

Since about 90% of the water in the West is used for irrigation, the problems of waste are easily identified with irrigation. First, given that the place and the purpose of a particular use are legitimate and beneficial, the amount of water diverted frequently is excessive and wasteful. The maximum rate of flow covered by an appropriation right is usually greater than necessary for certain times of the growing season, but the threat of having to forfeit the unused part of the right will cause the appropriator to take the water without a real need for it. Second, given that the purpose of a particular use is beneficial, its location often is such that the same use in another location would require a smaller amount of water because of fewer channel losses. Third, even if the location and the amount used are appropriate for the particular purpose to which the water is being applied, the same amount of water used for a different purpose might constitute a more beneficial use. The uses a junior appropriator can make may be quite limited by the existence of senior downstream rights, since irrigation is a highly consumptive use. A fuller use of stream flows could often be achieved by greater upstream use and successive reuse by lower appropriators. Nevertheless, the interdependency that exists where water is successfully used and reused by a number of junior appropriators frequently means that a change cannot be made because existing conditions of supply must be preserved and subsequent rights not impaired (Fischer 1958).

Another aspect of the problem of wasted water in an appropriation system is that an appropriation right allows water to be applied to the same purpose forever. This has the tendency to freeze in place the initial patterns of resource allocation. It has been suggested that the West's future may not be as bright as it could be because of devotion to an antiquated priority system in water use (U.S. President's Material Policy Commission, 1952, p. 94). These frozen water-use patterns may seriously restrain economic and industrial growth (Engelbert 1953, p. 90).

With the frozen water-use patterns of the prior appropriation doctrine (a system based on the characteristics of water flowing on the surface), many users have turned to groundwater as a supplemental source. Consequently, depletion in some groundwater aquifers has occurred, and the associated flow of natural streams has been reduced. A conflict has thus developed between the owners of surface water rights (who are senior in the priority system) and groundwater users. This conflict is brought into sharp focus whenever jurisdictions following the prior appropriation doctrine attempt to maximize the use of their limited water supply. No matter how desirable from an analytical point of view, the maximum utilization principle does not lend itself to a system of water rights administered under the appropriation doctrine in which protection of vested rights is the paramount concern. Maximum utilization involves a sharing of water resources among senior and junior users to foster intensive and efficient use of water for the overall benefit of the state (Carlson 1974, pp. 529, 537).

17.6 GROUNDWATER RIGHTS

Groundwater, that water which is below the surface of the land, is generally classified either as an *underground stream* or *percolating water*. Before water can be "legally" treated as a subsurface stream, it must be discoverable from the surface of the ground (*Logan Gas Co.* v. *Glasgo*, 170 N.E. 874-1930). If excavation is required in order to determine the direction and course of the subterranean waters, the water is classified as percolating. If the waters under consideration are determined to run in an underground stream, the overlying landowners have the same rights with respect to the subterranean stream as riparian proprietors have with respect to streams on the surface (*Evans* v. *City of Seattle*, 47 P. 2d 984-1935).

In many states the burden of establishing the existence of an underground stream is placed on the party asserting the fact. Unless it can be shown that underground water flows in a defined and known channel, it is presumed to be percolating water (*Higday* v. *Nickolaus*, 469 S.W. 2d 859—1971). The presumption that water is percolating must be overcome, and this may be difficult (*Clinchfield Coal Corp.* v. *Compton*, 139 S.E. 308-1927).

Percolating waters have been defined as:

> waters which slowly percolate or infiltrate their way through the sand, gravel, rock, or soil, which do not then form a part of any body of water or the flow of any watercourse, surface or subterranean, but which may eventually find their way by force of gravity to some watercourse or other body of water, with whose waters they mingle, and thereby lose their identify as percolating water [Kinney 1912, p. 2150].

It makes no difference whether the source of these waters is rain infiltrating the soil or seepage from the bed and banks of a stream into subterranean waters.

Except in a few cases where statutes have attempted to make the appropriation doctrine applicable to groundwaters, the law governing waters beneath the surface is usually administered according to one of three common law doctrines: absolute ownership (English rule), reasonable use (American rule), or correlative rights.

Under the *absolute ownership doctrine*, the percolating waters are considered part of the land in which they are found and belong absolutely to the owners of such land. These owners can divert or capture this water as they see fit and they are not liable for any action that might result in loss or injury to other landowners, except that they may not use the water in a malicious manner. Under the English rule, the person who owns the surface is almost completely immune from the impact of his or her actions on others. In addition to freedom from liability, the landowner is not restricted to the overlying land in using the water that has been captured. The fact that the water is used away from the premises from which it is pumped does not in any way increase the liability to others who are injured by the pumping of the wells.

The *reasonable use doctrine* has been adopted to provide some measure of protection to adjoining landowners. Although the owner of the land is still not liable for loss or injuries to others from the use of groundwater, this immunity is available only when the use of the water is reasonable in relationship to the needs and necessities of the owner's own tract and will not extend to uses away from the overlying land. The reasonable use rule means that an overlying landowner may use underground water free of liability, but only if its use is incidental to the beneficial enjoyment of the overlying land from which the water is taken (*Higday* v. *Nickolaus*, 469 S.W. 2d 859 (1971)).

The *correlative rights doctrine* is based on the theory of proportionate sharing of withdrawals among overlying landowners. Under this doctrine, the rights of landowners to percolating water are coequal and proportional to their overlying ownership. Thus, a landowner may not extract more than his or her share even for beneficial use on the person's own land when the rights of other overlying landowners will be injured by such use.

17.7 DIFFUSED SURFACE WATER RIGHTS

Surface water can be divided into two categories: water with bed and banks and diffused water which flows over the surface of the ground. Diffused waters follow no defined course or channel over the surface of the ground and have not gathered into or formed a natural body of water. These waters continue to retain their character as diffused surface waters until they reach some well-defined channel and become part of a watercourse.

Unlike waters with bed and banks, diffused waters can be captured by the owners of land over which they move and as such become the property of the landowner. No riparian rights are attached to these waters and in states where surface waters are held to belong to the public, no public property interest is found in them. In the case of diffused waters, the property interest is based on actual possession of the corpus of the property itself.

Most of the problems surrounding diffused waters are not caused by their allocation among users, but are concerned more with drainage problems resulting from land activities of adjoining landowners.

Over the years the courts have evolved three basic property rules to govern the management of diffused surface waters. The first, the *common enemy rule*, was stated in a California case as follows:

Stated in its extreme form, the common enemy doctrine holds that as an incident to the use of his own property, each landowner has unqualified right by operations on his own lands, to fend off surface waters as he sees fit without being required to take into account the consequences to other landowners, who have a right to protect themselves as best they can [*Keys* v. *Romely*, 412 P. 2d 529, 531, 1966].

The second rule, the *civil law rule,* seeks to preserve the status quo with respect to the flow of diffused surface waters. It gives the right of action against anyone who interferes with the natural conditions and causes water to be discharged in a greater quantity or in a different manner than would have occurred under natural conditions. (*Andrew Jargens Co.* v. *The City of Los Angeles*, 229 P. 2d 472, 1951). There have been some modifications in the civil law rule, and it has not been applied uniformly to public and private ownerships in some jurisdictions.

The last rule, the *reasonable use rule,* attempts to blend these two rules, one of which permits unrestricted action while the other makes any action that modifies the drainage pattern actionable. This rule attempts to define the rights of the parties by an assessment of all the relevant factors.

In jurisdictions where the common law provides the only guidance governing conduct with respect to diffused surface waters, the planners seeking to influence or prescribe land use changes should examine very carefully the applicable law, lest they recommend land use changes with severe impacts on landowners when diffused surface water drainage changes.

17.8 INTERSTATE LEGAL ISSUES

Although some interstate boundaries follow the course of streams and other interstate boundaries follow the divides that separate one watershed from another, political boundaries of the states generally do not correspond well with drainage basins. The disparity between hydrologic boundaries and political boundaries makes the management of the various water resources difficult.

From a legal standpoint, agreement between individual water users is not a satisfactory means of resolving interstate problems. Even if such agreements contained a framework for resolving future disputes and binding successive individual users, these private users would not represent the "public interest" of their respective states and thus the agreement could be unenforceable. The principal ways to resolve interstate water controversies are:

1. Federal legislation
2. An original action in the U.S. Supreme Court between two or more states
3. Litigation between citizens of two or more states
4. An agreement between two or more states without a formal compact
5. Interstate compacts

The legal basis for all federal action, including federal legislation to resolve interstate controversies, is found in those powers delegated to the federal government by the U.S. Constitution. The authority for much of the federal government's activity in water issues is found in Article 1, Section 8, of the Constitution, which gives Congress the power to regulate commerce among the states. The courts have interpreted "commerce" to include transportation, which encompasses navigation. Yet, even with this very liberal interpretation of the Constitution, there has been considerable question as to whether Congress does, in fact, have the power to apportion water among the states. In 1963, the U.S. Supreme Court resolved this issue by holding that Congress does have the power to apportion water among contending states in a suit precipitated by the passage of the Boulder Canyon Project Act of 1928 (*Arizona* v. *California*, 373 U.S. 546). It is not yet clear whether this congressional power extends to nonnavigable water, although it is likely to be held that Congress does have the power to apportion nonnavigable streams. Earlier court decisions have held that Congress can regulate nonnavigable tributaries by declaring that such regulations affect the navigable portions of streams.

Unresolved is the question of whether congressional apportionment of water can destroy vested rights under state law and thus give the owner of such rights a claim of action under the Fifth Amendment of the U.S. Constitution, which forbids the taking of property without just compensation. The courts have held consistently that Congress, acting pursuant to the commerce clause of the Constitution, is not required to compensate for vested water rights taken, since all such rights are held contingent to an assertion of power by the federal government.

In addition to federal legislation, interstate controversies may be resolved by lawsuits between contending states before the U.S. Supreme Court. In cases involving water rights, the Supreme Court has developed a special set of rules for resolving controversies between states, known as the doctrine of *equitable apportionment*. The need for this special set of rules lies in the fact that there is no federal law of water rights, and the various state laws on the subject differ from one another in many respects. Indeed, it is more likely than not that the states find themselves in the Supreme Court because of some difference in their laws or policies that impedes the resolution of their dispute. The Supreme Court first announced the principle of equitable apportionment in a suit between one state following the riparian rights doctrine and another state following the prior appropriation doctrine, but equitable apportionment has been applied subsequently to cases where both states adhere to either riparian rights or prior appropriation principles.

Under the doctrine of equitable apportionment, the Supreme Court attempts to fairly apportion the flow of an interstate stream between the states in controversy on a case-by-case basis. The Court may or may not look to the principles of existing riparian rights or appropriation law to help decide the case. There are no strict rules of priority.

Another way to resolve interstate controversies involves litigation between citizens of different states, but the impact of a divergence between the general rules of the two states is not clear. Conceivably, the federal courts would apply the equitable apportionment rule, but there is very little case law on the subject (Clark 1967).

Another method of resolving interstate water disputes is by means of an interstate compact. More often than not, initiation of a compact involves enactment of identical or substantially identical legislation by each participating state, followed by congressional approval, although congressional consent may be obtained in advance. For example, in 1952 Congress gave prior approval to interstate compacts concerning water pollution control agreements which conformed to prescribed criteria.

The compact has become the favored method of dealing with interstate water problems, with literally hundreds of compacts in effect concerning water resources. There are 15 or more compacts involving water rights; a dozen or more involving water pollution control; numerous compacts establishing public authorities to operate commercial-type facilities, such as the Port Authority of New York and New Jersey; and a limited number of multipurpose compacts, such as one establishing the Delaware River Basin Commission.

As a means of resolving interstate disputes and problems, the compact has certain obvious advantages over the alternative or original suits in the Supreme Court. It tends to focus on elements of harmony and mutuality instead of divisive factors which are highlighted by litigation. It provides a framework for a dynamic and ongoing approach to interstate problems, rather than a static approach.

On the other hand, the compact approach itself has certain disadvantages. It has often been criticized because of a tendency to foster agencies that are not responsive to democratic political control. Also, compact agencies typically have serious financing and fiscal problems, and other technical and practical problems, which tend to restrict their utility for program administration. Finally, the compact agency frequently has a built-in bias against one or more of the potential parties to the compact, which makes it very difficult to secure agreement on initiating the compact. For example, in a water pollution context, an interstate compact is almost inherently a means of benefiting the downstream water users at the expense of the upstream users.

17.9 INSTITUTIONAL STRUCTURES AND POWERS

Chapter 1 indicated that many institutions in the United States are involved in the water resources development process. This section will consider the necessary institutional structure to plan, construct, and operate an effective organization.

Criteria for evaluating institutional structures have been developed by URS Company (1975), Wendell and Schwann (1972), and the Institute of Public Administration (1972). Minton et al. (1980) reviewed the literature bearing on the subject and prepared a set of criteria for evaluating alternative types of institutional arrangements. The following list is based on this work:

1. *Public Acceptability.* Is the institutional structure directly accountable to the consituency for its needs? Is the public willing to pay the costs and make the social changes required for plan implementation?

2. *Political Feasibility.* Are officials willing to refer plan implementation to recommended organizations which are willing to implement the plan?

3. *Adequate Legal Authority.* Are the organizations and agencies legally able to

carry out assignments? Are appropriate interorganization agreements, such as contracts or memoranda of understanding, available for assigning responsibilities? Are geographic jurisdictions of implementing organizations of sufficient size to include the area of impact?

4. *Adequate Financial Resources.* Do assigned participants have sufficient access to financing to implement the recommended plan?

5. *Fairness and Equitability.* Are implementation costs fairly and equitably distributed among participating agencies and water consumers? Do those who derive benefits and/or create costs also contribute?

6. *Technical Capabilities.* Do the organizations assigned responsibilities have the appropriate technical staff?

7. *Stability/Reliability/Flexibility.* Are the organizations being assigned responsibilities already established? Can they be expected to remain in authority for the planning period? Are there sufficient allowances for future contingencies?

8. *Conservation Suitability.* Will the institutional structure adopted be suitable for implementing equitable conservation measures if area-wide emergencies should demand them?

9. *Efficiency.* Is the size of the implementing agency sufficient to realize economies of scale? Will the structure result in efficient allocation and operation and avoid duplication of services and excess capacity?

10. *Enforcement Authority.* Do the organizations assigned responsibility have the authority to enforce policies?

17.10 INTERNATIONAL LEGAL ISSUES

The "Second National Water Assessment" by the U.S. Water Resources Council (1978) lists some of the terms of agreements concerning international waters in which the United States has participated. There are six treaties between the United States and Canada and three between the United States and Mexico that establish respective rights and responsibilities to waters flowing in streams crossing the international boundaries. In addition to these treaties, laws and regulations have been enacted by the Congress, states, and public agencies that affect the use of waters within specified distances from the coast for the discharge of wastewaters, dumping of solid wastes, fishing, development of oil fields, navigation, and other water uses. The United States also is a signatory to a number of international conventions dealing with such matters.

Stone (1980) has analyzed the problems that arise because political jurisdictions do not coincide with river basins and has identified elements that characterize the international planning process. She found the following distinguishing features:

• Nations pursue distinctive, noncomparable, and often multiple development objectives.
• Nations are limited in their ability to act autonomously.

- Development decisions involve a strategic choice to share conflicting and mutual interests.

Stone has suggested a methodology for a systems approach to water resource allocation in international river development. Another approach involving a decision matrix that stresses environmental aspects has been suggested by Yapijakis (1981). A river basin systems analysis by TAMS (1978) involving the preparation of a master plan for water resources development in an international river basin is described in Chapter 6 and 13.

Guidelines for allocating costs of multipurpose projects in an international river basin may include the separable cost/remaining benefits technique and other methods discussed in Chapter 8 for U.S. federal government projects. A method of allocations for a reservoir benefiting two countries, based on proportioning costs according to the net benefits gained by each country, is also described in Chapter 8. Guidelines for "equitable utilization" of the waters of an international drainage basin have been prepared by the International Law Association (1966).

Other problems in addition to the sharing of costs and the allocaton of waters include provisions for the monitoring of quantity and quality of water, the lands and rights-of-way traversed by water conveyances, and the operation and maintenance of projects.

17.11 EMINENT DOMAIN

Eminent domain is the right to take private property for public use or, in more descriptive terms, it is the use of coercive machinery of a government to effectuate an exchange of ownership.

The source of the power for either the state or federal government is the power inherent in and a necessary attribute of "sovereignty." The power is inherent in the very concept of a "state" and exists independently of any constitutional provision. In the case of the federal government, which is one of delegated powers, the prerogative of eminent domain is not explicitly granted. However, early in the history of the country, the U.S. Supreme Court held that the power to acquire property is necessary for the exercise of the delegated powers of the federal government (*Kohl* v. *United States,* 91 U.S. 367, 1876).

The two critical issues in any eminent domain proceeding are whether the property sought is for a "public use" and, if it is, the value of it. In general, there are no exact definitions of the term "public use." In the narrowest sense, "public use" is equated with "use by the public." There are many examples where the definition applied to "public use" has been much more liberal. The fact that there are incidental private benefits has not, in many situations, overridden the paramount public interest which gave rise to the eminent domain proceeding. An early 1905 case arising in Utah is an excellent example. In this controversy the U.S. Supreme Court upheld a Utah statute permitting the exercise of eminent domain by a private party in order to widen a ditch by 1 foot *(Clark* v. *Nash*, 198 U.S. 361). Even the Fourteenth

Amendment of the federal Constitution does not forbid the exercise of eminent domain by a private party in his or her own behalf when the purpose is of both public and private importance. Water is so important in the western states that it is not uncommon for statutes to declare either that certain uses of water are "public" or that eminent domain may be exercised for specific private uses. Examples might involve ditch rights or other rights-of-way.

In any eminent domain preceeding involving a water right, the value of the right taken is usually subject to considerable differences of opinion. The courts usually speak in terms of market value of the water taken, but it is not uncommon for the original owner of the water right to have the depreciated value of the land considered as an element of his or her damages. Another question that frequently arises is whether the original owner of a water right is entitled to a larger compensation award because the special adaptability of the land coincides with the condemnor's purpose for condemning. Some courts prohibit this consideration, but most decisions are not explicit as to whether the taker's need has been included or excluded in establishing the market value of the water right (Hale 1931, pp. 1, 17).

REFERENCES

CARLSON, JOHN U., "Has the Doctrine of Appropriation Outlived Its Usefulness?" Rocky Mountain Mineral Law Institute, vol. 19, 1974, pp. 529–554.

CLARK, ROBERT EMMET, ed., *Water and Water Rights*, vol. II, Allen Smith Co., Indianapolis, 1967, pp. 310–314.

ENGLEBERT, ERNEST, "Political Aspects with Future Water Resource Development in the West," Committee on Economics of Water Resource Development, 1, Western Agricultural Economics Research Council, 1953.

FISCHER, CLYDE O., JR., "Western Experience and Eastern Appropriation Proposals" in *The Law of Water Allocation in the Eastern United States,* D. Haber and S. W. Bergen, eds., Conservation Foundation, Washington, D.C., 1958.

HALE, R.L., "Value to the Taker in Condemnation Cases," *Columbia Law Rev.,* vol. 31., 1931, pp. 1–31.

INSTITUTE OF PUBLIC ADMINISTRATION, "Organizational, Legal and Public Finance Aspects of Regional Water Supply," vol. I, report to North Atlantic Division, U.S. Army Corps of Engineers, 1972.

INTERNATIONAL LAW ASSOCIATION, "International Rivers—The Helsinki Rules," International Law Association, 1966 (reprinted in Kuiper, 1971).

KINNEY, CLESSON S., *A Treatise on the Law of Irrigation and Water Rights*, vol. 2, 2nd ed., Bender-Moss Co., San Francisco, 1912.

KUIPER, EDWARD, *Water Resource Project Economics,* Butterworth, Kent, England, 1971.

LAUER, T.E., "The Riparian Right as Property," in *Water Resources and the Law*, University of Michigan Law School, Ann Arbor, 1958, pp. 131–268.

MINTON, GARY R, RICHARD WILLIAMS, and THOMAS MURDOCK, "Institutional Analysis Criteria for Water Supply Planning," *Water Resources Bull.,* vol. 16, no. 3, June 1980.

STONE, PAULA J., "A Systems Approach to Water Resource Allocation in International River Basin Development," *Water Resources Res.,* vol. 16, no. 1, February 1980.

TAMS (Tippetts-Abbett-McCarthy-Stratton, New York, and Massachusetts Institute of Technology, Cambridge), "Integrated Development of the Vardar/Axios River Basin-Yugoslavia-Greece," United Nations, December 1978.

URS COMPANY, "Institutional Analysis," Technical Memorandum, Metropolitan Anchorage Urban Study/Water, U.S. Army Corps of Engineers, 1978.

U.S. President's Material Policy Commission, "Water for Industry," Rpt. 9 in *Resources for Freedom,* vol. 5, 1952.

U.S. Water Resources Council, "The Nation's Water Resources 1975–2000—Second National Water Assessment," 1978.

WENDELL and SCHWANN, "Intergovernmental Relations in Water Resources Activities," Washington, D.C., September 1972.

WIEL, S.C., "Water Rights in the Western States," 3rd ed., vol. 1, Sec. 93, 1911.

YAPIJAKIS, CONSTANTINE, "A Comprehensive Methodology for Project Appraisal and Environmental Protection in a Multinational Context," Ph.D. thesis, Polytechnic Institute of New York, 1981.

EIGHTEEN

Administration of Planning Programs

18.1 SCHEDULING OF PLANNING SERVICES

Professional services in the water resources planning and development field are usually characterized by the following:

- Interdisciplinary staff
- Interagency effort, if public works project
- More than one principal phase of work
- Many tasks, some of which overlap whereas others require the completion of one or more tasks before they can start
- Benchmark dates for starting and completing the work and at intermediate points when policy decisions or other important actions are required

Because of the obvious complexities introduced by these characteristics, graphical and analytical aids are useful to facilitate the process of providing professional services and improve its efficiency.

An *activity chart* showing personnel assignments for various components of a screening study is shown in Figure 18.1. For a large and complicated project, the manpower estimated for the activities would be distributed to various departments and then to individuals.

A schedule of major engineering tasks phased according to the construction requirements for the Pond Hill, Pennsylvania, cooling water reservoir serving a thermal electric power plant is shown in Figure 18.2 in the form of a *bar chart*.

Activities	Partners and Division Head	Project Manager	Staff Consultant — Hydroelectric	Staff Consultant — Geology	Staff Consultant — Planning	Principal Hydroelectric Engineer	Senior Geotechnical Engineer	Principal Hydromechanical Engineer	Geotechnical Engineer	Geologist	Engineers	Junior Engineers and Draftsmen	Totals
Presentation on Proposed Approach		16	16		16						16	32	96
Site Screening Phase (12 Sites)													
1. Collection and review of existing reports and other information		16	16			16			16	16	16	16	112
2. "Windshield surveys" to establish general characteristics of site			64	64									192
3. Utilizing published information to establish geology						16			16	16	16	16	80
4. Establish preliminary layouts		32	32				32		16	16	304	32	480
5. Preliminary identification of sources of construction materials					16	16			48	16	16		80
6. Material quantities rough estimate		16									64		80
7. Development of preliminary area-capacity curves										48	16		64
8. Preparation of preliminary layouts		32	16		32	16	16		16		224	240	575
9. Preparation of order of magnitude estimated costs		16			16			32			32	80	96
10. Preparation of report — Draft		48	48		80	16	32	16			112	80	336
Review by Utilities		64								16	16		80
Final		16	16		16						32	48	112
Site Selection Phase (4 Sites)													
1. Establishing geotechnical design criteria							32		32				64
2. Preparation of geologic maps and sections of the sites							16		48	64		80	160
3. Confirmation of construction material availability and quantities		32	48				48				16	16	144
4. Defining of optimum site developments and the associated land requirements		32	48			32				48	96	96	256
5. Development of more detailed conceptual designs and cost estimates		32	16			16	32	16	16	16	208	240	576
6. Development of area-capacity curves		16								32	16	32	48
7. Development of cost versus installed capacity curves for the sites			16		32			32			48		96
8. Preparation of report — Draft		48	48		80	16	16				80	80	304
Review by Utilities		32			32						16	80	48
Final		16	16		16	16	16	16			32	48	112
Attendance at Meetings and Superv. by Partners and Div. Head	128	96	32	64	32	16	16	16	16	64	64	64	384
Totals	128	560	240	64	224	208	272	80	192	208	1456	944	4576

Figure 18.1 Activity chart for screening of pumped-storage projects.

523

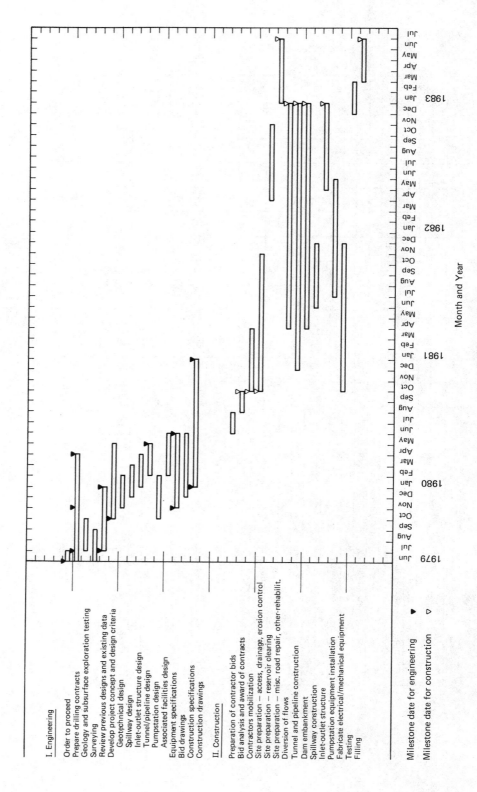

Figure 18.2 Engineering and construction schedule for Pond Hill reservoir. (From TAMS, 1979a.)

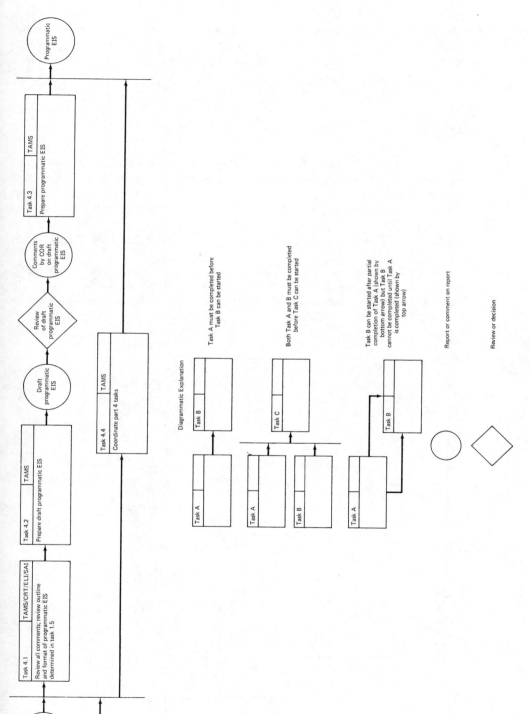

Figure 18.3 Portion of flowchart for preparing EIS. (From TAMS, 1979b.)

When a planning project involves a number of complicated interrelationships among the professional tasks, it is often useful to prepare a *flowchart*. Figure 18.3 shows the final portion of a flowchart for the study of a programmatic environmental impact statement for a public agency.

18.2 NETWORK ANALYSIS (CPM AND PERT)

For many complex projects, the rational scheduling of professional activities can benefit from the application of mathematical techniques. The approach often adopted is network analysis, using the "critical path method" (CPM) or the "program evaluation and review technique" (PERT). These methods were developed in parallel in the 1950s, CPM for the planning, scheduling, and cost control of chemical plants and PERT for measuring and controlling the progress of the Polaris Fleet ballistic program in the United States.

With CPM, the first step is to identify the various tasks, or *activities*, making up the project. The next step is to identify the *events* that constitute the start of the project and the completion of one or more activities. The activities and events may be

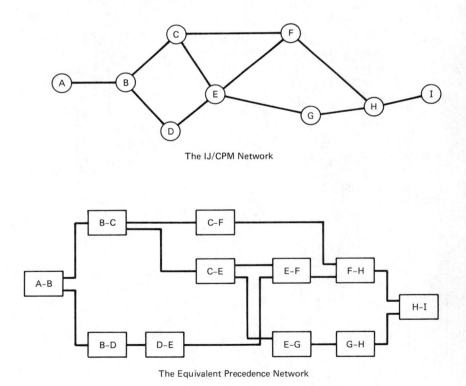

The IJ/CPM Network

The Equivalent Precedence Network

Figure 18.4 Outlines of CPM processing. (From IBM, 1971.)

Administration of Planning Programs   Chap. 18

set out in the form of a network of branches and nodes, respectively, also known as the "system flow plan." For processing, the equivalent "precedence network" may be needed. Figure 18.4 shows these representations. Once the project has begun, the times to arrive at important "milestone events" and to complete the project depend on the chain of "critical activities" lying along the "critical path."

An illustration of a critical path analysis is shown in Figure 18.5. A project starts at event 1 and is completed at event 6, and has seven activities (1–2, 2–3, 2–4, 3–4, 3–5, 4–5, and 5–6). The values shown along the branches indicate the number of units of time or *durations* estimated for the activities. For this case, the critical path is determined by inspection to be 1–2–3–5–6, with a minimum total time of 15 units. It is clear that there is "slack" or *float* on each branch that does not lie along the critical path, which permits a later start without delaying the final completion date. Thus, to reach point 6 via the path 1–2–4–5–6 requires 13 units, whereas the path 1–2–3–4–5–6 requires 14 units.

A CPM analysis is carried out before a project begins and at various points in time in order to monitor the project to: (1) identify bottlenecks where special management efforts are needed; (2) evaluate any modifications in the schedule that are required to accommodate actual progress on activities; and (3) make any changes that are caused by the reduction, addition, or modification of activities.

The IBM 1130 PCS System, Fifth Edition (1971), produces 14 standard reports for project control. A bar graph, prepared by this system and plotted by means of computer control for a river basin systems study, is shown in Figure 18.6. Note that this chart and the one in Figure 18.2, both developed by CPM methods, show tasks in a logical order (which may be different from the order originally assumed by the planner as indicated by the task numbers). The project control system can also present information on the progress of the component tasks, utilization of manpower and other resources, costs, and other subjects of importance to project analysts and managers.

PERT differs from CPM primarily in its capability to estimate the probability of meeting deadlines or milestone dates. The original version of PERT made the assumption that the duration time for each activity is a random variable characterized by a probability distribution having a mean and variance. These statistical parameters could be determined from records of similar activities or by judgment of experienced analysts. Versions now in use establish these parameters based on input values of "most likely," "optimistic," and "pessimistic" durations. Discussions of PERT are available in a number of references (e.g., Hillier and Lieberman 1980, Gillett 1976).

18.3 SOURCES OF WATER RESOURCES PLANNING INFORMATION

The body of published literature in the water resources planning and related fields is enormous and growing rapidly. There are also many reports issued by government agencies and other entities with limited distribution. This poses a difficult problem of access and identification of pertinent previous and ongoing investigations, when the

Figure 18.5 Critical path determinations. (From Mussivand, 1972.)

ACTIVITY (i - j)	DURATION (t)	EPO (1)	LPO (8)	EARLIEST START (Y) $Y=\propto-t$ (3=4-t)	EARLIEST FINISH ($\propto$) $\propto=EPO+t$ (4=1+t)	LATEST START (δ) $\delta=LPO-t$ (5=2-t)	LATEST FINISH (B) $B=\delta+t$ (6=6-t)	TOTAL FLOAT (T_f) $T_f=B-\propto$ (7=6-4)	FREE FLOAT (F_f) $F_f=EPO-\propto$ (8=1-4)	INTERFERING FLOAT (I_f) $I_f=T_f-F_f$ (9=7-8)	REMARKS
1 - 2	1	0	0	0	1	0	1	0	0	0	CRITICAL
2 - 3	6	1	1	1	7	1	7	0	0	0	CRITICAL
2 - 4	8			1	9	3	11	2	1	1	
3 - 4	3			7	10	8	11	1	0	1	
3 - 5	7	7	7	7	14	7	14	0	0	0	CRITICAL
4 - 5	3	10	11	10	13	11	14	1	1	0	
5 - 6	1	14	14	14	15	14	15	0	0	0	CRITICAL
6		15	15								

A CHOOSE LARGEST SUM FOR EPO
B CHOOSE SMALLEST SUM FOR LPO

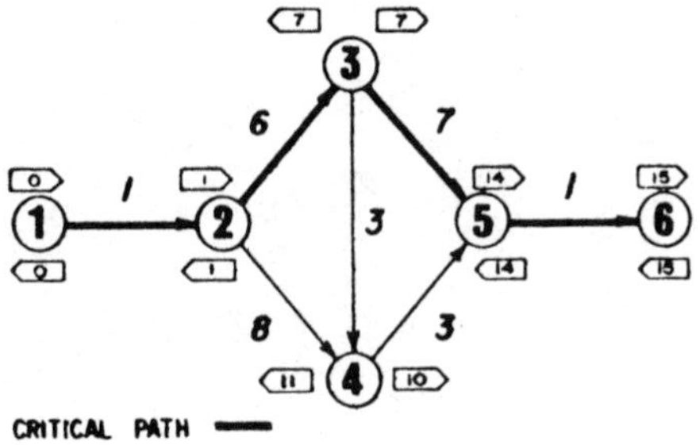

ABBREVIATIONS

EPO EARLIEST POSSIBLE OCCURANCE
LPO LATEST POSSIBLE OCCURANCE
i   INITIAL EVENT OF ACTIVITY
j   END EVENT OF ACTIVITY
t   DURATION
I_f INTERFERING FLOAT

$\propto$ EARLIEST FINISH TIME
B   LATEST FINISH TIME
Y   EARLIEST START TIME
δ LATEST START TIME
T_f TOTAL FLOAT
F_f FREE FLOAT

PREPARED: T V MUSSIVAND
DRAWN: L Cunningham

CRITICAL PATH ——

528

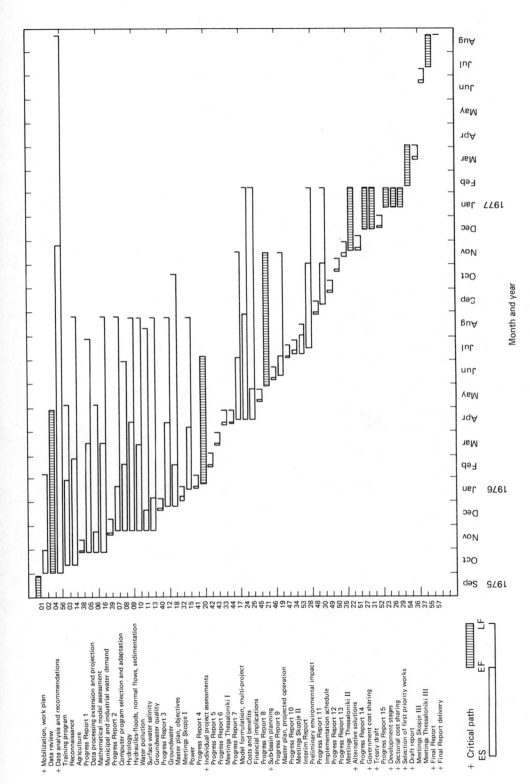

Figure 18.6 Critical path chart for Vardas/Axios River Basin study. (From TAMS, 1975.)

planning of a project can benefit from the experience of others. Fortunately, methods exist for the dissemination of information through establishments set up by government agencies. International agencies like the World Bank and United Nations regularly produce publications describing the materials that are available. In the United States, there are many sources of information presented in an organized way, of which the following are considered to be the most useful.

Since the later 1960's, a federal center in the U.S. Department of the Interior has prepared the bimonthly publication *Selected Water Resources Abstracts*, which is available from the Superintendent of Documents, Government Printing Office. This publication provides abstracts based on a comprehensive review of books, periodicals of the various professional societies, and groups and reports of governmental agencies, according to a systematic classification of water resources subjects. The center has also developed a computerized system for its abstracts whereby it can provide a search of the *Selected Water Resources Abstracts* and produce a printed listing of the abstracts for any subject that has been identified by key words.

All federal governmental agencies and many state agencies and other public and private entities, especially those supported by government funds, participate in the National Technical Information Service. As the central information source to federally sponsored research, NTIS receives some 250 research reports daily, and in 1980 had more than 750,000 document/data records covering federally sponsored research from 1964. More than 1000 Published Searches were listed in fall 1979, and NTIS was in a position to provide a customized search of its data base to retrieve abstracts for any subject area. NTIS could also make available already prepared subject searches from the data bases of the *Engineering Index*, the American Petroleum Institute, the Institute of Paper Chemistry, and the Technology Application Center.

The *Engineering Index* is published each month and it is an important source of worldwide engineering information from over 3500 sources.

The Science Information Exchange of the Smithsonian Institution can provide information on ongoing research based on the abstracts that must be provided in connection with every project sponsored by the federal government.

The Library of Congress, the Government Printing Office, and numerous university and public libraries are additional sources of information. Many of these organizations are able to carry out computerized searches.

Published and unpublished information is, of course, available from the numerous federal, state, regional, and local governmental agencies that exist. Various federal agencies, and their state and local counterparts, publish directories and other documents that provide descriptions of agency areas of interest and responsibility, and addresses where the agencies and their components may be contacted.

18.4 ARRANGEMENTS FOR PROFESSIONAL SERVICES

Large public organizations in the United States such as the federal design and construction agencies (Bureau of Reclamation, Corps of Engineers, Soil Conservation Service, and Tennessee Valley Authority) often have full rosters of specialists on their own staffs who are qualified to provide all the professional services for a project. They often have need for employing other firms and individuals, however, to supplement their own capabilities and capacity to perform work. Other public agencies and most utilities and private companies prefer to maintain small staffs and to engage consultants for most projects.

If professional services are performed in part or whole by outside consulting firms or individuals, the selection process may range from a simple designation based on previous experience with an entity to an elaborate scheme of inviting and evaluating tenders. The procedure used by many government agencies for selecting outside consultants is outlined in the following:

1. Advertisement or informational meeting with selected consulting firms.
2. Prequalification—review of material already on file or based on formal submission of qualifications.
3. Selection of consultants from whom proposals are requested—"short list."
4. Receipt and evaluation of formal proposals—methods for doing work; organization; personnel; etc. May or may not include prices; if prices are included, they may or may not be in a separate document.
5. Ranking of proposals in order of technical merit, or of a combination of technical merit and price factors.
6. Final negotiations with highest-ranked firm. If unsuccessful, negotiations with next-ranked firm.

The following are the principal methods used for reimbursement of the consulting firm:

1. Per diem payment of a fixed amount per day of services in each of several categories of professionals and subprofessionals
2. Retainer—fixed amount for services whether called on to perform them or not, or fixed amount for an expected level of services beyond which extra payments are expected
3. Salary cost times a multiplier, plus direct nonsalary expenses
4. Actual cost of services plus a fixed payment
5. Fixed lump sum for defined services
6. Percentage of construction cost
7. "Turnkey" arrangement, in which the engineering and other professional services are included as part of the payments to the construction contractor and may not be separately identified

18.5 TYPICAL COSTS OF STUDIES

A typical sequence of reports, documents, and actions for an individual water resources development has been discussed in Chapter 3. For such a project, the following are approximate guides to the cost of primarily engineering services in terms of percentage of estimated construction cost:

- Preliminary report based on reconnaissance studies—¼ to ½%
- Feasibility report—1 to 2%
- Design—4 to 6%
- Construction supervision on behalf of sponsor—5 to 10%
- Overall for the above—8 to 15%

The American Society of Civil Engineers has analyzed fees for engineering services in its *Manual 45* (1981). Median compensation is estimated for "basic services" in terms of percentage of construction cost. These services emphasize design work for an individual construction project whose general location, concept, and feasibility have already been determined, and include tasks defined in the manual for three distinct and sequential phases as follows:

Phase	Scope
1. Preliminary	Preliminary studies, layouts, and cost estimates
2. Design	Preparation of design drawings, specifications, and contract documents
3. Construction	Basic representation of client during construction

For projects of average complexity, median compensation for basic services ranges from 9.0% for a $100,000 project to 4.6% for a $100,000,000 project in 1980 dollars. For projects of above-average complexity, the values range from 11.6% to 5.6%.

Additional costs would be incurred for "special services" for field investigations, land surveys, materials testing, studies of water treatment processes, other very specialized engineering studies, and for most nonengineering activities.

Regional studies would involve costs that can be estimated only after the scope of work, level of analysis, and expected reports are defined. They could not be classified in the categories of "basic" or "special" services as used by the ASCE for individual projects.

REFERENCES

AMERICAN SOCIETY OF CIVIL ENGINEERS, "Consulting Engineering—A Guide for the Engagement of Engineering Services," Manual 45, rev. ed., 1981.

GILLETT, BILLY E., *Introduction to Operations Research*, McGraw-Hill, New York, 1976.

HILLIER, FREDERICK S., and GERALD J. LIEBERMAN, *Introduction to Operations Research*, 3rd ed., Holden-Day, San Francisco, Calif., 1980.

IBM (International Business Machines), "IBM 1130 Project Control System," Version 2, 5th ed., August 1971.

MUSSIVAND, T. V., "Application of Critical Path Method to Water Resources Planning," *Water Resources Bull.*, vol. 8, no. 4, August 1972.

TAMS (Tippets-Abbett-McCarthy-Stratton, New York), "Integrated Development of Vardar/Axios River Basin," 1975 (unpublished proposal).

TAMS (Tippets-Abbett-McCarthy-Stratton, New York), "Design of Pond Hill Reservoir," 1979a (unpublished proposal).

TAMS (Tippets-Abbett-McCarthy-Stratton, New York), "An Assessment of Environmental Impacts and Issues Concerning Hydropower Development and Operation," 1979b (unpublished proposal).

APPENDIX

Compounding and Discounting Tables

The following tables are taken from the 1973 publication "Compounding and Discounting Tables for Project Evaluation" of the Economic Development Institute, International Bank for Reconstruction and Development, Washington, D.C. This publication was edited by J. Price Gittinger and is distributed by the Johns Hopkins University Press.

Left Table — RATE 1%

Year	COMPOUNDING FACTOR FOR 1 — What an initial amount becomes when growing at compound interest	COMPOUNDING FACTOR FOR 1 PER ANNUM — Growth of equal year-end deposits all growing at compound interest	SINKING FUND FACTOR — Level deposit required each year to reach 1 by a given year
1	1.010 000	1.000 000	1.000 000
2	1.020 100	2.010 000	.497 512
3	1.030 301	3.030 100	.330 022
4	1.040 604	4.060 401	.246 281
5	1.051 010	5.101 005	.196 040
6	1.061 520	6.152 015	.162 548
7	1.072 135	7.213 535	.138 628
8	1.082 857	8.285 671	.120 690
9	1.093 685	9.368 527	.106 740
10	1.104 622	10.462 213	.095 582
11	1.115 668	11.566 835	.086 454
12	1.126 825	12.682 503	.078 849
13	1.138 093	13.809 328	.072 415
14	1.149 474	14.947 421	.066 901
15	1.160 969	16.096 896	.062 124
16	1.172 579	17.257 864	.057 945
17	1.184 304	18.430 443	.054 258
18	1.196 147	19.614 748	.050 982
19	1.208 109	20.810 895	.048 052
20	1.220 190	22.019 004	.045 415
21	1.232 392	23.239 194	.043 031
22	1.244 716	24.471 586	.040 864
23	1.257 163	25.716 302	.038 886
24	1.269 735	26.973 465	.037 073
25	1.282 432	28.243 200	.035 407
26	1.295 256	29.525 631	.033 869
27	1.308 209	30.820 888	.032 446
28	1.321 291	32.129 097	.031 124
29	1.334 504	33.450 388	.029 895
30	1.347 849	34.784 892	.028 748
31	1.361 327	36.132 740	.027 676
32	1.374 941	37.494 068	.026 671
33	1.388 690	38.869 009	.025 727
34	1.402 577	40.257 699	.024 840
35	1.416 603	41.660 276	.024 004
36	1.430 769	43.076 878	.023 214
37	1.445 076	44.507 647	.022 468
38	1.459 527	45.952 724	.021 761
39	1.474 123	47.412 251	.021 092
40	1.488 864	48.886 373	.020 456
41	1.503 752	50.375 237	.019 851
42	1.518 790	51.878 989	.019 276
43	1.533 978	53.397 779	.018 727
44	1.549 318	54.931 757	.018 204
45	1.564 811	56.481 075	.017 705
46	1.580 459	58.045 885	.017 228
47	1.596 263	59.626 344	.016 771
48	1.612 226	61.222 608	.016 334
49	1.628 348	62.834 834	.015 915
50	1.644 632	64.463 182	.015 513

Right Table — RATE 1%

DISCOUNT FACTOR — How much 1 at a future date is worth today	PRESENT WORTH OF AN ANNUITY FACTOR — How much 1 received or paid annually for X years is worth today	CAPITAL RECOVERY FACTOR — Annual payment that will repay a $1 loan in X years with compound interest on the unpaid balance	Year
.990 099	.990 099	1.010 000	1
.980 296	1.970 395	.507 512	2
.970 590	2.940 985	.340 022	3
.960 980	3.901 966	.256 281	4
.951 466	4.853 431	.206 040	5
.942 045	5.795 476	.172 548	6
.932 718	6.728 195	.148 628	7
.923 483	7.651 678	.130 690	8
.914 340	8.566 018	.116 740	9
.905 287	9.471 305	.105 582	10
.896 324	10.367 628	.096 454	11
.887 449	11.255 077	.088 849	12
.878 663	12.133 740	.082 415	13
.869 963	13.003 703	.076 901	14
.861 349	13.865 053	.072 124	15
.852 821	14.717 874	.067 945	16
.844 377	15.562 251	.064 258	17
.836 017	16.398 269	.060 982	18
.827 740	17.226 008	.058 052	19
.819 544	18.045 553	.055 415	20
.811 430	18.856 983	.053 031	21
.803 396	19.660 379	.050 864	22
.795 442	20.455 821	.048 886	23
.787 566	21.243 387	.047 073	24
.779 768	22.023 156	.045 407	25
.772 048	22.795 204	.043 869	26
.764 404	23.559 608	.042 446	27
.756 836	24.316 443	.041 124	28
.749 342	25.065 785	.039 895	29
.741 923	25.807 708	.038 748	30
.734 577	26.542 285	.037 676	31
.727 304	27.269 589	.036 671	32
.720 103	27.989 693	.035 727	33
.712 973	28.702 666	.034 840	34
.705 914	29.408 580	.034 004	35
.698 925	30.107 505	.033 214	36
.692 005	30.799 510	.032 468	37
.685 153	31.484 663	.031 761	38
.678 370	32.163 033	.031 092	39
.671 653	32.834 686	.030 456	40
.665 003	33.499 689	.029 851	41
.658 419	34.158 108	.029 276	42
.651 900	34.810 008	.028 727	43
.645 445	35.455 454	.028 204	44
.639 055	36.094 508	.027 705	45
.632 728	36.727 236	.027 228	46
.626 463	37.353 699	.026 771	47
.620 260	37.973 959	.026 334	48
.614 119	38.588 079	.025 915	49
.608 039	39.196 118	.025 513	50

CAPITAL RECOVERY / PRESENT WORTH / DISCOUNT (RATE 2%)

Year	CAPITAL RECOVERY FACTOR — Annual payment that will repay a $1 loan in X years with compound interest on the unpaid balance	PRESENT WORTH OF AN ANNUITY FACTOR — How much 1 received or paid annually for X years is worth today	DISCOUNT FACTOR — How much 1 at a future date is worth today
1	1.020 000	.980 392	.980 392
2	.515 050	1.941 561	.961 169
3	.346 755	2.883 883	.942 322
4	.262 624	3.807 729	.923 845
5	.212 158	4.713 460	.905 731
6	.178 526	5.601 431	.887 971
7	.154 512	6.471 991	.870 560
8	.136 510	7.325 481	.853 490
9	.122 515	8.162 237	.836 755
10	.111 327	8.982 585	.820 348
11	.102 178	9.786 848	.804 263
12	.094 560	10.575 341	.788 493
13	.088 118	11.348 374	.773 033
14	.082 602	12.106 249	.757 875
15	.077 825	12.849 264	.743 015
16	.073 650	13.577 709	.728 446
17	.069 970	14.291 872	.714 163
18	.066 702	14.992 031	.700 159
19	.063 782	15.678 462	.686 431
20	.061 157	16.351 433	.672 971
21	.058 785	17.011 209	.659 776
22	.056 631	17.658 048	.646 839
23	.054 668	18.292 204	.634 156
24	.052 871	18.913 926	.621 721
25	.051 220	19.523 456	.609 531
26	.049 699	20.121 036	.597 579
27	.048 293	20.706 898	.585 862
28	.046 990	21.281 272	.574 375
29	.045 778	21.844 385	.563 112
30	.044 650	22.396 456	.552 071
31	.043 596	22.937 702	.541 246
32	.042 611	23.468 335	.530 633
33	.041 687	23.988 564	.520 229
34	.040 819	24.498 592	.510 028
35	.040 002	24.998 619	.500 028
36	.039 233	25.488 842	.490 223
37	.038 507	25.969 453	.480 611
38	.037 821	26.440 641	.471 187
39	.037 171	26.902 589	.461 948
40	.036 556	27.355 479	.452 890
41	.035 972	27.799 489	.444 010
42	.035 417	28.234 794	.435 304
43	.034 890	28.661 562	.426 769
44	.034 388	29.079 963	.418 401
45	.033 910	29.490 160	.410 197
46	.033 453	29.892 314	.402 154
47	.033 018	30.286 582	.394 268
48	.032 602	30.673 120	.386 538
49	.032 204	31.052 078	.378 958
50	.031 823	31.423 606	.371 528

RATE 2%

COMPOUNDING FACTORS / SINKING FUND (RATE 2%)

Year	COMPOUNDING FACTOR FOR 1 — What an initial amount becomes when growing at compound interest	COMPOUNDING FACTOR FOR 1 PER ANNUM — Growth of equal year-end deposits all growing at compound interest	SINKING FUND FACTOR — Level deposit required each year to reach 1 by a given year
1	1.020 000	1.000 000	1.000 000
2	1.040 400	2.020 000	.495 050
3	1.061 208	3.060 400	.326 755
4	1.082 432	4.121 608	.242 624
5	1.104 081	5.204 040	.192 158
6	1.126 162	6.308 121	.158 526
7	1.148 686	7.434 283	.134 512
8	1.171 659	8.582 969	.116 510
9	1.195 093	9.754 628	.102 515
10	1.218 994	10.949 721	.091 327
11	1.243 374	12.168 715	.082 178
12	1.268 242	13.412 090	.074 560
13	1.293 607	14.680 332	.068 118
14	1.319 479	15.973 938	.062 602
15	1.345 868	17.293 417	.057 825
16	1.372 786	18.639 285	.053 650
17	1.400 241	20.012 071	.049 970
18	1.428 246	21.412 312	.046 702
19	1.456 811	22.840 559	.043 782
20	1.485 947	24.297 370	.041 157
21	1.515 666	25.783 317	.038 785
22	1.545 980	27.298 984	.036 631
23	1.576 899	28.844 963	.034 668
24	1.608 437	30.421 862	.032 871
25	1.640 606	32.030 300	.031 220
26	1.673 418	33.670 906	.029 699
27	1.706 886	35.344 324	.028 293
28	1.741 024	37.051 210	.026 990
29	1.775 845	38.792 235	.025 778
30	1.811 362	40.568 079	.024 650
31	1.847 589	42.379 441	.023 596
32	1.884 541	44.227 030	.022 611
33	1.922 231	46.111 570	.021 687
34	1.960 676	48.033 802	.020 819
35	1.999 890	49.994 478	.020 002
36	2.039 887	51.994 367	.019 233
37	2.080 685	54.034 255	.018 507
38	2.122 299	56.114 940	.017 821
39	2.164 745	58.237 238	.017 171
40	2.208 040	60.401 983	.016 556
41	2.252 200	62.610 023	.015 972
42	2.297 244	64.862 223	.015 417
43	2.343 189	67.159 468	.014 890
44	2.390 053	69.502 657	.014 388
45	2.437 854	71.892 710	.013 910
46	2.486 611	74.330 564	.013 453
47	2.536 344	76.817 176	.013 018
48	2.587 070	79.353 519	.012 602
49	2.638 812	81.940 590	.012 204
50	2.691 588	84.579 401	.011 823

Year	COMPOUNDING FACTOR FOR 1 — What an initial amount becomes when growing at compound interest	COMPOUNDING FACTOR FOR 1 PER ANNUM — Growth of equal year-end deposits all growing at compound interest	SINKING FUND FACTOR — Level deposit required each year to reach 1 by a given year
1	1.030 000	1.000 000	1.000 000
2	1.060 900	2.030 000	.492 611
3	1.092 727	3.090 900	.323 530
4	1.125 509	4.183 627	.239 027
5	1.159 274	5.309 136	.188 355
6	1.194 052	6.468 410	.154 598
7	1.229 874	7.662 462	.130 506
8	1.266 770	8.892 336	.112 456
9	1.304 773	10.159 106	.098 434
10	1.343 916	11.463 879	.087 231
11	1.384 234	12.807 796	.078 077
12	1.425 761	14.192 030	.070 462
13	1.468 534	15.617 790	.064 030
14	1.512 590	17.086 324	.058 526
15	1.557 967	18.598 914	.053 767
16	1.604 706	20.156 881	.049 611
17	1.652 848	21.761 588	.045 953
18	1.702 433	23.414 435	.042 709
19	1.753 506	25.116 868	.039 814
20	1.806 111	26.870 374	.037 216
21	1.860 295	28.676 486	.034 872
22	1.916 103	30.536 780	.032 747
23	1.973 587	32.452 884	.030 814
24	2.032 794	34.426 470	.029 047
25	2.093 778	36.459 264	.027 428
26	2.156 591	38.553 042	.025 938
27	2.221 289	40.709 634	.024 564
28	2.287 928	42.930 923	.023 293
29	2.356 566	45.218 850	.022 115
30	2.427 262	47.575 416	.021 019
31	2.500 080	50.002 678	.019 999
32	2.575 083	52.502 759	.019 047
33	2.652 335	55.077 841	.018 156
34	2.731 905	57.730 177	.017 322
35	2.813 862	60.462 082	.016 539
36	2.898 278	63.275 944	.015 804
37	2.985 227	66.174 223	.015 112
38	3.074 783	69.159 449	.014 459
39	3.167 027	72.234 233	.013 844
40	3.262 038	75.401 260	.013 262
41	3.359 899	78.663 298	.012 712
42	3.460 696	82.023 196	.012 192
43	3.564 517	85.483 892	.011 698
44	3.671 452	89.048 409	.011 230
45	3.781 596	92.719 861	.010 785
46	3.895 044	96.501 457	.010 363
47	4.011 895	100.396 501	.009 961
48	4.132 252	104.408 396	.009 578
49	4.256 219	108.540 648	.009 213
50	4.383 906	112.796 867	.008 865

DISCOUNT FACTOR — How much 1 at a future date is worth today	PRESENT WORTH OF AN ANNUITY FACTOR — How much 1 received or paid annually for X years is worth today	CAPITAL RECOVERY FACTOR — Annual payment that will repay a $1 loan in X years with compound interest on the unpaid balance	Year
.970 874	.970 874	1.030 000	1
.942 596	1.913 470	.522 611	2
.915 142	2.828 611	.353 530	3
.888 487	3.717 098	.269 027	4
.862 609	4.579 707	.218 355	5
.837 484	5.417 191	.184 598	6
.813 092	6.230 283	.160 506	7
.789 409	7.019 692	.142 456	8
.766 417	7.786 109	.128 434	9
.744 094	8.530 203	.117 231	10
.722 421	9.252 624	.108 077	11
.701 380	9.954 004	.100 462	12
.680 951	10.634 955	.094 030	13
.661 118	11.296 073	.088 526	14
.641 862	11.937 935	.083 767	15
.623 167	12.561 102	.079 611	16
.605 016	13.166 118	.075 953	17
.587 395	13.753 513	.072 709	18
.570 286	14.323 799	.069 814	19
.553 676	14.877 475	.067 216	20
.537 549	15.415 024	.064 872	21
.521 893	15.936 917	.062 747	22
.506 692	16.443 608	.060 814	23
.491 934	16.935 542	.059 047	24
.477 606	17.413 148	.057 428	25
.463 695	17.876 842	.055 938	26
.450 189	18.327 031	.054 564	27
.437 077	18.764 108	.053 293	28
.424 346	19.188 455	.052 115	29
.411 987	19.600 441	.051 019	30
.399 987	20.000 428	.049 999	31
.388 337	20.388 766	.049 047	32
.377 026	20.765 792	.048 156	33
.366 045	21.131 837	.047 322	34
.355 383	21.487 220	.046 539	35
.345 032	21.832 252	.045 804	36
.334 983	22.167 235	.045 112	37
.325 226	22.492 462	.044 459	38
.315 754	22.808 215	.043 844	39
.306 557	23.114 772	.043 262	40
.297 628	23.412 400	.042 712	41
.288 959	23.701 359	.042 192	42
.280 543	23.981 902	.041 698	43
.272 372	24.254 274	.041 230	44
.264 439	24.518 713	.040 785	45
.256 737	24.775 449	.040 363	46
.249 259	25.024 708	.039 961	47
.241 999	25.266 707	.039 578	48
.234 950	25.501 657	.039 213	49
.228 107	25.729 764	.038 865	50

RATE 4%

Year	COMPOUNDING FACTOR FOR 1 — What an initial amount becomes when growing at compound interest	COMPOUNDING FACTOR FOR 1 PER ANNUM — Growth of equal year-end deposits all growing at compound interest	SINKING FUND FACTOR — Level deposit required each year to reach 1 by a given year
1	1.040 000	1.000 000	1.000 000
2	1.081 600	2.040 000	.490 196
3	1.124 864	3.121 600	.320 349
4	1.169 859	4.246 464	.235 490
5	1.216 653	5.416 323	.184 627
6	1.265 319	6.632 975	.150 762
7	1.315 932	7.898 294	.126 610
8	1.368 569	9.214 226	.108 528
9	1.423 312	10.582 795	.094 493
10	1.480 244	12.006 107	.083 291
11	1.539 454	13.486 351	.074 149
12	1.601 032	15.025 805	.066 552
13	1.665 074	16.626 838	.060 144
14	1.731 676	18.291 911	.054 669
15	1.800 944	20.023 588	.049 941
16	1.872 981	21.824 531	.045 820
17	1.947 900	23.697 512	.042 199
18	2.025 817	25.645 413	.038 993
19	2.106 849	27.671 229	.036 139
20	2.191 123	29.778 079	.033 582
21	2.278 768	31.969 202	.031 280
22	2.369 919	34.247 970	.029 199
23	2.464 716	36.617 889	.027 309
24	2.563 304	39.082 604	.025 587
25	2.665 836	41.645 908	.024 012
26	2.772 470	44.311 745	.022 567
27	2.883 369	47.084 214	.021 239
28	2.998 703	49.967 583	.020 013
29	3.118 651	52.966 286	.018 880
30	3.243 398	56.084 938	.017 830
31	3.373 133	59.328 335	.016 855
32	3.508 059	62.701 469	.015 949
33	3.648 381	66.209 527	.015 104
34	3.794 316	69.857 909	.014 315
35	3.946 089	73.652 225	.013 577
36	4.103 933	77.598 314	.012 887
37	4.268 090	81.702 246	.012 240
38	4.438 813	85.970 336	.011 632
39	4.616 366	90.409 150	.011 061
40	4.801 021	95.025 516	.010 523
41	4.993 061	99.826 536	.010 017
42	5.192 784	104.819 598	.009 540
43	5.400 495	110.012 382	.009 090
44	5.616 515	115.412 877	.008 665
45	5.841 176	121.029 392	.008 262
46	6.074 823	126.870 568	.007 882
47	6.317 816	132.945 390	.007 522
48	6.570 528	139.263 206	.007 181
49	6.833 349	145.833 734	.006 857
50	7.106 683	152.667 084	.006 550

DISCOUNT FACTOR — How much 1 at a future date is worth today	PRESENT WORTH OF AN ANNUITY FACTOR — How much 1 received or paid annually for X years is worth today	CAPITAL RECOVERY FACTOR — Annual payment that will repay a $1 loan in X years with compound interest on the unpaid balance	Year
.961 538	.961 538	1.040 000	1
.924 556	1.886 095	.530 196	2
.888 996	2.775 091	.360 349	3
.854 804	3.629 895	.275 490	4
.821 927	4.451 822	.224 627	5
.790 315	5.242 137	.190 762	6
.759 918	6.002 055	.166 610	7
.730 690	6.732 745	.148 528	8
.702 587	7.435 332	.134 493	9
.675 564	8.110 896	.123 291	10
.649 581	8.760 477	.114 149	11
.624 597	9.385 074	.106 552	12
.600 574	9.985 648	.100 144	13
.577 475	10.563 123	.094 669	14
.555 265	11.118 387	.089 941	15
.533 908	11.652 296	.085 820	16
.513 373	12.165 669	.082 199	17
.493 628	12.659 297	.078 993	18
.474 642	13.133 939	.076 139	19
.456 387	13.590 326	.073 582	20
.438 834	14.029 160	.071 280	21
.421 955	14.451 115	.069 199	22
.405 726	14.856 842	.067 309	23
.390 121	15.246 963	.065 587	24
.375 117	15.622 080	.064 012	25
.360 689	15.982 769	.062 567	26
.346 817	16.329 586	.061 239	27
.333 477	16.663 063	.060 013	28
.320 651	16.983 715	.058 880	29
.308 319	17.292 033	.057 830	30
.296 460	17.588 494	.056 855	31
.285 058	17.873 551	.055 949	32
.274 094	18.147 646	.055 104	33
.263 552	18.411 198	.054 315	34
.253 415	18.664 613	.053 577	35
.243 669	18.908 282	.052 887	36
.234 297	19.142 579	.052 240	37
.225 285	19.367 864	.051 632	38
.216 621	19.584 485	.051 061	39
.208 289	19.792 774	.050 523	40
.200 278	19.993 052	.050 017	41
.192 575	20.185 627	.049 540	42
.185 168	20.370 795	.049 090	43
.178 046	20.548 841	.048 665	44
.171 198	20.720 040	.048 262	45
.164 614	20.884 654	.047 882	46
.158 283	21.042 936	.047 522	47
.152 195	21.195 131	.047 181	48
.146 341	21.341 472	.046 857	49
.140 713	21.482 185	.046 550	50

Year	COMPOUNDING FACTOR FOR 1 — What an initial amount becomes when growing at compound interest	COMPOUNDING FACTOR FOR 1 PER ANNUM — Growth of equal year-end deposits all growing at compound interest	SINKING FUND FACTOR — Level deposit required each year to reach 1 by a given year
1	1.050 000	1.000 000	1.000 000
2	1.102 500	2.050 000	.487 805
3	1.157 625	3.152 500	.317 209
4	1.215 506	4.310 125	.232 012
5	1.276 282	5.525 631	.180 975
6	1.340 096	6.801 913	.147 017
7	1.407 100	8.142 008	.122 820
8	1.477 455	9.549 109	.104 722
9	1.551 328	11.026 564	.090 690
10	1.628 895	12.577 893	.079 505
11	1.710 339	14.206 787	.070 389
12	1.795 856	15.917 127	.062 825
13	1.885 649	17.712 983	.056 456
14	1.979 932	19.598 632	.051 024
15	2.078 928	21.578 564	.046 342
16	2.182 875	23.675 492	.042 270
17	2.292 018	25.840 366	.038 699
18	2.406 619	28.132 385	.035 546
19	2.526 950	30.539 004	.032 745
20	2.653 298	33.065 954	.030 243
21	2.785 963	35.719 252	.027 996
22	2.925 261	38.505 214	.025 971
23	3.071 524	41.430 475	.024 137
24	3.225 100	44.501 999	.022 471
25	3.386 355	47.727 099	.020 952
26	3.555 673	51.113 454	.019 564
27	3.733 456	54.669 126	.018 292
28	3.920 129	58.402 583	.017 123
29	4.116 136	62.322 712	.016 046
30	4.321 942	66.438 848	.015 051
31	4.538 039	70.760 790	.014 132
32	4.764 941	75.298 829	.013 280
33	5.003 189	80.063 771	.012 490
34	5.253 348	85.066 959	.011 755
35	5.516 015	90.320 307	.011 072
36	5.791 816	95.836 323	.010 434
37	6.081 407	101.628 139	.009 840
38	6.385 477	107.709 546	.009 284
39	6.704 751	114.095 023	.008 765
40	7.039 989	120.799 774	.008 278
41	7.391 988	127.839 763	.007 822
42	7.761 588	135.231 751	.007 395
43	8.149 667	142.993 339	.006 993
44	8.557 150	151.143 006	.006 616
45	8.985 008	159.700 156	.006 262
46	9.434 258	168.685 164	.005 928
47	9.905 971	178.119 422	.005 614
48	10.401 270	188.025 393	.005 318
49	10.921 333	198.426 663	.005 040
50	11.467 400	209.347 996	.004 777

DISCOUNT FACTOR — How much 1 at a future date is worth today	PRESENT WORTH OF AN ANNUITY FACTOR — How much 1 received or paid annually for X years is worth today	CAPITAL RECOVERY FACTOR — Annual payment that will repay a $1 loan in X years with compound interest on the unpaid balance	Year
.952 381	.952 381	1.050 000	1
.907 029	1.859 410	.537 805	2
.863 838	2.723 248	.367 209	3
.822 702	3.545 951	.282 012	4
.783 526	4.329 477	.230 975	5
.746 215	5.075 692	.197 017	6
.710 681	5.786 373	.172 820	7
.676 839	6.463 213	.154 722	8
.644 609	7.107 822	.140 690	9
.613 913	7.721 735	.129 505	10
.584 679	8.306 414	.120 389	11
.556 837	8.863 252	.112 825	12
.530 321	9.393 573	.106 456	13
.505 068	9.898 641	.101 024	14
.481 017	10.379 658	.096 342	15
.458 112	10.837 770	.092 270	16
.436 297	11.274 066	.088 699	17
.415 521	11.689 587	.085 546	18
.395 734	12.085 321	.082 745	19
.376 889	12.462 210	.080 243	20
.358 942	12.821 153	.077 996	21
.341 850	13.163 003	.075 971	22
.325 571	13.488 574	.074 137	23
.310 068	13.798 642	.072 471	24
.295 303	14.093 945	.070 952	25
.281 241	14.375 185	.069 564	26
.267 848	14.643 034	.068 292	27
.255 094	14.898 127	.067 123	28
.242 946	15.141 074	.066 046	29
.231 377	15.372 451	.065 051	30
.220 359	15.592 811	.064 132	31
.209 866	15.802 677	.063 280	32
.199 873	16.002 549	.062 490	33
.190 355	16.192 904	.061 755	34
.181 290	16.374 194	.061 072	35
.172 657	16.546 852	.060 434	36
.164 436	16.711 287	.059 840	37
.156 605	16.867 893	.059 284	38
.149 148	17.017 041	.058 765	39
.142 046	17.159 086	.058 278	40
.135 282	17.294 368	.057 822	41
.128 840	17.423 208	.057 395	42
.122 704	17.545 912	.056 993	43
.116 861	17.662 773	.056 616	44
.111 297	17.774 070	.056 262	45
.105 997	17.880 066	.055 928	46
.100 949	17.981 016	.055 614	47
.096 142	18.077 158	.055 318	48
.091 564	18.168 722	.055 040	49
.087 204	18.255 925	.054 777	50

RATE 6%

Year	COMPOUNDING FACTOR FOR 1 — What an initial amount becomes when growing at compound interest	COMPOUNDING FACTOR FOR 1 PER ANNUM — Growth of equal year-end deposits all growing at compound interest	SINKING FUND FACTOR — Level deposit required each year to reach 1 by a given year
1	1.060 000	1.000 000	1.000 000
2	1.123 600	2.060 000	.485 437
3	1.191 016	3.183 600	.314 110
4	1.262 477	4.374 616	.228 591
5	1.338 226	5.637 093	.177 396
6	1.418 519	6.975 319	.143 363
7	1.503 630	8.393 838	.119 135
8	1.593 848	9.897 468	.101 036
9	1.689 479	11.491 316	.087 022
10	1.790 848	13.180 795	.075 868
11	1.898 299	14.971 643	.066 793
12	2.012 196	16.869 941	.059 277
13	2.132 928	18.882 138	.052 960
14	2.260 904	21.015 066	.047 585
15	2.396 558	23.275 970	.042 963
16	2.540 352	25.672 528	.038 952
17	2.692 773	28.212 880	.035 445
18	2.854 339	30.905 653	.032 357
19	3.025 600	33.759 992	.029 621
20	3.207 135	36.785 591	.027 185
21	3.399 564	39.992 727	.025 005
22	3.603 537	43.392 290	.023 046
23	3.819 750	46.995 828	.021 278
24	4.048 935	50.815 577	.019 679
25	4.291 871	54.864 512	.018 227
26	4.549 383	59.156 383	.016 904
27	4.822 346	63.705 766	.015 697
28	5.111 687	68.528 112	.014 593
29	5.418 388	73.639 798	.013 580
30	5.743 491	79.058 186	.012 649
31	6.088 101	84.801 677	.011 792
32	6.453 387	90.889 778	.011 002
33	6.840 590	97.343 165	.010 273
34	7.251 025	104.183 755	.009 598
35	7.686 087	111.434 780	.008 974
36	8.147 252	119.120 867	.008 395
37	8.636 087	127.268 119	.007 857
38	9.154 252	135.904 206	.007 358
39	9.703 507	145.058 458	.006 894
40	10.285 718	154.761 966	.006 462
41	10.902 861	165.047 684	.006 059
42	11.557 033	175.950 545	.005 683
43	12.250 455	187.507 577	.005 333
44	12.985 482	199.758 032	.005 006
45	13.764 611	212.743 514	.004 700
46	14.590 487	226.508 125	.004 415
47	15.465 917	241.098 612	.004 148
48	16.393 872	256.564 529	.003 898
49	17.377 504	272.958 401	.003 664
50	18.420 154	290.335 905	.003 444

DISCOUNT FACTOR — How much 1 at a future date is worth today	PRESENT WORTH OF AN ANNUITY FACTOR — How much 1 received or paid annually for X years is worth today	CAPITAL RECOVERY FACTOR — Annual payment that will repay a $1 loan in X years with compound interest on the unpaid balance	Year
.943 396	.943 396	1.060 000	1
.889 996	1.833 393	.545 437	2
.839 619	2.673 012	.374 110	3
.792 094	3.465 106	.288 591	4
.747 258	4.212 364	.237 396	5
.704 961	4.917 324	.203 363	6
.665 057	5.582 381	.179 135	7
.627 412	6.209 794	.161 036	8
.591 898	6.801 692	.147 022	9
.558 395	7.360 087	.135 868	10
.526 788	7.886 875	.126 793	11
.496 969	8.383 844	.119 277	12
.468 839	8.852 683	.112 960	13
.442 301	9.294 984	.107 585	14
.417 265	9.712 249	.102 963	15
.393 646	10.105 895	.098 952	16
.371 364	10.477 260	.095 445	17
.350 344	10.827 603	.092 357	18
.330 513	11.158 116	.089 621	19
.311 805	11.469 921	.087 185	20
.294 155	11.764 077	.085 005	21
.277 505	12.041 582	.083 046	22
.261 797	12.303 379	.081 278	23
.246 979	12.550 358	.079 679	24
.232 999	12.783 356	.078 227	25
.219 810	13.003 166	.076 904	26
.207 368	13.210 534	.075 697	27
.195 630	13.406 164	.074 593	28
.184 557	13.590 721	.073 580	29
.174 110	13.764 831	.072 649	30
.164 255	13.929 086	.071 792	31
.154 957	14.084 043	.071 002	32
.146 186	14.230 230	.070 273	33
.137 912	14.368 141	.069 598	34
.130 105	14.498 246	.068 974	35
.122 741	14.620 987	.068 395	36
.115 793	14.736 780	.067 857	37
.109 239	14.846 019	.067 358	38
.103 056	14.949 075	.066 894	39
.097 222	15.046 297	.066 462	40
.091 719	15.138 016	.066 059	41
.086 527	15.224 543	.065 683	42
.081 630	15.306 173	.065 333	43
.077 009	15.383 182	.065 006	44
.072 650	15.455 832	.064 700	45
.068 538	15.524 370	.064 415	46
.064 658	15.589 028	.064 148	47
.060 998	15.650 027	.063 898	48
.057 546	15.707 572	.063 664	49
.054 288	15.761 861	.063 444	50

RATE 7% — Left Table

Year	COMPOUNDING FACTOR FOR 1 — What an initial amount becomes when growing at compound interest	COMPOUNDING FACTOR FOR 1 PER ANNUM — Growth of equal year-end deposits all growing at compound interest	SINKING FUND FACTOR — Level deposit required each year to reach 1 by a given year
1	1.070 000	1.000 000	1.000 000
2	1.144 900	2.070 000	.483 092
3	1.225 043	3.214 900	.311 052
4	1.310 796	4.439 943	.225 228
5	1.402 552	5.750 739	.173 891
6	1.500 730	7.153 291	.139 796
7	1.605 781	8.654 021	.115 553
8	1.718 186	10.259 803	.097 468
9	1.838 459	11.977 989	.083 486
10	1.967 151	13.816 448	.072 378
11	2.104 852	15.783 599	.063 357
12	2.252 192	17.888 451	.055 902
13	2.409 845	20.140 643	.049 651
14	2.578 534	22.550 488	.044 345
15	2.759 032	25.129 022	.039 795
16	2.952 164	27.888 054	.035 858
17	3.158 815	30.840 217	.032 425
18	3.379 932	33.999 033	.029 413
19	3.616 528	37.378 965	.026 753
20	3.869 684	40.995 492	.024 393
21	4.140 562	44.865 177	.022 289
22	4.430 402	49.005 739	.020 406
23	4.740 530	53.436 141	.018 714
24	5.072 367	58.176 671	.017 189
25	5.427 433	63.249 038	.015 811
26	5.807 353	68.676 470	.014 561
27	6.213 868	74.483 823	.013 426
28	6.648 838	80.697 691	.012 392
29	7.114 257	87.346 529	.011 449
30	7.612 255	94.460 786	.010 586
31	8.145 113	102.073 041	.009 797
32	8.715 271	110.218 154	.009 073
33	9.325 340	118.933 425	.008 408
34	9.978 114	128.258 765	.007 797
35	10.676 581	138.236 878	.007 234
36	11.423 942	148.913 460	.006 715
37	12.223 618	160.337 402	.006 237
38	13.079 271	172.561 020	.005 795
39	13.994 820	185.640 292	.005 387
40	14.974 458	199.635 112	.005 009
41	16.022 670	214.609 570	.004 660
42	17.144 257	230.632 240	.004 336
43	18.344 355	247.776 496	.004 036
44	19.628 460	266.120 851	.003 758
45	21.002 452	285.749 311	.003 500
46	22.472 623	306.751 763	.003 260
47	24.045 707	329.224 386	.003 037
48	25.728 907	353.270 093	.002 831
49	27.529 930	378.999 000	.002 639
50	29.457 025	406.528 929	.002 460

RATE 7% — Right Table

DISCOUNT FACTOR — How much 1 at a future date is worth today	PRESENT WORTH OF AN ANNUITY FACTOR — How much 1 received or paid annually for X years is worth today	CAPITAL RECOVERY FACTOR — Annual payment that will repay a $1 loan in X years with compound interest on the unpaid balance	Year
.934 579	.934 579	1.070 000	1
.873 439	1.808 018	.553 092	2
.816 298	2.624 316	.381 052	3
.762 895	3.387 211	.295 228	4
.712 986	4.100 197	.243 891	5
.666 342	4.766 540	.209 796	6
.622 750	5.389 289	.185 553	7
.582 009	5.971 299	.167 468	8
.543 934	6.515 232	.153 486	9
.508 349	7.023 582	.142 378	10
.475 093	7.498 674	.133 357	11
.444 012	7.942 686	.125 902	12
.414 964	8.357 651	.119 651	13
.387 817	8.745 468	.114 345	14
.362 446	9.107 914	.109 795	15
.338 735	9.446 649	.105 858	16
.316 574	9.763 223	.102 425	17
.295 864	10.059 087	.099 413	18
.276 508	10.335 595	.096 753	19
.258 419	10.594 014	.094 393	20
.241 513	10.835 527	.092 289	21
.225 713	11.061 240	.090 406	22
.210 947	11.272 187	.088 714	23
.197 147	11.469 334	.087 189	24
.184 249	11.653 583	.085 811	25
.172 195	11.825 779	.084 561	26
.160 930	11.986 709	.083 426	27
.150 402	12.137 111	.082 392	28
.140 563	12.277 674	.081 449	29
.131 367	12.409 041	.080 586	30
.122 773	12.531 814	.079 797	31
.114 741	12.646 555	.079 073	32
.107 235	12.753 790	.078 408	33
.100 219	12.854 009	.077 797	34
.093 663	12.947 672	.077 234	35
.087 535	13.035 208	.076 715	36
.081 809	13.117 017	.076 237	37
.076 457	13.193 473	.075 795	38
.071 455	13.264 928	.075 387	39
.066 780	13.331 709	.075 009	40
.062 412	13.394 120	.074 660	41
.058 329	13.452 449	.074 336	42
.054 513	13.506 962	.074 036	43
.050 946	13.557 908	.073 758	44
.047 613	13.605 522	.073 500	45
.044 499	13.650 020	.073 260	46
.041 587	13.691 608	.073 037	47
.038 867	13.730 474	.072 831	48
.036 324	13.766 799	.072 639	49
.033 948	13.800 746	.072 460	50

RATE 8%

Year	COMPOUNDING FACTOR FOR 1 — What an initial amount becomes when growing at compound interest	COMPOUNDING FACTOR FOR 1 PER ANNUM — Growth of equal year-end deposits all growing at compound interest	SINKING FUND FACTOR — Level deposit required each year to reach 1 by a given year
1	1.080 000	1.000 000	1.000 000
2	1.166 400	2.080 000	.480 769
3	1.259 712	3.246 400	.308 034
4	1.360 489	4.506 112	.221 921
5	1.469 328	5.866 601	.170 456
6	1.586 874	7.335 929	.136 315
7	1.713 824	8.922 803	.112 072
8	1.850 930	10.636 628	.094 015
9	1.999 005	12.487 558	.080 080
10	2.158 925	14.486 562	.069 029
11	2.331 639	16.645 487	.060 076
12	2.518 170	18.977 126	.052 695
13	2.719 624	21.495 297	.046 522
14	2.937 194	24.214 920	.041 297
15	3.172 169	27.152 169	.036 830
16	3.425 943	30.324 283	.032 977
17	3.700 018	33.750 226	.029 629
18	3.996 019	37.450 244	.026 702
19	4.315 701	41.446 263	.024 128
20	4.660 957	45.761 964	.021 852
21	5.033 834	50.422 921	.019 832
22	5.436 540	55.456 755	.018 032
23	5.871 464	60.893 296	.016 422
24	6.341 181	66.764 759	.014 978
25	6.848 475	73.105 940	.013 679
26	7.396 353	79.954 415	.012 507
27	7.988 061	87.350 768	.011 448
28	8.627 106	95.338 830	.010 489
29	9.317 275	103.965 936	.009 619
30	10.062 657	113.283 211	.008 827
31	10.867 669	123.345 868	.008 107
32	11.737 083	134.213 537	.007 451
33	12.676 050	145.950 620	.006 852
34	13.690 134	158.626 670	.006 304
35	14.785 344	172.316 804	.005 803
36	15.968 172	187.102 148	.005 345
37	17.245 626	203.070 320	.004 924
38	18.625 276	220.315 945	.004 539
39	20.115 298	238.941 221	.004 185
40	21.724 521	259.056 519	.003 860
41	23.462 483	280.781 040	.003 561
42	25.339 482	304.243 523	.003 287
43	27.366 640	329.583 005	.003 034
44	29.555 972	356.949 646	.002 802
45	31.920 449	386.505 617	.002 587
46	34.474 085	418.426 067	.002 390
47	37.232 012	452.900 152	.002 208
48	40.210 573	490.132 164	.002 040
49	43.427 419	530.342 737	.001 886
50	46.901 613	573.770 156	.001 743

Year	DISCOUNT FACTOR — How much 1 at a future date is worth today	PRESENT WORTH OF AN ANNUITY FACTOR — How much 1 received or paid annually for X years is worth today	CAPITAL RECOVERY FACTOR — Annual payment that will repay a $1 loan in X years with compound interest on the unpaid balance
1	.925 926	.925 926	1.080 000
2	.857 339	1.783 265	.560 769
3	.793 832	2.577 097	.388 034
4	.735 030	3.312 127	.301 921
5	.680 583	3.992 710	.250 456
6	.630 170	4.622 880	.216 315
7	.583 490	5.206 370	.192 072
8	.540 269	5.746 639	.174 015
9	.500 249	6.246 888	.160 080
10	.463 193	6.710 081	.149 029
11	.428 883	7.138 964	.140 076
12	.397 114	7.536 078	.132 695
13	.367 698	7.903 776	.126 522
14	.340 461	8.244 237	.121 297
15	.315 242	8.559 479	.116 830
16	.291 890	8.851 369	.112 977
17	.270 269	9.121 638	.109 629
18	.250 249	9.371 887	.106 702
19	.231 712	9.603 599	.104 128
20	.214 548	9.818 147	.101 852
21	.198 656	10.016 803	.099 832
22	.183 941	10.200 744	.098 032
23	.170 315	10.371 059	.096 422
24	.157 699	10.528 758	.094 978
25	.146 018	10.674 776	.093 679
26	.135 202	10.809 978	.092 507
27	.125 187	10.935 165	.091 448
28	.115 914	11.051 078	.090 489
29	.107 328	11.158 406	.089 619
30	.099 377	11.257 783	.088 827
31	.092 016	11.349 799	.088 107
32	.085 200	11.434 999	.087 451
33	.078 889	11.513 888	.086 852
34	.073 045	11.586 934	.086 304
35	.067 635	11.654 568	.085 803
36	.062 625	11.717 193	.085 345
37	.057 986	11.775 179	.084 924
38	.053 690	11.828 869	.084 539
39	.049 713	11.878 582	.084 185
40	.046 031	11.924 613	.083 860
41	.042 621	11.967 235	.083 561
42	.039 464	12.006 699	.083 287
43	.036 541	12.043 240	.083 034
44	.033 834	12.077 074	.082 802
45	.031 328	12.108 402	.082 587
46	.029 007	12.137 409	.082 390
47	.026 859	12.164 267	.082 208
48	.024 869	12.189 136	.082 040
49	.023 027	12.212 163	.081 886
50	.021 321	12.233 485	.081 743

Year	COMPOUNDING FACTOR FOR 1 What an initial amount becomes when growing at compound interest	COMPOUNDING FACTOR FOR 1 PER ANNUM Growth of equal year-end deposits all growing at compound interest	SINKING FUND FACTOR Level deposit required each year to reach 1 by a given year
1	1.090 000	1.000 000	1.000 000
2	1.188 100	2.090 000	.478 469
3	1.295 029	3.278 100	.305 055
4	1.411 582	4.573 129	.218 669
5	1.538 624	5.984 711	.167 092
6	1.677 100	7.523 335	.132 920
7	1.828 039	9.200 435	.108 691
8	1.992 563	11.028 474	.090 674
9	2.171 893	13.021 036	.076 799
10	2.367 364	15.192 930	.065 820
11	2.580 426	17.560 293	.056 947
12	2.812 665	20.140 720	.049 651
13	3.065 805	22.953 385	.043 567
14	3.341 727	26.019 189	.038 433
15	3.642 482	29.360 916	.034 059
16	3.970 306	33.003 399	.030 300
17	4.327 633	36.973 705	.027 046
18	4.717 120	41.301 338	.024 212
19	5.141 661	46.018 458	.021 730
20	5.604 411	51.160 120	.019 546
21	6.108 808	56.764 530	.017 617
22	6.658 600	62.873 338	.015 905
23	7.257 874	69.531 939	.014 382
24	7.911 083	76.789 813	.013 023
25	8.623 081	84.700 896	.011 806
26	9.399 158	93.323 977	.010 715
27	10.245 082	102.723 135	.009 735
28	11.167 140	112.968 217	.008 852
29	12.172 182	124.135 356	.008 056
30	13.267 678	136.307 678	.007 336
31	14.461 770	149.575 217	.006 686
32	15.763 329	164.036 987	.006 096
33	17.182 028	179.800 315	.005 562
34	18.728 411	196.982 344	.005 077
35	20.413 968	215.710 755	.004 636
36	22.251 225	236.124 723	.004 235
37	24.253 835	258.375 948	.003 870
38	26.436 680	282.629 783	.003 538
39	28.815 982	309.066 463	.003 236
40	31.409 420	337.882 445	.002 960
41	34.236 268	369.291 865	.002 708
42	37.317 532	403.528 133	.002 478
43	40.676 110	440.845 665	.002 268
44	44.336 960	481.521 775	.002 077
45	48.327 286	525.858 734	.001 902
46	52.676 742	574.186 021	.001 742
47	57.417 649	626.862 762	.001 595
48	62.585 237	684.280 411	.001 461
49	68.217 908	746.865 648	.001 339
50	74.357 520	815.083 556	.001 227

DISCOUNT FACTOR How much 1 at a future date is worth today	PRESENT WORTH OF AN ANNUITY FACTOR How much 1 received or paid annually for X years is worth today	CAPITAL RECOVERY FACTOR Annual payment that will repay a $1 loan in X years with compound interest on the unpaid balance	Year
.917 431	.917 431	1.090 000	1
.841 680	1.759 111	.568 469	2
.772 183	2.531 295	.395 055	3
.708 425	3.239 720	.308 669	4
.649 931	3.889 651	.257 092	5
.596 267	4.485 919	.222 920	6
.547 034	5.032 953	.198 691	7
.501 866	5.534 819	.180 674	8
.460 428	5.995 247	.166 799	9
.422 411	6.417 658	.155 820	10
.387 533	6.805 191	.146 947	11
.355 535	7.160 725	.139 651	12
.326 179	7.486 904	.133 567	13
.299 246	7.786 150	.128 433	14
.274 538	8.060 688	.124 059	15
.251 870	8.312 558	.120 300	16
.231 073	8.543 631	.117 046	17
.211 994	8.755 625	.114 212	18
.194 490	8.950 115	.111 730	19
.178 431	9.128 546	.109 546	20
.163 698	9.292 244	.107 617	21
.150 182	9.442 425	.105 905	22
.137 781	9.580 207	.104 382	23
.126 405	9.706 612	.103 023	24
.115 968	9.822 580	.101 806	25
.106 393	9.928 972	.100 715	26
.097 608	10.026 580	.099 735	27
.089 548	10.116 128	.098 852	28
.082 155	10.198 283	.098 056	29
.075 371	10.273 654	.097 336	30
.069 148	10.342 802	.096 686	31
.063 438	10.406 240	.096 096	32
.058 200	10.464 441	.095 562	33
.053 395	10.517 835	.095 077	34
.048 986	10.566 821	.094 636	35
.044 941	10.611 763	.094 235	36
.041 231	10.652 993	.093 870	37
.037 826	10.690 820	.093 538	38
.034 703	10.725 523	.093 236	39
.031 838	10.757 360	.092 960	40
.029 209	10.786 569	.092 708	41
.026 797	10.813 366	.092 478	42
.024 584	10.837 950	.092 268	43
.022 555	10.860 505	.092 077	44
.020 692	10.881 197	.091 902	45
.018 984	10.900 181	.091 742	46
.017 416	10.917 597	.091 595	47
.015 978	10.933 575	.091 461	48
.014 659	10.948 234	.091 339	49
.013 449	10.961 683	.091 227	50

RATE 10%

Year	COMPOUNDING FACTOR FOR 1 — What an initial amount becomes when growing at compound interest	COMPOUNDING FACTOR FOR 1 PER ANNUM — Growth of equal year-end deposits all growing at compound interest	SINKING FUND FACTOR — Level deposit required each year to reach 1 by a given year
1	1.100 000	1.000 000	1.000 000
2	1.210 000	2.100 000	.476 190
3	1.331 000	3.310 000	.302 115
4	1.464 100	4.641 000	.215 471
5	1.610 510	6.105 100	.163 797
6	1.771 561	7.715 610	.129 607
7	1.948 717	9.487 171	.105 405
8	2.143 589	11.435 888	.087 444
9	2.357 948	13.579 477	.073 641
10	2.593 742	15.937 425	.062 745
11	2.853 117	18.531 167	.053 963
12	3.138 428	21.384 284	.046 763
13	3.452 271	24.522 712	.040 779
14	3.797 498	27.974 983	.035 746
15	4.177 248	31.772 482	.031 474
16	4.594 973	35.949 730	.027 817
17	5.054 470	40.544 703	.024 664
18	5.559 917	45.599 173	.021 930
19	6.115 909	51.159 090	.019 547
20	6.727 500	57.274 999	.017 460
21	7.400 250	64.002 499	.015 624
22	8.140 275	71.402 749	.014 005
23	8.954 302	79.543 024	.012 572
24	9.849 733	88.497 327	.011 300
25	10.834 706	98.347 059	.010 168
26	11.918 177	109.181 765	.009 159
27	13.109 994	121.099 942	.008 258
28	14.420 994	134.209 936	.007 451
29	15.863 093	148.630 930	.006 728
30	17.449 402	164.494 023	.006 079
31	19.194 342	181.943 425	.005 496
32	21.113 777	201.137 767	.004 972
33	23.225 154	222.251 544	.004 499
34	25.547 670	245.476 699	.004 074
35	28.102 437	271.024 368	.003 690
36	30.912 681	299.126 805	.003 343
37	34.003 949	330.039 486	.003 030
38	37.404 343	364.043 434	.002 747
39	41.144 778	401.447 778	.002 491
40	45.259 256	442.592 556	.002 259
41	49.785 181	487.851 811	.002 050
42	54.763 699	537.636 992	.001 866
43	60.240 069	592.400 692	.001 688
44	66.264 076	652.640 761	.001 532
45	72.890 484	718.904 837	.001 391
46	80.179 532	791.795 321	.001 263
47	88.197 485	871.974 853	.001 147
48	97.017 234	960.172 338	.001 041
49	106.718 957	1,057.189 572	.000 946
50	117.390 853	1,163.908 529	.000 859

RATE 10%

DISCOUNT FACTOR — How much 1 at a future date is worth today	PRESENT WORTH OF AN ANNUITY FACTOR — How much 1 received or paid annually for X years is worth today	CAPITAL RECOVERY FACTOR — Annual payment that will repay a $1 loan in X years with compound interest on the unpaid balance	Year
.909 091	.909 091	1.100 000	1
.826 446	1.735 537	.576 190	2
.751 315	2.486 852	.402 115	3
.683 013	3.169 865	.315 471	4
.620 921	3.790 787	.263 797	5
.564 474	4.355 261	.229 607	6
.513 158	4.868 419	.205 405	7
.466 507	5.334 926	.187 444	8
.424 098	5.759 024	.173 641	9
.385 543	6.144 567	.162 745	10
.350 494	6.495 061	.153 963	11
.318 631	6.813 692	.146 763	12
.289 664	7.103 356	.140 779	13
.263 331	7.366 687	.135 746	14
.239 392	7.606 080	.131 474	15
.217 629	7.823 709	.127 817	16
.197 845	8.021 553	.124 664	17
.179 859	8.201 412	.121 930	18
.163 508	8.364 920	.119 547	19
.148 644	8.513 564	.117 460	20
.135 131	8.648 694	.115 624	21
.122 846	8.771 540	.114 005	22
.111 678	8.883 218	.112 572	23
.101 526	8.984 744	.111 300	24
.092 296	9.077 040	.110 168	25
.083 905	9.160 945	.109 159	26
.076 278	9.237 223	.108 258	27
.069 343	9.306 567	.107 451	28
.063 039	9.369 606	.106 728	29
.057 309	9.426 914	.106 079	30
.052 099	9.479 013	.105 496	31
.047 362	9.526 376	.104 972	32
.043 057	9.569 432	.104 499	33
.039 143	9.608 575	.104 074	34
.035 584	9.644 159	.103 690	35
.032 349	9.676 508	.103 343	36
.029 408	9.705 917	.103 030	37
.026 735	9.732 651	.102 747	38
.024 304	9.756 956	.102 491	39
.022 095	9.779 051	.102 259	40
.020 086	9.799 137	.102 050	41
.018 260	9.817 397	.101 860	42
.016 600	9.833 998	.101 688	43
.015 091	9.849 089	.101 532	44
.013 719	9.862 808	.101 391	45
.012 472	9.875 280	.101 263	46
.011 338	9.886 618	.101 147	47
.010 307	9.896 926	.101 041	48
.009 370	9.906 296	.100 946	49
.008 519	9.914 814	.100 859	50

RATE 11% — Compounding Factors / Sinking Fund

Year	COMPOUNDING FACTOR FOR 1 — What an initial amount becomes when growing at compound interest	COMPOUNDING FACTOR FOR 1 PER ANNUM — Growth of equal year-end deposits all growing at compound interest	SINKING FUND FACTOR — Level deposit required each year to reach 1 by a given year
1	1.110 000	1.000 000	1.000 000
2	1.232 100	2.110 000	.473 934
3	1.367 631	3.342 100	.299 213
4	1.518 070	4.709 731	.212 326
5	1.685 058	6.227 801	.160 570
6	1.870 415	7.912 860	.126 377
7	2.076 160	9.783 274	.102 215
8	2.304 538	11.859 434	.084 321
9	2.558 037	14.163 972	.070 602
10	2.839 421	16.722 009	.059 801
11	3.151 757	19.561 430	.051 121
12	3.498 451	22.713 187	.044 027
13	3.883 280	26.211 638	.038 151
14	4.310 441	30.094 918	.033 228
15	4.784 589	34.405 359	.029 065
16	5.310 894	39.189 948	.025 517
17	5.895 093	44.500 843	.022 471
18	6.543 553	50.395 936	.019 843
19	7.263 344	56.939 488	.017 563
20	8.062 312	64.202 832	.015 576
21	8.949 166	72.265 144	.013 838
22	9.933 574	81.214 309	.012 313
23	11.026 267	91.147 884	.010 971
24	12.239 157	102.174 151	.009 787
25	13.585 464	114.413 307	.008 740
26	15.079 865	127.998 771	.007 813
27	16.738 650	143.078 636	.006 989
28	18.579 901	159.817 286	.006 257
29	20.623 691	178.397 187	.005 605
30	22.892 297	199.020 878	.005 025
31	25.410 449	221.913 174	.004 506
32	28.205 599	247.323 624	.004 043
33	31.308 214	275.529 222	.003 629
34	34.752 118	306.837 437	.003 259
35	38.574 851	341.589 555	.002 927
36	42.818 085	380.164 406	.002 630
37	47.528 074	422.982 490	.002 364
38	52.756 162	470.510 564	.002 125
39	58.559 340	523.266 726	.001 911
40	65.000 867	581.826 066	.001 719
41	72.150 963	646.826 934	.001 546
42	80.087 569	718.977 896	.001 391
43	88.897 201	799.065 465	.001 251
44	98.675 893	887.962 666	.001 126
45	109.530 242	986.638 559	.001 014
46	121.578 568	1,096.168 801	.000 912
47	134.952 211	1,217.747 369	.000 821
48	149.796 954	1,352.699 580	.000 739
49	166.274 619	1,502.496 534	.000 666
50	184.564 827	1,668.771 152	.000 599

RATE 11% — Capital Recovery / Present Worth / Discount

Year	CAPITAL RECOVERY FACTOR — Annual payment that will repay a $1 loan in X years with compound interest on the unpaid balance	PRESENT WORTH OF AN ANNUITY FACTOR — How much 1 received or paid annually for X years is worth today	DISCOUNT FACTOR — How much 1 at a future date is worth today
1	1.110 000	.900 901	.900 901
2	.583 934	1.712 523	.811 622
3	.409 213	2.443 715	.731 191
4	.322 326	3.102 446	.658 731
5	.270 570	3.695 897	.593 451
6	.236 377	4.230 538	.534 641
7	.212 215	4.712 196	.481 658
8	.194 321	5.146 123	.433 926
9	.180 602	5.537 048	.390 925
10	.169 801	5.889 232	.352 184
11	.161 121	6.206 515	.317 283
12	.154 027	6.492 356	.285 841
13	.148 151	6.749 870	.257 514
14	.143 228	6.981 865	.231 995
15	.139 065	7.190 870	.209 004
16	.135 517	7.379 162	.188 292
17	.132 471	7.548 794	.169 633
18	.129 843	7.701 617	.152 822
19	.127 563	7.839 294	.137 678
20	.125 576	7.963 328	.124 034
21	.123 838	8.075 070	.111 742
22	.122 313	8.175 739	.100 669
23	.120 971	8.266 432	.090 693
24	.119 787	8.348 137	.081 705
25	.118 740	8.421 745	.073 608
26	.117 813	8.488 058	.066 314
27	.116 989	8.547 800	.059 742
28	.116 257	8.601 622	.053 822
29	.115 605	8.650 110	.048 488
30	.115 025	8.693 793	.043 683
31	.114 506	8.733 146	.039 354
32	.114 043	8.768 600	.035 454
33	.113 629	8.800 541	.031 940
34	.113 259	8.829 316	.028 775
35	.112 927	8.855 240	.025 924
36	.112 630	8.878 594	.023 355
37	.112 364	8.899 635	.021 040
38	.112 125	8.918 590	.018 955
39	.111 911	8.935 666	.017 077
40	.111 719	8.951 051	.015 384
41	.111 546	8.964 911	.013 860
42	.111 391	8.977 397	.012 486
43	.111 251	8.988 646	.011 249
44	.111 126	8.998 780	.010 134
45	.111 014	9.007 910	.009 130
46	.110 912	9.016 135	.008 225
47	.110 821	9.023 545	.007 410
48	.110 739	9.030 221	.006 676
49	.110 666	9.036 235	.006 014
50	.110 599	9.041 653	.005 418

Year	COMPOUNDING FACTOR FOR 1 — What an initial amount becomes when growing at compound interest	COMPOUNDING FACTOR FOR 1 PER ANNUM — Growth of equal year-end deposits all growing at compound interest	SINKING FUND FACTOR — Level deposit required each year to reach 1 by a given year
1	1.120 000	1.000 000	1.000 000
2	1.254 400	2.120 000	471 698
3	1.404 928	3.374 400	296 349
4	1.573 519	4.779 328	209 234
5	1.762 342	6.352 847	157 410
6	1.973 823	8.115 189	123 226
7	2.210 681	10.089 012	099 118
8	2.475 963	12.299 693	081 303
9	2.773 079	14.775 656	067 679
10	3.105 848	17.548 735	056 984
11	3.478 550	20.654 583	048 415
12	3.895 976	24.133 133	041 437
13	4.363 493	28.029 109	035 677
14	4.887 112	32.392 602	030 871
15	5.473 566	37.279 715	026 824
16	6.130 394	42.753 280	023 390
17	6.866 041	48.883 674	020 457
18	7.689 966	55.749 715	017 937
19	8.612 762	63.439 681	015 763
20	9.646 293	72.052 442	013 879
21	10.803 848	81.698 736	012 240
22	12.100 310	92.502 584	010 811
23	13.552 347	104.602 894	009 560
24	15.178 629	118.155 241	008 463
25	17.000 064	133.333 870	007 500
26	19.040 072	150.333 934	006 652
27	21.324 881	169.374 007	005 904
28	23.883 866	190.698 887	005 244
29	26.749 930	214.582 754	004 660
30	29.959 922	241.332 684	004 144
31	33.555 113	271.292 606	003 686
32	37.581 726	304.847 719	003 280
33	42.091 533	342.429 446	002 920
34	47.142 517	384.520 979	002 601
35	52.799 620	431.663 496	002 317
36	59.135 574	484.463 116	002 064
37	66.231 843	543.598 690	001 840
38	74.179 664	609.830 533	001 640
39	83.081 224	684.010 197	001 462
40	93.050 970	767.091 420	001 304
41	104.217 087	860.142 391	001 163
42	116.723 137	964.359 478	001 037
43	130.729 914	1,081.082 615	000 925
44	146.417 503	1,211.812 529	000 825
45	163.987 604	1,358.230 032	000 736
46	183.666 116	1,522.217 636	000 657
47	205.706 050	1,705.883 752	000 586
48	230.390 776	1,911.589 803	000 523
49	258.037 669	2,141.980 579	000 467
50	289.002 190	2,400.018 249	000 417

DISCOUNT FACTOR — How much 1 at a future date is worth today	PRESENT WORTH OF AN ANNUITY FACTOR — How much 1 received or paid annually for X years is worth today	CAPITAL RECOVERY FACTOR — Annual payment that will repay a $1 loan in X years with compound interest on the unpaid balance	Year
892 857	892 857	1.120 000	1
797 194	1.690 051	591 698	2
711 780	2.401 831	416 349	3
635 518	3.037 349	329 234	4
567 427	3.604 776	277 410	5
506 631	4.111 407	243 226	6
452 349	4.563 757	219 118	7
403 883	4.967 640	201 303	8
360 610	5.328 250	187 679	9
321 973	5.650 223	176 984	10
287 476	5.937 699	168 415	11
256 675	6.194 374	161 437	12
229 174	6.423 548	155 677	13
204 620	6.628 168	150 871	14
182 696	6.810 864	146 824	15
163 122	6.973 986	143 390	16
145 644	7.119 630	140 457	17
130 040	7.249 670	137 937	18
116 107	7.365 777	135 763	19
103 667	7.469 444	133 879	20
092 560	7.562 003	132 240	21
082 643	7.644 646	130 811	22
073 788	7.718 434	129 560	23
065 882	7.784 316	128 463	24
058 823	7.843 139	127 500	25
052 521	7.895 660	126 652	26
046 894	7.942 554	125 904	27
041 869	7.984 423	125 244	28
037 383	8.021 806	124 660	29
033 378	8.055 184	124 144	30
029 802	8.084 986	123 686	31
026 609	8.111 594	123 280	32
023 758	8.135 352	122 920	33
021 212	8.156 564	122 601	34
018 940	8.175 504	122 317	35
016 910	8.192 414	122 064	36
015 098	8.207 513	121 840	37
013 481	8.220 993	121 640	38
012 036	8.233 030	121 462	39
010 747	8.243 777	121 304	40
009 595	8.253 372	121 163	41
008 567	8.261 939	121 037	42
007 649	8.269 589	120 925	43
006 830	8.276 418	120 825	44
006 098	8.282 516	120 736	45
005 445	8.287 961	120 657	46
004 861	8.292 822	120 586	47
004 340	8.297 163	120 523	48
003 875	8.301 038	120 467	49
003 460	8.304 498	120 417	50

RATE 13% — Present Worth and Recovery Factors

DISCOUNT FACTOR — How much 1 at a future date is worth today	PRESENT WORTH OF AN ANNUITY FACTOR — How much 1 received or paid annually for X years is worth today	CAPITAL RECOVERY FACTOR — Annual payment that will repay a $1 loan in X years with compound interest on the unpaid balance	Year
.884 956	.884 956	1.130 000	1
.783 147	1.668 102	.599 484	2
.693 050	2.361 153	.423 522	3
.613 319	2.974 471	.336 194	4
.542 760	3.517 231	.284 315	5
.480 319	3.997 550	.250 153	6
.425 061	4.422 610	.226 111	7
.376 160	4.798 770	.208 387	8
.332 885	5.131 655	.194 869	9
.294 588	5.426 243	.184 290	10
.260 698	5.686 941	.175 841	11
.230 706	5.917 647	.168 986	12
.204 165	6.121 812	.163 350	13
.180 677	6.302 488	.158 667	14
.159 891	6.462 379	.154 742	15
.141 496	6.603 875	.151 426	16
.125 218	6.729 093	.148 608	17
.110 812	6.839 905	.146 201	18
.098 064	6.937 969	.144 134	19
.086 782	7.024 752	.142 354	20
.076 798	7.101 550	.140 814	21
.067 963	7.169 513	.139 479	22
.060 144	7.229 658	.138 319	23
.053 225	7.282 883	.137 308	24
.047 102	7.329 985	.136 426	25
.041 683	7.371 668	.135 655	26
.036 888	7.408 556	.134 979	27
.032 644	7.441 200	.134 387	28
.028 889	7.470 088	.133 867	29
.025 565	7.495 653	.133 411	30
.022 624	7.518 277	.133 009	31
.020 021	7.538 299	.132 656	32
.017 718	7.556 016	.132 345	33
.015 680	7.571 696	.132 071	34
.013 876	7.585 572	.131 829	35
.012 279	7.597 851	.131 616	36
.010 867	7.608 718	.131 428	37
.009 617	7.618 334	.131 262	38
.008 510	7.626 844	.131 116	39
.007 531	7.634 376	.130 986	40
.006 665	7.641 040	.130 872	41
.005 898	7.646 938	.130 771	42
.005 219	7.652 158	.130 682	43
.004 619	7.656 777	.130 603	44
.004 088	7.660 864	.130 534	45
.003 617	7.664 482	.130 472	46
.003 201	7.667 683	.130 417	47
.002 833	7.670 516	.130 369	48
.002 507	7.673 023	.130 327	49
.002 219	7.675 242	.130 289	50

RATE 13% — Compounding and Sinking Fund Factors

Year	COMPOUNDING FACTOR FOR 1 — What an initial amount becomes when growing at compound interest	COMPOUNDING FACTOR FOR 1 PER ANNUM — Growth of equal year-end deposits all growing at compound interest	SINKING FUND FACTOR — Level deposit required each year-end to reach 1 by a given year
1	1.130 000	1.000 000	1.000 000
2	1.276 900	2.130 000	.469 484
3	1.442 897	3.406 900	.293 522
4	1.630 474	4.849 797	.206 194
5	1.842 435	6.480 271	.154 315
6	2.081 952	8.322 706	.120 153
7	2.352 605	10.404 658	.096 111
8	2.658 444	12.757 263	.078 387
9	3.004 042	15.415 707	.064 869
10	3.394 567	18.419 749	.054 290
11	3.835 861	21.814 317	.045 841
12	4.334 523	25.650 178	.038 986
13	4.898 011	29.984 701	.033 350
14	5.534 753	34.882 712	.028 667
15	6.254 270	40.417 464	.024 742
16	7.067 326	46.671 735	.021 426
17	7.986 078	53.739 060	.018 608
18	9.024 268	61.725 138	.016 201
19	10.197 423	70.749 406	.014 134
20	11.523 088	80.946 829	.012 354
21	13.021 089	92.469 917	.010 814
22	14.713 831	105.491 006	.009 479
23	16.626 629	120.204 837	.008 319
24	18.788 091	136.831 465	.007 308
25	21.230 542	155.619 556	.006 426
26	23.990 513	176.850 098	.005 655
27	27.109 279	200.840 611	.004 979
28	30.633 486	227.949 890	.004 387
29	34.615 839	258.583 376	.003 867
30	39.115 898	293.199 215	.003 411
31	44.200 965	332.315 113	.003 009
32	49.947 090	376.516 078	.002 656
33	56.440 212	426.463 168	.002 345
34	63.777 439	482.903 380	.002 071
35	72.068 506	546.680 819	.001 829
36	81.437 412	618.749 325	.001 616
37	92.024 276	700.186 738	.001 428
38	103.987 432	792.211 014	.001 262
39	117.505 798	896.198 445	.001 116
40	132.781 552	1,013.704 243	.000 986
41	150.043 153	1,146.485 795	.000 872
42	169.548 763	1,296.528 948	.000 771
43	191.590 103	1,466.077 712	.000 682
44	216.496 816	1,657.667 814	.000 603
45	244.641 402	1,874.164 630	.000 534
46	276.444 784	2,118.806 032	.000 472
47	312.382 606	2,395.250 816	.000 417
48	352.992 345	2,707.633 422	.000 369
49	398.881 350	3,060.625 767	.000 327
50	450.735 925	3,459.507 117	.000 289

Year	DISCOUNT FACTOR How much 1 at a future date is worth today	PRESENT WORTH OF AN ANNUITY FACTOR How much 1 received or paid annually for X years is worth today	CAPITAL RECOVERY FACTOR Annual payment that will repay a $1 loan in X years with compound interest on the unpaid balance
1	.877 193	.877 193	1.140 000
2	.769 468	1.646 661	.607 290
3	.674 972	2.321 632	.430 731
4	.592 080	2.913 712	.343 205
5	.519 369	3.433 081	.291 284
6	.455 587	3.888 668	.257 157
7	.399 637	4.288 305	.233 192
8	.350 559	4.638 864	.215 570
9	.307 508	4.946 372	.202 168
10	.269 744	5.216 116	.191 714
11	.236 617	5.452 733	.183 394
12	.207 559	5.660 292	.176 669
13	.182 069	5.842 362	.171 164
14	.159 710	6.002 072	.166 609
15	.140 096	6.142 168	.162 809
16	.122 892	6.265 060	.159 615
17	.107 800	6.372 859	.156 915
18	.094 561	6.467 420	.154 621
19	.082 948	6.550 369	.152 663
20	.072 762	6.623 131	.150 986
21	.063 826	6.686 957	.149 545
22	.055 988	6.742 944	.148 303
23	.049 112	6.792 056	.147 231
24	.043 081	6.835 137	.146 303
25	.037 790	6.872 927	.145 498
26	.033 149	6.906 077	.144 800
27	.029 078	6.935 155	.144 193
28	.025 507	6.960 662	.143 664
29	.022 375	6.983 037	.143 204
30	.019 627	7.002 664	.142 803
31	.017 217	7.019 881	.142 453
32	.015 102	7.034 983	.142 147
33	.013 248	7.048 231	.141 880
34	.011 621	7.059 852	.141 646
35	.010 194	7.070 045	.141 442
36	.008 942	7.078 987	.141 263
37	.007 844	7.086 831	.141 107
38	.006 880	7.093 711	.140 970
39	.006 035	7.099 747	.140 850
40	.005 294	7.105 041	.140 745
41	.004 644	7.109 685	.140 653
42	.004 074	7.113 759	.140 573
43	.003 573	7.117 332	.140 502
44	.003 135	7.120 467	.140 440
45	.002 750	7.123 217	.140 386
46	.002 412	7.125 629	.140 338
47	.002 116	7.127 744	.140 297
48	.001 856	7.129 600	.140 260
49	.001 628	7.131 228	.140 228
50	.001 428	7.132 656	.140 200

Year	COMPOUNDING FACTOR FOR 1 What an initial amount becomes when growing at compound interest	COMPOUNDING FACTOR FOR 1 PER ANNUM Growth of equal year-end deposits all growing at compound interest	SINKING FUND FACTOR Level deposit required each year to reach 1 by a given year
1	1.140 000	1.000 000	1.000 000
2	1.299 600	2.140 000	.467 290
3	1.481 544	3.439 600	.290 731
4	1.688 960	4.921 144	.203 205
5	1.925 415	6.610 104	.151 284
6	2.194 973	8.535 519	.117 157
7	2.502 269	10.730 491	.093 192
8	2.852 586	13.232 760	.075 570
9	3.251 949	16.085 347	.062 168
10	3.707 221	19.337 295	.051 714
11	4.226 232	23.044 516	.043 394
12	4.817 905	27.270 749	.036 669
13	5.492 411	32.088 654	.031 164
14	6.261 349	37.581 065	.026 609
15	7.137 938	43.842 414	.022 809
16	8.137 249	50.980 352	.019 615
17	9.276 464	59.117 601	.016 915
18	10.575 169	68.394 066	.014 621
19	12.055 693	78.969 235	.012 663
20	13.743 490	91.024 928	.010 986
21	15.667 578	104.768 418	.009 545
22	17.861 039	120.435 996	.008 303
23	20.361 585	138.297 035	.007 231
24	23.212 207	158.658 620	.006 303
25	26.461 916	181.870 827	.005 498
26	30.166 584	208.332 743	.004 800
27	34.389 906	238.499 327	.004 193
28	39.204 493	272.889 233	.003 664
29	44.693 122	312.093 725	.003 204
30	50.950 159	356.786 847	.002 803
31	58.083 181	407.737 006	.002 453
32	66.214 826	465.820 186	.002 147
33	75.484 902	532.035 012	.001 880
34	86.052 788	607.519 914	.001 646
35	98.100 178	693.572 702	.001 442
36	111.834 203	791.672 881	.001 263
37	127.490 992	903.507 084	.001 107
38	145.339 731	1,030.998 076	.000 970
39	165.587 293	1,176.337 806	.000 850
40	188.883 514	1,342.025 099	.000 745
41	215.327 206	1,530.908 613	.000 653
42	245.473 015	1,746.235 819	.000 573
43	279.839 237	1,991.708 833	.000 502
44	319.016 730	2,271.548 070	.000 440
45	363.679 072	2,590.564 800	.000 386
46	414.594 142	2,954.243 872	.000 338
47	472.637 322	3,368.838 014	.000 297
48	538.806 547	3,841.475 336	.000 260
49	614.239 464	4,380.281 883	.000 228
50	700.232 988	4,994.521 346	.000 200

548

Year	COMPOUNDING FACTOR FOR 1 — What an initial amount becomes when growing at compound interest	COMPOUNDING FACTOR FOR 1 PER ANNUM — Growth of equal year-end deposits all growing at compound interest	SINKING FUND FACTOR — Level deposit required each year to reach 1 by a given year
1	1.150 000	1.000 000	1.000 000
2	1.322 500	2.150 000	.465 116
3	1.520 875	3.472 500	.287 977
4	1.749 006	4.993 375	.200 265
5	2.011 357	6.742 381	.148 316
6	2.313 061	8.753 738	.114 237
7	2.660 020	11.066 799	.090 360
8	3.059 023	13.726 819	.072 850
9	3.517 876	16.785 842	.059 574
10	4.045 558	20.303 718	.049 252
11	4.652 391	24.349 276	.041 069
12	5.350 250	29.001 667	.034 481
13	6.152 788	34.351 917	.029 110
14	7.075 706	40.504 705	.024 688
15	8.137 062	47.580 411	.021 017
16	9.357 621	55.717 472	.017 948
17	10.761 264	65.075 093	.015 367
18	12.375 454	75.836 357	.013 186
19	14.231 772	88.211 811	.011 336
20	16.366 537	102.443 583	.009 761
21	18.821 518	118.810 120	.008 417
22	21.644 746	137.631 638	.007 266
23	24.891 458	159.276 384	.006 278
24	28.625 176	184.167 841	.005 430
25	32.918 953	212.793 017	.004 699
26	37.856 796	245.711 970	.004 070
27	43.535 315	283.568 766	.003 526
28	50.065 612	327.104 080	.003 057
29	57.575 454	377.169 693	.002 651
30	66.211 772	434.745 146	.002 300
31	76.143 538	500.956 918	.001 996
32	87.565 068	577.100 456	.001 733
33	100.699 829	664.665 524	.001 505
34	115.804 803	765.365 353	.001 307
35	133.175 523	881.170 156	.001 135
36	153.151 852	1,014.345 680	.000 986
37	176.124 630	1,167.497 532	.000 857
38	202.543 324	1,343.622 161	.000 744
39	232.924 823	1,546.165 485	.000 647
40	267.863 546	1,779.090 308	.000 562
41	308.043 078	2,046.953 854	.000 489
42	354.249 540	2,354.996 933	.000 425
43	407.386 971	2,709.246 473	.000 369
44	468.495 017	3,116.633 443	.000 321
45	538.769 269	3,585.128 460	.000 279
46	619.584 659	4,123.897 729	.000 242
47	712.522 358	4,743.482 388	.000 211
48	819.400 712	5,456.004 746	.000 183
49	942.310 819	6,275.405 458	.000 159
50	1,083.657 442	7,217.716 277	.000 139

DISCOUNT FACTOR — How much 1 at a future date is worth today	PRESENT WORTH OF AN ANNUITY FACTOR — How much 1 received or paid annually for X years is worth today	CAPITAL RECOVERY FACTOR — Annual payment that will repay a $1 loan in X years with compound interest on the unpaid balance	Year
.869 565	.869 565	1.150 000	1
.756 144	1.625 709	.615 116	2
.657 516	2.283 225	.437 977	3
.571 753	2.854 978	.350 265	4
.497 177	3.352 155	.298 316	5
.432 328	3.784 483	.264 237	6
.375 937	4.160 420	.240 360	7
.326 902	4.487 322	.222 850	8
.284 262	4.771 584	.209 574	9
.247 185	5.018 769	.199 252	10
.214 943	5.233 712	.191 069	11
.186 907	5.420 619	.184 481	12
.162 528	5.583 147	.179 110	13
.141 329	5.724 476	.174 688	14
.122 894	5.847 370	.171 017	15
.106 865	5.954 235	.167 948	16
.092 926	6.047 161	.165 367	17
.080 805	6.127 966	.163 186	18
.070 265	6.198 231	.161 336	19
.061 100	6.259 331	.159 761	20
.053 131	6.312 462	.158 417	21
.046 201	6.358 663	.157 266	22
.040 174	6.398 837	.156 278	23
.034 934	6.433 771	.155 430	24
.030 378	6.464 149	.154 699	25
.026 415	6.490 564	.154 070	26
.022 970	6.513 534	.153 526	27
.019 974	6.533 508	.153 057	28
.017 369	6.550 877	.152 651	29
.015 103	6.565 980	.152 300	30
.013 133	6.579 113	.151 996	31
.011 420	6.590 533	.151 733	32
.009 931	6.600 463	.151 505	33
.008 635	6.609 099	.151 307	34
.007 509	6.616 607	.151 135	35
.006 529	6.623 137	.150 986	36
.005 678	6.628 815	.150 857	37
.004 937	6.633 752	.150 744	38
.004 293	6.638 045	.150 647	39
.003 733	6.641 778	.150 562	40
.003 246	6.645 025	.150 489	41
.002 823	6.647 848	.150 425	42
.002 455	6.650 302	.150 369	43
.002 134	6.652 455	.150 321	44
.001 856	6.654 293	.150 279	45
.001 614	6.655 907	.150 242	46
.001 403	6.657 310	.150 211	47
.001 220	6.658 531	.150 183	48
.001 061	6.659 592	.150 159	49
.000 923	6.660 515	.150 139	50

RATE 16% — Present Worth and Capital Recovery

Year	DISCOUNT FACTOR — How much 1 at a future date is worth today	PRESENT WORTH OF AN ANNUITY FACTOR — How much 1 received or paid annually for X years is worth today	CAPITAL RECOVERY FACTOR — Annual payment that will repay a $1 loan in X years with compound interest on the unpaid balance	Year
1	862 069	862 069	1.160 000	1
2	743 163	1.605 232	622 963	2
3	640 658	2.245 890	445 258	3
4	552 291	2.798 181	357 375	4
5	476 113	3.274 294	305 409	5
6	410 442	3.684 736	271 390	6
7	353 830	4.038 565	247 613	7
8	305 025	4.343 591	230 224	8
9	262 953	4.606 544	217 082	9
10	226 684	4.833 227	206 901	10
11	195 417	5.028 644	198 861	11
12	168 463	5.197 107	192 415	12
13	145 227	5.342 334	187 184	13
14	125 195	5.467 529	182 898	14
15	107 927	5.575 456	179 358	15
16	093 041	5.668 497	176 414	16
17	080 207	5.748 704	173 952	17
18	069 144	5.817 848	171 885	18
19	059 607	5.877 455	170 142	19
20	051 385	5.928 841	168 667	20
21	044 298	5.973 139	167 416	21
22	038 188	6.011 326	166 353	22
23	032 920	6.044 247	165 447	23
24	028 380	6.072 627	164 673	24
25	024 465	6.097 092	164 013	25
26	021 091	6.118 183	163 447	26
27	018 182	6.136 364	162 963	27
28	015 674	6.152 038	162 548	28
29	013 512	6.165 550	162 192	29
30	011 648	6.177 198	161 886	30
31	010 042	6.187 240	161 623	31
32	008 657	6.195 897	161 397	32
33	007 463	6.203 359	161 203	33
34	006 433	6.209 792	161 036	34
35	005 546	6.215 338	160 892	35
36	004 781	6.220 119	160 769	36
37	004 121	6.224 241	160 662	37
38	003 553	6.227 794	160 571	38
39	003 063	6.230 857	160 492	39
40	002 640	6.233 497	160 424	40
41	002 276	6.235 773	160 365	41
42	001 962	6.237 736	160 315	42
43	001 692	6.239 427	160 271	43
44	001 458	6.240 886	160 234	44
45	001 257	6.242 143	160 201	45
46	001 084	6.243 227	160 174	46
47	000 934	6.244 161	160 150	47
48	000 805	6.244 966	160 129	48
49	000 694	6.245 661	160 111	49
50	000 599	6.246 259	160 096	50

RATE 16% — Compounding and Sinking Fund

Year	COMPOUNDING FACTOR FOR 1 — What an initial amount becomes when growing at compound interest	COMPOUNDING FACTOR FOR 1 PER ANNUM — Growth of equal year-end deposits all growing at compound interest	SINKING FUND FACTOR — Level deposit required each year to reach 1 by a given year
1	1.160 000	1.000 000	1.000 000
2	1.345 600	2.160 000	462 963
3	1.560 896	3.505 600	285 258
4	1.810 639	5.066 496	197 375
5	2.100 342	6.877 135	145 409
6	2.436 396	8.977 477	111 390
7	2.826 220	11.413 873	087 613
8	3.278 415	14.240 093	070 224
9	3.802 961	17.518 508	057 082
10	4.411 435	21.321 469	046 901
11	5.117 265	25.732 904	038 861
12	5.936 027	30.850 169	032 415
13	6.885 791	36.786 196	027 184
14	7.987 518	43.671 987	022 898
15	9.265 521	51.659 505	019 358
16	10.748 004	60.925 026	016 414
17	12.467 685	71.673 030	013 952
18	14.462 514	84.140 715	011 885
19	16.776 517	98.603 230	010 142
20	19.460 759	115.379 747	008 667
21	22.574 481	134.840 506	007 416
22	26.186 398	157.414 987	006 353
23	30.376 222	183.601 385	005 447
24	35.236 417	213.977 607	004 673
25	40.874 244	249.214 024	004 013
26	47.414 123	290.088 267	003 447
27	55.000 382	337.502 390	002 963
28	63.800 444	392.502 773	002 548
29	74.008 515	456.303 216	002 192
30	85.849 877	530.311 731	001 886
31	99.585 857	616.161 608	001 623
32	115.519 594	715.747 465	001 397
33	134.002 729	831.267 059	001 203
34	155.443 166	965.269 789	001 036
35	180.314 073	1,120.712 955	000 892
36	209.164 324	1,301.027 028	000 769
37	242.630 616	1,510.191 352	000 662
38	281.451 515	1,752.821 968	000 571
39	326.483 757	2,034.273 483	000 492
40	378.721 158	2,360.757 241	000 424
41	439.316 544	2,739.478 399	000 365
42	509.607 191	3,178.794 943	000 315
43	591.144 341	3,688.402 134	000 271
44	685.727 436	4,279.546 475	000 234
45	795.443 826	4,965.273 911	000 201
46	922.714 838	5,760.717 737	000 174
47	1,070.349 212	6,683.432 575	000 150
48	1,241.605 086	7,753.781 787	000 129
49	1,440.261 900	8,995.386 873	000 111
50	1,670.703 804	10,435.648 77	000 096

RATE 18% — CAPITAL RECOVERY FACTOR / PRESENT WORTH OF AN ANNUITY FACTOR / DISCOUNT FACTOR

Year	DISCOUNT FACTOR — How much 1 at a future date is worth today	PRESENT WORTH OF AN ANNUITY FACTOR — How much 1 received or paid annually for X years is worth today	CAPITAL RECOVERY FACTOR — Annual payment that will repay a $1 loan in X years with compound interest on the unpaid balance
1	.847 458	.847 458	1.180 000
2	.718 184	1.565 642	.638 716
3	.608 631	2.174 273	.459 924
4	.515 789	2.690 062	.371 739
5	.437 109	3.127 171	.319 778
6	.370 432	3.497 603	.285 910
7	.313 925	3.811 528	.262 362
8	.266 038	4.077 566	.245 244
9	.225 456	4.303 022	.232 395
10	.191 064	4.494 086	.222 515
11	.161 919	4.656 005	.214 776
12	.137 220	4.793 225	.208 628
13	.116 288	4.909 513	.203 686
14	.098 549	5.008 062	.199 678
15	.083 516	5.091 578	.196 403
16	.070 776	5.162 354	.193 710
17	.059 980	5.222 334	.191 485
18	.050 830	5.273 164	.189 639
19	.043 077	5.316 241	.188 103
20	.036 506	5.352 746	.186 820
21	.030 937	5.383 683	.185 746
22	.026 218	5.409 901	.184 846
23	.022 218	5.432 120	.184 090
24	.018 829	5.450 949	.183 454
25	.015 957	5.466 906	.182 919
26	.013 523	5.480 429	.182 467
27	.011 460	5.491 889	.182 087
28	.009 712	5.501 601	.181 765
29	.008 230	5.509 831	.181 494
30	.006 975	5.516 806	.181 264
31	.005 911	5.522 717	.181 070
32	.005 009	5.527 726	.180 906
33	.004 245	5.531 971	.180 767
34	.003 598	5.535 569	.180 650
35	.003 049	5.538 618	.180 550
36	.002 584	5.541 201	.180 466
37	.002 190	5.543 391	.180 395
38	.001 856	5.545 247	.180 335
39	.001 573	5.546 819	.180 284
40	.001 333	5.548 152	.180 240
41	.001 129	5.549 281	.180 204
42	.000 957	5.550 238	.180 172
43	.000 811	5.551 049	.180 146
44	.000 687	5.551 737	.180 124
45	.000 583	5.552 319	.180 105
46	.000 494	5.552 813	.180 089
47	.000 418	5.553 231	.180 075
48	.000 355	5.553 586	.180 064
49	.000 300	5.553 886	.180 054
50	.000 255	5.554 141	.180 046

RATE 18% — COMPOUNDING FACTOR FOR 1 / COMPOUNDING FACTOR FOR 1 PER ANNUM / SINKING FUND FACTOR

Year	COMPOUNDING FACTOR FOR 1 — What an initial amount becomes when growing at compound interest	COMPOUNDING FACTOR FOR 1 PER ANNUM — Growth of equal year-end deposits all growing at compound interest	SINKING FUND FACTOR — Level deposit required each year to reach 1 by a given year
1	1.180 000	1.000 000	1.000 000
2	1.392 400	2.180 000	.458 716
3	1.643 032	3.572 400	.279 924
4	1.938 778	5.215 432	.191 739
5	2.287 758	7.154 210	.139 778
6	2.699 554	9.441 968	.105 910
7	3.185 474	12.141 522	.082 362
8	3.758 859	15.326 996	.065 244
9	4.435 454	19.085 855	.052 395
10	5.233 836	23.521 309	.042 515
11	6.175 926	28.755 144	.034 776
12	7.287 593	34.931 070	.028 628
13	8.599 359	42.218 663	.023 686
14	10.147 244	50.818 022	.019 678
15	11.973 748	60.965 266	.016 403
16	14.129 023	72.939 014	.013 710
17	16.672 247	87.068 036	.011 485
18	19.673 251	103.740 283	.009 639
19	23.214 436	123.413 534	.008 103
20	27.393 035	146.627 970	.006 820
21	32.323 781	174.021 005	.005 746
22	38.142 061	206.344 785	.004 846
23	45.007 632	244.486 847	.004 090
24	53.109 006	289.494 479	.003 454
25	62.668 627	342.603 486	.002 919
26	73.948 980	405.272 113	.002 467
27	87.259 797	479.221 093	.002 087
28	102.966 560	566.480 890	.001 765
29	121.500 541	669.447 450	.001 494
30	143.370 638	790.947 991	.001 264
31	169.177 353	934.318 630	.001 070
32	199.629 277	1,103.495 983	.000 906
33	235.562 547	1,303.125 260	.000 767
34	277.963 805	1,538.687 807	.000 650
35	327.997 290	1,816.651 612	.000 550
36	387.036 802	2,144.648 902	.000 466
37	456.703 427	2,531.685 705	.000 395
38	538.910 044	2,988.389 132	.000 335
39	635.913 852	3,527.299 175	.000 284
40	750.378 345	4,163.213 027	.000 240
41	885.446 447	4,913.591 372	.000 204
42	1,044.826 807	5,799.037 818	.000 172
43	1,232.895 633	6,843.864 626	.000 146
44	1,454.816 847	8,076.760 258	.000 124
45	1,716.683 879	9,531.577 105	.000 105
46	2,025.686 977	11,248.260 98	.000 089
47	2,390.310 633	13,273.947 96	.000 075
48	2,820.566 547	15,664.258 59	.000 064
49	3,328.268 525	18,484.825 14	.000 054
50	3,927.356 860	21,813.093 67	.000 046

RATE 20% — Present Worth, Discount, and Capital Recovery

Year	DISCOUNT FACTOR — How much 1 at a future date is worth today	PRESENT WORTH OF AN ANNUITY FACTOR — How much 1 received or paid annually for X years is worth today	CAPITAL RECOVERY FACTOR — Annual payment that will repay a $1 loan in X years with compound interest on the unpaid balance
1	.833 333	.833 333	1.200 000
2	.694 444	1.527 778	.654 545
3	.578 704	2.106 481	.474 725
4	.482 253	2.588 735	.386 289
5	.401 878	2.990 612	.334 380
6	.334 898	3.325 510	.300 706
7	.279 082	3.604 592	.277 424
8	.232 568	3.837 160	.260 609
9	.193 807	4.030 967	.248 079
10	.161 506	4.192 472	.238 523
11	.134 588	4.327 060	.231 104
12	.112 157	4.439 217	.225 265
13	.093 464	4.532 681	.220 620
14	.077 887	4.610 567	.216 893
15	.064 905	4.675 473	.213 882
16	.054 088	4.729 561	.211 436
17	.045 073	4.774 634	.209 440
18	.037 561	4.812 195	.207 805
19	.031 301	4.843 496	.206 462
20	.026 084	4.869 580	.205 357
21	.021 737	4.891 316	.204 444
22	.018 114	4.909 430	.203 690
23	.015 095	4.924 525	.203 065
24	.012 579	4.937 104	.202 548
25	.010 483	4.947 587	.202 119
26	.008 735	4.956 323	.201 762
27	.007 280	4.963 602	.201 467
28	.006 066	4.969 668	.201 221
29	.005 055	4.974 724	.201 016
30	.004 213	4.978 936	.200 846
31	.003 511	4.982 447	.200 705
32	.002 926	4.985 372	.200 587
33	.002 438	4.987 810	.200 489
34	.002 032	4.989 842	.200 407
35	.001 693	4.991 535	.200 339
36	.001 411	4.992 946	.200 283
37	.001 176	4.994 122	.200 235
38	.000 980	4.995 101	.200 196
39	.000 816	4.995 918	.200 163
40	.000 680	4.996 598	.200 136
41	.000 567	4.997 165	.200 113
42	.000 472	4.997 638	.200 095
43	.000 394	4.998 031	.200 079
44	.000 328	4.998 359	.200 066
45	.000 273	4.998 633	.200 055
46	.000 228	4.998 861	.200 046
47	.000 190	4.999 051	.200 038
48	.000 158	4.999 209	.200 032
49	.000 132	4.999 341	.200 026
50	.000 110	4.999 451	.200 022

RATE 20% — Compounding and Sinking Fund

Year	COMPOUNDING FACTOR FOR 1 — What an initial amount becomes when growing at compound interest	COMPOUNDING FACTOR FOR 1 PER ANNUM — Growth of equal year-end deposits all growing at compound interest	SINKING FUND FACTOR — Level deposit required each year to reach 1 by a given year
1	1.200 000	1.000 000	1.000 000
2	1.440 000	2.200 000	.454 545
3	1.728 000	3.640 000	.274 725
4	2.073 600	5.368 000	.186 289
5	2.488 320	7.441 600	.134 380
6	2.985 984	9.929 920	.100 706
7	3.583 181	12.915 904	.077 424
8	4.299 817	16.499 085	.060 609
9	5.159 780	20.798 902	.048 079
10	6.191 736	25.958 682	.038 523
11	7.430 084	32.150 419	.031 104
12	8.916 100	39.580 502	.025 265
13	10.699 321	48.496 603	.020 620
14	12.839 185	59.195 923	.016 893
15	15.407 022	72.035 108	.013 882
16	18.488 426	87.442 129	.011 436
17	22.186 111	105.930 555	.009 440
18	26.623 333	128.116 666	.007 805
19	31.948 000	154.740 000	.006 462
20	38.337 600	186.688 000	.005 357
21	46.005 120	225.025 600	.004 444
22	55.206 144	271.030 719	.003 690
23	66.247 373	326.236 863	.003 065
24	79.496 847	392.484 236	.002 548
25	95.396 217	471.981 083	.002 119
26	114.475 460	567.377 300	.001 762
27	137.370 552	681.852 760	.001 467
28	164.844 662	819.223 312	.001 221
29	197.813 595	984.067 974	.001 016
30	237.376 314	1,181.881 569	.000 846
31	284.851 577	1,419.257 883	.000 705
32	341.821 892	1,704.109 459	.000 587
33	410.186 270	2,045.931 351	.000 489
34	492.223 524	2,456.117 621	.000 407
35	590.668 229	2,948.341 146	.000 339
36	708.801 875	3,539.009 375	.000 283
37	850.562 250	4,247.811 250	.000 235
38	1,020.674 700	5,098.373 500	.000 196
39	1,224.809 640	6,119.048 200	.000 163
40	1,469.771 568	7,343.857 840	.000 136
41	1,763.725 882	8,813.629 408	.000 113
42	2,116.471 058	10,577.355 29	.000 095
43	2,539.765 269	12,693.826 35	.000 079
44	3,047.718 323	15,233.591 62	.000 066
45	3,657.261 988	18,281.309 94	.000 055
46	4,388.714 386	21,938.571 93	.000 046
47	5,266.457 263	26,327.286 31	.000 038
48	6,319.748 715	31,593.743 58	.000 032
49	7,583.698 458	37,913.492 29	.000 026
50	9,100.438 150	45,497.190 75	.000 022

COMPOUNDING FACTOR / SINKING FUND FACTOR — RATE 25%

Year	COMPOUNDING FACTOR FOR 1 — What an initial amount becomes when growing at compound interest	COMPOUNDING FACTOR FOR 1 PER ANNUM — Growth of equal year-end deposits all growing at compound interest	SINKING FUND FACTOR — Level deposit required each year to reach 1 by a given year
1	1.250 000	1.000 000	1.000 000
2	1.562 500	2.250 000	.444 444
3	1.953 125	3.812 500	.262 295
4	2.441 406	5.765 625	.173 442
5	3.051 758	8.207 031	.121 847
6	3.814 697	11.258 789	.088 819
7	4.768 372	15.073 486	.066 342
8	5.960 464	19.841 858	.050 399
9	7.450 581	25.802 322	.038 756
10	9.313 226	33.252 903	.030 073
11	11.641 532	42.566 129	.023 493
12	14.551 915	54.207 661	.018 448
13	18.189 894	68.759 576	.014 543
14	22.737 368	86.949 470	.011 501
15	28.421 709	109.686 838	.009 117
16	35.527 137	138.108 547	.007 241
17	44.408 921	173.635 684	.005 759
18	55.511 151	218.044 605	.004 586
19	69.388 939	273.555 756	.003 656
20	86.736 174	342.944 695	.002 916
21	108.420 217	429.680 869	.002 327
22	135.525 272	538.101 086	.001 858
23	169.406 589	673.626 358	.001 485
24	211.758 237	843.032 947	.001 186
25	264.697 796	1,054.791 184	.000 948
26	330.872 245	1,319.488 980	.000 758
27	413.590 306	1,650.361 225	.000 606
28	516.987 883	2,063.951 531	.000 485
29	646.234 854	2,580.939 414	.000 387
30	807.793 567	3,227.174 268	.000 310
31	1,009.741 959	4,034.967 835	.000 248
32	1,262.177 448	5,044.709 793	.000 198
33	1,577.721 810	6,306.887 242	.000 159
34	1,972.152 263	7,884.609 052	.000 127
35	2,465.190 329	9,856.761 315	.000 101
36	3,081.487 911	12,321.951 64	.000 081
37	3,851.859 889	15,403.439 56	.000 065
38	4,814.824 861	19,255.299 44	.000 052
39	6,018.531 076	24,070.124 30	.000 042
40	7,523.163 845	30,088.655 38	.000 033
41	9,403.954 807	37,611.819 23	.000 027
42	11,754.943 51	47,015.774 03	.000 021
43	14,693.679 39	58,770.717 54	.000 017
44	18,367.099 23	73,464.396 93	.000 014
45	22,958.874 04	91,831.496 16	.000 011
46	28,698.592 55	114,790.370 2	.000 009
47	35,873.240 69	143,488.962 7	.000 007
48	44,841.550 86	179,362.203 4	.000 006
49	56,051.938 57	224,203.754 3	.000 004
50	70,064.923 22	280,255.692 9	.000 004

DISCOUNT FACTOR / PRESENT WORTH / CAPITAL RECOVERY — RATE 25%

DISCOUNT FACTOR — How much 1 at a future date is worth today	PRESENT WORTH OF AN ANNUITY FACTOR — How much 1 received or paid annually for X years is worth today	CAPITAL RECOVERY FACTOR — Annual payment that will repay a $1 loan in X years with compound interest on the unpaid balance	Year
.800 000	.800 000	1.250 000	1
.640 000	1.440 000	.694 444	2
.512 000	1.952 000	.512 295	3
.409 600	2.361 600	.423 442	4
.327 680	2.689 280	.371 847	5
.262 144	2.951 424	.338 819	6
.209 715	3.161 139	.316 342	7
.167 772	3.328 911	.300 399	8
.134 218	3.463 129	.288 756	9
.107 374	3.570 503	.280 073	10
.085 899	3.656 403	.273 493	11
.068 719	3.725 122	.268 448	12
.054 976	3.780 098	.264 543	13
.043 980	3.824 078	.261 501	14
.035 184	3.859 263	.259 117	15
.028 147	3.887 410	.257 241	16
.022 518	3.909 928	.255 759	17
.018 014	3.927 942	.254 586	18
.014 412	3.942 354	.253 656	19
.011 529	3.953 883	.252 916	20
.009 223	3.963 107	.252 327	21
.007 379	3.970 485	.251 858	22
.005 903	3.976 388	.251 485	23
.004 722	3.981 111	.251 186	24
.003 778	3.984 888	.250 948	25
.003 022	3.987 911	.250 758	26
.002 418	3.990 329	.250 606	27
.001 934	3.992 263	.250 485	28
.001 547	3.993 810	.250 387	29
.001 238	3.995 048	.250 310	30
.000 990	3.996 039	.250 248	31
.000 792	3.996 831	.250 198	32
.000 634	3.997 465	.250 159	33
.000 507	3.997 972	.250 127	34
.000 406	3.998 377	.250 101	35
.000 325	3.998 702	.250 081	36
.000 260	3.998 962	.250 065	37
.000 208	3.999 169	.250 052	38
.000 166	3.999 335	.250 042	39
.000 133	3.999 468	.250 033	40
.000 106	3.999 575	.250 027	41
.000 085	3.999 660	.250 021	42
.000 068	3.999 728	.250 017	43
.000 054	3.999 782	.250 014	44
.000 044	3.999 826	.250 011	45
.000 035	3.999 861	.250 009	46
.000 028	3.999 888	.250 007	47
.000 022	3.999 911	.250 006	48
.000 018	3.999 929	.250 004	49
.000 014	3.999 943	.250 004	50

CAPITAL RECOVERY FACTOR — Annual payment that will repay a $1 loan in X years with compound interest on the unpaid balance	PRESENT WORTH OF AN ANNUITY FACTOR — How much 1 received or paid annually for X years is worth today	DISCOUNT FACTOR — How much 1 at a future date is worth today	Year
1.300 000	.769 231	.769 231	1
.734 783	1.360 947	.591 716	2
.550 627	1.816 113	.455 166	3
.461 629	2.166 241	.350 128	4
.410 582	2.435 570	.269 329	5
.378 394	2.642 746	.207 176	6
.356 874	2.802 112	.159 366	7
.341 915	2.924 702	.122 589	8
.331 235	3.019 001	.094 300	9
.323 463	3.091 539	.072 538	10
.317 729	3.147 338	.055 799	11
.313 454	3.190 260	.042 922	12
.310 243	3.223 277	.033 017	13
.307 818	3.248 675	.025 398	14
.305 978	3.268 211	.019 537	15
.304 577	3.283 239	.015 028	16
.303 509	3.294 800	.011 560	17
.302 692	3.303 692	.008 892	18
.302 066	3.310 532	.006 840	19
.301 587	3.315 794	.005 262	20
.301 219	3.319 842	.004 048	21
.300 937	3.322 955	.003 113	22
.300 720	3.325 350	.002 395	23
.300 554	3.327 192	.001 842	24
.300 426	3.328 609	.001 417	25
.300 327	3.329 700	.001 090	26
.300 252	3.330 538	.000 839	27
.300 194	3.331 183	.000 645	28
.300 149	3.331 679	.000 496	29
.300 115	3.332 061	.000 382	30
.300 088	3.332 355	.000 294	31
.300 068	3.332 581	.000 226	32
.300 052	3.332 754	.000 174	33
.300 040	3.332 888	.000 134	34
.300 031	3.332 991	.000 103	35
.300 024	3.333 070	.000 079	36
.300 018	3.333 131	.000 061	37
.300 014	3.333 177	.000 047	38
.300 011	3.333 213	.000 036	39
.300 008	3.333 241	.000 028	40
.300 006	3.333 262	.000 021	41
.300 005	3.333 279	.000 016	42
.300 004	3.333 291	.000 013	43
.300 003	3.333 301	.000 010	44
.300 002	3.333 308	.000 007	45
.300 002	3.333 314	.000 006	46
.300 001	3.333 319	.000 004	47
.300 001	3.333 322	.000 003	48
.300 001	3.333 325	.000 003	49
.300 001	3.333 327	.000 002	50

COMPOUNDING FACTOR FOR 1 — What an initial amount becomes when growing at compound interest	COMPOUNDING FACTOR FOR 1 PER ANNUM — Growth of equal year-end deposits all growing at compound interest	SINKING FUND FACTOR — Level deposit required each year to reach 1 by a given year	Year
1.300 000	1.000 000	1.000 000	1
1.690 000	2.300 000	.434 783	2
2.197 000	3.990 000	.250 627	3
2.856 100	6.187 000	.161 629	4
3.712 930	9.043 100	.110 582	5
4.826 809	12.756 030	.078 394	6
6.274 852	17.582 839	.056 874	7
8.157 307	23.857 691	.041 915	8
10.604 499	32.014 998	.031 235	9
13.785 849	42.619 497	.023 463	10
17.921 604	56.405 346	.017 729	11
23.298 085	74.326 950	.013 454	12
30.287 511	97.625 036	.010 243	13
39.373 764	127.912 546	.007 818	14
51.185 893	167.286 310	.005 978	15
66.541 661	218.472 203	.004 577	16
86.504 159	285.013 864	.003 509	17
112.455 407	371.518 023	.002 692	18
146.192 029	483.973 430	.002 066	19
190.049 638	630.165 459	.001 587	20
247.064 529	820.215 097	.001 219	21
321.183 888	1,067.279 626	.000 937	22
417.539 054	1,388.463 514	.000 720	23
542.800 770	1,806.002 568	.000 554	24
705.641 001	2,348.803 338	.000 426	25
917.333 302	3,054.444 340	.000 327	26
1,192.533 293	3,971.777 642	.000 252	27
1,550.293 280	5,164.310 934	.000 194	28
2,015.381 264	6,714.604 214	.000 149	29
2,619.995 644	8,729.985 479	.000 115	30
3,405.994 337	11,349.981 12	.000 088	31
4,427.792 638	14,755.975 46	.000 068	32
5,756.130 429	19,183.768 10	.000 052	33
7,482.969 558	24,939.898 53	.000 040	34
9,727.860 425	32,422.868 08	.000 031	35
12,646.218 55	42,150.728 51	.000 024	36
16,440.084 12	54,796.947 06	.000 018	37
21,372.109 35	71,237.031 18	.000 014	38
27,783.742 16	92,609.140 53	.000 011	39
36,118.864 81	120,392.882 7	.000 008	40
46,954.524 25	156,511.747 5	.000 006	41
61,040.881 53	203,466.271 8	.000 005	42
79,353.145 98	264,507.153 3	.000 004	43
103,159.089 8	343,860.299 3	.000 003	44
134,106.816 7	447,019.389 0	.000 002	45
174,338.861 7	581,126.205 8	.000 002	46
226,640.520 2	755,465.067 5	.000 001	47
294,632.676 3	982,105.587 7	.000 001	48
383,022.479 2	1,276,738.264	.000 001	49
497,929.223 0	1,659,760.743	.000 001	50

Year	CAPITAL RECOVERY FACTOR — Annual payment that will repay a $1 loan in X years with compound interest on the unpaid balance	PRESENT WORTH OF AN ANNUITY FACTOR — How much 1 received or paid annually for X years is worth today	DISCOUNT FACTOR — How much 1 at a future date is worth today
1	1.400 000	714 286	714 286
2	816 667	1.224 490	510 204
3	629 358	1.588 921	364 431
4	540 766	1.849 229	260 308
5	491 361	2.035 164	185 934
6	461 260	2.167 974	132 810
7	441 923	2.262 839	094 865
8	429 074	2.330 599	067 760
9	420 345	2.378 999	048 400
10	414 324	2.413 571	034 572
11	410 128	2.438 265	024 694
12	407 182	2.455 904	017 639
13	405 104	2.468 503	012 599
14	403 632	2.477 502	008 999
15	402 588	2.483 930	006 428
16	401 845	2.488 521	004 591
17	401 316	2.491 801	003 280
18	400 939	2.494 144	002 343
19	400 670	2.495 817	001 673
20	400 479	2.497 012	001 195
21	400 342	2.497 866	000 854
22	400 244	2.498 476	000 610
23	400 174	2.498 911	000 436
24	400 124	2.499 222	000 311
25	400 089	2.499 444	000 222
26	400 064	2.499 603	000 159
27	400 045	2.499 717	000 113
28	400 032	2.499 798	000 081
29	400 023	2.499 855	000 058
30	400 017	2.499 897	000 041
31	400 012	2.499 926	000 030
32	400 008	2.499 947	000 021
33	400 006	2.499 962	000 015
34	400 004	2.499 973	000 011
35	400 003	2.499 981	000 008
36	400 002	2.499 986	000 005
37	400 002	2.499 990	000 004
38	400 001	2.499 993	000 003
39	400 001	2.499 995	000 002
40	400 001	2.499 996	000 001
41	400 000	2.499 997	000 001
42	400 000	2.499 998	000 001
43	400 000	2.499 999	000 001
44	400 000	2.499 999	000 000
45	400 000	2.499 999	000 000
46	400 000	2.500 000	000 000
47	400 000	2.500 000	000 000
48	400 000	2.500 000	000 000
49	400 000	2.500 000	000 000
50	400 000	2.500 000	000 000

Year	COMPOUNDING FACTOR FOR 1 — What an initial amount becomes when growing at compound interest	COMPOUNDING FACTOR FOR 1 PER ANNUM — Growth of equal year-end deposits all growing at compound interest	SINKING FUND FACTOR — Level deposit required each year to reach 1 by a given year
1	1.400 000	1.000 000	1.000 000
2	1.960 000	2.400 000	416 667
3	2.744 000	4.360 000	229 358
4	3.841 600	7.104 000	140 766
5	5.378 240	10.945 600	091 361
6	7.529 536	16.323 840	061 260
7	10.541 350	23.853 376	041 923
8	14.757 891	34.394 726	029 074
9	20.661 047	49.152 617	020 345
10	28.925 465	69.813 664	014 324
11	40.495 652	98.739 129	010 128
12	56.693 912	139.234 781	007 182
13	79.371 477	195.928 693	005 104
14	111.120 068	275.300 171	003 632
15	155.568 096	386.420 239	002 588
16	217.795 334	541.988 334	001 845
17	304.913 467	759.783 668	001 316
18	426.878 854	1,064.697 136	000 939
19	597.630 396	1,491.575 990	000 670
20	836.682 554	2,089.206 386	000 479
21	1,171.355 576	2,925.888 940	000 342
22	1,639.897 806	4,097.244 516	000 244
23	2,295.856 929	5,737.142 322	000 174
24	3,214.199 700	8,032.999 251	000 124
25	4,499.879 581	11,247.198 95	000 089
26	6,299.831 413	15,747.078 53	000 064
27	8,819.763 978	22,046.909 94	000 045
28	12,347.669 57	30,866.673 92	000 032
29	17,286.737 40	43,214.343 49	000 023
30	24,201.432 36	60,501.080 89	000 017
31	33,882.005 30	84,702.513 24	000 012
32	47,434.807 42	118,584.518 5	000 008
33	66,408.730 38	166,019.326 0	000 006
34	92,972.222 54	232,428.056 3	000 004
35	130,161.111 6	325,400.278 9	000 003
36	182,225.556 2	455,561.390 4	000 002
37	255,115.778 6	637,786.946 6	000 002
38	357,162.090 1	892,902.725 2	000 001
39	500,026.926 1	1,250,064.815	000 001
40	700,037.696 6	1,750,091.741	000 001
41	980,052.775 2	2,450,129.438	000 000
42	1,372,073.885	3,430,182.213	000 000
43	1,920,903.439	4,802,256.099	000 000
44	2,689,264.815	6,723,159.538	000 000
45	3,764,970.741	9,412,424.353	000 000
46	5,270,959.038	13,177,395.09	000 000
47	7,379,342.653	18,448,354.13	000 000
48	10,331,079.71	25,827,696.79	000 000
49	14,463,511.60	36,158,776.50	000 000
50	20,248,916.24	50,622,288.10	000 000

RATE 50% — Right table

Year	DISCOUNT FACTOR — How much 1 at a future date is worth today	PRESENT WORTH OF AN ANNUITY FACTOR — How much 1 received or paid annually for X years is worth today	CAPITAL RECOVERY FACTOR — Annual payment that will repay a $1 loan in X years with compound interest on the unpaid balance
1	666 667	666 667	1.500 000
2	444 444	1.111 111	900 000
3	296 296	1.407 407	710 526
4	197 531	1.604 938	623 077
5	131 687	1.736 626	575 829
6	087 791	1.824 417	548 120
7	058 528	1.882 945	531 083
8	039 018	1.921 963	520 301
9	026 012	1.947 975	513 354
10	017 342	1.965 317	508 824
11	011 561	1.976 878	505 848
12	007 707	1.984 585	503 884
13	005 138	1.989 724	502 582
14	003 425	1.993 149	501 719
15	002 284	1.995 433	501 144
16	001 522	1.996 955	500 762
17	001 015	1.997 970	500 508
18	000 677	1.998 647	500 339
19	000 451	1.999 098	500 226
20	000 301	1.999 399	500 150
21	000 200	1.999 599	500 100
22	000 134	1.999 733	500 067
23	000 089	1.999 822	500 045
24	000 059	1.999 881	500 030
25	000 040	1.999 921	500 020
26	000 026	1.999 947	500 013
27	000 018	1.999 965	500 009
28	000 012	1.999 977	500 006
29	000 008	1.999 984	500 004
30	000 005	1.999 990	500 003
31	000 003	1.999 993	500 002
32	000 002	1.999 995	500 001
33	000 002	1.999 997	500 001
34	000 001	1.999 998	500 001
35	000 001	1.999 999	500 000
36	000 000	1.999 999	500 000
37	000 000	1.999 999	500 000
38	000 000	2.000 000	500 000
39	000 000	2.000 000	500 000
40	000 000	2.000 000	500 000
41	000 000	2.000 000	500 000
42	000 000	2.000 000	500 000
43	000 000	2.000 000	500 000
44	000 000	2.000 000	500 000
45	000 000	2.000 000	500 000
46	000 000	2.000 000	500 000
47	000 000	2.000 000	500 000
48	000 000	2.000 000	500 000
49	000 000	2.000 000	500 000
50	000 000	2.000 000	500 000

RATE 50% — Left table

Year	COMPOUNDING FACTOR FOR 1 — What an initial amount becomes when growing at compound interest	COMPOUNDING FACTOR FOR 1 PER ANNUM — Growth of equal year-end deposits all growing at compound interest	SINKING FUND FACTOR — Level deposit required each year to reach 1 by a given year
1	1.500 000	1.000 000	1.000 000
2	2.250 000	2.500 000	400 000
3	3.375 000	4.750 000	210 526
4	5.062 500	8.125 000	123 077
5	7.593 750	13.187 500	075 829
6	11.390 625	20.781 250	048 120
7	17.085 938	32.171 875	031 083
8	25.628 906	49.257 812	020 301
9	38.443 359	74.886 719	013 354
10	57.665 039	113.330 078	008 824
11	86.497 559	170.995 117	005 848
12	129.746 338	257.492 676	003 884
13	194.619 507	387.239 014	002 582
14	291.929 260	581.858 521	001 719
15	437.893 890	873.787 781	001 144
16	656.840 836	1,311.681 671	000 762
17	985.261 253	1,968.522 507	000 508
18	1,477.891 880	2,953.783 760	000 339
19	2,216.837 820	4,431.675 640	000 226
20	3,325.256 730	6,648.513 460	000 150
21	4,987.885 095	9,973.770 190	000 100
22	7,481.827 643	14,961.655 29	000 067
23	11,222.741 46	22,443.482 93	000 045
24	16,834.112 20	33,666.224 39	000 030
25	25,251.168 29	50,500.336 59	000 020
26	37,876.752 44	75,751.504 88	000 013
27	56,815.128 66	113,628.257 3	000 009
28	85,222.692 99	170,443.386 0	000 006
29	127,834.039 5	255,666.079 0	000 004
30	191,751.059 2	383,500.118 5	000 003
31	287,626.588 8	575,251.177 7	000 002
32	431,439.883 3	862,877.766 6	000 001
33	647,159.824 9	1,294,317.650	000 001
34	970,739.737 4	1,941,477.475	000 001
35	1,456,109.606	2,912,217.212	000 000
36	2,184,164.409	4,368,326.818	000 000
37	3,276,246.614	6,552,491.227	000 000
38	4,914,369.920	9,828,737.841	000 000
39	7,371,554.881	14,743,107.76	000 000
40	11,057,332.32	22,114,662.64	000 000
41	16,585,998.48	33,171,994.96	000 000
42	24,878,997.72	49,757,993.44	000 000
43	37,318,496.58	74,636,991.17	000 000
44	55,977,744.87	111,955,487.8	000 000
45	83,966,617.31	167,933,232.6	000 000
46	125,949,926.0	251,899,849.9	000 000
47	188,924,889.0	377,849,775.9	000 000
48	283,387,333.4	566,774,664.9	000 000
49	425,081,000.1	850,161,998.3	000 000
50	637,621,500.2	1,275,242,998.	000 000

Index

DATE DUE

PRINTED IN U.S.A.